MODERN JAPANESE NOVELISTS

A BIOGRAPHICAL DICTIONARY

JOHN LEWELL

KODANSHA INTERNATIONAL
New York · Tokyo · London

Kodansha America, Inc.
114 Fifth Avenue
New York, New York 10011, U.S.A.

Kodansha International Ltd.
17–14 Otowa 1-chome
Bunkyo-ku, Tokyo 112, Japan

Published in 1993 by Kodansha America, Inc.

Printed in the United States of America

93 94 95 96 7 6 5 4 3 2 1

Library of Congress Cataloging-in-Publication Data
    Lewell, John.
        Modern Japanese novelists : a biographical dictionary / John
    Lewell. — 1st ed.
            p. cm.
        Includes bibliographical references.
        ISBN 4-7700-1649-2
        1. Japanese fiction—1868– —History and criticism. 2. Japanese
    fiction—1868– —Translations into English—Bibliography.
    I. Title.
    PL747.55.L48 1992
    895.6'3409—dc20   92-11324
    [B]   CIP

The text of this book was set in Palatino.
Composed by Photo-graphics,
Honiton, Devon,
United Kingdom

The jacket was printed by
Phoenix Color Corporation,
Long Island City, New York

Printed and bound by
R. R. Donnelley & Sons Company,
Harrisonburg, Virginia

CONTENTS

PREFACE

A few years ago, in the midst of researching *Modern Japanese Novelists*, I made an impromptu visit to a company dealing in rare books and asked the receptionist if the company had any works by Japanese writers. She thought for a moment and then said: "Oh, do you mean that man who killed himself? What *was* his name? He must have been as mad as a hatter."

Having already heard her speak with another customer, I guessed that she had a university education and maybe even a degree in literary studies. Yet her ignorance of Japanese literature was absolute and complete. She reminded me of myself when I was at college many years ago, sitting at the feet of Dr. Frank Leavis and learning why, in his opinion, *Hard Times* was a better novel than *Bleak House*. If he, who was certainly the most influential English critic of this century, had suddenly suggested that we turn our attention to the works of NATSUME SŌSEKI or MORI ŌGAI, I would have considered that he had taken leave of his senses. Of course, he never *did* mention any Japanese writers, and I was always slightly suspicious when never once did he refer to my favorite English writer, John Cowper Powys. I might have guessed that Dr. Leavis and his colleagues, in their common pursuit of true judgment, were inadvertently concealing much of the world's finest literature from us.

It is now more than twenty years since I left Cambridge, carrying with me the idea that the art of reading is every bit as important to civilization as the art of writing. For that, at least, I had Dr. Leavis to thank. Because of it I possessed sufficient confidence to form my own opinions without constant reference to the prevailing canons of good taste. I was also more adventurous in my reading than I might otherwise have been, if slow to realize that anyone east of the Ural Mountains had ever set pen to paper. When I eventually discovered Japanese literature it was by way of reading a novel from a writer whose work I had often seen but until then had studiously avoided. MISHIMA YUKIO, whose name would later escape the memory of the girl in the bookstore, was the writer, and the novel was his 1954 romance *Shiosai (The Sound of Waves)*.

Perhaps it was the fact that I was living in San Clemente within

audible distance of the Pacific Ocean, but there is no doubt that
The Sound of Waves made an extraordinary impression on me. It
was not the best novel I had ever read, but it excited me as no
other book had done for many years. It made me feel like a dweller
in the desert who discovers a leaf and from it extrapolates the
existence of a tree. Needless to say it also made me feel slightly
foolish in having avoided Mishima's work for so long, and I began
to question why I had done so. The answer, I decided, after reading
other Japanese writers with equal enjoyment, was that we lacked
accurate images of them both as people *and* as writers. For the
general reader it is surely the image of a writer that determines
whether or not his or her work is worth beginning. Word-of-
mouth recommendation, reviews, dust-jacket endorsements, and the
perceived reputation of the novelist in question are just some of
the factors that persuade us to address one writer rather than
another. Most people prefer novels that are either entertaining,
enlightening, or in some way relevant to their own lives. In
Mishima's case, his reputation as a rightwing militarist whose
exhibitionistic suicide was scandalously out-of-tune with the times
was enough to put me off him for years. That image, as I
subsequently discovered, was completely misleading.

The reader will gather that I am not a linguist, nor am I affiliated
with any academic institution. During the course of researching
Modern Japanese Novelists I have inevitably acquired a Japanese
vocabulary, but I have neither the patience nor the inclination to
make a systematic study of the Japanese language. I do not consider
this to be a disadvantage. My subject is Japanese literature *in
translation*, and I suspect that the majority of readers likewise do
not have time to gain sufficient fluency in Japanese to fully
appreciate, say, TANIZAKI JUN'ICHIRŌ in the vernacular. Nearly all
the research for this book has therefore been conducted in English,
and I have relied upon the work of many scholars whose painstaking
translations have been such a joy to read. Occasionally, and with
expert help, I have resorted to Japanese sources for certain
biographical details that were not available in English. I am therefore
greatly indebted, firstly to the Japanese novelists themselves whose
work has been such an inspiration, secondly to their translators
who have made it available to a wider public, and thirdly to the
many literary historians, biographers, and critics who have written
about this subject in English.

My method of working has been as follows: I began my research
by reading nearly every Japanese novel and story that had been
translated. Fearing that I might eventually forget even their plots, I
wrote an essay on each one as soon as I had finished it. As time

went by and I filled up disk after disk on my word processor, I began to wonder whether or not I might publish the resulting text. My agents, to whom I sent it, suggested that I add some biographical sketches about each writer. Gradually, these sketches became more and more elaborate, until I was obliged to plunder some of my original critical material on the novels and stories themselves. Five years into the project I discarded my original notes and retained the biographical format, addressing the major writers from A to Z.

That, briefly, is an outline of how *Modern Japanese Novelists* came to be written. As the project progressed I became motivated by a desire to share my discoveries with other people, especially when I came across novels and stories that appeared to be underrated by other critics. Thus, throughout this book I have not attempted to conceal my personal likes and dislikes, for they, after all, are the indicators of a literary sensibility. However, I have tried to reflect accurately the status of individual writers, both in Japan and in the West, noting the regard in which they are held, quite apart from my own opinion of them.

I have intended *Modern Japanese Novelists* to be a book in which readers can explore the topics that interest them, rather than one which demands being read from beginning to end. Nonetheless, it *is* a book to be read, explored, and enjoyed, and I should hate to think of it being used solely as a reference work. The bibliographies are appended as a convenient guide to the many English translations that have been published, and each one includes a short list of "recommended reading" as well as a more comprehensive guide. The latter would ideally be a complete listing, but inevitably there will be one or two translations that I have overlooked. If the reader notices any glaring omissions I should be grateful to hear about them. Please write to me, care of the publisher.

I am pleased to note that the availability of Japanese literature in English translation is improving all the time. The chain bookstores in the U.S. and U.K. carry works by the most popular and enduring authors, including Tanizaki Jun'ichirō, ABE KŌBŌ, Mishima Yukio, and ENDŌ SHŪSAKU. Useful as the chain stores are, however, you will find a much wider choice of Japanese literature in Japanese bookstores, nearly all of which have an English-language section.

Although the texts themselves are more widely available there are still one or two barriers you may have to overcome before feeling completely at ease with Japanese literature. The first concerns names. Japanese names are still largely unfamiliar to people in the West. In Japan, the family name is placed first, followed by a person's given name. Many American and English publishers (my own included) often reverse the traditional order to make the names sound more intelligible to the Western reader. University presses and scholars, meanwhile, usually retain the traditional order, with the result that the reader is initially confronted with two people instead of one. We meet Abe Kōbō and Kōbō Abe; YOSHIYUKI JUNNOSUKE and Junnosuke Yoshiyuki. The Japanese have avoided this problem and do *not* say Warren Penn Robert when they mean Robert Penn Warren. For my own part I have retained the traditional name order except, for example, when I refer to a publication such as *Death in Midsummer, and Other Stories by Yukio Mishima*. Fortunately, this "barrier" disappears very quickly when one gains some familiarity with the authors concerned. (For a complete explanation of how names are used in this book, see the separate note on page xii).

The other hurdle is the tendency of some Japanese novelists to invent titles which do not read well in English translation. Alas, NATSUME SŌSEKI – arguably the greatest of all modern Japanese novelists – was the worst offender in this respect. Today's American or English reader, confronted by a novel called *And Then*, is most unlikely to suppose that it could be a masterpiece. He or she may be equally baffled by seeing others called *Mon* and *Kokoro*, while the completely uninitiated may take *I Am a Cat* to be a kindergarten textbook. Yet having now discovered all these works by Sōseki, I, for one, should be reluctant to trade them for any cleverly titled novel by Jane Austen. Fortunately, many Japanese authors have since become adept at naming their works with a view to overseas sales. For example, translator John Nathan once asked Mishima to improve upon *Gogo no eikō*, which literally means "Glory (or Towing) in the Afternoon." Apparently, Mishima responded by reeling off a dozen titles in English, including the one he soon seized upon as the best: *The Sailor Who Fell from Grace with the Sea*. It was a brilliant title for a novel that went on to become a best-seller and the basis for a Hollywood film. Yet I suspect many people would prefer Sōseki's *And Then*, if only it were called something different.

I am hoping that the present volume will help break down any barriers that remain. Modern Japanese fiction offers something for everyone, and the purpose of this book is to guide individual readers towards the novels and stories that will appeal to them most.

I should like to express my thanks to those who have helped me directly and in various ways during the course of this project. My thanks are due, firstly, to my agents Michael Larsen and Elizabeth Pomada for their original suggestion. Equally, I am grateful to all the editors and consultants at Kodansha International: especially to my editors Chikako Noma and Dawn Lawson for the long hours they have spent in reading and checking; to Hirohisa Shibuya of the Photo Library at Kodansha Ltd. in Tokyo for combing the archives and collecting so many fine photographs of the authors; and to Editorial Director Paul De Angelis, whose personal encouragement and advice have been invaluable.

Modern Japanese Novelists is dedicated to my wife, Pornchan, whom I did not meet until halfway through the project; and to our son Jonathan who arrived even more recently. I thank them dearly for allowing literature and life to coexist so happily side-by-side.

John Lewell
London, 1992

How to Use This Book

Modern Japanese Novelists is arranged alphabetically with chapters on each author followed in each instance by a bibliography. There is no index, as such, but the alphabetical arrangement and an extensive system of cross-referencing should help readers locate the information they require.

Authors' names at the head of each chapter are printed with the family name first, in observance of traditional Japanese name order, and usually in capitals, except when an author is more commonly called by his or her given name – or in some cases by a literary sobriquet – in which case that name is shown in capitals. The exact choice of name has been determined by consulting two standard Japanese reference works: the 1990 edition of *Nihon Kindai Bungaku Daijiten* (published by Kodansha Ltd.) and the 1988 *Shincho Nihon Bungaku Jiten* (published by Shincho-sha).

Within the text the first reference to a writer other than the current subject of the essay is set in small capitals if he or she has an individual entry in the book. Other important figures who need further explanation have entries in the Glossary, indicated by an asterisk next to their names. Likewise, general topics and some terminology which may be unfamiliar to the reader are also treated in the Glossary, and this, in turn, refers back to other chapters of the book if the topic is discussed there at greater length.

The system of romanization for Japanese used in this dictionary is the older version of the Hepburn or Standard system, which prescribes using an *m* instead of an *n* before *p*, *b*, or *m*. Long vowels are indicated by macrons (e.g. Natsume Sōseki) except for common place-names (i.e. Tokyo, not Tōkyō).

The bibliographies are largely self-explanatory. For the purposes of categorization, texts over 100 pages are deemed to be "novels," whereas those of fewer than 100 pages are called "short fiction." One hastens to add that this is not intended to be an indication of literary merit or historical importance, but it does help to differentiate the longer works from the many short stories in translation. Page counts refer to the most representative translation and may vary slightly for others that are also listed. Dates immediately following Japanese titles are those of original publication in Japan, *given in italics for serial publication* and in roman type for book publication. This is also the case within the text, where dates in brackets refer to each work's first appearance in Japan. Publication dates of the translations are given in the bibliographies, where the unconventional if more readable practice of printing the publisher's name *before* the city has been deliberately adopted.

MODERN JAPANESE NOVELISTS

INTRODUCTION

From the ribald humor of NOSAKA AKIYUKI to the lofty purity of
SHIGA NAOYA the literature of Japan is remarkable for its diversity.
Far from being an "acquired taste" it offers something for everyone,
as may be expected from the world's most literate culture. It offers
detective and science fiction, historical novels of both the remote
and recent past, chronicles of war, socialist and proletarian fiction,
comedies, tragedies, and romances. To the present writer its
crowning glories are the collected works of TANIZAKI JUN'ICHIRŌ,
the psychological novels of NATSUME SŌSEKI, and the short stories
of AKUTAGAWA RYŪNOSUKE – but that is a personal choice. Other
readers may prefer the refined art of KAWABATA YASUNARI or the
austere perfection of MORI ŌGAI.

Whatever one's personal preference, the fact remains that Japanese
literature is still a subject treated cautiously in English-speaking
countries. This is largely because, in the public consciousness,
Japanese authors are rarely preceded by their reputations; even the
most eminent of them have to earn a readership alongside first-
time novelists in the West. Such a general lack of awareness is only
to be expected, since less consideration is given to literature than
to most other aspects of Japan's culture in the pages of Western
newspapers and magazines. From these sources one can more easily
acquire a familiarity with sumō wrestling or bonsai cultivation than
an introduction to the rich and varied landscape of modern Japanese
fiction.

Nonetheless, interest in Japan and in the Japanese is growing
rapidly on both sides of the Atlantic. It is only a matter of
time before those who enjoy good fiction begin to discover the
extraordinary virtuosity of Japanese writers, several of whom are
among the best storytellers one is ever likely to encounter. Moreover,
in exploring the literature of another country one inevitably discovers
new insights into the nature of literature itself. In this respect
modern Japanese fiction is especially revealing, for it is founded
upon an intensive study of theory and of Western literary forms,
while retaining many influences from Japan's own heritage.

Having already drawn attention to the diversity of Japanese

1

literature one hesitates to make generalizations of any kind. The risks inherent therein are well known to perceptive critics, not least because creative writers tend to cultivate any idiosyncrasies that have made them famous. However, one feels that having addressed so many novels, stories, and plays on an individual basis, one might be allowed to make some broad generalizations which could prove helpful to the reader. At the same time it will be worthwhile noting a few outstanding exceptions, if only to show that there are always writers who depart radically from the prevailing tradition.

Modern Japanese novelists display at least six characteristics which are likely to strike the Western reader most forcibly. They are as follows: a strongly developed visual sense; the use of juxtapositioning for poetic effect; a preference for understatement; a love of brevity; a tendency to "undramatize" even those subjects that lend themselves to high drama; and a deliberate avoidance of finality in their endings. These characteristics, together with many references to indigenous cultural traditions, account for the exotic flavor of Japan's literature as experienced by foreign readers.

The strongly developed visual sense of the Japanese is the one characteristic that is almost universal. It extends even to music in the work of Takemitsu Tōru, a composer who readily admits to painting pictures in sound. In literature nearly every major Japanese author draws upon the visual imagination to achieve emotional and aesthetic effects which are too subtle to be otherwise expressed. Rarely is a descriptive passage mere padding or scene-setting. Descriptions often lie at the very heart of a story or novel: evoking mood, advancing or resolving the narrative, or symbolizing the writer's philosophical ideas.

Perhaps one would least expect to find a strong visual sense in proletarian writing, which is, after all, chiefly concerned with political issues and with the ways of life forced upon the least fortunate members of society. Yet in the work of HIRABAYASHI TAIKO, a proletarian writer born in 1905, one finds the literary equivalent of photojournalism. Her 1950 story, "A Man's Life," about a convicted murderer awaiting his execution, is so vividly imagined that readers recalling it from memory may feel they have dreamed it. Elsewhere, in the work of ABE KŌBŌ, an experimental novelist and playwright who is greatly admired in the West, the reader is made aware of unfamiliar, invented worlds largely through visual impressions. Abe is often compared to Kafka, and he is equally adept at painting mental landscapes which he fills with everyday objects to create uniquely disturbing effects. Although his master-piece *The Woman in the Dunes* was turned into a highly successful film, the novel itself was conceived and executed as though its author were describing a film which had already been made. The experimentalist's reliance on visual impressions, like that of the proletarian Hirabayashi, is an indication of how universal is this most distinctive characteristic of Japanese fiction.

Juxtaposing images follows naturally from a heightened visual sensitivity. The entire œuvre of Japan's Nobel Prize-winning author, Kawabata Yasunari, is a succession of unpredictable juxtapositions. Take for example his famous story "The House of the Sleeping Beauties," which was described by Mishima as an "esoteric masterpiece." Here, an elderly but not entirely impotent man seeks the services of a procuress in order to lie with young women who have been drugged into deep sleep. As the procuress stoops to unlock the door to a secret room our attention is immediately drawn to the odd design of her waistband. "There was a large, strange bird on the knot of her *obi*. He did not know what species it might be. Why should such realistic eyes and feet have been put on a stylized bird?" In itself, the ominous design of the *obi* is a juxtaposition within a general technique of juxtaposing images, and the story continues as though an invisible narrator were turning the pages of a photograph album. Kawabata's unique style of storytelling, deliberately hesitant and lingering until he suddenly jumps to another image, extracts emotional meaning by the subtle contrast of old age and youth, death and eroticism, beauty and sadness. His texts are consistently interwoven with complex visual correspondences. In Eguchi's secret room not only do the curtains appear to be a deeper crimson in the dim light, but even the blood in the girl whom he fondles seems "to grow richer towards the tips of her fingers."

Understatement, often thought to be the prerogative of the English, is frequently a controlling factor in Japanese expression. The most famous understatement in history is surely Emperor Hirohito's proclamation signaling the end of World War II. After defeats across the entire Pacific, and only days after suffering the complete devastation of two cities by atomic weapons, the emperor declared: ". . . the war situation has developed not necessarily to Japan's advantage." Such an extreme form of understatement is heavily laden with irony, and a similar example of it may be found in Tanizaki's historical novel *A Blind Man's Tale*. In this complex narrative set in the samurai era, the warlord Hideyoshi is made to remark to the Lady Oichi, a widow from the opposing side: "I am sure your Ladyship has been greatly inconvenienced by the difficulties of wartime." Hideyoshi knows full well that the Lady's son has been murdered, her husband's body decapitated, and the severed head, together with that of a reliable family ally, lacquered with vermilion and served up as a New Year's table decoration. These events would certainly be a great inconvenience to the wife of a military commander. They might even be fatally traumatic.

Most understatement in Japanese fiction is not as extreme as it is in the examples given above. It could more accurately be described as obliqueness, most writers preferring to express themselves obliquely rather than directly or obviously. Again, this appears to be linked to the visual sense, for, as readers will know, Oriental painting is noted equally for what it excludes as for what it depicts. Like painters, Japanese writers prefer to suggest or imply their meanings rather than spell them out in obvious detail. The technique becomes especially effective when some extremity of human experience is the focus of attention.

Any extremity, in passion, courage, depravity, or suffering, is an appropriate subject for literature. Writers must explore the boundaries of human experience if they are to give an accurate rendering of life in its entirety. Yet Japanese writers, more than most, are aware of the gap that necessarily exists between reality and literature. They know that if they try to put extreme experience into words, the result can often be the kind of vulgarity which reduces, say, tragedy to melodrama. Much the same sentiment was expressed by George Steiner in *The Death of Tragedy* when he spoke of the difficulties writers have had in addressing the facts of the Holocaust.

In the middle of the twentieth century, Japan suffered a crushing military defeat that was accompanied by an atomic holocaust of horrific proportions. It was no easier for Japanese writers to depict these events than for Jewish writers to set their novels in the concentration camps of Europe. Both ran the risk of understating the subject. Thus it is all the more remarkable that IBUSE MASUJI, a man known chiefly for his humorous short stories, was able to take the subject of the Hiroshima bombing and by the sustained application of understatement create one of the truly great novels of the century: *Black Rain*.

Understatement is at the heart of Ibuse's novel, and nowhere else has it been used more effectively. Its hero is Shigematsu, an ordinary citizen who has kept a "Journal of the Bombing" during the days immediately following the event. In it he describes the explosion and its aftermath with unsparing detail, setting down the facts as they come to light. We know him to be a reliable and utterly truthful witness. However, the main action of the "present-day" narrative takes place some years later, when Shigematsu is hoping to find a husband for his niece, Yasuko. Like other young Hiroshima residents who were contaminated by "black rain" after the bombing, Yasuko is having difficulty in finding a family who will accept her. Ibuse's masterstroke in telling the story is to make Shigematsu, the obsessively truthful chronicler, deliberately withhold from the reader information concerning the true state of Yasuko's health. His omission is not only crucial to the emotional impact of the novel but it also echoes the author's underlying intent and its method of expression. For *Black Rain* is a profoundly religious work even though religion is never mentioned directly. Ibuse's interpretation of Buddhism is entirely implied. It is absorbed into everyday life, into the *particularities* of existence.

Thus far we have looked at three distinguishing characteristics of modern Japanese fiction: its visual emphasis; its juxtapositioning of images, ideas, and motifs; and its subtle use of understatement. A fourth characteristic is surely brevity. Nearly all major writers in Japan this century have been masters of the short story, and some of their stories are very short indeed. One thinks immediately of Kawabata's *tanagokoro no shōsetsu* (literally: "stories that fit into the palm of one's hand"), many of which encapsulate themes developed at greater length in his novels. Produced at various intervals throughout his life these miracles of miniaturization often need to be read and reread to extract their full meaning. Yet Kawabata is by no means the only writer who has created important works of prose in very small format. Akutagawa's "Rashōmon" (the basis, with one other story, for Kurosawa's classic film of the same name) is but nine pages long. And even at the most popular level of literature, in science fiction, the ingenious *Hoshi Shin'ichi has written hundreds of "short-shorts," described by one critic as the *haiku* of science fiction.

Ever since the eighth century the Japanese have demonstrated their brilliance at expressing complex thoughts in economical language. Indeed, the fact that brevity is still regarded as a virtue in Japan is testimony to the continuing influence of long-established literary traditions. The actual length of a prose work is not only seen as giving no indication of its quality but, in direct contrast to Western practice, is rarely adjusted to fit such rigid categories as "novel" or "short story." A work of Japanese fiction can be of any length, from one page to a thousand, in one-page increments. Thus there are many stories of an intermediate length: too short to be classified as novellas and too long to be called short stories. One doubts if they would be successful if originated in English because they require from the author an exceptional ability to condense a mass of material into some forty or fifty pages of text. Western writers and their publishers have always preferred to see such material developed into full-length novels.

Short works of fiction are much more popular in Japan than they are in the West. Moreover, a writer may establish a considerable reputation on the strength of a single story published in a prominent literary magazine. This is quite unlike the Western system which demands at least a substantial novel before anyone will take an author seriously. Japanese writers are also fortunate to have so many outlets for their work; a vast number of magazines and newspapers provide a ready market for stories of any chosen length. Prestigious prizes, too, are awarded for shorter works of fiction; and they are another factor ensuring that brevity remains a marketable commodity.

On the subject of brevity one might draw the reader's attention to an exceptionally fine story by Akutagawa called "Absorbed in Letters." It is not as famous as "Hell Screen" or "Rashōmon," but like all of this author's work it has both a personal and a universal meaning. Its central character is the great writer of the pre-modern era, *Takizawa Bakin: a man who wrote moralistic novels of quite exceptional length. Akutagawa pictures him in old age when he is partially blind and fearful that he is losing his creative powers. During the daytime, after wandering down to the public baths, Bakin is challenged by a tradesman who accuses of him of being unable to compose *haiku*. Returning home, the old writer is troubled. Is he merely, after all, an inferior artist? Does he avoid composing *haiku* because he is garrulous and undisciplined? Not until late at night do his spirits begin to rise. In an intensely moving passage that owes everything to Akutagawa's genius for brevity, Bakin coaxes his flagging inspiration into life and continues writing in his accustomed manner.

As readers will guess, Akutagawa has cleverly substituted Bakin's fear of *haiku* for his own fear of the long novel. Never choosing to compose at length, Akutagawa was severely criticized by Tanizaki for his lack of attention to the structural component of fiction. It was an argument that Tanizaki won completely. Japan's fiction would never match the Western achievement if its writers continued to ignore architectural qualities. Yet, so many years after this famous controversy, can one really say that Akutagawa's short stories are in any way inferior to novels many times their length? The brevity of "Absorbed in Letters" does not detract from its power. On the contrary, it shows us that a person should do what he is best at doing, and only then will the darkness around him be dispelled.

Looking for further characteristics of modern Japanese fiction one discovers a widespread reluctance to depict open confrontation. This is chiefly because novelists reflect the mechanisms they see at work in society around them. Japanese society goes to great lengths to avoid conflict between families and individuals. When disagreements arise, innumerable go-betweens are employed to bring aggrieved parties back together. The whole process can take a very long time, and ends, invariably, in either stalemate or a happy restoration of the status quo.

Given such deliberately undramatized material the Japanese novelist may appear to be severely hindered in his efforts to excite and entertain the reader with descriptions of conflict. Fortunately, quite the opposite is true. Conflict is never eradicated, but merely shifted from the social arena to the individual psyche. The novelist is therefore able to show exactly how social pressures affect the individual and how each person responds to them in his own way. As a result, Japanese fiction is frequently an expression of inner conflict, often based upon the author's own experience. Far from being flat or undramatic, it is acutely sensitive to the ups and downs of personal life. Its triumphs include such engaging novels as FUTABATEI's *Ukigumo* (arguably Japan's first modern novel), Sōseki's *Kokoro*, and all of DAZAI's autobiographical writings, culminating in *The Setting Sun* and *No Longer Human*.

In a hierarchy of literary values Japanese writers usually place aesthetic qualities above dramatic qualities, their desire for beauty overriding their desire for dramatic contrast. Time and again the reader will come across plots which promise some fatal dramatic encounter between protagonists, only to find that the tension is rapidly dispersed and the encounter avoided. A prime example of this can be found in ARIYOSHI SAWAKO's novel *The River Ki*. At one point in the story it becomes necessary for the head of the household, a man who aspires to a political career, to confront his truculent younger brother and insist that he be more prudent in his love life. In a novel by an English or American author one would expect a major scene, perhaps accompanied by lost tempers and violence. Yet Ariyoshi leaves out the scene completely and moves her story forward to a time when the younger brother has already been brought to heel. Her reason for doing so is not only a typical avoidance of confrontation but a deliberate suppression of drama in the interests of aesthetics. After all, *The River Ki* is chiefly concerned with the feminine psyche, being a portrait of a woman's life that spans several phases of recent Japanese history. Undue emphasis on a male confrontation would only draw attention away from the central character and thus alter the perspective of the book. Aesthetic principles are therefore given justifiable supremacy, for in the literature of Japan there can only be one "meta-principle" and that is beauty. Whatever constraints are placed upon it by realism, or indeed by any other objective, the meta-principle remains pure, shining, and immutable. It is the only unchanging concept in a land where change and transience are themselves considered beautiful.

Given the different attitude to dramatic confrontation – and the constant awareness of transience as a prized phenomenon – it is not surprising that Japanese authors resist making the endings of their stories too pronounced. They like to leave the reader with the impression that the life of a novel continues indefinitely even though the book itself has come to an end. The extent to which individual readers approve this device can be a test of how much they will enjoy Japanese literature as a whole. However, even the most knowledgeable experts can sometimes balk at what they perceive to be a particularly loose ending, as some scholars have with Tanizaki's *Diary of a Mad Old Man*.

One of the greatest writers of the century, Tanizaki Jun'ichirō embodied in his work most of the "general characteristics" put forward here. While other writers were struggling to develop fiction from less fertile theories of literature, Tanizaki was an unashamed aesthete. It would not, however, be appropriate to dismiss him as such by ascribing only a Western meaning to the word "aesthetic." To Tanizaki, all of Japan's traditional moral and cultural values were implicit in his appreciation of beauty. His brilliant essay, "In Praise of Shadows," was written with a passionate sense of the mysteries and harmonies of Old Japan. In his historical novels, whether of medieval times or of just a few years past, he uncovered a treasure trove of material and organized it with miraculous skill. No other writer could so consistently strike the pleasure centers of the mind with every unexpected twist of his plots.

In the 1980s, Tanizaki's works were still being translated into English and became widely available throughout the world. *Naomi*, an early work written in 1924, was published on both sides of the Atlantic as late as 1985. It was one of his most popular works: the story of how a young engineer takes a teenage mistress who gradually grows into a tormenting *femme fatale*. Throughout the later novels there are similar Naomi-like figures, always inflicting cruelty on their male victims, yet inspiring them, too, with a perverse desire for life. In Tanizaki's last novel, *Diary of a Mad Old Man*, the elderly protagonist's refusal to die prevents the novel from being neatly resolved to suit Western taste. The old man is simply too busy hatching another scheme to gain a glimpse of his young daughter-in-law's body. One may admire or deplore the absence of resolution, but Tanizaki's obsessional theme remains triumphant to the end.

If visual effects, poetic juxtapositions, understatement, brevity, undramatization, and unresolved endings are typical characteristics of modern Japanese fiction, which novels stand out as exceptions to the mainstream tradition? Very little emphasis is placed upon visual effects by SHIMAZAKI TŌSON in *The Family*, his monumental record of daily life. Despite the sheer number of aunts, uncles, and cousins in the two separate branches of the family, Tōson does not even attempt to delineate one character from another by describing their visual appearance. He makes no appeal to the mind's eye and fails, ultimately, to achieve the overall effect of realism that he appears to seek.

Writers who create strong narratives are often less reliant on juxtaposing images than those who create evocative or poetic fiction. ENDŌ SHŪSAKU is well known in the West for his vigorous stories about the history of Catholicism in Japan. His novels are entirely Western in their structure and relatively free from the disjointed effect which juxtapositioning can produce. Strongly influenced by French literature in his youth, Endō is exceptional for the smoothness of his narrative line. However, even he grows more experimental in his old age, using more complex imagery in his 1986 novel, *Scandal*. In a sense this work contains the ultimate juxtaposition, for its central character may or may not be leading a double life, depending on whether his *doppelgänger* is imagined or real. Perhaps for this reason *Scandal* seems more original in form, more daring in technique – and more Japanese – than Endō's previous works.

If the majority of Japanese writers prefer understated emotion, here the one outstanding exception is surely ARISHIMA TAKEO. Never much admired in his own country until recently, Arishima injected such strong emotions into his first novel, *A Certain Woman*, that it came dangerously close to melodrama. Resembling *Madame Bovary* on the high seas, it is the story of a love affair between a wayward woman and a ship's purser, conducted while the woman is fleeing from her first husband in Japan to marry a second one in America. Disregarding social convention she plunges into a vortex of passion, much as if seeking the magic elixir of life. Her story is described with complete frankness by Arishima, in sharp contrast to other Japanese writers who often expect us to "read between the lines."

Many more exceptions apply in the category of brevity, including a novel by one of the great masters of the short story, Shiga Naoya. Famous for such miniatures as "Seibei's Gourds," "Han's Crime," and "The Shop-boy's God," Shiga wrote only a single extended work: *A Dark Night's Passing*. Originally conceived in 1912 as an autobiographical account of a disagreement with his father, Shiga's novel took so many years in its execution that its author unexpectedly reached an impasse when he and his father became reconciled. Eventually completed in 1937 it runs to over four hundred pages in

English translation and has long been the most highly acclaimed *"I-Novel" in the Japanese language.

All of Natsume Sōseki's major novels are available in English, and these, too, are exceptional for their length and depth. Sōseki's art demanded a larger canvas than the restricted realm of the short story. He began his writing career with the long-running serial *I Am a Cat*, and concluded it with *Light and Darkness*, a Jamesian novel left unfinished at page 375. Although some of his early works (such as "Ten Nights of Dream") exemplify all of the characteristics noted here, Sōseki had a profound understanding of human psychology and discovered his own way of expressing it at length. Some of his insights predate those of Carl Jung, and they are all the more remarkable for being embodied in realistic fiction. Indeed, no one should approach Japanese literature expecting it to be composed entirely of fragile cameos and short, evocative tales. Japanese writers have been ambitious in undertaking projects on a monumental scale, and they have often succeeded in spite of their ability to miniaturize. The most notable achievements in this respect are Sōseki's two great trilogies, Tōson's *Before the Dawn*, Mishima's *The Sea of Fertility*, Ibuse's *Black Rain*, and Tanizaki's *The Makioka Sisters*.

The tendency to remove drama in the interests of aesthetics is not a charge that can be leveled at many of Japan's most popular writers. In the twentieth century popular fiction has provided the basis for films, and they by their very nature are usually dramatic. The Japanese, however, have traditionally taken a high-minded attitude towards literature, dividing it rigorously into "pure" and various "impure" categories. Popular fiction suitable for dramatic treatment in motion pictures was inevitably excluded from the former category for much of the century. Thus such a fine writer as KIKUCHI KAN, author of the brilliant short story "The Realm Beyond," was greatly criticized when he turned to popular fiction, theater, and film.

Finally, one looks for exceptions to the general rule that Japanese writers have a greater than average tolerance for problematic endings. The person who immediately springs to mind is Mishima Yukio, who ended his works – and his life – with predetermined finality. Unlike many writers Mishima rarely started a project without having a good idea for bringing it to a satisfactory conclusion. Even *The Sea of Fertility*, vast though it is, travels inexorably to its mystical climax. Mishima's most highly acclaimed work, *The Temple of the Golden Pavilion*, ends with one of the few, truly memorable, closing lines in modern Japanese fiction. The narrator, a Zen acolyte who has just destroyed his temple by fire, comments: "I felt like a man who settles down for a smoke after finishing a job of work. I wanted to live." After all that has gone before, the line has an unexpected resonance, making us see the whole novel from a different perspective. It is a strong, triumphant ending, totally at odds with the laconic tone in which it is expressed. Indeed, it is the same tone as that used by Meursault at the ending of Albert Camus' *The Outsider*. One can even imagine Mishima himself, in exactly the same spirit, coming to the opposite conclusion and declaring: "I wanted to die." Or in Meursault's words: ". . . all that remained was to hope that on the day of my execution there should be a large crowd of spectators and that they should greet me with howls of execration."

Mishima's violent death in 1970 did not spell the end of modern Japanese fiction. A new generation of writers, more in tune with the mood of the times, have continued to produce literature of outstanding quality – if never quite matching the genius of their predecessors. That, at least, is the only fair assessment one can make in the last decade of the twentieth century. Ten years later the fiction of the 1970s and 1980s will be seen differently, and many more biographies may need to be added to a volume such as this.

ABE Kōbō
(1924–93)

Novelist and playwright. Born in Tokyo. Grew up in Mukden, Manchuria. Lived on the outskirts of Tokyo.

It is often said of Abe Kōbō that he was the first truly international writer produced by Japan. His experimental works, although strongly influenced by Franz Kafka, have no specific cultural location. In them you will find no references to Shintō, Buddhism, Mount Fuji, or the *"floating world." Rather, they are compilations of the many kinds of spiritual anguish afflicting modern man. Their collector was both a symbolist and a surrealist, gifted with a powerful imagination and a cruel sense of comedy. He most often set his stories in a vast urban landscape, where a labyrinth of unremarkable streets echoes the mental landscape shared by the author, his characters, and, by implication, the reader. His plots have a sinister complexity and are sometimes so bizarre that they spoil otherwise brilliant conceptions. For example, in *Hakobune Sakuramaru* (1984, *The Ark Sakura*), the central character gets his foot trapped inside a flush lavatory and brings the novel to a standstill. Never was a masterpiece more deliberately ruined. In fact, Abe's perversity often prevented him from producing work of the highest order. Only a few short stories such as *"Yume no heishi"* (*1957*, "The Dream Soldier"), some passages from *Hako otoko* (*1973*, *The Box Man*), and his famous novel *Suna no onna* (1962, *The Woman in the Dunes*) are truly outstanding in English translation.

Of his background and upbringing Abe Kōbō himself once wrote: "I was born in Tokyo and brought up in Manchuria. The place of family origin on my papers, however, is Hokkaidō, and I lived there too for a few years. In short, my place of birth, the place where I was brought up, and the place of origin of my family are all distinctly different. Due to this fact, it is a difficult matter for me to write even an abbreviated list of important dates in my life. Essentially I am a man with no hometown. That is one thing I can say. And the feeling of hometown phobia which flows at the base of my emotions may be attributable to such a background. I am put off by anything which is valued only because it is stationary." (Translated by Andrew Horvat.)

The son of a physician, Abe Kōbō was persuaded to study medicine and actually graduated from Tokyo University Medical School in 1948. It would be an understatement to say that his heart was never in it. Not only did he refuse to practice medicine but he began publishing fiction in the very same year that he completed his university studies. Along with Takeda Taijun and Umezaki Haruo, he was invited to join the predominantly Marxist group that published the magazine *Kindai bungaku* (*Modern Literature*). He also joined the Communist Party and for a while showed signs of pursuing an active career in politics. However, the success of his writing soon propelled him in another direction: to the forefront of Japan's literary avant-garde. His early short stories, such as *"Akai mayu"* (*1950*, "Red Cocoon"), were brilliant examples of a uniquely personal genre and they contained many of the ideas that he would later develop at length in his novels.

"Red Cocoon" immediately addresses the question of rootlessness which lies at the heart of Abe's creations. The story's narrator can find no reason for living and would gladly hang himself if only he could comprehend why he has no home. Perhaps, he thinks, he has simply forgotten which house belongs to him, yet he has no means of identifying the correct one. The story then flows smoothly into a dream narrative as the unfortunate man snatches at "a bit of sticky silk thread," pulls, and begins to unravel his leg. Of its own accord the thread forms a cocoon around him, all the while diminishing his body. "Yes, I have a house now," says the man, "but there is no me to come home to it." In the words of William

Currie (who analyzes "Red Cocoon" in *Approaches to the Modern Japanese Short Story*): "Abe has seized upon the perfect metaphor for an alienated person who labors to secure a place in society, but loses himself in the process."

To read "Red Cocoon" is to approach the artistic essence of Abe Kōbō, for despite its brevity and lack of development it expresses a vision of alienated man which runs through all of his later work. In writing it Abe brushed aside the aesthetic preoccupations of his literary predecessors to create a new genre based on the work of Franz Kafka. As MISHIMA YUKIO pointed out (in his introduction to *New Writing in Japan*), Abe took exactly what he needed from Kafka, then continued on his own way through "a literary no-man's-land" without further reference to Western literature. That he could not return, either, to Japanese tradition was also apparent to Mishima. After calling Abe's poetic sensibility "the hollow, desiccated and blank glare of high noon," he made this often-quoted comment: "In the history of Japanese literature since the *Tale of Genji*, a thousand years ago, it would be difficult to find any writer who has eradicated so successfully the high 'humidity' content of traditional Japanese literature."

Despite the mixed reactions of other writers, Abe's reputation was already secure as early as 1951 when he was awarded the Akutagawa Prize for his novella "Kabe – Esu Karuma shi no hanzai" ("The Wall – The Crime of Mr. S. Karma"). Like "Red Cocoon" and other early stories, including *"Baberu no tō no tanuki"* (*1951*, "A Badger in the Tower of Babel") and *"Mahō no chōku"* (*1950*, "The Magic Chalk"), it deals with the subject of metamorphosis in human beings. No English version exists, which is surprising in view of the fact that Abe has since gained such a wide following in the West.

By far the best-known of all of Abe's works is *Suna no onna* (1962, *The Woman in the Dunes*). In 1963 it was made into a film by Teshigahara Hiroshi, whose interpretation has become recognized as one of the classics of the Japanese cinema. Indeed, many English and American people who have never read *any* Japanese literature have seen the film version of *The Woman in the Dunes* and have been mesmerized by its intensity.

Although it is not as extreme in its abstraction as some of Abe's other novels, *The Woman in the Dunes* is the work of a skilled reductionist. Two of the author's early obsessions – mathematics and insect collecting – are woven neatly into the plot. The central figure, Niki Jumpei, is a schoolteacher who collects sand insects, mainly because he is fascinated by the restless instability of sand and its apparent unsuitability for supporting life. He questions whether a stationary condition is absolutely indispensable for existence, and reasons: "Didn't unpleasant competition arise precisely because one tried to cling to a fixed position?" With this thought in mind he travels to a lonely promontory in the hope of discovering some new specimens of sand beetle. As night falls he asks the villagers – who appear to live among the dunes – whether they can find him somewhere to stay. Obligingly, they lower him into a deep hole where, at the bottom, lives a thirty-year-old widow in a ramshackle hut. Only when the rope ladder is withdrawn does Jumpei realize he is trapped.

For the remainder of the novel the author examines Jumpei's behavior much as a scientist observes the behavior of an insect. Will he escape and return to the real world, or will he adapt to living in his new, inhospitable environment? Throughout much of the novel Abe applies a reductionist technique, seeking the essence of human experience in the modern world by reducing both characters and their settings to symbolic terms. To live like an insect in shifting sand may be seen as an existential metaphor: a state of living which differs from everyday life only in degree, not in its essential conditions.

Mocking humor underlies *The Woman in the Dunes*, and indeed most of Abe's work. Such humor should be a signal for the critic to be wary of assigning specific meanings to this author's inventions, for very often they hover just on the verge of meaning yet still beyond the reach of a rational mind. In *Crisis in Identity*, Arthur G. Kimball makes a good attempt at analyzing the social, sexual, and metaphysical dimensions of *The Woman in the Dunes*, yet even he would admit that Abe – unlike an insect – is not easily pinned down. Setting problems for critics soon came to replace insect collecting as Abe's favorite pastime.

Tanin no kao (1964, *The Face of Another*) is one of Abe's least appealing novels. Overwritten and underdramatized it is the story of a man who fashions a realistic mask to conceal the facial injuries he sustained in a laboratory experiment. When he comes to wear the mask he not only suffers an identity crisis but discovers some unwelcome truths about modern society that would otherwise, and perhaps best, remain hidden. The novel is divided into three "notebooks" which are left, at the beginning of the narrative, in an empty apartment where they await the reader. As one later discovers, the "reader" is intended to be the narrator's wife, for it is she who has been the chief victim of the mask over the past few months. Having rejected her husband ever since his accident, she is subsequently seduced by him when he wears the "face of another." The notebooks contain a full explanation – and an apology, of sorts.

Chiefly they dwell upon the narrator's anguish, especially in those moments when he is overcome by jealousy while playing the twin roles of seducer and cuckold simultaneously.

Written as though its author were in a mood of resignation and despair (one can never be sure with Abe), *The Face of Another* only rarely enlightens and scarcely ever entertains. It is a sour novel, culminating in the truly poisonous remark: "Perhaps the act of writing is necessary only when nothing happens." Readers who are prepared to pay the author several hours of their lives are given in exchange a few flashes of brilliance, often expressed as one-line slogans ("Man's soul is in his skin") or disturbing similes (wearing the mask is "like having the house taken over when one has let but one room"). Apart from these isolated sugar pills the novel is a bitter and woefully meandering polemic which condemns modern society for its failure to see beneath surface appearances.

A lifelong interest in the stage prompted Abe to create several theatrical plays, one of the most notable of which is *Tomodachi* (*1967, Friends*), available in English translation. Highly inventive and well-crafted, *Friends* is very reminiscent of Pirandello. Indeed, it might be called "Eight Relatives in Search of a Ninth," for it depicts an aggressively benevolent family hell-bent on befriending a lonely bachelor. In the process they completely disrupt his life, seduce his fiancée, and bring about his untimely death. They are, of course, ghosts from the past: memories of tightly knit Family Units that still haunt the waking dreams of urban man. The hero's failure to keep them at bay is almost an admission by the author that his ideal – the condition of rootlessness – is sometimes impossible to defend.

Abe's determined defense of rootlessness is well argued in an essay that may be found, in English, in *Japan Quarterly* (vol. 22, nos. 2–3, 1975). Titled *"Uchi naru henkyō,"* ("The Frontier Within"), it discusses the tension between rooted and uprooted peoples, focusing on the historical position of the Jews in Western society and giving reasons for Abe's lifelong love affair with Jewish culture. He suggests that Jews were persecuted because they never developed "ties to the soil" – the deep, emotional ties of place which prevailing human orthodoxy demands. Instead they clustered into the cities to take those jobs available to them, becoming in the process thoroughly urbanized and dissociated from any links to the land. As a result, Abe claims, Jewish people were seen as representing all the evils of the city: encroaching into the countryside and threatening centuries-old ways of life.

Whether or not one agrees with Abe's analysis, one has to admire its quirky ingenuity. He dismisses the obvious objection (that the

Jews were sustained in their rootlessness because they had a clear idea of their ancestral homeland) by saying that Israel is a modern invention. Furthermore, he goes on to claim that Japan has an incipient "Jewish problem" even though it has no Jewish population of any significant size. There, he says, tension between city and land was clearly apparent when provincial lords took over the cities during the *Meiji Restoration. The tension is now largely undefined because there are no convenient scapegoats to focus upon, but it still exists as an abstract, embryonic form of "anti-Semitism."

According to Abe, "all orthodoxies are bound together by an agrarian motif." He seemed to dislike agrarian motifs with a special passion, and being habitually unorthodox he could not abide the idea that high culture evolves naturally from a love of the land. Indeed, so often in his novels did he reveal a distaste even for the force of gravity, that one may very well question whether he thought a love of the Earth – let alone love for any specific part of it – a necessary condition for artistic expression. In non-Israeli Jewish culture he detected a mode of thought liberated from the land and consequently heretical, subversive, and irresistible. Most of all he admired the apparent ease with which Jewish writers appear to touch a universal plane of significance in their work. That, at last, may be the crux of the matter. Abe, like his fellow existentialist Albert Camus, was an ambitious writer: and he probably found the way of Kafka an easier route to artistic success than the way of Tolstoy.

In addition to the aforementioned play, Abe's second major work of 1967 was *Moetsukita chizu* (*The Ruined Map*), a tale of urban alienation told in the manner of a detective thriller. Not an easy novel to read, it is nonetheless gripping and suspenseful, describing how the unnamed narrator – a private detective – tries to locate an applicant's missing husband. Scarcely any clues are available: only a crumpled newspaper and a worn-out matchbox containing two different sorts of matches. The man is one of thousands who vanish in the city every year, but in this instance there is no body, no murder, no motive, no crime. In fact, the whole novel is the antithesis of a detective story in all but its manner of telling. After some dreamlike sequences, in which the city's population fades from view leaving only the buildings intact, the narrator himself goes missing. It is a somewhat predictable ending, devised by a storyteller whose sense of irony is almost mathematical.

For most of his career Abe chose to remain with the surreal and the Kafkaesque rather than delve directly into science fiction. An exception is *Dai yon kampyō-ki* (*1958–59, Inter Ice Age 4*), one of his early works which is, incidentally, one of his most satisfying. It unfolds a delightfully implausible scenario with the aim of examining present-day attitudes toward the future. In a postscript Abe said: "The real future, I think, manifests itself like a 'thing,' beyond the abyss that separates it from the present, beyond the value judgments of the present . . ." And in the story itself he raised many ethical questions, which, by his own admission, are impossible to answer.

Professor Katsumi, the central figure of *Inter Ice Age 4*, discovers that a government institution is secretly purchasing large numbers of human fetuses. Understandably appalled, not least because his own wife has been tricked into aborting their child to swell the numbers even further, he investigates and comes across a project of enormous dimensions. Human beings up to the age of eight have been bred to exist underwater: a feat achieved by diverting evolutionary growth from the point at which gills develop in the embryo. And not only human beings, but fishlike dogs, pigs, and cows have also been created – all with the object of preserving land-based creatures when the polar ice caps finally melt. If the reader is sufficiently shocked into thinking the whole scenario absurd, then Abe would probably be well pleased. His purpose is to show how, under the stimulus of potential extinction, the human race would inevitably try to create a variation of itself to survive a changed environment. Moreover, in looking back toward the present from the vantage point of the future, he projects himself into the minds of the aquatic people and finds them surprisingly tolerant of their ancestors. Acceptance of the eternal present, he suggests, tends to override our sense of continuity with the past.

Hako otoko (1973, *The Box Man*) suffers from having a disjointed narrative line, but is well worth reading for the power of its final chapter. The narrator, a thirty-year-old photographer, opens the story by firing an air rifle at a mysterious stranger who wears a large cardboard box. Feeling guilty, but at the same time fascinated, the photographer casually begins to make his own portable "shell" from the carton in which his new freezer has been delivered. He cuts the appropriate observation window, equips it with a vinyl curtain, and subsequently takes to living in the streets until he, too, is hit by an air rifle bullet.

Moving on from the niggling details which always occur in Abe's most shipshape novels, the story finally gets under way. The box man, having photographed his assailant, is able to identify him as the doctor who treats him in hospital. Even more strange is the fact that the doctor's beautiful young nurse has offered him 50,000 yen if only he will stop wearing the box. After many twists, turns, and temporary changes of narrator the story culminates in the termination of a love affair between the box man and the nurse. Now the meaning of the novel becomes a little more clear. It deals with the relationship of self to others, depicting how modern man conceals himself in a labyrinth of his own creation. An intensely sad conclusion shows the box man projecting his problem onto the girl, fondly imagining that she searches for him in the labyrinth. In reality, she has left.

Similarities between *The Face of Another* and *The Box Man* will be all too apparent to the reader. In both of them the hero spends a lot of time concealing himself from the gaze of others. He wishes to see without being seen: the classic syndrome of the voyeur. The repetition of the idea, with its great emphasis on fashioning the mask in the first novel and equipping the box in the second, leads one to suppose that Abe was writing to a formula. It is as though his underlying thoughts remained stationary while only the metaphors were changed from one novel to the next.

Mikkai (1977, *Secret Rendezvous*) was Abe's next important novel and it dropped voyeurism in favor of eavesdropping, which is not even superficially different. Its setting is a vast, Kafkaesque hospital where every room and corridor is bugged with secret transmitters. Private conversations of patients and staff are relayed to a central security resource where they are taped by a bank of endlessly running tape recorders. However, despite gaining access to this information, the hero is quite unable to trace his wife, who, like the husband in *The Ruined Map*, has completely disappeared: kidnapped by hospital staff in the dead of night. The narrator-hero not only compiles notebooks reminiscent of the chronicles in *The Face of Another*, but stumbles upon a scandalous project that might have surprised even Professor Katsumi in *Inter Ice Age 4*. As so often happens in Abe's novels, the plot becomes cluttered with its own richness and confused with half-remembered echoes from the author's previous works. Yet this is probably what Abe intended. When a minor character turns into cotton (and is subsequently woven into a quilt and placed in a museum), we are witnessing the original metaphor of "Red Cocoon" making a guest appearance.

A merciful silence reigned for eight years after the publication of *Secret Rendezvous*. During this time Abe concentrated on experimental film, video and theater, touring the United States with his own theater company in 1979. He broke his "silence" with the eagerly awaited novel *Hakobune Sakuramaru* (1984, *The Ark Sakura*). For the first two hundred pages it appears to have been his best work since *The Woman in the Dunes*, but when the narrator traps his foot in the lavatory it is as though the author himself has suffered a seizure of the imagination. The narrator's plight must surely be seen as a symbol of the author's inability to advance the action of an otherwise promising novel.

The lavatory in question is actually the centerpiece of the Ark Sakura, the underground fallout shelter that Mole, the narrator, has built in a disused stone mine. Years ago, when the mine was still in use, Mole was traumatized because his father chained him to the lavatory for days on end. Now, erroneously believing he has overcome his childhood fears, he turns the mine into his private domain, equipped with weapons, food, and booby traps to deter trespassers. When the "ark" is almost finished to his satisfaction he searches for suitable people to whom he can give "tickets for survival." Those who appeal most strongly to him are an insect dealer and his two *sakura* ("shills" who pose as customers to encourage trade): a quick-witted young man and his delectable girlfriend. Mole is attracted to them on account of their unusual product, the tiny insect *eupcaccia*, that does nothing except move endlessly in anticlockwise circles consuming its own excrement. In fact, the disposal of waste matter is of consuming interest to Mole, who is later revealed to be financing his venture by flushing industrial wastes, illegally, down his monstrous underground lavatory.

Alas, in *The Ark Sakura*, Abe the storyteller is at odds with Abe the symbolist. It is essential to his initial concept that Mole should gradually turn into the *eupcaccia* insect, even though the metamorphosis is bound to ruin the story. When Mole becomes stuck in his own waste disposal unit, the novel goes so badly awry that even its imagery seems threadbare. Gone is the subtle dialogue indicating the tense relationships of the four main characters, and in its place is a confusion of activity. The insect dealer takes control of an army of fascist pensioners ... Mole's father is killed and brought to the cavern ... a group of high school girls is presumed lost in the lower bowels of the mine. Eventually, Abe is forced to abandon his nightmarish realism for a misty, dreamlike ending – perhaps the only possible escape for author and reader alike.

Abe Kōbō had the ability to create a supreme masterpiece of surrealist fiction to add to his fine achievement, *The Woman in the Dunes*, yet he never did. Like John Fowles in England he was compulsively experimental, often to the detriment of the quality of his work. He refused to be constricted by tried and tested forms, saying: "To specify a form – any form – for prose is to circumscribe the potential of the genre." Here once again Abe was standing in direct opposition to orthodox opinion. Had he not been part of Japan's literary establishment he might well have been called the

Novelist in Opposition, a writer whose function it is to disagree with others.

In real life, far from the claustrophobic world of his imagination, Abe Kōbō lived on the outskirts of Tokyo and was married to the artist, Abe Machi, who illustrated many of his works with her accomplished drawings. Abe died in Tokyo Hospital on January 22, 1993, after a short illness.

RECOMMENDED READING

Novels

The Ark Sakura. *Hakobune Sakuramaru.* 1984. 336 pages. Tr. Juliet W. Carpenter. Knopf, NY, 1988; Secker and Warburg, London, 1988; Vintage Paperback, NY, 1989. Abe's longest work in English translation, elegantly produced in Knopf version.
Inter Ice Age 4. *Dai yon kampyō-ki.* 1958–59. 228 pages. Tr. E. Dale Saunders. Knopf, NY, 1969; Tuttle, Tokyo, 1971; Berkley Pub., NY, 1972; G.P. Putnam's Sons, NY, 1981. One of Abe's most entertaining novels. Pure science fiction.
The Woman in the Dunes. *Suna no onna.* 1962. 241 pages. Tr. E. Dale Saunders. Knopf, NY, 1964; Secker and Warburg, London, 1965; Berkley Pub., NY, 1965; Tuttle, Tokyo, 1967; Random House, NY, 1972; Oxford University Press, Oxford, 1987; Vintage Paperback, NY, 1991. Abe's classic novel, filmed by Teshigahara Hiroshi.

WORKS IN ENGLISH TRANSLATION

Novels

The Ark Sakura. Hakobune Sakuramaru. 1984.
The Box Man. Hako otoko. 1973. 178 pages. Tr. E. Dale Saunders, Knopf, NY, 1974; Tuttle, Tokyo, 1975; G.P. Putnam's Sons, NY, 1980; North Point Press, San Francisco, 1991 paperback.
The Face of Another. Tanin no kao. 1964. 237 pages. Tr. E. Dale Saunders. Knopf, NY, 1966; Weidenfeld & Nicholson, London, 1969; Penguin, Harmondsworth, 1972; G.P. Putnam's Sons, NY, 1980; Kodansha International, Tokyo, NY, 1992.
Inter Ice Age 4. Dai yon kampyō-ki. 1958–59.

The Ruined Map. Moetsukita chizu. 1967. 299 pages. Tr. E. Dale Saunders. Knopf, NY, 1966; G.P. Putnam's Sons, NY, 1980, 1981 paperback; Kodansha International, Tokyo, NY, 1993.
Secret Rendezvous. Mikkai. 1977. 179 pages. Tr. Juliet W. Carpenter. Knopf, NY, 1979; Secker and Warburg, London, 1980; G.P. Putnam's Sons, NY, 1980, 1981 paperback.
The Woman in the Dunes. Suna no onna. 1962.

Short Fiction Collection

Beyond the Curve. 247 pages. Tr. Juliet Winters Carpenter. Kodansha International, Tokyo and

NY, 1991. Includes: "The Crime of S. Karma," "The Dream Soldier," "Beyond the Curve."

Short Fiction

"Beguiled." "Yūwakusha." 1957. 16 pages. Beyond the Curve.

"The Bet." "Kake." 1960. 30 pages. Beyond the Curve.

"Beyond the Curve." "Kābu no mukō." 1966. 25 pages. Beyond the Curve.

"The Cliff of Time." "Toki no gake." 1964. 29 pages. Tr. Andrew Horvat. Four Stories by Kōbō Abe. Hara Shobo, Tokyo, 1973.

"The Crime of S. Karma." "S. Karuma-shi no hanzai." Extract from "Kabe" ("The Wall"). 1951. 8 pages. Beyond the Curve.

"The Deaf Girl." "Oshi musume." 1949. 27 pages. Four Stories by Kōbō Abe.

"The Dog." "Inu." 1954. 7 pages. Tr. Andrew Horvat. Japan Quarterly, vol. 19, no. 1, 1972; Four Stories by Kōbō Abe.

"The Dream Soldier." "Yume no heishi." 1957. 6 pages. (1) Tr. Andrew Horvat. Japan Quarterly, vol. 19, no. 1, 1972; Four Stories by Kōbō Abe; Murder in Japan, ed. John L. Apostolou and Martin H. Greenberg. Dembner Books, NY, 1987. (2) Beyond the Curve.

"The Flood." "Kōzui." 1976. 6 pages. Tr. Lane Dunlop. A Late Chrysanthemum. North Point Press, San Francisco, 1986.

"Dendrocacalia." "Dendorokaka-riya." 1949. 22 pages. Beyond the Curve.

"Intruders." "Chinnyūsha." 1951. 34 pages. Beyond the Curve.

"An Irrelevant Death." "Mukankei na shi." 1961. 15 pages. Beyond the Curve.

"The Life of a Poet." "Shijin no shōgai." 1951. 14 pages. Beyond the Curve.

"The Magic Chalk." "Mahō no chōku." 1950. 12 pages. Tr. Alison Kibrick. The Shōwa Anthology, vol. 1. Kodansha International, Tokyo, 1985.

"Noah's Ark." "Noa no hakobune." 1952. 15 pages. Beyond the Curve.

"Record of a Transformation." "Henkei no kiroku." 1954. 22 pages. Beyond the Curve.

"Red Cocoon." "Akai mayu." 1950. 3 pages. (1) Tr. John Nathan. Japan Quarterly, vol. 13, no. 2, 1966; New Writing in Japan, ed. Mishima Yukio and Geoffrey Bownas. Penguin Books, Harmondsworth, 1972. (2) Tr. Lane Dunlop. A Late Chrysanthemum.

"Song of a Dead Girl." "Shinda musume ga utatta." 1954. 14 pages. Tr. Stuart A. Harrington. The Journal of Literary Translation, no. 17, 1986; The Mother of Dreams. Kodansha International, Tokyo, 1986.

"The Special Envoy." "Shisha." 1958. 16 pages. Beyond the Curve.

"Stick." "Bō." 1955. 5 pages. Details as for "Red Cocoon."

"Uniform." "Seifuku." 1955. 20 pages. Tr. Noah S. Brannen. Japan Christian Quarterly, vol. 45, no. 4, 1979.

Plays

Friends. Tomodachi. 1967. 55 pages. Tr. Donald Keene. Grove Press, NY, 1969; Tuttle, Tokyo, 1971. Contemporary Japanese Literature, ed. Howard Hibbett. Knopf, NY, 1977.

The Man Who Turned into a Stick. Bō ni natta otoko. 1969. 84 pages. Tr. Donald Keene. University of Tokyo Press, Tokyo, 1975.

You, Too, Are Guilty. Omae nimo tsumi ga aru. First performed

Jan. 1, 1965, at the Actor's Theater, Tokyo, and also published in 1965. Revised version completed 1978. 38 pages. Tr. Ted T. Takaya. *Modern Japanese Drama, An Anthology*. Columbia University Press, NY, 1979.

CRITICAL STUDIES

Currie, William Joseph. "Abe Kōbō: 'Red Cocoon,' 'Stick.'" *Approaches to the Modern Japanese Short Story*, ed. Thomas E. Swann and Kinya Tsuruta. Waseda University Press, Tokyo, 1982.

———. "Abe Kōbō: *The Woman in the Dunes*." *Approaches to the Modern Japanese Novel*, ed. Thomas E. Swann and Kinya Tsuruta. Sophia University, Tokyo, 1976.

———. "Metaphors of Alienation: The Fiction of Abe, Beckett and Kafka." Ph.D. diss., University of Michigan, Ann Arbor, 1973.

Hardin, Nancy S. "An Interview with Abe Kōbō." *Contemporary Literature*, no. 15, 1974.

Korges, James. "Abe and Ōoka: Identity and Mind-Body." *Critique: Studies in Modern Fiction*, vol. 10, no. 2, 1968.

Lidin, Olof G. "Abe Kōbō's *Mikkai*: A Discussion." *Man and Society in Japan Today*, 1984.

———. "Abe Kōbō's Philosophy of Box." *Transcultural Understanding and Modern Japan*, 1983.

McDonald, Keiko I. "Contemporary Man's Plight: An Analysis of *The Box Man*." *Literature East and West*, no. 21, 1977.

Morishige, Alyce Hisae Kawazoe. "The Theme of the Self in Modern Japanese Fiction: Studies on Dazai, Mishima, Abe, and Kawabata." Ph.D. diss., Michigan State University, East Lansing, 1970.

Richter, Frederick. "A Comparative Approach to Abe Kōbō's 'S. Karuma-shi no hanzai.'" *Journal of the Association of Teachers of Japanese*, vol. 9, nos. 2–3, 1974.

Taeusch, Carl F. "Abe Kōbō and the Absurd Image." *Dodder*, no. 2, 1970.

Tsuruta, Kinya. "An Interpretation of *The Ruined Map* by Kōbō Abe." *Postwar Trends in Japan*, 1975.

Yamamoto, Fumiko. "Metamorphosis in Abe Kōbō's Works." *Journal of the Association of Teachers of Japanese*, vol. 15, no. 2, 1980.

Yamanouchi, Hisaaki. "Abe Kōbō and Ōe Kenzaburō: The Search for Identity in Modern Japanese Literature." *Modern Japan: Aspects of History, Literature and Society*, 1975.

Essays

"The Frontier Within." "*Uchi naru henkyō*." 17 pages. Tr. Andrew Horvat. *Japan Quarterly*, vol. 22, nos. 2–3, 1975.

AKUTAGAWA Ryūnosuke
(1892–1927)

Writer of short fiction. Born and educated in Tokyo, and a lifelong resident there.

One of the most compelling writers of the twentieth century, Akutagawa Ryūnosuke was also the first from modern Japan to gain a reputation in the West during his own lifetime. He wrote more than a hundred short stories, two of which were brought to the screen by Kurosawa Akira in the 1950 film classic *Rashōmon*. Yet even though his works have been frequently translated into many Western languages since the 1920s, the details of Akutagawa's life – other than the fact of his suicide in 1927 – are not widely known. If they were, he might well acquire overseas the legendary status he has long held in Japan. There, not only is his name enshrined in the twice-yearly Akutagawa Prize awarded to up-and-coming writers for works of fiction, but his own extraordinary attempt to become the supreme modern writer is accepted as an inspiration, even though, by his own admission, it ended in failure.

Perhaps it is paradoxical to say that a writer has "failed" when he has so obviously made a substantial contribution to world literature. Be that as it may, paradox is scarcely a phenomenon which is unfamiliar to anyone who studies Akutagawa. For a start, his work positively invites a variety of interpretations while negating any single, definitive interpretation. This is a quality he himself identified as a hallmark of great literature when he said: ". . . a good work is like Mount Lu; it is many-sided, and therefore encourages viewing from many angles." Indeed, his art is first and foremost the embodiment of ambiguity. The meanings of his stories often seem to be balanced on a knife edge, wavering between hope and despair, beauty and ugliness, free will and determinism. Such poised ambiguity makes for a literature that is never tedious or dull, yet its very suggestiveness awakens a desire for further explanation. One wishes that Akutagawa could have written at length like his mentor, NATSUME SŌSEKI. But then again one feels – is *made* to feel – the absurdity of applying quantitative yardsticks in matters of art. After all, as one of Japanese literature's most committed aesthetes, Akutagawa stated: "Human life cannot compare with a single line from Baudelaire."

Born in Tokyo, the son of a dairyman called Niihara Toshizō, Akutagawa was adopted by his uncle (Akutagawa Dōshō) because his mother went insane nine months after his birth. She was, he recalled, "an extremely well-behaved lunatic," and she paid him no attention whatsoever. If we are to believe one of his late, autobiographical works he was raised exclusively on cow's milk rather than feeding from his mother's breast. That the cow's milk was supplied by his father, the dairyman, seems probable – and from Niihara he also received his only other parental gift, the given-name Ryūnosuke which means "dragon-helper," because he was born at the dragon hour on a dragon day in the dragon month of a dragon year. Yet by being welcomed into his Uncle Dōshō's cultured household he cannot have been entirely underprivileged in his infancy. He developed an exceptional intelligence and was soon devouring the stories of Bakin (*Takizawa Bakin, 1767–1848), the great writer of popular fiction in the late Edo period.

It is easy to underestimate the influence of Bakin on the young Akutagawa. That he was an early role model is strongly suggested by Akutagawa's vivid portrait of him in one of his best works, *"Gesaku zammai"* (1917, "Absorbed in Letters"). In this story, the aging Bakin, his eyesight failing after a lifetime of writing *gesaku fiction, is troubled when an aggressive stranger in the public baths accuses him of not being able to write *haiku*. Worse still, he overhears someone say that his works are a sham and completely without substance. On returning home he finds his publisher waiting impatiently for his next manuscript, and later he recalls being criticized by a student for not keeping a resident disciple. The cumulative effect of all this external pressure is echoed by the encroaching darkness as Bakin's seemingly wasted day draws to a close. But before it does so, the old man is briefly caught up in the everyday trivialities of his household. He plays with his grandson, Tarō, who impishly tells him to be more patient, because "the Kwannon of Asakusa said so." Finally, when the house is quiet, and as if inspired by Tarō's message from the gods, Bakin works through the night on his manuscript *The Tale of Eight Dogs*. This description of Bakin at work is one of the most moving in Japanese literature, for there, in the flickering lamplight, is not only Bakin but Akutagawa himself – and indeed every man who struggles to keep back the darkness by becoming absorbed in letters.

Akutagawa's renowned "bookishness" is completely vindicated by *Gesaku zammai*. Even as a student he believed that art was supreme and immaculate: existing on a higher plane, beyond the corruption of the real world. Books, in particular, he loved with a religious intensity and his later stories often contained scenes in which the narrator visits a bookshop for spiritual renewal. His personal reading at high school included de Maupassant, Anatole France, Strindberg, and Dostoievsky. He then went on to discover Ōgai and Sōseki, the two giants of Japanese literature in the late Meiji period.

In 1913 Akutagawa entered the English Literature department of Tokyo Imperial University where his closest friends were KIKUCHI KAN and Kume Masao. All three were aspiring writers, who, despite their differing personalities and abilities, were in agreement on the need to challenge the dominance of *Naturalism with its narrow emphasis on real-life observation. More sophisticated than most of their contemporaries, they believed that fiction should be fictional and not restricted to reproducing reality. In working toward this end, Akutagawa, unlike his friends, gained almost immediate recognition. His first story, "*Rōnen*" (*1914*, "Old Age"), was published in one of the university's literary magazines, *Shinshichō*. It was followed by "*Rashōmon*" in the November 1915 issue of *Teikoku Bungaku*, and by "*Hana*" ("The Nose") in *1916*. Natsume Sōseki (whom Akutagawa idolized to the extent of becoming tongue-tied in Sōseki's classes) was so impressed by "*Hana*" that he took the unusual step of praising it in public. Reprinted in *Shinshōsetsu*, "*Hana*" was widely read as a consequence of Sōseki's generous endorsement.

Looking back on Akutagawa's early work, one is struck most of all by the author's versatility. Where "*Rashōmon*" is grim, intense, and visionary, *"Hana"* is light, ironic, and genuinely funny. Even in English translation both stories are as impressive today as when Akutagawa first penned them seventy years ago. *"Rashōmon,"* in particular, gives ample evidence of its author's exceptional powers of visualization. He later wrote a critical essay on this very topic, entitled "Composition That Makes One Visualize." In it he quoted a line from Sōseki's "Spring Miscellanies": "As I opened the wooden door and stepped outside, I saw a horse's tracks, large and brimming with rainwater." Akutagawa commented: "With just one sentence, the impression of a country road full of rain puddles is vividly created. I like this type of writing."

Visualization apart, it is worth noting that Akutagawa prefaces the above statement by saying "with just one sentence." In other words, he favored brevity, and as a skilled *haiku* poet he was unlikely ever to become long-winded in his prose. During the mid-1920s when he came to admire SHIGA NAOYA's vast and rambling *An'ya kōro* (1921–37, *A Dark Night's Passing*), his comments betray just a hint of professional envy quite unrelated to the feelings of spiritual inferiority which that work provoked in him. For in Shiga he witnessed an Oriental artist composing on a grand scale: a feat he would have dearly loved to emulate. In a famous argument with TANIZAKI JUN'ICHIRŌ he tried to defend his own idea of literature against Tanizaki's call for larger, architectural structures, but he knew that his art would never accommodate such elements. Highly ambitious, Akutagawa wanted to hold center stage, but with his carefully wrought miniatures he found it hard to compete with the longer rhythms of Western fiction, let alone Tanizaki's elaborate structures or the recorded harmony between life and art exemplified by Shiga. He could only resign himself to remaining a miniaturist, albeit one who often practiced a cunning manipulation of his own literary method. For example, in the above-mentioned story "Absorbed in Letters," he transfers his so-called problem of "short-windedness" into the "long-windedness" for which Bakin is criticized by the stranger. By neatly reversing the problem, Akutagawa gives us yet another indication of his mastery of multilayered meanings, encapsulated in just a few lines of prose.

Akutagawa had no illusions about the difficulties of writing a novel – or for that matter any other sort of fiction – and he considered them to be almost insuperable. On the one hand the novelist had to pay attention to the everyday texture of life, to the details of people's actions and behavior – and hence compose his work with the dry, meticulous methods of an historian. On the other hand he needed to transmit a sense of life's essence, a sense of its primal energy – without which a novel would be as flat as (he claimed) was Flaubert's *Madame Bovary*. Since lyric poetry came much closer than any other literary form to expressing the spirit of life, the novelist had first to be a poet and only then an historian.

These ideas correspond very closely to those held by MORI ŌGAI, and, like so many modern insights, they came directly from Nietzsche. But whereas Ōgai merely acknowledged the importance of what Nietzsche called the Dionysian element in art (and then went his own, Apollonian way), Akutagawa wanted to bring the two elements into balance. He tried to do it stylistically, by creating a beautiful, polished style that always suggests pure, Apollonian control, while loading the content of his works with unadulterated Dionysian energy.

Ultimately, this technique failed him. Instead of bringing Dionysus and Apollo into harmony, he put them at odds with each other. Rarely did he try, as perhaps he should have done, to harmonize the Nietzschean elements within his style and within his themes separately. Had he not despised the Naturalists he might have listened to TAYAMA KATAI's dictum: ". . . blunt words for blunt ideas." Rather, he preferred Akutagawa's method, which might be called "elegant words for energetic ideas."

In matters of style, Akutagawa always emphasized precision and control. He disbelieved artists who claimed that their ideas sprang directly from their unconscious minds, and said: "So-called unconscious creative activities remind me of the imaginary seashell vainly sought by the nobleman in the old tale." Clearly, he was not willing to compromise on this issue, and probably saw no reason for doing so because his writing gave every appearance of being the product of a powerful imagination. In fact, Akutagawa seems to have had no inkling of what Aldous Huxley called the "fictional plane" of the mind: that often garrulous brokerage department in the brain which can be opened or closed at will by the skilled writer of fiction. With no great powers of invention, Akutagawa took much of his material from little-known texts, especially the book of 1,100 stories (written in the twelfth century) called *Konjaku monogatari* (*Tales of Times Now Past*). From this book came the settings for both "Rashōmon" and "Hana," and throughout his career Akutagawa continued to plunder ancient tales like a magpie stealing objects for its nest. (Indeed, he suggested in "Cogwheels" – his autobiographical masterpiece – that the magpie was his muse. "Whenever [the magpies] came," he said, "the words came to me too.") So, unlike Tanizaki who always gave his imagination a long leash, Akutagawa made his own imagination the guide dog of the intellect. He knew exactly what he wanted to say, and saw the literary process as being none other than finding (chiefly from books) the right words, settings, and plots which would enable him to say it.

The result, far from being what he may have hoped for at the outset of his career, was the exact opposite. Instead of building great and beautiful literary structures in which the life-spirit gives strength and suppleness to the whole, Akutagawa wrote stories that are fragile mosaics, often brittle in their texture, and distinctly odd. Each one seems to contain unlimited potential imprisoned in a slender cage, while each reading extracts an ever-increasing number of open-ended ambiguities. To read Akutagawa is like entering a hall of mirrors. It can be a very disorienting experience.

Even in describing Akutagawa the man, critics are often defeated by paradox. Howard Hibbett, in his introduction to Takashi Kojima's 1952 selection, *Rashomon and Other Stories*, says: "To sketch the background and temperament of Akutagawa Ryūnosuke is to risk a melancholy cliché." Going on to say that he was "brilliant, sensitive, cynical, neurotic . . . ," he adds that he was also "aloof, elusive, individual," and to the reader "remains withdrawn behind the polished facade of his collected works." Obviously no one can be an individual cliché (a contradiction in terms), so Akutagawa is left remote and mysterious.

The above comments are insufficient to give Western readers an image of Akutagawa as a person. Glenn W. Shaw does better in quoting Kikuchi Kan, who, writing in 1921, said that during their schooldays together the first thing he noticed about Akutagawa was "the bright spot his red lips made in his pale white face." After describing how his friend tended "to pepper his conversation with paradoxes," Kikuchi tells of how, in 1923, Akutagawa turned down several offers of professorships at prestigious universities in order to have more time to read. Constantly hanging on his door was a sign saying: "Sick. Compliments to Callers."

Perhaps, after all, Akutagawa really *was* aloof and elusive, and "played with life with silver tweezers" as his friends would have us believe. Yet he is also known to have had a six-month love affair while still an undergraduate, and later in life (in 1918) he married and became the father of three sons, born in 1920, 1922, and 1925. One of these sons became an accomplished actor. There is also plenty of evidence to suggest that Akutagawa, unlike the physically robust Tayama Katai, was never shy with women and enjoyed making new sexual conquests even after his marriage. He was rumored to have had an affair with the poet Kujō Takeko, although his reluctance to confide personal secrets – even to his closest friend Kume Masao – is demonstrated in his brief, impressionistic works of autobiography.

Akutagawa moved in mysterious ways, motivated by an intense desire to be the supreme god of literature. Unfortunately, the complete fulfillment of this desire was made more difficult by his refusal to address any conflicts in the society around him. He deliberately placed himself above and apart from society in order to create his art. Always highly self-conscious, he was probably aware of the dangers of failing to come to terms with contemporary life. Nonetheless he continued to act the role of the isolated artist who alone carries the torch of human culture. If we are to judge him from the portrait photographs that survive, Akutagawa, with his high forehead, his long, expressive fingers, and those intelligent, hooded eyes, looks like a man who would relish a complex role in life. Even when he was on the edge of insanity he could inject subtle humor into his own prose-portrait: sketching the paranoid genius who wanders around Tokyo's coffee bars only to panic when total strangers speak about him in hushed whispers. Such is the price of fame, but he enjoyed it, and wanted more of it.

For three years following his graduation in 1916, Akutagawa pursued the relatively humdrum occupation of teaching English at the Engineering Naval College in Yokosuka. But in the same manner as when he set aside his personal feelings (that unhappy love affair) to write "*Rashōmon*" and "*Hana*," he also largely ignored all the life experience he must have gained while teaching. In 1917 he wrote what he later called his "worst story," "*Chūtō*" ("The Robbers"), an exciting tale filled with lurid and sometimes exaggerated imagery. Nonetheless, it is technically a *tour de force*: well-plotted and well-resolved. Again set in twelfth-century Kyoto, it concerns two brothers, both of whom are in love with Shakin, a beautiful woman who leads a band of robbers. Among the characters a conflict between brotherly love and sexual passion is acted out on the stage of the decaying city. As in "*Rashōmon*," it is moral darkness that becomes the greatest threat to the protagonists. The one-eyed hero, Tarō, can barely see the difference between good and evil on the occasion of being tempted to leave his brother to face certain death. ("What he saw was but limitless night, he saw the depths of love and hate, like the night itself.") Yet instead of riding headlong into night by returning to the gate Rashōmon (the portal of darkness itself), Tarō, "his one eye shining like a light from a face that had been dark and grim," asserts his inner spark of conscience and rescues his brother.

Melodramatic though it may be, "The Robbers" is indicative of Akutagawa's great interest in Christianity. Not that he makes any direct reference to it in a story with a twelfth-century setting, but in making Tarō give up his opportunity to win Shakin by foul means, he imparts a Christian flavor which is unusual in Japanese literature. Indeed, Akutagawa greatly admired the Christian martyrs of Japan, and, in later stories, turned his attention to sixteenth-century Nagasaki where Christianity once flourished.

As a truth-seeker himself, Akutagawa regarded Christ as a great Romantic hero. At the same time he seems to have held the Japanese view that at least *some* social pressure is needed before an individual conscience can be triggered. For example, in his children's fable "*Shiro*" (*1923*, "The Dog Shiro"), a cowardly white dog fails to warn a neighboring animal that he is in imminent danger of being trapped by the dogcatcher. Bitterly ashamed, Shiro finds himself suddenly turned from white to black, and is promptly driven from his home by owners who fail to recognize him. As if in parody of the "doctrine of redemption by good works," Shiro is shown as leading the life of a Good Samaritan. His heroic adventures, now as a black dog bent on rescuing everyone in a crisis, become legendary – until, at last, after praying to the moon, he is restored to his original color. "*Shiro*" is a brilliant story, and one which strongly suggests that the threat of darkness – indeed, the *stigma* of darkness – can stimulate life's energies and turn them to a good purpose. Akutagawa's friend Kikuchi Kan made much the same point in his masterpiece "The Realm Beyond," while MISHIMA YUKIO (one of Akutagawa's greatest admirers) made it a central principle of his life.

Especially noticeable in Akutagawa's analysis of life's moral mechanisms is the implication of commonality as well as differences between Eastern and Western codes of behavior. They are, he seems to suggest, similar in essence but different in their expression. In "*Hankechi*" (1916, "The Handkerchief"), a professor contends that the samurai code of *bushidō* might, in essence, be profitably identified with the Christian spirit in order to help "revitalize Japan." But faced with a grieving woman who exemplifies the *bushidō* attitude of emotional concealment, the professor reconsiders his idea. Westerners would never understand. From their point of view, *bushidō* would seem mannered and inauthentic – like bad acting as described by Strindberg in a book he is reading. As always in Akutagawa's work, many interpretations are possible – but if one is inclined to regard the author as gently chiding the professor for doubting his native culture, the story gains immeasurably in power and conviction. Mishima called it "the ultimate short story," and one has to agree it ranks with the best.

No introduction to Akutagawa would be complete without reference to his masterpiece of fiction, "*Jigokuhen*" (*1918*, "Hell Screen"). As in "The Handkerchief," where the problem of interpretation hinges on the extent to which the author identifies with the central character, so, in "Hell Screen," one must judge whether any aspect of Akutagawa is represented by Yoshihide – the artist who kills the only person he loves (his daughter) in order to complete his painting of hell. On both counts the answer is surely the same.

Akutagawa is utterly detached from his story. No part of him is present in either the professor or the artist. Rather, they are figures in his own "painting of hell" – his portrayal of other people who do not share his vision of aesthetic truth. Far from being like Akutagawa, Yoshihide is not only his physical opposite but a complete realist in artistic style. Akutagawa abhorred realism. He thought it gave little opportunity for revealing the presence of what really exists: namely the vital spirit which informs life and gives it meaning and purpose. That is why he was so impressed by Van Gogh and Gauguin among modern artists, although he came to prefer Renoir for his "elegant beauty." Of course, an ambiguity is also present in "Hell Screen": in Akutagawa's vision of himself as a painter of hell, painting pictures of people who paint pictures . . . etc. But only in this sense is he Yoshihide. In other respects he is Yoshihide's polar opposite.

Akutagawa's oblique approach to literature, whereby he could remain unusually detached from his fictional actors, was one that was clearly suited to satirical writing. He was a gifted satirist, in the tradition of Voltaire and Swift. Every critic comments on the Swiftian mode he used for "*Kappa*" (*1927*, "The Kappa"), the story of how a man becomes a guest of strange, mythological creatures whose behavior parodies that of human beings. In fact, the story owes more to Anatole France's *Penguin Island* than to Swift's *Gulliver's Travels*, but it reads more like Swift than any other work that springs to mind. Part of its charm is the author's implied suggestion that his narrator sees the "other side" of life: the peculiar world of the life-worshiping Kappa. Among them is the poet Tokk who goes against Kappa religion by committing suicide. He is said to have lacked Faith, one of the three deciders of Kappa destiny, the others being Circumstance and Chance. In a conversation with Tokk's departed spirit, the narrator is told: "Really I have no regrets. If I get tired of this spiritual existence, I shall take a pistol and suicide back to life."

Akutagawa explored multiple points of view in "The Kappa" as in many of his more serious works. The most famous of these is "Yabu no naka" (*1922*, "In a Grove"), which provides most of the plot for Kurosawa's film *Rashōmon*. Told in the manner of a sophisticated detective story (not unlike those by the Swiss writer Friedrich Dürrenmatt, born 1921), it presents three conflicting versions of events leading up to the death of a samurai near the Yamashima stage road. Both the testimony of the bandit who is suspected of the crime, and that of the dead man's wife, are plausible, if contradictory. Yet when the victim's spirit speaks through a medium, he explains how his wife willingly cooperated in being raped by the stranger and how she subsequently suggested the murder of her husband. Even then the mystery is impenetrable, for neither wife nor robber can be identified as the killer, nor is it clear that the samurai dies as a result of stabbing himself after the others have left. In fact, he dies when an "invisible hand" removes the dagger – and this is the masterstroke of the story. For the unseen hand is surely that of the author, withdrawing his pen from the scene of a perfect crime. In teasing out the facts of the story, Akutagawa turns our attention away from the literal question of who has actually killed the samurai, towards the moral problem of who is to blame.

"In a Grove" portrays a perfect crime because all three characters share the moral burden equally (or, as we shall see, not at all). The samurai's greed in accepting the bandit's initial invitation to visit the grove where treasures are buried, the wife's betrayal of her husband, and the robber's natural criminality are all contributory causes of the samurai's death. Yet even together they do not completely determine his destiny, because in trying to commit suicide he is motivated by feelings of humiliation and an inability to bear the shame of returning to normal society. When the author himself withdraws the dagger, he does so as if on behalf of society, and lets him die. Since the author's sympathies lie, if anywhere, with the bandit (who alone takes responsibility for his actions) the real murderer turns out to be society – in other words, the reader! It is the reader who has been lured into the grove of the author's imagination in the hope of discovering some insight into life. There he discovers a "magpie's collection" of objects, characters, and events – culled from ancient texts and so arranged as to communicate the message that the spirit of life is altogether too energetic to be held in check by normal codes of social conduct. He is given no alternative but to identify with the unseen hand that sends the samurai to the spirit world.

Not all of Akutagawa's stories match the quality of "In a Grove," but many of them do. *"Hina"* (1923, "The Dolls"), *"Kareno-shō"* (1918, "Withered Fields"), *"Kesa to Moritō"* (1919, "Kesa and Moritō"), *"Kumo no ito"* (1918, "The Spider's Thread"), and *"Shūzanzu"* (1921, "Autumn Mountain") are brilliant examples of his fictional art. Unhappily, however, Akutagawa was under constant pressure to turn his attention to autobiographical writing. Not only had the Naturalist movement given rise to the *shishōsetsu* (the *I-Novel) but the new proletarian writers were gaining popularity by depicting the hardships they suffered. Akutagawa was becoming increasingly isolated. On one side he had to contend with the supreme genius of Tanizaki, whom he could tolerate, while on the other he felt compelled to challenge the fame of Shiga Naoya whom he found deeply disturbing. He wrote the Shiga-esque story *"Mikan"* (*1919*, "The Tangerines") as a prelude to launching himself into direct autobiography.

Akutagawa produced two sets of personal writings, the first of which, *"Daidōji Shinsuke no hansei"* (*1924*,"The Early Life of Daidōji Shinsuke"), has never been translated into English and is generally considered to be an inferior work. In his second autobiographical period, however, he produced two masterpieces shortly before his death. With their restrained passion and impressionistic style, *"Haguruma"* (*1927*, "Cogwheels") and *"Aru ahō no isshō"* (*1927*, "A Fool's Life") are his best and most revealing works.

"Cogwheels" is the story of the artist's encroaching madness and paranoia. It explains how he lives on a plane of coincidence where everything seems to have menacing significance. One by one the touchstones of his life begin to dissolve until reality is almost entirely replaced by fantasy. Anything suggestive of the duality of light and darkness causes him to panic, while even his favorite books seem to accuse him of some terrible sin. Wherever he glances he sees phantom cogwheels, mechanically turning of their own accord. Astonishingly, the whole of this paranoid vision is expressed with elegant lucidity. He even backs up his argument by mentioning that Napoleon, as a student, made a last entry into his geography notebook: "Saint Helena – a small island." Akutagawa's narrator remarks: "It might have been, as we say, a coincidence. But it must have made even Napoleon shiver eventually. . . ."

Always the master of the macabre, Akutagawa took a terrible risk in making himself the subject of his art. When he did so, said the critic Itō Sei: "It was simply a case of self-destruction like a snake devouring its own tail." "Cogwheels" ends with the plaintive words: "I haven't the strength to go on writing . . . . Isn't there anyone to come and strangle me quietly in my sleep?"

Written over a longer period than "Cogwheels" and covering all his adult years, "A Fool's Life" begins appropriately with books. Surveying the works of his favorite authors, Akutagawa sees not books but the *fin de siècle* itself. He seems to suggest that he belongs to an era which has now passed. Going on to relate many other incidents, mostly in chronological order, he quickly assembles a patchwork quilt of impressions, meetings, loves, and departures. Most moving is the (five-line) chapter entitled "Mentor." He recalls sitting under a large oak tree (the strength of which suggests the scale of Sōseki's achievement) reading his mentor's book. "Somewhere off in the far sky a pair of glass pans hung from a balance, in perfect equilibrium."

If only Akutagawa could have achieved that balance of Sōseki's – that harmony of subjective experience and social observation, of inner and outer worlds – he might not have been compelled to take his own life. His suicide in 1927, planned and carried out with utmost efficiency, stunned the literary world. It brought about the close of a brilliant period in Japanese letters: *Taishō aestheticism. More than any other movement it was dominated by a single figure, and even now one wishes that Akutagawa, like the poet Tokk, could somehow "suicide back to life."

RECOMMENDED READING

Short Fiction Collections

Exotic Japanese Stories. 431 pages. Tr. Takashi Kojima and John McVittie. Liveright, NY, 1964; paperback 1972. Includes: "The Robbers," "The Handkerchief," "The Dolls," "The Faith of Wei Sheng," "The Kappa," "Absorbed in Letters," "Heresy," etc. To date, the best of Akutagawa anthologies in English. Contains 40-page intro. by John McVittie.

Japanese Short Stories. 224 pages. Tr. Takashi Kojima. Liveright, NY, 1961; Avon Books, NY, 1963; Tuttle, Tokyo, 1981. Includes such famous stories as: "The Hell Screen," "The Spider's Thread," "The Nose," "The Tangerines," etc. Contains woodcut illustrations by Masakazu Kuwata. Easily obtainable.

Hell Screen, Cogwheels, A Fool's Life. 145 pages. Tr. various. Eridanos Press, Hygiene, CO, 1987. No. 2 in the Eridanos Library. Contains a foreword by Jorge Luis Borges. Paperback.

WORKS IN ENGLISH TRANSLATION

Other Short Fiction Collections

Hell Screen and Other Stories. 177 pages. Tr. W. H. H. Norman. Greenwood Press, Westport, CT, 1970. Includes: "Heresy," "The General," "Mensura Zoilii." Reprint of 1948 edition by The Hokuseido Press, Tokyo.

Rashomon and Other Stories. 119 pages. Tr. Takashi Kojima. C.E. Tuttle, NY, 1952; Liveright, New York, 1970, paperback; Tuttle, Tokyo, 1952, 1954. Includes: "In a Grove," "Yam Gruel," "Kesa and Morito."

Hell Screen, Cogwheels, A Fool's Life. 145 pages. Tr. Takashi Kojima, Cid Corman, and Will Petersen. David Godine Publishers, Boston, 1992.

Short Fiction

"Absorbed in Letters." *"Gesaku zammai."* 1917. 36 pages. *Exotic Japanese Stories*.

"The Ajari." *"Dōso mondō."* 1917. 4 pages. Tr. R. E. Morrell. *Young East*, vol. 12, no. 48, 1963.

"Akutagawa's Last Note: To My Old Friends." *"Aru kyūyū e okuru shuki." 1927.* Suicide note. 4 pages. (1) Tr. John Mortimer. *Japan Times,* July 26, 1927. (2) As "A Note Forwarded to a Certain Old Friend." Tr. Akio Inoue. *Posthumous Works of Ryūnosuke Akutagawa.* Tenri Jihosha, Tenri, 1961.

"Ano Koro no Jibun no Koto." *1919. "Ano koro no jibun no koto."* Tr. W. J. Whitehouse. *Eigo no kenkyu to kyoju.* Tokyo, 1938.

"Autumn." *"Aki." 1920.* 13 pages. (1) Tr. E. Omiya. *Eigo Seinen,* vol. 58, nos. 10–12, vol. 59, nos. 2–9, 1928. (2) As "The Autumn." Tr. Eric S. Bell and Eiji Ukai. *Eminent Authors of Contemporary Japan,* vol. 2, Kaitakusha, Tokyo, 1931. (3) Tr. Hisao Kitajima and Thomas H. Carter. *Shenandoah,* Winter 1954. (4) Tr. Norimitsu Antoko. *Eigo Eibungaku Ronshu,* vol. 11, no. 3, 1970.

"The Badger." *"Mujina." 1917.* 7 pages. (1) Tr. Glenn W. Shaw. *Tales Grotesque and Curious.* Hokuseido, Tokyo, 1930. (2) *Exotic Japanese Stories.*

"The Ball." *"Butōkai." 1919.* 11 pages. Tr. Glenn W. Shaw. *Tales Grotesque and Curious.* Hokuseido, Tokyo, 1930.

"The Christ of Nankin." *"Nankin no Kirisuto." 1920.* 6 pages. (1) Tr. W. M. Bickerton. *Eigo Seinen,* vol. 65, nos. 1–7, 1931. (2) As "Christ in Nankin." Tr. Saburo Haneda. *The Reeds,* vol. 6, 1960.

"A Clod of Soil." *"Ikkai no tsuchi." 1923.* (1) As "A Clod of Earth." Tr. Richard McKinnon. *The Heart Is Alone.* Hokuseido, Tokyo, 1957. (2) Tr. Takashi Kojima. *Eibungaku Kenkyu,* no. 19, 1961; *Japanese Short Stories.*

"Cogwheels." *"Haguruma." 1927.* 35 pages. (1) As "The Cogwheel." Tr. Beongcheon Yu. *Chicago Review,* vol. 18, no. 2, 1965. (2) Tr. Cid Corman and Susumu Kamaike. *Hell Screen, Cogwheels, A Fool's Life.*

"Cold." *"Samusa." 1924.* 5 pages. *Stone Lion Review,* no. 10, 1983.

"Dialogue in Darkness." *"Anchū mondō." 1927.* Tr. Beongcheon Yu. *East–West Review,* vol. 4, no. 1, 1971.

"The Dog Shiro." *"Shiro."* Composed 1923. 11 pages. (1) As "White the Dog." Tr. Takamasa Sasaki. *The Three Treasures, and Other Stories for Children.* Hokuseido, Tokyo, 1944. (2) *Exotic Japanese Stories.* (3) As "Whitie." Tr. Dorothy Britton. *The Spider's Thread and Other Stories.* Kodansha International, Tokyo, 1987.

"The Dolls." *"Hina."* Composed 1923. (1) *Exotic Japanese Stories.* (2) *The Spider's Thread and Other Stories.*

"The Dragon." *"Ryū." 1919.* 17 pages. (1) *Rashomon and Other Stories.* (2) Tr. Norimitsu Antoku. *Eigo Eibungaku Ronshu,* vol. 10, no. 2, 1969.

"The Faith of Wei Sheng." *"Bisei no shin."* Composed 1919. 4 pages. *Exotic Japanese Stories.*

"The Feud Between the Monkey and the Crab." *"Saru kani gassen." 1923.* 4 pages. Tr. Thomas E. Swann. *Monumenta Nipponica,* vol. 24, no. 4, 1969.

"A Fool's Life." *"Aru ahō no isshō." 1927.* 57 pages. (1) As "Life of a Certain Fool." Tr. Akio Inoue. *Posthumous Works of Ryūnosuke Akutagawa.* Tenri Jihosha, Tenri, 1961. (2) Tr. Will Petersen. Mushinsha, Tokyo, 1970; Grossman, NY, 1970. (3) Tr. Cid Corman and Susumu Kamaike. *Hell Screen, Cogwheels, A Fool's Life.*

"Futari Komachi." *1923.* 10 pages. (1) Tr. Glenn W. Shaw. *Tokyo Nichinichi,* May 15, 1923. (2) Tr. Jihei Hashiguchi. *Tokyo Nichinichi,* May 15–18, 1926. (3) Tr. Thomas E. Swann. *Monumenta Nipponica,* vol. 23, nos.3–4, 1968.

"The Garden." *"Niwa."* Composed 1922. 11 pages. *Exotic Japanese Stories.*

"The General." *"Shōgun."* 1922. 33 pages. *Hell Screen and Other Stories.*

"Genkaku-Sanbo." *"Genkaku-sambō."* 1927. 17 pages. *Japanese Short Stories.*

"The God of Agni." *"Aguni no kami."* 1920. 23 pages. (1) As "God Agni." Tr. Taro Ito. *Eigo Kenkyu,* vol. 21, nos. 4–11, 1928–29. (2) Tr. Takamasa Sasaki. *The Three Treasures, and Other Stories for Children.* Hokuseido, Tokyo, 1944.

"Gratitude." *"Hōonki."* Composed 1922. 22 pages. *Exotic Japanese Stories.*

"The Greeting." *"Ojigi."* Composed 1923. 6 pages. (1) Tr. Takashi Kojima. *Eibungaku Kenkyu,* no. 21, 1963. (2) *Exotic Japanese Stories.* (3) As "Greeting." Tr. Norimitsu Antoku. *Eigo Eibungaku Ronshu,* vol. 8, no. 1, 1967.

Haiku. (20 Haiku). Poetry. 9 pages. Tr. Makoto Ueda. *Modern Japanese Haiku, An Anthology.* University of Tokyo Press, Tokyo, 1976.

"The Handkerchief." *"Hankechi."* Composed 1916. 11 pages. (1) Tr. Glenn W. Shaw. *Tales Grotesque and Curious.* Hokuseido, Tokyo, 1930; *Rashomon and Other Stories.* Hara Shobo, Tokyo, 1964. (2) As "Handkerchief." Tr. Kiyoshi Morikuro. *Asia and the Americans,* vol. 43, 1943. (3) Tr. Takashi Kojima. *Eibungaku Kenkyu,* no. 21, 1963. (4) *Exotic Japanese*

Stories. (5) Tr. Norimitsu Antoku. *Eigo Eibungaku Ronshu,* vol. 7, no. 2, 1966.

"Heichu, The Amorous Genius." *"Kōshoku."* 1921. 20 pages. *Japanese Short Stories.*

"Hell Screen." *"Jigokuhen."* 1918. 25 pages. (1) As "The Horrors of Hell." Tr. Einosuke Omiya. *Eigo Seinen,* vol. 76, nos. 4, 6, 8, 10, 12, 1937; and vol. 77, nos. 1–5, 7–10, 12, 1937. (2) *Hell Screen and Other Stories; Modern Japanese Literature,* ed. Donald Keene. Grove Press, NY, 1956; Tuttle, Tokyo, 1957; Grove Weidenfeld, NY, 1989 paperback. (3) As "The Hell Screen." *Japanese Short Stories.* (4) Tr. Cid Corman and Susumu Kamaike. *Hell Screen, Cogwheels, A Fool's Life.*

"Heresy." *"Jashūmon."* 1918. 60 pages. (1) As "Jashumon." *Hell Screen and Other Stories.* (2) *Exotic Japanese Stories.*

"Hyottoko." *"Hyottoko."* 1915. 6 pages. Tr. Paul McCarthy. *Monumenta Nipponica,* vol. 24, no. 4, 1969.

"In a Grove." *"Yabu no naka."* 1922. 14 pages. *Rashomon and Other Stories; Masterpieces of the Orient.* Norton, NY, 1961, 1976 paperback; Avon Books, NY, 1963; *The Mentor Book of Modern Asian Literature.* Philosophical Library, NY, 1969; *Murder in Japan,* ed. John L. Apostolou and Martin H. Greenberg. Dembner Books, NY, 1987.

"The Kappa." *"Kappa."* 1927. 56 pages. (1) As "Kappa." Tr. Seiichi Shiojiri. Akitaya, Osaka, 1947; Hokuseido, Tokyo, 1949; Perkins, Pasadena, 1950; Greenwood Press, NY, 1970. (2) *Exotic Japanese Stories.* (3) Tr. Geoffrey Bownas. Peter Owen, London, 1970; Tuttle, Tokyo, 1970. (4) *"Kappa: A Satire."* Tr. Geoffrey

Bownas. Tuttle, Boston, 1971.
"Kesa and Morito." "Kesa to Mor-itō." 1919. 6 pages. (1) Rashomon and Other Stories. (2) Tr. Howard Hibbett. Modern Japanese Literature. Grove Press, NY, 1956; Tuttle, Tokyo, 1957; Grove Weidenfeld, NY, 1989 paperback. (3) Tr. Shigeru Tadokoro. Jimbun Kagaku, no. 9, 1959. (4) As "Lady Kesa and Imperial Guardsman Morito." Tr. Ryozo Matsumoto. Japanese Literature, New and Old. Hokuseido, Tokyo, 1961.
"The Lady Roku-no-Miya." "Roku-nomiya no himegimi." Composed 1922. 11 pages. (1) Exotic Japanese Stories. (2) As "Lady Roku no Miya." Tr. Cameron Hurst. Journal of Oriental Literature, no. 7, 1966.
"Lice." "Shirami." 1916. Tr. Glenn W. Shaw. Eigo Seinen, vol. 47, nos. 1–4, 1922; Tales Grotesque and Curious. Hokuseido, Tokyo, 1930; Rashomon and Other Stories. Hara Shobo, Tokyo, 1964.
"Lilies." "Yuri." 1922. 3 pages. Tr. Marvin J. Suomi. Solidarity, vol. 8, no. 2, 1973.
"Magic." "Majutsu." 1920. 19 pages. (1) As "Magic Art." Tr. Seizo Mori. Osaka Mainichi, Sept. 23–26, 1927. (2) Tr. Takamasa Sasaki. The Three Treasures, and Other Stories for Children. Hokuseido, Tokyo, 1944.
"The Marshland." "Numachi." 1919. 3 pages. (1) As "The Picture of a Quagmire." Tr. Yoshimatsu Suzuki. Eigo Seinen, vol. 44, no. 8, 1921. (2) As "Marsh." Tr. Kazuo Yamada. Eigo Seinen, vol. 81, no. 9, 1939. (3) Tr. Beongcheon Yu. Chicago Review, vol. 18, no. 2, 1965. (4) As "A Marsh." Tr. Norimitsu Antoku. Eigo Eibungaku Ronshu, vol. 10, no. 1, 1969.
"The Martyr." "Hōkyōnin no shi."

1918. 15 pages. Rashomon and Other Stories.
"Mensura Zoilii." "Mensura Zoilii." 1917. 10 pages. (1) Tr. Tadao Katayama. The Reeds, vol. 12, 1968. (2) Hell Screen and Other Stories.
"Mirage." "Shinkirō."1927. 6 pages. Tr. Beongcheon Yu. Chicago Review, vol. 18, no. 2, 1965.
"Momotaro." "Momotarō." 1924. 3 pages. Tr. Akira Funasaka. The Reeds, vol. 15, 1981.
"The Monkey." "Saru." 1916. 6 pages. Japan Chronicle, 1919.
"Mujina." "Mujina." 1917. 5 pages. Tr. Yutaka Kato. Osaka Kyoiku Daigaku Eibun Gakkaishi, no. 9, 1964.
"Nezumi Kozo, The Japanese Robin Hood." "Nezumi kozō Jirokichi." 1920. 26 pages. Japanese Short Stories.
"The Nose." "Hana." 1916. 6 pages. (1) As "Hana." Tr. A. Spann and A. Ennenberg. Japan Times, Sept. 4, 1927. (2) As "Hana." Tr. Haruo Endo and Eric S. Bell. Osaka Mainichi, Sept. 6–20, 1927. (3) Tr. Glenn W. Shaw. Tales Grotesque and Curious. Hokuseido, Tokyo, 1930; Rashomon and Other Stories. Hara Shobo, Tokyo, 1964. (4) Tr. Eric S. Bell and Eiji Ukai. Eminent Authors of Contemporary Japan, vol. 2. Kaitakusha, Tokyo, 1931. (5) As "Hana". Tr. Shigejiro Ichikawa. The Current of the World, vol. 27, no. 10, 1950. (6) As "The Nose of Naigu Zenchi." Tr. T. Fukuda. Eigo Seinen, vol. 98, no. 7, 1952. (7) Tr. Ivan Morris. Japan Quarterly, vol. 2, no. 4, 1955. (8) Japanese Short Stories. (9) The Spider's Thread and Other Stories.
"Notes on Bashō." "Bashō zakki." 1923. Tr. Cid Corman and Susumu Kamaike. Origin, vol. 8, Jan. 1968.

"The Old Murder." "*Kaika no satsujin.*" *1918*. 4 pages. *Orient–West*, vol. 6, no. 9, 1961.

"Otomi's Virginity." "*Otomi no teisō.*" *1922*. 15 pages. (1) As "Otomi's Virtue." Tr. Kazuo Nishida. *Asia Scene*, Dec. 1955. (2) *Japanese Short Stories*.

"The Painting of an Autumn Mountain." "*Shūzanzu.*" *1921*. 8 pages. (1) As "Autumn Mountains." *Living Age*, vol. 308, Feb. 5, 1921. (2) Tr. Ivan Morris. *Japan Quarterly*, vol. 2, no. 4, 1955; *Modern Japanese Stories*. Eyre and Spottiswoode, London, 1961; Tuttle, Tokyo, 1962.

"The Pipe." "*Kiseru.*" *1916*. 13 pages. Tr. Glenn W. Shaw. *Tales Grotesque and Curious*. Hokuseido, Tokyo, 1930; *Rashomon and Other Stories*. Hara Shobo, Tokyo, 1964.

"Rashomon." "*Rashōmon.*" *1915*. 9 pages. (1) Tr. Glenn W. Shaw. *Eigo Seinen*, vol. 44, nos. 1–6, 1920; *Tales Grotesque and Curious*. Hokuseido, Tokyo, 1930; *Rashomon and Other Stories*. Hara Shobo, Tokyo, 1964. (2) *Rashomon and Other Stories; Treasury of World Literature*. Philosophical Society, NY, 1956; *Masterpieces of the Orient*. Norton, NY, 1961, 1976 paperback; *The Mentor Book of Modern Asian Literature*. New American Library, NY, 1969.

"The Robbers." "*Chūtō.*" Composed 1917. 73 pages. *Exotic Japanese Stories*.

"Saigo Takamori." "*Saigō Takamori.*" Composed 1917. 14 pages. *Exotic Japanese Stories*.

"San Sebastian." "*Yūwaku.*" *1927*. Film scenario. 11 pages. Tr. Arthur Waley. *Horizon*, no. 20, Sept. 1949; *The Real Tripitaka, and Other Pieces*. Allen and Unwin, London, 1952.

"The Seashore." "*Umi no hotori.*" *1925*. 5 pages. Tr. Susan Orpett. *Voices*, vol. 3, no. 1, 1971.

"Sennin." "*Sennin.*" *1916*. (1) Tr. Takamasa Sasaki. *Eigo Kenkyu*, vol. 39, no. 5, 1950; *The Three Treasures, and Other Stories for Children*. Hokuseido, Tokyo, 1951. (2) Tr. Norimitsu Antoku. *Seinan Gakuin University; Eigo Eibungaku Ronshu*, vol. 9, no. 3, 1969. (3) Tr. Akira Funasaka. *The Reeds*, vol. 15, 1981.

"The Shadow of Death." *Shisō*. 1943. 2 pages. Tr. Thomas E. Swann. *Monumenta Nipponica*, vol. 26, nos. 1–2, 1971.

"The Sick Infant." "*Kodomo no byōki.*" *1923*. 7 pages. Tr. Norimitsu Antoku. *Eigo Eibungaku Ronshu*, vol. 9, no. 1, 1968.

"The Spider's Thread." "*Kumo no ito.*" *1918*. 9 pages. (1) As "The Spider's Web." Tr. Eric S. Bell and Eiji Ukai. *Japan Times*, Sept. 11, 1927; *Eminent Authors of Contemporary Japan*, vol. 2, Kaitakusha, Tokyo, 1931. (2) Tr. Glenn W. Shaw. *Tales Grotesque and Curious*. Hokuseido, Tokyo, 1930; *Rashomon and Other Stories*. Hara Shobo, Tokyo, 1964; *The Mentor Book of Modern Asian Literature*. New American Library, NY, 1969. (3) As "Spider-Thread." Tr. F. J. Daniels. *Japanese Prose*. Lund Humphries, London, 1944. (4) Tr. Takamasa Sasaki. *The Three Treasures, and Other Stories for Children*. Hokuseido, Tokyo, 1944. (5) Tr. Yoshimatsu Suzuki. *Eigo Seinen*, vol. 96, no. 2, 1950. (6) Tr. Umeyo Hirano. *Young East*, no. 10, 1954; *Buddhist Plays from Japanese Literature*. CIIB Press, Tokyo, 1963. (7) Tr. Takashi Kojima. *Eibungaku Kenkyu*, no. 19, 1959; *Japanese Short Stories*. (8) Tr. Norimitsu Antoku.

Seinan Gakuin Joshi Tanki Daigaku Kenkyu Kiyo, no. 10, 1964. (9) As "Spider's Thread." Tr. Akira Funasaka. *The Reeds*, vol. 15, 1981. (10) *The Spider's Thread and Other Stories*.

"The Story of a Fallen Head." "*Kubi ga ochita hanashi.*" *1918*. 26 pages. Tr. Eric S. Bell and Eiji Ukai. *Japan Times*, Sept. 25, 1927; *Eminent Authors of Contemporary Japan*, vol. 1. Kaitakusha, Tokyo, 1930.

"The Story of Yonosuke." "*Yonosuke no hanashi.*" *1918*. 6 pages. Tr. Takashi Kojima. *Eibungaku Kenkyu*, vol. 1, no. 2, 1954; *Eigo Seinen*, vol. 101, nos. 9–11, 1955; *Japanese Short Stories*; *Pacific Spectator*, vol. 9, no. 2, 1965.

"A Strange Story." "*Myō na hanashi.*" *1921*. 1 page. Tr. Taro Ito. *Eigo to Eibungaku*, vol. 4, nos. 3–4, 1929.

"The Tangerines." "*Mikan.*" *1919*. (1) As "The Mandarin Oranges." Tr. T. Yuasa. *Contemporary Japan*, vol. 6, no. 4, 1938. (2) As "Tangerines." Tr. Ineko Sato. *Eigo Seinen*, vol. 93, no. 3, 1949. (3) As "Tangerines." *Orient–West*, vol. 6, no. 9, 1961. (4) *Japanese Short Stories*. (5) As "The Oranges." Tr. Norimitsu Antoku and Gunichi Antoku. *Seinan Gakuin Joshi Tanki Daigaku Kenkyu Kiyo*, no. 10, 1964. (6) Tr. Norimitsu Antoku. *Eigo Eibungaku Ronshu*, vol. 9, no. 2, 1969. (7) As "Tangerines." *The Spider's Thread and Other Stories*.

"The Three Treasures." "*Mittsu no takara.*" *1922*. 22 pages. Tr. Takamasa Sasaki. *The Three Treasures, and Other Stories for Children*. Hokuseido, Tokyo, 1944.

"Tobacco and the Devil." "*Tabako to akuma.*" *1917*. 25 pages. Tr. Glenn W. Shaw. *Tales Grotesque and Curious*. Hokuseido, Tokyo, 1930; *Rashomon and Other Stories*. Hara Shobo, Tokyo, 1964.

"Torokko." "*Torokko.*" *1922*. (1) As "The Track." Tr. Tomokazu Nishira. *English Society Review*, 1930. (2) As "The Wagon." Tr. S. G. Brickley. *The Writing of Idiomatic English*. Kenkyusha, Tokyo, 1951. (3) As "Flatcar." Tr. Richard McKinnon. *The Heart is Alone*. Hokuseido, Tokyo, 1957. (4) As "The Flatcar." Tr. Takashi Kojima. *Eibungaku Kenkyu*, no. 27, 1964. (5) As "Torokko, or the Handcart." Tr. Norimitsu Antoku. *Eigo Eibungaku Ronshu*, vol. 9, no. 1, 1966. (6) As "The Wagon." *The Spider's Thread and Other Stories*.

"Tu Tze-Chun." "*To Shishun.*" *1920*. 30 pages. (1) As "Tu Tsuchun." Tr. Eric S. Bell and Eiji Ukai. *Eibun Tokyo Nichinichi*, Nov. 27–Dec. 3, 1926; *Eminent Authors of Contemporary Japan*, vol. 1, Kaitakusha, Tokyo, 1930. (2) As "Tu Tzu-Chun." Tr. Takamasa Sasaki. *The Three Treasures, and Other Stories for Children*. Hokuseido, Tokyo, 1944. (3) Tr. Takashi Kojima. *Eibungaku Kenkyu*, no. 29, 1964. (4) Tr. Dorothy Britton. Kodansha International, Tokyo, 1965; Ward Lock, London, 1965; *The Spider's Thread and Other Stories*. (5) As "Tu Tzu-Chun." Tr. Norimitsu Antoku. *Eigo Eibungaku Ronshu*, vol. 8, no. 2, 1968.

"Western Man." "*Saihō no hito.*" *1919*. 20 pages. (1) Tr. Akio Inoue. *Posthumous Works of Ryūnosuke Akutagawa*. Tenri Jihosha, Tenri, 1961. (2) As "Man of the West." Tr. Tadao Katayama. *The Reeds*, vol. 8, 1962.

"Western Man Continued." "*Zoku saihō no hito.*" *1920*. 11 pages. Tr. Akio Inoue. *Posthumous Works of Ryūnosuke Akutagawa*. Tenri

Jihosha, Tenri, 1961.
"The Wine Worm." *"Shuju no kotoba."* *1923.* 25 pages. (1) Tr. Glenn W. Shaw. *Tales of the Grotesque and Curious.* Hokuseido, Tokyo, 1930; *Rashomon and Other Stories.* Hara Shobo, Tokyo, 1964. (2) As "Told by a Pigmy." Tr. Tadao Katayama. *The Reeds,* vol. 9, 1963.
"Withered Fields." *"Kareno-shō."*

Composed 1918. 11 pages. (1) *Exotic Japanese Stories.* (2) As "Winter Field." Tr. Hiroaki Sato. *Chanoyu Quarterly,* vol. 9, 1974.
"A Woman's Body." *"Nyotai."* Composed 1917. 3 pages. *Exotic Japanese Stories.*
"Yam Gruel." *"Imogayu."* *1916.* 24 pages. Tr. Takashi Kojima. *Rashomon and Other Stories.*

CRITICAL STUDIES

Hibbett, Howard. "Akutagawa Ryūnosuke and the Negative Ideal." *Personality in Japanese History,* 1970.

Lippit, Noriko Mizuta. "Akutagawa's 'Toshishun' and the Chinese 'Tu Tzu-ch'un.'" *Asian Cultural Quarterly,* vol. 6, no. 4, 1978.

Morris, Ivan. "Introductory Note: Shiga and Akutagawa." *Japan Quarterly,* vol. 2, no. 4, 1955.

O'Brien, James A. *Akutagawa and Dazai: Instances of Literary Adaptation.* Arizona State University Press, Tempe, 1988.

Tsuruta, Kinya. "Akutagawa: His Concepts of Life and Art." Ph.D. diss., University of Washington, Seattle, 1967.

———. "Akutagawa: 'Hell Screen,' 'In a Grove,' 'Kappa.'" *Approaches to the Modern Japanese Short Story,* ed. Thomas E. Swann and Kinya Tsuruta. Waseda University Press, Tokyo, 1982.

———. "Akutagawa and the I-Novelists." *Monumenta Nipponica,* vol. 25, no. 1, 1970.

———. "Akutagawa's 'In a Grove.'" *Essays on Japanese Literature,* 1975.

Yu, Beongcheon. *Akutagawa: An Introduction.* Wayne State University Press, Detroit, 1972.

ARISHIMA Takeo
(1878–1923)

Novelist. Born in Tokyo. Moved to Sapporo in Hokkaidō to study, then traveled extensively in the West.

"Reading Arishima's novels is just like listening to a record of Western music," said AKUTAGAWA RYŪNOSUKE, in conversation with the writer Eguchi Kiyoshi. When asked by Eguchi to elaborate he added: "I can't help feeling how wonderful it would be if they were the real thing."

From the vantage point of today, a Western reader can acknowledge the truth of Akutagawa's remark yet at the same time contradict it. For two of the best works written by Arishima Takeo, a relatively poor stylist in his own language, have since been rendered into English. In 1955, John Morrison translated *"Kain no matsuei"* (*1917*, "Descendants of Cain"), while in 1978 Kenneth Strong published a complete version of *Aru onna* (*1911–19, A Certain Woman*). By any standard they are "the real thing," works written in a full awareness of Western literary traditions. If they emulate but do not quite match the best creations of Flaubert, Ibsen, or Tolstoy, they nonetheless contain unique qualities of their own. "Descendants of Cain" is a timeless classic of peasant life. Set in a desolate landscape in Hokkaidō it seems to touch a fundamental process of nature in its description of Nin'emon's struggle for survival, despite all the odds stacked against him. By contrast, *A Certain Woman* switches our attention to the opposite sex, discovering there a woman who, though like Nin'emon in being governed by instinct, has the sophistication to rise above her culture and seek her destiny overseas. Both works are tragedies, and if they remind one of "listening to a record" it is because they are born in the spirit of music in the full Nietzschean sense.

Arishima Takeo was the eldest son of Arishima Takeshi, a wealthy man who was in charge of the Customs Bureau at the Ministry of Finance. Takeshi had achieved this position (in 1881 at the age of forty) largely through his own abilities, having come from a relatively humble samurai family serving the Satsuma fief in Kyūshū. His wife, Yukiko, Takeo's mother, was a northerner whose family had opposed the removal of the shōgun and the Restoration of the emperor in 1868. In temperament she was cool and rational, unlike her husband who tended to be emotional and obsessive. Takeo, by his own admission, was a blend of the two: a shy intellectual, constantly frustrated by the difficulty of asserting his abundant energies.

Arishima's upbringing was one of spartan discipline, imposed on him by his father because he was the oldest son. It was made even more rigorous by the addition of English-language lessons from the age of six onward, his father quite correctly judging that Japan's future leaders would need to have an intimate knowledge of Western culture. Takeo was thus enrolled at the En'wa Mission School in Yokohama where most of the other pupils were foreigners, and where, for the first time, he was introduced to Christianity. Somewhat surprisingly he seems to have enjoyed this experience, recalling his memories of the American schoolmistress with considerable warmth in his children's story *"Hitofusa no budō"* (1920, "A Bunch of Grapes").

As Arishima grew older, the demands placed upon him became heavier. In a letter to a friend he once wrote: "Only he who has experienced it can know the burden of being an eldest son in Japan." By contrast, his four brothers and two sisters were relatively free from paternal pressure, directed solely at Takeo because it was he who would one day bear the responsibility of being head of the family. Though less gifted than himself, two of his brothers, the painter Arishima Ikuma and the writer SATOMI TON, were allowed to pursue careers in the arts without being hindered by their father.

Takeo, however, was being groomed for the "higher" calling of either scholarship or government. When he entered the Peers' School in 1887 he was already a model pupil: clever, diligent, and well-behaved. Although it would be many years before he could aspire to being a leading writer of the *Taishō period, he was, ironically, selected at around this time to be a "special friend" of the Crown Prince Yoshihito. Every Saturday he was taken to the Fukiage Palace to play with this boy, who, in 1912, became the Emperor Taishō, the one hundred and twenty-third ruler of Japan.

In 1896 at age nineteen, Arishima found an ingenious way of alleviating parental pressure by choosing to go to the Sapporo Agricultural College in distant Hokkaidō. Other factors also may have influenced his choice, including a romantic notion that Hokkaidō was still a virgin territory where a docile person, such as himself, might more easily find self-expression. Once there, he lodged with *Nitobe Inazō, an old family friend who has since become well-known in the West for his famous book, *Bushidō, The Soul of Japan*. Although fervently Christian, Nitobe made no attempt to impose his religion on Arishima. This came quickly enough when Takeo became the intimate of Morimoto Kōkichi, a fellow student who had graduated from a Christian college in Tokyo. So close was their friendship that many scholars believe it to have been motivated by homosexual feelings. Whether or not this was true, it is clear that Morimoto exercised great influence over Arishima, often making him feel guilty, and persuading him to become a member of the Sapporo Independent Church.

In Sapporo, Arishima was virtually surrounded by Christianity. The college itself had been started by an American Christian, Dr. William Clark, an educator who had converted not only Nitobe Inazō but also *Uchimura Kanzō, whose influence on the new generation of writers was especially strong. Arishima would have been well aware that he was following in Uchimura's footsteps by attending the college, while in Morimoto he had a friend who had actually been taught by him. Together the two students attended Nitobe's lectures, read Uchimura's *Dokuritsu zasshi* (*Independent Magazine*), and became united in their determination to overcome the wickedness of the world, the flesh, and the devil.

Never quite as fervent as Morimoto, Arishima tried to make amends by teaching at the Enyū Yagakkō, a night school for the poor, organized and supported by the church. For the first time in his life he was brought into contact with genuine poverty, and the experience played its part in a reevaluation of his life's goals and ambitions. Humanitarian by nature, he usually placed the needs of others before those of himself, and was overcome with guilt when, on one occasion, he failed to visit Morimoto who was sick. In fact, he was trying to distance himself from Morimoto's unpopularity with the other students, which was having an adverse effect on his own standing in the college. When Morimoto accused him of being neglectful, Arishima decided, on February 15, 1899, to kill himself. He even went so far as to buy a gun, and paid a last visit to his friend to bid him farewell. The whole scene then began to develop like one from Arishima's later novels, for Morimoto insisted on dying with him, and together they journeyed to a remote spot to end their lives. At this point Morimoto called a halt to the melodrama by citing some Christian arguments against suicide. Arishima concurred, and from then on became more resolutely Christian than before. To celebrate their graduation, he and Morimoto jointly wrote *Ribingusuton-den* ("A Biography of David Livingstone"), which was published by Keiseisha in 1901.

After a year of compulsory military service Arishima was offered several attractive career choices. He could have become a private secretary to the Minister of the Interior, or, alternatively, might have served as aide to his old playmate, the Crown Prince. In rejecting both offers he had in mind another path which would take him even further into the mainstream of Western culture. Now completely fluent in English, he had been studying intensively during early 1903, reading the English Romantics and the great figures of Western literature: Shakespeare, Dante, and Goethe. It seemed obvious to him that he should continue his studies in the West. Thus, in late summer of the same year he sailed for America, having chosen Haverford College, Pennsylvania, as the place where he would conduct his graduate studies.

Arishima was overseas for nearly three and a half years, beginning with intensive study at Haverford on diverse subjects ranging from labor relations to European history and politics. Many intellectuals residing in a foreign country tend to immerse themselves in their work, and Arishima, like NATSUME SŌSEKI in England, was no exception. He wrote the longest college thesis of his year on the origins of Japanese culture, with special reference to Indian and Chinese influences. He studied the great Russian and French authors, and came upon Ibsen whose portrayal of anguished individuals impressed him greatly. He even found time to keep an English-language diary, one of the true delights of Arishima studies today. No account of his life is complete without one or two quotations from his diary, which (unaccountably) has never been published in the West.

Towards the end of Arishima's course at Haverford, the Russo–Japanese War broke out at home. Not unnaturally he was very concerned by this serious turn of events, and was disturbed by the reactions of his American colleagues who regarded it as an amusing diversion. But even though the Japanese were successfully bear-baiting the Russians, Arishima was appalled at the unnecessary loss of life. He rejoiced only in Tolstoy's condemnation of the war, finding in it an affirmation of Christianity which otherwise he felt was declining in the West.

Having obtained his M.A. in 1904, Arishima took self-sacrifice a step further by becoming a male nurse at the Friends' Asylum for the Insane in Frankford, near Philadelphia. Again, he was following in the footsteps of Uchimura Kanzō who had undertaken similar work twenty years previously at the Pennsylvania State Mental Hospital. For both men it was a difficult task admirably performed, but in Arishima's case it was also the beginning of his disillusionment with Christianity. During his two months at the hospital he became a close acquaintance of one of the patients, a certain Dr. Scott, who killed himself after Arishima left. Deeply upset by the incident, Arishima found himself in need of spiritual support – and discovered it in a most unusual quarter.

An obscure Boston lawyer called Peabody unwittingly played a significant role in Japanese literary history by reciting Walt Whitman's poetry to his lodger, Arishima Takeo, in January 1905. As Arishima later recalled: "Whitman's great hand struck me on the shoulder," jolting him into an awareness that sensual and spiritual freedom were, after all, within his grasp. Although Whitman's works were considered offensive at the time and Arishima had some difficulty in buying a copy of *Leaves of Grass*, he later translated the book into Japanese. Thirteen years previously, Sōseki had written an undergraduate essay called "On the Poems of Walt Whitman, a Representative Egalitarian Writer," but because it appeared in a philosophical journal it had not been widely noted. However, Arishima's promotion of Whitman in Japan was extremely influential, and among those who welcomed the American's optimism was OSARAGI JIRŌ (1897–1973), one of the most popular novelists of the *Shōwa period.

After a brief spell at Harvard College, Arishima joined his friend Morimoto in Washington, D.C. No longer as close as they had been in Sapporo, they disagreed on several issues, particularly in regard to pacifism. Arishima was now the more extreme of the two, and was rapidly becoming a radical socialist as a result of reading the works of Gorki. While in Washington he wrote his first work of fiction, a short story called *"Kankan mushi"* (1906, published 1910, "The Rust Chippers"). Scarcely the product of personal experience it depicted the lives of laborers who chipped the rust off ships' hulls in the harbor of Kherson on the Dnieper River. The author's choice of subject completely baffled Japanese critics who could never understand why the Crown Prince's former playmate, resident of mysterious Hokkaidō, teacher of the poor, and one-time nurse to insane Americans should suddenly start writing about Ukrainian laborers. Nonetheless, influenced by Gorki, Arishima demonstrated a powerful imagination of his own, and showed that any future work he might produce was unlikely to be restricted by Japanese literary conventions.

On Arishima's remarkable independence from the traditions of Japanese literature, Donald Keene is most enlightening. In *Dawn to the West* he says: "Arishima alone, not only among the *Shirakaba* writers but among all writers of the Japan of his day, possessed a range and intensity of emotional expression that might be described as European." Whereas others merely hinted at their deepest feelings, Arishima "tended to overemphasize rather than understate his emotions, and the vocabulary he used was definitely not in the Japanese tradition." By writing *"Kankan mushi"* Arishima took a courageous step in aligning himself with Western avant-garde thought.

Traveling from New York to Naples in September 1906, Arishima was greeted on arrival by his brother Ikuma who was studying art in Italy. Together they toured the museums, then moved north into Switzerland. There, without realizing it at the time, Arishima fell in love with Mathilda, the daughter of a hotel keeper in Schaffhausen. Their poignant friendship, conducted entirely by correspondence after only a week together, is described in some detail by Kenneth Strong in his introduction to one of Arishima's novels. Long after the novelist's death, "Tildi" remained faithful to his memory, twice traveling to Japan to see his grave and to acquire copies of his books. She died at age eighty-four in 1970 (Kenneth Strong reports) "surrounded by Arishima's books, none of which, of course, she could read."

In London in 1907 at the end of his overseas tour, Arishima enjoyed quite a different sort of encounter, this time with Prince Kropotkin (1842–1921) the celebrated anarchist. It was a high note on which to end, for he was so impressed by the Russian theorist of international revolution that he listened to him (he said in a 1916 essay) "like a docile child sitting by the knee of an aged parent." During the two-month voyage home, Arishima read *Anna Karenina* and many other Western books before the mountains of Japan finally appeared over the horizon. In what is perhaps the most famous passage of his English-language diary he wrote: "I could not help admiring in spite of all my intellectual objection the beauty and loveliness of my birthplace. . . . I must be frank and love this country until one day her degradation disgusts me thoroughly or my behavior enrages her deeply."

He had achieved much while away from home, but at age twenty-nine was still a single man in need of a job and a wife. He returned to Sapporo where he was offered a post as lecturer in English at his old college, now Tōhoku Imperial Agricultural University. His father bought him some 800 acres of land in Hokkaidō, and he was married to Kamio Yasuko, the daughter of an army general, in 1908. Still afraid of his father, he had agreed to this marriage despite a preference for Nitobe Inazō's niece, whom his father rejected because of her inferior social status. In the years that followed, three sons were born, although Arishima could never permit himself to enjoy sex without feeling a Puritan guilt, even within marriage. He wrote little during this period (1908–10), working only on a translation of Turgenev's *Fathers and Sons*, while contributing articles and essays to the first issues of *Shirakaba*. His two-part essay *"Futatsu no michi"* (1910, "Two Ways") expressed his vision of the human condition as eternal conflict between the flesh and the spirit, passion and reason: between which polarities man vacillates like Hamlet. No "middle way" was possible, and these, he claimed, were "the only two paths to salvation."

Arishima projected all his longing for freedom into Yōko, the central character of *A Certain Woman*. He published the first part of this, his first full-length novel, in the *Shirakaba* during the years 1911–12. It was called *Aru onna no gurimpusu* (*Glimpse of a Certain Woman*). The complete novel, finished in 1919 and published by Sōbunkaku, is a masterpiece of modern Japanese literature. It is all the more astonishing when one considers how little Arishima had written up till then, and how dangerously his mind was overstocked with theoretical knowledge. Intellectuals often make poor novelists, but this was not at all true in Arishima's case. Basing his characters on people with whom he was acquainted, he wove a story of exceptional power, giving it a tragic dimension which is rarely attained in Japanese fiction. Not until the postwar novels of MISHIMA YUKIO does one encounter a similar vortex of energy generated by a Japanese writer.

Unlike Mishima, however, Arishima does not appear to have predetermined the ending of his novel. In common with many great writers he developed his story intuitively, moving it unpredictably towards either a confirmation or a denial of Yōko's ideals. The first half displays the optimism and confidence of a woman who is determined to liberate herself from social convention; while in the second half, hysteria and paranoia begin to dominate and the story draws to an inevitable, tragic conclusion.

Satsuki Yōko, the eldest of three sisters in a Christian family, has offended society by backing out of her marriage to a young war reporter only a few weeks after their wedding. These incidents correspond exactly to the real-life scandal of Sasaki Nobuko leaving her husband, the war reporter KUNIKIDA DOPPO (who, by the time the book was published, had died, having first become one of Japan's best-loved writers of autobiographical fiction). Arishima kept close to the facts in showing how Yōko, in traveling to America to join her new fiancé, Kimura, falls in love *en route* with the ship's purser, Kuraji. As she sets out to win Kuraji's affections she plunges headlong into unrestrained passion, almost eliminating any "watchful self" that would normally inhibit her behavior.

In Yōko's story Arishima embodied what he believed to be a war between the sexes, brought about by the oppression of women in a male-dominated society. In a revealing letter (to Ishizaka Yōhei, Oct. 19, 1919) he spoke of how women, using sex as their only means of influence, had separated themselves from their maternal nature. Consequently, the man-hating seductress became "torn between those two conflicting instincts, hatred and love."

For all its bleakness there is an element of truth in Arishima's vision, and in *A Certain Woman* he created a character who confirmed the force of his argument by her lifelike qualities. He never equaled this achievement although his 1917 work, "Descendants of Cain," was more popular in its day. It was written during a period of intensive productivity following the death of his wife from tuberculosis in 1916, and of his father, who died of cancer at around the same time.

Although somber in tone, "Descendants of Cain" is exhilarating to read, and in its rustic fatalism reminds one of the work of Thomas Hardy. The hero, Nin'emon, is a brutish man: surly towards his neighbors, ignorant of the larger world, and violent even with woman and children. Yet while he is not a likable character, he has one redeeming feature which endears him to the reader and almost turns his vices into virtues. He has a sense of purpose. He wants to be rich.

When we first meet Nin'emon he is trudging through a desolate landscape with his wife, their child, and a few belongings, searching for the manager's office on a remote farm. He is faced with the dismal prospect of becoming a tenant farmer, knowing full well that the job will entail backbreaking labor for very little reward. However, he has no intention of "playing fair" with the landlord, but will use his great physical strength to intimidate those who stand between him and prosperity.

There is a grim inevitability to Nin'emon's rapid rise and fall. Yet although tragedy strikes the family, the hero is never completely defeated. He even seems to delight in the prospect of repeating the same mistakes elsewhere. Like Yōko in *A Certain Woman* he is assertive by nature, and in this sense is quite in harmony with his rugged surroundings.

Following his father's death Arishima was completely free to follow his own inclinations. He produced a succession of stories and essays, including *"Kurara no shukke"* (*1917*, "Clara Takes the Vows"); *"Umare izuru nayami"* (*1918*, "The Agony of Coming into the World"); *"Chiisaki mono e"* (*1918*, "To My Little Sons"); and *"Oshiminaku ai wa ubau"* (*1917*, "Love Takes All Without Regret"). Together with his two brothers who participated in the *Shirakaba-ha (White Birch Society), Arishima enjoyed his new prominence as a writer. The entire November 1917 issue of *Chūō kōron* (*Literary Review*) was devoted to the works of Arishima, his brother, Satomi Ton and the Tanizaki brothers (TANIZAKI JUN'ICHIRŌ, and his brother Seiji who was a professor of English and American literature at Waseda University).

As an humanitarian with Christian sympathies, Arishima regarded as singularly depressing the newspaper reports of the Great War that was taking place in Europe (1914–18). He was not to know that this war, more than any other event in history, would destroy the social order that he so much detested. Yet while he had no especial knowledge or understanding of international affairs, his awareness of inequality and social injustice was such that he was prepared to act upon his socialist beliefs when the opportunity arose. With astonishing generosity early in 1923 he gave away his entire estate in Hokkaidō to the tenant farmers who worked upon it.

Having thus assuaged his conscience, the author of "Descendants of Cain" was, one might suppose, a happier man. Nothing could be further from the truth. In private life he had become hopelessly entangled in a relationship with Hatano Akiko, a married woman whose husband threatened to ruin the lovers with public disgrace. For a man of high moral principle it was an impossible situation; and for a Japanese man in such a position there was only one logical solution. Of their own free will, he and Akiko resolved to commit suicide. They carried out their plan in the holiday resort of Karuizawa on June 8, 1923.

Arishima's life had been a series of frustrations, culminating in his awareness that he could be neither a true Christian nor a true socialist. His many-sided personality made him impatient with the

Church, while his class prevented him from sharing the struggle of the proletariat. Now once again he was frustrated in love, and perhaps momentarily lost the will to continue.

Many years were to pass before Arishima was accorded his rightful status as one of the great writers of his era. However, when Japanese critics became more familiar with Western styles, they recognized the quality of his work. Anyone who enjoys European literature will admire the taut structure of Arishima's novels, their vivid imagery, and, above all, their emotional intensity. For his fiction, still vibrant with life, he will be long remembered.

RECOMMENDED READING

Novel

A Certain Woman. Aru onna. 1911–19. 388 pages. Tr. Kenneth Strong. University of Tokyo Press, Tokyo, 1978. Contains 25-page introduction by the translator; is in the UNESCO Collection of Representative Works, Japanese Series.

Short Fiction

"Descendants of Cain." "Kain no matsuei." 1917. 54 pages. Tr. John W. Morrison. In *Modern Japanese Fiction.* University of Utah Press, Salt Lake City, Utah, 1955. Is the only translated story in this volume, which otherwise discusses early modern Japanese literature and, separately, the career of *Fukuzawa Yukichi.

WORKS IN ENGLISH TRANSLATION

Novel

A Certain Woman. Aru onna. 1911–19.

Short Fiction

"The Agony of Coming into the World." "*Umare izuru nayami.*" 1918. 97 pages. Tr. Seiji Fujita. *Eigo Seinen,* vol. 97, no. 5, 1951; complete: Hokuseido, Tokyo, 1955.

"A Bunch of Grapes." "*Hitofusa no budō.*" 1920. Tr. Hideichi Ono and John McVittie. *The Japanese Image,* vol. 2, ed. M. Schneps and A. D. Coox. Orient West, Tokyo, 1966.

"Descendants of Cain." "*Kain no matsuei.*" 1917.

Letter

"To My Little Sons." "*Chiisaki mono e.*" 1918. 16 pages. Tr. Yoshikazu Ueno. *The Reeds,* vol. 13, 1972.

Play

Death. Shi to sono zengo. 1917. 56 pages. Tr. Yozan T. Iwasaki and Glenn Hughes. *New Plays from Japan.* Ernest Benn, London, 1930.

CRITICAL STUDIES

Anderer, Paul James. *Other Worlds: Arishima Takeo and the Bounds of Modern Japanese Fiction.* Columbia University Press, NY, 1984.

———. "Other Worlds: A Study of Arishima Takeo." Ph.D. diss., Yale University, New Haven, 1979.

Kodama, Koichi. "Walt Whitman and Takeo Arishima." *Aoyama Gakuin Daigaku Eibungaku Shicho,* vol. 32, no. 1, 1959.

McClellan, Ryoko Toyama. "The White Birch School (*Shirakaba-ha*) of Japanese Literature: Some Sketches and Commentary." *Occasional Paper,* no. 2, University of Oregon, 1975.

Morrison, John Wilson. "A Study in Modern Japanese Literature with a Translation of Arishima Takeo's 'Descendants of Cain.'" Ph.D. diss., University of Washington, Seattle, 1948.

Morton, Leith D. "A Comparison of Arishima Takeo's '*Kankan Mushi*' and '*Kain no matsuei.*'" *Transactions of the International Conference of Orientalists in Japan,* no. 22, 1977.

———. *Divided Self: A Biography of Arishima Takeo.* Allen and Unwin, Sydney, 1988.

———. "An Introduction to Arishima Takeo: A Comparative Study of '*Kankan mushi*' and '*Kain no matsuei.*'" *Journal of the Oriental Society of Australia,* no. 12, 1977.

———. "Review Article of *A Certain Woman* by Arishima Takeo." *Journal of the Oriental Society of Australia,* no. 13, 1978.

Nabeshima, Norihiro. "Takeo Arishima and Walt Whitman." *Ochanomizu University Studies in Arts and Culture,* no. 10, 1967.

ARIYOSHI Sawako
(1931–84)

Novelist and playwright. Born in Wakayama City, south of Osaka. Early years spent mostly in Java.

A born storyteller who could unfailingly hold the attention of her readers from the outset of a novel, Ariyoshi Sawako was one of the most prolific and popular of Japan's modern novelists. Although, as an exponent of the fictional mode of writing, she rarely expressed her personal experiences directly, she nonetheless put deep feeling into her work and always appeared to display an admirable tolerance towards her fellow human beings. Her novels, short stories, and plays were written over a twenty-five-year period and they clearly demonstrated her two great preoccupations: firstly, with the traditions and arts of Old Japan, and secondly – but becoming dominant in her later career – with the many social, racial, and environmental issues that confront today's society.

A representative selection of Ariyoshi's works is available in English translation, including the first novel of her famous *River Trilogy*, the generational story *Ki no kawa* (1959, *The River Ki*). Here, as elsewhere in her work, her focus was upon the Japanese woman – a subject that she always brought to life by imparting a complete and rounded individuality to her central character. To her eternal credit the essentially nonpolitical Ariyoshi never reduced social issues to mere abstractions but always showed exactly how individual people – women in particular – were affected by them.

Ariyoshi Sawako was born in Wakayama City, which lies some thirty-five miles to the south of Osaka. The second of three children, she was brought up in Japan until 1937 when the whole family moved to the island of Java where her father was working. They remained there for nearly four years, returning briefly to Japan in 1940 and, then, permanently in 1941. As a consequence, much of Ariyoshi's knowledge of her own country during this period was gleaned from books, through which she developed a romantic longing for the grace and sensibility of Old Japan. Even when she entered the Faculty of English Literature at the Tokyo Women's College she seems to have been chiefly interested in traditional Japanese theater, especially the *Kabuki to which she was irresistibly attracted.

On leaving college, Ariyoshi worked as a reporter for a theatrical magazine and subsequently as a secretary to the *Azuma Kabuki* troupe, assisting with productions. Her literary career did not begin properly until 1956 when her story *"Jiuta"* ("Jiuta Ballad," tr. as "Jiuta") was published in *Bungakukai* (*Literary World*). It brought her immediate recognition as one of the most accomplished prose stylists of her generation. Nonetheless, nominated for the Akutagawa Prize, *"Jiuta"* was considered by the judges to be "too old-fashioned" in its theme to be declared the winner, a comment which the young Ariyoshi never forgot.

Guaranteed to provoke a wide range of emotions, "Jiuta" tells of how Toshihisa, one of the most revered masters of traditional Japanese music, has disinherited his daughter, Kunie, for marrying a *nisei* (second-generation Japanese-American). Kunie, too, is an accomplished musician and is deeply hurt by her father's stubbornness, yet, because she really loves her husband, she is quite unable to bow to her father's wishes. She often remembers how she and her father once communicated through music, he being completely blind but possessing an uncanny ability to visualize the "colors" that she would paint in sound with her *koto*.

If, early on in "Jiuta," one is inclined to regard the old man as utterly unreasonable in his rejection of Kunie, one may well come to admire his uncompromising stance as the story progresses. He rejects all foreign influences, especially the cold, mechanical aspects of modern civilization, and knows in his heart that his daughter will never become a great musician if she leaves Japan with her American husband. As the hour for her departure draws closer, Toshihisa still refuses to see her, remaining at home with Niizeki, a new and promising disciple whom Kunie believes has replaced her in his affections. Of course, nothing could be further from the truth, for the old man will not even allow Niizeki to touch Kunie's last letter bidding him farewell. Hurrying to the airport on the pretext of seeing someone else, he meets Kunie and asks her – almost helplessly – if she will ever return. She says she will, but both of them know that she is leaving Japan and its age-old cultural tradition forever.

"Jiuta" is a story of great power and subtlety in which Ariyoshi shows a true dramatist's talent for identifying a nexus of human conflicts and turning them into art. She appears to take the view that cultural transmission has all the intimacy of a parent–child relationship, a theme which she developed in later stories such as "Sumi" (1961, "The Ink Stick"). Indeed, one has the feeling that if the heroine of "Jiuta" had no instinctive genius for Japanese music, her father would not mind whom she married or where she traveled. But he feels betrayed by her because he fears that his new disciple, promising though she is, will never master the most difficult secrets of his art. Thus, the story's tragedy is intact and inevitable. Even if Niizeki *does* continue the unbroken tradition of music, Toshihisa will be obliged to recognize that he once held expectations of his daughter that were quite unnecessary.

Among Ariyoshi's other early stories, "Eguchi no sato" (1958, "The Village of Eguchi") is outstanding. Here again she identifies the dramatic tension generated when cultural traditions collide, exploring it in a gently probing manner that prefers understatement to the depiction of outright conflict. In her portrait of the foreign priest, Father Gounod, and his relationship to his Japanese congregation, she also displays a remarkable talent for seeing the world from two different points of view. From Father Gounod's point of view, the Japanese Catholics are unnecessarily zealous, demanding ever longer sermons from him while remaining quite oblivious to his message of tolerance and understanding. To Mrs. Sakurai, however, one of the church's main supporters, the priest is gravely at fault in giving instruction to the *geisha* Kofumi who visits the church on impulse after returning from her mother's Buddhist memorial service.

Ariyoshi's genius in "The Village of Eguchi" becomes apparent at the end of the story, when, instead of falling prey to the dangers of drink, Father Gounod is uplifted in spirit by seeing the beautiful Kofumi dance. The description of the priest enraptured by this timeless scene from Old Japan is deeply moving, for it suggests that the cultural barrier is not entirely insurmountable. Momentarily it becomes irrelevant, and Father Gounod thanks the Lord for His blessings and resolves to repay them.

Of the three novels in Ariyoshi's *River Trilogy*, *Ki no kawa* (1959, *The River Ki*), *Arita-gawa* (1963, *Arita River*), and *Hidaka-gawa* (1965, *Hidaka River*), only the first has been translated into English. It is a masterpiece of storytelling, tracing the life of Kimoto Hana from the occasion of her marriage at the beginning of the century to her final years after the end of World War II. Spanning five generations it reveals the enormous changes that have taken place in Japan during that period, and although it is largely conventional in style it has an immense vitality that makes it very enjoyable to read.

Hana's wedding with which *The River Ki* opens is in one sense the climax of the story. Brought up by Toyono, her strict but kindly grandmother, Hana is being married to Matani Keisaku, an ambitious young landowner who lives many miles downstream on the River Ki. The fact that he lives downstream rather than upstream has been of great significance to the old-fashioned Toyono. Indeed, she has selected him to be Hana's husband, in preference to another suitor from a more illustrious family, simply because superstition dictates that women must never "go against nature" by moving upstream on their wedding day.

As it turns out, Toyono's choice has been a wise one, even though the Matani family has none of the refinements of the Kimotos. Hana herself, exceptionally beautiful and intelligent, has been brought up by Toyono to believe wholeheartedly in all the traditional virtues of Old Japan. She departs for her wedding lavishly equipped with a magnificent dowry, and is floated downriver in a palanquin toward her new home. Not only does the scene have a wonderful sense of age-old traditions, it is also an extraordinary affirmation of these traditions by the strong-willed Toyono, who has had to go against other members of the family in order to ensure Hana's future happiness.

No other novel readily springs to mind in which the aging of its characters is accomplished with greater skill. Taking the River Ki as the continuing metaphor of the story, the author exactly matches Hana's development to the gradual broadening of the river as it moves towards the ocean. Whereas, at the beginning, we seem to be observing Hana objectively, by the end we are viewing all the events of the novel from her unique perspective.

It becomes apparent that Ariyoshi's intention in *The River Ki* is to identify and emphasize the strength of women in Japanese society. She also tries to show how the traditional role of women does not necessarily reduce their influence in what is certainly a patriarchal system. Conventional to the point of being hidebound, Toyono and Hana nonetheless have the strength of will to dominate those around them, whereas Hana's rebellious daughter, Fumio, has a more easily exhausted source of vitality. Unlike her mother, she believes that women should be independent of men: free to stand or fall by their own decisions. Throughout the novel a constant battle rages between Fumio and her mother, and it is resolved only by the appearance of a granddaughter, Hanako, to whom Hana, at a critical point in the story, is able to pass some of her strength.

The River Ki unfolds in a manner that might serve as a classic example of Japanese storytelling technique. Slow-moving on the surface, it sometimes advances rapidly and unexpectedly but without ever changing its ultimate destination. There is, perhaps, a certain sleight of hand in the skill with which Ariyoshi keeps her narrative within the control of her female characters, not allowing the men to assume center stage for very long. But the river itself stands for the female principle and its flow must necessarily be undiminished by men's activities.

In 1966, Ariyoshi published *Hanaoka Seishū no tsuma* (*The Doctor's Wife*), as a single installment in a magazine. This chilling story – of how two women, the wife and the mother of an eighteenth-century doctor, vie with each other to be human guinea pigs in his efforts to discover a general anesthetic – confirmed the author's popularity. It was immensely successful and was not only adapted for stage and screen, but, in translation (as *Kae*) became a best-seller in France some twenty years later.

Western readers of *The Doctor's Wife* will probably not query why two beautiful and intelligent women should behave in such a self-sacrificing manner, for that is fully explained in the story. More astonishing is the fact that a responsible doctor should consent to using his own wife and mother as subjects for a dangerous experiment. Fortunately, the author is at pains to portray him not only as a man with a driving ambition, but also as one who tends to be cautious. Hanaoka waits until he is reasonably confident that any new technique has a good chance of success before trying it. Indeed, as so often in Ariyoshi's work, there is an untold story attached to the male character: in this instance the doctor's implicit struggle with the whole issue of medical ethics, balancing potential benefits to mankind with potential dangers to those on whom he experiments.

As the English translators note in their introduction, *The Doctor's Wife* is based on the personal records, diaries, and biography of Hanaoka Seishū, one of Japan's most celebrated physicians

(1760–1835). Part of the book's popularity in Japan may have been the reminder that Seishū developed a general anesthetic some forty years before chloroform and ether were used in the West. The supposed Japanese lack of originality (one of the world's most misleading half-truths) is here dealt a resounding denial, despite Hanaoka's lending an Oriental aura of respectability to his research by citing the ancient Chinese physician, Hua Tu, as a precedent. "I want to be the Hua Tu of Japan," he says, noting that his great predecessor performed many elaborate surgical operations that could scarcely have been done without anesthetic. In itself, this desire to unite Oriental and Western knowledge is a significant theme, and one which naturally evokes a response among Japanese readers. Equally appealing is the contrast between the semi-Westernized doctor and the courageous women who apply their "samurai" discipline to help him. On this level the novel is simply a duel between two women, both of whom hold to traditional values in a world that is being changed irrevocably by Western science.

While addressing moral issues of universal significance in *The Doctor's Wife*, Ariyoshi also went further, examining specific social issues in works that were far removed from whatever was then understood by "women's fiction." *Hishoku (1963–64, Colorless)* focused on racial tensions in the United States, a country she had visited in 1959 at the invitation of the Rockefeller Foundation. *"Fukugō osen" (1974–75, Compound Pollution)* discussed the problem of environmental pollution: an issue which Ariyoshi had touched upon in passing in *The River Ki* and which was clearly one of her major concerns.

Because of its translated version, *Kōkotsu no hito (1972, The Twilight Years)* has been in the West the best-known of Ariyoshi's *shakai shōsetsu* (novels dealing with social issues). Its theme is the problem of senility, a problem that is regarded in Japan with a mixture of horror and fascination. Indeed, senility has been the subject of several important works of modern Japanese literature, including INOUE YASUSHI's *Chronicle of My Mother*, TANIZAKI's *Diary of a Mad Old Man*, and NIWA FUMIO's remarkable short story "The Hateful Age." No author, however, looks at the social problem of senility more comprehensively than Ariyoshi in *The Twilight Years*. With this novel she achieved the difficult feat of including an immense amount of factual information without spoiling the entertaining qualities of the narrative.

There is a curious ambiguity at the heart of *The Twilight Years*, and it is to this that the novel owes much of its power. Both Shigezō, the eighty-four-year-old widower, and Akiko, his hard-pressed daughter-in-law, vie to be the central character of the story.

One might attribute this to the author's desire to show conflict between the elderly and those who have the responsibility of caring for them, yet the story has a further dimension, too. On another level it is a feminist novel: one in which men can be freely caricatured while only women inhabit a world of feeling and sensitivity.

Throughout his life, Shigezō has certainly been a monster: obsessed with his own well-being, bad tempered, and callously uncaring about his wife's feelings. He has been equally unpleasant to his daughter-in-law, to the extent that she and her husband have rarely visited even though the old couple have been living in a small cottage attached to their home. When her mother-in-law dies suddenly, Akiko is appalled to discover that Shigezō suffers from advanced senility. His eccentricities are at once pitiful and exasperating, leading Akiko to wonder how her mother-in-law, even with her old-fashioned stoicism, could have endured them for so long.

Shigezō develops a voracious appetite, demanding to be fed at all hours of the day. On occasions, possessed by some unexplained obsession, he runs away from home and walks so rapidly along the main thoroughfares of the city that Akiko can scarcely catch up with him. He is quite unable to recognize either of his children, Kyōko or Akiko's husband, Nobutoshi, and hardly ever speaks except to express his alarm at being left alone with Nobutoshi whom he thinks is a burglar. His robust physique is in sharp contrast to his feeble mind, and he shows every sign of being a burden to his family for many years to come.

Akiko copes magnificently with the old man, aided by the fact that now, in his advanced years, his unpleasant personality has completely changed. Although still demanding, he has become simple, gentle, and particularly well-disposed towards Akiko. Her son, Satoshi, cynically observes that this is only because Shigezō's continued survival is dependent on her, and Akiko is inclined to agree. Nonetheless, she develops a real affection for him, and it is this unexpected change in feeling that raises the novel to a higher plane than its documentary approach would seem to allow.

In her subsequent novel, *Compound Pollution*, Ariyoshi decided to abandon nearly all the elements of the conventional novel in favor of a documentary style. The *Asahi shimbun*, Japan's second-largest newspaper with a circulation of over twelve million copies, invited her to write a serial novel on any subject she cared to choose. At first she thought she would write about the growth of the women's movement in Japan, but the intended focus of her work, the suffragette Ichikawa Fusae, decided to run again for office

at the advanced age of eighty-one. Not wishing to interfere with
the political process, Ariyoshi turned her attention elsewhere: to
the subject of environmental pollution, which had concerned her
for many years.

Her decision to write about pollution was remarkably courageous,
given that she was neither a chemist nor a biologist. It was quite
possible that she would appear foolishly ignorant when she
committed herself to writing about such scientific matters. In the
event, her work was a triumph. When it ran in the *Asahi* between
October 1974 and June 1975 the series created a sensation, the effects
of which are still reverberating through Japanese society. Indeed,
commentators have remarked that the impact of Ariyoshi's "novel"
was greater than that of the *sum total* of all previous Japanese
writings on environmental pollution. In book form, *Compound
Pollution* sold a million copies, volume one appearing even before
the newspaper series had finished its run. With this single work,
Ariyoshi did much to dispel public apathy and as a consequence
prompted the introduction of corrective measures which have gone
at least some way towards cleaning up the environment.

Ariyoshi was by no means the first person to write about pollution
in Japan. The Ashio Mine Pollution Incident at the end of the
nineteenth century provided a subject for a novella by SHIGA NAOYA,
while other, individual disasters had been addressed by various
writers at different times. Ariyoshi's original contribution lay in the
fact that she wrote about *compound* pollution, that is, pollution
caused gradually and by a variety of factors rather than by a single
act or accident. As many people are now aware, compound pollution
is the most insidious kind: that gradual accumulation of toxins in
air, water, and food that poses a new threat to human survival as
serious as the older ones of war, famine, and pestilence. For her
theme, Ariyoshi took virtually the *whole* of compound pollution,
describing it in such a way that its causes, dangers – *and* its possible
remedies – were comprehensible to the average reader.

At first, she had no intention of addressing such a vast
subject. Realizing that a novelistic structure demanded a focus, she
considered writing about the development of a new factory town,
describing how it becomes not only prosperous but severely
polluted. At the end of this novel she planned to have her main
character (the "man of vision" who has instigated the project)
desperately trying to prove that the water supply is safe by drinking
it in front of the media. Perhaps inevitably, real events stole her
thunder. Before she could write the book, factory owners up and
down the country were already quaffing effluent in the presence of

the media – and doing it so frequently that any inclusion of such a scene would have been a mere cliché.

Ariyoshi therefore embarked on a much more diffuse, but in many ways more powerful work about pollution in general. She divided it into fifteen sections of varying length, coming to grips with the technical issues while using her novelist's skill to make them understandable. For example, in order to avoid patronizing the reader she invented just one fictional character, an Old Man, with whom she discusses the issues in an anecdotal manner. This brilliant device not only links the past with the present but adds a literary dimension to an otherwise undiluted exposition of facts.

For historical reasons, pollution of land, air, water, and food has been even more severe in Japan than in the West, and thus the facts presented by Ariyoshi were devastating. With an unerring touch she revealed the cynicism and incompetence of government bureaucrats, identified many of the dangerous practices of modern agriculture (such as using chemicals to make fruit and vegetables look more attractive to the eye), and pointed to Japan's lack of expertise in natural history as one of the reasons why the nation's agricultural methods were failing. Although her attacks did not go unrebuffed, various bureaucrats were eventually obliged to admit their mistakes, while many farmers came to be among her most ardent supporters.

One of Ariyoshi's most telling examples of wholly unnecessary pollution was gathered on a trip to Kyoto. Inquiring on behalf of the Old Man, who complains that *tsukemono* (pickled vegetables) no longer taste as they should, she discovers where she can purchase genuine *tsukemono* that have not been treated with modern preservatives. In fact, they are available only in a small pickle shop, the proprietress of which was formerly a wholesaler who found herself unable to compete when her rivals started using additives. The woman describes to Ariyoshi how pickles are made traditionally by compressing salted vegetables. Modern methods, she explains, are quite different. Because compressed vegetables lose water – and water adds weight – suppliers who sell by weight now add water. Water reduces the product's shelf life, so they add preservatives, which in turn reduce the flavor . . . so the suppliers add flavoring agents. It is a classic instance of marketing logic being taken to extremes – and it is of a kind that is certainly not restricted to Japan alone. In this episode, too, with its references to traditional culture, one senses that the author is essentially the same person who wrote "Jiuta" and "The Ink Stick," however different those elegant works may seem when compared to *Compound Pollution*.

Unfortunately, *Compound Pollution* has not been fully translated into English. Readers who are interested in it, however, are urged to examine Karen Colligan-Taylor's brilliant analysis of it in *The Emergence of Environmental Literature in Japan* (Garland, NY, 1990), which has provided the basis for the above discussion. As the author notes, two years after *Compound Pollution* was completed, a further volume was issued, called *Fukugō osen, sono go* (1977, *Fukugo Osen, The Aftermath*). It contained transcripts of various discussions between Ariyoshi and both her critics and supporters.

In 1984, Ariyoshi died peacefully in her sleep at the age of fifty-three. In her time she had been one of the most famous women in Japan and had acquired considerable wealth from her writing. Yet she had always placed work before personal happiness, and her marriage in 1962 lasted only two years before it broke down. It is possible that she would have had a longer life had she not worked so hard, but one suspects that, given a few extra years, she might have written a best-selling book on the subject of overwork (long identified as an acute Japanese social problem).

Throughout her career, Ariyoshi's interest in drama was sustained by seeing many of her novels adapted to stage and screen, and she herself translated and directed Father Daniel Berrigan's anti-war play *The Trial of the Catonsville Nine* in 1972. One of her last major achievements was in winning the Mainichi Cultural Prize for her novel *Kazunomiyasama Otome* (1979, *Her Highness Princess Kazu*). Since then, her fame has spread to the West through the sensitive translations of Mildred Tahara in English, Yoko Sim and Jean Christian Bouvier in French, Lydia Origlia in Italian, and many more. It appears likely that Ariyoshi's popularity overseas will continue to grow, while her reputation as a writer of polemical but highly readable fiction is already assured.

RECOMMENDED READING

Novels

The Doctor's Wife. *Hanaoka Seishū no tsuma.* 1966. 174 pages. Tr. Wakako Hironaka and Ann Siller Kostant. Kodansha International, Tokyo, 1978. The remarkable story of a pioneering doctor and his family, drawn from true life.

The River Ki. *Ki no kawa.* 1959. 243 pages. Tr. Mildred Tahara. Kodansha International, Tokyo and NY, 1980. Ariyoshi's best novel in translation. Highly recommended.

WORKS IN ENGLISH TRANSLATION

Novels

The Doctor's Wife. Hanaoka Seishū no tsuma. 1966.

The River Ki. Ki no kawa. 1959.

The Twilight Years. Kōkotsu no hito. 1972. 216 pages. Tr. Mildred Tahara. Peter Owen, London, 1984; reprint of paperback edition by Kodansha International, Tokyo, 1992.

Short Fiction

"The Ink Stick." "*Sumi.*" *1961.* 18 pages. Tr. Mildred Tahara. *Japan Quarterly*, vol. 22, no. 4, 1975.

"Jiuta." "*Jiuta.*" *1956.* 18 pages. Tr. Yukio Sawa and Herbert Glazer. *Japan Quarterly*, vol. 22, no. 1, 1975.

"Prayer." "*Kitō.*" *1959.* 33 pages. Tr.

John Bester. *Japan Quarterly*, vol. 7, no. 4, 1960.

"The Tomoshibi." "*Tomoshibi.*" *1961.* 17 pages. Tr. Keiko Nakamura. *The Mother of Dreams, and Other Short Stories*, ed. Makoto Ueda. Kodansha International, Tokyo, 1985.

"The Village of Eguchi." "*Eguchi no sato.*" *1958.* 15 pages. Tr. Yukio Sawa and Herbert Glazer. *Japan Quarterly*, vol. 18, no. 4, 1971.

Miscellaneous

Extract from the novel: *Her Highness Princess Kazu. Kazunomiyasama Otome* 1979. 18 pages. Tr. Mildred Tahara. *Journal of Literary Translation*, no. 17, 1976.

CRITICAL STUDIES

Allen, Louis. "A Critique of Ariyoshi Sawako: *Hanaoka Seishū no tsuma.*" *Proceedings of the British Association for Japanese Studies*, no. 9, 1984.

McClain, Yoko. "Ariyoshi Sawako: Creative Social Critic." *Journal of the Association of Teachers of Japanese*, vol. 12, no. 2, 1977.

Uyttendaele, Francis. "Love the Old as Yourself: Ariyoshi Sawako's *Kōkotsu no hito.*" *Japan Missionary Bulletin*, vol. 26, no. 10, 1972.

DAZAI Osamu
(1909–1948)

Novelist and writer of short fiction. Real name, Tsushima Shūji. Born in Kanagi, Tsugaru, Aomori Prefecture. Lived in Tokyo.

No modern Japanese writer inspires so much affection as Dazai Osamu, and both his life and work have long held legendary status in Japan. As the author of *Shayō* (*1947, The Setting Sun*) and *Ningen shikkaku* (*1948, No Longer Human*) he must surely be ranked among the elite of the world's novelists. Although his work contains none of the inventiveness of a TANIZAKI, MISHIMA, or Dostoievesky, it has all the emotional force of the greatest literature. That much of it is subjective, being based on Dazai's dramatization of himself and his relationship to society, is testimony to his unique qualities as a writer.

Dazai, Tsushima Shūji, was born into a wealthy, bourgeois family in Tsugaru, the northernmost part of Honshū. Around thirty people lived in the huge Tsushima mansion, including the three older brothers and four sisters of the new infant, Shūji. Their father, Tsushima Gen'emon, served in the National Diet from 1912 until

64

his death in 1923. He was thus away in Tokyo during most of
Dazai's childhood years. Nor was Shūji's mother any more attentive.
A semi-invalid, she delegated her parental role to wet nurses who
came and went with confusing frequency. If Dazai can be said to
have regarded anyone as his "mother," she would be Take, a girl
who was fourteen when she became his nursemaid, and eighteen
when she left to get married. Dazai's description (albeit an
embroidered one, according to scholars) of being reunited with
Take, in May 1944, is one of the most moving passages in Japanese
literature.

By the time Dazai entered Hirosaki High School in 1927, he was
already showing a strong interest in creative writing. At Aomori
Junior High School he had worked on a literary magazine, and,
within the family, had started a journal called *Shinkirō* (*Mirage*). But
now his eldest brother, Bunji, disapproved of his more serious
attempts at writing, fearing that he might neglect his studies. In
this, at least, Bunji was right. Dazai began his inexorable drift
towards a bohemian life-style, partly modeled on the Paris example,
partly an expression of his alienation from his family. He also began
a long career of womanizing at around this time, falling in love
with a young *geisha*, Oyama Hatsuyo, whom he was later to marry.

Dazai's sense of alienation was not wholly attributable to his
family background, although he often claimed that it was. He
was unusually self-conscious, and always hypersensitive in his
relationship to others. Like Mishima after him, he was quite correct
in diagnosing his own genius, while those around him had little
conception of the value or status of literature. Furthermore, his
feelings of rejection were exaggerated by failing to find comradeship
even among the leftwing students whose politics he shared. As a
rich man's son he felt like a charlatan in their company. Depression
overtook him. He failed in his studies and attempted to commit
suicide in 1929, the year prior to entering Tokyo Imperial University.

Dazai gained admittance to the French department of the
university without any qualifications and without knowing a word
of French. His professor is said to have been amused by his audacity
in making the application. With equal audacity, Dazai also sought
the acquaintance of IBUSE MASUJI, a writer he greatly admired.
Ibuse's support and guidance were to be the most positive factors
counterbalancing Dazai's self-destructive tendencies. The older man
recognized his potential, even though Dazai had published only a
few stories, such as "*Mugen naraku*" (*1928*, "Bottomless Hell");
"*Aware ga*" (*1928*, "Poor Mosquito"); and "*Jinushi ichidai*" (*1929–30*,
"A Landlord's Life").

Dazai's personal life became even more confused in 1930. After heavy drinking with a bar hostess from the Ginza he took the lady in question to the resort of Kamakura where they flung themselves into the sea in a love suicide attempt. The girl drowned, and Dazai was thoroughly disgraced. Charges against him were dropped only after his eldest brother (the dreaded Bunji) intervened. After recuperating, Dazai married Hatsuyo and continued his political activities under constant harrassment from the authorities. In 1932 he was devastated to learn the true facts of his wife's career as a *geisha*, but achieved a reconciliation and began writing his most significant work so far. This was *"Omoide"* ("Recollections"), which he completed and published in 1933.

"Recollections" was Dazai's seminal work. In a brilliant study (with translations), *The Saga of Dazai Osamu*, Phyllis I. Lyons refers to it as: "Dazai's first step in his development of his most characteristic autobiographical method of storytelling, a method perfected in *No Longer Human*, where the narrator reveals his desperate need to cling to a hope of self-worth through a statement of seeming worthlessness." It is a story of childhood and adolescence, told with a rare sense of detachment. As Professor Lyons says, it restructures the reality of Dazai's experience and presents an "historical tale as much about his own fragmentary perceptions as about events."

The real beginning of Dazai's literary career was in 1933. Not only did he make contact with the young writers who were publishing *Kaihyō* (*The Sea Lion*), a literary journal in Tokyo, but he also won a competition in an Aomori newspaper with his story, *"Ressha"* ("The Train"). It was the first work to be published under his new pen name, Dazai Osamu. In the same year he also received favorable notices for his story *"Gyofukuki"* ("Metamorphosis"), and its publication in *Kaihyō* was followed by the serialization of "Recollections." Dazai went on to write for several other journals, becoming quite prolific in his output.

However, in 1935, Dazai suffered serious setbacks that were to affect him for the rest of his life. He gave up his attempt to graduate from Tokyo University; failed an entrance examination to work on the newspaper *Miyako shimbun* (*Capital News*); made his third suicide attempt; and, in April, he contracted peritonitis and became addicted to the painkilling drugs given him in hospital. Worse still, he was just beaten by ISHIKAWA TATSUZŌ in the competition for the first Akutagawa Prize established by the journal *Bungei shunjū* (*Literary Seasons*). It was the most cruel blow of all, for despite his dissipation, Dazai remained intensely ambitious. He craved fame, perhaps as a substitute for the affection he had never received as a child.

Dazai finally separated from Hatsuyo, bringing to an end a relationship that culminated in her affair with one of his friends, a brief reconciliation, and a love suicide attempt in 1937. When Dazai published his first short-story collection, *Bannen* (1936, *Final Years*), he intended the title seriously. His life seemed to be drawing to a tragic, premature end. Seriously ill with tuberculosis, alcoholism, and drug addiction, and with a failed marriage, a disastrous academic record, and many personal debts, it is not surprising that one of the judges for the Akutagawa Prize, KAWABATA YASUNARI, referred publicly to the "unfortunate cloud" over Dazai's life. It fell to Ibuse Masuji to rescue the twenty-nine-year-old author in 1938.

As Dazai's mentor, Ibuse was contacted by the Tsushima family and asked to arrange a new marriage for his delinquent protégé. Accordingly, Dazai and an attractive twenty-six-year-old school-teacher, Ishihara Michiko, were married at Ibuse's house on January 8, 1939. The new stability was highly beneficial. Dazai won his first literary prize for "*Ōgon fūkei*" (*1939*, "A Golden Picture") and the Kitamura Tōkoku Award for "*Joseito*" (*1939*, "Schoolgirl"). He began traveling and lecturing, and, on a visit to Izu, wrote his important autobiographical summary, "*Tokyo hakkei*" (*1941*, "Eight Views of Tokyo"). Furthermore, his 1939 piece, "*Fugaku hyakkei*" ("One Hundred Views of Mount Fuji") was selected by Shinchōsha for a series called *The Best of Shōwa Period Literature*.

Most of Dazai's works available in English translation are the autobiographical writings for which he is chiefly known. However, in his productive wartime period (poor health exempted him from serving even as a journalist) he wrote many stories based on historical material. They included "*Udaijin Sanetomo*" (1943, "Sane-tomo, Minister of the Right") and "*Shinshaku shokoku banashi*" (1945, "New Tales of the Provinces").

Like most successful writers, Dazai was presented with projects that were commercially attractive but potentially time-wasting and tedious. One such project was to write a travel book about his home province in northern Japan. Again, Ibuse Masuji was an inspiration. He suggested to Dazai that the travelogue might be turned into a vehicle for self-expression. Thus, after a momentous trip to see his family and tour the province, Dazai produced a masterpiece, filled with anecdote, reminiscence, comment, and observation. It was called simply *Tsugaru* and was translated into English as *Return to Tsugaru* in 1985.

Overwork and the stress of wartime probably contributed to the return of Dazai's nihilism and self-destructive life-style. Disaster provided the stimulus he needed to produce his best work. He became involved with two married women, Ōta Shizuko and

Yamazaki Tomie – the latter, an obsessive disciple who has been described as Dazai's "angel of death." She was most likely the model for Kazuko, an aristocratic woman who abandons her class, in his greatest novel, *Shayō* (*1947, The Setting Sun*).

The Setting Sun was an immediate best-seller when it was serialized in *Shinchō* in four installments. It brilliantly evoked the atmosphere of contemporary postwar Japan: a nation with a Western facade and an Eastern spirit. The character of Kazuko, the determined survivor, caught the imagination of the public.

Dazai was never again to equal the quality of *The Setting Sun*. In his next novel, *No Longer Human*, he appeared to retrace his steps, going over material he had used previously in "Recollections" and "Eight Views of Tokyo". It is the story of Yōzō, who, "disqualified as a human being," acts as the yardstick by which Dazai makes a final judgment of life in all its ugliness and beauty. Only weeks after compiling it, and while still working on another novel entitled *Guddo-bai* (*Goodbye*), Dazai committed suicide with Yamazaki Tomie. Their bodies were recovered from the Tamagawa Canal on June 19, 1948: Dazai's fortieth birthday by Japanese reckoning.

RECOMMENDED READING

Novels

No Longer Human. *Ningen shikkaku*. *1948*. 177 pages. Tr. Donald Keene. Peter Owen, London, 1957; New Directions, NY, 1958, 1977; Four Square Press, London, 1961. Contains 7-page translator's introduction.

The Setting Sun. *Shayō*. *1947*. 189 pages. Tr. Donald Keene. New Directions, NY, 1956; Peter Owen, London, 1958; Four Square Press, London, 1961; Rupa, Calcutta, 1961; Hara Shobo, Tokyo, 1965; Tuttle, Tokyo, 1981. Dazai's masterpiece and a postwar classic. Contains translator's 10-page introduction.

Short Fiction Collections

Crackling Mountain and Other Stories. Tr. James O'Brien. Tuttle, Tokyo and Boston, 1989. 255 pages. Includes: "Monkey Island," "On the Question of Apparel," "A Poor Man's Got His Pride," "Recollections," and "The Sound of Hammering."

The Saga of Dazai Osamu, A Critical Study with Translations. By Phyllis I. Lyons. Stanford University Press, Stanford, 1985. 410 pages. A critical study of Dazai's semi-autobiographical writings, with translations of five stories, "Recollections," "Eight Views of Tokyo," "Going Home," "Hometown," and "An Almanac of Pain," and the travel memoir *"Return to Tsugaru,"* tr. as *"Tsugaru."* Highly recommended to the serious reader.

Self-Portraits. Tr. with a 16-page introduction by Ralph F. McCarthy. Kodansha International, Tokyo and NY, 1991. 230 pages. A fine selection of Dazai's autobiographical writings, including "My Elder Brothers" (as "My Older Brothers" elsewhere), "One Hundred Views of Mount Fuji," "Early Light," and fifteen other stories. The volume is profusely illustrated with black-and-white photographs. Again, highly recommended.

WORKS IN ENGLISH TRANSLATION

Novels

No Longer Human. Ningen shikkaku. 1948.
Return to Tsugaru. Tsugaru. 1944. 172 pages. (1) Tr. James Westerhoven. Kodansha International, Tokyo, 1985. (2) As *Tsugaru. The Saga of Dazai Osamu.*
The Setting Sun. Shayō. 1947.

Short Fiction

"An Almanac of Pain." *"Kunō no nenkan."* 1946. 9 pages. *The Saga of Dazai Osamu.*
"Canis Familiaris." *"Chikukendan."* Composed 1939. 16 pages. *Self-Portraits.*
"Cherries." *"Ōtō.* 1947. 6 pages. (1) Tr. Edward Seidensticker. *Encounter*, vol. 1, no. 1, 1953. (2) *Self-Portraits.*
"Cherry Leaves and Whistler." *"Hazakura to mateki."* 1939. 11 pages. Tr. Ralph F. McCarthy. *Run, Melos, and Other Stories.* Kodansha International, Tokyo, 1988.
"Chiyojo." *"Chiyojo."* 1941. 12 pages. Tr. Lane Dunlop. *Michigan Quarterly Review*, vol. 21, no. 4, 1982; *A Late Chrysanthemum.* Tr. Lane Dunlop. North Point Press, San Francisco, 1986; Tuttle, Boston, 1991 paperback.

"The Courtesy Call." *"Shin'yū kōkan."* 1946. 15 pages. Tr. Ivan Morris. *Modern Japanese Short Stories.* Eyre and Spottiswoode, London, 1961; Tuttle, Tokyo, 1962; *The World of Japanese Fiction.* Dutton, NY, 1973; As "The Visitor." *The Japanese Image*, ed. M. Schneps and A. D. Coox. Orient West, Tokyo, 1965.
"Crackling Mountain." *"Kachikachiyama."* 1945. 26 pages. *Crackling Mountain and Other Stories.*
"The Criminal." *"Hannin."* 1948. 10 pages. Tr. Takashi Kojima. *Ei-Bei Bungaku (English and American Literature)*, no. 2, Meiji University, 1956.
"Currency." *"Kahei."* 1946. 7 pages. Tr. James O'Brien. *Dazai Osamu: Selected Stories and Sketches.* East Asia Papers, no. 33. China–Japan Program. Cornell University Press, Ithaca, NY, 1983.
"Das Gemeine." *"Dasu Gemaine."* 1935. 24 pages. *Dazai Osamu: Selected Stories and Sketches.*
"Early Light." *"Hakumei."* Composed c. 1947. 12 pages. *Self-Portraits.*
"Eight Views of Tokyo." *"Tokyo hakkei."* 1941. 23 pages. (1) *Dazai Osamu: Selected Stories and Sketches.* (2) *The Saga of Dazai Osamu.* (3) As "Eight Scenes

from Tokyo." *Run, Melos, and Other Stories; Self-Portraits.*

"Fallen Flowers." *"Sange."* 10 pages. Tr. Thomas E. Swann. *Monumenta Nipponica*, vol. 24, nos. 1–2, 1969.

"The Father." *"Chichi."* 1947. Tr. David J. Brudnoy and Kazuko Shimizu. *Monumenta Nipponica*, vol. 24, no. 4, 1969.

"Fulfillment of a Vow." *"Mangan."* 1938. 3 pages. (1) Tr. David J. Brudnoy and Kazuko Shimizu. *Monumenta Nipponica*, vol. 24, nos. 1–2, 1969. (2) As "A Promise Fulfilled." *Self-Portraits.*

"Garden." *"Niwa."* Composed c. 1946. 5 pages. *Self-Portraits.*

"A Garden Lantern." *"Tōrō."* 1937. 7 pages. (1) As "The Magic Lantern." Tr. Tomone Matsumoto. *The Shōwa Anthology*, vol. 1, Kodansha International, Tokyo, 1985. (2) *A Late Chrysanthemum.*

"Going Home." *"Kikyorai."* 1942. 15 pages. *The Saga of Dazai Osamu.*

"A Golden Picture." *Ōgon fūkei.* 1939. 4 pages. (1) *A Late Chrysanthemum.* (2) As "Seascape with Figures in Gold." *Self-Portraits.*

"Handsome Devils and Cigarettes." *"Bidanshi to tabako."* 1948. 6 pages. *Self-Portraits.*

"Hometown." *"Kokyō."* 1943. 11 pages. (1) As "Homecoming." *Dazai Osamu: Selected Stories and Sketches.* (2) *The Saga of Dazai Osamu.*

"I Accuse." *"Kakekomi uttae."* 1940. 19 pages. (1) Tr. Tadao Katayama. *The Reeds*, vol. 4, 1958. (2) As "Heed My Plea." *Crackling Mountain and Other Stories.*

"I Can Speak." *"I Can Speak."* Composed 1939. 3 pages. (1) Tr. David Brudnoy and Kazuko Shimizu. *Monumenta Nipponica*, vol. 24, no. 3, 1969. (2) *Self-Por-*

traits.

"The Lady Who Entertained." *"Kyōō fujin."* 1948. 8 pages. Tr. Karen Kaya Shimizu. *The Mother of Dreams, and Other Short Stories*, ed. Makoto Ueda. Kodansha International, Tokyo, 1986.

"Leaves." *"Ha."* 1934. 10 pages. Tr. Eric Gangloff. *Chicago Review*, vol. 20, 1968.

"A Lie." *"Uso."* 1946. 6 pages. Tr. Toshihiko Sato. *Today's Japan*, vol. 5, May–June, 1960; *The Japanese Image*, vol. 2.

"A Little Beauty." *"Bishōjo."* Composed 1939. 9 pages. *Self-Portraits.*

"Melos, Run!" *"Hashire Merosu."* 1940. 15 pages. (1) *Crackling Mountain and Other Stories.* (2) As "Run, Melos!" *Run, Melos, and Other Stories.*

"Merry Christmas." *"Merii Kurisumasu."* Composed late 1946. 10 pages. *Self-Portraits.*

"Metamorphosis." *"Gyofukuki."* 1933. 4 pages. (1) Tr. Thomas J. Harper. *Japan Quarterly*, vol. 17, no. 3, 1970. (2) As "Undine." *Crackling Mountain and Other Stories.*

"Monkey Island." *"Sarugashima."* 1936. 6 pages. (1) Tr. Aileen Gatten. *Voices*, vol. 3, no. 1, 1971. (2) As "The Island of the Monkeys." *Dazai Osamu: Selected Stories and Sketches.* (3) *Crackling Mountain and Other Stories.*

"Morning." *"Asa."* 1947. 4 pages. Tr. David J. Brudnoy and Yumi Oka. *Monumenta Nipponica*, vol. 24, no. 4, 1969.

"Mother." *"Haha."* 1947. 9 pages. Tr. David J. Brudnoy and Yumi Oka. *Monumenta Nipponica*, vol. 24, no. 3, 1969.

"The Mound of a Monkey's Grave." *"Saruzuka."* 8 pages. (1) *Dazai Osamu: Selected Stories and*

Sketches. As "The Monkey's Mound." (2) *Crackling Mountain and Other Stories.*

"No Kidding." *"Zakyō ni arazu."* Composed c. 1937. 3 pages. *Self-Portraits.*

"My Older Brothers." *"Anitachi."* 1940. 9 pages. (1) *Dazai Osamu: Selected Stories and Sketches.* (2) As "My Elder Brothers." *Self-Portraits.*

"Of Women." *"Mesu ni tsuite."* 1936. 3 pages. (1) Tr. Edward Seidensticker. *Encounter*, vol. 1, no. 1, 1953; *Atlantic Monthly*, Jan. 1955. (2) As "Female." *Self-Portraits.*

"One Hundred Views of Mount Fuji." *"Fugaku hyakkei."* Composed 1939. 31 pages. (1) *Run, Melos, and Other Stories; Self-Portraits.*

"On the Question of Apparel." *"Fukusō ni tsuite."* 1941. 13 pages. *Dazai Osamu: Selected Stories and Sketches; Crackling Mountain and Other Stories.*

"Osan." *"Osan."* 1947. 13 pages. Tr. Edward Seidensticker. *Japan Quarterly*, vol. 5, no. 4, 1958; *Modern Japanese Short Stories.* Japan Publications Trading Co., 1960; revised edition, 1970. *Dazai Osamu: Selected Stories and Sketches.*

"A Poor Man's Got His Pride." *"Hin no ij."* 1945. 10 pages. *Dazai Osamu: Selected Stories and Sketches; Crackling Mountain and Other Stories.*

"Putting Granny Out to Die." *"Ubasute."* Composed 1938. 16 pages. *Dazai Osamu: Selected Stories and Sketches.*

"Recollections." *"Omoide."* 1933. 34 pages. (1) As "Memories." *Dazai Osamu: Selected Stories and Sketches; Crackling Mountain and Other Stories.* (2) *The Saga of Dazai Osamu.* (3) As "Memor-

ies." *A Late Chrysanthemum.*

"A Record of the Autumn Wind." *"Shūfūki."* 1939. 9 pages. Tr. Keiko McDonald. *Denver Quarterly*, vol. 12, no. 2, 1977.

"Romanesque." *"Romanesuku."* 1934. 15 pages. Tr. John Nathan. *Japan Quarterly*, vol. 12, no. 3, 1965.

"Schoolgirl." *"Joseito."* 1939. 58 pages. *Run, Melos, and Other Stories.*

"A Sound of Hammering." *"Toka-tonton."* 1947. 9 pages. (1) Tr. Frank Motofuji. *Japan Quarterly*, vol. 16, no. 2, 1969. (2) As "The Sound of Hammering." *Dazai Osamu: Selected Stories and Sketches; Crackling Mountain and Other Stories.*

"A Snowy Night's Tale." *"Yuki no yo no hanashi."* 5 pages. (1) Tr. Thomas E. Swann. *Monumenta Nipponica*, vol. 22, nos. 1–2, 1967. (2) As "One Snowy Night." *Run, Melos, and Other Stories.*

"Taking the Wen Away." *"Kobu-tori."* 1945. 13 pages. *Dazai Osamu: Selected Stories and Sketches; Crackling Mountain and Other Stories.*

"Toys." *"Gangu."* 1935. 6 pages. *Dazai Osamu: Selected Stories and Sketches.*

"Thinking of Zenzo." *"Zenzō o omou."* 1939. 19 pages. *Self-Portraits.*

"Train." *"Ressha."* Composed 1932 or before. 4 pages. *Self-Portraits.*

"Twilight." *"Hakumei."* 1946. 11 pages. Tr. Michael C. Brownstein. *Journal of Literary Translation*, no. 17, 1986.

"Two Little Words." *"Oya to iu niji."* Composed c. 1946. 5 pages. *Self-Portraits.*

"Villon's Wife." *"Viyon no tsuma."* 1947. 17 pages. Tr. Donald Keene. *New Directions*, no. 15, 1955; *Modern Japanese Literature*,

Grove Press, NY, 1956; Tuttle, Tokyo, 1957.
"Waiting." "*Matsu*." 3 pages. Tr.

David J. Brudnoy and Kazuko Shimizu. *Monumenta Nipponica*, vol. 24, nos. 1–2, 1969.

CRITICAL STUDIES

Brudnoy, David. "The Immutable Despair of Dazai Osamu." *Monumenta Nipponica*, vol. 23, no. 3, 1968.

Chia, Joseph. *Dazai Osamu: Life and Art*. National University of Singapore, Singapore, 1988.

Gunn, Giles B. "Traditions and Modernity in Modern Japanese Fiction: Variations on a Theme in Natsume Sōseki, Tanizaki Jun'ichirō and Dazai Osamu." *Japan Christian Quarterly*, no. 35, 1969.

Hoaglund, Alan N. "Dazai's Novels: Mirror for Postwar Japan." *Japan Christian Quarterly*, no. 33, 1967.

Keene, Donald. "The Artistry of Dazai Osamu." *East West Review*, vol. 1, no. 3, 1965.

Lyons, Phyllis I. "Art Is Me: Dazai Osamu's Narrative Voice as a Permeable Self." *Harvard Journal of Asiatic Studies*, vol. 41, no. 1, 1981.

———. "The Osamu Saga: The Autobiographical Fiction of Dazai Osamu." Ph.D. diss., University of Chicago, Chicago, 1975.

———. *The Saga of Dazai Osamu, A Critical Study with Translations*. Stanford University Press, Stanford, 1985.

Morishige, Alyce Hisae Kawazoe. "The Theme of the Self in Modern Japanese Fiction: Studies on Dazai, Mishima, Abe, and

Kawabata." Ph.D. diss., Michigan State University, East Lansing, 1970.

O'Brien, James A. *Akutagawa and Dazai: Instances of Literary Adaptation*. Arizona State University Press, Tempe, 1988.

———. "A Biographical and Literary Study of Dazai Osamu." Ph.D. diss., Indiana University, Bloomington, 1969.

———. *Dazai Osamu*. Twayne Publishers, NY, 1975.

———. "Dazai Osamu: Comic Writer." *Critique*, 1970.

———. "Dazai's *The Setting Sun*." *Approaches to the Modern Japanese Novel*, ed. Thomas E. Swann and Kinya Tsuruta. Sophia University, Tokyo, 1976.

Rolf, Robert. "The Turn of the Narrative Screw in Dazai's *No Longer Human*." *Approaches to the Modern Japanese Novel*, ed. Thomas E. Swann and Kinya Tsuruta. Sophia University, Tokyo, 1976.

Wolfe, Alan. "Dazai Osamu: Man, Artist, Symbol." Ph.D. diss., Columbia University, NY, 1971.

———. *Suicidal Narrative in Modern Japan: The Life of Dazai Osamu*. Princeton University Press, Princeton, NJ, 1990.

Yanagida, Tomotsune. "The Consciousness of Sin in Osamu Dazai." *Japan Christian Quarterly*, no. 24, 1958.

ENCHI Fumiko
(1905–86)

Novelist, playwright, and essayist. Maiden name, Ueda Fumiko. Born in Asakusa, Tokyo.

Arguably the most accomplished female writer in Japan this century, Enchi Fumiko began to give full expression to her genius during the 1950s, when she was already middle-aged. Although in the pre-war years she had established a reputation as a playwright of some distinction, it was as a prose writer that she truly excelled. Noted equally for her insight into the female psyche and for the skill with which she could weave classical allusions into modern-day narrative, Enchi produced dozens of novels and short stories of the highest quality. Her precise use of language and the uncompromising realism of her characterizations were hallmarks of her fiction throughout the latter part of her career. As a scholar of classical literature she translated *The Tale of Genji into modern Japanese and was also the author of many critical works and essays. In English translation she is best known for Onna-men (1958, Masks) and Onnazaka (1957, The Waiting Years), although these two novels represent only a fraction of her achievement. In November 1985 she was given the ultimate recognition by being awarded the Bunka Kunshō, or "Cultural Medal," which is the highest honor that can be bestowed upon an individual in Japan.

As the second daughter of the distinguished scholar of the Japanese language Ueda Kazutoshi (1867–1937), Enchi Fumiko was brought up in a household where books and classical knowledge were accepted as a normal part of everyday life. Prone to sickness as a child, she spent much of her time engrossed in the Japanese classics, discovering the pleasures of the Edo school of writing and, later, the modern masters TANIZAKI and NAGAI KAFŪ. Her greatest love was the theater, especially the *Kabuki* and *shingeki* forms of drama, and not unnaturally she soon developed an ambition to become a playwright herself. High school, on the other hand, was never entirely to her liking. After the age of sixteen she opted to continue her studies at home under the guidance of private tutors.

At age twenty-one Enchi Fumiko published her first play, *Furusato* (*1926, Native Land*) and, two years later, she saw another of her plays, *Banshun sōya* (*1928, Tumultuous Spring*), produced on the stage of the Tsukiji Little Theater. These early works were praised for their fine construction and psychological insight, and Enchi soon became known as the leading member of the so-called Women Playwright Trio, the other members being her friends Okada Teiko and Miyake Yukiko.

After her marriage in 1930 to the journalist and political commentator Enchi Yoshimatsu, Enchi herself turned to writing fiction. Her stories were published in such magazines as *Nichireki* (*Solar Calendar*) and *Jimmin bunko* (*People's Library*), both of which were quite prominent in the 1930s. However, she never attained the highest standards with her pre-war fiction, even though she succeeded in defining her central theme: the deprivation of Japanese women. Towards the end of the decade she published a collection of short stories called *Kaze no gotoki kotoba* (1939, *Words Like the Wind*) and wrote several novels, including *Onna no fuyu* (*1939, Women's Winter*) and *Nippon no yama* (1940, *The Mountains of Japan*). Apart from her writing, much of her time was spent in bringing up her daughter, born in 1932.

Enchi wrote and published little during the war. Her home was destroyed in an air raid in 1945, and during the following year she fell seriously ill with cancer of the womb. For several years she was bedridden and on occasions nearly died from her illness. The only positive aspect of her life at this time was the close relationship she developed with her mother, with whom she once again started living. As a child, Enchi had been so dazzled by the brilliance of her father that she had never really appreciated her mother, who was from rural Kyūshū. Now, the proximity of her mother helped her to define her identity as a woman, and this influence was certainly carried over into her work. However, not until 1949 was she strong enough to continue writing, eventually publishing an excellent story about the frustrations of two plain sisters called "*Kōmyō Kōgō no e*" (*1951*, "Portrait of the Empress Kōmyō").

Enchi's first major success with a work of fiction was "*Himojii tsukihi*" (*1953*, "The Starving Years"), which first appeared in the *Chūō kōron* (*Literary Review*). Its description of a woman trapped in her marriage to a domineering and faithless man was immediately recognized as the expression of unique voice in women's literature. For this work Enchi was awarded the sixth Women's Literary Award.

With recognition Enchi experienced a surge of confidence and a great desire to work as hard as possible at her fiction. Between 1952 and 1957 she issued various installments of a major work entitled *Onnazaka* (*1957*, *The Waiting Years*). Describing the humiliation of a woman who suffers under her husband's absolute authority, it was based on true stories told to the author by her maternal grandmother. The narrative opens with a visit to the city by Tomo, the wife of a wealthy provincial bureaucrat, for the express purpose of finding a suitable concubine for Yukitomo, her husband. Few tasks could be more distasteful, yet Tomo stifles her jealousy on this occasion, as indeed she always does. She believes that the presence of a single concubine within the home will be more bearable than having to endure the public shame of Yukitomo's many infidelities with women of the town.

Alas, as the "waiting years" tick by, Tomo's decision to bear the unbearable proves to be a violation of her own, indelible feminine identity. If, at first, harmony is restored by her introduction of Suga, a fifteen-year-old beauty with a placid temperament, then the later addition of a second concubine by Yukitomo puts a further strain on her emotional resources. More years pass and a wife is found for her son, Michimasa, a dull-witted young man whose very presence in the novel compels us to see his father in a new light. Yukitomo's understanding of women makes him an even more formidable character: an irresistible force pitted against Tomo's unshakable determination to show not the slightest trace of resentment. However, having long been sustained by a steady influx of beautiful women, Yukitomo now begins to gain the upper hand in his perpetual but unspoken battle of wills with his wife. He seduces his new daughter-in-law and virtually makes her his third concubine. Ultimately, when Tomo falls ill, all the pent-up anger of a lifetime is released in her violent condemnation of her husband. Her outburst is quite shocking, for it goes against the code by which she has lived and reveals the extent to which she believes that Yukitomo "got the better of me after all."

Novels that are a long time in the making are often flawed in their construction, but this is not the case with *The Waiting Years*. It shows both a mastery of structure and a fine sense of drama. If it has a single fault it is in the lack of vitality that comes from telling the story exclusively from the point of view of a frustrated and unhappy woman. Indeed, all the vitality of the women appears to be siphoned away by the wily Yukitomo, whose own thoughts, emotions, and actions are rarely described in detail. In this respect alone, one feels that Enchi sacrificed the quality of her novel, in much the same spirit as Tomo tries to sacrifice her feminine identity.

Also from the same period and available in English translation is Enchi's fine short story "Yō" (1956, "Enchantress"), which, within just a few pages, contains a complete portrait of a woman in middle age. Its heroine, Chikako, has long been estranged from her husband, Keisaku, even though she continues to live with him. Earning her own income by making English translations of Japanese classics, she has added an extension to their home and lives there in virtual isolation, leaving her husband to pursue his own interests as an antiques dealer in the older part of the house. Their children having married and moved away, the couple gradually become more aware of each other despite their mutual coolness. In the end, an incident – in which two young lovers accidentally ring their doorbell while kissing – signals a thaw in their relationship. The story is so adroitly handled that one can forgive Enchi her habitual insistence upon telling it entirely from the woman's point of view.

In English translation, *Onna-men* (1958, *Masks*) represents Enchi at her best. It is a virtuoso performance in construction and in this respect could be described as an exercise in triangulation: themes, characters, scenes, and narrative being woven together as a series of interlocking triangles. The novel itself has three sections, each entitled with the name of a female mask from the Nō theater. (Literally translated the novel's title is *Female Masks*.) Events within the story take place in three eras: ancient, recent past, and present, and even the relationships of the characters can be interpreted in sets of three, for this is the pattern in which they have been conceived.

Two men, Ibuki (a young professor of Japanese literature) and Mikame (a psychiatrist), are both in love with Yasuko, a beautiful young widow with whom they have become acquainted through their common interest in folklore studies. Yasuko's late husband, Akio, died on a climbing expedition, leaving her under the spell of his mother, the mysterious Toganō Mieko. It is Mieko who is the "gray eminence" of the novel, manipulating people and events with her strong psychic powers. She is described by Yasuko as being a woman whose heart is "as secretive as a garden of flowers at night: the mingled scent of unseen blossoms trailed from her every gesture."

Neither Ibuki who initiates a passionate affair with Yasuko, nor Mikame who proposes marriage to her, is aware that her husband had a twin sister. Brought up in secret, Harume is severely retarded, and, although attractive, is most unlikely to marry and bear children. However, for reasons of her own, Mieko wishes to have a single grandchild, a boy who will be the very image of her lost son. To this end she uses her daughter-in-law Yasuko as the "medium" for her plan, persuading her to seduce Ibuki and substitute Harume while he is either drugged or drunk. By these devious means Mieko achieves her objective – and in doing so may have outwitted a vengeful ghost (the spirit of a female rival) from her own past.

In outline, the plot of *Masks* appears to be an overgrown garden of fantasies, but the novel itself is distinguished by its clarity and precision. It was clearly inspired by the episode of the Rokujō lady in *The Tale of Genji*, of whom Enchi's female protagonist Mieko has secretly written an essay, quoted in full at a key point in the story. Mieko's suggestion (and by implication it is Enchi's suggestion also) is that the archetypal woman is not only an object of man's eternal love but can also be the object of his eternal fear. The Rokujō lady who continues to haunt Prince Genji's lovers long after he has rejected her is, Mieko/Enchi claims, "an embodiment of this archetype." While not being especially original, the theory certainly underlines Enchi's feminist belief that the oppression of women must surely have its origin in the male psyche.

Enchi's major achievement at the peak of her career was her autobiographical trilogy of novels published by Shinchōsha between 1955 and 1968: *Ake o ubau mono* (1956, *The Pilferer of Vermilion*), *Kizu aru tsubasa* (1960, *The Injured Wing*), and *Niji to shura* (1968, *Rainbow and Carnage*). Portraying a woman novelist who finds herself locked into a loveless marriage, the trilogy goes on to explore her relationships with other men, her struggle with cancer, and how she comes to terms with the encroachment of old age. Enchi herself always denied that these novels were autobiographical, but when her own account of her life, *Uso makoto shichi-jū-yonen* (*Lies and Truth: More than Seventy Years*), was published in 1984 it was clear that the trilogy was based largely on personal experience. For the three novels in question she was awarded the Tanizaki Jun'ichirō Prize in 1969.

In translating *The Tale of Genji* into modern Japanese, Enchi made a major contribution to classical studies in Japan. *Enchi Genji*, as it is called by students, is a very accessible text that puts *Murasaki's great novel within reach of the general reader. It was completed in 1972, having taken five years (and a lifetime's experience) to translate.

Turning her attention once more to contemporary society, Enchi wrote *Shokutaku no nai ie* (1979, *A Family Without a Dining Table*), a long novel based on an incident that occurred during the student rebellions of 1968. Its central figure is a senior manager of a large corporation who refuses to take responsibility for the actions of his son, a student agitator accused of murdering renegade members of his group. The story's theme may seem to be utterly different from those addressed in previous works, but in fact there is continuity in Enchi's promotion of the concept of individualism. After all, she strongly suggested in *The Waiting Years* that the plight of women in pre-modern society was aggravated because people had obligations to family, clan, and country rather than to themselves as individual moral beings. In expressing a new awareness of the individual as a self-contained moral entity Enchi spoke directly to the postwar generation, and the acclaim given to her work is one indication that her message was clearly understood.

RECOMMENDED READING

Novels

Masks. *Onna-men.* 1958. 141 pages. Tr. Juliet W. Carpenter. Knopf, NY, 1983; Random House, NY, 1983. A sophisticated novel that has proved to be very popular in the West. The Random House edition is an Aventura paperback in the Vintage Library of Contemporary World Literature.

The Waiting Years. *Onnazaka.* 1957. 203 pages. Tr. John Bester. Kodansha International, Tokyo and NY, 1971 and 1980, paperback; Fontana, London, 1992.

WORKS IN ENGLISH TRANSLATION

Novels

Masks. Onna-men. 1958.
The Waiting Years. Onnazaka. 1957.

Short Fiction

"Blind Man's Buff." *"Mekura oni."*
1962. 12 pages. Tr. Beth Cary.
*The Mother of Dreams, and Other
Short Stories.* ed. Makoto Ueda.
Kodansha International, Tokyo,
1986.
"Boxcar of Chrysanthemums."
"Kikuguruma." 1967. 28 pages.
Tr. Yukiko Tanaka and Elizabeth
Hanson. *This Kind of Woman,
Ten Stories by Japanese Women
Writers.* Putnam Publishing
Group, NY, 1982.
"Enchantress." *"Yō."* 1956. 21
pages. Tr. John Bester. *Japan
Quarterly*, vol. 5, no. 3, 1958;
Modern Japanese Short Stories.
Japan Publications Trading Co.,
Tokyo, 1960; revised edition,
1970.
"Love in Two Lives: The Rem-
nant." *"Nisei no en shūi."* 1957.
15 pages. (1) Tr. Noriko Mizuta
Lippit. *Stories by Contemporary
Japanese Women Writers.* M.E.
Sharpe, Armonk, MY, 1982;
reissued as *Japanese Women Wri-
ters*, 1991. (2) As "A Bond for
Two Lifetimes: Gleanings." Tr.
Phyllis Birnbaum. *Rabbits,
Crabs, Etc., Stories by Japanese

Women. University of Hawaii
Press, Honolulu, 1982.
"Skeletons of Men." *"Otoko no
hone."* 1956. 29 pages. Tr. Susan
Matisoff. *Japan Quarterly*,
vol. 35, no. 4, 1988.

CRITICAL STUDIES

Bargen, Doris, G. "Twin Blossoms
on a Single Branch: The Cycle
of Retribution in *Onna-men."*
Monumenta Nipponica, vol. 46,
no. 2, 1991.
Carpenter, Juliet Winters. "Enchi
Fumiko: A Writer of Tales."
Japan Quarterly, vol. 37, no. 3,
1990.
Gessel, Van C. "The 'Medium' of
Fiction: Fumiko Enchi as Nar-
rator." *World Literature Today*,
vol. 62, no. 3, 1988.
McClain, Yoko. "Eroticism and the
Writings of Enchi Fumiko." *Jour-
nal of the Association of
Teachers of Japanese*, vol. 15,
no. 1, 1980.
Pounds, Wayne. "Enchi Fumiko
and the Hidden Energy of the
Supernatural." *Journal of the
Association of Teachers of
Japanese*, vol. 24, no. 2, 1989.
Reiger, Naoko Alisa. *Enchi Fumiko's
Literature: The Portrait of Women
in Enchi Fumiko's Selected Works.*
Gesellschaft für Natur/ Völker-
kunde Ostasiens, Hamburg,
1986.

ENDŌ Shūsaku
(1923–   )

Novelist. Born and resides in Tokyo. Has traveled widely, especially in Europe.

Extremely popular in English translation, Endō Shūsaku is invariably described by Western critics as "the Japanese Graham Greene." Given the high status accorded the British novelist the epithet is meant kindly. Endō, being a Roman Catholic who addresses such issues as guilt, betrayal, and the anguish of faith, positively invites comparison to Graham Greene. Yet many of his admirers would say that he is the better writer. He is the author of several masterpieces, including *The Sea and Poison*, *Silence*, and *The Samurai*, and has proved himself consistently as a creator of tense, meaningful fiction. His insights into the unique Japanese interpretation of Christianity would alone ensure his reputation in the West.

Endō was born in Tokyo in 1923. After his parents were divorced, both he and his mother were baptized into the Catholic Church. When the time came for him to enter Keiō University he gave his father the impression that he would be studying medicine, which was his father's wish. In fact he had applied to study French literature, a subject in which he excelled, and was accepted by the university on that understanding.

Even as a young man Endō suffered from ill health, having contracted pleurisy, and was unable to pass the medical tests for a period of compulsory military service. Instead he was obliged to perform assembly work in a Kawasaki factory until he was free to continue his studies overseas. He moved to Lyons, France, in 1950, and remained there for two and a half years. During this time he concentrated on reading twentieth-century French Christian literature. However, on a visit to Paris, he fell seriously ill and had to endure the first of his many long periods of hospitalization.

Returning to Japan in 1953, Endō gradually recovered some of his strength and began writing his first story, *"Aden made"* (1954, "To Aden"). He met with success very quickly, winning the Akutagawa Prize in 1955 for his novella *"Shiroi hito"* (1955, "White Men"). Set in France during the German occupation it is a story of faith, guilt, and betrayal within the French Resistance. He followed it with *Kiiroi hito* (1956, *Yellow Man*), a novel written in the form of a student's letter to his pastor, a French missionary. Already, Endō was addressing some of his most characteristic themes, especially that of the difference between European and Japanese religious sensibilities. His firsthand acquaintance with Christian thought in France gave him a unique, dual perspective on East and West. Almost alone among Japanese writers he would later create genuinely believable foreign characters in his novels.

Not until 1958, however, did Endō gain a national reputation. In that year he won both the Mainichi and Shinchō prizes for his novel *Umi to dokuyaku* (*The Sea and Poison*). Here he dealt with a notorious war crime in which a team of doctors vivisected a captive American soldier. The power of the book lies not only in its grimly realistic atmosphere, but, more especially, in the author's futile quest to find "guilt" in the individual Japanese soul.

Endō's output now increased, and he worked simultaneously on *Kazan* (1959, *Volcano*) and *Obaka san* (1959, *Wonderful Fool*). In *Volcano* he contrasted the character of a complacent Japanese vulcanologist with that of a fervent French priest (the same priest, Durand, who had appeared in *Yellow Man*). The practical and spiritual implications of whether or not a particular volcano might be extinct, Endō exploited to the full. On the other hand, in *Wonderful Fool*, he showed his versatility by creating a genuinely comic novel. This time, a foreign visitor exemplifies Christianity by "foolishly" identifying with outcast (and often dangerous) elements of Japanese society, much to the distress and inconvenience of his young hosts.

The two 1959 novels are strikingly different in both mood and texture. *Volcano* is a subdued, thoughtful, and highly polished text, its theme the perception of good and evil in the human soul. It contains two parallel storylines that are directly linked in only one brief incident. The first concerns Suda Jimpei, a senior employee of the Weather Station, who, as the novel opens, is celebrating his retirement. He is known to his colleagues, slightly ironically, as the Akadake Demon because of his fascination with Akadake, the local volcano to which he has dedicated a lifetime of study. Suda, however, is no scholar. His sentimental theory that the volcano, like himself, is reaching old age and becoming extinct is merely the echo of some vivid off-the-cuff remarks by his old teacher. Younger and better-qualified men believe Akadake to be very much alive and in imminent danger of erupting.

The novel's second storyline features Durand, the retired foreign priest who continues to be an embarrassment to the Church in Japan. Now old and ill, he is constantly at odds with Father Satō, whom he considers to be typically Japanese in his lack of insight into the true nature of conscience and original sin. When he learns that Father Satō is to build a quiet mountain retreat for his congregation, Durand insists: "Akadake is absolutely going to explode. Because Evil itself is a volcano that will never be extinct."

Volcano is exciting to read because one longs to discover whether the vulcanologist, Suda, or the priest, Durand, is correct about Akadake. Will it erupt or not? Without giving away the story's resolution one can identify its message. Endō implies that evil can be considered either as a weakness inherent in the very structure of nature, akin to the inability of the Earth's crust to contain the forces below, or as the demonic force itself. The two ways of regarding it are demonstrated, respectively, by the two strands of the novel. Convergence occurs when the two characters meet, and Duran tells Suda: "Your defense of Akadake is true form for the Japanese who consider nature itself to be a god." In his remark is a tacit acknowledgment of the strength and vitality of the Japanese spirit, however alien that spirit may be to him. The author, standing with a foot in both camps, offers no clue as to which concept of evil is correct, implying that they are simply two ways of viewing the same phenomenon.

Wonderful Fool is a more spontaneous, more amusing novel than *Volcano* and is readily accessible to Western readers in both its structure and content. It is particularly brilliant for its evocation of modern Tokyo: an evocation which, as translator Francis Mathy notes, is not unlike Dickens's London. Endō applies a similar method of caricature, brings an equal measure of compassion, and shows an identical preference for leading us down the backstreets of his town. Like Dickens, too, he has a realistic concern for everyday economics. All the characters, with one notable exception, are clearly seen to earn their living and indeed are defined by their occupations of secretary, gangster, priest, or prostitute. Only Gaston, the French simpleton who suddenly visits his old pen pal Takamori, has no ostensible occupation, and for this very reason the mystery that surrounds him is magnified.

There is something saintly about Gaston although he is far from being as noble a character as Dostoievsky's "Idiot." He is an impulsive but somewhat fearful man. Immediately on his arrival he befriends a stray dog and quite unwittingly becomes enmeshed in Tokyo's dangerous underworld. Kidnapped by a professional killer, ironically called Endō, Gaston soon recognizes that his mission in Japan is to prevent a murder from taking place – and to this end he makes frequent appeals to Endō's (*fictional* Endō's) conscience. Meanwhile, his Japanese hosts, Takamori and sister Tomoe, follow him around the city like two ineffectual guardian angels.

In common with most of Endō's novels *Wonderful Fool* is characterized by its philosophical simplicity and formal complexity. The author clearly identifies the central conflict: between the killer who is driven by his paranoid inability to trust anyone, and Gaston, whose actions flow naturally from his total trust in everyone. While at no time is Gaston's mission expressed in such theological terms as "the saving of a soul," that, in effect, is what it is. It is also the extent of the novel's "message." Literary qualities, on the other hand, are abundant and can be found in the novel's complex texture, in its subtle observation of behavior, in its unpredictable dialogue, and especially in its satirical but compassionate humor.

Bedridden for three years after writing *Wonderful Fool*, Endō underwent three major operations in 1961. On his recovery he began writing "rehearsals" for what is generally considered his greatest work, *Silence*. Some of these preliminary stories were collected in *Aika* (1965, *Elegies*), and among them, "Unzen" contains a detailed sketch of Kichijirō, the Judas-like character of the longer novel. Again, as in much of his work, Endō looked for the essence of Christianity and found it in compassion for those who are weak, downtrodden, and suffering.

In his introduction to the 1989 English translation of *Ryūgaku* (1965, *Foreign Studies*) Endō refers to the last part of this three-part novel as another "prelude" to *Silence*. A common theme – the inability of the Japanese to absorb the essence of Western culture when they study in Europe – runs through the three parts, which otherwise are entirely separate stories. The first, set in 1950, concerns a young Japanese Christian who is embarrassed by the generosity of his French hosts. Various incidents justify his suspicion that their apparent goodwill is at least partly an expression of contempt for other cultures, especially his own, of which they know nothing. The second part outlines the story of Araki Thomas, a Japanese Catholic priest educated in Europe at the end of the sixteenth century. Church elders who had first welcomed him with open arms were quick to condemn him when he avoided martyrdom on his return to Japan during the shōgun Hideyoshi's purges. Both introductory parts of *Foreign Studies* add religious and historical dimensions to what is to follow: a longer and much more entertaining story set in France during the mid-1960s.

Traveling alone, a young Japanese scholar called Tanaka arrives in Paris with an ambitious project to study the life of the Marquis de Sade. From the moment he lands he realizes he is out of his depth, overawed by the alien spirit of European culture. He meets another student who has become physically ill in trying to come to terms with it, and Tanaka fears a similar fate. Eventually he discovers that his obsession with the Marquis de Sade springs from a desire "to confront a writer who was totally foreign to him in all senses of the word" and the insight gives him renewed energy. He visits Sade's ruined chateau at La Coste and there he experiences a kind of ecstasy, feeling for the first time a deep sense of connection with a fragment of European history. Of course, the reason that Tanaka feels as he does is that the Marquis had sufficient strength, recklessness, and depravity to oppose the great flow of Christian culture – a "lava flow" that tends to destroy everything in its wake. Suddenly, the reader is inclined to recall the earlier stories in the novel and all the pieces of Endō's magnificent construction fall into place.

In his next major novel, Endō moved away from the sharp criticism of Christianity expressed in *Foreign Studies* and tried a new approach. *Chimmoku (Silence)* is a monumental work that deals with the martyrdom of Christians in Japan in the late sixteenth and early seventeenth centuries. Although it was extremely controversial when it was published in 1966, it won the Tanizaki Prize. Its central incident is the apostasy of the Portuguese Jesuit, Ferreira, a priest who "betrays" Christ by stamping on the crucifix. He does so in order to end the torture of innocent people, having been ingeniously driven into a philosophical corner by a toughminded magistrate. Serious in tone, as befitting its subject matter, *Silence* is regarded by many as Endō's greatest novel. In writing it he was continuing a lifelong quest, in his own words: "To take the Christian religion which was so uncongenial to me as a Japanese, analyze why it was so uncongenial, and in some way to make it something more compatible . . ."

Switching back to a contemporary, medical theme, Endō published *Kuchibue o fuku toki* (*When I Whistle*) in 1974. Although brilliantly constructed, as indeed are all his works, the novel confirms the impression that in technique, if not in outlook, he is closer to Western than Japanese tradition. Moral content ranks above aesthetic effect in Endō's hierarchy of literary values. However, that he can be a first-rate storyteller was again proven with *Samurai* (1980, *The Samurai*), a long historical tale of a samurai's mission to establish trade with Nueva España (Mexico). It received high praise in the West and helped to build Endō's readership to a point where he could, with a subsequent novel, be acclaimed in London newspapers as a fashionable contender for the Nobel Prize.

The British launch of *Sukyandaru* (1986, *Scandal*), Endō's eighth volume to be translated into English, was helped considerably by a television documentary on the author himself. In it he again admitted that Christianity – like Western clothes – did not always fit him as comfortably as he wished. He also commented on the Japanese aesthetic: "Places where we draw nothing are not empty places. They are energy!" And again on his meticulous method of writing: "I use a tape recorder to check the rhythm of a sentence. If the sentence is not right I rewrite it." These comments, together with the unusual sight of a distinguished novelist singing in his own (deliberately dreadful) operatic productions, must have fascinated the public – for a copy of *Scandal* suddenly became harder to obtain than a 1905 edition of OZAKI KŌYŌ's *The Gold Demon*.

Scandal is an extraordinary novel, not least because in technique it is a virtuoso performance: unusual for an author in his sixties. Being an exploration of the nature of evil, it surprisingly features a sixty-five-year-old Catholic novelist not unlike Endō himself. One might even say that Suguro is Endō's double, were this character not also plagued by a *doppelgänger* who threatens his reputation as an upstanding citizen and Christian writer. Suguro's double, it transpires, often frequents the city's "red light" district, engaging in unspecified acts of sadomasochistic pleasure. Gradually, the thesis of the novel becomes clear. Evil, we are told, is a natural phenomenon which nonetheless runs counter to life's natural processes of growth and survival. It is born of a death wish: a desire to regain that state of perfect happiness experienced by the human embryo in the womb. Supporting his thesis, Endō weaves an immensely entertaining plot involving a beautiful widow who is not only sexually aroused by dreaming of horrific atrocities, but who nearly corrupts the central character himself. In other words, Suguro is brought face to face with his double and can either accept or reject what he sees.

Ultimately, the reader may feel that *Scandal* does not really succeed in addressing the problem of evil, chiefly because it draws upon the subjective imagination of a kind and gentle man. Yet in making an original, if almost schizophrenic, contribution to the *I-Novel tradition, Endō enjoyed a literary triumph which did not go unnoticed. In 1987 he received an honorary doctorate from George-town University, one of many awards by which the West has acknowledged his international reputation.

To modern Japanese literature Endō Shūsaku has brought a new, if sometimes clinical, professionalism, and has produced a body of work remarkable for its variety, technical virtuosity, and its many insights into the Japanese experience of Christianity. In translation he is a novelist to whom most readers can relate without much difficulty, chiefly because his novels are so Western in their construction. Yet even though his qualities far outweigh his faults, Endō never really allows life to express itself directly in his novels. Rather, he filters it through his intellect, satirizing its comic aspects, while lamenting its stupidities and cruelties. For this reason his novels seem to fall short of the very highest achievements in literature, although they may well win their author the highest accolade.

RECOMMENDED READING

Novels

Foreign Studies. *Ryūgaku.* 1965. 219 pages. Tr. Mark Williams. Peter Owen, London, 1989; Tuttle, Tokyo, 1989; Sceptre (Hodder & Stoughton), 1990; Simon & Schuster, NY, 1990. Contains author's 7-page introduction. Endō's books are becoming collectible (according to one London dealer) and this volume is surely one to be treasured in its hardcover edition.

Scandal. *Sukyandaru.* 1986. 237 pages. Tr. Van C. Gessel. Peter Owen, London, 1988; Dodd, Mead & Co. NY, 1988; Dufour Editions, Chester Springs, PA, 1988; Penguin Books, Harmondsworth, 1989; Vintage Paperback, NY, 1989. Highly entertaining; has inspired best dust wrapper design ever seen on a Peter Owen book.

Silence. *Chimmoku.* 1966. 306 pages. Tr. William Johnston. Sophia University, Tokyo, 1969; Tuttle, Tokyo, 1969; Prentice-Hall, NY,

1970; Peter Owen, London, 1976; Quartet, London, 1978; Taplinger, NY, 1979, 1980 paperback; Penguin Books, Harmondsworth, 1988. Endō's masterpiece; somber but magnificent.

Volcano. *Kazan.* 1959. 175 pages. Tr. Richard A. Schuchert. Peter Owen, London, 1978; Tuttle, Tokyo, 1979; Taplinger, NY, 1980, 1985 paperback; Quartet, London, 1980; Sceptre, London, 1990. A good starting point for an exploration of Endō; a serious but very readable work.

Wonderful Fool. *Obaka san.* 1959. 237 pages. Tr. Francis Mathy. Peter Owen, London, 1974; Tuttle, Tokyo, 1975; Quartet, London, 1979; Harper & Row, NY, and Kodansha International, Tokyo, 1983; Penguin Books, Harmondsworth, 1990. Contains 4-page introduction by Julian Moynahan. Another good starting point for discovering Endō.

WORKS IN ENGLISH TRANSLATION

Novels

Foreign Studies. Ryūgaku. 1965.

The Samurai. Samurai. 1980. 272 pages. Tr. Van C. Gessel. Kodansha International, Tokyo, 1982; Peter Owen, London, 1982; Penguin Books, Harmondsworth, 1983; Random House, NY, 1984.

Scandal. Sukyandaru. 1986.

The Sea and Poison. Umi to dokuyaku. 1958. 164 pages. Tr. Michael Gallagher. Peter Owen, London, 1972; Tuttle, Tokyo, 1973; Taplinger, NY, 1980; W. W. Norton, NY, 1992 paperback.

Silence. Chimmoku. 1966.

Volcano. Kazan. 1959.

When I Whistle. Kuchibue o fuku toki. 1974. 277 pages. Tr. Van C. Gessel. Peter Owen, London, 1979; Tuttle, Tokyo, 1980; Taplinger, NY, 1980; Quartet, London, 1980.

Wonderful Fool. Obaka san. 1959.

Short Fiction Collection

Stained Glass Elegies. Selections from *Aika* (1965, *Elegies*) and *Jūichi no iro garasu* (1979, *Eleven Stained-Glass Segments*). 165 pages. Tr. Van C. Gessel. Peter Owen, London, 1984; Dufour Editions, Chester Springs, PA, 1984; Penguin Books, Harmondsworth, 1986. Includes: "Fuda-no-Tsuji," "Retreating Figures," and "Old Friends."

Short Fiction

"The Day Before." *"Sono zenjitsu."* 1963. 11 pages. Tr. Van C. Gessel. *Stained Glass Elegies; The Shōwa Anthology,* vol. 2, ed. Van C. Gessel and Tomone Matsumoto. Kodansha International, Tokyo, 1985.

"Despicable Bastard." *"Iyana yatsu."* 1959. 15 pages. *Stained Glass Elegies.*

"A Forty Year Old Man." *"Yonjussai no otoko."* 1964. 21 pages. (1) As "A Man Forty." Tr. Lawrence Rogers. *Translations,* vol. 9, 1982. (2) *Stained Glass Elegies.*

"Fuda-no-Tsuji." *"Fuda no Tsuji."* *1963.* 9 pages. (1) Tr. Frank Hoff and James Kirkup. *Japan P.E.N. News,* no. 14, Jan. 1965. (2) As "Fuda-no-Tsuji." *Stained Glass Elegies.*

"Incredible Voyage." *1968.* 15 pages. *Stained Glass Elegies.*

"Mine." *"Watashi no mono."* *1963.* 13 pages. (1) Tr. Peter W. Schumacher. *Japan Christian Quarterly,* vol. 40, no. 4, 1974. (2) As "Something of My Own." Tr. John Bester. *Japan Echo,* vol. 27, special issue, 1984. (3) As "My Belongings." *Stained Glass Elegies.*

"Mothers." *"Haha naru mono."* *1969.* 27 pages. (1) Tr. Francis Mathy. *Japan Christian Quarterly,* vol. 40, no. 4, 1974. (2) *Stained Glass Elegies.*

"Old Friends." *1977.* 7 pages. *Stained Glass Elegies.*

"Retreating Figures." *1976.* 11 pages. *Stained Glass Elegies.*

"The Shadow Figure." *"Kageboshi."* *1968.* 16 pages. (1) As "The Shadow of a Man." Tr. Shoichi Ono and Sanford Goldstein. *Bulletin of the College of Biomedical Technology,* Niigata University, vol. 1, no. 1, 1983. (2) Tr. Thomas Lally, Oka Yumiko, and Dennis J. Doolin. *Japan Quarterly,* vol. 31, nos. 2–3, 1984.

"Unzen." *"Unzen."* 1965. 11 pages. *Stained Glass Elegies.*

"The War Generation." *"Aru senchūha."* 1977. 13 pages. *Stained Glass Elegies.*

Biography

A Life of Jesus. Iesu no shōgai. 1973. 179 pages. Tr. Richard A. Schuchert. Paulist Press, NY, 1978, 1979 paperback; Peter Owen, London, 1989.

Play

The Golden Country. Ōgon no kuni. 1966. 128 pages. Tr. Francis Mathy. Tuttle, Tokyo, 1970; Peter Owen, London, 1989; Dufour Editions, Chester Springs, PA, 1989.

CRITICAL STUDIES

Boscaro, Adriana. "Man in the Novels of Endō Shūsaku." *Man and Society in Japan Today,* 1984.

———. "The Meaning of Christianity in the Works of Endō Shūsaku." *Tradition and Modern Japan,* 1981.

Durfee, Richard E., Jr. "Portrait of an Unknowingly Ordinary Man: Endō Shūsaku, Christianity and Historical Consciousness." *Japanese Journal of Religious Studies,* vol. 16, no. 1, 1989.

Gessel, Van Craig. "The Literature of Kojima Nobuo, Yasuoka Shōtarō and Endō Shūsaku: Cripples, Clods and Cowards in Contemporary Japanese Fiction." Ph.D. diss., Columbia University, NY, 1979.

———. "Salvation of the Weak: Endō Shūsaku." *The Sting of Life.* Columbia University Press, New York, 1989.

———. "War and Postwar in the Writings of Kojima Nobuo, Yasuoka Shōtarō and Endō Shūsaku." *Transactions of the International Conference of Orientalists in Japan,* no. 23, 1978.

———. "Voices in the Wilderness: Japanese Christian Authors." *Monumenta Nipponica,* vol. 37, no. 4, 1982.

Lee, Ban. "Endō Shūsaku's *Chinmoku* and the Potentiality of Korean Christian Literature." *Japan Christian Quarterly,* vol. 54, no. 3, 1988.

Mathy, Francis. "Shūsaku Endō:

Japanese Catholic Novelist." *Thought*, no. 42, 1967.

———. "Shūsaku Endō: The Second Period." *Japan Christian Quarterly*, vol. 40, no. 4, 1974.

Saito, Masako. "Contemporary Japanese Theater: Symbolism in Shūsaku Endō's *Ōgon no Kuni*." *Modern Drama*, 1968.

Uyttendaele, Francis. "Shūsaku Endō." *Japan Christian Quarterly*, vol. 38, no. 4, 1972.

FUTABATEI Shimei
(1864–1909)

Novelist and translator. Real name, Hasegawa Tatsunosuke. Born in Ichigaya, Tokyo. Lifelong resident of Tokyo.

One of the most important contributors to modern Japanese literature, Futabatei Shimei is now generally regarded as the author of Japan's first modern novel. Even today, over a century later, *Ukigumo* (1887–89, *The Drifting Cloud*) engages one's attention and compels the reader to identify with its main protagonist. Among its many qualities is the way in which the author presents both social and psychological conflict, and in so doing injects life into his characters and into the novel as a whole.

How tragic it was, therefore, that Futabatei could not sustain his vocation as a novelist. A gifted translator of Russian literature, he was personally disappointed that his own fiction did not match the quality achieved by Gogol, Turgenev, or Dostoievsky. From today's perspective, this seems absurd. One can compare Futabatei to thousands of other modern writers, few of whom match the great nineteenth-century Russians, and place him among that exclusive group whose work remains perpetually "alive." Yet Futabatei was relentless in his self-criticism. Although he followed *Ukigumo* in 1906 with *Sono omokage*, (literally: "In his image," translated under the title *An Adopted Husband*), he was again dissatisfied with the result.

In trying to understand Futabatei's lack of self-confidence – while noting that it was, after all, a key ingredient of his art – one must look at the historical context in which he wrote. Only then can his extraordinary achievement, so surprisingly hidden from the man himself, be accurately assessed.

By the late 1880s and 1890s, Japanese writers had created a largely independent community known as the Meiji *bundan*. Dominated by OZAKI KŌYŌ, who founded the literary society *Ken'yūsha* in 1885, the *bundan* paid only lip-service to the radical ideas advanced by the great critic, TSUBOUCHI SHŌYŌ. Their stories were relatively limited in scope, concentrating on love themes while ignoring the larger issues of the time. Futabatei, however, was a close disciple of Shōyō, and had a deep understanding of the Western literature on which Shōyō had based his thesis of realism. As a later critic, Itō Sei, commented: "[Futabatei] went beyond the illusion of the *risshin shusse* (literally: "cult of advancement in life and social success") spirit, bringing forth the problems of the inner life of people in the *Meiji period."

Unfortunately, there was no Japanese precedent for the elevated ideal of literature which Futabatei attempted to put into practice. He was, as a result, uncomfortably isolated: unable to earn a living from his work and reluctant to associate with writers whom he considered grossly inferior to himself. His knowledge of Russian only worsened his dilemma. Even had he succeeded in emulating Turgenev or Dostoievsky, he would still have been unappreciated and misunderstood. Furthermore, his Confucian beliefs prevented him from accepting second best. He could not, in all honesty, write the sort of popular fiction which would have earned him a handsome living.

Born to a samurai family at the close of the samurai era, Futabatei was aware of insecurity even as a child. Because of the social upheavals that accompanied the Restoration, his father, Hasegawa Yoshikazu, sent him away from Tokyo to the family home in Nagoya to be educated. There Futabatei made his first acquaintance with Western literature and displayed an early obsession with writing. On his father's appointment to the Shimane prefectural government, the family moved to Matsue where Futabatei was enrolled at Sōchōsha, a private school directed by the distinguished Confucianist, Uchimura Rokō (1821–1901). Under Uchimura's tutelage, as

Futabatei himself recalled: "The Confucian concept of living according to one's ideals was strongly implanted in my mind."

When he left Matsue for Tokyo in 1879, the adolescent Futabatei was unusually mature in his political views. Nationalistic by inclination, he considered Russia to be Japan's main threat from overseas. His study of Russian was therefore motivated by a desire to make himself useful to the nation, either in the foreign service or in some military capacity. In the event, he came under the spell of the Russian authors, fascinated by how they observed and analyzed the social phenomena of their era. He later commented: ". . . soon my nationalistic fervor was quieted and my passion for literature alone burned on."

Futabatei's understanding of the Russian language was greatly enhanced by one of his teachers at Tokyo Gaigo Gakkō, the foreign-language school he attended. Himself a Russian, Nicholas Gray read Goncharov and Dostoievsky aloud, going through each novel from beginning to end. As the American scholar Marleigh Grayer Ryan has noted in her excellent commentary on *Ukigumo*: "Hearing his teacher's voice, the young man sharpened his perception of the musical or lyrical possibilities of language. When he began to write and translate himself, he tried to create a Japanese style which would be as euphonious as the language of the Russian master novelists." In 1886, when Futabatei left the language school intent on becoming a writer, he sought the encouragement of Tsubouchi Shōyō. Their highly creative friendship lasted until Futabatei's death, some twenty-three years later.

In *Shōtsetsu shinzui* (1885, *The Essence of the Novel*), Shōyō had identified all the weaknesses of contemporary Japanese fiction and recommended radical changes. He wanted to see tightly constructed, realistic plots and better characterization; both of which should embody the author's insights into human nature. However, despite his brilliance as a critic, Shōyō had only a modest creative talent and was quite unable to write the sort of fiction he had in mind. Futabatei, on the other hand, not only had models from Russian literature with which Shōyō was unfamiliar, but many creative gifts of his own. His fine sense of dialogue, his skill at fashioning a style appropriate to realistic fiction, and his inner conflicts which in retrospect seem so typical of the Meiji period: all combined to produce *Ukigumo*, a novel which introduced an entirely new spirit into Japanese literature.

The central character of *Ukigumo* is Bunzō, a young man who, at the beginning of the narrative, is dismissed from his job as a clerk. Not unlike the author himself, Bunzō has held to his own principles of behavior rather than act blindly on the instructions of his superior. However, the personal repercussions are serious, for the loss of his job means that he will be perceived in a bad light by his aunt, with whom he lodges, and perhaps even by his aunt's daughter, Osei, with whom he is deeply in love.

Having imposed the conditions of the story with great skill, Futabatei allowed the characters to develop a life of their own. This is the great strength of *Ukigumo*, and also the cause of the author's difficulties with it. Bunzō's intelligence and generosity are set against the salesman-like smoothness of his rival-in-love, Noboru, and found to be entirely ineffectual in practice. Noboru is a winner, Bunzō a loser; and Futabatei could find no satisfactory resolution to the story.

Published in three parts in June 1887, February 1888, and July/August 1889, *Ukigumo* brought Futabatei considerable fame, but insufficient money on which to live. After a short period of working in a bank and teaching in a girls' school, he turned to translation, producing a brilliant version of Turgenev's *Fathers and Sons*. This was followed by an even better translation of the same author's *The Rendezvous* (1850) under the Japanese title *Aibiki*. Marleigh Grayer Ryan has commented: "The delicacy and pathos of Turgenev's story, as it describes now a helpless lovelorn maiden, now a callous, indifferent young man, are fully conveyed in the Japanese." Like Futabatei's subsequent translations, it greatly influenced the stylistic awareness of the writers who succeeded him.

Not until 1906 did Futabatei commence another original work of fiction. In that year he wrote *Chasengami* (*Widow's Hair*), but, as he failed to complete it, the manuscript was not published until after his death. He did complete *An Adopted Husband*, a novel that deals with the common Japanese practice of adopting a prospective son-in-law into a family that has no son-and-heir. Translated into English in 1919, it lacks the energy of *Ukigumo* but is nonetheless highly convincing in its social analysis.

More bitter and more directly autobiographical was Futabatei's last work of fiction, *Heibon* (*Mediocrity*), published in the *Asahi shimbun* at the end of 1907. It summarizes the author's hostile attitude to the literary climate of his day, an attitude which, in a sense, is encapsulated by his own pseudonym. Long ago he had chosen the name "Futabatei Shimei" because it sounded like the profanity *kutabatte shimae* ("go to hell" or "you might as well be dead"). There is even evidence to suggest that Futabatei had a greater admiration for men of business or politics than for those who spent their lives studying or creating literature. After all, can the reader of *Ukigumo* wholly deny Noboru's qualities, antipathetic though they are to everything one associates with literary sensibilities?

Futabatei withdrew from literary circles completely in 1889 and took up a government post. In the last five years of his life, between 1904 and 1909, he wrote articles on Japanese and Russian literature, on social problems, and on various aspects of his experience. An isolated genius, he was so far ahead of his time that he had no context in which to continue his creative career. To the generation that followed, however, his legacy was invaluable. For modern Japanese literature he initiated a great tradition: one which, though it climaxed in the early *Shōwa period, still continues to this day.

RECOMMENDED READING

Novels

Ukigumo. *Ukigumo. 1887–89.* 160 pages. (1) Extract as "The Drifting Cloud." Tr. Donald Keene. *Modern Japanese Literature.* Grove Press, NY, 1956. (2) As *Japan's First Modern Novel:* Ukigumo *of Futabatei Shimei.* Tr. Marleigh Grayer Ryan. Columbia University, NY, 1967; Greenwood Press, London, 1983. Marleigh Ryan's volume, 381 pages in total, contains a full critical biography of Futabatei. It was published in both clothbound and paperbound editions.

WORKS IN ENGLISH TRANSLATION

Novels

An Adopted Husband. Sono omokage. 1906–07. 275 pages. Tr. Buhachiro Mitsui and Gregg M. Sinclair. Knopf, NY, 1919; Hutchinson & Co., London, 1919; Eigo Kenkyusha, Tokyo, 1926; Greenwood Press, NY, 1969.

Mediocrity. Heibon. 1907–08. 195 pages. Tr. Glenn Shaw. Hokuseido, Tokyo, 1927.

Ukigumo. Ukigumo. 1887–89.

CRITICAL STUDIES

Ryan, Marleigh Grayer. "Futabatei Shimei and the Creation of *Ukigumo.*" Ph.D. diss., Columbia University, NY, 1965.

———. "Futabatei Shimei and the Superfluous Hero." *Journal Newsletter of the Association of Teachers of Japanese,* vol. 4, no. 1, 1966.

———. *Japan's First Modern Novel:* Ukigumo *of Futabatei Shimei.* Columbia University Press, NY, 1967.

———. "A Study of Futabatei Shimei." *Researches in the Social Sciences of Japan,* no. 2, 1959.

Hayashi FUMIKO
(1903–1951)

Novelist and poet. Born in Shimonoseki, in Yamaguchi Prefecture. Had an itinerant childhood but eventually settled in Tokyo.

A famous photographic portrait of Hayashi Fumiko graces the cover of *To Live and To Write* (Seal Press, 1987), an anthology of stories by Japanese women writers in English translation. It is a picture which speaks eloquently of the author, for the woman seated at her desk, pen in hand, emanates an aura of exceptional dedication to her art. She is not posing for the photograph. She is writing; and to Fumiko, the act of writing was as much a part of life as eating or sleeping.

Although she died at the relatively early age of forty-eight, Fumiko wrote over 30,000 pages, including 278 books. She was the most successful Japanese woman writer of the twentieth century, acclaimed by critics and fêted by an adoring public. Many of her novels became best-sellers, and no less than nine were made into films.

Indeed, Fumiko's own story reads like popular legend, for although she was to become one of the wealthiest and best-known women in Japan, she spent her early years in extreme poverty. Visited by the editor of *Nyonin geijutsu* (*Woman and the Arts*), an influential magazine for aspiring women writers, she is said to have received him in her bathing dress, "the only clothing she had to wear," according to translator Yukiko Tanaka. However, the story Fumiko gave to the editor on that occasion in 1928 was *"Hōrōki"* (1930, "Vagabond's Song"). Reprinted on its own, it sold 600,000 copies and established her reputation as a writer of fiction with wide popular appeal.

In "Vagabond's Song," Fumiko wrote: "I am by fate a wanderer. I have no native place. My father was a man of Iyo in Shikoku, an itinerant peddler of dry goods. My mother was a maid at a hot-springs inn in Sakurajima of Kyūshū. Since she had married an outlander, she was driven out of her hometown. The couple came to rest in a place called Shimonoseki in Yamaguchi Prefecture. That Shimonoseki is where I was born." (Translated by Lane Dunlop, in his introduction to *A Late Chrysanthemum*, North Point Press, 1986.)

Fumiko's mother, Kiku, was clearly a source of great strength to her daughter. A warm, spirited woman, she was quite oblivious to convention, and she had several children by different lovers: Fumiko herself being an illegitimate child conceived before her mother married the peddler. Yet perhaps because the family's history was not generally known, Fumiko did not suffer as a result. She maintained a close and loving relationship with her mother, as depicted in "Vagabond's Song," throughout her life.

There is no question, however, but that Fumiko's adolescence was marked by rootlessness and poverty. She worked at many menial jobs as a maid and factory girl, eventually moving to Tokyo in 1922. There she was jilted by her lover, a man with whom she lived for a short time, and was forced to support herself as a waitress, shop girl, and in many other badly paid jobs. It was a difficult time, but one in which Fumiko accumulated experiences to draw upon in her writing. Indeed, one good example of Fumiko's skill at evoking "life on the margin" is the 1948 story *"Shitamachi,"* variously translated as "Tokyo" (in Donald Keene's anthology, *Modern Japanese Literature*) and as "Downtown" (in Ivan Morris's collection, *Modern Japanese Stories*).

Fumiko's career might easily have followed the pattern set by so many of her contemporaries. More than a few women writers, beset by poverty, sacrificed their careers after being influenced by Marxist revolutionaries who cared little for the arts. But Fumiko was fortunate in meeting and marrying Tezuka Ryokutoshi, an art student who was not only good company but moderate in his politics. Equally important, he possessed the strength of character to withstand Fumiko's spectacular success when it finally arrived.

The critical acclaim for Fumiko's 1931 story *"Seihin no sho"* ("The Poor") matched the commercial success of "Vagabond's Song." It was again strongly autobiographical and drew upon scenes from her life with Ryokutoshi. Not until later, with such stories as *"Kaki"* (*1935*, "The Oyster") and *"Toki"* (*1935*, "The Crested Ibis") did Fumiko begin to show her imaginative skills as a creator of pure fictions.

Perhaps through habit, Fumiko could not give up her passion for travel, even while married. She made long trips to Europe, China, and Southeast Asia, including participation in a trip to Manchuria to comfort soldiers in 1941, organized by the publishers of the *Mainichi shimbun*. Like a war reporter, she sent back dispatches from the front, where she was obviously extending her experience of hardship and deprivation. These trips, too, helped her to create one of the great masterpieces of wartime fiction, *Ukigumo* (*1949–51*, *Floating Cloud*), a finely structured novel that has secured her reputation in literary history.

Fumiko will continue to be read, however, not only for *Ukigumo* but for those stories that depict women on the fringes of society. By far the greatest in English translation is *"Bangiku"* (*1948*, "A Late Chrysanthemum"), for which Fumiko won the Women's Literary Award in 1949. It is a vivid portrait of an aging *geisha* who, now living in isolation, reluctantly receives one of her former lovers. There is a worldly wisdom contained in this story that was always unlikely to find expression in the work of Fumiko's female contemporaries – and scarcely ever did. Those who had the talent were too sheltered by their social position; while those with extensive life experience had neither the skill nor the artistic dedication to bring their art to this level of perfection.

RECOMMENDED READING

Novels

Floating Cloud. *Ukigumo*. *1949–51*. 110 pages. (1) Tr. Yasushi Wuriu. *Info*, vol. 2, nos. 4–12, 1956. (2) Tr. Yoshiyuki Koitabashi. Information Pub., Tokyo, 1957. (3) As *The Floating Clouds*. Tr. Yoshiyuki Koitabashi and Martin C. Collcott. Hara Shobo, Tokyo, 1965. Not to be confused with FUTABATEI's novel of the same name, Fumiko's *Ukigumo* is out of print in translation at the time of writing and is not easily obtainable.

WORKS IN ENGLISH TRANSLATION

Novels

Floating Cloud. Ukigumo. 1949–51.

Short Fiction

"Bones." *"Hone."* 1949. 21 pages. Tr. Ted T. Takaya. *The Shadow of Sunrise.* Kodansha International, Tokyo, 1966; Ward Lock, London, 1966. Same volume issued as *The Catch and Other War Stories.* Kodansha International, Tokyo, 1981.

"Downtown." *"Shitamachi."* 1949. Tr. Ivan Morris. As "Tokyo." *Modern Japanese Literature,* ed. Donald Keene. Grove Press, NY, 1956; Grove Weidenfeld, NY, 1989 paperback; *Modern Japanese Stories.* Spottiswoode, London, 1961; Tuttle, Tokyo and Boston, 1962, 1977 paperback.

"Late Chrysanthemum." *"Bangiku."* 1948. 20 pages. (1) Tr. John Bester. *Japan Quarterly,* vol. 3, no. 4, 1956; *Modern Japanese Short Stories.* Japan Publications Trading Co., Tokyo, 1960; revised edition, 1970. (2) Tr. Lane Dunlop. *A Late Chrysanthemum, Twenty-One Stories from the Japanese.* North Point Press, San Francisco, 1986; Tuttle, Boston, 1991 paperback.

"Narcissus." *"Suisen."* 1949. 12 pages. Tr. Kyoko Iriye Selden. *Stories by Contemporary Japanese Women Writers.* M. E. Sharpe, Armonk, NY, 1982; reissued as *Japanese Women Writers,* 1991.

"Vagabond's Song." *"Hōrōki."* 1930. Extracts; up to 22 pages. (1) As "Journal of a Vagabond." Tr. S. G. Brickley. *The Writing of Idiomatic English.* Kenkyusha, Tokyo, 1951. (2) Tr. Elizabeth Hanson. *To Live and To Write, Selections by Japanese Women Writers 1913–1938,* ed. Yukiko Tanaka. The Seal Press, Seattle, 1987.

Poems

"Song in Despair," *An Anthology of Modern Japanese Poetry,* ed. and tr. Ichiro Kono and Rikutaro Fukuda. Kenkyusha, Tokyo, 1957.

"Homecoming." Tr. Hisakazu Kaneko. *Orient West,* vol. 8, no. 1, 1963; *The Japanese Image,* ed. M. Schneps and A. D. Coox. Orient West, Tokyo, 1965; *London Magazine,* vol. 7, no. 7, 1967.

"The Lord Buddha." *The Burning Heart,* ed. and tr. Kenneth Rexroth and Ikuko Atsumi. Seabury Press, NY, 1977.

CRITICAL STUDIES

Brown, Janice. "Hayashi Fumiko, 'Late Chrysanthemum.'" *Approaches to the Modern Japanese Short Story,* ed. Thomas E. Swann and Kinya Tsuruta. Waseda University Press, Tokyo, 1982.

Higuchi ICHIYŌ
(1872–1896)

Writer of short fiction, also poet and diarist. Real name, Higuchi Natsuko. Born in and a resident of Tokyo.

In the years 1895 and 1896 no Japanese writer was producing fiction of a higher quality than Higuchi Ichiyō. According to Donald Keene she was "not only the first woman writer of distinction for centuries but, thanks to 'Growing Up,' the finest writer of her day." Her contemporaries thought so, too. In a famous review of *"Takekurabe"* (*1895–96*, "Growing Up," also translated as "Child's Play"), MORI ŌGAI said: "This author, who has painted the local coloring of the Daionji-mae so effectively that one might say it has ceased to exist apart from 'Growing Up' . . . must truly be called a woman of rare ability."

Since her death at the early age of twenty-four, Ichiyō's life and works have become the subject of intense scrutiny by many Japanese critics, most notably Wada Yoshie and Shioda Ryōhei. There is universal agreement that she was an exceptional writer. Even the scholar Hisamatsu Sen'ichi, a man rarely inclined to be generous in his praise of women novelists, said: "She appeared and vanished like a comet ... yet she enjoys a special place in the history of *Meiji literature as a writer whose work shows a degree of perfection that borders on genius." And if one expects a writer actually to cross the border and dwell exclusively in the realms of genius, Nakamura Mitsuo had this to add: "No novel equals 'Growing Up' in its poetic and yet accurate description of the subtle feelings of boys and girls in the transition from childhood to adulthood."

All the praise for Higuchi Ichiyō centers on her masterpiece, "Growing Up." She was also the author of some four thousand classical poems, many essays, twenty other fictional stories, and a long, rambling diary. Were it not for her diary and her premature death, one doubts if the literary world would have sustained its interest in her for so many years. Her achievements in fiction were soon eclipsed by those of Mori Ōgai and NATSUME SŌSEKI, and most people would agree that her contemporary, OZAKI KŌYŌ, was a far more productive and entertaining writer. Yet the more closely one comes to know the details of Ichiyō's life, the more meaningful, and indeed beautiful, her stories become. Chiefly for this reason, her reputation has risen in the West since the publication of Robert Lyons Danly's *In the Shade of Spring Leaves* (1981), an English-language biography with many translations; its title is taken directly from that given by Ichiyō to her famous diary.

Ichiyō's real name was Higuchi Natsuko, and she was born in Tokyo, the second daughter of a minor official in the city's municipal government. Although she was proud of her "samurai heritage," her father, Noriyoshi, was actually the son of a scholarly peasant from the nearby province of Kai. Noriyoshi had married Furuya Ayame in 1857 and had immediately left his hometown for Tokyo, hoping to be admitted to the ranks of the samurai. For ten years the couple worked hard to raise the money they needed to petition the authorities, Ayame even becoming a nursemaid on the Yushima estate of Inaba Daizen (one of the shōgun's personal retainers), despite having children of her own. Their efforts culminated in a short-lived success. Noriyoshi became a samurai in 1867 but was able to draw his stipend for one year only. The clan system was abolished after the Restoration of 1868, whereupon Noriyoshi was compelled to find work to support his growing family. When his fourth child, Natsuko, was born on May 2, 1872 (by the European calendar), he was already forty-two, and, if far from being wealthy, at least better off than many of the other *rōnin* (disbanded samurai) of that era.

Noriyoshi doted on his precocious daughter, encouraging her aptitude for reading even though his wife often disapproved. He sent her to a private school run by a Buddhist priest, later transferring her to the Seikai Gakkō, a similar establishment, when the family moved from Hongō to Shitaya in 1881. Natsuko, who much preferred reading books to playing games, was heartbroken when her mother withdrew her from the school three years later. Believing that her daughter was becoming altogether too learned, Taki (as Ichiyō's mother was universally called since her nursemaid days) was worried lest she impair her chances of making an advantageous marriage. In this respect Mrs. Higuchi was probably right, but eventually ceded to Noriyoshi's wishes and allowed Natsuko to enroll at the Haginoya ("Bush-clover Cabin"), the most prestigious poetry school in Tokyo.

Run by the poet Nakajima Utako, the Haginoya was a world in microcosm, completely divorced from the everyday realities of Meiji Tokyo. It was located in Mrs. Nakajima's luxurious home, where it offered a genteel and highly specialized education to young ladies of a wealthy or upper-class background. As Robert Lyons Danly says: "The Haginoya so emulated the gossamer world of the *Heian romances, where breeding and taste and literary sense were all synonymous, that Natsuko soon imagined herself living in some latter-day court." Needless to say, she also felt socially inferior to the other girls and tried exceptionally hard to impress them with her knowledge. Her natural reticence would suddenly switch to exhibitionism, but when her confidence grew stronger her natural gifts and tenacious temperament proved more than a match for the others. She won the first poetry contest she entered.

Disaster befell the Higuchi family in 1887. In that year not only did Noriyoshi lose his job, but his eldest son Sentarō died suddenly. The family moved to Shiba where Noriyoshi went into business with some unreliable friends and lost what little capital he had. All at once the harsh realities of life in an unfamiliar world pressed heavily on the shoulders of the former samurai. He became ill under the strain and died in 1889 when Natsuko was seventeen.

In order to help the family's finances, Natsuko became an apprentice at the Haginoya, a position that meant spending more time in the kitchen performing menial work than in the front parlor composing poetry. She was disillusioned, especially with Mrs. Nakajima who was now revealed both as an opportunist and as an aging widow who consorted with disreputable men. Meanwhile, Natsuko's attempts to start a career as a writer were going badly. Far from being a meteoric talent of Meiji letters, she was making slow progress and becoming increasingly frustrated. "I am like a little cart huffing and puffing its way up the hill," she wrote in her diary.

Ever competitive, Natsuko was amazed when one of her genteel rivals at the Haginoya, a Miss Tanabe, became extremely successful as a novelist. The girl in question was only twenty years old and would later assume the pen name Miyake Kaho (1868–1943). A disciple of TSUBOUCHI SHŌYŌ, she had written "Yabu no uguisu" (1888, "A Songbird in the Grove"), for which she had been paid a not inconsiderable sum of money. With her imperious manner, stylish dress, and penetrating wit she resembled a latter-day *Sei Shōnagon (the author of the Pillow Book in the early eleventh century) and was clearly making her way in the literary world with far more assurance than Natsuko.

Inspired by the example of Miyake Kaho, Natsuko turned her attention to fiction and fastened upon Nakarai Tōsui, a writer of popular newspaper serials, to be her mentor. At their first meeting she fell in love with him, for Tōsui was a strikingly handsome man who greatly enjoyed the company of women. However, he tended to be wary of his new pupil, not only because she was a member of respectable society rather than a geisha, but also because his brother had recently created a scandal. Fearing further trouble, Tōsui did not encourage Natsuko's feelings even if he was aware of them, which is doubtful. Instead, he coached her in *Edo fiction and emphasized the importance of entertaining the reader: an approach to writing that Natsuko, the classicist, found distinctly unpalatable. She remained adamant in her refusal to write ephemeral entertainments, saying: "I have no use for brocades, for stately mansions. A name that may last for a thousand years I am not about to sully for the advantage of the moment."

The name to which Natsuko was referring was her new literary sobriquet, Ichiyō, assumed by her at the end of 1891. Literally translated it means "one leaf," suggesting that its possessor clings to the tree of life, or, more probably, the tree of literature. In fact, its origin was delightfully obscure, as Ichiyō was well aware. She loved to pepper her writing with conceits and classical allusions, and her pen name referred to the boat, made from a single reed, on which the Zen patriarch Bodhidarma crossed the Yangtze River after his argument with the Emperor Wu-ti. His voyage to poverty and enlightenment was the lofty ideal Ichiyō wished to suggest in her choice of a name.

After her initial meetings with Tōsui, Ichiyō was left to make her own way as best she could. People were beginning to gossip about the long hours they spent in each other's company, and she had little option but to cool their growing friendship. However, all the evidence suggests that it was now Tōsui who was more in love with Ichiyō than vice versa. Her brilliance and quietly domineering character were taking their toll on the *gesaku* writer, making him feel inadequate to the task she had set him. In 1892 he started a new magazine called *Musashino* (*Musashi Plain*), hoping to rival the Ken'yūsha's *Garakuta bunko* (*Literary Trash*) and YAMADA BIMYŌ's *Miyako no hana* (*Flower of the Capital*). The first issue appeared on March 23, and contained Ichiyō's first published story "*Yamizakura*" ("Flowers at Dusk").

Inevitably, the magazine failed because Tōsui's whole conception of literature was out of date. Only Ichiyō's story attracted favorable attention, a factor that may have strained their relationship even further. Realizing he could be of little further help, Tōsui offered to introduce her to Ozaki Kōyō, but Ichiyō backed out at the last moment. Politics were rife in the Meiji *bundan*, and Ichiyō, perhaps aware that Kōyō and Bimyō were at loggerheads, opted for publication in *Miyako no hana*. Two of her stories appeared in this magazine, commencing with "*Umoregi*" (*1892*, "In Obscurity"), a work which made her reputation and brought her eleven, much-needed yen.

Written in imitation of KŌDA ROHAN's *Gojū no tō* (*1891–92, The Five-Storied Pagoda*), "In Obscurity" addresses the theme of artistic integrity, a subject which was close to Ichiyō's heart. The story featured an idealized portrait of her brother Toranosuke, who was proving to be such a disappointment in real life. In fiction he became a noble craftsman: a painter of porcelain who alone is dedicated to his art amid the crass commercialism of the day. In reality, however, Toranosuke was a ne'er-do-well who contributed little to the family's income. Survival depended largely on the efforts of Taki and her daughters, Kuniko and Ichiyō.

Gradually making her way in the literary world, Ichiyō established the themes for which she would later become famous. Now writing for *Bungakukai* (*The World of Literature*), the magazine of the Romantic movement to which the poet Kitamura Tōkoku (1868–94) and the novelist SHIMAZAKI TŌSON belonged, she produced the stories "*Yuki no hi*" (*1892–93*, "A Snowy Day"); "*Koto no ne*" (*1893*, "The Sound of the Koto"); and "*Yamiyo*" (*1894*, "Encounters on a Dark Night"). The second of these stories, "The Sound of the Koto," inaugurated what critics call the "beauty in the valley" tradition of Ichiyō's fiction. When it was refined in her later works it typically featured a beautiful but lonely woman living in some isolated spot, bravely enduring the neglect of a handsome man whom she loves. Invariably a "waif" becomes attracted to her, thus completing a triangle of pathos. In "The Sound of the Koto," however, there is no handsome man waiting in the wings. The waif, an embittered and loveless orphan, becomes entranced when he hears the "beauty" playing the *koto*. Her music banishes "the clouds in his heart," and it will, says the impersonal narrator, become "his friend for a hundred years."

Like many Japanese authors before and since, Ichiyō sought to create and define a mood rather than construct dramatic frameworks in the Western tradition. Neither she nor Kōda Rohan, whom she much admired, explored any literature west of China. "The Sound of the Koto," for example, is wholly Japanese in form and content, and although its mood of yearning may reflect a universal emotion, Ichiyō expresses this mood in the stylized manner that is peculiar to Japanese art. In Ichiyō's stories, the raw material of human feelings is made to crystallize into a pattern: hence the waif, the beauty, and the handsome man waiting in the wings. Had she lived Ichiyō might well have produced a modern prose version of the *Nō, for that was one direction left open to her in her pre-Saikaku period.

Two major events prompted changes in Ichiyō's life and work in the years 1893–94. In July 1893, the Higuchi women sold their possessions and moved to a cheaper, downtown area of the city. In 1894, the complete works of *Ihara Saikaku (1642–93) were reprinted; and highly praised by Ōgai, Kōyō, and Rohan as being the best antidote to Europeanization. The influence of these events lasted for the remainder of Ichiyō's short life, contributing both new raw material and a new literary model on which she could base her best works of fiction.

Ryūsenji was the area chosen by the Higuchis for their new home. Located to the southeast of the more respectable parts of the city, it fringed a notorious "red light" district called the *Yoshiwara. In this unpromising venue the three women opened a shop selling candy and other low-cost items to the impoverished population. Woefully undercapitalized, they made an average profit of less than five yen per month. Realizing that this was half as much as she had received for her story "In Obscurity," Ichiyō began to regret the move, particularly since running the shop left her very little time for writing. She imagined various other schemes for making money, including a plan to join forces with her old classmate from the Haginoya, Tanaka Minoko, to open a new poetry establishment. Miyake Kaho, the latter-day Sei Shōnagon, had done exactly that – much to Mrs. Nakajima's annoyance. In the event, Ichiyō pursued no money-making schemes but once more resumed her fiction, this time drawing upon her experiences in Ryūsenji, and writing in the manner of Saikaku.

In the 1890s the first wave of European realism had receded, or perhaps "been repelled" would be a more accurate way of putting it. The great instigators of the craze, Tsubouchi Shōyō and FUTABATEI SHIMEI, had not been forgotten but their influence had waned. The stage belonged to Ozaki Kōyō and the *Ken'yūsha, and to one or two individuals such as Rohan and Ōgai. They all admired Ihara Saikaku, the Edo author of *kōshoku bon* ("love books") and other types of fiction, whose brand of realism was essentially Japanese. Robert Lyons Danly comments: "When Ichiyō happened on these works in the second half of her career, Saikaku's earthy approach to fiction liberated her from her classical prejudices, and in fact made it possible for her to return to the classical tradition and draw from it what had made the poets and the Heian women writers truly great: passion, frankness and honesty."

Ichiyō's transitional work bridging her early and mature periods was "Ōtsugomori" (1894 "On the Last Day of the Year"). Even its title was derived from Saikaku, from the subtitle of his novel *Seken Munezan'yō* (1692, *Worldly Reckonings*). Ichiyō's story tells of how Omine, a young maid in a rich household, steals two yen from her employer in order to rescue her uncle from a loan shark. Fortunately, the theft is concealed from the severe mistress of the house when Ishinosuke, her ne'er-do-well stepson, borrows the remainder of the money and leaves a note to that effect. The reader is given to understand that Ishinosuke has seen Omine take the money. For all his dissolute ways he has, perhaps, taken pity on her and deliberately covered up the theft. With its inconclusive ending and swiftly moving narrative, "On the Last Day" opened up a new direction in Ichiyō's writing.

From Saikaku, Ichiyō learned how to derive fiction from poetry, creating prose structures that paralleled *haikai, the comic linked-poetry mastered by Saikaku early in his career. In the work of both writers the technique was used for painting a shifting tableau, a panoramic view of society that draws one's attention first to one character, then to another. This approach reached perfection in "Growing Up," but it may also be seen in other stories of Ichiyō's mature period.

Although she was inclined to be more compassionate than Saikaku, Ichiyō shared his sense of irony. As Robert Lyons Danly explains: "In her hands, Saikaku's broadsides are balanced with a new and deft understatement. Here is the *haikai* juxtaposition, the blend of humor and pathos the critics talk about. Lines of thought shoot out like arrows. Some suddenly converge and others evaporate. As with Saikaku we don't bother asking where Ichiyō is taking us. We sit back and enjoy the ride."

Yet perhaps the most striking of the many qualities to be found in Ichiyō's masterpiece is her sense of locale, remarked upon (as mentioned above) by Mori Ōgai. The sights, sounds, and smells of the Yoshiwara are all preserved in her tale, and nothing of any consequence escapes her attention. Indeed, "Growing Up" works on many levels. It is at once a shrewdly observed portrait of children on the verge of adulthood, and an elegy about the passing of an age of innocence in Japanese society. It captures the spirit of the 1890s: an era when the joyful enthusiasms of the previous decade were stifled by such authoritarian demands as the Imperial Rescript on Education (1890) and the dispatch of an army to China in 1894. Yet for all its contemporary relevance, "Growing Up" took its central theme from an incident in *The Tales of Ise*, the ninth-century collection of prose and poetry that had a similar randomness of narrative progression.

In Episode Twenty-three of *The Tales of Ise*, a young man and a young woman exchange notes, recalling how they played at comparing their heights when they were children. The woman writes to say that her hair has now grown to below her shoulders, and concludes: "If it is not to be you, who then best should tie it up?" Subsequently the two of them are married, and it is in reference to this passage that Ichiyō's "Growing Up" derives much of its bitter-sweet irony. Her heroine, Midori, is inevitably destined to become a prostitute, yet as a child she is completely in control of her immediate destiny. In any other quarter she would stand a good chance of marrying her childhood sweetheart, but here in the Yoshiwara no such option is open to her. Although hers is only one of the stories in Ichiyō's intricate tapestry, it is by far the most compelling. Midori's tragedy is in having to reverse her imperious, willful nature once she has discovered the greater power of sexuality. For although (like the young woman in *The Tales of Ise*) she signals to her sweetheart, she finds no response. She will never enjoy a natural progression to married bliss.

Ichiyō was now writing at the peak of her powers. She followed "Growing Up" with *"Nigorie"* (*1895*, "Troubled Waters"), the story of a faded courtesan who is forced by circumstances to move to a cheaper quarter of the pleasure district. *"Jūsan'ya"* (*1895*, "The Thirteenth Night") describes the effects of a loveless marriage on a young wife; while *"Wakare-michi"* (*1896*, "Separate Ways") depicts the heroine, Okyō, deserting her waiflike friend in order to marry a wealthy man. "Separate Ways" was Ichiyō's last completed story.

For a brief period at the end of her life, Ichiyō enjoyed remarkable fame. The most celebrated writers of the day beat a path to her door. Kōda Rohan used all his charm to persuade her to co-write a novel with himself and his friends. Both he and Mori Ōgai even wanted to share with her their monthly column in the magazine

Mesamashigusa (*The Eye-Opener*). But none of their plans came to fruition. Ichiyō fell victim to tuberculosis and died on November 23, 1896. The only fact one may add in mitigation of this tragic event is to record that her sister, Kuniko, who had done so much to support the family through its greatest hardships, went on to make the happiest of marriages. She raised eleven children, each of whom, apparently, had a successful career.

RECOMMENDED READING

Short Fiction Collection

In the Shade of Spring Leaves, The Life and Writings of Higuchi Ichiyō, A Woman of Letters in Meiji Japan. By Robert Lyons Danly. Yale University Press, New Haven, 1981. Highly recommended, this book contains 164 pages of critical biography, many fine photographs, and nine translated stories, including "Child's Play," "Separate Ways," and "The Sound of the Koto." They are all, with some alternative translations, listed in full below.

WORKS IN ENGLISH TRANSLATION

Short Fiction

"Child's Play." "Takekurabe." 1895–96. 33 pages. (1) As "They Compare Heights." Tr. W. M. Bickerton. *Transactions of the Asiatic Society of Japan*, 2nd Series, vol. 7, 1930. (2) As "Growing Up." Tr. Edward Seidensticker. *Modern Japanese Literature*, ed. Donald Keene. Grove Press, NY, 1965; Tuttle, Tokyo, 1957. (3) As "Teenagers Vying for Tops." Tr. Seizo Nobunaga. *Takekurabe*. Information Pubs., Tokyo, 1960. (4) *In the Shade of Spring Leaves*.

"Encounters on a Dark Night." "Yamiyo." 1894. 25 pages. *In the Shade of Spring Leaves*.

"Flowers at Dusk." "Yamizakura." 1892. 8 pages. *In the Shade of Spring Leaves*.

"On the Last Day of the Year." "Ōtsugomori." 1894. 13 pages. (1) As "The Last Day of the Year." Tr.

Tei Fujiu. *Hanakatsura*. Ikuseikai, Tokyo, 1903. (2) *In the Shade of Spring Leaves*.

"Separate Ways." "Wakare-michi." 1896. 8 pages. *In the Shade of Spring Leaves*.

"A Snowy Day." "Yuki no hi." 1892–93. 4 pages. *In the Shade of Spring Leaves*.

"The Sound of the Koto." "Koto no te." 1893. 4 pages. *In the Shade of Spring Leaves*.

"The Thirteenth Night." "Jūsan'ya." 1895. 13 pages. (1) Tr. Hisako Tanaka. *Monumenta Nipponica*, vol. 14, nos. 3–4, 1960–61. (2) *In the Shade of Spring Leaves*.

"Troubled Waters." "Nigorie." 1895. 23 pages. (1) As "Muddy Bay." Tr. Hisako Tanaka. *Monumenta Nipponica*, vol. 14, nos. 1–2, 1958. (2) As "In the Gutter." Tr. Seizo Nobunaga. *Takekurabe*. (3) *In the Shade of Spring Leaves*.

CRITICAL STUDIES

Danly, Robert Lyons. *In the Shade of Spring Leaves*. Yale University Press, New Haven, 1981.

Keene, Donald. "The Diary of Higuchi Ichiyō." *Japan Quarterly*, vol. 36, no. 2, 1989.

Takagi, Kyoko. "Religion in the Life of Higuchi Ichiyō." *Japanese Journal of Religious Studies*, vol. 10, nos. 2 and 3, 1983.

Tanaka, Hisako. "Higuchi Ichiyō." *Monumenta Nipponica*, vol. 12, no. 3, 1956.

————. "Women Writers of Meiji and Western Literature." *Transactions of the International Congress of Orientalists in Japan*, no. 1, 1956.

Ueda, Makoto. "Higuchi Ichiyō: 'Growing Up.'" *Approaches to the Modern Japanese Short Story*, ed. Thomas E. Swann and Kinya Tsuruta. Waseda University Press, Tokyo, 1982.

Vernon, Victoria. *Daughters of the Moon*. Institute of East Asian Studies, U.C. Berkeley, 1988.

Hirabayashi TAIKO
(1905–1972)

Writer of short fiction. Born in Suwa, Nagano (central Japan). Lived in Tokyo.

Most of Japan's pre-war proletarian writers were at best mediocre; a few were skillful and conscientious. Only two of them – KOBAYASHI TAKIJI and Hirabayashi Taiko – possessed real genius. As a woman, Taiko had perhaps the greater struggle to equip herself with the education she needed to pursue her art. Her subsequent political activities increased the odds against her, but, unlike Kobayashi, she survived a period of imprisonment, eventually becoming one of the great writers of her generation.

Brought up in a small village in central Japan, Taiko was a precocious student. Although her parents discouraged her, she read widely in Western literature: absorbing the French and Russian authors who were so admired in Japan's literary circles. The influence of Dostoievsky from these early studies was always to be a positive presence in her work.

Great strength of will and a sense of idealism guided Taiko,

109

bringing her quickly to confront the moral issues of poverty and freedom. After reading *Das Kapital* she joined a group of leftwing revolutionaries, effectively cutting herself off from following a "safe" career as a teacher. She went instead to Tokyo, where she embarked on a series of disastrous love affairs with unsuitable and wholly disreputable anarchists and leftists. Moving from one city to another with her first love, she eventually arrived in occupied Manchuria. Here, her friend was imprisoned for criticizing the emperor, while Taiko herself gave birth to – and lost – her only child. She returned from Manchuria alone in 1924, later to write of the experience in the powerful story "*Azakeru*" (*1927*, "Self-Mockery").

In Tokyo's bohemian underworld, the young Taiko met a woman who was in many ways not unlike herself. An aspiring writer, working in menial jobs and similarly exploited by a succession of lovers, HAYASHI FUMIKO became a lifelong friend. She taught Taiko how to sell stories to magazines, and, by example, was an inspiration to her. But whereas Fumiko found stability in a lasting relationship and soon became self-supporting as a writer, Taiko had greater difficulty. If the life of an artist has three basic needs – to earn a living, to form a relationship, and to pursue a chosen art – Taiko became ensnared in the conflict so often created by these largely separate activities.

In 1925, Taiko started writing for *Bungei sensen* (*Literary Front*), a journal in which she would later publish her prize-winning story "*Seryōshitsu nite*" (*1927*, "In a Charity Hospital"), again based on her Manchurian experiences. Between these events, she joined the Proletarian Art Association, and married Kobori Jinji, a working-class activist. An improvement on her previous lovers, Kobori had been introduced to her because she frankly requested her friends to play matchmaker. The marriage, however, was not a great success, and Taiko felt betrayed when Kobori had a child with another woman.

Artistically, 1927 was a productive year for Taiko. She won the New Writer's Award contest for "Self-Mockery," and wrote "*Hikambu-ha no nikki*" ("Diary of Members of the Opposition Faction"), a story which expressed her distrust of rigid socialist dogma. For Taiko, the end did not necessarily justify the means, and she was appalled by the idea of putting human feelings aside in the fight for social justice. As translator Yukiko Tanaka says in the anthology *To Live and To Write*: "In . . . 'Sorrowful Love' (1931, "*Kanashiki aijō*"), Taiko examined the dilemmas of love and class struggle, presenting the difficult conflicts between human emotion and political ideology. Taiko's own sympathies in this story are clearly on the side of love."

In the late 1930s, Hirabayashi Taiko entered the darkest phase of her life: one which lasted until the end of World War II. Imprisoned and brutally interrogated by the military authorities, she became critically ill with tuberculosis and was bedridden for eight years. During this time, too, she was forced to remain silent, being unable to publish fiction that would inevitably be unacceptable to the government. Only in 1946 did she resume her career with "*Kōyū onna*" ("A Woman Like This"), winning the Women's Literary Award for what was clearly one of the few outstanding works of fiction in the immediate postwar era.

Translator George Saito refers to Taiko as "transcending class consciousness and moving toward humanism" in the next phase of her career. In the March issue of *Sekai bunka* (*World Culture*) she published one of her most brilliant stories: "*Mō Chūgoku hei*" ("Blind Chinese Soldiers"), since translated into English in the anthology *Stories by Japanese Women Writers* (M. E. Sharpe, 1982; reissued as *Japanese Women Writers*, 1991). It is a moving and horrifying account of those wartime atrocities so rarely addressed in Japanese literature.

For documentary realism, scarcely anyone can match Taiko's uncanny, pictorial intensity. At full strength, as in "*Hito no inochi*" (*1950*, "A Man's Life"), she creates an atmosphere of Dostoievskian compulsiveness, concentrating on vivid details which bring the story to life.

Far too little of Taiko's work has been translated for a full evaluation from an English perspective, but, judging by what is available, her work is among the very best of modern Japanese literature. Her (untranslated) autobiographical novel *Sabaku no hana* (1957, *Flower in the Desert*) gives a full account of her life in all its vitality, hardship, and uncompromising struggle for freedom, justice, and independence.

Hirabayashi Taiko died in 1972 of pneumonia.

RECOMMENDED READING

Short Fiction

"Blind Chinese Soldiers." "*Mō Chūgoku hei*." 1946. 5 pages. Tr. Noriko Mizuta Lippit. *Bulletin of Concerned Asian Scholars*, vol. 12, no. 4, 1980; *Stories by Contemporary Japanese Women Writers*. M.E. Sharpe, Armonk, NY, 1982; reissued as *Japanese Women Writers*, 1991.

"A Man's Life." "*Hito no inochi*." 1950. 16 pages. Tr. George Saito. *Modern Japanese Stories*, ed. Ivan Morris. Spottiswoode, London, 1961; Tuttle, Tokyo and Boston, 1962 and 1977, paperback. One of the best stories in a superlative anthology.

WORKS IN ENGLISH TRANSLATION

Short Fiction

"The Black Age." "*Kuroi nenrei*." *1962*. 14 pages. Tr. Edward Seidensticker. *Japan Quarterly*, vol. 10, no. 4, 1963; *Comment*, no. 20, 1963; *Solidarity*, March 1958.

"Blind Chinese Soldiers." "*Mō Chūgoku hei*." *1946*.

"The Goddess of Children." "*Kishimojin*." *1946*. 7 pages. Tr. Ken Murayama. *Pacific Spectator*, vol. 6, no. 4, 1952.

"A Man's Life." "*Hito no inochi*." *1950*.

"I Mean to Live." "*Watashi wa ikiru*." *1947*. 10 pages. Tr. Edward Seidensticker. *Japan Quarterly*, vol. 10, no. 4, 1963; *Asian P.E.N. Anthology*, ed. F. S. Jose. Taplinger, NY, 1966; *Solidarity*, vol. 8, no. 2, 1973.

"Secret." "*Himitsu*." *1967*. 4 pages. *Japan P.E.N. News*, no. 24, 1971.

"Self-Mockery." "*Azakeru*." *1927*. 22 pages. Tr. Yukiko Tanaka. *To Live and To Write: Selections by Japanese Women Writers 1913–1938*, ed. Yukiko Tanaka. The Seal Press, Seattle, WA, 1987.

"A Woman To Call Mother." "*Haha to iu onna*." *1966*. 15 pages. Tr. Richard Dasher. *The Mother of Dreams*, ed. Makoto Ueda. Kodansha International, Tokyo, 1986.

IBUSE Masuji
(1898–   )

Novelist, essayist, and writer of short fiction. Born in Kamo, Hiroshima Prefecture. Lived in Tokyo for much of his life.

As more people in the West come to appreciate the forms and conventions of modern Japanese literature, so they will increasingly admire the unique qualities of Ibuse Masuji. Even in translation his style is instantly recognizable, and he is, in many ways, the "archetypal modern Japanese writer." He has addressed some of the great moral dilemmas of the twentieth century, most notably in his monumental novel *Kuroi ame* (*1965–66, Black Rain*), which deals with the bombing of Hiroshima. He has also drawn themes from the more distant past, producing a substantial body of historical literature that rivals that of TANIZAKI JUN'ICHIRŌ in the ingenuity of its telling. A countryman at heart who has experienced the alienation of life in a modern city, he projects first and foremost a sense of compassion for his fellowman. There is an elegiac quality about much of his writing, as if one compelling purpose of his literature is to rescue from oblivion those who would otherwise be forgotten.

Ostensibly apolitical and of no declared religious faith, he nonetheless makes one acutely aware of political and religious issues. Bitter irony, biting sarcasm, and a deep, reverberating sense of humor are all combined in Ibuse's work to produce a literature, not of suffering but of healing. In a long career in which first painting and then poetry were his initial inclinations, Ibuse Masuji has won nearly every major Japanese literary prize.

For the first nineteen years of his life Ibuse lived where he was born, in the village of Kamo which is now part of Fukuyama in the eastern reaches of Hiroshima Prefecture. His well-off, farming family had long been established in that area, their records dating back to the fifteenth century. However, neither his father, Ikuta, nor his mother, Miya, was especially affectionate towards him. Theirs was a marriage full of trials and tensions, at least partially caused by the fact that Ikuta was an "adopted husband," that is, a man who becomes adopted into his wife's family in order to continue their name. Ibuse's maternal grandfather, Tamizaemon, was therefore the patriarch, a situation that made his father feel inferior. Young Masuji probably made matters worse by being drawn to his grandparents, enjoying both his grandmother's stories of the peasant uprisings that occurred when she was small and his grandfather's even more exciting stories about the medieval period. A sensitive, intelligent man who took Masuji on trips each year to the Inland Sea, Grandfather Tamizaemon was the formative influence of his early years.

An uneventful school career, during which Masuji developed a great interest in becoming a painter, ended in disappointment when he was rejected by an established artist whose apprentice he had hoped to become. As an alternative he decided to go to Waseda University in Tokyo to study literature. Consequently, in August 1917 he traveled from the provinces to this, one of the world's great capital cities: a rite of passage for many an aspiring writer or artist, even to the present day. At his destination, however, he found no welcoming arms but merely a city largely indifferent to his fate. Moving from one lodging house to another he began a decade of rootlessness, the experience of which influenced his writing for the rest of his life.

Ibuse attended the lectures on Shakespeare given by TSUBOUCHI SHŌYŌ and those on Bashō given by Yoshida Genjirō. He avoided all the student strikes which were rife at the time, but mixed freely with the many aspiring writers who attended, however intermittently, Waseda University. His most valued friend was his classmate Aoki Nampachi, who constantly encouraged him to write. Hoping to please Aoki he actually wrote seven stories while on a summer vacation, each of them based on a particular animal. Among them was one about a salamander which later became his first published work, under the title *"Yūhei"* (*1923*, "Confinement"). Tragically, Aoki died after a short illness, leaving Ibuse – who already suffered from depression – with a desperate feeling of bereavement. Partly out of a sense of duty to his friend he began to take his writing more seriously. His career began in the pages of a small literary magazine called *Seiki* (*The Century*), published by Waseda students, and it was there that "Confinement" first appeared.

To all but the literary historian, "Confinement" and *"Sanshōuo"* (*1929*, "Salamander") are essentially one and the same work. Throughout his career Ibuse tended to revise his earlier writings, and indeed he even made further changes to this particular story as late as 1985 so that it reads very much like the original. Textual niceties aside, it is unquestionably his seminal work: the tale of a salamander who insists on remaining idly in his rocky cave until, having grown much larger, he can no longer escape from it. He curses his fate and grows sad at the sight of fish and other creatures cavorting outside. Eventually he traps a frog, compelling him to share his confinement with him. Years pass, by which time the frog, too, is reduced to a similar state of mind. Yet at the end of this brief (7-page) story the frog says to the salamander, with the utmost diffidence: "Even now I'm not really annoyed with you."

Reviewed in the light of Ibuse's later works, "Salamander" has all kinds of meanings and implications. One is struck, first of all, by its allegorical tone. In one passage the salamander observes a shoal of killifish and mocks them because they all behave slavishly as a group, each imitating the one immediately in front "for fear of being left behind." It is an image that obviously has a symbolic meaning in a society where strict hierarchies are rigorously applied. For example, in the army an aspiring corporal may imitate his sergeant who in turn imitates an officer, and so on up the chain of command. It is "the system" in operation, and one will find further examples of it scattered not only throughout Ibuse's stories but again in "Salamander" itself. Here the main protagonist, the amphibian with whom the author appears to identify, is guilty of imposing his own fate on that of the poor frog. He does so in order to create a microcosmic world within the cave, a world which becomes no different in its rules from that which exists outside. Because the frog seems to appreciate this fact he is unable to become really annoyed with his captor.

With its sharp irony and delightful touches of humor, "Salamander" is not an apprentice work but a fully fledged Ibuse story containing many of his most characteristic qualities. It may be seen not only as a metaphor of the existential condition – a condition, the author implies, which is so appalling that one's only option is to join in the cosmic humor which created it – but also as an indication of his state of mind at the time of writing it. In the latter case, the cave and its occupants are a complex symbol of the author's creative self. Depressed and isolated, with little room for maneuver, the salamander nonetheless has acute powers of observation and an awareness of a vast emptiness whenever he closes his eyes. The frog, on the other hand, represents the compassionate side of Ibuse's nature with his extraordinary capacity to forgive his captor. There is only one other occupant (who has not so far been mentioned), namely the tiny shrimp who laughs and laughs at the salamander's predicament. He represents both the humorous element in Ibuse's psychology and the author's instinct for survival when the going gets tough. As the story tells us: "There is no creature quite like a shrimp for laughing in muddy water."

"Salamander" in its original version as "Confinement" made little impact on the literary scene. Waseda University was the focus for the *Naturalist movement, and while it was clear that Ibuse was not a Naturalist it was not at all clear into which category he should be fitted. In any case, much of Tokyo was destroyed by the *Great Kantō Earthquake shortly after the story's appearance, so it is not surprising that favorable comment was strictly limited. Ibuse went home to Kamo, returning to Tokyo a month later. It was around this time that he met the writer Tanaka Kōtarō (1880–1941), an essayist and composer of stories with supernatural themes, who agreed to become his mentor. Tanaka provided both material and psychological support during a very difficult period of Ibuse's life, behaving towards his disciple in much the same way that Ibuse himself would later behave toward the younger writer DAZAI OSAMU. Working as a proofreader in various publishing firms, Ibuse was grateful when Tanaka's support enabled him to spend more time writing. He produced some further stories of the highest quality, including "Yofuke to ume no hana" (1925, "Plum Blossom by Night") and "Koi" (1926, "Carp"), both of them written in the first person and this time featuring human rather than animal protagonists.

In "Plum Blossom by Night" the narrator is plagued by feelings of guilt when he finds himself unable to return a five-yen note given to him by a drunk. Perhaps influenced by Tanaka Kōtarō, he introduces an element of almost supernatural mystery into the story, implying that he must first break down some psychic barrier within himself before he can return the money. "Carp" has an even greater intensity. An autobiographical piece commemorating his late friend Aoki, it describes how the author cares for a large white carp that his friend once gave him. The story introduces another characteristic that is elaborated in Ibuse's later work, namely the importance he attaches to ritual. In this case it is the personal ritual of caring for the carp that is the focus of the story. The narrator removes the fish from a pond belonging to Aoki's former mistress and places it into a larger pool on the Waseda University campus. He goes to watch over it during both summer and winter. In summer he sees students swimming and sunbathing, while in winter he sees nothing but the pool itself frozen over. When snow falls on the ice he uses a stick to draw a large picture of a fish "close to twenty feet long," and says: "In my mind it was my white carp." The narrator concludes by expressing his complete satisfaction: "I was utterly content."

Throughout Ibuse's work the carp is a symbol of life and regeneration, its most notable appearance – apart from this early story – being at the climax of his novel *Black Rain*. It is highly effective in both works because Ibuse succeeds in communicating the force of his personal belief that the well-being of the carp is vitally important. Here we see Ibuse in the act of inventing a ritual, just as elsewhere in his work – for example in his late story "*Kenkōji no ike*" (1978, "The Pond at Kenkōji Temple") – we see him observing the commemorative rituals of others. One possible interpretation of the early story is that Ibuse, by means of ritual, had in some way internalized Aoki's spirit, and with this additional creative force was able to proceed with more confidence as a writer.

Ibuse was still virtually unknown in the literary world, despite having produced several first-rate stories. For this reason, his mentor, Tanaka Kōtarō, felt obliged to introduce him to another, perhaps more influential writer, Satō Haruo. The author of the novel *Den'en no Yūutsu* (1918, *Rural Melancholy*), Satō had an established reputation and was well-connected in literary circles. He helped Ibuse by introducing him to editors and publishers, enabling his work to appear in prominent journals. For example, "Carp," which had first appeared in Tanaka's journal *Kagetsu* (*Beautiful Moon*), made a second appearance two years later in the more widely read *Mita bungaku* (*Mita Literature*).

In 1927 Ibuse's grandfather died, thus severing one of the young writer's most vital links with home. As a consequence Ibuse was more inclined to make his home in the capital than he might have been otherwise. He became engaged to Akimoto Setsuyo; received his first payment for a story – for "*Ibitsu na zuan*" (1927, "An Elliptical Design"); and borrowed some money from his elder brother Fumio to help build a small house in Ogikubo, a cheap area outside Tokyo (now much more expensive and very much *inside* Tokyo). The transformation of Ibuse from country boy to sophisticated urban dweller was now complete. Or was it? Only the themes and textures of his works could give the answer, and the evidence is overwhelming that Ibuse's imagination was fed by his experiences in the country and not by those he gained in the city.

Perhaps subconsciously Ibuse was thinking of the country when he wrote *"Yane no ue no Sawan"* (*1929*, "Savan on the Roof"). It is a story in which the narrator finds a wounded wild goose and becomes reluctant to part with it even when it has regained its health. Like the earlier hero who feels guilty about failing to return the five-yen note, he determines to rectify the matter, but before he can do so, Savan (as he calls the goose) unexpectedly escapes to join his flock in the wild. Again, the story carries the force of having a personal meaning over and above its anecdotal value. It may be said to represent another step in the liberation of Ibuse's imagination from a narrow world of alienation and confinement to the boundless vistas of the world at large. Equally, it suggests that the writer was now aware that he did not necessarily have to address his immediate surroundings, but could fly in his imagination to the countryside around Kamo for his future works.

That is exactly what Ibuse did. He ignored the proletarian movement, whose writers described mainly the oppressive nature of urban life, and joined with others who published the nonproletarian magazine (and therefore, it has to be said, the nonfashionable magazine) *Bungei toshi* (*Literary City*). "Salamander" appeared in it, as did some of his other stories. An exception was his 1929 work, which is now readily available in English translation, called *"Kuchisuke no iru tanima"* ("Kuchisuke's Valley"), which appeared in *Sōsaku gekkan* (*Creative Writing Monthly*). It contains a brilliant portrait of an elderly man, the first of many such portraits in Ibuse's stories. A countryman of great natural wisdom, Kuchisuke is an old family retainer whom the narrator goes to visit in the mountains. The story's great drama derives from the fact that the old man's valley is about to be flooded as a result of a new dam that has been constructed some miles away. Inexorably, the day of the cataclysm arrives, and the crux of the story is to be found in Kuchisuke's search for some glimmer of hope amid the destruction.

Ibuse was among those who founded the *Shinkō Geijutsuha Kurabu* (*New Artists Club*) in 1930, and he also joined the journal *Sakuhin* (*Works*), the first issue of which appeared in April 1930. These activities brought him into close contact with writers who were exploring avenues of creativity other than those trodden by the proletarians. His stories in the 1930s became more complex and much longer. To sustain his fiction he used traditional techniques of "linked ficiton" – fiction in which different vignettes are linked at the level of ideas and imagery rather than through any dictate of the plot. In this manner he produced *"Kawa"* (*1931*, "The River"), which describes many tragic incidents that happen alongside (and then mostly in) the River Ashida that runs near to Kamo in his home province; and *"Sazanami gunki"* (*1930–38*, "Waves: A War Diary"), an extraordinary historical tale over which he deliberately lingered for nearly a decade.

"Waves: A War Diary" is readily available in English translation, having been issued in 1986 in a volume that contains one other famous Ibuse story: *"Wabisuke"* (*1946*, "Isle-on-the-Billows"). For readers of English there is no better introduction to his historical fiction than this volume (*Waves, Two Short Novels*), which incidentally contains a useful list of twenty-four historical works written by Ibuse between 1930 and 1961. In most of Ibuse's historical writings there is a sense of powerful yet impersonal forces at work, shaping the destiny of the world. His heroes are not the movers and shakers of history but ordinary people who take part in events chiefly with survival in mind. In their survival, Ibuse suggests with incontestable logic, lies the future of the world.

Set in the twelfth century, "Waves: A War Diary" describes the misfortunes of the Heike clan after their expulsion from the capital by Kiso Yoshinaka. Subsequently pursued by the military genius Yoshitsune, the doomed Heike were scattered to the Western Isles, where, even today, their descendants are said to remember the shame of defeat. Supposedly, it was from an actual war diary kept by "a fairly highly placed member of the Heike clan" that the author derived his story. The family who owned this important historical document were, we are led to believe, so reluctant to reveal their lineage that they kept it hidden, the narrator hearing of its contents only via a third party. However, even this tenuous (and undoubtedly fictitious) link with the past is sufficient to give the story an uncanny authenticity. "Waves: A War Diary" is a masterpiece of storytelling: episodic in form like an ancient chronicle, and, not least because it is told from the point of view of the defeated clan, highly poignant in feeling. Moreover, even in English translation it bears all the inimitable characteristics of Ibuse's mature style. It has his unique rhythm of narration, typified by a perfect timing whenever he switches our attention from momentous historical events to examine some minor phenomenon of nature.

As Ibuse continued his exploration of historical events he began to address certain themes with such frequency that they can be said to constitute whole genres of his fiction. For example, disasters and catastrophes figured largely in his work long before he wrote *Black Rain*. The various ways in which ordinary men and women cope with wars, erupting volcanoes, floods, and earthquakes form an inexhaustible subject and one to which his style was becoming ideally suited. Indeed, without these frequent appearances of disaster, his work as a whole would be that of a miniaturist – entertaining and highly polished but scarcely the product of a literary giant. By placing his deeply sympathetic portrayals of individual people against the enormities of natural and man-made disasters he created the potential for literature of the highest order.

"Aogashima taigaiki" (1934, "A General Account of Aogashima") is a work that seems to anticipate the events of World War II and is an early example of Ibuse's disaster genre. Set in the 1780s, it takes the form of a letter, written by the inhabitants of Aogashima, thanking the authorities for their help during volcanic disturbances which devastated the island. By this means the author builds a precise picture of what actually happened, noting the various ill omens that appeared before the event and describing the inhabitants' evacuation to a neighboring island. The whole story is told in retrospect, in a documentary, "deadpan" style which Ibuse usually favored for this type of subject. The essential point of the story is that life regenerates itself after even the most cataclysmic disturbance, implying that it may perhaps be a force equal or superior to the forces of destruction.

All disaster stories run the danger of making human beings appear ant-like in their behavior, but Ibuse's protagonists are so idiosyncratic that they never seem less than human. Even so, he sought other ways of enhancing their role, of making them larger on the canvas without necessarily eradicating the element of disaster. He succeeded by developing one particular genre and making it all his own: that of the "castaway novel" in which ships' crews are blown off-course to various unexpected destinations. An essay, two stories, and a novel, all written in the mid-1930s, launched his long and productive exploration of the castaway genre.

The essay was called *"Nihon hyōmin"* (1933, "Japanese Castaways"), and it drew attention to the many *hyōryūki* ("castaway accounts") that survive in archives from the *Edo period. During Japan's long period of isolation the only people to have contact with the outside world were the sailors who were accidentally blown into foreign waters. If these men were fortunate enough to return home they would always have to undergo a comprehensive interrogation by the authorities, not only to pass on useful information but also to make sure they had not become foreign spies. The accounts of these interrogations were the aforementioned *hyōryūki*, and they were a great inspiration to Ibuse, a writer who could easily identify with the sailors' rootless, alienated existence.

The first two stories in the castaway genre were *"Mujintō Chōhei"* (1936, "Chōhei on an Uninhabited Island") and *"Chōhei no haka"* (1936, "Chōhei's Grave"). Chōhei himself was one of five sailors from the Tosa domain who were marooned on Marcus Island, nearly a thousand miles south of Tokyo. He was the only one of his crew to survive and return to Japan to tell of his experiences. In the first story he describes how he and his comrades devise a new calendar, using a "first day, second day" chronology instead of counting by reigns and emperors. Their improvised calendar gives them a feeling of presence on the island, a place that would otherwise seem unbearably distant from home. However, despite ingenuity of this kind (they also become adept at catching birds and fish), one by one the castaways die until only Chōhei is left. Fortunately for him, two other ships are wrecked and their crews join him on the island. In "Chōhei's Grave" the story is told of how, having saved their tools, the sailors of the last vessel are able to construct a boat that will take them, eventually, back to Japan.

The cornerstone of Ibuse's first batch of castaway literature is *"Jon Manjirō hyōryūki"* (1937, "John Manjirō: A Castaway's Chronicle"). Translated by Anthony Liman and David Aylward, it is one of Ibuse's most important works available to English readers. It is by far the most entertaining of his translated works, telling the true story of a young Japanese fisherman who is shipwrecked and subsequently rescued by a friendly American whaling captain. Bearing in mind that war clouds were already gathering when Ibuse wrote the novel, the reader may well suspect him of intending some oblique political message in portraying a foreigner in such a favorable light. Yet even without its symbolic overtones "John Manjirō: A Castaway's Chronicle" would be a triumph of historical fiction. No reader can fail to be gripped by the accounts of Manjirō's three epic voyages across the world, or fail to be moved by the very peculiarity of his personal destiny. Educated in the United States at a time when no other Japanese had contact with Americans, Manjirō came to play a key role for his country in the years that followed Commodore Perry's visits (in 1853–54) to Edo harbor. As an interpreter he accompanied the first Japanese delegation to San Francisco and was charged with the responsibility of teaching his compatriots about the science and customs of the West. He discharged his duties with admirable patience, all the time longing to return to the high seas as a whaler like his American benefactor, Captain Whitfield.

Ibuse was approaching middle age when the war in the Pacific began, and even though he was now a respected novelist he was not exempted from active service. He was actually on a fishing trip to Kōfu with his friend Oda Takeo when his wife sent word that he had been called up. Typically, he finished the trip in a leisurely fashion, then returned to face whatever fate awaited him. He recorded all the experiences of the following year in the army in his memoir *Chōyōchū no koto* (*1977–80, Under Arms*).

After some brief training in Osaka, Ibuse was assigned to one of several "writers' units" – propaganda units that were intended to win the acceptance of people in countries defeated by the Japanese army. He was shipped off to an unidentified destination, actually Southeast Asia, where he traveled down the Malay Peninsula to witness the fall of Singapore. Throughout this period Ibuse kept a war diary which he used as the basis for various memoirs, including *Nankō taigaiki* (1943, *An Account of My Voyage South*). In describing the battle for Singapore, however, he resorted to another source for *Aru shōjo no senji nikki* (1943, *A Young Girl's Wartime Diary*). It is based, he claims, on the experiences of a fourteen-year-old Eurasian girl, whose diary he obtained after seeking just such a document. As an outsider with no affiliations to either of the warring sides (the British and the Japanese), the girl speaks as an innocent bystander who wishes only to survive. At one stage, Ibuse himself intervenes in the narrative to describe the spectacular destruction of the city. The image of a city on fire becomes, in his eloquent, detailed prose, one of horrifying beauty – akin to the great natural disasters that he had so often depicted.

Ibuse's attitude to the war is best described as one of implicit opposition, although he was never able to state his views openly. Even before the war he had written stories, such as "*Kokki*" (1934, "The Flag"), that contained a sly, subversive humor. During hostilities he was greatly restricted by military censorship, and cited this as the main reason for discontinuing *An Account of My Voyage South* in March 1942. In "*Kane kuyō no hi*" (1943, "The Day of a Memorial Service for a Bell") he described how a temple bell was requisitioned for its metal content – and how a special service was held to mark the transformation of its soul. Again, there was no overt criticism of the authorities, and the story was actually published in a military magazine. After completing it, Ibuse stopped writing for two years and maintained a dignified silence, like Tanizaki Jun'ichirō and NAGAI KAFŪ at the time, and indeed like the bell of his own story. In the postwar years, however, his talent for directing bitter irony against the authorities won him the affection of a vast readership. There are many examples of it in translation, the most notable being *"Noriai jidōsha"* (*1952*, "The Charcoal Bus") and *"Yōhai taichō"* (*1950*, "Lieutenant Lookeast").

A strong element of anti-establishment feeling enters also into Ibuse's brilliant historical story "Isle-on-the-Billows," which appeared in 1946. It can even be read as an allegory of the recent war although it deals with events of the late seventeenth century. In 1687, Shōgun Tsunayoshi (the so-called Dog Shōgun) issued an edict that no one was to kill any living creature, a law which fishermen and bird-catchers – like the narrator Wabisuke – found impossible to obey. Those found guilty of breaking the law were sent into exile, one penal colony being on the "island" of Hadakajima, which is actually a sandbank in the middle of a river. Ibuse's story concentrates on the experiences of the oppressed convicts, leaving the reader in no doubt that their rulers are both cruel and hypocritical. At the end, the whole island is suddenly hit by an earthquake, causing it to disappear completely under the water.

During the 1950s Ibuse's fame spread from the literary world to the general public. He won the first Yomiuri Prize for his story, *"Honjitsu kyūshin"* (*1949–50*, "No Consultation Today"). Later, this work was also made into a film, as were his novels *Ekimae ryokan* (*1956–57*, *The Station Hotel*) and *Chimpindō shujin* (*1959*, *The Curio-Shop Proprietor*). Ibuse's translations from English were also very popular and over a period of fourteen years (1941–55) he published translations of all Hugh Lofting's Doctor Dolittle stories for children. One other translation is also worth noting: that of Daniel Defoe's *Robinson Crusoe*, which he published in 1961. A prime example of "castaway literature," albeit from a foreign source, it confirmed his dominance of this unusual genre.

In 1960 Ibuse was made a member of the Japan Art Academy, and at the age of sixty-two he could look back on a career of remarkable achievements. However, his best work was yet to come. *Black Rain* is not merely one of the finest works of modern Japanese literature; it is one of the world's great novels. Based on the bombing of Hiroshima on August 6, 1945, it is a book that constantly surprises any reader who may be inclined to anticipate a depressing catalogue of tragedy. *Black Rain* addresses one of the most horrific subjects available to a writer but it does not itself add to the sum of the world's misery. There is no sentiment in the novel, only compassion; no violent protest, only factual account. Ibuse pieced together a tapestry of details, setting down ordinary, everyday events which assume a religious significance when seen against the inhuman catastrophe inflicted on Hiroshima.

Structurally, *Black Rain* is the most complex of Ibuse's works. Had he taken a more straightforward approach to the subject – for example, by describing events in strict chronological order – he would have failed. Instead, he chose to sustain a sense of the immediacy of the explosion throughout the whole book, returning to it frequently while using as his main character a man who kept a "Journal of the Bombing" during the weeks following the event.

Shigematsu Shizuma is a senior employee at a factory which makes clothing for the military, and it is through his eyes that we observe the catastrophe and to whose account we keep returning, even though several years have elapsed in the main narrative. In fact, Shigematsu's "Journal" gradually takes over from the third-person narrative with which the book begins. In this way the great conception of the novel slowly unfolds. Although Shigematsu suffers some effects of radiation, neither he nor his wife, Shigeko, is badly injured. Their chief concern after the war has ended is to find a suitable husband for their niece, Yasuko, who lives with them. Even though she is in apparent good health, everyone knows that she walked through the ruins on the outskirts of the city and was stained with the "black rain" that fell later during the day. People are distrustful, fearing that Yasuko will fall victim to the mysterious illness which has already affected so many others. Shigematsu refuses to believe that his niece is in danger, while she, as if to spite the rumors, makes herself more attractive in subtle ways, hoping that a husband may be found.

Alongside the major strand of the novel described above is another, to which it is closely related. In order to avoid being criticized for self-indulgence, Shigematsu tries to find a good excuse for his fishing expeditions. Fishing is the ideal recreation for him, for it brings him into contact with the natural world, so essential to the spirit after the horrors of war. Moreover, it is not physically demanding, for any strenuous work brings on symptoms of radiation sickness. He thus decides to breed carp, in partnership with some friends. They breed and raise them with great care, the exercise being documented in loving detail. It soon becomes clear that the novel's two major themes are linked by implication: Shigematsu has faith that the carp will breed – and they do – but no one has faith that Yasuko will find a husband.

Not until near the end of the novel do we reach a vantage point from which its pattern can be seen. Up to that point the tapestry has been almost "flat" – like the ruins of the city. Yet there comes a sudden heightening of emotion when Shigematsu speaks openly about the number of people who have died of radiation sickness. He says: "Having no need to keep silent any longer, I have described these things ... just as they occurred. ..." And he goes on to explain that his niece has begun to show symptoms of the disease. The words "having no need to keep silent any longer" are the key to *Black Rain* as a work of literature. Shigematsu, the obsessive chronicler who has been so exceptionally diligent in setting down the terrible consequences of the bomb, is now revealed as being capable of keeping some things to himself. Only a great master of literature could conceive this device, telling us by implication that the full story of Hiroshima has not, will not, and can never be told.

Black Rain was serialized in *Shinchō* (*New Currents*) between January 1965 and September 1966, finally appearing as a complete volume in 1966. In that year, too, Ibuse won the Noma Prize and was awarded the Order of Cultural Merit, the highest award that can be given to a Japanese citizen. Naturally, he continued to work, producing many more stories and essays throughout the 1970s and 1980s. His 1981 collection *Umiagari* (*Up from the Sea*) contained one notable story (mentioned earlier) called "The Pond at Kenkōji," an elegy in which he depicts himself observing how some villagers mourn the men from their locality who have been lost at war. It is typical of his style: clear, detailed, and utterly concerned with the immediacy of his subject.

The West has no writer directly comparable to Ibuse Masuji, for he writes essentially as an essayist who has extended his work into the realm of the novel by applying many traditional Japanese literary techniques. His liberal use of notebooks, diaries, postulated chroniclers, vignettes, linked stories, and the perennial "I" of the narrator are elements that are used less frequently in the West than in Japan. Yet how successfully Ibuse orchestrates them, all the time allowing his voice, personality, and sometimes genial, sometimes acerbic, humor to speak directly to the reader.

First and foremost an artist who delights in the uniqueness of individual life, whether that of a human being, a bird, or a fish, Ibuse was called upon by history to write his masterpiece, *Black Rain*. Although that particular novel is of a different magnitude from his other work, he will long be remembered also for the subtlety and humor of his short stories and novellas. Few writers have shown such a sharp perception of everyday life, or expressed it with more wit, warmth, and humility.

RECOMMENDED READING

Novel

Black Rain. *Kuroi ame. 1965–66.* 300 pages. Tr. John Bester. *Japan Quarterly*, vol. 14, nos. 2–4, 1967; vol. 15, nos. 1–3, 1968; Kodansha International, Tokyo and NY, 1969, 1979 paperback; Secker and Warburg, London, 1971; Bantam, NY, 1985 paperback; Fontana, London, 1990. Ibuse's best-known work; readily obtainable.

WORKS IN ENGLISH TRANSLATION

Novel

Black Rain. Kuroi ame. 1965–66.

Short Fiction Collections

Castaways, Two Short Novels. 159 pages. Tr. Anthony Liman and David Aylward. Kodansha International, Tokyo, 1987.
Lieutenant Lookeast and Other Stories. 247 pages. Tr. John Bester. Kodansha International, Tokyo, 1971; Secker and Warburg, London, 1971.
Salamander and Other Stories. 134 pages. Tr. John Bester. Kodansha International, Tokyo and NY, 1981 paperback.
Waves, Two Short Novels. 171 pages. Tr. David Aylward and Anthony Liman. Kodansha International, Tokyo, 1986.

Short Fiction

"Carp." *"Koi." 1926.* 5 pages. (1) Tr. John Bester. *Lieutenant Lookeast and Other Stories; Salamander and Other Stories.* (2) As "The Carp." Tr. Lane Dunlop. *Literary Review*, vol. 28, no. 1, 1984.
"The Cat." *"Neko." 1959.* 4 pages. Tr. Lawrence Rogers. *Japan Quarterly*, vol. 32, no. 1, 1985.
"Catching a Kappa." *"Kappa sōdō."* 1956. 24 pages. Tr. Kiyoaki

Nakao. *Two Stories by Masuji Ibuse.* Hokuseido, Tokyo, 1971; Secker and Warburg, London, 1971.
"The Charcoal Bus." *"Noriai jidō-sha." 1952.* 10 pages. Tr. Ivan Morris. *Modern Japanese Stories*, ed. I. Morris. Spottiswoode, London, 1961; Tuttle, Tokyo and Boston, 1961 and 1977, paperback.
"A Cold Night." *"Kan'ya." 1948.* 5 pages. Tr. George Saito. *Japan P.E.N. News*, no. 18, March 1966.
"The Crazy Iris." *"Kakitsubata." 1951.* 19 pages. Tr. Ivan Morris. *Encounter*, vol. 6, no. 5, 1956; *Fire from the Ashes*, 1985; *The Crazy Iris, and Other Stories of the Atomic Aftermath*, ed. Ōe Kenzaburo. Grove Press, NY, 1985.
"A Geisha Remembers." *"Oshima no zonnengaki." 1951.* 41 pages. *Castaways, Two Short Novels.*
"Isle-on-the Billows." *"Wabisuke." 1946.* 27 pages. *Waves, Two Short Novels.*
"John Manjirō, A Castaway's Chronicle." *"Jon Manjirō hyōr-yūki." 1937.* 136 pages. (1) As *"John Manjirō, The Castaway."* Tr. Hisakazu Kaneko. Hokuseido, Tokyo, 1944. (2) *Castaways, Two Short Novels.*
"Kuchisuke's Valley." *"Kuchisuke*

no iru tanima." *1929.* 20 pages. *The Shōwa Anthology*, vol. 1, ed. Van C. Gessel and Tomone Matsumoto. Kodansha International, Tokyo, 1985.

"Kuro, the Fighting Cock." *"Iwata kun no Kuro." 1938.* 7 pages. Tr. Yokichi Miyamoto, with Frederick Will. *Chicago Review*, vol. 19, no. 1, 1966.

"Lieutenant Lookeast." *"Yōhai taichō." 1950.* 28 pages. (1) As "A Far-Worshipping Commander." Tr. Glenn Shaw. *Japan Quarterly*, vol. 1, no. 1, 1954; *No Consultation Today*. Hara Shobo, Tokyo, 1964. (2) Tr. John Bester. *The Shadow of Sunrise: Lieutenant Lookeast and Other Stories; Salamander and Other Stories*.

"Life at Mr. Tange's." *"Tange shi tei." 1931.* 15 pages. (1) As "At Mr. Tange's." Tr. Sadamichi Yokoo and Sanford Goldstein. *Literature East and West*, vol. 13, nos. 1–2, 1969. (2) *Lieutenant Lookeast and Other Stories; Salamander and Other Stories*.

"The Life of Mutsugoro of Noheji." *"Noheji no Mutsugorō ryakuden."* 40 pages. Tr. Kiyoaki Nakao. *Two Stories by Masuji Ibuse*. Hokuseido, Tokyo, 1970.

"No Consultations Today." *"Honjitsu kyūshin." 1949.* 28 pages. Tr. Edward Seidensticker. *Japan Quarterly*, vol. 8, no. 1, 1961; *No Consultation Today*. Hara Shobo, Tokyo, 1964.

"Old Ushitora." *"Ushitora jiisan." 1950.* 22 pages. *Lieutenant Lookeast and Other Stories; Salamander and Other Stories*.

"Pilgrim's Inn." *"Henro yado. 1940.* 6 pages. *Lieutenant Lookeast and Other Stories; Salamander and Other Stories*.

"Plum Blossom by Night." *"Yofuke to ume no hana." 1925.* 11 pages. *Lieutenant Lookeast and Other Stories; Salamander and Other Stories*.

"The Salamander." *"Sanshōuo."* 13 pages. (1) Tr. Tadao Katayama. *The Reeds*, vol. 2, 1956. (2) Tr. Leon Zolbrod. *The East*, vol. 1, no. 2, 1964. (3) As "Salamander." Tr. Sadamichi Yokoo and Sanford Goldstein. *Japan Quarterly*, vol. 13, no. 1, 1966. (4) *Lieutenant Lookeast and Other Stories; Salamander and Other Stories*.

"Savan on the Roof." *"Yane no ue no Sawan." 1929.* 6 pages. (1) As "Sawan on the Roof." Tr. Yokichi Miyamoto, with Frederick Will. *Chicago Review*, vol. 19, no. 1, 1966. (2) As "Sawan on the Rooftop." Tr. Tadao Katayama. *The Reeds*, vol. 11, 1967. (3) *Lieutenant Lookeast and Other Stories; Salamander and Other Stories*.

"Swan Song." *"Hakuchō no uta." 1955.* Tr. G. W. Sargent. *Eigo Seinen*, vol. 102, nos. 9–12, 1956.

"Tajinko Village." *"Tajinko mura." 1939.* 112 pages. *Lieutenant Lookeast and Other Stories; Salamander and Other Stories*.

"Urashima Tarō." *"Urashima Tarō."* 4 pages. *Nippon*, vol. 3, 1933.

"Waves: A War Diary." *"Sazanami gunki."* Composed 1930–38. 77 pages. *Waves, Two Short Novels*.

"Yosaku, The Settler." *"Kaikon mura no Yosaku." 1955.* 16 pages. *Lieutenant Lookeast and Other Stories; Salamander and Other Stories*.

CRITICAL STUDIES

Dorsey, John T. "The Theme of Survival in John Hersey's *Hiroshima* and Ibuse Masuji's *Black Rain.*" *Tamkang Review*, vol. 14, no. 1, 1983–84.

Liman, Anthony V. "Ibuse's *Black Rain.*" *Approaches to the Modern Japanese Novel*, ed. Thomas E. Swann and Kinya Tsuruta. Sophia University, Tokyo, 1976.

——. "Ibuse Masuji: 'Carp' and 'Pilgrim's Inn.'" *Approaches to the Modern Japanese Short Story*, ed. Thomas E. Swann and Kinya Tsuruta. Waseda University Press, Tokyo, 1982.

——. "The River: Ibuse's Poetic Cosmology." *Essays on Japanese Literature*, 1975.

Treat, John Whittier. *Pools of Water, Pillars of Fire: The Literature of Ibuse Masuji.* University of Washington Press, Seattle, 1988.

INOUE Yasushi
(1907–1991)

Author of novels, historical fiction, and poetry. Born in Asahikawa, Hokkaidō.

A prolific and versatile writer, Inoue Yasushi is one of the leading figures of postwar Japanese literature. He is well known in the West through the many translations of his brilliant historical novels: fiction that captures the imagination by its superb reconstruction of the distant past. *Tempyō no iraka* (1957, *The Roof Tile of Tempyō*) is set in the era of "Heavenly Calm" (*Tempyō*: the early eighth century), when the Japanese sent expeditions to China to bring back a Buddhist master. *Tonkō* (*1959, Tun-Huang*) is an adventure tale which gives a plausible reason why, in the eleventh century, thousands of Buddhist scrolls were concealed in a cave in Western China. "*Rōran*" (*1959,* "Lou-Lan") describes the fate of a city caught between the two great warring peoples: the Chinese and the Hsiung-nu, in the first century B.C.

From these English translations one forms a distinctive impression of Inoue. He is clearly a master storyteller, a painstaking and meticulous scholar who seems quite uncompromising in his dedication to serious historical fiction. However, this impression does not take into account the full range of his life's work. For Inoue has also been a newspaper reporter, a poet of some distinction, a popular novelist who once resurrected the *Ken'yūsha mode of romantic fiction, and the author of many works on contemporary themes.

Inoue Yasushi was born in 1907, the son of an army medical officer. Because his parents spent much of their time moving between military bases, he was brought up largely by his grandmother at the family home in Izu. He attended a high school in Kanazawa, afterwards enjoying some years of freedom until entering university. In 1932 he left Kyūshū Imperial University, enrolled at Kyoto Imperial University, and graduated from the latter with a degree in aesthetics in 1936.

Already nearly thirty, Inoue might easily have continued as a dilettante had he not become a professional journalist on the *Mainichi shimbun*, first in Osaka and then in Tokyo. His decision to join the newspaper seems admirably "out of character," and is the first evidence in his career of that rare ability to transform oneself – so necessary in achieving anything exceptional in life.

At university Inoue had written his thesis on "The Pure Poetry of Valéry," scarcely the normal interest of a newspaperman. He had even written much poetry of his own and had published a play called *Meiji no tsuki* (1935, *Moon of Meiji*) which had been staged by a well-respected theater. Nonetheless, on joining the *Mainichi* he dedicated himself to becoming a good reporter, and, except for six months in the army, remained with the newspaper for the next twelve years.

At the age of forty-three, Inoue again transformed his career by turning seriously to writing fiction. During 1950 he published a dozen short stories, an anthology of poetry, and two full-length novels. Clearly, this second transformation had been happening gradually. The poetry had been written over a number of years, and in 1948 he had shown his classic story *"Ryōjū"* ("Shotgun," also translated as "The Hunting Gun") to Satō Haruo, and had received some encouragement. His debut, therefore, was spectacular when it occurred. With his story *"Tōgyū"* (*1949*, "The Bullfight") he won the Akutagawa Prize, while, with "Black Tide" he found a contemporary theme – the mystery surrounding the death of a public figure – and became simultaneously a popular and fashionable author.

Examined closely, Inoue's first serious stories do not reveal any great genius for mainstream fiction. Although beautifully structured, "Shotgun" is somewhat static in its narrative, quite lacking in that magical transference of "life-as-lived" into "life-on-the-page" that we find, say, in a novel by FUTABATEI, TANIZAKI, or MISHIMA. Rather, it is closer to a poem in conception, and indeed many of Inoue's stories are based on powerful poetic images that do not readily lend themselves to dramatic treatment.

Perhaps aware of this aspect of his writing, Inoue concentrated more on popular fiction in the mid-1950s, producing a long novel called *Hyōheki* (*1957, The Ice Cliff*). Concerning a love triangle, and serialized in 270 daily issues of the *Asahi shimbun*, the novel helped Inoue to win the Academy of Arts Prize in 1959. Undoubtedly, the long narrative helped him to develop his storytelling skills, preparing him for the next phase of his remarkable career.

The Roof Tile of Tempyō was Inoue's first major historical novel and is still regarded as his best. While not a brilliant scholar in his college days, Inoue now addressed himself to researching eighth-century China and Japan, and succeeded where many professional scholars might have failed. All the dialogue is, of course, pure invention, but the whole story is rooted in facts that have been meticulously sifted. In writing *The Roof Tile of Tempyō*, Inoue discovered a genre which he could make his own: in much the same sense as (for example) the British writer John le Carré has made the spy thriller into a distinguished form of literature.

Apart from the Asian novels already mentioned, Inoue went on to write historical fiction in a more popular vein with *Yodo-dono nikki* (*The Diary of Lady Yodo*) in 1961. He followed it with *Fūtō* (*1963, Wind and Waves*), an account of how Kublai Khan tried to use Korea as a means of conquering Japan. The first of these novels in the early 1960s won Inoue the Noma Literary Prize; the second, the Yomiuri Newspaper Award. In 1964 he was elected to membership of the Japanese Academy of Arts, one of the highest national distinctions in letters.

Although most of Inoue's work is highly objective fiction, far from the Japanese *I-Novel tradition, he has also written on subjects to which he has strong emotional ties. *Waga haha no ki* (*1964–74, Chronicle of My Mother*) is at once a portrait of his aging mother and a description of how the family coped with her increasingly eccentric behavior. It is a moving and intimate recollection, of value to anyone who faces a similar family situation.

Still active in the 1970s and 1980s, Inoue produced a major work in *Wadatsumi* (*1977, God of the Sea*), an account of Japanese immigration into the United States. In 1981, he published *Honkakubō ibun* (*Papers Left by the Priest Honkaku*), based on the final days of the tea master, *Sen no Rikyū.

Throughout Inoue's writing there is a recurrent mood of what might be called "heroic loneliness." It appears not only in such obvious guise as the central character of "The Hunting Gun," but in the historical fiction, too. In essence, it is a vision of Man set in a vast landscape: either an individual like Josuke of "The Hunting Gun," or the ant-like armies doing battle in the open plains of central Asia.

There is, too, an elegaic note of regret in nearly everything Inoue has written. This is most apparent in such stories as "The Counterfeiter," which, like "The Hunting Gun," has a disturbing, subjective quality that comes close to being an admission of defeat. However, counterbalanced by often exciting narratives, even the "notes of regret" contribute to a distinctive body of literature that will long be read with pleasure.

RECOMMENDED READING

Novels

The Roof Tile of Tempyō. *Tempyō no iraka.* 1957. 140 pages. Tr. James T. Araki. University of Tokyo Press, Tokyo, 1975. Columbia University Press, NY, 1982. Contains 10-page translator's introduction; finely printed with extra wide margins; dust jacket photo shows statue of Ganjin, the monk who is featured in the novel.
Tun-Huang. *Tonkō.* 1959. 201 pages. Tr. Jean Oda Moy. Kodansha International, Tokyo and NY, 1978 and 1983. Contains both author's preface and translator's introduction.

WORKS IN ENGLISH TRANSLATION

Novels

The Roof Tile of Tempyō. Tempyō no iraka. 1957.
Tun-Huang. Tonkō. 1959.
Wind and Waves. Fūtō. 1963. 200 pages. Tr. James T. Araki. University of Hawaii Press, Honolulu, 1989.

Reminiscences

Chronicle of My Mother. Waga haha no ki. 1964–74. 152 pages. Tr. Jean Oda Moy. Kodansha International, Tokyo, 1982 and 1985. Is divided into three parts: "Under the Blossoms" (written 1964), "The Light of the Moon" (1969), and "The Surface of the Snow" (1974).

Journey Beyond Samarkand. Saiiki monogatari. 1967–69. 130 pages. Tr. Gyo Furuta and Gordon Sager. Kodansha International, Tokyo, 1971.

Shirobamba: An Izu Boyhood. Shirobamba. Tr. Jean Oda Moy. Peter Owen, London, 1991.

Short Fiction Collections

The Counterfeiter, and Other Stories. 112 pages. Tr. Leon Picon. Tuttle, Tokyo and Boston, 1965; Prentice-Hall, London, 1965; Peter Owen, London, 1989. Contains "Obasute," "The Full Moon," and "The Counterfeiter."

Lou-Lan, and Other Stories. 160 pages. Tr. Edward Seidensticker and James T. Araki. Kodansha International, Tokyo and NY, 1979 and 1981. Includes "Princess Yung-t'ai's Necklace," "The Opaline Cup," and "Passage to Fudaraku."

Mixed Anthology

The Izu Dancer, and Other Stories. 144 pages. Tr. Leon Picon (Inoue), Edward Seidensticker (Kawabata). Tuttle, Tokyo and Boston, 1974, paperback. Contains all the contents of *The Counterfeiter, and Other Stories* (see above) plus title story by KAWABATA YASUNARI.

Prose Poem Anthology

The Modern Japanese Prose Poem. An Anthology of Six Poets. Tr. with an introduction by Dennis Keene. Princeton University Press, Princeton, 1980. Contains 25 prose poems by Inoue, published between 1958–76. Also features works by Miyoshi Tatsuji, Anzai Fuyue, Tamura Ryūichi, Yoshioka Minoru, and Tanikawa Shuntarō.

Letters

Letters of Four Seasons. Shiki no gansho. Correspondence between Ikeda Daisaku and Inoue Yasushi. Written 1975–76. 123 pages. Tr. Richard L. Gage. Kodansha International, Tokyo, 1980.

Short Fiction

"The Azaleas of Hira." *"Hira no shakunage."* 1950. 34 pages. Tr. Edward Seidensticker. *Japan Quarterly*, vol. 2, no. 3, 1955; *Modern Japanese Short Stories.* Japan Publications Trading Co., Tokyo, 1960; revised edition 1970; as "The Rhododendrons." *Lou-Lan, and Other Stories.*

"The Counterfeiter." *"Aru gisakka no shōgai."* 1951. 54 pages. *The Counterfeiter, and Other Stories.*

"Flood." *"Kōzui."* 1959. 67 pages. Tr. John Bester. *Japan P.E.N. News*, no. 4, Dec. 1959; *Flood.* Hara Shobo, Tokyo, 1964.

"The Full Moon." *"Mangetsu."* 1958. 25 pages. *The Counterfeiter, and Other Stories.*

"God of the Sea." *"Wadatsumi."* 1977. Tr. John Bester. *The East*, vol. 2, nos. 5–6, 1966; vol. 3, nos. 2–6; vol. 4, nos. 1–6.

"How Came Ceylon to Be Founded." *"Sokara kuni engi."* 11 pages. Tr. Yutaka Kato. *Konan Joshi Daigaku Eibungaku Kenkyu*, no. 5, 1969.

"The Hunting Gun." *"Ryōjū. 1949.* 74 pages. (1) Tr. Sadamichi Yokoo and Sanford Goldstein. Tuttle, Tokyo, 1961; Prentice-Hall, London, 1961; Peter Owen, London, 1989. (2) As "Shotgun." Tr. George Saito. *Modern Japanese Stories*, ed. I. Morris.

Spottiswoode, London, 1961; Tuttle, Tokyo, 1962.

"Kobandai." *"Kobandai." 1961.* 11 pages. (1) Tr. Laurie Berman. *Japan Echo*, vol. 22, 1985. (2) As "Under the Shadow of Mt. Bandai." Tr. Stephen W. Kohl. *The Shōwa Anthology*, vol. 2, ed. Van C. Gessel and Tomone Matsumoto. Kodansha International, Tokyo, 1985.

"Lou-Lan." *"Rōran."* 1959. 38 pages. Tr. Edward Seidensticker. *Japan Quarterly*, vol. 6, no. 4, 1959; *Lou-Lan, and Other Stories.*

"A Marriage Interview." *"Miai no hi."* 1963. 14 pages. Tr. Sara Dillon. *The Mother of Dreams, and Other Short Stories*, ed. Makoto Ueda. Kodansha International, Tokyo, 1986.

"Obasute." *"Obasute."* 1955. 23 pages. *The Counterfeiter, and Other Stories.*

"The Opaline Cup." *"Gyoka wan ki."* 1951. 20 pages. *Lou-Lan, and Other Stories.*

"Passage to Fudaraku." *"Fudaraku tokaiki."* 21 pages. *Lou-Lan, and Other Stories.*

"Princess Yung-T'ai's Necklace." *"Eitai koshu no kubikazari."* 1964. 20 pages. *Lou-Lan, and Other Stories.*

"The Sage." *"Seija."* 19 pages. *Lou-Lan, and Other Stories.*

"The Wind." *"Kaze."* 1974. 11 pages. Tr. Tsutomu Fukuda. *Eigo Kenkyu*, vol. 55, nos. 4–6, 1966.

Essays

"My Thoughts on Chanoyu." *Chanoyu Quarterly*, vol. 1, no. 1, 1970.

"The Writer's Role in the Nuclear Age." 3 pages. Tr. Juliet Winters Carpenter. *Japan Quarterly*, vol. 32, no. 2, 1984.

Miscellaneous

Extract from novel: *Icy Crag. Hyōheki.* 1957. 18 pages. Tr. Jukichi Suzuki. *Jigo Eigo Kenkyu*, vol. 22, nos. 4–7, 1967. (Full novel is available in French and German translations).

CRITICAL STUDIES

Araki, James T. "Yasushi Inoue and His *Tempyō." Books Abroad*, vol. 44, no. 1, 1970.

Kimball, Arthur G. "Inoue's 'Hunting Gun': The Irony of Deception." *Japan Christian Quarterly*, vol. 41, no. 2, 1975.

Ishikawa TATSUZŌ
(1905–1985)

Novelist and war reporter. Born in Akita Prefecture. Lived in Tokyo.

Best known to English readers for his 1954 novel *Aku no tanoshisa* (*Evil for Pleasure*), Ishikawa Tatsuzō was the winner of the very first Akutagawa Prize in 1935. It was awarded for *"Sōbō"* ("The Common People"), a story based on the author's experiences in Brazil among Japanese emigrants. The pathetic sight of these people, mostly poor farmers unable to make a living in Japan, prompted him to address the social issues of his country, however unpleasant the facts might be. Nonetheless, he never became a radical or so-called proletarian writer, preferring instead to take a moral but politically neutral stance. As a war reporter, sending stories to the *Chūō kōron* from the Chinese front in the late 1930s, he was vehemently anti-militaristic: an attitude that incurred the displeasure of the Ministry of the Interior which immediately prohibited the sale of the magazine. After serving a short prison sentence, Tatsuzō resumed his literary career, going on to write numerous popular and serious novels depicting the darker side of human life.

Born in the northern snow country, Tatsuzō was the third of eight
brothers and no stranger to hardship even as a child. He was forced
to become self-reliant at an early age and was largely self-taught in
the art of literature. He left the Department of English Literature at
Waseda University before graduating, but continued to study in his
spare time while working for a magazine publisher. Unlike most
aspiring authors he never sought the help of an established writer
for gaining entry to the literary world. To this extent he was, as his
writing often reflects, an outsider who could be freely critical of the
society around him.

Winning the Akutagawa Prize was undoubtedly the event which
catapulted Tatsuzō to prominence. The editors of *Chūō kōron*,
impressed by his journalistic skills, sent him to report from Nanking
in 1937. Already convinced that war was "brutal, miserable, and
idiotic," Tatsuzō found nothing in the Japanese-occupied city to
change his attitudes. He quickly wrote a short novella called *"Ikite-
iru heitai"* (1938, "Living Soldiers") and sent it back for publication.
As Donald Keene estimates, it "must have had the force of a
bombshell," for it depicted Japanese atrocities exactly as they
happened. To the public, who were more accustomed to newspaper
reports of heroic and even godlike soldiers, the arrest of Tatsuzō
and his editor came as no surprise. The two men were tried and
found guilty of being unpatriotic. No one from the literary world
came to their defense, and only by suggesting that the author
redeem himself by writing a "more positive" book about the war
did the editors of the magazine secure his release.

Without completely compromising his integrity, Tatsuzō wrote
Bukan sakusen (1939, *The Wuhan Operation*), a novel which described
the war in strategic and political terms rather than focusing on
individual incidents or moral issues. The text was published without
censorship, and, by the end of 1941, Tatsuzō was fully back in favor
with the military authorities.

Perhaps because he was not always allowed to express his views
directly, Tatsuzō began writing popular fiction during World War
II. Objective in style and quite unrelated to the *I-Novel tradition,
these works often contained elements of crime fiction, as instanced
by his story (readily available in English) called "The Affair of the
Arabesque Inlay." Even here, however, there is a strong sense of
human evil unleashed by wartime experiences. It is worth noting, too,
that Genjirō Nakane, the miserable anti-hero of *Evil for Pleasure*, is
mentioned as having killed many people while serving as a soldier.
Although Tatsuzō does not belabor the point, it is clearly an important
clue to understanding Nakane's peculiar deadness of spirit.

Dozens of works followed Tatsuzō's wartime chronicles. Many
were serialized in newspapers, among them *Kaze ni soyogu ashi*

(*1949–51, Reeds Swaying in the Wind*), which examined the social impotence of the intellectual classes; and *Ningen no kabe* (*1957–59, The Human Wall*), which criticized the pressures of Japan's educational system. Although neither of the above works has been translated into English, Tatsuzō's 1956 novel, *Shijū hassai no teikō* was published as *Resistance at Forty-Eight* in 1960. It is a story of midlife crisis: a "novel of manners" whose title, in Japan, became a fashionable phrase for describing an all-too-familiar phenomenon.

Though intelligent, readable, and popular in their time, Tatsuzō's works cannot be classed as fictions of the highest order. Modeled on Western forms, they do not (in translation, at least) show sufficient command of dramatic structure. Equally, the author's moderate political views often seem to be at odds with his social observations, as though a more carefully considered philosophy were needed to match the realities shown. Nonetheless, in Japan Tatsuzō's work has for many years represented a significant and not unsuccessful challenge to prevailing literary traditions.

RECOMMENDED READING

Novel

Evil for Pleasure. *Aku no tanoshisa.* 1954. 356 pages. Tr. Paul T. Konya. Yohan Publications, Tokyo, 1972. Contains 3-page translator's introduction.

WORKS IN ENGLISH TRANSLATION

Novels

Evil for Pleasure. Aku no tanoshisa. 1954.

Resistance at Forty-Eight. Shijū hassai no teikō. 1956. 343 pages. Tr. Kazuma Nakayama. Hokuseido, Tokyo, 1960.

Short Fiction

"The Affair of the Arabesque Inlay." 12 pages. Tr. Makoto Momoi and Jan Gluck. *Ukiyo,* ed. Jay Gluck. Vanguard Press, NY, 1963; *Murder in Japan,* ed. John L. Apostolou and Martin H. Greenberg. Dembner Books, NY, 1987.

"The Emigrants." *"Sōbō." 1935–39. The East,* vol. 21, nos. 4–6, 1985; vol. 22, no. 1, 1986.

"New Folk Tales of Japan." *Shin Nihon minwashū.* 21 pages. Tr. Kohji Oi. *The Reeds,* vol. 5, 1959.

"Young Mischief." *"Seishun no satetsu."* 5 pages. *Japan P.E.N. News,* no. 24, 1971.

Essays

"Thoughts in the Dark." 4 pages. Tr. Brewster Horwitz. *New World Writing 3,* 1953.

Izumi KYŌKA
(1873–1939)

Novelist and playwright. Real name, Izumi Kyōtarō. Born in Kanazawa. Resident of Tokyo.

Izumi Kyōtarō, who is always referred to by his pseudonym, Kyōka, was the author of over three hundred novels, short stories, and plays, half of them dealing with the supernatural. Greatly admired by AKUTAGAWA, TANIZAKI, and MISHIMA, his work set an example for the aesthetic movement that blossomed in the *Taishō era (1912–26). Much of his work is brilliantly structured, and, though written in a lively modern idiom, contains many influences from *Kabuki* and from Chinese classical literature. Staunchly feudal in his morality, Kyōka relied upon the traditional conflict between *giri* (social obligation) and *ninjō* (human feeling) as the basis for his often farfetched plots. Yet the eerie atmosphere of his stories, so marvelously evoked, was entirely the product of his own poetic imagination. Sadly neglected by translators despite his achievements, Kyōka can be read in English only in three works: his masterpiece,

"*Kōya hijiri*" (*1900*, "The Kōya Priest"), "*Sannin no mekura no hanashi*" (1912, "A Tale of Three Who Were Blind"), and "*Uta andon*" (1910, "The Song of the Troubadour"). Both of them are well worth seeking if one enjoys (for example) the work of Tanizaki, where Kyōka's considerable influence can be clearly seen.

Born in Kanazawa, the son of a metal engraver, Kyōka was only nine years old when his mother died in 1882. A devotee of the *Nō theater, his mother is thought to have been the model for many of the women of his novels: the older women with whom his heroes fall desperately in love. Another formative influence was the city of Kanazawa itself. A center for traditional arts and crafts, it must surely have stimulated his youthful imagination, for the Izumi family actively continued the local tradition. In 1884 Kyōka entered a mission school where he remained for three years, excelling in English literature and acquiring a great enthusiasm for the contemporary Japanese works of OZAKI KŌYŌ. It was his greatest ambition to become a disciple of this man, whose fame and dominance of the *Meiji literary world were legendary.

In 1890 Kyōka moved to Tokyo with high hopes of joining Kōyō's literary circle, the *Ken'yūsha. The best he might have expected would have been a menial position in the writer's household, but even making such a request was beyond him when he first arrived. Living in great poverty, he put off his proposed visit to Kōyō until 1891, when at his first attempt he was readily accepted. Moreover, he soon became Kōyō's favored disciple, and by 1893 had written his first novel, *Kammuri Yazaemon*, which was serialized in a Kyoto newspaper. Not until the following year, however, did he write anything with real quality. Returning home for his father's funeral, he drafted *Giketsu kyōketsu* (1894, Noble Blood, Heroic Blood), a novel that was largely rewritten by Kōyō in the master's own style. Its melodramatic plot, featuring a *geisha* in love with the law student who later becomes her judge at a murder trial, hinges upon the *giri-ninjō* conflict traditional in popular Japanese literature. Although the exact nature of this conflict has been questioned by Doi Takeo (in 1971, *The Anatomy of Dependence*), it is clearly an inexhaustible source of moral dilemmas. Kyōka's hero, faced with the problem of deciding where his duty lies, has to choose between persuading the *geisha* to confess to her crime or else allowing it to pass unsolved; the latter being an attractive choice because the woman has murdered a rich couple in order to acquire funds to support his legal career. In the event, the hero opts for social duty. He convicts the *geisha*, but commits suicide as a gesture of his love for her. Feudal morality thus triumphant, the author leaves the reader to ponder its implications. Kyōka often posed problems in this manner, and, along with Kawakami Bizan (1869–1908), is credited with inventing the *kannen shōsetsu*: the "problem novel."

Kyōka was an incorrigible romantic in both life and art. His one and only dispute with Kōyō, whom he practically worshipped, was over a love affair with a *geisha*, and he was unable to marry her until after Kōyō's death in 1903. In the meantime, he became a prolific writer and was soon being hailed as the most talented member of the junior Ken'yūsha circle. Among his closest friends was TOKUDA SHŪSEI, who also came from Kanazawa but whose work differed sharply from his own. Shūsei went on to become the best of the Naturalist writers and espoused *Naturalism even after it fell from favor. Kyōka, on the other hand, was never interested in depicting life in a realistic manner. He was a fantasist who actually believed in the supernatural. In the words of the writer Minakami Takitarō, he wanted "to give an impression of truth not by describing things just as they are, but by describing impossibilities."

In *Writers and Society in Modern Japan* (1983), Irena Powell places Kyōka alongside MORI ŌGAI as providing one of the two basic models of literary method for the writers of the aesthetic school. Whereas Ōgai showed how the writer's personal views could be kept apart from his logical analysis of the hero's thoughts and actions, Kyōka drew attention to suitable material and showed how it could be used. He took his ideas from "tales of old mystery," embellished them with dream sequences and sensuous imagery, and then organized this material into elaborate plots – some of which operate in an almost cinematic style of rapid cross-cutting. His literary method certainly influenced Tanizaki, Satō Haruo, Murō Saisei, and SATOMI TON, and was eventually adopted in their later works by YOKOMITSU and KAWABATA.

Kyōka was very active in the years 1895–96, moving from Kōyō's house to the home of Ōhashi Otowa (1869–1901), a Ken'yūsha member who had married into an influential publishing family. He also joined the *Sōsha* (literally the "Sea-Weed Group"), an embryonic *bundan*, or literary group, that consisted chiefly of himself, Yanagawa Shun'yō, Oguri Fūyō, and his constant friend Tokuda Shūsei. In those years, too, he wrote *"Yakō junsa"* (*1895*, "Night Patrolman"), the story of how a policeman sacrifices his life in order to save his girlfriend's father, even though the man has been trying to keep the couple apart. *"Gekashitsu"* (*1895*, "The Operating Room") was his most popular early story, a lurid account of how a surgeon (much like the hero of *Noble Blood . . .*) is obliged to operate on a beautiful countess who loves him. In this case, unable to marry the hero, the countess commits suicide on the operating table.

"*Teriha kyōgen*" ("Teriha Play") followed in 1896, together with "*Ichinomaki*" ("The First Volume"). Also in that year Kyōka scored one of his biggest triumphs by having his work "*Biwa den*" (1896, "The Legend of Biwa") published in the New Year supplement of *Kokumin no tomo*. According to TAYAMA KATAI, the supplement conferred "the hallmark of status as a major writer, rather like the *Chūō kōron* . . . nowadays" (i.e., 1917, when Katai wrote *Thirty Years in Tokyo*, reminiscences in which, incidentally, he revealed no small degree of envy of Kyōka's success).

Kyōka wrote his most realistic works when he concentrated on what he knew best. For example, the descriptions of *geisha* costumes in "*Yushima mōde*" (1899, "Worship at Yushima") are derived from firsthand knowledge, which can scarcely be said for the remarkable images of his best-known story, "The Kōya Priest." Published at the turn of the century, the novella perfectly illustrates the "world of impossibilities" towards which Kyōka was taking his art. Set in a remote part of the country, it tells of how a priest tries to rescue a peddler whom he thinks is in danger of losing his life on a flooded road. But in searching for the man, he meets an enchantress who is half-woman, half-snake. When she assumes a completely human form she tries, without success, to seduce the priest. Unlike the peddler who succumbed to her charms and has been turned into a horse, the priest survives his ordeal. In this he is alone, for the countryside thereabouts is populated by numerous monkeys, toads, and bats, all of them once men who proved to be unsatisfactory lovers for the enchantress.

Exactly why Kyōka, a quiet, bespectacled man with a strong respect for authority, should have been so strongly attracted by escapist fantasy is unclear. Irena Powell suggests that the Japanese language itself tended to drive writers away from reality, mainly because it could never be used as a common currency suitable for describing all the social classes of the day. Rather, it had a decorative function ideally suited to revealing a world of sensuous beauty. A great stylist, Kyōka used the language to brilliant effect, and was supreme among modern Japanese writers in his ability to evoke ghostly, Nō-like atmospheres.

Content to go his own way, Kyōka rejected the new methods of Naturalism that appeared in the first decade of the century. His melodramatic plots lent themselves readily to the stage, and many of them became a staple diet of the low-brow *Shimpa* theater. However, the process of adaptation tended to destroy their literary merit by eliminating Kyōka's distinctive style. More successful artistically were his original plays, such as *Tenshu monogatari* (1917,

The Castle Tower), a drama that was not performed until 1951, long after the author's death.

Both *"Onna keizu"* (*1907*, "A Woman's Pedigree") and *"Shirasagi"* (*1909*, "Snowy Heron") were well received, but of all his works, *"Uta andon"* (*1910*, "The Song of the Troubadour) was the one most highly praised by critics in Japan. It first appeared in the January issue of *Shinshōsetsu* and was written in the elegant *gembun-itchi (unified speech and writing) style originally pioneered by FUTABATEI SHIMEI. Donald Keene in *Dawn to the West* singles out *"Uta andon"* as exemplifying Kyōka's fine sense of structure. Indeed, Kyōka was considered by Tanizaki to be the only contemporary Japanese novelist who had any talent whatsoever for plot construction.

Most accessible to English readers by virtue of its inclusion in the anthology *Modern Japanese Literature* (1956) is "A Tale of Three Who Were Blind." It is a complex fantasy in which the protagonist, Sakagami, is accosted by three blind people – two men and a woman – while on his way to meet a lover. They tell him that if he should continue his journey he will be pursued by a demon that "takes the shadows of men, snatches and devours them." Dimly aware that the three figures are none other than himself, his rival, and the woman he loves, he goes on to his destination and tells his lover to "look to her own conscience." In doing just that, the woman begins to live in terror of her shadow, and, like Sakagami's rival – her blind admirer who is the only "demon" among the three figures – loses her sight. Sakagami, determined to be with her in love, drives a needle into his own eyes. Now the eternal triangle is complete: all three people becoming "phantoms in the fading gaslight." By retaining a tenuous link with the real world the story has all the power of a vivid dream.

Kyōka went on to write many other stories of mystery and imagination, including *"Mayu kakushi no rei"* (*1924*, "The Ghost with Hidden Eyebrows") and *"Sankai hyōbanki"* (1929, "Comparative Views of Land and Sea"). His final work, *"Rukō shinsō"* (*1939*, "A Web of Crimson Thread") was published shortly before his death. Stephen W. Kohl in *Far Eastern Literatures in the 20th Century* says: "[It] combines all the elements for which [Kyōka's] work is known: ghosts from the past, the beautiful temptress, the distorting power of passion, and the redeeming power of mercy."

In a long and prolific career, Kyōka – a mild-mannered man who according to Donald Keene "lived in mortal dread of dogs and lightning" – extracted beauty from terror and treated the supernatural as though it were a contiguous extension of the real world. Much more of his work should be made available in English.

RECOMMENDED READING

Short Fiction Collection

The Saint of Mt. Kōya and The Song of the Troubadour. Tr. Stephen W. Kohl. 184 pages. Takakuwa Bujutsu Insatsu. Kanazawa, 1990. Can be found in specialist libraries. Produced by a Japanese committee dedicated to promoting the works of Izumi Kyōka in English translation.

Short Fiction

"A Tale of Three Who Were Blind." *"Sannin no mekura no hanashi."* *1912.* 12 pages. Tr. Edward Seidensticker. *Modern Japanese Literature from 1968 to the Present Day,* ed. Donald Keene. Grove Press, NY, 1956; Tuttle, Tokyo, 1957; Grove Weidenfeld, NY, 1989, paperback.

WORKS IN ENGLISH TRANSLATION

Novels

Of a Dragon in the Deep. Ryūtan den. 1896. 113 pages. Tr. M. Cody Poulton. Publishing Committee, Kanazawa, 1987.

Short Fiction

"The Kōya Priest." *Kōya hijiri. 1900.* 78 pages. (1) 4-page extract as "The Kōya Mendicant." *Introduction to Classic Japanese Litera-* ture, 1956. (2) Tr. Eiichi Hayashi. *The Reeds,* vol. 5, 1959; vol. 6, 1960. (3) As "The Saint of Mt. Kōya." *The Saint of Mt. Kōya and The Song of the Troubadour.*

"The Song of the Troubadour." *"Uta andon."* 1910. *The Saint of Mt. Kōya and The Song of the Troubdaour.*

"A Tale of Three Who Were Blind." *"Sannin no mekura no hanashi." 1912.*

CRITICAL STUDIES

Carpenter, Juliet Winters. "Izumi Kyōka: Meiji-Era Gothic." *Japan Quarterly,* vol. 31, no. 2, 1984.

Funatsu, Jean Akemi. "Through the Colored Looking Glass of Izumi Kyōka: Reflections of the Kusazoshi." Ph.D. diss., Harvard University, Cambridge, 1972.

Yamada, Yusaku. "Modern Labyrinth: The Literary Style of Izumi Kyōka." *Transactions of the International Conference of Orientalists in Japan,* no. 26, 1981.

KAIKŌ Takeshi
(1930–1989)

Novelist and journalist. Often referred to as Kaikō Ken. Born in Osaka. Married the poet Maki Yōko, in 1953. Lived in Tokyo.

A man of many abilities, Kaikō Takeshi was, in turn, a public relations manager for Suntory Whiskey, a war correspondent whose reports from Vietnam once gained him considerable fame in Japan, and a leading novelist of the postwar era. He appeared frequently on television, wrote at length on angling, and was renowned as a brilliant conversationalist who enjoyed gourmet cooking and a largely Western life-style. In his writing he made a radical departure from Japanese literary tradition. He filled his stories with action and individual psychology, sometimes in the style of superior thriller-writing in the West. Yet his sharp intelligence and unique, anecdotal mode of introspection gave his work a distinctiveness which has been equally appealing to Japanese readers. His best novel, *Kagayakeru yami* (1968, *Into a Black Sun*), was awarded the Mainichi Cultural Prize.

Born in Osaka in 1930, Kaikō Takeshi grew up amid the turmoil and confusion of World War II. He graduated from the law school of Osaka City University and survived the immediate postwar era by working in a variety of different jobs. From Osaka he would commute to Tokyo to work one day a week in the public relations department of Suntory Whiskey, and (so he claimed) earn sufficient money to support himself as a six-day-a-week writer. Such practice would only be possible in an economic boom period, yet Kaikō always seemed peculiarly ungrateful. Much of his work is cynical and pessimistic, and he frequently expressed his distaste for anything Japanese.

Kaikō's first story to attract wide attention was *Panikku* (1957, *Panic*), a short disaster novel describing bureaucratic incompetence in dealing with a plague of rats. Yet, even though it was well-crafted, thoughtful, and inventive, it gave little indication that its author would go on to produce such a powerful novel as, say, *Into a Black Sun*. Dry and unemotional, *Panic* not only lacked the essential elements of serious literature but even those qualities which characterize good popular fiction. Nonetheless, for reasons that have now faded into the history of fashion-prone sensibilities, the story established Kaikō on the Japanese literary scene.

At the end of 1957 Kaikō produced a far superior work called "*Hadaka no ōsama*" ("The Naked King"). First published in the December issue of *Bungakukai*, it tells of how a man teaching art to small children exacts his revenge on what he believes to be an unholy alliance between big business and education. The story is ingenious in the extreme, and its narrative structure has all the satisfying precision of clockwork. Moreover, through some feat of the imagination, Kaikō combined a mastery of plot with believable characters whose behavior is properly motivated. Even today "The Naked King" remains one of Kaikō's best works, while in 1958 it won him the Akutagawa Prize.

Kaikō's experience of the commercial world was turned to good advantage in the novella "*Kyojin to gangu*" (*1957*, "Giants and Toys"). This has since been anthologized as a "business novel," not only in Japan where it appeared in Shiroyama Saburō's collection *Keizai shōsetsu meisaku-sen* (1980, *Selected Business Novels*), but also in Tamae K. Prindle's *Made in Japan and Other Japanese Business Novels* (1989), a collection in English translation. It should be noted that these so-called business novels (*keizai shōsetsu*) constitute a popular genre that emerged in the late 1950s, growing in variety and sophistication ever since. Typified by the works of Shiroyama himself, its novels afford the reader various entertaining insights into the machinations of the banks, the stock market, and every conceivable type of business, large or small. Kaikō, of course, was never a writer who could be categorized easily, and was certainly not a "business novelist" as such. Indeed, "Giants and Toys" takes a particularly jaundiced view of Japanese merchandising, describing how an ordinary and somewhat unappealing teenage girl is turned into a media star in order to rescue the fortunes of an ailing candy manufacturer. The story is brilliantly told and contains a wonderful portrait of an advertising executive whose cynical professionalism is not unlike that of, say, Edward G. Robinson in the film classic *Double Indemnity*.

Other novels followed in rapid succession, for Kaikō wrote quickly and rarely revised his work. Eventually, a leading daily newspaper invited him to become a special correspondent. As a first assignment he was sent to cover the Eichmann trial in Israel, and thence to Vietnam, Biafra, and other trouble spots around the globe. His life was often at risk, yet he seemed to relish the danger as if it were an addictive drug. In his 1972 novel *Natsu no yami* (*Darkness in Summer*), he evoked what were surely his own ambivalent feelings of that period with great skill and insight, even though the novel itself is not one of his best. In English translation its style has the surface intensity of Joan Didion's prose, and its narrative is so oblique as to be infuriating. Set in an unnamed European location, the novel describes the feelings of a former war reporter on being reunited with his expatriate lover. Whereas the girl's pathetic alienation fails to supply the exhausted narrator with energy, mere word of an imminent attack in Vietnam galvanizes him into action and gives him back his habitual, if neurotic, reason for living.

In contrast to *Darkness in Summer*, *Into a Black Sun* addresses the Vietnam war directly. It is Kaikō's most moving and original work: a novel in which the dividing line between journalism and literature has been completely eradicated. Here, Kaikō himself is the mercilessly introspective narrator who is nonetheless gifted with acute powers of objective observation. He gathers his material by using all five senses, re-creating the camps and jungles of Vietnam with reference to sight, sound, touch, taste, and smell. As a Japanese journalist attached to an American unit he also displays an ambivalent attitude towards the war, seeing it from an Asian perspective while having certain obvious (if superficial) cultural affinities with the Americans. Thus, both the novel and its author appear to be paradoxical in spirit: a phenomenon reflected in a sinewy prose style which is packed with energy even when Kaikō is describing lethargy.

As an exploration of the contradictions that are inherent in human behavior, *Into a Black Sun* is especially remarkable. For example, Kaikō exposes the self-deception of soldiers who cannot bear to see their enemies tortured yet will readily drop napalm on them from a distance. "They're hypocrites, sentimental hypocrites," comments a South Vietnamese colonel with whom Kaikō seems to agree. Indeed, Kaikō's sympathies are with the Asiatic Vietnamese – the stoic, intelligent peasants who are caught in the midst of historical turmoil – rather than with either of the warring sides. He is less inclined than a Western writer to make clear distinctions between Communist and non-Communist ideals, seeing the conflict as almost nonsensical in its complexity. Moreover, he has no qualms about using the war for his own artistic purposes, all the time measuring himself against the people he meets, and trying, often successfully, to simulate within his own mind their peculiar psychologies and attitudes.

Unlike many of Japan's great writers, Kaikō Takeshi is the biographer's ideal subject – and no doubt an English-language biography of his action-packed life will one day become available. He was a Japanese Ernest Hemingway: a man who preferred foreign cultures, who sought adventure for adventure's sake, and who was no stranger to war. But perhaps the most striking similarity to Hemingway was Kaikō's obsession with angling. He was renowned throughout Japan for his remarkable fishing expeditions in various parts of the world. His essays describing them became best-sellers in Japan, collected under such titles as "Opa! Opa! Opa," "Farther!" and "Grander!"

Kaikō's works have been extensively translated into English by Cecilia Segawa Seigle, who once claimed that Kaikō, more than any other writer in Japan, deserved to win a Nobel Prize in literature. Although many honors were given to Kaikō in his long and distinguished career, it was not surprising that he did not become the second Japanese to receive the highest international award (the first was KAWABATA YASUNARI). His output was surely too varied, and consequently lacking any coherent artistic vision. Nonetheless, for all his eccentricity – perhaps because of it – Kaikō was a champion of individualism in a society that prefers its members to behave less flamboyantly. In this respect Kaikō was remarkably consistent. His willingness to side with the individual is the factor which most endears him to his readers. Kaikō died in 1989 at the age of fifty-nine.

RECOMMENDED READING

Novel

Into a Black Sun. *Kagayakeru yami.* 1968. 214 pages. Tr. Cecilia Segawa Seigle. Kodansha International, Tokyo, 1980; Fontana, London, 1990; Kodansha International, Tokyo, 1983, paperback. Kaikō's excellent war novel, set in Vietnam.

Short Fiction

"The Naked King." *"Hadaka no ōsama."* 1957. 40 pages. Tr. Howard Curtis. *Japan Quarterly*, vol. 24, no. 2, 1977. A brilliant story, well worth obtaining from a good library.

WORKS IN ENGLISH TRANSLATION

Novels

Darkness in Summer. Natsu no yami. 1972. 210 pages. Tr. Cecilia Segawa Seigle. Knopf, NY, 1973; Tuttle, Tokyo, 1974; Peter Owen, London, 1988; Dufour Editions Inc., PA, 1989.

Into a Black Sun. Kagayakeru yami. 1968.

Short Fiction Collections

Five Thousand Runaways. Gosennin no shissōsha. Tr. Cecilia Segawa Seigle. Dodd, Mead and Co., NY, 1987; Peter Owen, London, 1987. Contains eight stories, including: "Duel," "Laughing Stock," and "The Crushed Pellet." Dufour Editions Inc., PA, 1990.

Panic, and The Runaway. Tr. Charles Dunn. University of Tokyo Press, Tokyo, 1977.

Short Fiction

"Building a Shell Mound." 25 pages. *Five Thousand Runaways.*

"A Certain Voice." *"Aru koe."* 1955. 13 pages. Tr. Maryellen Toman Mori. *The Mother of Dreams, and Other Stories,* ed. Makoto Ueda. Kodansha International, Tokyo, 1986.

"The Crushed Pellet." *"Tama kudakeru."* 1978. 12 pages. (1) As "The Gray Ball Has Broken into Powder." Tr. Hiroo Tagawa. *The Reeds,* vol. 15, 1981. (2) Tr. Cecilia Segawa Seigle. *The Shōwa Anthology,* vol. 2. Kodansha International, Tokyo, 1985; *Five Thousand Runaways.*

"Duel." *"Kettō."* 1968. 9 pages. *Five Thousand Runaways.*

"Festivities by the River." *"Kishibe no matsuri."* 1967. 46 pages. *Five Thousand Runaways.*

"The Fishing Hole." *"Ana."* 1959. 20 pages. *Five Thousand Runaways.*

"Five Thousand Runaways." *"Gosennin no shissōsha."* 1964. 30 pages. *Five Thousand Runaways.*

"Giants and Toys." *"Kyojin to gangu."* 1957. 37 pages. Tr. Tamae K. Prindle. *Made in Japan and Other Japanese "Business Novels,"* ed. Tamae K. Prindle. M. E. Sharpe, NY, 1989.

"The Laughingstock." 1963. 33 pages. *Five Thousand Runaways.*

"Monster and Toothpick." *1979.* 16 pages. *Five Thousand Runaways.*
"The Naked King." *"Hadaka no ōsama."* *1957.*

"Panic." *"Panikku."* *1957.* 57 pages. *Panic, and The Runaway.*
"The Runaway." *"Rubōki."* *1959.* 63 pages. *Panic, and The Runaway.*

CRITICAL STUDY

Yoshida, Sanroku. "Takeshi Kaikō's Paradox of Light and Darkness."   *World Literature Today,* vol. 62, no. 3, 1988.

KAWABATA Yasunari
(1899–1972)

Novelist. Born in Osaka. Lived in Kamakura. Won Nobel Prize for
Literature in 1968.

As one of only four Japanese novelists whose works are invariably
stocked by large Western bookstores (the others, incidentally, are
NATSUME SŌSEKI, MISHIMA and TANIZAKI), Kawabata Yasunari has
long enjoyed a reputation as a representative writer of modern
Japan. Even in translation his style is instantly recognizable. Its
very simplicity evokes both depth of emotion and complexity of
meaning, while the extraordinary texture of his prose – the
unpredictable progression of images and allusions, dialogue and
narrative – is a unique source of aesthetic delight to those who
discover it. That many thousands of readers *have* discovered it is
due chiefly to the efforts of Edward Seidensticker, whose eloquent
English translations must surely have helped Kawabata win the
1968 Nobel Prize for Literature. Even if the opening lines of *Snow
Country* ("The train came out of the long tunnel into the snow

150

country. The earth lay white under the night sky . . .") are not yet
on every Westerner's list of familiar quotations, they are at least
better known than, say, the actual titles of many other modern
Japanese classics. Moreover, Kawabata's future reputation seems
assured, for his popularity in the West is still growing.

In his youth, Kawabata was not merely modern but Modernist,
having been profoundly influenced by such Western writers as
James Joyce and Virginia Woolf. Along with YOKOMITSU RIICHI he
was a leading figure of the *Shinkankakuha* movement, the "new
sense-impression" school which sought to find a method for
transcribing the immediacy of personal experience, chiefly by using
stream-of-consciousness techniques. For all his later espousal of
traditional aesthetics Kawabata remained true to his early ambitions,
never hesitating to make a daring experiment whenever he thought
it necessary. Just as he could lure the reader into the dreamlike,
transcendental world of the "snow country" and go on to tell a story
in relatively conventional terms, so too could he invent bizarre,
surrealist narratives that departed completely from realism in all
but their symbolic content. In the last analysis, as many critics have
observed, Kawabata was purely a Symbolist striving to express the
fleeting, melancholic beauty that is the predominant feature of
traditional Japanese art.

Kawabata was born in Osaka, the son of a physician who took
an interest in literature and the arts. However, neither his father
nor his mother played any role in forming his own artistic tastes,
for tragically they both died before their son reached the age of
four. Over a half century later Kawabata would be nicknamed "the
Master of Funerals" for the excellence of the many obituaries he
would write in commemoration of famous authors. Perhaps his
childhood experiences fortified him for the task, for he lost not only
his parents but also his grandmother (when he was seven) and his
sister two years later. By the time he was fourteen he was reduced
to just one close relative, his grandfather, whom he was obliged to
nurse through a terminal illness. The cumulative experience of so
many deaths is said to have scarred Kawabata's psyche throughout
his life, although he himself rejected any such idea. He preferred
to believe that he had overcome all his early misfortunes, even
claiming that he had possessed the emotional maturity to chronicle
his grandfather's death at the time it occurred.

Scholars are divided on the veracity of Kawabata's claim. "*Jūrokusai
no nikki*" (1925, "Diary of a Sixteen-Year-Old") was almost certainly
rewritten ten years later, shortly before its publication, because it
contains many passages that are typical of his Modernist style.
Nearly everyone is agreed, however, that the chronicle is an

exceptional work of art. Donald Keene calls it "an extraordinary evocation of the relations between the boy and the dying old man," going on to describe how Kawabata "by an unerring choice of detail" expresses both the love – and the disgust – the dying grandfather arouses in the boy.

In 1920, Kawabata enrolled for the Japanese literature course at Tokyo Imperial University, having already discovered that he wanted to become a writer. His first published story, "Shōkonsai ikkei" (1921, "A View of the Yasukuni Festival"), came to the attention of KIKUCHI KAN, whose influential position in Japanese letters was not unlike that occupied by Kawabata many years later. Kikuchi was highly perceptive of new talent and did much to encourage young authors setting out on their careers. He was astonished at Kawabata's sophisticated, Modernist style, admiring in particular its sharp objectivity – so different from the stale, subjective narratives of contemporary *Naturalists. He offered to introduce Kawabata to other influential figures in the literary world, keeping true to his promise by arranging a meeting with Yokomitsu Riichi. As a consequence the two younger men became close friends, and there is little doubt that Kawabata gained much from Yokomitsu's enthusiasm and penetrating intellect.

When Kawabata graduated from university in 1924 he joined Yokomitsu and others including Kataoka Teppei in founding the magazine Bungei jidai (Literary Age). As self-styled members of the avant-garde they believed in the elevation of form above content: a stance which often led to the creation of overwrought prose verging on obscurity. None of Kawabata's early Modernist works has stood the test of time, and it was the success of "Izu no odoriko" (1926, "The Izu Dancer"), a novella couched in a more conventional idiom, that may have persuaded him to modify his ideas.

"The Izu Dancer" made Kawabata famous. It was based on material he had written four years earlier in 1922, describing his walking tour of the Izu Peninsula in 1918. Some historians have suggested that he made the original trip in order to recover his spirits after being jilted by his fifteen-year-old girlfriend, but this cannot be true because the latter incident (which certainly is true) did not occur until 1921. However, his emotions may well have been heightened when he wrote his 1922 notes, for he was deeply upset by the girl's rejection of him. The experience seems to have reminded him of having been "deserted" by his family earlier in his life. Under these circumstances, recalling the happier times of his carefree vacation on the peninsula would have been a welcome diversion. There, amid the windswept scenery, he had made friends with a troupe of strolling entertainers, among whom was a teenage girl who attracted him. The joys and agonies of adolescent love thus became the main focus of the novel, although Kawabata's lyrical evocation of the landscape is every bit as memorable.

At the climax of "The Izu Dancer," the lovelorn student is talking to the man of the group when he notices that the women are bathing naked in the public bath. The dancer to whom he is attracted runs out into the sunlight – and for the first time he realizes that she is much too young to be considered seriously as a sexual partner. "She was a child, a mere child, a child who could run out naked into the sun and stand there on her tiptoes in her delight at seeing a friend." In a magical way the moment is a catharsis, and the realization that the dancer is unobtainable seems to confirm rather than deny the author's vision of purity. His hero returns home in tears, but they are tears of joy rather than of grief. "It was as though my head had turned to clear water, it was falling pleasantly away drop by drop; soon nothing would remain."

Kawabata's triumph was complete, for he had created a mature work of art out of the emotions of adolescence. In order to do so he had plundered his autobiographical account "*Yugashima no omoide*" ("Memories of Yugashima"), a work that remained unpublished because he destroyed the manuscript at a later date. But in the process of writing and rewriting he established both a literary method and a style that were all his own. The delicate juxtaposition of ideas and images, the shy eroticism and the theme of unobtainable love, the wandering and rootlessness, the awareness of purity and ephemerality, the subtle changes of mood, the longing and loneliness, the sense of incompleteness and the curiously unexpected transitions from one episode to another – all are features of "The Izu Dancer," and all are developed in Kawabata's later novels.

It took Kawabata three years of research to gather material for his next major work, *Asakusa kurenai dan* (1929–30, *The Asakusa Crimson Gang*). The new novel was eagerly awaited, appearing eventually as a serial in the Tokyo *Asahi shimbun*, where, despite its Modernist style, it was extremely popular. It was simply a chronicle of a man's perceptions and experiences while walking around the rundown neighborhood of Asakusa. In fact, the "walking around" accounted for the whole of Kawabata's leisurely schedule of research, and in all of that time he hardly ever spoke to an Asakusa resident. Nonetheless, in following the activities of Yumiko, the heroine who assumes many different guises throughout the novel, Kawabata created quite a plausible character from his personal scrapbook of detached observations. Although the novel was left unfinished, its linear structure enabled him to cease writing at any point without spoiling the work's overall quality.

Structure, or more precisely the lack of structure, is a vexed issue in Kawabata studies – for his work must never be approached in the expectation of finding a strict adherence to Aristotelian unities. In his critical writings he tended to echo conventional Western ideas similar to those expressed by E. M. Forster in *Aspects of the Novel*. But in practice Kawabata rarely structured his novels with a beginning, a middle, and an end, preferring to develop a rich, linear texture somewhat in the manner of linked verse. His use of this technique gives his work a distinct, Oriental flavor, closer in spirit to *The Tale of Genji* or *The Pillow Book* than to the Modernist novels of Joyce or Woolf.

Kawabata, who spoke no foreign languages, could read English with some difficulty and had actually attempted to read James Joyce's original text of *Ulysses*. He relied chiefly, however, on translations made by Itō Sei in the early 1930s. As a result, his own most Joycean works appeared at around this time, and included the story "*Hari to garasu to kiri*" (1930, "Needles, Glass and Fog") and *Suishō gensō* (1931, *Crystal Fantasies*), an unfinished novel in two parts. In both of these works the stream-of-consciousness of the central character is indicated by parentheses, between which the author's technique of free association is given full rein. The passages are particularly notable for their startling visual imagery: further confirmation, if any were needed, that Kawabata viewed the world with the eyes of a painter.

In 1933 Kawabata joined the staff of *Bungakukai* (*Literary World*) and in the following year was appointed to the *Bungei kondan kai* (Literary Discussion Group), a quasi-governmental organization through which the authorities kept a watchful eye on the arts. He seems to have had no qualms about the sinister implications of such a body, and being himself a "pure" artist untainted by political ideology he was readily accepted by the government as a safe representative of the artistic community. His participation in public life grew even wider when he was also appointed to be a judge of the Akutagawa Prize, a position which carried considerable authority in Japan's literary world. Among the other judges were Tanizaki, Yokomitsu, Satō Haruo, and, from the sponsoring publishers Bungei Shunjūsha, Kawabata's old friend and mentor Kikuchi Kan.

Controversy surrounded the award of the first Akutagawa Prize in 1935. The most obvious candidate was DAZAI OSAMU for his story "*Gyakkō*" (1935, "Losing Ground"), but largely because of staunch opposition from Kawabata the committee gave the prize to another author, ISHIKAWA TATSUZŌ. Dazai was furious – and with some justification because Kawabata made some cruel remarks about Dazai's personal life that were wholly uncalled for. He virtually denounced Dazai's work, saying that it was the product of an unhealthy mind. Not one to sit idly by without a fight, Dazai retaliated by calling Kawabata "a scoundrel through and through." He also made a sly reference to Kawabata's own 1933 story *"Kinjū"* ("Of Birds and Beasts"), which, in depicting a man who hoarded dead animals in a cupboard, was far more neurotic than anything Dazai ever wrote. The whole episode of the first Akutagawa Prize was sad and confusing at the time, although in retrospect it serves to remind us that Kawabata was not infallible in his judgment of literature.

Kawabata tended to assume that a novel would naturally be uplifting if its author displayed fine spiritual qualities in real life. Dazai's life was notoriously chaotic, plagued with debts, drugs, and abortive attempts at suicide. Therefore, thought Kawabata, his work must be spiritually inferior. By the same token, Kawabata had little regard for Tanizaki's novels, for Tanizaki was a notorious womanizer quite lacking in the gravity of mind that was supposedly the hallmark of a great artist. SHIGA NAOYA, by contrast, exemplified everything that Kawabata most admired – and, predictably, he regarded Shiga as the greatest of his contemporaries. Unfortunately, there was a flaw in Kawabata's reasoning, for the fact remains that nearly everything written by Tanizaki and Dazai is spiritually uplifting, whereas most works by Shiga – and indeed by Kawabata himself – are profoundly depressing.

In his chapter on Kawabata in *Modern Japanese Writers*, Makoto Ueda remarks that many of his stories could be renamed "Beauty and Sadness," which is actually the title of only one novel, written in 1961–63. This is a fair comment, for on those rare occasions when Kawabata was not evoking the sadness of beauty he was usually describing the beauty of sadness. Not surprisingly, such a vision tends to become depressing when pursued to extremes, and Kawabata's work – brilliant though it is – lacks the physical vigor which would otherwise counterbalance its pervasive melancholy.

All the foregoing comments may be applied to Kawabata's most famous novel, *Yukiguni* (*Snow Country*, written 1935–37 but not completed until 1947). It contains four main characters: Shimamura, a dilettante who occasionally likes to escape from his wife and family to visit a hot-spring resort in the mountains; Komako, a country *geisha* who falls deeply in love with Shimamura; Yōko, a demure teenager whose haunting beauty captivates Shimamura; and Yukio, Komako's former lover and Yōko's current lover, who is seriously ill and destined for an early death. With great ingenuity Kawabata derives beauty from their tragic relationships, portraying each individual's love as being freely given without any hope of reward. The same theme is repeated in the background: in Shimamura's purely gratuitous studies of Occidental ballet, in Komako's annotations of popular novels, and especially in the labor-intensive production of Chijimi cloth – on which many a snow country maiden once expended her youth. The sum total of all this "wasted" effort is a powerful symbol of existence, offered by the author to the reader in the manner of a priest offering a flower to his disciple.

Intellectually one may agree with Kawabata entirely. In *Snow Country* he identifies not only an existential truth but the very essence of culture. Each of his characters is the exact opposite of Oscar Wilde's celebrated cynic: they know the value of everything and the price of nothing. They inhabit the pure world of the snow country where behavior is not a means to an end but an end in itself. If transported to the utilitarian West they would melt into thin air immediately – as, in a sense, they do when one compares them to the full-bodied characters of Western fiction. Yet for all the dazzling intellectual clarity of *Snow Country* it is not an emotionally satisfying novel. Instead of stirring one's passions it depresses them, putting the reader in much the same state of mind as that felt by the student at the end of "The Izu Dancer."

During the war years Kawabata was engaged on a project so far removed from such useful activities as winning and losing empires that one begins to suspect his true motives. He had long taken an interest in the Oriental game of *go* and was reputed to be a skilled player. In 1938 the Mainichi newspaper group commissioned him to write a series of reports on a championship match between the reigning Master, Shūsai, and his challenger Kitani Minoru. It was a memorable occasion, its tense atmosphere much like that surrounding championship chess matches in the West. After some three months of play the outcome of the contest was finally decided in Kitani's favor. Kawabata described the entire process in detail, eventually returning home to meditate on what he had experienced. However, not until Shūsai died in 1940 did it seem that the final act of the drama had been played. Shūsai's death prompted Kawabata to turn his newspaper reports into a novel, a task which occupied him until well after the end of the war. The result was *Meijin* (*1942–54, The Master of Go*), a novel of immense power and perception which Kawabata himself regarded as his personal favorite.

The Master of Go captures perfectly the qualities of Japanese culture that Kawabata most admired. Its narrative has vigor, dignity, and subtlety, and no one reading it without prior knowledge of how it came to be written could suspect it of being an amalgam of fact and fiction rather than a soaring triumph of the imagination. Kawabata added several elements of fiction, notably those which elevate Shūsai's personal character. He also allocated a fictitious name – Otake – to Shūsai's opponent, and gave the whole story a political dimension by hinting at a battle between the last remnants of feudalism (in the Master's imperious attitudes) and the brave new world of democracy (in the game's increasingly rigid rules). Indeed, *The Master of Go* is the only one of Kawabata's major works to contain any sort of political content.

Kawabata's other wartime writings consisted of the autobiographical novel *Koen* (1943–45, *Birthplace*), and *Tōkaidō* (1943–44), an unfinished, quasi-fictional discussion of Japanese culture. His awareness and appreciation of traditional culture in all its forms were exceptional, and having written a *go* novel there was every reason to suppose that he might go on to write a "tea" novel and perhaps a whole series of works featuring one or other of Japan's great cultural traditions. In fact, a tea novel (of sorts) did appear even before he finished *The Master of Go*. It was called *Sembazuru* (1949–51, *Thousand Cranes*) and is one of his most prominent works in English translation.

Tea merely provides a convenient context for the story of *Thousand Cranes*, the main emphasis being placed on the contrast between the longevity of art versus the brevity of life. However, unlike the other novels discussed above, it is fiction of a lower order and contains a melodramatic plot designed to appeal to readers of women's magazines. Critics have offered various explanations of why Kawabata occasionally produced this type of work, the most plausible being that he needed the money to finance his growing art collection. Yet there is also the acceptable excuse that ideal plots for his particular vision of literature were few and far between. He may even have toyed with the idea that plots were irrelevant to his art, believing he could dress any kind of story in the clothes of his renowned style. If so, he was wrong – because *Thousand Cranes* is marred irretrievably by its unrealistic dramatic action.

For some unexplained reason the hero of *Thousand Cranes* is dominated by his late father's discarded mistress. Mitani Kikuji is a young man in the process of discovering women when his life is completely disrupted by Chikako, a venomous crone who harbors evil intent toward the sentimental Mrs. Ōta: the second "other woman" who once replaced Chikako in the affections of Kikuji's father. Both Chikako and the young girl she introduces to Kikuji are identified emblematically, the first by a hideous birthmark on her chest; the second by an exquisite thousand-crane-patterned kimono indicative of springlike beauty. Somewhat predictably,

Kikuji falls in love with the girl but is loath to do anything about it because Chikako is the go-between. Instead he falls into a sexual relationship with Mrs. Ōta.

The story continues in the manner described, but its impact is quite different from what one might expect. This is because Chikako, Mrs. Ōta, and even Mrs. Ōta's daughter (who is a plausible rival to the thousand-crane girl) are all devotees of the tea ceremony. By cloaking such melodrama in the sacred trappings of tea, Kawabata was deliberately showing his disapproval of the way in which the tea ceremony had lost its sense of meaning in modern times.

The early 1950s were Kawabata's most productive period. In 1948 he had become the fourth president of the Japanese P.E.N. Club, a post which gave him the opportunity to meet and correspond with many overseas writers. At the same time he was influential on behalf of young Japanese novelists, especially Mishima Yukio who became his friend and disciple. The impact of fresh ideas was undoubtedly beneficial, for Kawabata completed what many believe to be his greatest work, *Yama no oto* (*The Sound of the Mountain*) in 1950.

The Sound of the Mountain is a beautifully textured novel, weaving ordinary domestic life together with philosophical messages – many of which are introduced into the narrative by means of newspaper reports, much as if they were dispatches from some distant battlefront of human experience. There is a timeless sense of security and well-being in the household of Shingo, the novel's aging patriarch, and the very cosiness of his domestic arrangements is a perfect receptor for one or two chilly harbingers of fate. In his rare moments of solitude Shingo hears "the sound of the mountain," clearly a premonition of death that is banished only when a member of his family brings him some fresh, domestic problem to be solved. With considerable sensitivity Shingo addresses each problem in his own good time, and in so doing wins the affection of the reader. Indeed, he is much closer in spirit to IBUSE MASUJI's genial heroes than to the shadowy figures of Kawabata's other novels.

If *The Sound of the Mountain* reminds one of Ibuse, *Mizuumi* (*1954, The Lake*) reads like a collaboration between ABE KŌBŌ and *Togawa Masako. It evokes ugliness rather than beauty, its central figure being a sad, twisted character called Gimpei Momoi whose self-loathing is epitomized by a curious hatred of his misshapen feet. Once a schoolteacher who was dismissed for seducing a female student, he has become a voyeur, following young girls around the neighborhood and perhaps only dimly aware that he is heading for complete degradation. Surprisingly, the novel is a reasonably sympathetic study of a psychopathic mind, chiefly because Kawabata reveals in flashback the true story of Gimpei's love affair with the student. As Mishima once pointed out, Kawabata wrote alternately in esoteric and exoteric modes, and *The Lake* is surely a prime example of the dark, esoteric mode which probed the negative aspects of the author's own sexual psychology. In short, Kawabata's attitude towards his hero is: "There, but for the grace of God, go I."

No story is more dark and esoteric than *"Nemureru bijo"* (1960–61, "The House of the Sleeping Beauties"). It is a memorable work: the story of an elderly man who frequents a brothel where he spends the night with girls who are drugged into deep sleep. From the moment when Eguchi sees the deathlike emblem on the *obi* belonging to the brothel's madam – until the searing climax when a girl is killed in actuality – the narrative is gripping and profound. The novella won Kawabata the Mainichi Cultural Prize, one of many such honors bestowed on him in a long writing career.

In a highly productive period at the beginning of the 1960s Kawabata published not only "The House of the Sleeping Beauties" but *Utsukushisa to kanashimi to* (1961–63, *Beauty and Sadness*) and *Koto* (1962, *The Old Capital*). *Beauty and Sadness* is a complex melodrama exploring the idea that true beauty is always to be found in pathos, and vice versa. The result is highly entertaining, not least because the main ingredients are lust, jealousy, and revenge. However, the novel's very liveliness tends to detract from the author's guiding aesthetic, the latter being expressed in only one or two episodes which stand apart from the main narrative. Chief among them is a newspaper report (Kawabata was an avid reader of newspapers) describing the discovery of Princess Kazu's skeleton. Princess Kazu, forced to marry the last shōgun shortly before his fall from power, was forbidden to see the man she really loved. Yet when archaeologists opened her coffin they found her clutching a man's photograph. As if by magic, the image faded so quickly that no one was able to identify the figure. Was it a picture of her husband, or was it the lover she was not allowed to see when she was alive? Nobody ever discovered the truth, but the whole episode contains so much "beauty and sadness" that it makes the rest of the novel seem inferior by comparison.

There is nothing inferior about *The Old Capital*, a novel that by some oversight of scholars was not translated into English until 1987. It was one of the three works cited when Kawabata won the Nobel Prize for Literature: a completely harmonious composition in the muted colors of traditional Japanese taste. Set in postwar Kyoto it tells of how Chieko, the adopted daughter of a kimono trader, discovers her lost twin sister, Naeko. In a sense, it is a wholly feminine love story, written with a lightness of touch that perfectly echoes its theme. The focus of the novel gradually moves from one character to another, from the father Takichirō to Chieko, and thence to Naeko who works in the cedar forests on the edge of the city. The plot is simple and delightfully inconclusive. Hideo, a skilled weaver whose father supplies Takichirō's store with fabric, is in love with Chieko. He wants to make her a special gift of an *obi* woven by himself, but Chieko insists that he weave it for Naeko. When Hideo eventually asks Naeko to marry him, the "country twin" is disturbed because she feels his love is an illusion. For her part Chieko has no desire to marry Hideo and can see no reason why Naeko should not accept. Moreover, she is deeply distressed when Naeko decides to return to the forest where she was brought up, perhaps never again to see her sister in the city.

If Naeko's dilemma seems artificially contrived it is because the whole novel is an affectionate gesture to old Japan. Naeko intuitively believes that she cannot, and should not, cut loose from her proper place in the world: the forest that has nurtured and, in a sense, created her. Such a passive, plantlike philosophy is a beautiful relic of the past. In fact, in its entirety, *The Old Capital* is a deliberate anachronism. It is essentially a "novel of place," Kawabata's vision of all the most charming aspects of Kyoto, a city that was once the capital of Old Japan.

Kawabata wrote only one important work of fiction after completing *The Old Capital*: a short, surrealist novella called *"Kataude"* (1964, "One Arm"). This extraordinary tale of a man's experiences with a woman's disembodied arm (it begins: "'I can let you have one of my arms for the night," said the girl . . .'") is reminiscent of Shimamura's fanciful comment to Komako in *Snow Country*, telling her that his finger remembered her "best of all." Indeed, the concept of "One Arm" is a logical extension of the original idea, and one which Kawabata exploits to the full. It contains a sense of love unfulfilled and unfulfillable: the recurrent theme of all Kawabata's work.

Taken as a whole, Kawabata's major novels are a magnificent achievement, especially notable for their consistency of style and vision. Yet like many Japanese writers he was most at home when working in a miniature format, as if he were a *haiku* poet newly experimenting in a world of prose. Even *Snow Country* is a "single-breath" novel, best absorbed in one sitting – while his longest work, the rambling newspaper serial *Tōkyō no hito* (1954–55, *Tokyo People*) is generally reckoned to be one of his least satisfactory creations. Perhaps the works most typical of his genius are the famous "palm-of-the-hand stories," the *tanagokoro no shōsetsu* which he produced throughout his career in odd moments of inspiration.

Although these are the shortest of short stories, some of them consisting of just a few lines of prose, they are by no means "minor." "*Batta to suzumushi*" (*1924*, "The Grasshopper and the Bell Cricket") is certainly a greater work of art than *Beauty and Sadness*, even though it is only four pages long. Kawabata wrote over a hundred palm-of-the-hand stories, and referred to them as his "youthful poetry," meaning that they were substitutes for poetry in which he developed his unique, attenuated style.

The scale of Kawabata's achievement, so much greater than the scale of his individual works, tends to eclipse the bare facts of his life. He had the bearing of a lonely man, who wrote mostly away from home while staying at various inns. Even his Nobel Prize acceptance speech, *Utsukushii Nihon no watakushi* (1948, *Japan, the Beautiful, and Myself*) was heavily reworked in his hotel room a few hours before its delivery. Although he married unofficially and in 1943 adopted a daughter, an air of homelessness always clung to him. At heart he was a bachelor-aesthete, not a family man like SHIMAZAKI TŌSON. That he was also a member of Japan's literary establishment for much of the century (the Japan P.E.N. Club, he said, was a society composed of unsociable men) is a welcome reminder that he formed many close friendships among his peers. He was deeply shaken when Mishima Yukio took his own life in 1970, and although he had once stated "I neither admire nor am I in sympathy with suicide," he too died, presumably by his own hand, on April 16, 1972.

Some scholars believe that Kawabata's death by inhalation of gas may have been a simple accident, and they point to the fact that he left no written explanation. However, one cannot help thinking that for Kawabata to have left a farewell note would have been completely out of character. He never did believe in accentuated endings.

RECOMMENDED READING

Novels

The Master of Go. *Meijin.* Composed 1942–54. 186 pages. Tr. Edward Seidensticker. Knopf, NY, 1972; Secker and Warburg, London, 1973; Tuttle, Tokyo, 1973; Berkley Pub., NY, 1974; Penguin Books, Harmondsworth, 1976; G. P. Putnam's Sons, NY, 1981, paperback. Novel contains several *go* diagrams and 4 pages of notes.

The Old Capital. *Koto.* 1961–62. 164 pages. Tr. J. Martin Holman. North Point Press, San Francisco, 1987, paperback; Tuttle, Tokyo, 1988.

Snow Country. Yukiguni. 1935–47. 188 pages. Tr. Edward Seiden-sticker. Knopf, NY, 1956; Secker and Warburg, London, 1957; Tuttle, Tokyo, 1957; Berkley Pub., NY, 1960; G. P. Putnam's Sons, NY, 1981, paperback; *Snow Country and Thousand Cranes.* Penguin Books, Harmondsworth, 1991. Kawabata's most famous novel, one of the most easily obtainable translations.

Short Fiction Collections

House of the Sleeping Beauties, and Other Stories. Tr. Edward Seidensticker. Kodansha International, Tokyo and NY, 1969 and 1980, 1982 paperback; Quadriga Press, London, 1969; Sphere, London, 1971; Ballantine Books, NY, 1970; Fontana, London, 1989. Book contains: title story, "One Arm," and "Of Birds and Beasts." *Palm-of-the-Hand Stories.* 238 pages. 70 very short stories. Tr. Lane Dunlop and J. Martin Holman. North Point Press, San Francisco, 1988, paperback; Tuttle, Tokyo, 1988; Picador Classics, Pan Books, London, 1989. Ranging in length from a few lines to a few pages, many of these stories are miniature masterpieces. The earliest in the collection is "A Sunny Place," "Hinata," 1923; while the last is "Gleanings from Snow Country," "Yukigunishō," 1972. For reasons of space – and because this volume is easily obtainable – individual titles are not listed in full here, although alternative translations *are* listed below under "Very Short Fiction."

WORKS IN ENGLISH TRANSLATION

Novels

Beauty and Sadness. Utsukushisa to kanashimi to. 1961–63. 206 pages. Tr. Howard Hibbett. Knopf, NY, 1975; Secker and Warburg, London, 1975; Penguin, Harmondsworth, London, 1979; G. P. Putnam's Sons, NY, 1981, paperback.

The Lake. Mizuumi. 1954. Tr. Reiko Tsukimura. Kodansha International, Tokyo and NY, 1974 and 1980, paperback; Peter Owen, London, 1977; Fontana, London, 1989.

The Master of Go. Meijin. Composed 1942–54.

The Old Capital. Koto. 1961–62.

Snow Country. Yukiguni. 1935–47.

The Sound of the Mountain. Yama no oto. 1950. 276 pages. Tr. Edward Seidensticker. Extract in: *Japan Quarterly,* vol. 11, nos. 3–4, 1964. Complete novel: Knopf, NY, 1970; Peter Owen, London, 1970; Tuttle, Tokyo, 1970; Secker and Warburg, London, 1971; Penguin Books, London, 1974; G. P. Putnam's Sons, NY, 1981, paperback.

Thousand Cranes. Sembazuru. 1949–51. 144 pages. Tr. Edward Seidensticker. Knopf, NY, 1958; Secker and Warburg, London, 1959; Tuttle, Tokyo, 1960; Berkley Pub., NY, 1964; G. P. Putnam's Sons, NY, 1981, paperback; *Snow Country and Thousand Cranes.* Penguin Books, Harmondsworth, 1991.

Short Fiction

"The Happiness of One Person."
"*Hitori no kōfuku.*" 8 pages. Tr.
Kiyoaki Nakao. *Eigo Kenkyu*,
vol. 55, nos. 8 and 9, 1966.

"House of the Sleeping Beauties."
"*Nemureru bijo.*" 1960–61. 86
pages. (1) As "The Sleeping
Beauty." Tr. J. I. Ackroyd and
Hiro Mukai. *Easter Horizon*,
vol. 4, March 1965. (2) *House of
the Sleeping Beauties, and Other
Stories.*

"The Izu Dancer." "*Izu no odoriko.*"
1926. 29 pages. (1) Tr. Edward
Seidensticker. *Atlantic Monthly*,
vol. 195, 1954; *The Izu Dancer.*
Hara Shobo, Tokyo, 1963; *The
Izu Dancer, and Other Stories.*
Tuttle, Tokyo, 1974. (2) As "The
Dancing Girl of Izu." Tr. Eiichi
Hayashi. *The Reeds*, vol. 3, 1957.

"Lyric Poem." "*Jojōka.*" 1932. 19
pages. Tr. Francis Mathy.
Monumenta Nipponica, vol. 26,
nos. 3–4, 1971.

"The Mole." "*Hokuro no tegami.*"
1940. 8 pages. Tr. Edward Seid-
ensticker. *Japan Quarterly*,
vol. 2, no. 1, 1955; *Modern
Japanese Literature*, Grove Press,
NY, 1956; Tuttle, Tokyo, 1957;
Modern Japanese Short Stories.
Japan Publications Trading Co.,
Tokyo, 1960; revised edition,
1970; *The Izu Dancer.* Hara
Shobo, Tokyo, 1963.

"The Moon on the Water." "*Sui-
getsu.*" 1953. 11 pages. (1) As
"The Moon in the Water." Tr.
George Saito. *United Asia*, vol. 8,
no. 4, 1956; *Diliman Review*,
vol. 6, nos. 2–4, 1958. (2) *Modern
Japanese Stories*, ed. Ivan Morris.
Spottiswoode, London, 1961;
Tuttle, Tokyo, 1962; *The Izu
Dancer*; *The World of Japanese
Fiction*, Dutton, NY, 1973.

"Of Birds and Beasts." "*Kinjū.*"

1933. 24 pages. *House of the
Sleeping Beauties, and Other Stories.*

"One Arm." "*Kataude.*" 1963. 22
pages. *House of the Sleeping
Beauties, and Other Stories*; *The
Shōwa Anthology*, ed. Van C.
Gessel and Tomone Matsumoto.
Kodansha International, Tokyo,
1985.

"Rediscovery." "*Saikai.*" 14 pages.
Tr. Leon Picon. *Orient West*,
vol. 8, no. 4, 1963; *The Japanese
Image.* Image West, Tokyo, 1965.
As "Reencounter." *The Izu
Dancer.* Hara Shobo, Tokyo,
1963.

Very Short Fiction

Note: a complete list of Kawabata's
palm-of-the-hand stories can be
found in *Shikon no genryū*,
Kawabata Bungaku Kenkyūkai,
pages 12–29. Most of the translated stories listed below – and
many others – can also be found
in *Palm-of-the Hand Stories*, tr.
Lane Dunlop and J. Martin Holman. (See "Recommended
Reading" above.)

"Autumn Rain." "*Aki no ame.*"
1962. 3 pages. Tr. Makoto Ueda.
*The Mother of Dreams, and Other
Short Stories.* Kodansha International, Tokyo, 1986.

"The Bamboo Leaves." "*Sasabune.*"
1950. 2 pages. Tr. Edward
Seidensticker. *Contemporary
Japanese Literature*, ed. Howard
Hibbett. Knopf, NY, 1977.

"Beyond Death." "*Fushi.*" 1963. 3
pages. Tr. Makoto Ueda. *The
Mother of Dreams, and Other
Stories.* As "Immortality." *Journal of Literary Translation*,
vol. 17, 1986.

"The Camellia." "*Sazanka.*" 1946. 5
pages. Tr. Edward Seiden-

sticker. *Contemporary Japanese Literature.*

"The Cereus." *"Gekka bijin."* 1963. 2 pages. Tr. Edward Seidensticker. *Contemporary Japanese Literature.*

"The Child's Standpoint." *"Kodomo no tachiba."* 1926. Half-page. Tr. P. Metevelis. *Japan Quarterly,* vol. 31, no. 4, 1984.

"The Dead Face Affair." *"Shinigao no dekigoto."* 1925. 1 page. Tr. P. Metevelis. *Japan Quarterly,* vol. 31, no. 4, 1984.

"The Death Mask." *"Shimen"* or *"Desu masuku."* 1932. 3 pages. Tr. George Saito. *Japan P.E.N. News,* vol. 23, Oct. 1970; *Asian and Pacific Short Stories.* Cultural and Social Centre for the Asian and Pacific Region, Seoul, 1974; Tuttle, Tokyo, 1974.

"A Girl Who Goes Toward the Fire." *"Hi ni yuku kanojo."* 1924. 2 pages. Tr. Minoru Kohda. *The Reeds,* vol. 14, 1976.

"Grasshopper and the Bell Cricket." *"Batta to suzumushi."* 1924. 5 pages. (1) Tr. Minoru Kohda. *The Reeds,* vol. 14, 1976. Tr. Lane Dunlop. *A Late Chrysanthemum.* North Point Press, San Francisco, 1986.

"The Hair." *"Kami."* 1924. 1 page. Tr. Minoru Kohda. *The Reeds,* vol. 14, 1976.

"The Harbor." *"Minato."* 1924. Half-page. Tr. P. Metevelis. *Japan Quarterly,* vol. 31, no. 4, 1984.

"A Hat Incident." *"Bōshi jiken."* 1926. 5 pages. (1) Tr. Shohei Shimada. *The Reeds,* vol. 6, 1960. (2) As "The Hat Incident." Tr. P. Metevelis. *Japan Quarterly,* vol. 31, no. 4, 1984.

"The Jay." *"Kakesu."* 4 pages. Tr. Edward Seidensticker. *Contemporary Japanese Literature.*

"Palm of the Hand Stories." *"Tana-gokoro no shōsetsu."* (Selection) 11 pages. Tr. Margaret F. Breer. *Japan Interpreter,* vol. 12, no. 3, 1979.

"The Plum." *"Kōbai."* 1948. 2 pages. Tr. Edward Seidensticker. *Contemporary Japanese Literature.*

"The Pomegranate." *"Zakuro."* 1945. 3 pages. Tr. Edward Seidensticker. *Contemporary Japanese Literature.*

"A Saw and Childbirth." *"Nokogiri to shussan."* 1924. 4 pages. Tr. Minoru Kohda. *The Reeds,* vol. 13, 1972.

"The Silverberry Thief." *"Gumi nusutto."* 1925. 4 pages. *A Late Chrysanthemum.*

"Socks." *"Tabi."* 1948. 3 pages. Tr. Makoto Ueda. *Journal of Literary Translation,* no. 17, 1986; *The Mother of Dreams, and Other Stories.*

"Summer and Winter." *"Natsu to fuyu."* 1949. 4 pages. Tr. Edward Seidensticker. *Contemporary Japanese Literature.*

"Summer Shoes." *"Natsu no kutsu."* 1926. 3 pages. Tr. Yamada Kazuo. *Eigo Seinen,* vol. 97, no. 2, 1951.

"The Sunny Place." *"Hinata."* 1923. 3 pages. Tr. Shohei Shimada. *The Reeds,* vol. 6, 1960.

"The Umbrella." *"Amagasa."* 1932. 2 pages. Tr. Minoru Kohda. *The Reeds,* vol. 14, 1976.

"Waterfall." *"Taki."* 3 pages. Tr. Leon Zolbrod. *The East,* vol. 2, no. 1, 1972.

"A Weak Vessel." *"Yowaki utsuwa."* 1924. 2 pages. Tr. Minoru Kohda. *The Reeds,* vol. 13, 1972.

"The Young Lady of Suruga." *"Suruga no reijō."* 1927. 3 pages. *A Late Chrysanthemum.*

Essays

"The Existence and Discovery of Beauty." "Bi no sonzai to hakken." 1969. 109 pages. Tr. V. H. Viglielmo. Mainichi Shimbunsha, Tokyo, 1969.
Japan, the Beautiful, and Myself.

Utsukushii Nihon no watakushi. Nobel Prize acceptance address. 1968. 74 pages. Tr. Edward Seidensticker. *Jiji Eigo Kenkyu,* vol. 24, no. 3, 1969; *Social Education,* vol. 33, no. 7, 1969; in book form: Kodansha International, Tokyo, 1969.

CRITICAL STUDIES

Akiyama, Masayuki. *A Comparative Study of James, Kawabata and Major Japanese Writers.* Nanundo, Tokyo, 1989.

Araki, James T. "Kawabata: Achievements of the Nobel Laureate." *Books Abroad,* no. 43, 1969.

———. "Kawabata and His *Snow Country.*" *Centennial Review,* no. 4, 1969.

Ashton, Elizabeth Ann. "Maboroshi: The Otherworldly Overtones in Kawabata Yasunari's *The Lake.*" *Proceedings of the Second International Symposium on Asian Studies,* 1980.

Brown, Sidney DeVere. "Kawabata Yasunari: Tradition Versus Modernity." *World Literature Today,* vol. 62, no. 3, 1988.

Buckstead, Richard C. "Eros, Aesthetics and Fate: Kawabata's *Beauty and Sadness.*" *Proceedings of the Fourth International Symposium on Asian Studies,* 1982.

———. "Kawabata Yasunari: The Cultural Tradition and the Divided Self." *International Congress of Orientalists,* 29th, 1976.

———. "Kawabata's 'One Arm': The Woman and the Circle." *Asian Profile,* vol. 10, no. 5, 1982.

———. "Mirror Symbolism in Kawabata's 'The Moon on the Water.'" *Asian Profile,* vol. 9, no. 1, 1981.

———. "The Search for a Symbol in Kawabata's *Snow Country.*" *Asian Profile,* vol. 1, no. 1, 1973.

Fukasawa, Margaret Benton. "Kawabata Yasunari's Style in *Yama no Oto.*" Ph.D. diss., Columbia University, NY, 1970.

Gupta, P.C. "Kawabata Yasunari." *Contemporary Indian Literature,* no. 9, 1969.

Iga, Mamoru. "Tradition and Modernity in Japanese Suicide: The Case of Yasunari Kawabata." *Journal of Asian and African Studies,* no. 10, 1975.

Kato, Muneyuki. "Yasunari Kawabata's *Snow Country*: Its Modernity Viewed in the Light of Comparative Literature." *Kyushu American Literature,* no. 10, 1967.

Liman, Anthony V. "Kawabata's Lyrical Mode in *Snow Country.*" *Monumenta Nipponica,* vol. 26, no. 3, 1971.

Loftus, Margaret. "Yasunari Kawabata: A Missionary Tribute." *Japan Missionary Bulletin,* vol. 26, no. 10, 1972.

Mathy, Francis. "Kawabata Yasunari, Bridge-builder to the West." *Monumenta Nipponica,* vol. 24, no. 3, 1969.

Morishige, Alyce Hisae Kawazoe. "The Theme of the Self in Modern Japanese Fiction: Studies on Dazai, Mishima, Abe, and Kawabata." Ph.D. diss., Michigan State University, East Lansing, 1970.

Obuchowski, Mary DeJong. "Theme and Image in Kawabata's *The Sound of the Mountain.*" *World Literature Today,* vol. 51, no. 2, 1977.

Peterson, Gwenn Boardman. *The Moon in the Water: Understanding*

Tanizaki, Kawabata and Mishima. University Press of Hawaii, Honolulu, 1979.

Rajakaruna, Don. "On Translating Kawabata's 'Izu no Odoriko.'" *Fourth Proceedings of the International Cultural Conference,* vol. 1, 1977.

Saeki, Shoichi. "The Paradox of Modern Japanese Literature, with Special Reference to Kawabata Yasunari." *Bulletin of Japanese Culture,* no. 96, 1969.

Seidensticker, Edward G. "Kawabata." *Hudson Review,* vol. 22, no. 1, 1969.

————. "On Kawabata Yasunari." *Bulletin of the Asiatic Society of Japan,* 1970; *This Country, Japan.* Kodansha International, Tokyo, 1979 and 1984.

Swann, Thomas E. "Kawabata Yasunari: 'The Izu Dancer,' 'The House of the Sleeping Beauties,' 'One Arm.'" *Approaches to the Modern Japanese Short Story,* ed. Thomas E. Swann and Kinya Tsuruta. Waseda University Press, Tokyo, 1982.

————. "Kawabata Yasunari: *The Master of Go.*" *Approaches to the Modern Japanese Novel,* ed. Thomas E. Swann and Kinya Tsuruta. Sophia University, Tokyo, 1976.

————. "Kawabata's "Thousand Cranes" and the Maelstrom of Time." *Proceedings of International Symposium on Asian Studies,* 1980.

————. "On Kawabata's *Sembazuru.*" *East West Review,* vol. 3, no. 2, 1967.

————. "A Study of Kawabata Yasunari's Major Works." Ph.D. diss., Harvard University, Cambridge, 1975.

————. "*Yukiguni:* One View." *East West Review,* no. 2, 1965.

Takeda, Katsuhiko. "Biblical Influence upon Yasunari Kawabata." *Neohelicon,* vol. 10, no. 1, 1983.

————. "Kawabata's Literature: Harmony and Conflict." *Essays on Japanese Literature,* ed. Katsuhiko Takeda. Waseda University Press, Tokyo, 1975.

Tsuruta, Kinya. "The Flow-dynamics in Kawabata Yasunari's *Snow Country.*" *Monumenta Nipponica,* vol. 26, no. 3, 1971.

————. "Two Journeys in *The Sound of the Mountain.*" *Approaches to the Modern Japanese Novel,* ed. Thomas E. Swann and Kinya Tsuruta. Sophia University, Tokyo, 1976.

Ueda, Makoto. "Kawabata Yasunari: *Snow Country.*" *Approaches to the Modern Japanese Novel,* 1976.

Kikuchi KAN
(1888–1948)

Novelist, playwright, and screenwriter. Born in Takamatsu in Kagawa Prefecture. Lived in Zōshigaya, Tokyo.

More than anyone else, Kikuchi Kan was a spokesman and champion for authors in the first half of the twentieth century. Himself an author and playwright of distinction, he wanted to see a higher status accorded to writers in Japan, along with greater remuneration for their work. Ironically, he was often criticized by the very people he tried to help. This was because, through turning to popular fiction and away from serious literature, he had amassed a great fortune of his own. In retrospect, however, it is not hard to see why Kan behaved as he did. His attitude was in many ways justifiable, and ultimately his work as a writer, publisher, and editor was enormously beneficial to Japanese literature as a whole.

Born in the castle town of Takamatsu on the island of Shikoku, Kan grew up in poverty. He developed a passion for reading, despite the difficulty of obtaining books. He is said to have read most of the books in his local library before he enrolled at Kyoto

Imperial University to study English literature. There he became acquainted with the works of George Bernard Shaw and John Galsworthy, both of whom were to become major influences in his writing. While still a student, he teamed up with his great contemporary, AKUTAGAWA RYŪNOSUKE, to publish the third and fourth issues of a magazine called *Shinshichō* (*New Thought Tides*). However, the brilliance of Akutagawa quite eclipsed Kan's earliest works, and the young man from Shikoku left college to start his career as a humble newspaper reporter on the Tokyo daily *Jiji Shimpō*.

Kan's real literary debut came in 1918 when, at the age of thirty, he had his story "*Mumei sakka no nikki*" ("Diary of an Unknown Writer") published in *Chūō kōron*. During the two years that followed he wrote what many consider to be his best works of fiction. Often, he would conceive and write a finely plotted story based on historical material, then later adapt it for the stage.

Kan's approach to writing was not, alas, in the mainstream of what was then considered to be the only serious literature. Along with TANIZAKI and Akutagawa he wanted to develop a detached and impersonal style of narrative. However, departing from the *I-Novel tradition was not easily done. Kan, less patient than Tanizaki and more pragmatic than Akutagawa, therefore decided to use his storytelling skills to write popular fiction. Before his inspiration faded he succeeded in producing several stories which, even in English translation, are minor classics: timeless in their appeal.

"*Onshū no kanata ni*" (*1919*, "The Realm Beyond") is surely one of the best short stories in any language. Based on an old traditional tale, it turns tradition on its head by revealing the absurdity that lies at the heart of revenge, as formalized in the cherished notion of *kataki-uchi* (revenge) during the *Tokugawa period. Equally paradoxical is the plot of "*Tadanao-kyō gyōjōki*" (*1918*, "On the Conduct of Lord Tadanao"), which shows how a feudal *daimyō* is turned into a cruel oppressor because no one dares to treat him as an equal in combat.

Stories such as these became highly influential, prompting other writers to address historical subjects in a similar fashion. The resulting works were known as *tēma shōsetsu* ("theme novels") because they contained a definite theme, or thesis, which acted as a focal element. As the epithet suggests, the idea was new to Japanese literature and was borrowed from the West.

In writing his plays, Kan was motivated by TSUBOUCHI SHŌYŌ's 1904 treatise, "*Shingakugekiron*" ("Treatise on a New Drama"). An advocate of Western realism in drama as in prose, Shōyō urged young playwrights to create a modern theater. Among others, Kan responded during and after World War I with such plays as *Okujō no kyōjin* (1916, *The Housetop Madman*) and *Chichi kaeru* (1917, *The Father Returns*), both of which are Western in their dramatic structure. These plays, and many others – including the adaptation of "The Realm Beyond," to which Kan gave the ingenious title *Katakiuchi ijō* (*Better Than Revenge*) – have been translated into English.

The *Great Kantō Earthquake of 1923 destroyed most of the theaters in Tokyo, and Kan was one of those who began writing for the so-called little theaters which sprang up to fill the gap. His plays were staged by the Tsukiji Shōgekijō (The Tsukiji Little Theater), one of the few that succeeded commercially.

Readers who seek out Kan's plays (and, admittedly, his works are not easily obtained except from specialist libraries) will find some of them surprisingly modern in feeling and technique. One example is *The Savior of the Moment*, a piece that would last for little more than half an hour as a stage production, but which, even today, would be appealing in the intimate surroundings of a small, lunchtime theater. It is an amusing and ingeniously constructed play, depicting a somewhat impoverished writer, Eisaku, and his demanding wife, Nuiko. Right at the beginning they quarrel about money. Nuiko packs her bags with the intention of returning to her parents, but, unexpectedly, her cousin Yoshiko arrives, having left her own husband under similar circumstances. Her visit is dreadfully inconvenient. Eisaku can no longer write with a guest in the house, and Nuiko can neither leave nor stay now that another woman has arrived. Determined to get rid of her, Eisaku hatches a plan which his wife agrees to help put into action. Together they pretend to be blissfully happy, thus making Yoshiko feel homesick and in need of affection. It works surprisingly well, and within a short time Yoshiko is pining for her husband and getting ready to leave. The point of the play is now revealed. In pretending to be a happily married couple Eisaku and Nuiko have actually convinced themselves that such a state might be possible. They decide to stay together and be more understanding of each other's needs. Ironically, their unwanted guest whom they have tricked into leaving has become "the savior of the moment" and appears to have rescued their marriage entirely.

Gaining in confidence, Kan was now beginning to develop some formidable business skills and apply them to the service of literature. In January 1923, he established *Bungei shunjū*, a magazine which was to become one of the most influential and widely read in Japan. It changed its format over the years, being at first simply a literary journal for Kan and his friends. In 1926, it broadened its horizons to become an entertaining rival to the more solemn *Chūō kōron*

(*Central Review*). Maintaining a conservative position on current affairs up to World War II, it survived the war as a literary magazine when many other "general interest" publications were forced to close. Most important, under Kikuchi Kan, it established the Akutagawa and Naoki prizes in 1935, and published the winning stories in its pages.

Ardent in his support of literature as an art form, Kan was opposed to proletarian writing unless it had special merit. He consequently made some enemies on the left who perceived him as being politically motivated. In fact, he was not. A simple patriot, he successfully steered a course that he believed would be most beneficial to literature during the new *Shōwa period. As a result, many of Japan's greatest writers won their literary reputations largely through being published in *Bungei shunjū*. Among them were YOKOMITSU RIICHI, Kume Masao, Akutagawa, and Kawabata Yasunari.

Kan's interests were wide-ranging and his activity tireless. In addition to his work on *Bungei shunjū* he was on the editorial staff of *Engeki shinchō* (*New Tides of Drama*); wrote popular fiction for the magazine *Kingu* (*King* – started by Kodansha in 1925); founded the Writers' Association; held the post of president at the Daiei Motion Picture Company; wrote many new books to satisfy his thousands of readers; and became by far the wealthiest author in Japan prior to World War II.

A humanist who disliked rigid dogma, Kan is remembered as a likable and friendly man by those who knew him. He died in 1948 at the age of sixty.

RECOMMENDED READING

Short Fiction

"Laughter." *"Warai."* *1910*. 18 pages. (1) Tr. A. L. Sadler. *Selections from Modern Japanese Writers*. Australian Medical Pub., Sydney, 1943. (2) Tr. Frank Daniels. *Adam International Review*, vol. 25, no. 261, 1957. Sadler's volume is a rare, collector's item, and includes an amusing article on insulting language by Dr. Motoda Sakunoshin.
"The Realm Beyond." *"Onshū no kanata ni."* *1919*. 26 pages. (1) As "The Serene World Beyond Passions." Tr. Kan'ichi Ando. *Eigo Seinen*, vol. 43, nos. 1–12, 1920; vol. 44, nos. 1–12, 1920–21; *The Serene Realm Beyond Passions*, Kenkyusha, Tokyo, 1922. (2) Tr. John Bester. *Japan Quarterly*, vol. 7, no. 3, 1960; *The Realm Beyond*. Hara Shobo, Tokyo, 1964. (3) As "Beyond the Pale of Vengeance." Tr. Teru Kikuchi. Karin Bunko, Ube, 1961. Most easily located in *Japan Quarterly*, this is Kan's finest story.

WORKS IN ENGLISH TRANSLATION

Novel

Victory or Defeat. Shōhai. 1931. 289 pages. Tr. Kiichi Nishi. Kairyudo, Tokyo, 1934.

Short Fiction

"The Actor Who Was Yuranosuke." "*Yuranosuke yakusha.*" 17 pages. Tr. S. G. Brickley. *The Writing of Idiomatic English.* Kenkyusha, Tokyo, 1951.

"Laughing at the Dead." "*Shisha o warau.*" 1918. 6 pages. Tr. Michael Y. Matsudaira. *The Heart Is Alone*, ed. Richard N. McKinnon. Hokuseido, Tokyo, 1957.

"Laughter." "*Warai.*" 1910.

"On the Conduct of Lord Tadanao." "*Tadanao-kyō gyōjōki.*" 1918. 24 pages. Tr. Geoffrey Sargent. *Today's Japan*, vol. 6, no. 3, 1961; *Modern Japanese Stories*, ed. Ivan Morris. Spottiswoode, London, 1961; Tuttle, Tokyo, 1962; *The Realm Beyond*, Hara Shobo, Tokyo, 1964.

"The Realm Beyond." "*Onshū no kanata ni.*" 1919.

Play Collection

Tojuro's Love, and Four Other Plays. Tr. Glenn W. Shaw. 138 pages. Hokuseido, Tokyo, 1925. Contains: *Tojuro's Love, Better than Revenge, The Housetop Madman, The Father Returns,* and *The Miracle.*

Plays

Better than Revenge. Katakiuchi ijō. 1910. 50 pages. *Tojuro's Love, and Four Other Plays.*

The Father Returns. Chichi kaeru. 1917. First performed 1920. 19 pages. (1) *Tojuro's Love, and Four Other Plays.* (2) As "Return of the Father." Tr. Ichiro Nishizaki. *Eigo Kenkyu*, vol. 54, nos. 4–9, 1965.

The Housetop Madman. Okujō no kyōjin. 1916. 19 pages (1) Tr. Glenn W. Shaw. *Eibun Mainichi*, May 1, 1923. *Tojuro's Love, and Four Other Plays.* (2) As *Madman on the Roof.* Tr. Yozan Iwasaki and Glenn Hughes. *Three Modern Japanese Plays.* Stewart Kidd, Cincinnati, 1923; *Modern Japanese Literature*, ed. Donald Keene. Grove Press, NY, 1956; Tuttle, Tokyo, 1957; Grove Weidenfeld, NY, 1989, paperback; *Treasury of World Literature*, ed. D. D. Runes. Philosophical Library, NY, 1956; *The Mentor Book of Modern Asian Literature*, ed. D. B. Shimer. New American Library, NY, 1969. (3) As *The Madman on the Roof.* Tr. Ichiro Nishizaki. *Helicon* (Ochanomizu University), no. 9, 1958.

The Miracle. Kiseki. 20 pages. Tr. Glenn W. Shaw. *Tokyo Nichinichi*, Jan. 13–17, 1925; *Tojuro's Love, and Four Other Plays.*

The Savior of the Moment. 29 pages. Tr. Noboru Hidaka. *The Passion, and Three Other Japanese Plays.* Oriental Literature Society, Honolulu, 1933; Greenwood, Westport, 1971.

Tojuro's Love. Tojūrō no koi. 1919. 24 pages. *Tojuro's Love, and Four Other Plays.*

Kinoshita NAOE
(1869–1937)

Novelist, political activist, and orator. Born in Matsumoto, Shinshū. Lived in Matsumoto, Tokyo, or Ikaho, in Gumma Prefecture.

Trained as a lawyer, Kinoshita Naoe wanted to be a politician but was prevented from holding office because of his radical views. He spent most of his life fighting for specific causes, such as universal suffrage for men and women, the elimination of poverty, and the prevention of industrial pollution. A Christian Socialist and a pacifist, he was consistently opposed to Japan's militarism during the war with Russia, and was equally disapproving of materialistic socialists who demanded violent revolution. Indeed, it would be difficult to exaggerate the variety and radicalism of Naoe's opinions, for he rejected most of Japan's socio-political traditions, including the family system and what he saw as its logical extension: the monarchy. Even his forthright manner of presentation was decidedly "un-Japanese." He was a brilliant orator, a crusading journalist, and, in the view of many critics, might have become one of the greatest modern novelists had he devoted more time to literature.

His two best novels, *Hi no hashira* (1904, *Pillar of Fire*) and *Ryōjin no jihaku* (1904–06, *The Confessions of a Husband*), have both been translated into English and are distinctly superior to most other Japanese leftwing fictions. In 1910, after constant harassment by the authorities, Naoe suddenly withdrew from political life. He met Okada Torajirō, the founder of *seiza* meditation (see p. 176), and became one of his most dedicated followers. Oriental quietism blended harmoniously with Naoe's peculiar brand of "samurai Christianity." When told in 1937 that he was suffering from terminal cancer, he composed this eloquent poem (translated by Kenneth Strong):

> *Nothing*
> *Is the memento*
> *To take home*
> *To the land of no-action.*

Matsumoto, the town where Kinoshita Naoe was born in 1869, is in the mountainous region of central Japan, about a hundred miles northwest of Tokyo. It was the traditional seat of the Matsumoto clan, in whose employ Naoe's father was retained as a lower-class samurai until the *Meiji Restoration of 1868. When the samurai were disbanded, Naoe's father became a policeman and was obliged to spend much of his time traveling around the country on duty. For this reason, his son rarely saw him.

At Matsumoto Middle School, Naoe studied Chinese history but became inspired by the example of the English nonconformist, Oliver Cromwell, whose life was recounted in *Wilson's English Reader*. When he graduated in 1886, Naoe promptly went to Tokyo with the ambitious idea of studying law and using it, as Cromwell had done against Charles I, to judge and destroy the monarchy. This proved to be more difficult than he supposed, not least because he found university education to be lacking in many respects. After three months at Igirisu Hōritsu Gakkō (School of English Law, later Chūō University) he moved to Tokyo Semmon Gakkō (now Waseda University) in pursuit of his legal studies. "I asked for bread," he said. "The wretches threw me a stone." In particular, he was disillusioned by the English themselves, who had not only reinstated their monarchy but had become a great imperial and mercantile power. He feared that Japan was set on a similar course and that it would ultimately prove detrimental to the majority of her citizens.

Although he pretended to despise literature, Naoe made several attempts to write fiction between 1886–90, some fragments of which survive. He was an avid reader of *Tokutomi Sohō's magazine *Kokumin no tomo* (*The People's Friend*), which appeared in the same year as FUTABATEI's *Ukigumo* (1887). He was also aware that both the status and content of literature had changed dramatically since the early years of the Meiji period, and that his early hero, *Fukuzawa Yukichi (1834–1901), may not have been entirely correct in supposing literature to be a frivolous occupation.

Two misfortunes, however, befell Naoe in 1887. An arranged marriage robbed him of the girl he loved, and his father died suddenly of cancer. In the following year, after his graduation, Naoe returned to Matsumoto where he began contributing articles to the *Shin'yō Nippō*, a newspaper which supported the Progressive Party. It was the beginning of a long and turbulent journalistic career, for he immediately became embroiled in local political issues, supporting the return of the prefectural offices to Matsumoto and denouncing corruption. Although his activities attracted opprobrium from many quarters, a chance reading of the Sermon on the Mount in his sister's Bible gave him renewed strength and determination. In a letter of 1937 he recalled: "For the first time in my life I knew true joy; all the world renewed itself before my eyes."

Forced to leave Matsumoto temporarily, Naoe returned in 1893 to become a country lawyer. He hated this profession and was preoccupied with the idea of starting a Christian movement which could eventually challenge the central government. Unfortunately, he was disillusioned when many Christians supported the Sino–Japanese War of 1894–95. On this issue, as on so many others, Naoe was attempting to swim against the tide of history. An extremely able and courageous man he might well have risen to a position of greatness in another time, another place.

Ironically, the champion of universal suffrage and the scourge of corrupt politicians was himself arrested for corruption in 1897. He was convicted (rightly, in the view of most historians) of being paid a thousand yen for keeping silent about the purchase of votes by a district councillor. After ten months in prison he was released on appeal and was fortunate to obtain a post on the *Mainichi shimbun*, an independent leftwing newspaper. From this prominent platform he addressed many controversial issues of the day, including the long-running scandal of industrial pollution at the Furukawa copper mine in Ashio. It was this same incident which provoked the celebrated conflict between the novelist SHIGA NAOYA and his father, Shiga having been taken to the site, along with many other students, by Naoe and the Christian leader *Uchimura Kanzō. The problem was eventually buried when the entire area became a reservoir serving the growing metropolis of Tokyo.

In 1900 Naoe married Misako, a disciple of the Christian nurse, Chikako Ozeki, who used to visit him in prison. He had already had several affairs, mostly with *geisha*, but had long desired the stability of marriage. Now, with a wife and a steady job on the *Mainichi*, he could look forward to the future with greater confidence, and it was at this point that he began writing fiction in earnest. Editors of the newspaper were worried about finding a new serial to replace Tolstoy's *Resurrection*, and Naoe volunteered to write a novel for this very purpose. Amused by the idea, the editors gave their approval, and *Pillar of Fire* began appearing in daily installments.

One of the most entertaining socialist novels of all time, *Pillar of Fire* is a plausible (if improbable) love story concerning Umeko, the daughter of a ruthless capitalist, and Shinoda, a charismatic Christian leader who edits a socialist newspaper. Naoe's plot is especially ingenious, because Yamaki, the capitalist, is shown to have been corrupted by his second wife, O-Kame. He is inclined to tolerate Umeko's disobedience only because her purity reminds him of her mother, his first wife. By this means, Naoe gives some depth and complexity to Yamaki's character and conceals one of the plot's potential weaknesses: Yamaki's reluctance to compel Umeko to marry Captain Matsushima who ardently pursues her. Strongly tipped to become the next Navy minister, Matsushima is scarcely a man whom Yamaki would wish to upset.

Naoe's aim in writing *Pillar of Fire* was to expose the conspiracy between power and money: that is, between the military and the capitalists, aided and abetted by the aristocracy. As an analysis of the power structure in Japan, it was uncomfortably close to the truth. Moreover, in describing the sort of people with whom he was acquainted, and by projecting himself into the person of Shinoda, Naoe created a novel of compelling realism. One feels that it has been grossly underrated by literary historians, partly because stylistic awkwardness concealed the vigor of its narrative, until being gracefully repaired in Kenneth Strong's excellent English translation.

Naoe's second novel, *The Confessions of a Husband*, lacked the force of *Pillar of Fire* but was more sophisticated in its plot and characterization. Again, the hero is an extension of the author himself, this time in his role as a Christian humanist dealing with the hidebound conventions of his clients (one is almost tempted to say "parishioners") in Matsumoto. Translated into English in 1905, some sixty-five years before *Pillar of Fire*, the novel shows Naoe's great talent for creating popular fiction with a serious message.

Among the most important of the many journals with which Naoe was associated was the weekly *Heimin shimbun* (*People's Newspaper*) which he co-founded with the socialist Kōtoku Shūsui in 1903.

Immediately prior to the Russo–Japanese War censorship was rife. The newspaper was banned and most of its staff imprisoned, although Naoe was among those who remained free. Eventually, after Japan's victory in the war and the appointment of Saionji Kimmochi as prime minister, restrictions were relaxed. In 1905, Naoe launched the Christian Socialist periodical, *Shinkigen* (*New Era*), soliciting contributions from such well-known writers as TOKUTOMI ROKA. Its publication underlined an ideological difference with the atheist Kōtoku, who was the leader of those executed after the celebrated Treason Trials of 1910. Influenced not only by the Christian faith but by the ideals of pre-Restoration Japan, Naoe wanted to promote a nonmaterialistic brand of socialism. Others, including Kōtoku, were more interested in the division of wealth and the classical Marxist doctrine: common ownership of the means of production.

Naoe was deeply affected by the death of his mother in May 1906, feeling that he had contributed to her suffering by attracting so much attention from the police. Resolving to give up politics he withdrew to Ikaho, in the mountains of Gumma Prefecture, to write *Zange* (1907, *Repentance*). He had come to the conclusion that Japan was incapable of radical social and political change, and said so in his characteristic, forthright manner. Over the next two years he produced three more novels: *Rei ka niku ka* (1908, *The Spirit and the Flesh*); *Kojiki* (1908, *The Beggar*); and *Kataku* (1910, *House of Fire*), the last of which showed his growing interest in Buddhist teaching. And it was in 1910 that he first met Okada Torajirō, the founder of the Zen-like technique of *seiza* meditation. The meeting changed Naoe's life completely.

Still practiced today, *seiza* is a form of silent meditation which emphasizes correct posture. Whether because of its inherent merits or because it put a brake on Naoe's hectic life of political action, it brought him a sense of transcendent peace. "Now, no man is my enemy," he said, going on to explain that even the capitalists whom he once reviled were just ordinary people, blind to the truth. He turned away from politics to write studies of the Buddhist priests, Nichiren, Hōnen, and Shinran (during 1910–11), then fell silent until after Okada's death in 1920. His reminiscences, *Kami, ningen, jiyū* (*God, Man, Freedom*) were published in 1934.

As Nakamura Mitsuo has pointed out, Japanese critics were once inclined to classify such writers as Naoe, Tokutomi Roka, and others of the period as occupying a "valley" between the peaks of *Ken'yūsha literature and *Naturalism. From the vantage point of the end of the century this seems unfair. The serious content of Naoe's work, his ability to interpret reality through fiction, and his intelligent, entertaining, and devastatingly accurate analysis of Japan's power structure have all helped to qualify him for reappraisal. His reputation has grown steadily since the 1950s, when *Pillar of Fire* was published in an uncensored form for the first time since 1910. Of course, subversive revolutionaries – however distinguished – are always an embarrassment in their hometowns (as witness the example of Thomas Paine, so long ignored in Thetford, England). But one day even the citizens of Matsumoto may be proud of being associated with Kinoshita Naoe, their sometime country lawyer.

RECOMMENDED READING

Novel

Pillar of Fire. *Hi no hashira*. 1904. 199 pages. Tr. Kenneth Strong. George Allen and Unwin, London, 1972. Contains excellent 52-page introduction by the translator. Was no. 6 in the UNESCO Asian Fiction Series. Jacket illustration: *Fuji Above the Lightning* by Hokusai.

WORKS IN ENGLISH TRANSLATION

Novels

The Confessions of a Husband.
   Ryōjin no jihaku. 1904–06. 2 vols.
   Tr. Arthur Lloyd. Yurakusha,
   Tokyo, 1905–06.
Pillar of Fire. Hi no hashira. 1904.

CRITICAL STUDY

Strong, Kenneth. "Kinoshita Naoe:
   Non-conformist." *Journal of Australian Oriental Society*, vol. 4,
   no. 1, 1966.

KITA Morio
(1927–   )

Novelist. Real name, Saitō Munekichi. Lives in Tokyo.

Born in the year of AKUTAGAWA's suicide, Kita Morio has brought to a fine art that aspect of fiction which, when overemphasized, Akutagawa most deplored. In his monumental, 760-page novel *Nireke no hitobito* (1962–64, *The House of Nire*), Kita shows the skills of a biographer and historian. He dwells exclusively on the factual details of life rather than seeking out and revealing its underlying energies. Although it is undoubtedly one of the landmarks of postwar literature, *The House of Nire* is a profoundly depressing work and appears to be the product of a cynical mind. Nonetheless, Kita has written other works which have quite the opposite effect, and he is always a meticulous and intelligent craftsman, gifted with a satirical sense of humor and an acute, observing eye.

Kita Morio is the pen name of Saitō Munekichi. He was the second son of Saitō Mokichi, a practicing psychiatrist who was also one of the most prominent Japanese poets of the early twentieth century. An austere, aloof man – on whom the character Tetsukichi in *The House of Nire* was loosely modeled – Mokichi became notorious for his support of the military regime when other, more enlightened artists were opposed to it. A traditionalist in poetry, he was highly regarded for his *tanka* verse even by those who disliked his outspoken political views. It is clear that his literary example set a very high standard for his son to emulate.

Although Kita entered medical school at Tōhoku University in 1948 he had already made up his mind to become a writer. He began writing stories in his first year at university, and by 1950 had published several poems and one piece of fiction. His first novel, *Yūrei* (*Ghosts*), was serialized in a magazine in 1953–54.

Ghosts stands midstream in the *I-Novel tradition and will strike the Western reader as being pure autobiography despite many elements of artifice that have been imposed on the author's material. It is chiefly the story of the narrator's attempts to discover in himself memories of his mother who disappeared during the war. Occasionally he feels her presence, yet never can he summon up a clear visual impression of her, and she remains until the end of the novel a ghostly figure composed of white vapor. By contrast, his other childhood memories are extremely vivid, and he describes at some length his obsessive interest in collecting insects, his trips to the mountains to catch them, and his interactions with a kindly uncle who liked to impress both him and his skeptical older cousin with conjuring tricks and obscure medical knowledge. A novel of great intensity, relieved here and there with touches of humor, *Ghosts* is a fine piece of writing and reads very well in Dennis Keene's recent translation. Certainly it is highly introspective and at times seems to verge on solipsism, but it nonetheless ends triumphantly when the narrator feels that he is finally able to join the rest of humanity on equal terms.

Much of Kita's early work shows the influence of DAZAI OSAMU, by far the most idolized novelist of the immediate postwar era. Yet Dazai's highly personal style did not lend itself to someone who wished to write objectively about the society around him. Kita discarded it, and, somewhat unpredictably, turned to the encyclopedic novels of Thomas Mann for inspiration. From Mann's example, he realized that it was possible to put intellectual theories, historical facts, and indeed a whole body of specialist knowledge into a work of fiction without necessarily ruining its form. With this in mind he began taking notes for the novel that would eventually become *The House of Nire*.

However, long before writing his masterwork, Kita produced many short stories – two of which have been translated into English. "*Iwaone ni te*" (1956, "On the Rock Ridge") describes how a lone climber in the mountains of central Japan comes face to face with a mild form of madness. He observes two people, one of whom lies dead at the foot of a precipice, the other climbing erratically away from the body. Later in the story the narrator meets the second climber and has a conversation with him. Both men agree that when they ascend the mountains they feel a "nameless apprehension" quite unrelated to any fear of falling. No further explanation is given, yet one is left with the impression that perfectly sane men can be made to feel a touch of insanity if they venture into an alien landscape such as the author so powerfully evokes.

"*Tanjō*" (*1959*, "Birth") is much more down to earth. It is a moving tale of a young student physician who goes to stay with his uncle, a provincial doctor who first inspired him to take up medicine. Now, having become disillusioned by years in the country with inadequate facilities, the older man has taken to drink and even refuses to answer an emergency call that coincides with his nephew's arrival. Going in his uncle's stead, the young physician is faced with a dying patient who is apparently untended by her relatives and impossible to save. He is bitterly depressed by the experience, and he begins to think that his uncle may have been right in telling him to wait until morning before making the visit. However, when he discovers the patient's family supervising the birth of a litter of pigs on their nearby farm, his spirits begin to rise. This simple renewal of life goes at least some way toward validating his youthful idealism.

"*Tanjō*" was actually written two years before its publication, in 1957. In the following year, Kita made a six-month trip to Europe as a ship's doctor, later using the experience as the basis for *Dokutoru Mambō kōkaiki* (1960, *Dr. Mambo's Voyage*). This humorous novel has enjoyed great popularity over the years and is still enjoyed by many Japanese readers. More somber is Kita's other 1960 work, "*Yoru to kiri no sumi de*" ("In the Corner of the Night and Mist"). Set in Nazi Germany it is a story of how psychiatrists collude with the authorities in their extermination policy for mental patients. The novella won the Akutagawa Prize, and Kita's reputation as a leading writer was virtually assured.

A man of remarkable energy and application, Kita continued to write essays and stories while still conducting his psychiatric studies. He received an M.D. in 1960 for a study of schizophrenics, and in 1961 wrote most of *The House of Nire*, a gargantuan task by any standards. It is for this work, translated by Dennis Keene and published by Kodansha in two volumes, that Kita is chiefly known in the West.

Writing in *Japan Book News*, the critic T. J. G. Harris praises the "humanity, humor and breadth of vision" of *The House of Nire*, claiming that it is "totally unlike the kind of Japanese novel to which the West is accustomed." Going further than the translator (who said: "It implies a respect for the everyday, for the way people actually feel, think and behave . . ."), Harris says: "It gives a far better idea of how Japanese people actually live, think and feel than do those many Japanese novels that are informed chiefly by a narrow aestheticism and a factitious gloom that seems primarily to derive from a misunderstanding of . . . existentialism." If this is a typical Western reaction (and there is some reason to suppose that it is), it betrays a tragic ignorance of the true nature of literature. For Kita's masterpiece is in reality little more than a magnificent documentary history of the twentieth century, observed from a Japanese perspective. Were it not for the brilliance of its opening chapters it would have none of the vitality which fiction at its best can embody, nor does it make the reader aware of any spiritual resources that might offset its unrelenting pessimism.

The House of Nire traces the lives and fortunes of three generations of the Nire family who own and run a psychiatric hospital on the outskirts of Tokyo. This bold venture was started by Nire Kiichirō, an amusing personification of the *Meiji period whose rise to wealth and fame is largely the result of his charming dishonesty. He is so supremely self-confident that patients rarely object to his ludicrous methods of diagnosis or treatment. In fact, people have such faith in his foreign qualifications that some of them even recover. Those who fail to get better merely help swell the coffers of the hospital, enabling Kiichirō to add fanciful towers and luxurious colonnades of his own design.

Kiichirō's large family – his wife, three daughters, two sons, and two adopted sons – are among the large cast of characters that includes various patients, friends, neighbors, and Nanny Shimoda, the children's beloved nurse. Unfortunately, not a single one of them has Kiichirō's vitality, and this is the chief weakness of the novel. When Kiichirō dies, the novel dies with him. Its delightful humor disappears, only to be replaced by a gathering storm of misery culminating in World War II.

One may well argue that literature must reflect life accurately, and one may hold up Kita's novel as a shining example which ridicules false optimism and shows life as it really is. Yet if that were the case, Japanese culture would have perished long ago, so lackluster are the second and third generations of the Nire family. Furthermore, only at the end of the novel, when the normally thin Shun'ichi returns home from war bloated, overweight, and hysterical, does one begin to appreciate the hideous depth of Kita's cynical humor. For the hospital family's son-and-heir has survived starvation on a Pacific island and should by rights be thinner than ever. There is a strong implication that he has consumed human flesh: perhaps the worst depravity to which a doctor may stoop. If one makes the connection (as readers are bound to do), one can imagine his grandfather Kiichirō congratulating him for his initiative, mouthing his patronizing catchphrase: "Well done!"

The House of Nire won the Mainichi Prize in 1964, and since then Kita has gone on to write many other stories, essays, science fiction, and some travel literature.

RECOMMENDED READING

Novels

The Fall of the House of Nire. *Nireke no hitobito.* (Part Three). 1964. 245 pages. Tr. Dennis Keene. Kodansha International, Tokyo, 1985. Be sure to read *The House of Nire* first.

The House of Nire. *Nireke no hitobito.* (Parts One and Two). 1962–64. 519 pages. Tr. Dennis Keene. Kodansha International, Tokyo and NY, 1984, 1991, paperback. Fontana, London, 1990. Kita's original work was published as a single volume by Shinchosha, Tokyo, but for reasons of length has been issued in translation in two volumes, i.e., this one and *The Fall of the House of Nire.*

WORKS IN ENGLISH TRANSLATION

Novels

The Adventures of Kupukupu the Sailor. Funanori Kupukupu no bōken. 224 pages. Tr. Ralph F. McCarthy. Kodansha International, Tokyo, 1985.

Doctor Mambo at Sea. Dokutoru Mambō kōkaiki. 1960. 359 pages. Tr. Ralph F. McCarthy. Kodansha International, Tokyo, 1987.

The Fall of the House of Nire. Nireke no hitobito. (Part Three). 1964.

Ghosts. Yūrei. 1953–54. 193 pages. Tr. Dennis Keene. Kodansha International, Tokyo, 1992.

The House of Nire. Nireke no hitobito. (Parts One and Two). 1964.

Short Fiction

"Birth." "*Tanjō.*" Composed 1957; published 1959. 9 pages. Tr. Clifton Royston. *Japan Quarterly*, vol. 16, no. 4, 1969.

"The Empty Field." "*Akichi.*" 12 pages. Tr. Kinya Tsuruta and Judith Merril. *The Empty Field.* Omega Fawcett, Greenwich, 1973; *The Best Japanese Science Fiction Stories*, 1989.

"On the Rock Ridge." "*Iwaone nite.*" 1956. 8 pages. Tr. Clifton Royston. *Japan Quarterly*, vol. 16, no. 4, 1969.

Kobayashi TAKIJI
(1903–1933)

Novelist. Born in Akita Prefecture, on the Japan Sea coast. Lived in Otaru in northwest Hokkaidō.

Highly revered in postwar Japan, Kobayashi Takiji was at once the outstanding figure and the most conspicuous martyr of the proletarian literature movement of the 1920s and early 1930s. Tortured to death in the Tsukiji Police Station on February 20, 1933, he had been a passionate spokesman for Japan's oppressed classes: the peasants and tenant farmers who were cruelly exploited by that historical anomaly, feudalistic capitalism. Always brave to a point of recklessness, Takiji was a competent writer whose works are now admired more for the powerful messages they contain than for the simple realistic style in which they were written. *Kani kosēn* (*1929, The Factory Ship*; also translated as *The Cannery Boat*) and *Fuzai jinushi* (*1929, The Absentee Landlord*) are his two major novels. Both are essential reading if one wishes to gain a complete picture of twentieth-century Japan from its literature.

Born to a poor farming family in Akita prefecture, Takiji grew up

in Otaru, a coastal city in Hokkaidō to which his uncle had brought
the whole family in 1907. Student unrest was rife when Takiji
attended Otaru Higher Commercial School. Inflation ran at an all-
time high; wages remained low; strikes and riots were common.
By the time he graduated in 1924, he had become gripped by
revolutionary fervor, feelings held in check only by the need to earn
a living.

In the year of his graduation, Takiji accepted a post with the
Hokkaidō Colonial Bank in Sapporo and was immediately transferred
to his hometown, Otaru. He was also active creatively, contributing
to a magazine called *Clarté*, after Barbusse's novel of the same name.
In fact, he was to continue these two oddly divergent careers of
banking and writing until his notoriety as a Marxist prompted the
bank to fire him in 1929. Scholars still find inexplicable the curious
fact that, in view of the substance of his work, the bank authorities
did not dismiss him sooner.

Many of Takiji's leftwing friends were arrested in a mass roundup
on March 15, 1928, accused of violating the Peace Preservation Law.
Subsequently, he wrote a story entitled *"1928 nen 3 gatsu 15 nichi"*
("The Fifteenth of March 1928") which was published in the
magazine *Senki* (*Battle Flag*) later that year. Banned, but secretly
distributed, the November and December issues of the magazine
brought him to the attention of a committed readership, and, less
welcomely, to the notice of the secret police.

Undeterred, Takiji set about writing his most celebrated work,
The Factory Ship, a fictionalized but highly accurate account of
conditions on board a cannery boat in the Okhotsk Sea. He had
found the idea for the story by reading a newspaper article two
years previously. As had been widely reported, workers on the
Hakuai Maru (literally: "ship of brotherly love") were not only paid
a pittance, but were brutally tortured if they infringed the rules.
All the facts were revealed in a court case, following a civil action
brought by the workers on their return to port.

The subject was a virtual gift to a writer who was now an orthodox
Marxist: one who was seeking to publicize the evils of the existing
system. Takiji collected many details about the daily life of the
workers on the ship and put them together in a tense, "cinematic"
narrative that was sure to be widely noticed. He concentrated on
action and dialogue rather than character development; a technique
generally disliked by critics, but one which in this instance
works extremely well. Nobody, other than the evil superintendent,
Asakawa, is given a name. The characters are called simply "the
student," or "the stutterer," or "the man from Shibaura." In this

way, Takiji achieved his aim of having "no heroes," only a "collective hero" in the motley group of workers.

The story, published in the May and June 1929 issues of *Senki*, was privately praised by SHIGA NAOYA with whom Takiji had been corresponding for several years. Shiga, however, was critical of Takiji's insistence on propagating Communist ideals in his work. "I believe that as art it is awkward and unattractive when a man expounds a particular philosophy in his writings," said Shiga, making one wonder why Takiji had chosen such an unsuitable mentor in the first place.

The Factory Ship sold fifteen thousand copies in book form before it, too, was banned by the authorities. Meanwhile, its author was already under contract with the *Chūō kōron (Central Review)* to write another story in a similar vein, this time addressing the plight of tenant farmers in Hokkaidō. Perhaps because it was much closer to home, the subject of *The Absentee Landlord* presented Takiji with greater creative problems. He wanted to show exactly how that pernicious Japanese phenomenon, capitalism grafted onto feudalism, worked in practice. In this he failed, although he gave a strong general impression of the evils of the system.

The tenants' landlord in Takiji's novel has the psychological advantage of being a feudal lord who receives the complete loyalty of his subjects as a matter of tradition. However, in the author's own words, the man is also "in the process of evolving into a member of the bourgeoisie." Being a capitalist who no longer lives on the estate, he can exploit it ruthlessly from a distance, quite oblivious to the suffering he causes.

As a novel, *The Absentee Landlord* has many qualities, not least of which is the superb evocation of the growing mood of solidarity among the peasants. The work, however, was not well received at the time of its publication. Critics found it loosely constructed and marred by ideological statements. Moreover, Takiji's own employers were displeased that he had mentioned some of their best customers by name. Dismissed by the bank (as noted previously), he left for Tokyo in March 1930.

From this point onwards, the young author was doomed to destruction. Already a "marked man," he was arrested two months later while on a lecture tour of Osaka. Released after interrogation and torture, he was rearrested when he returned to Tokyo and imprisoned for a further six months. This time the charge related to the passage in *The Factory Ship* where a worker, packing cans for the emperor, says he would like to mix some sand in with the crab meat. Less than a year after his release, Takiji formally joined the Communist Party and went underground.

In the last three years of his life, Takiji wrote "*Kōba saibō*" (*1930*, "The Factory Cell"); "*Orugu*" (*1931*, "The Organizer"); "*Yasuko*" (*1931*); "*Tenkeiki no hitobito* " (*1931*, "Men in Transition"); "*Numajiri-mura*" (*1932*, "Numajiri Village"); "*Tōseikatsusha*" (1932, "Life in the Communist Party"); "*Chiku no hitobito*" (*1932*, "Men of the Zone"); and several critical essays and articles.

"Life in the Communist Party" was especially controversial, and was not printed in uncensored form until 1945. It describes Takiji's own life as a party member, hunted by the police because he spreads anti-war propaganda, but ultimately successful in organizing a Communist cell. The "I" of the story claims that he is happy in his work, despite the obvious danger to his personal safety.

Within a year of writing "Life in the Communist Party," Takiji was dead, and with him began the death of the proletarian movement in literature. Forced underground, other writers could no longer circulate their work freely, while others remained silent or modified their views. Only a few, like HIRABAYASHI TAIKO, continued to put forward provocative ideas during the period of militarism that led to World War II.

RECOMMENDED READING

Novels

The Factory Ship, and The Absentee Landlord. 185 pages. Tr. Frank Motofuji. University of Tokyo Press, Tokyo, 1973; University of Washington Press, Seattle, 1973. In a single volume with a 31-page introduction by the translator, these two short novels represent the very best of Japan's proletarian literature. UTP edition has the same double-page picture of the author on both inside covers.

WORKS IN ENGLISH TRANSLATION

Novels

The Absentee Landlord. Fuzai jinushi. 1929. 100 pages. Tr. Frank Motofuji. *The Factory Ship, and The Absentee Landlord.*

The Factory Ship. Kani kosēn. 1929. 83 pages. (1) As "The Cannery Boat." Tr. (anonymous). *The Cannery Boat, and Other Japanese Short Stories.* International Publishers, NY, 1933; Martin Lawrence, London, 1933; Greenwood Press, NY, 1968. Extract in: *Modern Japanese Literature,* ed. Donald Keene. Grove Press, NY, 1956; Tuttle, Tokyo, 1957. (2) *The Factory Ship, and The Absentee Landlord.*

Short Fiction

"The Fifteenth of March 1928." *"1928 nen 3 gatsu 15 nichi."* 1928. 24 pages. *The Cannery Boat, and Other Japanese Short Stories.*

"For the Sake of the Citizens." *"Shimin no tame ni."* 9 pages. *The Cannery Boat, and Other Japanese Short Stories.*

Kōda ROHAN
(1867–1947)

Writer of short fiction, essays, and drama. Real name, Kōda Shigeyuki. Born in Kanda, Edo (now Tokyo).

Kōda Rohan was one of the most revered figures of Japanese literature, not only for his work but also for his character. A man of strong principles, he combined immense learning with a true poetic sensitivity and a profound sense of religious truth. It is no exaggeration to call him a Renaissance man, for like MORI ŌGAI he possessed multiple gifts and developed each of them to the full. Indeed, the famous literary critic TSUBOUCHI SHŌYŌ once compared him with Leonardo da Vinci, although, as his translator Chieko Mulhern has noted, the most appropriate epithet for him is probably that of *kunshi*, meaning a Confucian scholar-gentleman. Imbued with Confucianism from an early age, Rohan exemplified many of the traditional virtues of Japanese culture while retaining a keen awareness of contemporary life and the unique challenges that it posed.

He completed his best work early in his career, his acknowledged masterpiece being the short novel *Gojū no tō* (*1891–92, The Five-Storied Pagoda*). Later, he turned away from pure fiction to write essays and historical works in which he could more easily express his learning. If, with our vantage of hindsight, he appears to stand slightly outside the mainstream of modern Japanese literature, to his contemporaries Rohan was one of the towering figures of *Meiji letters. In the shorthand terminology of literary students, the 1890s were simply *Kō-Ro jidai*: "The Age of [OZAKI] KŌYŌ and Rohan."

Rohan himself was never entirely sure of his exact birthday, believing it to have been the twenty-third day of the seventh month of 1867 (which is probably correct). He was given the legal name Shigeyuki, together with the childhood name Tetsushirō, *shirō* meaning "fourth child." His mother, Yū, of whom he was greatly in awe, was the daughter of Kōda Ritei, a high-ranking shōgunate official in charge of ceremonies and protocol. His father, Shigenobu, was the son of another (lower-ranking) official who had taken his wife's family name.

It was the last year of the shogunate in 1867, and the new generation of the Kōda family was obliged to adapt itself to greatly changed circumstances. Remarkably, it succeeded to such an extent that it is hard to think of many other Japanese families that have surpassed the Kōdas in accomplishment. Rohan's three brothers pursued careers in commerce, military service, and academia, the eldest becoming president of a textile company, the second a naval lieutenant who was one of the most famous explorers of his day, and the third a professor of Japanese economic history. Moreover, Rohan's two sisters were both gifted musicians. Nobuko (1870–1946) studied Western music in Boston and Vienna, returning to become a highly acclaimed concert pianist and tutor to the empress. His younger sister, referred to by her married name Andō Kōko (1878–1963), was a violinist and music teacher to the crown princess. It is worth noting that the subsequent generation also produced high achievers. Rohan's nephew Takagi Taku (1907–74) was offered the Akutagawa Prize in 1940, but declined it on the grounds that he would have preferred to have received it for another work that had previously won him a nomination. Finally, and more relevant to students of Rohan, his own daughter, Kōda Aya, began her impressive literary career as his biographer, describing his life in a series of anecdotal works which enjoyed wide popularity.

After learning to read and write at a private school Rohan entered Ochanomizu Normal School, the first in Japan to experiment with Western educational methods. However, after the age of twelve when he attended Tokyo First Middle School in Kanda, Rohan found that his education was frequently interrupted because of the family's reduced financial circumstances. He spent just one year at the Tokyo English School, becoming passably proficient in the English language, and went on to become largely self-taught through intensive reading at the Tokyo Library. Fortunately, the family's funds allowed him to attend the Geigijuku, a private school of Chinese learning run by the Confucian scholar Kikuchi Shōken. There, Rohan became greatly influenced by the philosophy of Wang Yang-ming, a Ming dynasty thinker who proclaimed the doctrine of Unity of Knowledge and Action. The Eastern philosophies encountered by Rohan during this period (1880–83) were to be the formative influence of his life, despite his extensive acquaintance with Western thought.

Rohan's Establishment background, strict Confucian upbringing, and passionate love of scholarship may well suggest that his destiny was precisely defined. So it may come as a surprise to discover that he entered a government telegraphy school in 1883, graduated a year later, and accepted a post as a telegrapher in Yoichi, a remote "frontier" town near present-day Otaru in Hokkaidō. One needs no clearer illustration that the early Meiji period could play havoc with a young man's career, offering unusual opportunities while sweeping away the financial security of shōgunate stipends.

Rohan probably had the romantic notion that while operating the telegraphy station he would have plenty of time for reading, for in fact he took an entire trunk of books for that very purpose. Yet, lonely and isolated, he soon ran out of reading material and to occupy his mind was obliged to borrow *sutras* from a local temple. When in that same year (1885) Tsubouchi Shōyō published his treatise *The Essence of the Novel*, Rohan decided that he would forsake telegraphy and walk back to Tokyo to pursue a literary career. The decision gave him a great sense of liberation, and the long journey, too, was beneficial. It ended with his return home and the discovery that his father had, in his absence, been converted to Christianity. Indeed, Shigenobu had had the whole family baptized, Rohan alone being left to carry on the family's traditional faith in Nichiren Sect Buddhism.

Rohan's first printed work was an essay called *"Oto to kotoba"* (*1887*, "Sound and Words") which appeared in the January issue of *Kunshi to Shukujo* (*Gentlemen and Ladies*). It was a discussion of traditional music and an appeal to raise the status of the Japanese composer. Perhaps Rohan thought he could do for music what Shōyō was doing for literature, but the piece did not have the necessary breadth and weight.

With publication of his work came the opportunity to use his new pen name, Rohan ("Companion of the Dew"), which referred to his experience of hiking from northern Japan to Tokyo. It is the name by which he is universally known and to which he made further reference in the title of his first published work of fiction, "*Tsuyu dandan*" (*1889*, "Dewdrops"). Appearing in the February issue of YAMADA BIMYŌ's magazine *Miyako no hana*, this story established him as a writer of great promise. Quite unlike his later work, it is set chiefly in America and reads very much like a translation of a Western novel. In it, a millionaire advertises for a man to marry his daughter Rubina, hoping to test the affections of her existing fiancé, Mr. Sincere. He sets the condition that the man must never lose his good humor, a condition everyone fails except for a Japanese poet acting on behalf of his Chinese employer. Too embarrassed to marry the girl, the poet flees back to the East, pursued by the millionaire who now believes him to be an ideal companion for a forthcoming trip around the world.

Ingeniously, Rohan had plundered a popular Chinese story called "Master Ch'ien Wins Miss Feng Unexpectedly" for the plot of "Dewdrops." Transposed to a Western setting and with dialogue in the new *gembun itchi* (unified speech and writing) style, the story worked very well and earned Rohan a reputation as a modern and fashionable writer. It was not, however, a work that contained many of the elements for which Rohan is remembered today. For these one must look to his next story, "*Fūryūbutsu*" (1889, "Love Bodhisattva"), written for the series *Shincho hyakushu* (*A Hundred Best Stories*).

In "*Fūryūbutsu*" Rohan introduced the idea of the creative man who seeks artistic perfection and suggested that such a person was the ideal human being. His hero, a Buddhist sculptor called Shu'un, rescues Otatsu (the illegitimate daughter of a senior official) from a violent uncle who has been intending to sell her into prostitution. Later, when Shu'un falls ill, Otatsu nurses him back to health and they fall in love. However, she is called away by her father and in her absence the sculptor carves a statue of her. At first it is fully clothed, but Shu'un removes layer upon layer of wood until he is left with a magnificent nude statue of a bodhisattva. On hearing that Otatsu is to marry a nobleman Shu'un tries to destroy his work but cannot bring himself to do it. He turns away and suddenly the girl herself is there beside him. We are given to believe that the statue is so perfect that it has come to life, perhaps in response to having been spared by its creator.

"Love Bodhisattva" made an enormous impact when it was published, although today it seems both flawed and dated. Having read it, the poet Masaoka Shiki declared: "For some time afterward, I was almost delirious with a feverish wish to author even one novel like it in my lifetime." Quoting Shiki's comments, Rohan's translator, Chieko Mulhern, goes on to note that the author's striking style and poetic imagination were chiefly responsible for the story's success. In her critical biography *Kōda Rohan* she says: "Despite its first impression of classicism, this story deals with a new view of love, unexpectedly rendered in classical guise."

The word *love* does not adequately render the concept of *fūryū* which was central to Rohan's thinking for much of his career. In saying that he wished "to attain *fūryū* with all my being," Rohan had in mind an idea of poetic refinement in which love, faith, and beauty became united. He thought of *fūryū* as a state of mind that had the potential to achieve salvation for the individual. Creative artists who had shed all delusions and faced up to reality could attain *fūryū*, but only rarely. In the world of literature he found its expression in the later poems of Bashō, but nowhere else. Rather, it was exemplified by such an artist as the tea master *Sen no Rikyū (1522–91), and Rohan's story *"Rikyū no tsuma"* (1913, "Rikyū's Wife") described how the master and his wife were perfectly united in their elegant taste.

Given the seriousness of Rohan's aspirations it is astonishing that he wrote so many stories that could not possibly help him to achieve them. Of his other works in 1889, *"Kore wa, kore wa"* ("Surprise") and *"Ayashi yana"* ("How Suspicious!") were mystery stories, while *"Kidanji"* ("A Rare Man") was the first of many samurai tales. He also began a much longer work, *Yuki funpun* (*Snowflakes Dancing*), an epic tragedy based on the Ainu rebellion of the 1660s, but it remained unfinished until a disciple wrote the closing chapters many years later.

Rohan's greatest period was undoubtedly the decade of the 1890s, and it began with the minor masterpiece *Tai dokuro* (1890, *Encounter with a Skull*). Echoing the intricate structure, eerie atmosphere, and Buddhist philosophy of a ghostly *Nō play, the story is narrated by a young traveler called Rohan. During a long trek, Rohan's high spirits are dampened when he comes to a seemingly hostile part of the mountains. He calls at an isolated hut and is met there by a beautiful woman who invites him to stay the night. Being both cautious and highly moral, he refuses to sleep with her, instead requesting that she relate her story. She explains that she has retreated from the world because her rejection of a young nobleman has resulted in his death. Now, in her conversation with the young traveler – during which he has promised to tell her story to the world – she says she has found peace of mind. As dawn breaks, both the woman and her house "vanish like a cloud of mist," and the narrator sees only a bleached white skull lying at his feet. Later, at his destination, Rohan learns that a mad beggar woman in the advanced stages of a disfiguring disease strayed into the mountains a year ago. It was her skull he encountered and her spirit which he helped to release.

The narrator's promise to turn the woman's story into art is the key that liberates her spirit. In making this point the author demonstrated his belief that "the purifier of mankind is the poet ... the creator." He went on to elaborate it with great eloquence in many of his works, but nowhere better than in *The Five-Storied Pagoda*. In this powerful novel produced for serialization in the newspaper *Kokkai (Parliament)*, he depicted a feud between two master builders, both of whom aspire to be in charge of constructing a pagoda for the Kanno Temple. The two men are opposites in both personality and social standing. Genta, who has built most of the existing temple, is a true patrician: rich, born to lead, and highly regarded. By contrast his rival, Jūbei, is desperately poor, socially inept, and widely ridiculed for being slow-witted. When Jūbei puts in an earnest bid for the contract to build the pagoda, Genta, his employer, is deeply offended.

With great skill, Rohan portrayed both men as individuals, fully realizing Tsubouchi Shōyō's demands for improved characterization. Idealistic in essence the story is nonetheless realistic in effect, and the episode in which Jūbei goes to the temple to present his ideas to the Abbot is just one among many unforgettable scenes. Suddenly Jūbei is revealed in his true light: as a great craftsman who has hitherto been forced by circumstances into accepting relatively menial work.

Telling the two men to decide the matter between themselves, the Abbot emphasizes cooperation as the means of attaining enlightenment. Eventually Genta gives way with bad grace and the project is carried out entirely by Jūbei. His finished pagoda withstands even the onslaught of a furious typhoon, described with some extraordinary use of personification in a highly effective passage. Jūbei's skill wins even Genta's admiration and one is left with the impression that divine order has been restored in the face of overwhelming odds.

Fine though Rohan's characters are in *The Five-Storied Pagoda*, they do not strike every reader as being fully rounded and believable. Donald Keene mentions that "they tend to be two-dimensional, in the traditional manner of Japanese and Chinese fiction." Yet it is hard to agree entirely with the poet Miyoshi Tatsuji who first suggested that they lack "a dark side." After all, Genta is proud and quick to anger, his wife, Okichi, actually incites their employee, Seikichi, to injure Jūbei, and even Jūbei himself is a brooding figure whom one feels could be dangerous when cornered. A surfeit of human folly and sin are displayed in the story, yet, because goodness wins in the end, critics are inclined to be skeptical.

In 1896 Rohan married Yamamuro Kimiko, a woman of modest demeanor who gave him a son and two daughters before her premature death in 1910. All the evidence suggests that his first marriage was very happy – and quite unlike his second marriage to Kodama Yayoko in 1912. A fervent Christian, Yayoko quarreled constantly with him, on many occasions causing him to drown his anger in sake. Although Rohan came to be revered as a sage he was certainly not without human fallibilities, and his daily life did not always echo the calm, reflective world of Oriental philosophy.

As a man, Rohan captured people's imagination by his personality and bearing. In his late twenties he met the young writer HIGUCHI ICHIYŌ who described him thus: "He was fair complexioned, ruddy around the throat, not tall but stoutly built. He spoke serenely in a deep, dignified voice" (Tr. Chieko Mulhern). Rohan demonstrated a unity of personal style and writing style, for his prose – like his manner – was always very formal and is considered to be much easier for foreigners to read in translation than for Japanese to read in the original. There is a famous description of Rohan's style by MASAMUNE HAKUCHŌ, who said that it reminded him of an aged samurai walking under the weight of his heavy armor and helmet. The description was intended as a compliment.

It is the practice in Japanese studies to divide Rohan's career into various phases, the first of which, his Idealistic phase (1889–93), contained many of his best works. In his Mature phase (1893–96) he moved more closely to reflecting real life as it actually occurs, developing a new narrative technique for the purpose. The plot of his long novel *Fūryū mijinzō* (1893–95, *The Storehouse of Infinitesimal Life*) has an interlocking, chainlike structure and no determinate ending. Dissatisfied with it, he turned to writing shorter stories during his so-called Stagnant phase (1896–1903). This period has surely been misnamed, for in 1901 Rohan published two books of essays, *Rangen* (*Empty Words*) and *Chōgo* (*Unnecessary Words*), which some critics regard as his finest work.

Rohan never wrote any fiction superior to *The Five-Storied Pagoda* mainly because he deliberately turned away from fiction at the time of the Russo–Japanese War. With the beginning of his Syncretic phase (1903–19) came the publication of the first installment of *Sora utsu nami* (*Waves Striking the Sky*). However, he later abandoned the work, saying that the writing of fiction was incompatible with the national emergency. He explained himself fully in the long poem "*Shutsuro*" (1905, "Leaving the Hermitage"), in which he put forward a beguiling case for "art for art's sake" only to destroy it with an urgent plea to the artist to face reality. The poem is not widely read today, and copies of its English translation are hard to come by. Nonetheless, its scholarly references, clever imagery, and energetic language make it surprisingly enjoyable to read, however much one may regret Rohan's decision to abandon fiction.

Towards the latter part of his life Rohan once more began to write prolifically. One of his most notable works in this period was *Unmei* (*1919*, *Fate*), an account of the reign of the second Ming emperor, Chien Wen, who was defeated by his uncle in battle and subsequently became a monk. Grand in style and highly praised by TANIZAKI JUN'ICHIRŌ, *Fate* did not find a wide readership, and indeed Rohan's books were rarely best-sellers. Only *The Five-Storied Pagoda*, with 300,000 copies being printed over a thirty-year period, could be placed into that category.

In *Renkanki* (1940, *A Series of Records*) Rohan returned to the chainlink structure that he had used previously in *The Storehouse of Infinitesimal Life*. It is the story of Kamo no Yasutane, the tenth-century author of *Chiteiki* (*Chronicle of the Lakeside Residence*, 982, tr. as *Chiteiki* in 1971), and Ōe no Sadamoto (930–1036), both of whom become priests. Rohan was fascinated by those who retreat from the world to take up the religious life, although he himself believed that the pursuit of art could be a religious calling in itself.

Hyōshaku Bashō shichibu shū (1947, *Commentaries on the Verse of Bashō*) reveal Rohan's own outlook and sensibility as much as they reveal Bashō's. Each commentary is an independent essay, and the entire work provides many insights into the *Tokugawa period. It was published in the year of his death, and once more underlined the fact that Rohan was (and had always been) preoccupied with the continuance of traditional Oriental culture.

Greatly honored throughout his life, Rohan was awarded a Doctorate of Literature in 1911. In 1937 he received the first Award of Cultural Merit and became a member of the prestigious Japan Art Academy. His death in 1947 at the age of eighty was keenly felt by the entire literary world, even by whose who had never been influenced by him. Fortunately, his memory was kept very much alive in the postwar years by his surviving daughter, Kōda Aya, whose "Sōsō no ki" (*1947*, "Record of the Funeral") established her own reputation as a writer. It was followed by "Sugano no ki" (*1949*, "Record of Sugano"), "Konna koto" (1950, "Such Things") and "Misokkasu" (1951, "Good-for-Nothing"). Her essays, written for magazines and collected into a series of books, form a vivid portrait of a strict, erudite man: a true *kunshi* who focused on the past and yet was one of the founders of modern Japanese literature.

RECOMMENDED READING

Novels

Pagoda, Skull & Samurai. Tr. Chieko Irie Mulhern. Tuttle, Tokyo, 1985. These three short novels are an excellent introduction to Rohan's work. They are *The Five-Storied Pagoda* (translated elsewhere as *The Pagoda*); *Encounter with a Skull*; and *The Bearded Samurai*. The volume also contains 13-page introduction and 13-page afterword by the translator, with additional historical notes.

WORKS IN ENGLISH TRANSLATION

Fiction

The Bearded Samurai. Higeotoko. 1890–96. 108 pages. Tr. Chieko Irie Mulhern. *East Asia Papers.* Cornell University, Ithaca, 1982; *Pagoda, Skull & Samurai.*

Encounter with Skull. Tai dokuro. 1890. 45 pages. Tr. Chieko Irie Mulhern. *East Asia Papers.* Cornell University, Ithaca, 1982; *Pagoda, Skull & Samurai.*

Lodging for a Night. 30 pages. Tr. Miyamori Asataro. *Representative Tales of Japan.* Sanseido, Tokyo, 1914; Sanko Shoten, Tokyo, 1917.

The Pagoda. Gojū no tō. 1891–92. 167 pages. (1) Tr. Sakai Shioya. Okura Shoten, Tokyo, 1909. Extract as "The Gojiu no to, the Pagoda." *The Treasury of Japanese Literature*, ed. Tokichi Watanabe. Jippōkaku, Tokyo, 1933. (2) Extract as "Gozyuu-no-too" (chapters 31 and 32). Tr. F. J. Daniels. *Selections from Japanese Literature.* Lund Humphries, London, 1959. (3) As *The Five-Storied Pagoda.* Tr. Chieko Irie Mulhern. *East Asia Papers.* Cornell University, Ithaca, 1982; *Pagoda, Skull & Samurai.*

Poetry

"Leaving the Hermitage." "*Shu-tsuro*" or "*Kokoro no ato.*" 1905. Epic poem. 195 pages. Tr. Jiro Nagura. George Allen and Unwin, London, 1925.

CRITICAL STUDIES

Mulhern, Chieko Irie. *Kōda Rohan.* Twayne Publishers, NY, 1977.
———. "Kōda Rohan: A Study of Idealism". Ph.D. diss., Columbia University, NY, 1973.

KOJIMA Nobuo
(1915–   )

Novelist and writer of short fiction. Born in Gifu Prefecture in central Honshū. Moved to Tokyo in 1932. Posted to China in World War II.

A gifted satirist, Kojima Nobuo is best known for a very short but quite outstanding novella called *"Amerikan sukūru"* (*1954*, "The American School"), which won the Akutagawa Prize in the year of its publication. He wrote it several years after beginning his career, although his first published work, *"Kisha no naka"* ("On the Train"), appeared as late as 1948. Reacting strongly to the war and postwar Occupation period, he developed a compelling and often brutal form of satire that pictured the Japanese male as an ineffectual creature, crushed by society and increasingly dominated by women. His anti-heroes resemble those of FUTABATEI SHIMEI, and, like his great predecessor, Kojima has been greatly influenced by Russian literature, especially by Gogol. Indeed, Kojima has forged a vital link between the satirists of the past and those of the present, such as MARUYA SAIICHI and Inoue Hisashi who owe much to his pioneering work. His brilliant literary technique lures the reader into sharing the doubts and dilemmas of his characters, and its effect can sometimes be disturbing rather than enlightening. Nonetheless, in his concentration on the minutiae of everyday life, Kojima reveals himself as a true novelist who is intent on reflecting the truth as he sees it.

Born near the town of Gifu in central Japan, Kojima was the son of a craftsman who made Buddhist altars. Always clever as a student, he studied a wide range of world literature, including English, American, and Russian and graduated from the University of Tokyo in English Literature in 1941. His graduation essay was entitled: "Thackeray as a Humorist," a clear sign that he had already developed a preference for novels with a humorous element.

Although he had married a few years previously, Kojima now found himself obliged to serve in the army, and he joined a unit that would later be sent to its total destruction in the Philippines. He was fortunate in being singled out for intelligence service in northern China and was transferred to a communications unit in Peking in 1944, his job being that of intercepting American military radio transmissions. His reports, he later confessed, were often pure fiction.

In the chaotic period after the war, Kojima supported his family by teaching at various high schools while writing in his spare time. Recognition came quickly with the publication of "On the Train," a short story set on an overcrowded train going to Tokyo from Kyūshū amidst the devastation of the recent war. Its central character is a country schoolteacher, Sano, who, like Kojima at the time, moves his family to Tokyo. Married to a nagging wife who constantly undermines his already fragile ego, Sano is close to psychological collapse. Indeed, he is so uncertain about everything in life that he can scarcely speak to his own students above a whisper. Disaster strikes when all the family's possessions are stolen by a black marketeer, prompting Sano's wife to comment: "It's a wonder your own body wasn't stolen from you." In describing the weariness of the train's passengers and evoking a sense of them hurtling towards an unknown future, Kojima ensured that his story had significance beyond that of the individual. He was clearly a writer of great promise.

One of Kojima's earliest stories, "Shōjū" (1952, "The Rifle"), has been translated into English. Written in the mode of a fictional memoir it tells of how Shin, a soldier, becomes so savagely disillusioned by war that he begins to lose his grip on reality. Before he leaves for the front he falls in love with a married woman who, pregnant by her husband, will not allow Shin to make love to her. For his part, Shin is not at all downhearted. As if in compensation he transfers his affections to his army rifle, treating it with all the care that one would normally lavish on a valued mistress. Later, during the war, Shin is instructed to shoot a woman who reminds him of his love – using the very same rifle. From this point onwards his army career declines rapidly until defeat finally comes.

Shockingly, Kojima succeeds in making us feel a degree of sympathy for the narrator of "The Rifle," a man who is, after all, a common war criminal. He achieves this by having him tell his tale in a completely factual manner, without making any excuses for his behavior. That its one optimistic element – Shin's instinctive reaction against his crime – leads to his subsequent degeneration is evidence of the story's bleakness. For once in Kojima's work it is devoid of satire in the accepted sense.

In the January 1953 issue of *Bungakukai* a number of young Japanese writers were identified by Yamamoto Kenkichi in an article which bore the title *"Daisan no shinjin"* ("The Third Generation of New Writers"). The expression had a certain ring to it. YOSHIYUKI JUNNOSUKE, one of the writers so mentioned, thought it not unlike "third-rate" or even "third class" as applied to a train compartment. This interpretation notwithstanding, the editors of *Bungakukai* decided to organize regular meetings of the Third Generation in the hope that a new literary movement would begin to form. Thus the *Ichi-ni kai* (One-Two Association) was started, and, as its name implied, met regularly on the twelfth of each month. Kojima was one of its original members, as were YASUOKA SHŌTARŌ, Miura Shumon, Shimao Toshio, and also Gomi Yasusuke who had just won the Akutagawa Prize.

From the day of its artificial inception the One-Two Association was never a true literary school but merely a group of individual writers who occasionally met socially. It changed its name to *Kōsō no kai* (The Conceptions Society) in 1954, when it was greatly cheered up by the activities of ENDŌ SHŪSAKU who helped promote its members to the world of radio and television. Today, scholars regard the association as a phenomenon of interest chiefly because several members, Kojima among them, soon followed Gomi in being awarded the Akutagawa Prize.

Kojima's prize-winning story was "The American School," and without question it fully deserved the honor. Set in 1948 it describes a visit by a group of twenty-nine Japanese English-language teachers to one of the American schools established for children of the

Occupation forces. In depicting the various reactions of the group to their first direct experience of American culture Kojima created a classic satire, as moving as it is comic.

The central figure of "The American School" is Isa, who actually loathes the English language even though he teaches it. He believes, perhaps with some justification, that a knowledge of English tends to undermine one's identity as a Japanese. Indeed, much the same point was made by the late Marshall McLuhan in *The Gutenberg Galaxy*, when he spoke of the Japanese as "retaining the core of auditory tribal unity and total togetherness." Be that as it may, Isa's embarrassment at the prospect of being challenged to give a joint demonstration of teaching skills with the swaggering Yamada, a former army commander, is almost too real for the reader's comfort.

During the characters' eight-mile walk to the American School we are made to wonder what mysterious request Michiko, the only woman in the group, intends to make of Isa, her silent walking companion. Arriving at their destination the visitors are astounded by the school's luxury, yet they feel out of place and huddle together "like a flock of peasants being herded around the capital." Michiko, who feels especially drab in the shadow of a foreign lady, finally makes her request, asking Isa if she may borrow his chopsticks to eat her packed lunch. That Kojima is able to turn such a trivial matter into an event of heroic proportions is a remarkable achievement, and to this day "The American School" remains one of his finest works.

Kojima's other stories in 1954 included "*Bishō*" ("Smile"), "*Hoshi*" ("Stars"), and a longer work called "*Uma*" ("The Horse"). They all abound with irony, pain, and the dilemmas of men who have not yet found their bearings in postwar society. In "*Bishō*" a father returns home after four years at war to discover that his infant son is handicapped. Unable to accept it, he turns his anger against the boy, only to be shamed when a photographer asks him to "smile" and a falsely cheerful picture of father and son appears next morning in the newspaper.

"Stars" is readily available in English translation and is the story of a luckless Japanese–American who, while visiting Japan to see his grandfather, is drafted into the army to fight against his fellow countrymen in World War II. As a lowly "buck private," George Sugihara is reviled by the other soldiers who display their contempt for a man with a foreign education. Only his ugly comrade-in-arms, Hikida, receives worse treatment: a fact which gives Sugihara a certain feeling of security and comfort. Aware that the pecking-order of the army is established through rank, he becomes obsessed with insignia: with the stars that symbolize identities, values, and goals. Like Shin in "The Rifle" he sells his soul to the army and suffers for it when he is stripped of his insignia at the end of the war.

If Kojima's returning war veterans are crippled psychologically, those whom he depicts as making their lives in postwar Japan are equally afflicted by forces beyond their control. In "The Horse," the unnamed husband is completely dominated by his wife who insists on reconstructing their home at vast expense. Unable to stop her, he is appalled to discover that even as a provider he is superfluous, for she rents out the main room as a stable for a friend's horse. Ironically, the "horse" of the title may actually refer to the deposed master, and the story as a whole is a fine satire on the *mai-hōmu shugi* (homeownership ethic) which spread rapidly during Japan's economic recovery.

Kojima continued to write while teaching English and American literature at Meiji University. For several years, however, his work did not reach the standard he achieved in the early 1950s, and neither his long novel *Shima* (*1955, Island*) nor *Yoru to hiru no kusari* (*1960, The Chain Between Night and Day*) was well received. More popular were his translations of American short stories, including Irwin Shaw's "The Girls in Their Summer Dresses" and Dorothy Parker's "Big Blonde." The next milestone in his career as a writer of fiction did not come until the 1965 publication of *Hōyō kazoku* (*Embracing Family*), for which he became the first author to receive the newly established Tanizaki Prize.

Embracing Family has been variously described as "important," "gloomy," "harrowing," and even (by the critic Etō Jun) as "anthropocentric." The novel is narrowly focused on a single family, the head of which is Miwa Shunsuke, a university professor whose halfhearted struggle to keep his family together is doomed to failure. Moreover, his reputation as a pioneer of the latest Western ideas is largely misplaced because he is essentially old-fashioned in his psychology. Although he allows his wife to organize their home from top to bottom he is devastated when she takes her freedom a step further by having an affair with a young American soldier. As Kojima's translator, Van C. Gessel, has pointed out: "Now that her adultery has disqualified her in his [Shunsuke's] eyes as a source of values and judgments, he has nowhere else to turn." Ingeniously, the reader too is trapped because, in Professor Gessel's words: ". . . there is no narrative voice to provide answers."

Kojima's reputation in the West is unlikely to grow until some of his longer works have been translated. He has, however, been greatly honored in Japan where he received a prestigious humanities award for his collection of critical essays *Watashi no sakka henreki*

(1981, *My Journeys with Great Writers*), and the Noma Prize for his immense novel *Wakareru riyū* (*1982, Reasons for Parting*).

In Japan's fast-evolving society during this century, writers have always been in danger of being left behind. Kojima, in particular, has lived dangerously in this respect, for to Western eyes the Japanese male – prime mover of the world's most successful economy – is anything but ineffectual. Yet in digging beneath the surface this writer has found a host of uncertainties and has placed them on display. His stories, which must be read in a historical context, form a complete catalog of Japanese neuroses. Whether the expression of these feelings has significance beyond the borders of Japan is for the foreign reader to judge.

RECOMMENDED READING

Short Fiction

"The American School." "*Amerikan sukūru. 1954*. 30 pages. (1) Tr. Bernard Susser. *Japan Interpreter*, vol. 11, no. 4, 1977. (2) Tr. William F. Sibley. *Contemporary Japanese Literature*, ed. Howard Hibbett. Knopf, NY, 1977; Tuttle, Tokyo, 1978. Inclusion in Howard Hibbett's classic anthology has made this fine story one of Kojima's most easily obtainable works in the West.

WORKS IN ENGLISH TRANSLATION

Short Fiction

"The American School." "*Amerikan sukūru.*" 1954.

"Happiness." 13 pages. Tr. Tanaka Yukiko. *Japan Quarterly*, vol. 28, no. 4, 1981.

"The Rifle." "*Shōjū.*" 1952. 10 pages. (1) As "Shoju." Tr. Elizabeth Baldwin. *Fact and Fiction: The Modern Short Story*, ed. Robert Detweiler and Glenn Meeter.

William B. Eerdmans, Grand Rapids, MI, 1979. (2) Tr. Lawrence Rogers. *Japan Quarterly*, vol. 34, no. 1, 1987.

"Stars." "*Hoshi.*" 1954. 30 pages. Tr. Van C. Gessel. *The Shōwa Anthology*, vol. 1, ed. Van C. Gessel and Tomone Matsumoto. Kodansha International, Tokyo, 1985.

CRITICAL STUDIES

Gessel, Van C. "Human Handicapped." *The Sting of Life*. Columbia University Press, NY, 1989.
——. "The Literature of Kojima Nobuo, Yasuoka Shōtarō and Endō Shūsaku: Cripples, Clods and Cowards in Contemporary Japanese Literature." Ph.D. diss.,

Columbia University, NY, 1979.
——. "War and Postwar in the Writings of Kojima Nobuo, Yasuoka Shōtarō and Endō Shūsaku." *Transactions of the International Conference of Orientalists in Japan*, no. 23, 1978.

Tanaka, Yukiko. "The Fiction of Kojima Nobuo; A Study of Its Development in the Historical Perspective of Modern Japanese Prose Narrative." Ph.D.diss., University of California, Los Angeles, 1977.

Kunikida DOPPO
(1871–1908)

Novelist and poet. Real name, Kunikida Tetsuo. Born in Chōshi, in Chiba Prefecture. Moved to Tokyo in 1887.

The work of Kunikida Doppo is an acquired taste for Western readers, and not everyone perceives the strength that underlies it. For the author of "River Mist," "Musashino," and "The Self-Made Man" wrote stories that are filled with profound melancholy. His lonely, isolated heroes often appear to be overwhelmed by forces of nature which loom large by comparison to individual human destinies. Nonetheless, the perceptive reader will be aware of the conflicts that motivated Doppo, and will admire his tenacity in coming to terms with them.

There is no better description of Doppo's struggle than the comments made by AKUTAGAWA in his essay "Literary, Too Literary": "Doppo had a keen mind, and at the same time a gentle heart. But they were at odds with each other, which was tragic for him. Because of his sharp mind he couldn't help but look down at the earth, but because of his gentle heart he couldn't help but look up to heaven." In other words, Doppo had tendencies toward both realism and Romanticism, and his uniqueness lies in how he expressed the inner tension that resulted.

Doppo was born Kunikida Kamekichi, in the coastal town of Chōshi, due east of Tokyo. He changed his given name to Tatsuo in 1889, but is universally called by his pen name, Doppo, which means "One who walks alone." Although some controversy surrounds both his parentage and the date of his birth, he was certainly raised by Kunikida Sempachi, a dispossessed samurai who earned a living as a minor official in the judiciary. Sempachi's employment on the court circuit obliged him to move frequently from one part of the country to another. Doppo traveled with him, visiting many towns in Yamaguchi and Hiroshima prefectures before finally settling in the Iwakuni countryside in Yamaguchi.

Hoping to make a career in politics, Doppo moved to Tokyo in 1887 and began studying at a private law school. After only a year he left to join the English department of the college that was later to become Waseda University. There he studied Western literature, including the works of Carlyle, Tolstoy, Dostoievsky, and Wordsworth. He also became a baptized Christian, the ceremony taking place on January 4, 1891.

Inspired chiefly by Wordsworth, Doppo opened a private school in Matsushita, an experience which forms the background to his stories "Teacher Tomioka" and "The Sorrows of a Young Man." However, his growing literary ambition sent him back to Tokyo where he joined the staff of a political newspaper, the *Jiyū shimbun*. Paid very little for his efforts, he reverted once more to teaching, this time at the Tsuruya Gakken school in the town of Saeki in Kyūshū. Fervently idealistic, he had already decided to become a "teacher of mankind" through his writing, yet, by 1894, the year in which the Sino–Japanese war began, he could claim very little progress in this direction.

Readers of ARISHIMA TAKEO's great novel, *Aru onna* (1919, *A Certain Woman*), may know that the heroine who so resembles Emma Bovary was in fact based on Sasaki Nobuko, a *femme fatale* who was briefly married to a famous war reporter. That reporter was none other than Kunikida Doppo. After his pleasant year in Saeki he joined the *Kokumin shimbun* and attracted wide attention with his dispatches from the Japanese patrol vessel, the *Chiyoda-maru*. He met Nobuko on his return from the front, and married her, against her mother's wishes, in November 1895.

The couple had intended to live in sublime rusticity in Hokkaidō, but the fickle Nobuko left her husband in April 1896. Being sensitive and romantic, Doppo was heartbroken, but there was little he could do to win her back. He turned instead to creative writing, concentrating first on poetry, then on "prose-poetry" to express his feelings. Previously he had published only journalism and part one of a biography of Benjamin Franklin. Now, while on vacation with his friend, the novelist TAYAMA KATAI, he was able to write "Gen Oji" (1897, "Old Gen"), one among several stories that later would be frequently translated into English.

Doppo's work between 1897 and 1903 was chiefly Romantic prose-poetry that owed much to Wordsworth. It shows both a deep appreciation of nature and a sense of its "otherness" in a way that Wordsworth might have found disturbing. Doppo's central figures are lonely vagabonds who, despite their inner commitment, have been alienated by human society. They are all in a state of decline: becoming once more at one with nature by blending, physically and spiritually, into the landscape.

In 1897, Doppo remarried and acquired new financial responsibilities which forced him to return to journalism. He became editor of the *Tōyō gahō*, Japan's first pictorial magazine, in March 1903. His stories continued to enlarge his reputation, and he gradually drifted from pure lyricism to placing a greater emphasis on human frailties. One of his most brilliant stories, "Gyūniku to bareisho" (1901, "Meat and Potatoes"), contains a humorous debate between a group of men who favor ideals and others who prefer to compromise for the sake of worldly survival. Like all of Doppo's stories it addressed a subject that was close to his heart.

Kunikida Doppo died at the age of thirty-seven of tuberculosis. Unlike his friend, Tayama Katai, he had never been a member of a literary circle – part of the so-called *bundan that produced the literature of the period. Yet shortly before his death he was already being hailed as the progenitor of the new school of *Naturalism. His last stories included "Kyūshi" (1907, "Death in Poverty"); "Nami no oto" (1907, "The Sound of the Waves"); "Gōgai" (1907, "Extra"); "Take no kido" (1908, "Bamboo Door"); and "Ni-rōjin" (1908, "Two Old Men"). They were all first-rate stories, dealing with the lives of ordinary men.

Doppo himself, however, was by no means an ordinary man. He was one of the most gifted writers of the early modern period. His use of poetic imagery in prose fiction to express strong emotion has scarcely ever been surpassed, and the intensity of his vision is apparent even in translation. Though of a lesser stature than some of the writers who followed him, Doppo will always occupy a special place in the affections of Japanese readers.

RECOMMENDED READING

Short Fiction Collection

River Mist, and Other Stories by Kunikida Doppo. Tr. David Chibbett. Paul Norbuy Publications, Tenterden, Kent, England, 1983. Highly recommended. Contains a representative selection of Doppo's work, including: "The Bonfire," "Meat and Potatoes," "Musashino," and "Old Gen." Has 22-page introduction by the translator and is attractively presented in red boards with gold lettering. Gray dust wrapper features a brush painting by Irene Sanderson.

WORKS IN ENGLISH TRANSLATION

Short Fiction

"The Bamboo Gate." "*Take no kido.*" *1908.* 7 pages. (1) Tr. John Bester. *Japan P.E.N. News*, no. 13, Oct. 1964. (2) Tr. Jay Rubin. *Monumenta Nipponica*, vol. 27, no. 3, 1972.

"Bird of Spring." "*Haru no tori.*" *1904.* 8 pages. (1) As "Haru no tori." Tr. Takamasa Sasaki. *Eigo no kenkyu to kyoju.* Tokyo, 1940. (2) As "Spring Birds." Tr. Tsutomu Fukuda. *Pacific Spectator*, vol. 8, no. 3, 1954; *Sanshō Dayū, and Other Stories.* Hokuseido, Tokyo, 1970. (3) As "A Bird of Spring." Tr. Jean Funatsu. *Journal of Oriental Literature*, vol. 7, 1966. (4) As "The Spring Bird." Tr. Atsumu Kanayama. *The Reeds*, no. 10, 1965. (5) Tr. David Chibbett. *Monumenta Nipponica*, vol. 26, nos. 1–2, 1971; *River Mist, and Other Stories.*

"Death." "*Shi.*" *1908.* 10 pages. Tr. Thomas E. Swann. *Monumenta Nipponica*, vol. 24, no. 3, 1969.

"The Deer Hunt." "*Shikagari.*" *1898.* 8 pages. (1) Tr. Miyuki Tobe. *The Deer Hunt, Those Days.* Hyoronsha, Tokyo, 1982. (2) *River Mist, and Other Stories.*

"Driven to Death." "*Kyūshi.*" *1907.* 10 pages. Tr. Iwao Matsubara. *Tokyo Nichinichi*, Oct. 24, 1924.

"The Fatalist." "*Unmei ronja.*" *1903.* 20 pages. (1) Tr. Tsutomu Fukuda. *Eigo Kenkyu*, vol. 42, nos. 10–12, 1953; vol. 43, nos. 2–3, 1954. (2) As "The Man of Fate." Tr. Kenshiro Honma. *The Man of Fate and the Evils of Women.* Nanundo, Tokyo, 1981.

"A Friend on Horseback." "*Bajō no tomo.*" *1903.* Tr. Taro Ito. *Osaka Mainichi*, Feb. 7–12, 1928.

"An Honest Man." "*Shōjiki mono.*" *1903.* 10 pages. Tr. Jay Rubin. *Monumenta Nipponica*, vol. 27, no. 3, 1972.

"Letter from Yugahara." "*Yugahara yori.*" *1902.* 6 pages. (1) As "Letter from Yugawara." Tr. Arthur Lloyd. *Model Translations and Dialogues.* Eigo Kenkyusha. Tokyo, 1913. (2) *River Mist, and Other Stories.*

"Meat and Potatoes." "*Gyūniku to bareisho.*" *1901.* 16 pages. (1) As "Beef and Potatoes." Tr. Arthur Lloyd. *Model Translations and Dialogues.* (2) Tr. Leon Zolbrod. *The Heart Is Alone*, ed. Richard McKinnon, Hokuseido, Tokyo, 1957; *Orient West*, vol. 9, no. 3, 1964; *The Japanese Image*, vol. 2, ed. M. Schneps and A. D. Coox. Orient West, Tokyo, 1966; (3) *River Mist, and Other Stories.*

"Musashino." *"Musashino." 1898.* 16 pages. (1) Tr. Kyohei Yamamoto. *Living English,* 1932. (2) Extract as "A Diary of Musashino." Tr. Kazutomo Takahashi. *Eigo Seinen,* vol. 62, nos. 9–10, 1930. (3) *River Mist, and Other Stories.*

"Old Gen." *"Gen oji." 1897.* 12 pages. (1) As "Uncle Gen." Tr. Akira Ota. *New World,* Aug. 1946. (2) Tr. Sam Houston Brock. (Abridged). *Modern Japanese Literature,* ed. Donald Keene. Grove Press, NY, 1956; Tuttle, Tokyo, 1957; Grove Weidenfeld, NY, 1989 paperback. (3) Tr. Jay Rubin. *Monumenta Nipponica,* vol. 27, no. 3, 1972. (4) *River Mist, and Other Stories.*

"Phantoms." *"Maboroshi." 1898.* 5 pages. *River Mist, and Other Stories.*

"River Mist." *"Kawagiri." 1898.* 9 pages. *River Mist, and Other Stories.*

"The Self-Made Man." *"Hibon naru bonjin." 1903.* 8 pages. *River Mist, and Other Stories.*

"The Suburbs." *"Kōgai." 1900.* 12 pages. Tr. Jay Rubin. *Monumenta Nipponica,* vol. 27, no. 3, 1972.

"Sunbeams Through the Mist." *"Naki warai." 1907.* 5 pages. Tr. Iwao Matsubara. *Eigo Seinen,* vol. 58, nos. 7–9, 1928.

"Third Party." *"Daisansha." 1903.* 16 pages. (1) As "Love as Cruel as the Grave." Tr. Asataro Miyamori. *Representative Tales of Japan.* Sanko Shoten, Tokyo, 1917. (2) *River Mist, and Other Stories.*

"Those Days." *"Ano jibun." 1906.* 18 pages. Tr. Miyuki Tobe. *The Deer Hunt, Those Days.* Hyoronsha, Tokyo, 1982.

"Those Unforgettable People." *"Wasure-enu hitobito." 1898.* 11 pages. (1) As "Men I Shall Never Forget." Tr. Arthur Lloyd. *Japan Magazine,* vol. 1, 1910. (2) As "Unforgettable People." Tr. Jay Rubin. *Monumenta Nipponica,* vol. 27, no. 3, 1972. (3) *River Mist, and Other Stories.*

"Tomioka Sensei." *"Tomioka Sensei."* Composed 1902. 61 pages. Tr. Arthur Lloyd. *Model Translations and Dialogues.*

"Woman Trouble." *"Jonan." 1903.* 21 pages. (1) As "Petticoat Dangers." Tr. Arthur Lloyd. *Model Translations and Dialogues.* (2) As "The Evils of Women." Tr. Kenshiro Honma. *The Man of Fate and The Evils of Women.* Nanundo, Tokyo, 1981. (3) *River Mist, and Other Stories.*

Poems

"Freedom in the Mountains: Entering into the Woods." Tr. James R. Morita. *Journal of the Association of Teachers of Japanese,* vol. 10, nos. 2–3, 1975.

"In the Woodland Freedom Exists." Tr. Shigeshi Nishimura. *The Current of the World,* vol. 30, no. 1, 1953.

Prose Poetry

"The Bonfire." *"Takibi." 1896.* 5 pages. (1) Tr. Thomas E. Swann. *Asian Studies,* vol. 6, April 1968. (2) Tr. Jay Rubin. *Monumenta Nipponica,* vol. 25, nos. 1–2, 1970. (3) *River Mist, and Other Stories.*

"Poetic Images." *"Shisō." 1898.* 4 pages. *River Mist, and Other Stories.*

"The Stars." *"Hoshi." 1896.* 3 pages. *River Mist, and Other Stories.*

CRITICAL STUDIES

Atkins, Dennis H. "The Life and Short Stories of Kunikida Doppo." Ph.D. diss., University of Washington, Seattle, 1970.

Rubin, Jay. "Kunikida Doppo." Ph.D. diss., University of Chicago, Chicago, 1970.

Woods, Sharon E. "The Fiction of Kunikida Doppo." Ph.D. diss., Columbia University, NY, 1971.

MARUYA Saiichi
(1925–   )

Novelist, translator, and critic. Real name, Nemura Saiichi. Born in
Tsuruoka City, Yamagata Prefecture.

Maruya Saiichi is a writer who, while retaining a serious intent,
has swept away every trace of solemnity from the modern Japanese
novel. His truly outstanding talent for comedy is matched by an
equally acute sense of social observation. With his brilliant novel
Tatta hitori no hanran (1972, *Singular Rebellion*) he won much
admiration in the West, even though it appeared in translation a
full sixteen years after its original publication. As a scholar of
English literature, Maruya has translated works by Joyce, Graham
Greene, and Jerome K. Jerome into Japanese and has published
many volumes of critical essays. At times his wide knowledge of
other writers' works has intruded into his own creative territory,
an occupational hazard of well-read novelists. Nonetheless, even at
his most scholarly he is unfailingly entertaining. It is hoped that
many more of his works will appear in English during the coming
years.

Maruya was born Nemura Saiichi, the second son of a medical doctor who ran a private practice in Yamagata Prefecture. Growing up in the difficult period before World War II he found himself drafted into the army under the Students' Mobilization Law while he was still attending Niigata High School. He resumed his studies after the war, later entering the Department of English Literature at Tokyo University from which he graduated in 1950.

While lecturing at both Kokugakuin University and Tokyo University, Maruya acquired an enviable reputation as a translator. His main specialty was James Joyce, of whom he had made an intense study. In translating *Ulysses,* he ventured where few other scholars dared to tread, producing an excellent version of a novel that poses many challenges to the translator. Since then he has at various times rendered many of Graham Greene's novels into Japanese, ignoring the "great works" and concentrating on the famous "entertainments" such as *Loser Takes All.* That Maruya puts a high value on the idea of entertaining the reader, while writing with a serious purpose in mind, is shown by one of his early essays, *"Entāteinmento to wa nani ka?"* (1953, "What Is Entertainment?").

Maruya's first novel was called *Ehoba no kao o sakete* (1960, *To Flee the Face of Jehovah*) and, not surprisingly, was influenced by James Joyce whose work he had studied so assiduously. Based on the story of Jonah in the Old Testament it is a strange blend of ancient and modern ideas, depicting the plight of an individual who is lost in a mythical and largely irrational world. It was published serially in *Chitsujo (Order)* between the years 1952 and 1960.

Maruya developed his talent for short fiction with *"Okurimono"* (1966, "A Present"), published in *Fukei.* For his short stories he was three times runner-up for the Akutagawa Prize before eventually winning it in 1968 for *"Toshi no nokori"* ("Life's Remaining Year"). In the interim, however, he produced a work on a larger scale called *Sasa makura (Pillows of Grass),* published in book form in 1966.

In *Pillows of Grass* Maruya elaborated one of the themes for which he is now famous: that of dodging military service. There was certainly an element of wishful thinking in his espousal of such a theme, because, as already mentioned, he was himself drafted into the army when he was a teenager. The hero of his novel, Hamada Shōsuke, is somewhat more mature at twenty years of age, being an assistant section head in the General Affairs section of a university. He simply bows out, avoiding the authorities by wandering around the country, sleeping rough, and eventually by posing as the husband of Akiko, with whom he becomes acquainted on his travels. He lives with Akiko until the war is over, only then discovering that his mother has committed suicide in the interim and that both his father and brother have fallen ill. Faced with these new problems he draws strength from recalling his worst moment: being interrogated by the police during his absence without leave. Remembering how he tricked them into believing him innocent he philosophizes: "One has to be a traveler on a dangerous journey until the end."

If *Pillows of Grass* seems more somber than the stories by which Maruya is known to the West, it shows a darker side that is always present in his work but is usually cloaked in humor. Despite his affinities with English literature there is much evidence that his main influence has been KOJIMA NOBUO who pioneered a biting and realistic brand of satire during the postwar years. Ten years senior to Maruya, Kojima developed a literary technique which combined close attention to everyday detail with a notable absence of any judgmental narrative voice. Likewise, Maruya appears to create genuine fiction even when he includes one or two elements of his direct experience. He stands, if anything, at a greater distance from his material than Kojima from his, while his characters are generally much more resourceful and assured.

Maruya's maturing skills found their full expression in *Singular Rebellion*. A comic novel *par excellence*, it won the Tanizaki Prize in the year of its publication, 1972. Over the years it has become a modern classic, remaining as fresh today as when it was first written. Moreover, it reads exceptionally well in Dennis Keene's English translation. It is the sort of novel that one wishes Margaret Drabble could have written had she retained her Cambridge wit from the 1960s while analyzing London life in the 1970s.

The fictional narrator of *Singular Rebellion* is one Mabuchi Eisuke, a former civil servant who has successfully changed his career in midstream by joining a Tokyo-based electrical company. When the novel opens in 1969 Mabuchi has recently become a director of his new firm and has recovered his spirits after the death of his wife a year ago. He is ready to enjoy life if something interesting should come along, and, needless to say, it does. The first glimpse we have of Mabuchi's off-center relationship to conventional society is when he starts a love affair with Yukari, a fashion model half his age.

Delightful as the opening chapters are, *Singular Rebellion* does not reveal its greatest qualities until after Mabuchi has made an honest woman of Yukari. Only then does the novel's humor begin to vibrate in earnest. Suddenly, we are made aware that Yukari's father – an art historian with a devious intellect – has gently pressed Mabuchi into marrying his daughter before the unsuspecting company director discovers the truth. And the truth is simply that

Yukari's maternal grandmother is about to be released from jail where she has been serving a life sentence for murdering her ex-husband with a razor.

A plain synopsis of *Singular Rebellion* from this point onward, complete with student revolutions and purple-suited art critics, would only make it seem farfetched. However, no author is more careful than Maruya in making every step of his narrative seem plausible. It is even plausible that Mabuchi, although basically conservative and mindful of others' opinions, is quite unable to exclude the murderous Granny Utako from his new family home. She moves in with the newlyweds and proves to be a wonderfully convincing mixture of "refined old lady" and "survival-conscious ex-convict." In his weaker moments Mabuchi believes she has gate-crashed his home merely because he has that rarest of assets: an efficient family maid whose cooking is excellent.

The very idea of a middle-aged Japanese businessman as an habitual nonconformist may seem comic to the English and American readers. Yet although *Singular Rebellion* is essentially a humorous novel it also works on a serious level as a critical examination of social conventions. Nothing escapes Mabuchi's eye. Moreover, he remains almost absurdly calm in the midst of crisis, weighing difficult situations with his astute business mind. In trying to solve each of the problems thrust upon him he acts every bit as heroically (if not quite as recklessly) as NATSUME SŌSEKI's Botchan.

Since the publication of *Singular Rebellion* in the West, a volume of Maruya's shorter works has been translated and published under the title *Rain in the Wind*. The four stories represent a fair sampling of his work and are of a consistently high quality. The title story, "*Yoko shigure*" (1975), finds the author in a traditional and scholarly mood, depicting a narrator who uncovers a closely concealed family secret while engaged in an otherwise frivolous episode of literary detection. In "*Daradara zaka*" (*1975*, "The Gentle Downhill Slope") Maruya again shows his firm grasp of how things actually happen, while in "*Jueitan*" (1988, "Tree Shadows") he combines mystery with erudition in his most charming manner.

The fourth story of the collection, "*Yume o kaimasu*" (*1988*, "I'll Buy That Dream"), is slight by contrast, if highly original. In it, a prostitute called Rika, on having a dream described to her by a friend, repeats it to a customer (a theological professor) while pretending it to be true in actuality. The dream, in which a model wishes to reverse her cosmetic surgery so that she can return to her previous self, intrigues the professor greatly. Finding an old photograph of Rika he looks closely at it for similarities between her old and new faces. Naturally, he finds some and is delighted, for it confirms his favorite theological theory: that behind every angel with wings there is a divine messenger without them. If somewhat contrived, the story is urbane, witty, and entertaining, like most of Maruya's work.

One hopes that some of Maruya's critical writings might one day be translated, for, with one or two exceptions, there is very little Japanese criticism of any sort available to English readers. In Japan, many of Maruya's essays have been collected into books, which include *"Nashi no tsubute"* (1966, "Have Heard Nothing from Them"); *"Gotoba-in"* (1973, "The Retired Emperor Gotoba"); *"Nihongo no tame ni"* (1974, "For the Japanese Language"); and *"Bunshō dokuhon"* (1977, "The Composition Reader").

In more than one sense, Maruya Saiichi, represents a new peak of maturity in modern Japanese literature. First of all, he is unhampered by the *I-Novel tradition and has the imagination to create true fictions. Second, he has fully assimilated those parts of the Western tradition that are most useful to him. Finally, and perhaps most significantly, he has shaken off the self-doubt afflicting many of his generation and writes with great assurance and fluidity. Many Western readers, coming to Japanese literature for the first time, will find him congenial rather than exotic. He fully deserves his growing reputation in the West.

RECOMMENDED READING

Novel

Singular Rebellion. *Tatta hitori no hanran.* 1972. 412 pages. Tr. Dennis Keene. Andre Deutsch, London, 1988; Paladin, London, 1989. On Deutsch edition, Angus Wilson (who once wrote that modern Japanese fiction was "defeatist") is quoted as saying "I loved it."

Short Fiction Collection

Rain in the Wind, Four Stories. 234 pages. Tr. Dennis Keene. Kodansha International, Tokyo and NY, 1990; Andre Deutsch, London, 1990. The four stories are: "The Gentle Downhill Slope," "I'll Buy That Dream," "Tree Shadows," and "Rain in the Wind." An excellent adjunct to *Singular Rebellion*. Cover of Deutsch edition features *The Maples of Mama, Tekona Shrine*, by Hiroshige.

WORKS IN ENGLISH TRANSLATION

Novel

Singular Rebellion. Tatta hitori no hanran. 1972.

Short Fiction

"The Gentle Downhill Slope." *"Daradara zaka."* 1975. 19 pages. *Rain in the Wind, Four Stories.*

"I'll Buy That Dream." *"Yume o kaimasu."* 1988. 21 pages. *Rain in the Wind, Four Stories.*

"Rain in the Wind." *"Yoko shigure."* 1975. 122 pages. *Rain in the Wind, Four Stories.*

"Tree Shadows." *"Jueitan."* 1988. 62 pages. *Rain in the Wind, Four Stories.*

Miscellaneous

Three-page synopsis of the novel *Pillow of Grass. Sasa makura.* 1966. *Japan P.E.N. News,* no. 23, 1970.

Two-page synopsis of the novel *Sing the National Anthem in a Falsetto Voice. Uragoe de utae Kimigayo. Japanese Literature Today,* no. 8, 1983.

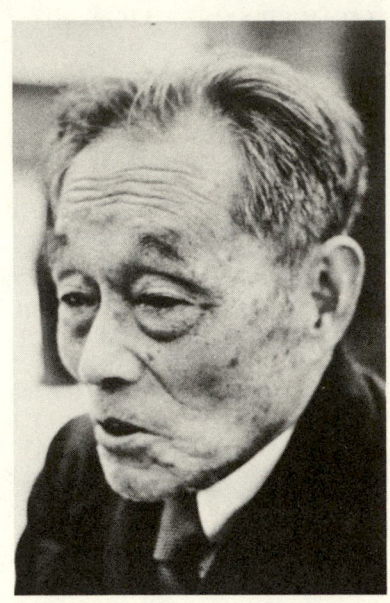

Masamune HAKUCHŌ
(1879–1962)

Critic, novelist, and playwright. Real name, Masamune Tadao. Born in Honami, Okayama Prefecture. Moved to Tokyo at age seventeen.

According to AKUTAGAWA, who rated him as being among the best of the *Naturalists, Masamune Hakuchō produced work that "began and ended with a negation." Such stories as "*Jin'ai*" (*1907*, "Dust") and "*Doro ningyō*" (*1911*, "The Mud Doll"), both of which have been translated into English, display a stark pessimism that falls not far short of despair. Greatly influenced by Zola in choosing to write about the lower classes rather than about those who shared his own wealthy background, he quickly became disillusioned with Christianity, the religion to which he had been converted in his youth. Like many Japanese he felt uncomfortable with alien beliefs, even though he always retained vestiges of a personal faith in Christ. His stories, more highly praised in Japan than elsewhere, tend to be regarded as "cynical" by Westerners, perhaps because they show poverty and hopelessness without much reference to any kind of inspirational belief. To the Japanese, however, they are recognized as accurately representing the hardships of life as experienced by the poor for countless generations. In his long career, Hakuchō wrote many such works, the best of which appeared before 1915. Although he also wrote plays he became especially prominent as the critic who documented the Naturalist movement. His critical works included *"Bundan jimbutsu hyōron"* (1932, "A Critique of Figures in the Literary World") and *Shizen shugi seisui shi* (1948, *The Rise and Fall of Naturalism*). In these and other essays he probed beneath the various "masks" of the Naturalist writers to examine their personal qualities and motivations.

Hakuchō was born, Masamune Tadao, in a fishing village in Okayama Prefecture where his family were wealthy landowners. He was a brilliant student who developed an early interest in literature, enjoying the works of *Bakin, *Chikamatsu, and other popular writers of the *Edo period. Like many other young intellectuals he was influenced by the Christian bias of the magazine *Kokumin no tomo* (*The People's Friend*), published by *Tokutomi Sohō from 1887 onwards. Thus, when he left Okayama at age seventeen to attend Tokyo Semmon Gakkō (now Waseda University) he was already acquainted with Christianity. He read the works of that most prominent Japanese Christian, *Uchimura Kanzō (1861–1930), whose lectures he attended prior to being baptized by Uemura Masahisa. Meanwhile he studied English literature, a course which included TSUBOUCHI SHŌYŌ's lectures on Shakespeare, and graduated in 1898.

The sudden outbreak of Christianity among Japanese intellectuals in the 1890s deserves a word of explanation. Many leading writers were affected by it, including SHIMAZAKI TŌSON, KUNIKIDA DOPPO, SHIGA NAOYA, KINOSHITA NAOE, and ARISHIMA TAKEO. It may be seen as an inevitable corollary of Westernization, even if those who had the deepest understanding of Western culture (such as NATSUME SŌSEKI and MORI ŌGAI) held firm to traditional beliefs. In fact, the movement lacked religious fervor to an almost astonishing degree. Far from being a latter-day Savonarola, Uchimura promoted a mild brand of New England Protestantism which appealed more as philosophy than as religion. Its emphasis upon the believer's personal relationship to God was attractive because it suggested that there was an authority higher than the state. It gave young writers a perspective from which they could criticize the recently founded Meiji state without appearing to be old-fashioned or "feudal."

Hakuchō, having no interest in politics whatsoever, had little practical use for Christianity and rejected it almost as soon as he was baptized. When he was seriously ill he was comforted by the idea of a personal God, but on recovery he began to dislike

Christianity's condemnation of worldly pleasure. In a letter dated January 1901 to his brother the poet Masamune Atsuo (translated here by Katō Shūichi), he said: "At heart I was unenthusiastic about martyrdom, and further, when I realize that I often feel towards mankind not a love but a hate, I can no longer pretend to be a Christian."

In 1901 Hakuchō began contributing to the literary supplement of the *Yomiuri shimbun*, and published his first fiction in 1904. He won a reputation as a new Naturalist writer when his story "Dust" was published in the magazine *Shumi* (*Taste*) in 1907. Describing the dreary life of a newspaper proofreader, it evokes an atmosphere of physical and spiritual aridity, symbolized by the dust which permeates the city. Like other Naturalist works it concentrates on the minutiae of daily existence, examined without the mediation of any sentimentality.

The Japanese literary movement of Naturalism (*shizen shugi*) was really quite unlike any movement in the West to which similar names might be applied. It began, essentially, with the publication of Kunikida Doppo's second collection of short stories, *Doppo-shū*, in 1905. Although it would be an exaggeration to call him a Naturalist writer as such, Doppo was certainly both realistic in his observations and completely ingenuous when describing his feelings. The fact that he "wore his heart on his sleeve" greatly endeared him to the younger generation who were tired of the artifice of OZAKI KŌYŌ and the *Ken'yūsha. All the optimism of the early *Meiji period had long since faded, and the mood among intellectuals was one of disillusionment and doubt. The soul-searching Naturalists who came after Doppo were thus inclined to reject fiction in favor of autobiography, and the imagination in favor of pure reportage of their immediate surroundings. Hakuchō helped them to define themselves and he enhanced their identity as an influential literary movement. In 1905 he praised Doppo highly in his essay "On Reading the *Doppo-shū*," and produced a theory of literature which emphasized the importance of re-creating objective reality. He attacked Kōyō for his lack of realism, and went on to write stories himself in a truly Naturalistic vein, including "Dust," mentioned above.

Centered on the campus of Waseda University, Japanese Naturalism reached its peak between 1906 and 1910 and began to decline after 1912. It was largely the product of young writers who had come to Tokyo from the provinces, and its most accomplished exponents were Shimazaki Tōson, TAYAMA KATAI and TOKUDA SHŪSEI. It was characterized chiefly by its pervasive gloom, its obvious sincerity, and the tendency of its authors to confess their most intimate secrets at every opportunity. It is important to note, however, that although it was the Naturalist writer Tayama Katai who produced the first *I-Novel, *Futon* (*1907, The Quilt*), the I-Novel tradition outlasted the Naturalist movement and in fact continues to this day. The distinction between the two is hard to grasp on first acquaintance, but this is not surprising because elements of Naturalism can sometimes recur when least expected. Yet in direct contrast to the movement which produced it, the I-Novel (*watakushi shōsetsu*) proved to be a very flexible form of expression and it permitted the novelist to venture into varying degrees of fiction that went far beyond the bounds considered proper by the Naturalists. For example, writers of the late Meiji period would have found DAZAI OSAMU's semi-autobiographical stories completely baffling in their deliberate mixing of fact and fiction. Yet Dazai was an I-Novelist, as indeed were many writers who were completely opposed to Naturalism.

In 1908 Hakuchō published a succession of works beginning with *"Doko-e"* ("Where To?"), and followed by *"Tamatsukiya"* ("Billiards Hall"), *"Satsuki-nobori"* ("May Streamer"), and *Nikazoku* ("Two Families"). *"Doko-e,"* generally reckoned to be the best of his stories, depicts a thoroughgoing nihilist who can find no pleasure in life whatsoever. The hero, Kenji, is undoubtedly a projection of the author himself, although his miseries may well have been exaggerated for literary effect.

Unlike many Naturalists, Hakuchō did not always write about himself. In *"Bikō"* (1910, "Glimmer of Light"), for example, he wrote about a woman who survives by becoming the mistress of one man after another. As a person she is no more sympathetic than most of Hakuchō's characters, but she "gets by" in the only way that she understands. "The Mud Doll" is a more personal work, describing the author's complete lack of feeling for his young wife; while *"Ushibeya no nioi"* (1916, "The Stench of the Cowshed") delves into the lives of three generations of women in a fishing village, not unlike the one in which the author was raised.

Like Tokuda Shūsei, Hakuchō continued to enhance his reputation with Naturalist stories long after the movement itself had declined. His work included *"Irie no hotori"* (1915, "By a Small Bay"), an autobiographical story describing his childhood home ("a large, old-fashioned house by an inlet") from which he was always anxious to escape: "Whenever I left the village my spirits lifted." For many years following 1915 he devoted himself to the theater – an early love, and one of the chief reasons why he had come to Tokyo in the first place. His plays included *Jinsei no kōfuku* (1924, *Happiness in Life*); *Azuchi no haru* (1926, *Spring in Azuchi*), and *Mitsuhide to Jōha* (1926).

As a critic, Hakuchō earned the respect of Japanese and Western scholars alike. In *The Rise and Fall of Naturalism* he produced a definitive work, and one to which scholars often refer when they discuss Tōson, Doppo, Shūsei, or *Iwano Hōmei. It was he who identified the period immediately following the Russo–Japanese War as being "an age of confession" when these writers, led by Tayama Katai with *The Quilt*, pioneered autobiographical fiction. Not overly impressed with *The Quilt* itself, Hakuchō acknowledged it nonetheless as a milestone. For his part, Katai mentioned Hakuchō in his memoir *Tokyo no sanjū-nen* (1917, *Thirty Years in Tokyo*), describing him as "a short, small-framed person with a rather cold manner." He admired many of his stories, including *"Rakujitsu"* (1909, "Setting Sun") and "Glimmer of Light," but thought they revealed a "dispirited, miserable author." Indeed, Hakuchō appears to have been a figure of fun in the Tayama household because of his habit of leaving abruptly without speaking whenever he found Katai absent. When he did speak (Katai noted): "His remarks were always negative."

Among Naturalists, Hakuchō is always most closely associated with Chikamatsu Shūkō (1876–1944), not because of any similarity in their work, but because, coming from the same district, they had known each other since childhood. Although Shūkō positively idolized women, the misogynist Hakuchō was said to have once stolen a mistress from him. It was this same woman who became the heroine of "Glimmer of Light."

Hakuchō's career declined in the late 1930s and continued to do so throughout the war. He refused to join any government-run literary organizations until he was virtually compelled to become a member of the Imperial Academy of Art in 1940. In 1943 he succeeded Shimazaki Tōson as the president of the Japan P.E.N. Club and was made head of the Japan Patriotic Literature Society in 1944. His only novel during this period was a long childhood reminiscence called *Nenashigusa* (1942, *Duckweed*) which he serialized for eight months before it was finally discontinued. As the war grew worse, life for Hakuchō and his wife became increasingly difficult and had they not moved to Karuizawa they would almost certainly have been killed, for their Tokyo home was destroyed in an air raid in May 1945. Hakuchō's literary output was reduced to zero. As his English-language biographer Robert Rolf describes it: "The life to which the militarists had led the Japanese in the last year of the war allowed no time for art; there was only survival."

In his later years, Hakuchō returned to writing fiction. "*Jinsei kyōfu zu*" (1956, "A Chart of the Dread of Life") contained elements of fantasy, while *Nihon dasshutsu* (*1950–53*, "Escape from Japan") was subtitled "A Tale for Children," but left unfinished. Having twice traveled to the West (in 1928–29 and 1936–37), Hakuchō may often have wished to leave Japan for good – just as he once wanted to leave his childhood home. But one doubts if he could ever have lived in the West like Sōseki or Ōgai. If he pretended to hate his fellow Japanese it was more likely because, familiarity breeding contempt, he regarded them as tiresome relatives rather than as hostile strangers. Essentially an intellectual whose cool objectivity aided his criticism as much as it hindered his creative writing, Hakuchō was an integral part of the literary scene for over half a century.

RECOMMENDED READING

Short Fiction

"Dust." "Jin'ai." 1907. 8 pages. Tr. Robert Rolf. *Monumenta Nipponica*, vol. 25, nos. 3–4, 1970.

WORKS IN ENGLISH TRANSLATION

Fiction

"Dust." "Jin'ai." 1907.
"Home." "Kikyō." 8 pages. *Contemporary Japan*, vol. 2, no. 3, 1933.
"The Mud Doll." "*Doro ningyō.*" 1911. 15 pages. Tr. Gregg M. Sinclair and Kazo Suita. *Tokyo People, Three Stories from the Japanese.* Keibunkan, Tokyo, 1925.
"Something for Nothing." "*Hisa san.*" 16 pages. Tr. Asataro Miyamori. *Representative Tales of Japan.* Sanko Shoten, Tokyo, 1917.

Essays

"The Guest of One Afternoon." *Japan Times*, Dec. 23, 1928.
"Review of Mr. Hosoda's Novel: *Shinri no Haru.*" Tr. Einosuke Omiya. *Eigo Seinen*, vol. 66, nos. 4–5, 1931.

CRITICAL STUDIES

Rolf, Robert. *Masamune Hakuchō.* Twayne Publishers, Boston, 1979.
———. "Shūsei, Hakuchō, and the Age of Literary Naturalism 1907–1911." Ph.D. diss., University of Hawaii, Honolulu, 1975.

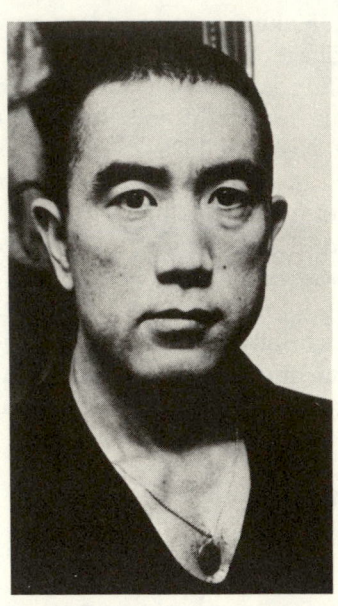

MISHIMA Yukio
(1925–1970)

Novelist, playwright, and essayist. Real name, Hiraoka Kimitake. Born and resided in Tokyo.

No Japanese person in the twentieth century, with the possible exception of the emperor himself, has achieved such fame in the West as Mishima Yukio. Even people who cannot name a single Japanese industrialist, banker, or prime minister will respond with a spark of recognition to a mention of his name. His spectacular suicide in 1970 continues to identify him in the popular imagination as representing everything that is different, strange, and inexplicable about Japan. After all, everyone knows that he was a famous writer, and yet no Western writer has ever been reported as having led a private army like that commanded by Mishima at the time of his death. Add to that his apparent rightwing fanaticism, his much-publicized body-building activities, and the plethora of magazine photographs confirming him as an outrageous exhibitionist, and one begins to acquire a fascinating but possibly repellent image of Mishima as a man. It can deter even the most broadminded person from approaching his art, for what can one possibly hope to learn from an artist who was clearly so misguided in life?

The truth about Mishima Yukio is therefore obscured by the sensationalism that usually accompanies the films, books, and articles about him. Even serious biographies are invariably adorned with pictures of the naked Mishima kissing a rose or brandishing a samurai sword, or of the fanatical Mishima addressing the troops Mussolini-style. Never in the history of literature has an author's reputation been so dramatically colored by his own mischievous publicity. In the book that made him famous, *Kamen no kokuhaku* (1949, *Confessions of a Mask*), he said that even as a boy he was intent on playing his part on the stage of life without ever revealing his true self. Yet something very close to the real truth about Mishima *can* be discovered. It can be found in his work, in the dozens of novels, stories, and plays that he produced during a career that blazed at full strength for a brief, quarter century.

To a perceptive reader, the essential truth about him can be gleaned from the opening pages of *Shiosai* (1954, *The Sound of Waves*), the novel he later called "that joke on the public." For whatever one's preconceptions of Mishima, they vanish instantly under the spell of his perfectly controlled imagination. His best works are fully formed and have a life of their own quite apart from all the half-understood details of his personal psychology. There need be no doubt whatsoever that many of his novels, stories, and plays are classics of modern literature and that his long-term literary reputation is secure.

In the opinion of most critics, Mishima's greatest novel is *Kinkakuji* (1956, *The Temple of the Golden Pavilion*), a mysterious yet perfectly sustained metaphor of beauty that invites detailed critical elucidation. *The Sound of Waves*, already mentioned, is more accessible and requires no explanation at all. Mishima's work is like that: it varies from one extreme to another and encompasses a wide spectrum of themes, styles, and ideas. For example, he wrote many short stories featuring incidents in the lives of ordinary people, yet he was at his best when depicting men and women who were in some ways exceptional, like himself. Arguably, his best short stories are "*Shigadera shōnin no koi* (1954, "The Priest of Shiga Temple and His Love") and "*Mikumano mōde*" (1965, "Act of Worship"), both of which demonstrate his feeling for traditional Japanese aesthetics. He could write with great insight about adolescence, as in the brief story "*Tabako*" (1946, "Cigarette"), or evoke with equal eloquence the horrors of old age, as at the end of his tetralogy *Hōjō no umi* (1965–71, *The Sea of Fertility*), the last installment of which he dispatched on the day of his suicide. In between these two extremes he produced such delightfully fashioned novels as *Utage no ato* (*1960, After the Banquet*) and, in a darker mood, *Gogo no eikō* (1963, *The Sailor Who Fell from Grace with the Sea*). All his work merits attention; the best of it holds our attention throughout with its life-enhancing energy, its vivid imagery, its clarity of thought, and its visionary power.

Mishima Yukio was born Hiraoka Kimitake on January 14, 1925. Both his father, Azusa, and his grandfather, Jōtarō, had been civil servants, the latter having served as the first civilian governor of Sakhalin (the island, off the north of Japan, which later reverted to the Soviet Union). Thus, the family in which Mishima was raised was relatively well-off, if not as prosperous as it had been before the turn of the century. It was also strongly matriarchal; Mishima was brought up largely by his strong-willed grandmother, Natsuko, a woman who was said to have occult powers, so great was the force of her personality.

Physically weak but intellectually precocious, Mishima learned to read and write by the time he was five. In 1931 he entered the Peers' School, an upper-class establishment with a strongly liberal tradition. His unusual home life had already helped to shape his complex psychology, described by some critics as a "dual personality" – both strong-willed and acutely introspective. School presented him with situations that forced him to develop his defenses, and he would frequently retreat into a world of fantasy, generated by a powerful imagination and fueled by literature.

Mishima's taste in literature ranged from ancient to modern and from Eastern to Western. He acquired an intimate knowledge of the Japanese classics, and, equally, enjoyed the contemporary lyric poetry of Tachihara Michizō. His Romantic leanings inclined him towards Novalis, who inspired the Romantic movement in Europe, but he was also strongly drawn to both the work and philosophy of Oscar Wilde. If one adds to these influences his love for all forms of theater, including the *Nō, *Jōruri, and *Kabuki styles, then one has at least some indication of the literary context that Mishima chose for his debut as a writer.

Just before the outbreak of war in the Pacific in 1941 the serialized publication of Mishima's first work began, in the highbrow magazine *Bungei bunka* (*Literary Culture*). Called *Hanazakari no mori* (*The Forest in Full Bloom*), it was a historical novel in five parts, couched in beautiful language and filled with nostalgia for Old Japan. A friend of the professor who taught Japanese to the sixteen-year-old Mishima referred to its author as "the blessed child of ancient history" – the first recorded praise of a writer for whom only war could postpone international acclamation.

War, and in particular the destruction of much of Tokyo, made an enormous impact on Mishima. While he was relieved that his frailty prevented him from being called up by the army, he also (he later said) relished the thought of being destroyed in the bombing. In fact, although he survived, Mishima found his career as a writer was in jeopardy when the war was finally over. He sent his new manuscripts to the most distinguished novelist of the day, SHIGA NAOYA, who dismissed them as romantic fantasies. Said Shiga: "They have no reality. They are no good."

Mishima was not easily deterred. Fully convinced of his own genius he also had an exceptional ability to strengthen himself in whatever areas he considered necessary. If his work lacked "reality" he would write an autobiography – a book that would totally eclipse Shiga's own confessional approach by its brilliance and emotive power. After an unsuccessful attempt to create a full-length novel with *Tōzoku* (1946–48, *The Thieves*), he produced *Confessions of a Mask*, ostensibly an account of his homosexual fantasies but, on a higher plane, a beautiful metaphor of lost innocence and youth. Whereas *The Thieves* had been a derivative piece written under the influence of Raymond Radiguet, *Confessions of a Mask* was strikingly original, and written, if not straight from the heart, then at least straight from a newly discovered and extremely potent literary persona. Before writing either of these works Mishima had already won the support and admiration of KAWABATA YASUNARI (who was forty-six when Mishima first approached him in 1945), and he was therefore well placed to take the literary world by storm.

Divided into four long chapters, *Confessions of a Mask* begins with the narrator's earliest childhood memories, continues with his discovery of a sexuality inextricably linked to "death, blood and muscular flesh," and concludes with a fully dramatized account of his relationship to Sonoko, a girl whom he can neither marry nor forget. By suppressing extraneous information, Mishima concentrates almost exclusively on the growth of his narrator's sexual psychology. He describes how as an infant he identified with figures in fairy tales, but only with those who met violent deaths. He recalls dressing up in feminine clothes in imitation of the actors whom he had seen at the theater. He savors "the soldiers' odor of sweat" and remembers how it aroused in him "a sensuous craving for such things as the destiny of soldiers, the tragic nature of their calling, the distant countries they would see, the ways they would die. . . ." Although he admits to being normal in most other respects, his "heart's leaning toward Death and Night and Blood would not be denied."

For all its absorption with the young man's sexual psychology,

Confessions of a Mask vividly recalls so many childhood incidents that the whole book seems alive with the perversity of youth. The thirteen-year-old narrator pictures himself at school, where, during playtime, obscene games break out "like a morbid disease." He notes how rebelliousness is expressed in subtle ways, as in the wearing of fancy gloves or brightly colored socks. Becoming more intense he goes on to describe how he begins to idolize one of the older boys, who is clearly, in both physique and temperament, his natural opposite. The narrator claims that his falling in love with Omi laid the foundation for his own "systematic structure of likes and dislikes." He says: "Because of him I began to love strength, an impression of overflowing blood, ignorance, rough gestures, careless speech, and the savage melancholy inherent in flesh not tainted in any way with intellect."

It was fortunate for literature that Omi was a love-object rather than a role model for Mishima, if indeed one can equate Mishima with the narrator of the story. Years later, when he had finally decided to join the ranks of muscular men rather than continue regarding them with love and envy, Mishima would again compare the mind unfavorably with the body. He said that during his athletic training he had come to realize that the body "could be intellectualized to a higher degree, could achieve a closer intimacy with ideas, than the spirit." In his youth, however, he lived an entirely cerebral existence, weaving grotesque fantasies that were certainly best kept within the confines of the mind. *Confessions of a Mask* rises to a crescendo of murderous daydreams, including one in which the narrator imagines a well-built classmate, lashed to "a large foreign-style platter" and served up, garnished with salad, to a party of impatient guests. "Holding the knife in my right hand, I began carving the flesh of the breast, gently, thinly at first . . ."

Many critics have questioned the meaning of the "mask" in the title of Mishima's confessions and they suggest that nowhere do we see the author's "real face." It seems impossible that a young man could contrive a work so sophisticated as to be the confession of a persona, yet that is precisely what Mishima appears to have achieved. His response to Shiga's *I-Novels was an I-Novel so revolutionary as to be the product of a Romantic genius of his own invention. He does, however, suggest quite clearly how this came about. His narrator states that in his everyday life he was "masquerading as a normal person," being so highly secretive about his sexuality that no one could possibly suspect him of being either homosexual or perverted. He then goes on to describe how his own knowledge of the deception has corroded any normality which he might have possessed originally. There is an implication, too, that he underwent a long period of introspection that he wishes to conceal from the reader. As a result, he has convinced even himself that his vestiges of original normality were themselves counterfeit and hence part of the mask. The idea is almost *too* clever, *too* paradoxical, and yet *Confessions of a Mask* is entirely plausible as a description of an emergent identity. It even allows glimpses of another self in the passages in which the narrator speaks of the mysterious feeling of grief which Sonoko triggers in him: ". . . a grief moreover that was no part of my masquerade." He knows that Sonoko loves him and that he is bound to lose her through his own equivocation. Overcoming this terrible loss of love is the single most important factor in his life.

The events described in *Confessions of a Mask* tally exactly with what is known of Mishima's early life. Both the realities and the fantasies were to be developed and used in his later work, fulfilling all the potential which is so strongly indicated by the confession. Examples abound, but one could note the "bizarre banquet" as the source for the climax of *The Sailor Who Fell from Grace with the Sea*, and the loss of Sonoko as that for Kiyoaki's loss of Satoko in *Spring Snow*.

By writing *Confessions of a Mask* Mishima developed a method of channeling his psychology into fiction that was to sustain him creatively for the rest of his career. The book moves from impotence to potency, culminating in a magnificent scene in which the "I-character" completely forgets Sonoko even though she is sitting beside him. Not only is the emotional power of her presence eclipsed by the sight of the young laborer in the bar, but the empty chair vacated by him is infinitely more suggestive in its potency as an image. The sunlight glistening on the table highlights the moment's significance, for it refers back to the very first image in the story: to the narrator's recollection of seeing sunlight reflected from the edge of a bath shortly after he is born. Needless to say, he is careful to note that this early memory may be entirely spurious since he was born during the night. No further indication should be needed to confirm that *Confessions* is essentially a novel rather than an autobiography.

Mishima was later to write, in "*Watakushi no henreki jidai*" (1961, "The Days of My Pilgrimage"), of how he conquered his inner monster by creating *Confessions of a Mask*. The monster was not homosexuality but self-deception – and perhaps not even that, but rather the *fear* of self-deception. By vanquishing his fear Mishima discovered his true vocation as a writer of fiction. As Noriko Mizuta Lippit has written (*Reality and Fiction in Modern Japanese Literature*, M. E. Sharpe, New York, 1980): "For Mishima, who preferred masks to real faces, structure to lyricism, and artificial effects to real facts, 'fiction' was the key term." The discovery inspired him with a tremendous will to live.

Along with the recognition he had always craved, Mishima found himself able to make money from his writing after the success of *Confessions of a Mask*. A year or two earlier he had been obliged to become an office worker at the Ministry of Finance, but those days were now gone forever. Editors demanded his work, and he satisfied them by writing a succession of stories and novels. However, not all of these works were intended as serious contributions to literature. Many, such as the novel *Jumpaku no yoru* (1950, *The Pure-White Night*), were "middle-brow" fiction aimed more at entertaining the public than widening the range of his expression. His next attempt at serious fiction was *Ai no kawaki* (1950, *Thirst for Love*), an intensely dramatic story of jealousy and unrequited passion.

Thirst for Love is not one of Mishima's best novels. Indeed, of all his novels in English translation, to which one is inclined to add his shorter fiction as well, it is almost certainly the worst. He endows his heroine, Etsuko, with a heavily adapted version of his own psychology, making her in some ways not unlike the narrator of *Confessions of a Mask*. She is a sophisticated but displaced Tokyoite, who, after the death of her husband, goes to live near Osaka as the mistress of her sixty-year-old father-in-law. On his farm, which enjoys a mouth-watering prosperity (surely aimed at inciting the passions of readers in 1950), Etsuko falls in love with Saburō. He, a bronzed but woefully slow-witted young man, proceeds to make another girl pregnant and in so doing arouses jealousy in Etsuko and envy in her impotent father-in-law. It appears that the author wishes to lock Etsuko into a plausible, if unusual, psychological trap, yet he fails because Etsuko is clearly too intelligent and too self-aware to convince us that she has no other options. One wonders why she remains with these insufferable people. Can it be for the food? Or is it because, as the instrument of the author's sexual fantasies, she must first gouge Saburō's magnificent torso with her nails as a prelude to killing him?

Thirst For Love was not the only mediocre novel that Mishima wrote in his early career. Also in 1950 was the publication of *Ao no jidai* (*The Blue Period*), a story about a student who becomes a moneylender while still at college. Soon afterwards, in 1951, Mishima's most ambitious project to date began its serial publication in *Gunzō* (*The Group*). Called *Kinjiki* (*Forbidden Colors*), it too is markedly inferior to his later work, although it was admired by many and considered very daring when it first appeared. Set among the bars and nightclubs of Tokyo's homosexual underworld,

Forbidden Colors contains little that is memorable except for the relationship between Yūichi and his aging mentor, Hinoki. Yūichi, "an amazingly beautiful young man," is persuaded by Hinoki, a novelist who has been married in turn to a spendthrift, a mad woman, and a slut, to take Yasuko as his wife even though he has no feelings for women. Indeed, Yūichi has no feelings for anyone except himself, and, like Saburō in *Thirst for Love*, his unappealing personality suggests that Mishima was having difficulty in bringing his sexual objects to life. After all, it is the distinguishing mark – the physical imperfection or quirk of behavior – that helps make a character real and believable. Pure Apollonian youths, especially soulless sophisticates who "smile bitter smiles," are excruciatingly dull to meet on the page.

If *Forbidden Colors* was by Mishima's own admission "an unnecessarily confused work," his next major novel, *The Sound of Waves*, was sublimely simple and direct. It was inspired by his visit to Greece in 1953, an experience which changed his life more dramatically than he could possibly have anticipated. Whereas before he had "hankered after Novalis's night and Yeatsian Irish twilights," he now "exchanged a reconciliatory handshake with the sun." (The phrases are taken directly from his 1968 essay "*Taiyō to tetsu*" ["Sun and Steel"]). As a result, *The Sound of Waves* is imbued with the warmth of the sun and a sense of unalloyed happiness that is rare in Mishima's work.

Based on the ancient Greek romance of Daphnis and Chloe, *The Sound of Waves* tells of a love affair between a young fisherman and a village girl on a remote Japanese island. The setting is important, for unlike those of his previous novels it is truly rustic and timeless. Equally, the novel's characters give the impression of being native to the place in which they live. Both of these factors impart an air of conviction and purpose to a story which is by no means as bland as a plot synopsis would suggest. In fact, it is astonishing that the author of *Confessions of a Mask* could produce such a pure vision of heterosexual love, albeit between two essentially androgynous beings like Shinji and Hatsue.

Despite his later disclaimers, Mishima took great pains in writing *The Sound of Waves*. He researched its setting by traveling to the island of Kamishima off the coast of Ise. There he befriended the lighthouse keeper, sailed out in the early mornings with the fishermen, and took copious notes during his ten-day visit. Returning to Tokyo he wrote the novel between September 1953 and April 1954. Even from the first few pages, two qualities are apparent that immediately capture the reader's attention. The first is the exceptional control which the author imposes on his narrative. The second is the descriptive richness of the novel, so unlike much Japanese writing where the simple naming of an object is believed to be sufficient for evoking its properties. At first sight, these two qualities may appear contradictory: with control moving towards greater simplicity and with richness adding greater complexity. Here, however, they are complementary. Far from adding to the novel's complexity, Mishima's "adjectival approach" helps to define more narrowly the world in which the action takes place.

In *The Sound of Waves*, Mishima tantalizes the reader not only by contriving to keep the lovers apart but also by leaving individual scenes unconsummated by any climax. The most famous scene is that in which the two lovers take shelter from a storm and find themselves alone together, completely naked, and kissing in front of a roaring fire. Not even then is there any end to Hatsue's virginity or Shinji's noble innocence, for the couple simply defer their union to a later date. The scenes that follow, too, are deliberately clipped short of their full potential. It is an appropriate device because it seems to echo the action of waves breaking on the shore. Each wave threatens with its energy and then disperses into gentle or playful ripples. Moreover, as each dramatic wave approaches, the author cleverly ensures that the reader will misjudge its size.

In his everyday life Mishima was now gradually shifting his internal balance – or *correcting* the balance, he would have said – from a cerebral to a physical self-awareness. His devotion to athletic training dates from this period: he began by taking up swimming in 1952, progressed to boxing in the following year (a sport at which he was so incompetent that he was nearly always beaten), and went on to serious weight lifting to improve his physical strength in 1955. According to his biographer, John Nathan, "he maintained a regimen of three workouts a week for fifteen years and allowed nothing to interfere." During this time he transformed his body from that of "a weak and anemic creature" (Mishima's words) to one of such muscularity that a photograph of him was requested to illustrate a body-building entry in a popular encyclopedia.

One can enjoy Mishima's novels without any knowledge that in real life he was dedicated to improving his physique. Nonetheless, another dimension is surely added to our understanding of his work from this period onwards if we bear in mind his body-building obsession. For example, Mishima not only transformed his body, he also transformed his prose style. He moved from the variety of ornate and delicate styles which characterize his early work towards an increasingly masculine style based on that of the soldier-writer MORI ŌGAI. For Mishima, a sparse, masculine style was the essential weapon he needed to tame his fertile imagination.

In "Sun and Steel" he said: "There was no telling when the sickly forces of an invisible imagination, still lying in wait, might launch their cowardly assault from without the carefully arrayed fortifications of style." In his brilliant chapter on Mishima in *Modern Japanese Writers*, Makoto Ueda states quite categorically: "He renovated his prose style by renovating his physique. In this respect he shared Tanizaki's view that one's style is rooted in one's physical constitution. Yet whereas Tanizaki believed that one's basic style of writing is physical and therefore cannot be changed, Mishima maintained that one's basic style is physical and therefore *can* be changed."

Not only in matters of style is Mishima's physical obsession relevant to a study of his work, but also in the matter of structure. Few authors have been so intent on shaping everything that suggested the chaotic, the mysterious, or the formless. He molded his body, his life, and his art with exceptional strength of will and a visionary zeal. However, whereas in his early work he believed that language alone was sufficient to impose order, he soon came to realize that the events he described must move according to predetermined structures. If his ideal style was restrained, noble, and austere, his ideal form was one that convinced the reader of the absolute inevitability of events as they unfolded. A story, he wrote in an essay about the art of the novel, should run like a train on schedule. Surprising or unexpected happenings should seem so perfectly natural that the reader, with hindsight, will feel he has always been waiting for them. Isolated coincidences that stand out so jarringly in their role as plot devices should be completely eliminated. Rather, the entire novel should be one huge and fascinating coincidence, its events and characters moving like the stars.

While not fully measuring up to Mishima's ideals, *The Temple of the Golden Pavilion* does at least approximate them. Nonetheless, it has eluded critical interpretation more successfully than most modern Japanese novels. Mishima himself is said to have listened with a "bowed head" while the famous Japanese critic Kobayashi Hideo insisted that it was not a novel at all since it contained no real interpersonal relationships or any dramatic structure derived from such relationships. Rather, said Kobayashi, it was a lyrical poem in which the author's own attitudes on the subject of beauty were stated in too direct a fashion.

For once, Kobayashi was wide of the mark. *The Temple of the Golden Pavilion* contains some brilliantly conceived and fully developed interpersonal relationships – all of them involving the novel's central figure, its narrator Mizoguchi. However, the novel does not depend on those relationships for its artistic success. Far stronger, and dominating the entire work, is the narrator's obsessive relationship to the Golden Temple. As Mishima himself said, in the same talk with Kobayashi: "I wrote about a man, the symbol of the artist, pursued by the idée fixe of beauty. A critic has told me it is an 'artist novel' – with not an artist but a priest as its hero, and that's what makes it unusual and interesting. My intention was something like that."

Mizoguchi is a young priest who has been brought up in a harsh coastal environment where the unreliable weather has, he believes, contributed to his own changeable disposition. He explains to the reader that his handicap – a severe stutter – has placed an obstacle between himself and the outside world: "When finally I reach the outer world after all my efforts, all that I find is a reality that has instantly changed color and gone out of focus – a reality that has lost the freshness that I had considered fitting for myself, and that gives off a half-putrid odor." At school he would imagine himself as a cruel tyrant, with retainers listening in an agony of anticipation to his every half-formed word. His father, a simple country priest, taught him that there is nothing on Earth more beautiful than the Golden Temple, an idea that Mizoguchi found disturbing. "At the thought that beauty should already have come into this world unknown to me, I could not help feeling a certain uneasiness and irritation. If beauty really did exist there, it meant that my own existence was a thing estranged from beauty." Eventually, when his father dies, Mizoguchi fulfills the old man's wishes by becoming an acolyte at the Golden Temple, and thus begins his complex relationship with the inanimate but strangely provocative building, culminating in his final destruction of it by arson.

Throughout the novel Mizoguchi flirts with evil, perhaps sensing a connection between evil and those forces of energy he needs to summon if he is to break down the barrier between his inner world and the world at large. Repeatedly, he makes attempts to get in touch with reality. He falls in love with a girl, Uiko, only to be prevented from reaching her by his last-minute fumbling for words. An image of the beautiful Golden Temple seems to interpose itself between him and the girl. He also acquires two friends, a "good angel" in the person of Tsurukawa and a "bad angel" in Kashiwagi. Because Tsurukawa accepts his stuttering, Mizoguchi's "stuttering identity" is temporarily stripped from him, leaving his real identity exposed. Even so, Tsurukawa constantly misinterprets him, causing him to comment: ". . . my dark, turbid feelings could become clear and radiant by being filtered through Tsurukawa's heart!"

Kashiwagi is the most Dostoievskian character in Mishima's

novels. Completely governed by his cynical intellect, he is similar to Mizoguchi only in respect of having a physical handicap. However, unlike his stuttering friend, he has been able to turn his clubfeet into a positive asset. In a long monologue (one of the most complex passages in the novel) he describes how he discovered his sexuality after being forced by his handicap to overcome his need to be loved. Once he had killed all expectation of love, "desire rose endlessly" within him. A similar transformation could, he suggests, take place in Mizoguchi, if only the younger man would follow his example.

Mizoguchi is "profoundly impressed" by Kashiwagi but he is never controlled by him. Women, on the other hand, are totally at the mercy of the clubfooted but otherwise handsome seducer, and one might suppose Mizoguchi to be envious of his friend's sexual success. This is not so. Rather, desire itself is blocked in Mizoguchi's complex psychology – and the only reason he can give for it is his obsessive fixation on the beauty of the Golden Temple. It is as though the temple is siphoning off all the natural desires of the world to which Mizoguchi might otherwise respond with normal desires of his own. Nonetheless, he recognizes that Kashiwagi has, by devious argument, urged him toward life. "It was Kashiwagi who had taught me the dark byway along which I could reach life from the back."

Deeply in trouble for neglecting his studies, Mizoguchi borrows money from Kashiwagi and takes the train to an area familiar from his childhood. Confronted by the turbulent Sea of Japan he realizes: "Here was the source of all my unhappiness, of all my gloomy thoughts, the origin of all my ugliness and all my strength." In other words, here is the reality of life in all its chaos: a reality to which he can no longer build any bridge whatsoever. It is at this point that he conceives the idea of setting fire to the Golden Temple.

Mizoguchi's relationship to the temple undergoes significant changes during the period described in the novel. During the war when an attack on Kyōto seems imminent, Mizoguchi looks forward to being destroyed along with the Golden Temple and therefore develops a feeling that they both share the same fate. When the danger passes, however, the temple appears to be more remote, even arrogant in its unchanging perfection. Gradually it becomes his mortal enemy, standing between him and life itself. With infinite cunning, he rejects the idea of murdering the superior, arguing: "Mortal things like human beings cannot be eradicated." But in destroying the temple he will be committing "an act of pure destruction, of irreparable ruin, an act which would truly decrease the volume of beauty that human beings had created in this world."

The Temple of the Golden Pavilion is peculiarly unyielding to interpretation even though it is greatly admired and discussed by critics. For example, it is not unreasonable to suggest that Mizoguchi represents the "anemic" Mishima in thrall to language, beauty, and art, while the Golden Temple represents the glorious self that Mishima wished to become. With this interpretation one may go on to note that, for Mishima, beauty must by definition be tragic and contain the seeds of its own destruction. As Mizoguchi says: "When people concentrate on the idea of beauty, they are, without realizing it, confronted with the darkest thoughts that exist in the world." One may then bring this line of reasoning to an end by suggesting that Mishima may have conceived his own suicide as early as 1956 when writing the novel. Alas, because there is not sufficient evidence for such a neat interpretation one looks for alternatives – of which there are many.

One possibility is that the temple is an embodiment of Mishima's art: an art that is created by bringing intellectual order to the chaos of the imagination. In the long descriptive passage at the climax of the novel the author refers to the lake beside the temple as being "the dwelling place of the abundant sensual power that had originally constructed the Golden Temple." He speculates that this power, brought under control in the architecture of the building, cannot bear to remain in its new form and must escape back to the pool from whence it came. Moreover, the beauty of every detail of the building is "filled with uneasiness," and though it dreams of perfection it knows no completion but is "invariably lured on to the next beauty, the unknown beauty." Can this be a metaphor of Mishima's creative life? Quite possibly, for he goes on to suggest that the contemplation of beauty is equally a contemplation of the nothingness that surrounds it. The most famous line in Ivan Morris's translation of the novel is: ". . . there arose automatically an adumbration of nothingness, and this delicate building, wrought of the most slender timber, was trembling in anticipation of nothingness, like a jeweled necklace trembling in the wind."

Mishima's recognition of opposites was more than a habit of thought, it was an insight that he wished to communicate to others. For example, in the terms of his philosophy a man must always be aware of nonexistence in order to appreciate those things that exist. Equally, the cerebral process of creating literature should be viewed as a feminine occupation that had to be offset in life by masculine, active pursuits. Mishima would always pit one idea against its direct opposite, out of perversity, insight, or a deep-seated compulsion. Throughout all his work runs a sense that the vital energies of life can be tapped only by facing squarely the beauty of death – a paradox which he undoubtedly derived from *bushidō*, the way of the samurai. The once secret document, *Hagakure*, written by Yamamoto Jōchō (1659–1719), was a constant inspiration to him and he always kept a copy of it on his desk. His 1967 commentary on it, *"Hagakure nyūmon* ("On Hagakure"), is a masterpiece of critical analysis and shows how passionately he believed in the samurai code.

Following *The Temple of the Golden Pavilion* Mishima suffered two setbacks, first by experimenting on a grand scale with his long novel *Kyōko no ie* (*1959, Kyōko's House*), and second by incurring a libel action for his novel with a political milieu, *Utage no ato* (*1960, After the Banquet*). Neither setback was fatal. The critical and commercial failure of *Kyōko's House* was something he half expected, while his earnings from *After the Banquet* far outstripped the damages he had to pay. A more lasting impact on his life was made in 1958 when he married the daughter of an artist. It was a surprising move in view of his stated sexual preference for men.

The story of his meticulous search for a wife, partly in order to satisfy the wishes of his parents, is entertainingly told in John Nathan's biography of him. In one anecdote the biographer notes that a women's magazine conducted a poll among its readers, inquiring whether, if obliged to make the choice, they would prefer to marry the crown prince or Mishima Yukio. More than fifty percent said they would rather commit suicide! Clearly, most women no more relished the prospect of marrying Mishima than spending a lifetime shackled to court etiquette. Yet in the event Mishima *did* discover an excellent wife in Sugiyama Yōko, whose father was a well-known painter of the traditional school. Yōko met all Mishima's conditions, and there is every reason to believe that the couple were genuinely attracted to each other. They went on to have two children, a daughter, Noriko, born in 1959, and a son, Iichirō, born in 1962.

Of all Mishima's novels *After the Banquet* is the most enjoyable to read. It has none of the difficulties of *The Temple of the Golden Pavilion*; none of the cruelty of *The Sailor Who Fell from Grace with the Sea*. It is the story of an explosive liaison between the proprietress of a famous restaurant and a retired politician whose career she decides to resurrect. They are both worldly people, not at all the sort one normally expects to find center-stage in a Mishima novel. Kazu is the flamboyant and dynamic owner of the Setsugoan, the "After-the-Snow Retreat," which is favored by the patronage of the ruling Conservative Party. In middle age she falls in love, not with a Conservative, but with Noguchi of the Radical Party, a man with lofty ideals and rigid principles. In doing so, Kazu, who has had to fight her way up the social ladder, senses that she may be able to fulfill one of her most deeply held ambitions: to marry a famous man and have the security of knowing that she will eventually be buried in a respectable family tomb.

The couple do indeed get married and their lives are little changed until members of the Radical Party invite Noguchi to run for the governorship of Tokyo. Divining their purpose, Kazu becomes filled with the new and exciting prospect of helping her husband win the election. She will spare no expense in this task and will use all the tricks she has learned, both from running her business and from her long acquaintance with the much more ruthless politicians of the opposing party.

Noguchi's attitude towards his wife's activities wavers between mild alarm and outright anger. His own moralizing speeches are as dry as dust, and he flies into a cold, aristocratic rage when he discovers some of the brash advertising materials produced by his wife. In a lesser novel, a wife would respond by being upset at such an outburst – for Noguchi even hits her and tries to trample on her body when she falls over – but here Kazu is delighted! By this time, enough has already been revealed of her complex psychology to make her response ring true. Kazu's deepest feeling is a death wish, and she delights in Noguchi's display of antiquated virtue. It confirms her destiny in the tomb of a morally impeccable family.

Two elements of suspense (the resolution of which will not be revealed here) provide the novel with its momentum. The first looks forward to the outcome of the election; the second to the fate of the Setsugoan, now perilously close to collapse under the financial strain of Kazu's reckless spending. Mishima brilliantly contrasts these two strands of the narrative, making the reader aware that the fate of the Setsugoan is of infinitely greater importance. Expressed in abstract terms, the novel portrays a clash between heart, in the person of Kazu, and logic, represented by Noguchi. Other polarities, too, are strongly emphasized: Kazu's pragmatism versus Noguchi's idealism; even life versus death. That these opposing states already coexisted in the daily life of the Setsugoan – the world in microcosm – is an indication that Kazu has upset the balance by her fantastic notion of salvation in Noguchi's tomb. In the end, balance is restored with great ingenuity by the author and to the great satisfaction of the reader.

At the time of its publication in Japan, *After the Banquet* was believed to be a satirical attack on Arita Hachirō, a former foreign minister. Like Noguchi, a man of liberal views, Arita was known to have had an affair with the proprietress of the Hannyaen, a restaurant identical to the Setsugoan of the novel. The members of the Arita family were so outraged by what they saw as Mishima's deliberate ridiculing of their most prominent member that they brought a libel suit against him. Mishima lost, but not before he had gained immense and valuable publicity that greatly helped the sales of *After the Banquet* and his previous novels as well.

By this time Mishima was already a great celebrity in Japan. He had written many plays that were performed in theaters across the country. Some of his novels had been adapted for the screen, including an excellent version of *The Temple of the Golden Pavilion*, directed by Ichikawa Kon. He entertained foreign journalists at the Western-style home he had built, in 1959, overlooking Tokyo Bay. Some of his work had already reached the West, and he had high hopes that his *Kindai Nōgakushū* (1956, a selection translated as *Five Modern Nō Plays*) would one day be performed in New York. By dint of his prodigious efforts he had achieved both critical acclaim and popular success, goals that nearly every creative writer wants but which few attain together.

In the last decade of his life, Mishima became even more productive despite devoting so much time to his athletic and quasi-military activities. The decade began with a remarkable story, written in the summer of 1960, called *"Yūkoku"* (*1961*, "Patriotism"). Many critics regard it as a "dress rehearsal" for his suicide ten years later, for it depicts a young army lieutenant committing *seppuku* after the failure of a rebellion against the government. The story has great drama, although some people may recoil at its essential spirit, a curious combination of glamour, agony, beauty, and obscenity. Looking beyond these aspects, one is nonetheless moved by the typically Japanese behavior of the lieutenant and his wife (for she decides to join him) as they prepare for death. Scenes like this, one feels, have been enacted thousands of times before – and on each occasion every trivial detail has acquired similar dimensions of grandeur.

There was undoubtedly a decline in Mishima's popularity in the first half of the 1960s. *The Sailor Who Fell from Grace with the Sea* sold only fifty thousand copies, prompting him to apologize to his Kodansha editor. His previous novel, one concerning global catastrophe, called *Utsukushii hoshi* (1962, *Beautiful Star*) sold a mere twelve thousand copies. It was apparent that he was losing his young audience of college students to a new generation of writers including ŌE KENZABURŌ and ABE KŌBŌ. Indeed, the twenty-five-year-old Ōe had only recently written a stinging satire of "Patriotism" in his story "Seventeen". It was a clear sign that Mishima was becoming out of step with the times.

If Mishima was out of step he had not, however, lost his talent for self-publicity. During 1965 he took a rare break from writing and concentrated on producing a film of "Patriotism" with the English-language title *The Rite of Love and Death*. In the film, Mishima himself played the role of the lieutenant, believing – rightly from an artistic point of view – that the character required no special individuality. Shown at the Tours Film Festival in 1966 the film created a sensation when many women in the audience fainted. It was subsequently shown in Japan to packed audiences, proving once again Mishima's skill in manipulating the media.

The film completed, Mishima cleared his desk to write what he fully expected to be his masterpiece: a tetralogy entitled *The Sea of Fertility*. The title was intended to be ironic, having been taken from one of the "seas" on the moon which are far from being fertile. Although each of the four novels can be enjoyed independently, the reader is strongly advised to approach them in their correct order, beginning with *Haru no yuki* (1965–67, *Spring Snow*); moving on to *Homba* (1967–68, *Runaway Horses*); *Akatsuki no tera* (1968–69, *The Temple of Dawn*); and *Tennin gosui* (1970, *The Decay of the Angel*). The four novels have a continuous narrative, spanning some seventy years, although most of the characters are different in each one. Only Honda, the childhood friend of the hero Matsugae Kiyoaki in *Spring Snow*, figures in every work. Kiyoaki dies, aged twenty, at the end of the first novel and is supposedly reincarnated in subsequent volumes, as a young patriot in *Runaway Horses*, as a Thai princess in *The Temple of Dawn*, and (although Honda comes to realize that the fourth reincarnation is false) as the ill-natured boy Tōru in *The Decay of the Angel*.

Critical opinion concerning Mishima's tetralogy is divided. Few scholars consider it to be his best work, partly because its sheer length gave him too much scope for making mistakes. The second volume usually attracts most attention because it elaborates themes that Mishima broached in "Patriotism." The third volume is uneven in structure, while the fourth seems at times hurried in its execution and obscure in its content. Nonetheless, taken in its entirety, *The Sea of Fertility* is a remarkable achievement and certainly the most comprehensive expression of Mishima's unique art. It is notable in particular for *Spring Snow*, the first volume, which alone of the four is a work of dazzling beauty and miraculous storytelling.

Spring Snow begins in the year 1913 with an evocation of life in the vast mansion of the aristocratic Matsugae family. The early scenes are as vivid as if recalled from the author's own memory and contain just the right amount of detail to bring them to life. Kiyoaki, the strikingly handsome son of the Marquis Matsugae, is a diffident and dreamy young man with an extremely melancholy disposition. He has been raised, not at home, but in Count Ayakura's more refined household because the Marquis "was conscious of his own family's lack of polish." Throughout his childhood Kiyoaki has been close to Satoko, the Ayakuras' daughter, who, at the beginning of the narrative is twenty years old to Kiyoaki's eighteen. She is very much in love with him, but her love does not seem to be reciprocated because Kiyoaki is too immature to acknowledge his real feelings. Only when she eventually agrees to marry someone else does he discover how much he loves her, but by then it is too late. Fearing disgrace, Satoko flees to a convent, putting herself beyond his reach. While waiting hopelessly outside the convent gates Kiyoaki catches pneumonia, which proves to be fatal. Just before he dies he promises his only friend, Honda Shigekuni, that they will meet again "beneath the waterfall." This proves to be an important clue that enables Honda to "rediscover" his friend in the person of Isao in the second novel of the tetralogy.

Entertaining, dramatic, and easily understood, the plot of *Spring Snow* puts it in the tradition of OZAKI KŌYŌ's *The Gold Demon*: middle-brow fiction with a highbrow appeal. One either loves it or hates it, but few could deny its exceptional quality as a fully achieved novel. Like *Confessions of a Mask* it contains within it the spirit of youth – perhaps not the raw spirit of the earlier work but one that has been filtered by the author's years of experience. There is a gentle sense of nostalgia throughout the early scenes, much as though Mishima were bidding farewell to the past before addressing the concerns of the present. Its characters are drawn with great psychological insight, the willful Kiyoaki in particular being one of his most vivid creations. Of all the novels mentioned in this biographical dictionary, *Spring Snow* is one of the most delightful and enduring.

The details of Mishima's suicide on November 25, 1970, have been documented so frequently that there is little need to repeat them here. Suffice it to say that he and some members of his so-called private army (an amateur but very serious cadet force which he sponsored and led) took hostage a general of the Self-Defense Forces. After making a speech to an assembled crowd of soldiers and reporters from a balcony, Mishima returned inside army headquarters and committed ritual suicide in the approved manner of *bushidō*. He was forty-five and at the peak of his physical, intellectual, and creative powers.

Innumerable reasons have been put forward to explain the dramatic manner, timing, and fact of Mishima's death. One may take at face value his statement that he died as a patriot in order to reawaken the true Japanese spirit. He certainly believed that the armed forces had been emasculated and were unworthy of a country with such a proud samurai tradition. Yet one must also consider the many personal reasons that prompted his action, chief among them his distaste for old age and his incurable romanticism. There is little doubt that he killed himself in triumph rather than despair. Moreover, he had long used the *bushidō* technique of "preparedness for death," of being ready to die at any moment, in order to enhance his awareness and to give his life a sense of urgency. In this he had been entirely successful and his uncompromising logic may have led him to believe that the time to die was sooner rather than later. There was some speculation that minor disappointments, such as failing to be awarded a Nobel Prize, may have swayed his decision, but it was wide of the mark. Mishima wanted immortality – and his perception of opposites would have told him that it was best achieved by death.

Since his death Mishima has been more popular in the West than in Japan where he is closely identified with the extreme political right. Any prospect of a "Mishima revival" in his native country would be seen as a reversion to pre-war militarism with rearmament high on the agenda. Alas, such outright identification of an author's life with his work is a relatively recent phenomenon, which, if applied to all the great artists of the past, would reduce considerably our enjoyment of art. It is not even necessary to "like Mishima as a person" to appreciate his work – and indeed one is unlikely to discover the real Mishima except in the stories, plays, and novels that he bequeathed to the world. The best of *them* could scarcely be better.

RECOMMENDED READING

Novels

After the Banquet. *Utage no ato. 1960.* 271 pages. Tr. Donald Keene. Knopf, NY, 1963; Secker and Warburg, London, 1963; Tuttle, Tokyo, 1963; Avon Books, NY, 1967; Berkley Pub., NY, 1971; G. P. Putnam's Sons, NY, 1980; Perigee Paperback, NY, 1981. Mishima's most entertaining novel in translation.

Confessions of a Mask. *Kamen no kokuhaku.* 1949. 255 pages. (1) Extract as "Omi." Tr. Meredith Weatherby. *Modern Japanese Literature*, ed. Donald Keene. Grove Press, NY, 1956; Tuttle, Tokyo, 1957. (2) Tr. Meredith Weatherby. New Directions, NY, 1958; Secker and Warburg, London, 1960; World Distributors, London, 1965; Sphere Books, London, 1967; New Directions, NY, 1968, paperback; Tuttle, Tokyo, 1970; Panther, London, 1972; Paladin, London, 1988. The autobiographical novel that first made Mishima famous.

The Sound of Waves. *Shiosai.* 1954. 182 pages. Tr. Meredith Weatherby. Knopf, NY, 1956; Tuttle, Tokyo, 1956; Secker and Warburg, London, 1957; Berkley Pub., NY, 1961; G. P. Putnam's Sons, NY, 1980; Perigee Paperback, NY, 1981. An idyllic romance.

Spring Snow. *Haru no yuki.* 1965–67. 392 pages. Tr. Michael Gallagher. Knopf, NY, 1971; Tuttle, Tokyo, 1972; Secker and Warburg, London, 1973; Pocket Books, NY, 1973; Penguin Books, Harmondsworth, 1976. *Sea of Fertility.* Penguin Books, 1985; Vintage International, NY, 1990 paperback. Arguably Mishima's finest work; a classic in its own right. The first book in the *Sea of Fertility* tetralogy. (Note: "tetralogy" in ancient Greece was a series of four dramas, three of them tragic, the fourth satyric. Mishima's work follows this pattern).

The Temple of the Golden Pavilion. *Kinkakuji.* 1956. 262 pages. Tr. Ivan Morris. Knopf, NY, 1959; Secker and Warburg, London, 1959; Tuttle, Tokyo, 1959; Avon Books, NY, 1959; Berkley Pub., NY, 1971. (Extract in *The Mentor Book of Modern Asian Literature,* ed. D. B. Shimer. New American Library, NY, 1969.) G. P. Putnam's Sons, NY, 1980; Perigee Paperback, NY, 1981; Penguin Books, Harmondsworth, 1987. Brilliant novel, much-interpreted by the critics.

WORKS IN ENGLISH TRANSLATION

Novels

After the Banquet. Utage no ato. 1960.

Confessions of a Mask. Kamen no kokuhaku. 1949.

The Decay of the Angel. Tennin gosui. 1970. 238 pages. Tr. Edward Seidensticker. Knopf, NY, 1974; Tuttle, Tokyo, 1974; Secker and Warburg, London, 1975; Pocket Books, NY, 1975; Penguin Books, Harmondsworth, 1977; *Sea of Fertility,* Penguin Books, 1985. Fourth and final novel of the *Sea of Fertility* tetralogy.

Forbidden Colors. Kinjiki. 1951–53. 403 pages. Tr. Alfred H. Marks. Knopf, NY, 1968; Secker and Warburg, London, 1968; Tuttle, Tokyo, 1969; Avon Books, NY, 1969; Berkley Pub., NY, 1971; Penguin Books, Harmond-sworth, 1971; G. P. Putnam's Sons, NY, 1980; Perigee Paperback, NY, 1981.

Runaway Horses. Homba. 1967–68. 421 pages. Tr. Michael Gallagher. Knopf, NY, 1973; Tuttle, Tokyo, 1973; Secker and Warburg, London, 1973; Pocket Books, NY, 1975; Penguin Books, Harmondsworth, 1977; *Sea of Fertility,* Penguin Books, 1985; Vintage International, NY, 1990, paperback. Second novel of the *Sea of Fertility* tetralogy.

The Sailor Who Fell from Grace with the Sea. Gogo no eikō. 1963. 181 pages. Tr. John Nathan. Knopf, NY, 1965; Secker and Warburg, London, 1966; Tuttle, Tokyo, 1967; Penguin Books, Harmondsworth, 1970 and 1982; Berkley Pub., NY, 1971; G. P. Putnam's

Sons, NY, 1980; Perigee Paperback, NY, 1981.

The Sound of Waves. Shiosai. 1954.

Spring Snow. Haru no yuki. 1965–67.

The Temple of Dawn. Akatsuki no tera. 1968–69. 334 pages. Tr. E. Dale Saunders and Cecilia Segawa Seigle. Knopf, NY, 1973; Secker and Warburg, London, 1974; Tuttle, Tokyo, 1974; Pocket Books, NY, 1974; Penguin Books, Harmondsworth, 1977; *Sea of Fertility.* Penguin Books, 1985. Third novel of the *Sea of Fertility* tetralogy.

The Temple of the Golden Pavilion. Kinkakuji. 1956.

Thirst for Love. Ai no kawaki. 1950. 200 pages. Tr. Alfred H. Marks. Knopf, NY, 1969; Secker and Warburg, London, 1969; Tuttle, Tokyo, 1970; Berkley Pub., NY, 1970; Penguin Books, Harmondsworth, 1978; G. P. Putnam's Sons, NY, 1980; Perigee Paperback, NY 1981.

Short Fiction Collections

Acts of Worship, Seven Stories. 205 pages. Tr. John Bester. Kodansha International, Tokyo and NY, 1989 and 1991 paperback; HarperCollins, London, 1991. Includes "Fountains in the Rain," "Martyrdom," "Cigarette," "Act of Worship," and 3 other stories.

Death in Midsummer, and Other Stories. 181 pages. Tr. Edward Seidensticker. New Directions, NY, 1966, paperback; Secker and Warburg, London, 1967; Penguin Books, Harmondsworth, 1971; Includes "The Priest of Shiga Temple and His Love," "The Seven Bridges," "Patriotism," and 7 other stories.

Short Fiction

"Act of Worship." "*Mikumano mōde.*" 1965. 60 pages. *Acts of Worship.*

"The Boy Who Wrote Poetry." "*Shi o kaku shōnen.*" 1954. 9 pages. Tr. Ian H. Levy. *Contemporary Japanese Literature,* ed. Howard Hibbett, Knopf, NY, 1977.

"Cigarette." "*Tabako.*" 1946. 18 pages. (1) Tr. Tadao Katayama. *The Reeds,* vol. 13, 1972. (2) *Acts of Worship.*

"Death in Midsummer." "*Manatsu no shi.*" 1952. 27 pages. Tr. Edward Seidensticker. *Death in Midsummer, and Other Stories.*

"Fountains in the Rain." "*Ame no naka no funsui.*" 1963. 10 pages. *Acts of Worship.*

"Love in the Morning." "*Asa no jun'ai.*" 1965. 5 pages. Tr. Leon Zolbrod. *The East,* vol. 2, no. 2, 1965.

"Martyrdom." "*Junkyō.*" 1948. 15 pages. *Acts of Worship.*

"The Monster." "*Kaibutsu.*" 1950. 14 pages. Tr. David O. Mills. *Occasional Papers,* no. 11, 1969. University of Michigan, Center for Japanese Studies.

"Onnagata." "*Onnagata.*" 1957. 22 pages. Tr. Donald Keene. *Death in Midsummer, and Other Stories.*

"Patriotism." "*Yūkoku.*" 1966. 30 pages. Tr. Geoffrey W. Sargent. *Death in Midsummer, and Other Stories; New Writing in Japan.* Penguin Books, Harmondsworth, 1972.

"The Peacock." "*Kujaku.*" 1965. 13 pages. Tr. David O. Mills. *Occasional Papers,* no. 11, 1969. University of Michigan, Center for Japanese Studies.

"The Pearl." "*Shinju.*" 15 pages. Tr. Geoffrey W. Sargent. *Death in Midsummer, and Other Stories.*

"The Priest of Shiga Temple and

His Love." *"Shigadera shōnin no koi."* *1954*. 18 pages. Tr. Ivan Morris. As "The Priest and His Love." *Modern Japanese Stories,* ed. Ivan Morris. Spottiswoode, London, 1961; Tuttle, Tokyo and Boston, 1962 and 1977, paperback. *Death in Midsummer, and Other Stories; The World of Japanese Fiction.* Dutton, NY, 1973.

"Raisin Bread." *"Budōpan."* *1963*. 18 pages. *Acts of Worship.*

"Revenge." *"Fukushū."* *1954*. 8 pages. Tr. Grace Suzuki. *Ukiyo.* Phoenix Books, Tokyo, 1954; *Ukiyo,* ed. J. Gluck. Vanguard Press, NY, 1963; Universal Library, London, 1964.

"Sea and Sunset." *"Umi to yūyake."* *1955*. 11 pages. *Acts of Worship.*

"The Seven Bridges." *"Hashi zukushi."* *1958*. 16 pages. Tr. Donald Keene. *Death in Midsummer, and Other Stories.*

"Swaddling Clothes." *"Shinbungami."* *1955*. 8 pages. Tr. Ivan Morris. *Today's Japan,* vol. 5, Jan.–Feb. 1960; *The Japanese Image,* ed. M. Schneps and A. D. Coox. Orient West, Tokyo, 1965; *Death in Midsummer, and Other Stories.*

"Sword." *"Ken."* *1963*. 54 pages. *Acts of Worship.*

"Tamago." *"Tamago."* *1953*. 7 pages. Tr. Adam Kabat. *Winds,* no. 12, 1985.

"Thermos Bottles." *"Mahōbin."* *1961*. 20 pages. Tr. Edward Seidensticker. *Japan Quarterly,* vol. 9, no. 2, 1962; *Death in Midsummer, and Other Stories.*

"Three Million Yen." *"Hyakuman' en sembei."* *1960*. 11 pages. Tr. Edward Seidensticker. *Japan Quarterly,* vol. 9, no. 2, 1962; *Death in Midsummer, and Other Stories; Asian P.E.N. Anthology,* ed. F. S. Jose. Taplinger, NY, 1966.

"Three Primary Colors." *"San genshoku."* *1955*. 20 pages. Tr. Miles K. McElrath. *Occasional Papers,* no. 11, 1969. University of Michigan, Center for Japanese Studies.

Play Collection

Five Modern Nō Plays. 1956. 198 pages. Tr. Donald Keene. Knopf, NY, 1957; Secker and Warburg, London, 1957; Tuttle, Tokyo, 1967; Vintage Books, NY, 1973. Contains 11-page introduction by the translator. The five plays are *Sotoba Komachi; The Damask Drum; Kantan; The Lady Aoi;* and *Hanjo.*

Plays

The Blind Young Man. Yoroboshi. 1965. 16 pages. Tr. Ted T. Takaya. *Modern Japanese Drama, An Anthology.* Columbia University Press, NY, 1979.

The Damask Drum. Aya no tsuzumi. First performed 1955. 40 pages. *Five Modern Nō Plays.*

Dojoji. Dōjōji. 1957. 20 pages. Tr. Donald Keene. *Death in Midsummer, and Other Stories.*

Hanjo. Hanjo. 23 pages. 1956. Tr. Donald Keene. *Encounter,* vol. 8, no. 1, 1957; *Five Modern Nō Plays.*

Kantan. Kantan. First performed 1950. 63 pages. *Five Modern Nō Plays.*

The Lady Aoi. First performed 1956. 25 pages. *Five Modern Nō Plays.*

Madame de Sade. Sado kōshaku fujin. 1965. 107 pages. Tr. Donald Keene. Grove Press, NY, 1967; Peter Owen, London, 1968; Tuttle, London, 1971.

My Friend Hitler. Waga tomo Hittorā. 1968. 47 pages. Tr. Hiroaki Sato. *St. Andrews Review,* vol. 4, nos. 3–4, 1977.

Sotoba Komachi. Sotoba Komachi. First performed 1952. 34 pages. Tr. Donald Keene. *Virginia Quarterly Review,* Spring 1957; *Five Modern Nō Plays.*

Tropical Tree. Nettaiju. Written 1959. 36 pages. Tr. Kenneth Strong. *Japan Quarterly,* vol. 11, no. 2, 1964.

Twilight Sunflower. Yoru no himawari. 1953. 143 pages. Tr. Shigeho Shinozaki and Virgil A. Warren. Hokuseido, Tokyo, 1958.

Essays

"An Appeal." 4 pages. Tr. Harris I. Martin. *Japan Interpreter,* vol. 7, no. 1, 1971; *Solidarity,* August 1971.

"An Ideology for an Age of Languid Peace." 2 pages. *Journal of Social and Political Ideas in Japan,* vol. 2, no. 2, 1964; *Japan Interpreter,* vol. 7, no. 1, 1971.

"Memorial Service for Prince Genji." "*Genji kuyō.*" 1962. 14 pages. Tr. Adam Kabat. *Journal of Literary Translation,* no. 17, 1986.

"On Hagakure." "*Hagakure nyūmon.*" 1967. 166 pages. Tr.

Kathryn Sparling. Basic Books, NY, 1977; Souvenir Press, London, 1977; Penguin Books, Harmondsworth, 1979.

"The Shield Society." "*Tate no Kai.*" (1) Tr. Ivan Morris. *Queen,* Jan. 7–20, 1970. (2) 2 pages. Tr. Andrew Horvat. *Solidarity,* Aug. 1971; *Japan Interpreter,* vol. 7, no. 1, 1971.

"Sun and Steel." "*Taiyō to tetsu.*" 1968. 104 pages. Tr. John Bester. Kodansha International, Tokyo, 1970; Secker and Warburg, London, 1971; Grove Press, NY, 1972; Kodansha, Tokyo, 1980.

"Testament of a Samurai." 4 pages. Tr. Michael Gallagher. *Sports Illustrated,* Jan. 1971.

"Yang-Ming Thought as Revolutionary Philosophy." "*Kōdōgaku nyūmon.*" 1970. 8 pages. Tr. Harris I. Martin. *Japan Interpreter,* vol. 7, no. 1, 1971.

Poetry

"A Bright Oak Tree." Tr. Junko Ohmagari. *Poetry Nippon,* nos. 35–36, 1976.

"Farewell Poems of Yukio Mishima." Tr. Alan Ireland. *Poetry Nippon,* no. 14, 1971.

CRITICAL STUDIES

Buckstead, Richard C. "The Role of Nature in Mishima's *The Sound of Waves.*" *Asian Profile,* vol. 5, no. 1, 1977.

Duus, Louise. "The Novel as Koan: Mishima Yukio's *The Temple of the Golden Pavilion.*" *Critique: Studies in Modern Fiction,* vol. 10, no. 2, 1968.

Fujimoto, Kazuko. "Mishima Yukio: Death of a Modernist." *Concerned Theatre Japan,* vol. 1, no. 4, 1971.

Goldie, Rosamund. "Mishima and the Military: A Sociological Study of Mishima's Novels and the Mili-

tary in Japan." *European Studies on Japan,* 1979.

Grenwood, Joan V. "After Mishima." *Literature East and West,* vol. 15, no. 2, 1971.

Ikeda, M. S. "Yukio Mishima: A Study of Personal Metamorphosis." Ph.D. diss., University of Chicago, Chicago, 1974.

Iwamoto, Yoshio. "Mishima Yukio: 'Death in Midsummer'; 'Onnagata'; 'Patriotism.'" *Approaches to the Modern Japanese Short Story,* ed. Thomas E. Swann and Kinya Tsuruta. Waseda University Press,

Tokyo, 1982.

Jewel, Mark. "A Comparative Study of Translations of Sōseki and Mishima." *Transactions of the International Conference of Orientalists in Japan*, no. 20, 1975.

Keene, Donald. "Mishima and the Modern Scene." *Times Literary Supplement*, no. 3,265, 1971.

———. "Mishima." *International Congress of Orientalists*, 28th, 1974.

Knapp, Bettina L. "Mishima's Cosmic Noh Drama: *The Damask Drum*." *World Literature Today*, no. 3, 1980.

Libra, Joyce C. "Mishima's Last Act." *Literature East and West*, vol. 15, no. 2, 1971.

McCarthy, Paul Francis. "Mishima Yukio's *Confessions of a Mask*." *Approaches to the Modern Japanese Novel*, ed. Thomas E. Swann and Kinya Tsuruta. Sophia University, Tokyo, 1976.

Miller, Henry. *Reflections on the Death of Mishima*. Capra Press, Santa Barbara, 1972.

Morishige, Alyce Hisae Kawazoe. "The Theme of the Self in Modern Japanese Fiction: Studies on Dazai, Mishima, Abe, and Kawabata." Ph.D. diss., Michigan State University, East Lansing, 1970.

Napier, Susan Jolliffe. "Death and the Emperor: Mishima, Ōe and the Politics of Betrayal." *Journal of Asian Studies*, vol. 48, no. 1, 1989.

———. "In Search of Intensity, Heroes of Action and Inaction in the Works of Mishima Yukio and Ōe Kenzaburō." Ph.D. diss., Harvard University, Cambridge, 1984.

Nathan, John. "The Life and Works of Yukio Mishima." Ph.D. diss., Harvard University, Cambridge, 1974.

———. *Mishima, A Biography*. Little, Brown, Boston, 1974.

Noguchi, Takehiko. "Mishima Yukio and Kita Ikki: The Aesthetics and Politics of Ultranationalism in Japan." Tr. Teruko Craig. *Journal of Japanese Studies*, vol. 10, no. 2, 1985.

Peterson, Gwenn Boardman. *The Moon in the Water: Understanding Tanizaki, Kawabata and Mishima*. University Press of Hawaii, Honolulu, 1979.

Pollack, David. "Action as Fitting Match to Knowledge: Language and Symbol in Mishima's *Kinkakuji*." *Monumenta Nipponica*, vol. 40, no. 1, 1985.

Razic, Dejan. "Mishima Yukio's Modern Nō Plays." Ph.D. diss., Australian National University, Canberra, 1967.

Scott Stokes, Henry. *The Life and Death of Yukio Mishima*. Farrar Straus and Giroux, NY, 1974; Tuttle, Tokyo, 1974; Penguin Books, Harmondsworth, 1985.

———. "Mishima, a Movie and Nakasone." *Japan Quarterly*, vol. 31, no. 1, 1984.

———. "Yukio Mishima: The Last Samurai." *Interplay*, vol. 4, no. 2, 1971.

Seidensticker, Edward G. "Mishima Yukio." *Hudson Review*, vol. 24, no. 2, 1971; *This Country, Japan*. Kodansha International, Tokyo, 1979 and 1984.

———. "Mishima Yukio: Life, Works and Death." *Pacific Community*, vol. 2, no. 3, 1971.

Swann, Thomas E. "What Happens in *Kinkakuji*." *Monumenta Nipponica*, vol. 27, no. 4, 1972.

Wagenaar, Dick. "Yukio Mishima: Dialectics of Mind and Body." (By Dick Wagenaar and Yoshio Iwamoto.) *Contemporary Literature*, vol. 16, no. 1, 1975.

Wilson, Michiko Niikuni. "The Artist as Critic as Mishima: Wilde and Mishima Yukio's 'The Peacock.'" *Literature East and West*, no. 21, 1977.

———. "The Fabrication of Beauty: The Art of Mishima Yukio." Ph.D. diss., University of Texas, Austin, 1977.

———. "Three Portraits of Women in Mishima's Novels." *Journal of the Association of Teachers of Japanese*, vol. 14, no. 2, 1979.

Wolfe, Peter. *Yukio Mishima*. Continuum, NY, 1989.

Yamaji, Katsuyuki. "Conradism and Japan Today: Mishima and Conrad." *Kagoshima Daigaku Bunka Hokoku*, no. 7, 1971; no. 8, 1972.

Yoshida, Sanroku. "Mishima' Modernist Treatment of Time and Space in *The Sea of Fertility*." *World Literature Today*, vol. 57, no. 3, 1983.

Yourcenar, Marguerite. *Mishima: A Vision of the Void*. Tr. Alberto Manguel. Aidan Ellis, Henley-on-Thames, 1985.

Miyamoto YURIKO
(1899–1951)

Novelist. Born in Koishikawa, Tokyo. Widely traveled, but was a resident of Tokyo for most of her life.

One of the few socialist writers to attempt to put forward radical views at the height of Japan's militarism, Miyamoto Yuriko suffered severely at the hands of the authorities. Her health was destroyed by constant imprisonment and frequent torture between the years 1932 and 1942. Yet she recovered sufficiently to make major contributions, both to Japanese letters and to various democratic and women's rights movements, before her death at the age of fifty-one.

Yuriko was the first child of a Cambridge-trained architect and the granddaughter of Nishimura Shigeki, one of the leading intellectuals of the *Meiji period. Precocious as a child, she developed her writing ability early in life, publishing her first novel *Mazushiki hitobito no mure* (*A Flock of Poor People*) in the September 1916 issue of *Chūō kōron* (the most prestigious magazine of the time) at the age of seventeen. Unlike her contemporary, HIRABAYASHI TAIKO, she was strongly encouraged by her well-educated parents. Both of them were gratified to hear their daughter being praised by no less a critic than TSUBOUCHI SHŌYŌ (arguably the founder of modern Japanese literature) while Yuriko was still a freshman at Japan Women's College.

Influenced by the work of Tolstoy, Yuriko often visited a small, rural village on her grandfather's estate in Fukushima Prefecture. Her contact with the impoverished farmers in this area provoked her to write her first novel. She made it clear that her sympathies were with the underprivileged peasants and completely against the ruling classes to whom she was more closely related by birth.

Yuriko rebelled against her middle-class parents, and, at the age of twenty, decided to travel to New York, a city which must have seemed suitably remote from her conventional upbringing. Enrolled at Columbia University, she met and married Araki Shigeru, a graduate student some fifteen years older than herself. After returning to Japan, the newly married couple proved to be so ill-matched that Yuriko, desperately trying to cling to her identity as a writer, finally divorced her husband after five nonproductive years. The story of their disastrous marriage became the subject of Yuriko's first significant autobiographical novel, *Nobuko* (1925), an extract of which has been published in English translation in *To Live and to Write*.

However, Yuriko's failed marriage may not have been entirely the fault of her husband, as some feminist translators have implied. Her latent bisexuality found expression when she met Yuasa Yoshiko, a scholar of Russian literature who encouraged her to divorce Araki. Afterward, the two women lived together for seven years, traveling to Russia in 1927 where Yuriko remained until 1930.

On her return to Japan, Yuriko was brimming over with enthusiasm for Marxism. She joined the All-Japan Proletarian Artists Association (NAPF), became coordinator of its Women's Committee and editor of the journal *Hataraku fujin* (*Working Women*). In the same year, 1930, she also became a member of the Japanese Communist Party, an institution through which she was to meet the leftwing literary critic Miyamoto Kenji. Her marriage to Kenji in 1932 ended her relationship with Yuasa.

In love with Kenji, Yuriko might have expected a longer period of happiness, but military oppression separated the couple after only a few months. First Kenji was sentenced to life imprisonment, then Yuriko herself was arrested. It was not until after World War II that their reunion took place: an occasion that would be recorded in Yuriko's novel "*Fūchisō*" (1946, *The Weathervane Plant*).

Direct personal experience forms the basis for Yuriko's best work. Her trilogy of autobiographical novels examines her life until the early

1930s. It begins with *Nobuko*; tells the story of her relationship with Yuasa in *Futatsu no niwa* (1947, *The Two Gardens*); and relates her Russian experiences in *Dōhyō* (*1950, Signpost*). Other works, too, are autobiographical, such as *Fūchisō* and *Banshū heiya* (1947, *Banshū Plain*), and to these works Japanese readers can add the many letters exchanged by Yuriko and Kenji, collected in *Jūninen no tegami* (1951, *Letters of Twelve Years*) for a complete picture of Yuriko's heroic and tragic life.

English readers are less fortunate, for although much of Yuriko's work has been translated into Russian (which is not surprising in view of her Soviet sympathies) relatively little is available in English. "*Koiwai no ikka*" (1938, "The Family of Koiwai"), an example of socialist realism, does not show Yuriko at her best. Nor is *Banshū Plain* (which, with "*Fūchisō*," won the Mainichi Publishing Culture Prize in 1947) easily obtainable. Only the few chapters of *Nobuko* in English translation reveal a fine stylist and an author gifted with exceptional ability to create character through dialogue.

However, Miyamoto Yuriko is far from being forgotten in Japan. Her work is, in a sense, a personal testament to the twentieth century. She will be remembered as one who stood steadfast in the face of oppression.

RECOMMENDED READING

Short Fiction

Excerpts from the novel **Nobuko**. *Nobuko*. *1924–1926*. 18 pages. Tr. Yukiko Tanaka. *To Live and To Write, Selections by Japanese Women Writers 1913–1938*, ed. Yukiko Tanaka. The Seal Press, Seattle, 1987.

WORKS IN ENGLISH TRANSLATION

Short Fiction

"The Family of Koiwai." "*Koiwai no ikka*." 1938. 19 pages. Tr. Noriko Mizuta Lippit. *Bulletin of Concerned Asian Scholars*, vol. 10, no. 2, 1978; *Stories by Contemporary Japanese Women Writers*, ed. Noriko Mizuta Lippit and Kyoko Iriye Selden. M.E. Sharpe, NY, 1982; reissued as *Japanese Women Writers*, 1991.

Miscellaneous

Excerpt from the novel *Banshū Plain*. *Banshū heiya*. 1947. 6 pages. Tr. Yukiko Sakaguchi and Jay Gluck. *Ukiyo*, ed. J. Gluck. Vanguard Press, NY, 1963; Universal Library, London, 1964.

Excerpts from the novel *Nobuko*. *Nobuko*. *1924–1926*.

Excerpt from the novel *The Weathervane Plant*. *Fūchisō*. 1946. 5 pages. Tr. Brett de Bary. *Journal of the Association of Teachers of Japanese*, vol. 19, no. 1, 1984–85.

Mori ŌGAI
(1862–1922)

Physician and man of letters. Real name, Mori Rintarō. Born and raised in Tsuwano, in modern-day Shimane Prefecture. Studied in Germany, lived in Kyūshū and Tokyo.

Although many well-educated Westerners have never heard of Mori Ōgai, the Japanese remember him as one of the greatest men of the modern era. However, even Japanese scholars admit that a full assessment of his career is difficult, not least because their frames of reference are restricted to their individual fields. Ōgai, by contrast, was a Renaissance man. Soldier, scientist, physician, government adviser, linguist, essayist, critic, novelist, historian: he was all of these, and he not only excelled in each profession, but, if one divides these roles broadly according to the conventions of lesser mortals, can be judged as having had few equals in either the sciences or the arts.

Surprisingly, Ōgai often said he was a dilettante, even going so far in his later years as to identify himself (in a story called "Saiki Kōi") with a dissolute rake of the *Tokugawa period. He did, there can be no denying, spread his energies widely. But dilettante? More than anyone else who springs to mind, he seems to have been the exact opposite: a man who put all his genius into his work but who had few talents remaining for the enjoyment of life itself. Ōgai's achievements are thus far more impressive than his personal biography, for in a sense, his biography is simply the summation of his achievements.

Born in what is now Shimane Prefecture, the son of an official physician to the Tsuwano clan, Ōgai graduated from the Department of Medicine at Tokyo Imperial University at the age of nineteen. He joined the army and was one of the first Japanese to be sent to Europe for an extended period of study. Between 1884 and 1888 he resided in Germany, studying at the universities of Leipzig, Munich, Dresden, and Berlin. There, quite apart from his medical interests, he began to read widely in Western literature, aided by his knowledge of Dutch (the language of Japanese medicine at the time) and German. When he returned home, confident in his abilities, he had both the satisfaction and the stress of seeing all of his careers take off simultaneously.

As a soldier and physician, Ōgai served in two wars, the Sino–Japanese war of 1894–1895 and the Russo–Japanese war of 1904–1905. He became, in turn, director of the Military Medical College, chief of medical staff to the Imperial Guard Division, and ultimately Surgeon-General of the whole Japanese Army. In his bureaucratic roles he applied his knowledge of public hygiene (which, rather than Western literature, had been his official subject of study in Germany) and was so vigorous in his activity that his superiors exiled him to Kyūshū between 1899 and 1902. Indeed, his progressive views stirred up such resentment that he was also forced to resign as editor-in-chief of the *Japanese Medical Journal* and start his own, rival publication. Always a keen exponent of Western medicine, Ōgai actually secured legislation to ban antiquated medical practices and led a battle to modernize the charter of the Japan Medical Association. Toward the end of his life, having finally retired from the army in 1916, he became director and curator of the Imperial Household Museum and Library, and head of the Imperial Art Academy.

It is scarcely credible that a man would be capable of pursuing alternative careers in parallel to the one described in outline above. Yet as a linguist and translator, there is no doubt that Ōgai was altogether more influential than he was in medicine. At an early age he became familiar with the Chinese and Japanese classics, and continued to draw upon his knowledge of Chinese throughout his life. When he gained access to the huge and unfamiliar range of

Western literature, he was prompted to address the problems of translating it into Japanese. In this activity he was supremely successful. Immediately on his return from Germany he published *Omokage* (1889, *Vestiges*), an anthology of seventeen poems by such authors as Shakespeare, Byron, Goethe, and Heine. Later, after the war with China, he published his translation of Hans Christian Andersen's 1835 novel *Improvisatoren*. As *Sokkyō shijin*, it was serialized over a long period (1892–1901) and came to be regarded as the finest translation ever made into Japanese. In all, Ōgai translated over 150 works of European literature, including Goethe's *Faust* (1911–1912), Ibsen's *Ghosts* (1912), *A Doll's House* (1913), Shakespeare's *Macbeth* (1913), and Strindberg's *Storm Weather* (1914).

At the turn of the century, the translation of Western literature required a willingness to experiment with the Japanese language: a task to which Ōgai, with his scientific mind, was ideally suited. As a prose stylist he was preeminent. Had he achieved nothing else in his career he would still rank among the greatest men of letters for his influence on the prose of AKUTAGAWA RYŪNOSUKE, TANIZAKI JUN'ICHIRŌ, and MISHIMA YUKIO. Scholars divide his styles into three clearly defined periods: the classical Japanese of his early works, the modern colloquial style which first appeared in his story "Hannichi" (1909, "Half a Day"), and, third, the blend of Japanese with classical Chinese which he adopted after 1912. Of all his styles, the most influential was the crisp, masculine prose of his middle period, and it was to this that Mishima Yukio (for example) turned when he sought a model for the prose of *Kinkakuji* (1956, *The Temple of the Golden Pavilion*). In passing, one might note how Mishima, the most versatile stylist of the modern period, came remarkably close to Ōgai's prose in "Taiyō to tetsu" (1968, "Sun and Steel"), a biographical work in which he reflected: "My ideal style would have had the grave beauty of polished wood in the entrance hall of a samurai mansion on a winter's day." Ōgai, one feels, would have approved of this noble sentiment, so austerely expressed yet containing the vitality of a disciplined Romanticism.

For all his mastery of the colloquial language Ōgai consistently opposed attempts to make Japanese entirely phonetic in its written form. His efforts prevented any changes in the language until after 1945, when a compromise was reached and the number of characters was reduced dramatically. Ōgai was well placed to be influential, being chairman of the Provisional Commission on the Japanese Language. His conservative stance in orthography must be counted as one of the formative influences on present-day Japanese culture.

In the foregoing paragraphs, little has been said of Ōgai's achievement as a creative writer even though that is the intended subject of this essay. But then, Ōgai himself once wrote a biography (*Shibue Chūsai, 1916*) in which the subject not only dies halfway through the book but is barely mentioned in the first eleven chapters. Therein lies a clue to the unique difficulties which face the Western reader who wants to become acquainted with Ōgai's work. To summarize the position first, one has to say that to the highly literate Western reader approaching Ōgai in English translation, some of the stories will appear utterly obscure and almost meaningless, while others will be seen as self-evident masterpieces. Most of the former may be found in volume 2 of David Dilworth's and J. Thomas Rimer's selection of Ōgai's stories, entitled *Saiki Kōi and Other Stories*. Most of the latter, the "self-evident masterpieces," are in volume 1, entitled *The Incident at Sakai and Other Stories*.

Why is Ōgai such a difficult writer, one may ask, remembering that his prose style is a model of clarity and precision? In a sense, the question arises only in the later, historical works mentioned above. The other stories and novels which are available in English translation are not at all obscure. In fact, they are sometimes so transparently obvious in their meaning that they give rise to a further difficulty, prompting the question: why would a man of Ōgai's intellectual abilities produce work of such apparently pedestrian quality? For example, the reader who picks up *Vita Sexualis* (*1909*), expecting psycho-sexual insights on a par with Mishima's *Confessions of a Mask*, will be sadly disappointed. Ōgai's hero appears to lack a sexual drive strong enough to give him problems of any sort, whether social, emotional, or spiritual. Equally, the novel seems to be an artistic failure, commencing like an early NATSUME SŌSEKI satire and then rambling into a mode of serious autobiography where the author was clearly ill at ease.

Ōgai's motives in writing *Vita Sexualis* were complex, but nonetheless well-defined. Firstly, he strongly disliked the *Naturalist school of writing in all its confessional self-centeredness. He belonged to no "school" of writing himself, and did not claim to be the leader of any kind of "movement." He argued against the critic TSUBOUCHI SHŌYŌ, complaining of his lack of ideals, and was savage in his dismissal of OZAKI KŌYŌ, the dominant force in Japanese letters in the 1890s. Ōgai had his own ideas. He was intent on going his own way, wherever that might lead.

Ōgai had already written three Romantic novellas on his return from Germany, namely *"Maihime"* (*1890*, "The Dancing Girl"), *"Utakata no ki"* (*1890*, "Foam on the Waves"), and *"Fumizukai"* (*1891*, "The Courier"). Sometimes critics point to *"Maihime"* as being the forerunner of the *I-Novel (the genre developed by the Naturalists) and, admittedly, this novel does contain a confessional account of his student days in Germany, concentrating on the classic opposition of *giri* (feudal loyalty) and *ninjō* (personal emotion). But Ōgai was not amused by the confessions of others. He seemed to find depressing and perhaps even a little ludicrous the way in which the Naturalists concentrated on the intimate details of their emotional lives with little regard for aesthetics. Thus, in *Vita Sexualis*, he set out quite consciously to poke fun at them, inventing a professor of philosophy, Mr. Kanai, who tries to write a book about sex even though he believes that other aspects of life are more important. Mr. Kanai's justifications for the project are witty and compelling. He dismisses Casanova's *Memoirs* as misleading because the rake's appetite for sex, like Napoleon's for power, "far surpassed that of the ordinary man." If one takes Kanai to represent the author, even in caricature, then one must conclude that Ōgai saw himself as speaking to the "ordinary man" on the subject of sex. He sincerely wanted to put the record straight for others like himself who might be confused by the introspections of the Naturalists. In other words, *Vita Sexualis* was a piece of practical sex education, written by an eminent medical man who "knew of such things" firsthand.

On the subject of sex, society of course has a will of its own. Ōgai's wholly innocuous book was immediately banned. The authorities feared it might pave the way for other, more salacious material to be published in its wake. This seems extraordinary, for only at the end of the narrative does the hero actually *have* sex, and even then it is not described in any detail. The hero merely mentions a visit to a prostitute to whom he loses his virginity, and says that although the experience cured him of his shyness with women he made no subsequent effort to pursue them.

Ōgai's sexual psychology is a fascinating topic in view of the protean nature of his career. In *Vita Sexualis* he finally rejects the idea, raised earlier in the novel, that self-knowledge has "blasted" his passion. Revealingly he mentions Michelangelo in the same line of thought, implying a diversion of sexual energy into creative endeavor. This appears to be the best explanation, even though, ironically, it shows how inappropriate was Ōgai's aim of educating the "ordinary man." Unless young readers of this brief biography are universal geniuses like Ōgai, they would surely do better to find a transcript of Carl Jung's 1922 lecture *The Love Problem of a Student*, which is everything *Vita Sexualis* claims to be, but is not.

Another extended work by Ōgai which is readily available in English translation is *Gan* (*The Wild Geese*), first published in twelve issues of *Subaru* (*The Pleiades*, virtually Ōgai's own literary magazine) in 1911–1913. This has always been Ōgai's most popular work, being a story of unrequited love and featuring a tragic heroine whom the author portrayed with great sensitivity and insight. Indeed he gave the novel a mythological dimension which one would not expect from such a rational, scientific mind.

The story begins: "This is an ancient tale . . ." yet it is set as recently as 1880, indicating that the events which take place exist within the larger time scales of mythology. The "Ōgai-figure" is Okada, an immature medical student who is predominantly concerned with his career. The heroine, Otama, is the very embodiment of femininity, but nonetheless a projection (as David Dilworth so rightly says) of Ōgai's own feminine *anima*. Although Otama falls in love with Okada she is completely unable to express her feelings. Strong as they are, her feelings must be set aside for the higher good of "duty," and thus Otama becomes the mistress of an insensitive moneylender, Suezō, in order to support her aging father.

While *The Wild Geese* is certainly "a highly nuanced, personal expression . . . full of an intense but subdued emotion" (Dilworth) it is by no means an artistic triumph. Donald Keene, who appreciates the novel's "evocative setting," is correct in noting the heavy-handedness of its symbolism. For example, when Okada kills a snake which has crept into a cage where Otama keeps two birds, the sexual symbolism is all too obvious. Equally, when Okada accidentally kills the wild goose the story seems to have entered a realm of farce, quite at odds with the intensity of emotion the author was trying to express.

For all its shortcomings, however, *The Wild Geese* was a noble failure. It shows, to quite an extraordinary extent, how much Ōgai had absorbed of Western literature. Underlying the plot is a plane of coincidence, which, in real life, one perceives only at times of heightened awareness. In a sense, the whole tragedy is "caused" by those trivial, everyday workings of fate which so fascinated (for example) Thomas Hardy. It was also a novel in which Ōgai strove to integrate the deeper workings of his creative imagination, using the very techniques later recommended by Carl Jung. He came to terms with the feminine in himself by objectifying his *anima* figure, acknowledging her "muteness" and recognizing that he had hitherto rejected her.

Restricted, as English readers are, chiefly to secondary sources in examining Ōgai's life, the man who emerges from the pages of *Vita Sexualis* and *The Wild Geese* does not easily correspond to the image we have of him. Was the author of these books, with all their evidence of inner sensitivity, really so austere and aloof as the critics would have us believe? Fortunately, there is now one primary source in English to which the reader can turn. Only a few pages long, it is a firsthand account by TAYAMA KATAI in his memoir *Thirty Years in Tokyo* (published by E. J. Brill as *Literary Life in Tokyo*, translated by Kenneth G. Henshall). It describes several meetings between Katai, who was incidentally the most daring of the Naturalist writers, and Ōgai, at the battlefront during the Russo–Japanese War.

Katai's recollection of Ōgai is vivid and extremely moving. It was, he says, "thanks to literature" that he, Katai, a lowly war correspondent, could gain access to the head of the medical corps with the rank of general. Furthermore, Ōgai proved to be affable, informal, and very pleased to see another literary man under such circumstances, despite the extraordinary pressure his work was then demanding of him. Katai, in noting that "the beauty of Ōgai's wife was a talking-point in the literary world of the time," says: "When I read Ōgai's *Verse Diary*, which was published later, I can appreciate how he himself felt on these plains, thinking of his young wife whom he'd left behind in Tokyo, along with his beloved newborn daughter."

Ōgai in fact married twice, with a long period of bachelorhood in between. He is said to have divorced his first wife, whom he wedded in 1889, because he resented the attitude of his in-laws toward his own family. He remained single from 1890 to 1902, then married a girl much younger than himself: the beautiful young wife to whom Katai was referring. Although the couple remained together until Ōgai's death, it is clear that a man of so many accomplishments cannot have spared much time to foster an ideal relationship. The novelist Mishima Yukio once remarked: "I believe it is true to say that Ōgai saw in his own household the failure of Japan's modern age" (Tr. Donald Keene).

Putting all of the above impressions together, one pictures a man with a highly developed persona, a "true gentleman" who placed duty above affection as a matter of principle. In exploring the deeper springs of his unconscious mind he was not seeking personal happiness but hoping to realize his full potential within the (virtually unbounded) confines of his work. In common with many other Japanese writers, and in accordance with Oriental tradition in general, he was also willing to accept the possibility of a "union of opposites" in the world. Here one might turn again to Jung for an additional insight. Jung said (in *Anima and Animus*): "To the degree that the world invites the individual to identify with the mask (i.e., the persona), he is delivered over to influences from within . . ."

That Ōgai did indeed wear a "mask" was freely admitted by him. In "*Mōsō*" (*1911*, "Delusion"), an autobiographical work written in the same year as *The Wild Geese*, he said he felt that ". . . the things

I do are no more than what an actor does, who comes upon the stage and performs a certain role . . . there must be something else behind this role I play." Being so brilliant, yet, as we have seen, so affable, it is not surprising that Ōgai could use his persona very effectively to make his way in life. But the further he went, the more necessary it became for him to address and accept the contradictory impulses of his unconscious. Since he scarcely ever faltered in any one of his simultaneous careers, he achieved even this difficult feat of self-analysis and control.

Expressed in mythological terms, two of the opposites in the world are the Apollonian and Dionysian aspects of the human spirit. Ōgai was well acquainted with Nietzsche's 1872 essay, "The Birth of Tragedy," in which these concepts appeared, and he noted in an essay of his own that he himself was wholly Apollonian in his work. "I have never exerted the kind of effort required to make a story 'Dionysian,'" he wrote. There is a touch of regret in this remark, as though he realized that an artist needs to awaken the "sleeping tigers" of desire and harness them to his chariot if he is to present a total picture of reality. On their own, intellect, cool appraisal, and refined expression are disembodied if cut off from the vital energies of life. Yet Ōgai had very specific literary ideals to which Dionysian energy would have been inappropriate. In any case, he channeled his energies elsewhere, putting into his literature only those elements which he felt were suited to it.

On September 13, 1912, Ōgai's friend and colleague General Nogi committed ritual suicide, using the excuse of having once lost a regimental flag as a reason for following the Emperor Meiji into death. Ōgai, who had done so much to import Western ideas to Japan, was thoroughly shaken by this example of pure samurai loyalty. It prompted him to turn his attention to the past in order to find some parallel which might help him come to terms with the anachronism. The resulting story, "*Okitsu Yagoemon no isho*" (1912, "The Last Testament of Okitsu Yagoemon"), was the first of his many historical works, written in a new and more elaborate style to which the closest Western equivalent would be something like a "biblical" style.

Throughout his historical writings, consisting of both fictional (*rekishi shōsetsu*) and biographical (*shiden*) pieces, Ōgai searched for universal values. Like many Japanese he found the ultimate value in beauty. True spiritual beauty is touched by each one of his heroes and heroines, often in self-sacrifice but frequently in resignation and acceptance of their fate. Although Westerners other than romantics or decadents rarely find beauty in the embrace of death, in the Japanese tradition such an act is often the only way to resolve fundamental moral issues. In Ōgai's story "*Abe ichizoku*" (*1913*, "The Abe Family") nearly everyone dies, and for reasons which seem quite incomprehensible until one examines the logic of Tokugawa ethics. Then the events have an undeniable beauty of their own.

One or two of Ōgai's historical stories are quite outstanding. The three finest are surely "*Jiisan baasan*" (*1915*, "The Old Man and the Old Woman"), "*Sanshō dayū*" (*1915*, "Sanshō the Steward"), and "*Takasebune*" (*1916*, "The Boat on the River Takase"). The last-named, in particular, is one of the best two or three Japanese stories in translation. It has been rendered into English eleven times since 1918, and is so clear in its statement that it can serve as a key to understanding Ōgai's other, more difficult works.

Set in the Tokugawa period on one of the *takase* boats which ferried prisoners into exile, the story contains just two characters: a lonely but strangely contented prisoner, and a constable in charge of him. The constable is disturbed by the man's apparent happiness and requests his story. Without spoiling the plot for the reader (who is strongly recommended to search out this extraordinary work), one can say that the man's reply has two aspects, one of which states the reason why he accepts his fate, the other touching upon a subject of fundamental importance in medical ethics. Here one can see how Ōgai brought together, in a burst of pure inspiration, different facets of his experience. Gone is the "malcontent" of which he complained in his earliest works. Gone is the unsatisfactory resignation of his middle period. In "*Takasebune*" the inner dialogue is resolved, maybe temporarily and in this instance only, but with complete realism, logic, and feeling. The story is a perfect fusion of Western and Oriental art.

A fusion of East and West is exactly what Ōgai always sought in his rich and productive life. He wanted to preserve what was best in Japan's past, particularly its spiritual and aesthetic values, while importing from the West science, medicine, and the best of its ideals. His belief that it could be done, and his prodigious efforts to do it, inspired confidence in his fellow countrymen. That is why he is held in such great affection in Japan.

Mori Ōgai, who was born Mori Rintarō and often used the pen names Sendagi Sanbō and Ōgai Gyoshi, died in 1922.

RECOMMENDED READING

Short Fiction Collections

The Incident at Sakai and Other Stories, ed. David Dilworth and J. Thomas Rimer. Volume One of *The Historical Literature of Mori Ōgai*. 228 pages. The University Press of Hawaii, Honolulu, 1977. University Microfilms International, Books on Demand, Ann Arbor. Contains 12-page introduction by J. Thomas Rimer, 11 stories, notes, and a glossary. Stories include: "Sansho the Steward," "The Old Man and the Old Woman," and "The Boat on the River Takase" (arguably Ōgai's finest work). Superbly produced like its matching companion volume (see below): black boards with silver lettering on spine; black and silver dust wrapper.

Saiki Kōi and Other Stories, ed. David Dilworth and J. Thomas Rimer. Volume Two of *The Historical Literature of Mori Ōgai*. 200 pages. The University Press of Hawaii, Honolulu, 1977. Contains 31-page essay, "The Significance of Ōgai's Historical Literature" by David Dilworth, 7 stories, notes, and a glossary. Title story is the best.

The Historical Fiction of Mori Ōgai, ed. David Dilworth and J. Thomas Rimer. 422 pages. University of Hawaii Press, Honolulu, 1991. This is the combined, single-volume paperback of the two books mentioned immediately above.

WORKS IN ENGLISH TRANSLATION

Novels

Vita Sexualis. Vita sekusuarisu. 1909. 153 pages. Tr. Kazuji Ninomiya and Sanford Goldstein. Tuttle, Tokyo and Boston, 1972, paperback.

The Wild Geese. Gan. 1911–13. 119 pages. (1) Extract as *The Wild Goose*. Tr. S. G. Brickley. *The Writing of Idiomatic English*. Kenkyusha, Tokyo, 1951. (2) Extract as *The Wild Goose*. Tr. Burton Watson. *Modern Japanese Literature*, ed. Donald Keene. Grove Press, NY, 1956; Tuttle, Tokyo and Boston, 1957 and 1974, paperback. (3) Tr. Kingo Ochiai and Sanford Goldstein. Tuttle, Tokyo, 1959; *The World of Japanese Fiction*. Dutton, NY, 1973.

Mixed Anthology

Sanshō dayū and Other Short Stories. 82 pages total; 65 devoted to two stories by Ōgai. Tr. Tsutomu Fukuda. Hokuseido, Tokyo, 1970. Contains title story and "The Boat on the River Takase." Also "Bird of Spring" (tr. as "Spring Birds") by KUNIKIDA DOPPO.

Biographical Writing

The Woman in the Crested Kimono. Shibue Chūsai. 1916. 148 pages. Tr. and adapted by Edwin

McClellan. Yale University Press, New Haven, 1985.

Short Fiction

"The Abe Family." "*Abe ichizoku.*" *1913.* 32 pages. Tr. David Dilworth. *The Incident at Sakai, and Other Stories.*

"As If." "*Ka no yō ni.*" *1912.* 57 pages. Tr. G. M. Sinclair and Kazo Suita. *Tokyo People, Three Stories from the Japanese.* Keibunkan, Tokyo, 1925.

"The Boat on the River Takase." "*Takasebune.*" *1916.* 11 pages. (1) As "Takase-bune." Tr. Torao Taketomo. *Paulownia, Seven Stories from Contemporary Japanese Writers.* Duffield, NY, 1918. (2) As "Takase River Boat." Tr. G. Ogura. *Japan Times,* July 15 and 16, 1934. (3) As "Takasebune." Tr. W. J. Whitehouse. *Eigo no kenkyu to kyoju,* June 1936. (4) As "Takase-bune." Tr. Tosiyosi. *Travel Bulletin,* 1940. (5) As "Takasebune." Tr. Akira Ota. *New World,* June 1946. (6) As "The Takase-Boat." Tr. Tsutomu Fukuda. *Sanshō Dayū, and Other Stories.* Hokuseido, Tokyo, 1952. (7) As "The Takase Boat." Tr. Eiichi Hayashi. *The Reeds,* vol. 2, 1956. (8) As "Takasebune." Tr. Garland W. Paschal. *The Heart Is Alone,* ed. Richard McKinnon, Hokuseido, Tokyo, 1957. (9) As "The Takase Boat." Tr. Edmund R. Skrzypczak. *Monumenta Nipponica,* vol. 26, nos. 1–2, 1971; as "The Boat on the River Takase." *The Incident at Sakai, and Other Stories.* (10) As "Takasebune." Tr. Tadashi Kikuoka. *Traditions,* vol. 3, no. 1, 1979.

"The Courier." "*Fumizukai.*" 1891. Tr. Karen Brazell. *Monumenta Nipponica,* vol. 26, nos. 1–2, 1971.

"Cups." "*Sakazuki.*" 7 pages. (1) Tr. Asataro Miyamori. *Representative Tales of Japan.* Sanseido. Tokyo. 1914. (2) Tr. John W. Dower. *Monumenta Nipponica,* vol. 26, nos. 1–2, 1971.

"Delusion." "*Mōsō.*" *1911.* 15 pages. Tr. John W. Dower. *Monumenta Nipponica,* vol. 25, nos. 3–4, 1970.

"Exorcising Demons." "*Tsuina.*" 6 pages. Tr. John W. Dower. *Monumenta Nipponica,* vol. 26, nos. 1–2, 1971.

"Gyogenki." "*Gyogenki.*" *1915.* 14 pages. *The Incident at Sakai, and Other Stories.*

"Hanako." "*Hanako.*" *1910.* 17 pages. (1) Tr. Yonejiro Noguchi. *Chugai Eigo,* Nov. and Dec. 1918. (2) Tr. Torao Taketomo. *Paulownia, Seven Stories from Contemporary Japanese Writers.*

"Hannichi." "*Hannichi.*" *1909.* 16 pages. Tr. Darcy Murray. *Monumenta Nipponica,* vol. 28, no. 3, 1973.

"The Incident at Sakai." "*Sakai jiken.*" *1914.* 22 pages. Tr. David Dilworth. *The Incident at Sakai, and Other Stories.*

"Ishida Jisaku." "*Ishida Jisaku.*" 3 pages. Tr. Shigeshi Nishimura. *The Current of the World,* vol. 21, no. 5, 1944.

"Kanzan Jittoku." "*Kanzan Jittoku.*" *1916.* 9 pages. (1) As "Han Shan and Shih-te." Tr. David Dilworth and J. Thomas Rimer. *Monumenta Nipponica,* vol. 26, nos. 1–2, 1971. (2) As "Han-shan and Shih-te." Tr. Hiroaki Sato. *Literature East and West,* vol. 15, no. 2, 1971. (3) *The Incident at Sakai, and Other Stories.* (4) As "Kanzan and Jittoku." Tr. Tadashi Kikuoka. *Traditions,* vol. 4, no. 2, 1980.

"Kuriyama Daizen." "*Kuriyama Daizen.*" *1915.* 25 pages. Tr. J.

Thomas Rimer. *Saiki Kōi, and Other Stories.*

"The Last Phrase." *"Saigo no ikku."* 1915. 13 pages. *The Incident at Sakai, and Other Stories.*

"The Last Testament of Okitsu Yagoemon." *"Okitsu Yagoemon no isho."* Two versions: 1912 and (with revisions) 1913. 15 pages. (1) Tr. William Ritchie Wilson. *Monumenta Nipponica*, vol. 26, nos. 1–2, 1971. (2) Tr. Richard Bowring and William Ritchie Wilson. *The Incident at Sakai, and Other Stories.*

"Maihime (The Dancing Girl)." *"Maihime."* 1890. 14 pages. (1) As "My Lady of the Dance." Tr. F. W. Eastlake. Saiunkaku, Tokyo, 1906. (2) As "The Girl Who Danced." Tr. Leon Zolbrod. *The Language of Love.* Bantam Books, NY, 1964. (3) As "Maihime (The Dancing Girl)." Tr. Richard Bowring. *Monumenta Nipponica*, vol. 30, no. 2, 1975.

"The Old Man and the Old Woman." *"Jiisan baasan."* 1915. 9 pages. *The Incident at Sakai, and Other Stories.*

"The Pier." *"Sambashi."* 1910. 5 pages. Tr. Torao Taketomo. *Paulownia, Seven Stories from Contemporary Japanese Writers; Treasury of World Literature*, ed. D. D. Runes. Philosophical Library, NY, 1956.

"Sahashi Jingoro." *"Sahashi Jingorō."* 1913. 10 pages. Tr. J. Thomas Rimer. *Saiki Koi, and Other Stories; The East*, vol. 20, nos. 3–4, 1984.

"Saiki Koi." *"Saiki Kōi."* 1917. 33 pages. Tr. William R. Wilson. *Saiki Koi, and Other Stories.*

"Sansho the Steward." *"Sanshō dayū."* 1915. 25 pages. (1) As "Sansho-Dayu." Tr. Tsutomu Fukuda. *Eigo Seinen*, vol. 97, no. 6, 1951; *Sanshō Dayū, and Other Stories.* Hokuseido, Tokyo, 1952. *Sanshō-dayū.* P. D. Perkins, South Pasadena, 1953. (2) As "Sanshōdayū." Tr. Masaki Seikai. *Asia Scene*, vol. 1, nos. 4–6, 1956. (3) Tr. J. Thomas Rimer. *The Incident at Sakai, and Other Stories.*

"Snake." *"Hebi."* 1911. 12 pages. Tr. John W. Dower. *Monumenta Nipponica*, vol. 26, nos. 1–2, 1971.

"Suginohara Shina." *"Suginohara Shina."* 1916. 11 pages. Tr. David Dilworth. *Monumenta Nipponica*, vol. 26, nos. 1–2, 1971; *Saiki Koi, and Other Stories.*

"Tokō Tahai." *"Tokō Tahei."* 1917. 12 pages. Tr. J. Thomas Rimer. *Saiki Koi, and Other Stories.*

"Tsuge Shirozaemon." *"Tsuge Shirozaemon."* 1915. 28 pages. Tr. Edmund R. Skrzypczak. *Saiki Koi, and Other Stories.*

"Under Reconstruction." *"Fushinchū."* 1910. 7 pages. Tr. Ivan Morris. *Modern Japanese Stories*, ed. Ivan Morris. Spottiswoode, London, 1961; Tuttle, Tokyo, 1962; *The Japanese Image*, ed. M. Schneps and A. D. Coox. Orient West, Tokyo, 1965.

"Utakata no Ki." *"Utakata no ki."* 1890. 15 pages. Tr. Richard Bowring. *Monumenta Nipponica*, vol. 29, no. 3, 1974.

"The Vendetta at Gojiingahara." *"Gojiingahara no katakiuchi."* 1913. 27 pages. Tr. David Dilworth. *The Incident at Sakai, and Other Stories.*

"Yasui Fujin." *"Yasui fujin."* 1914. 16 pages. *Saiki Koi, and Other Stories.*

Essay

"History as It Is and History Ignored." *"Rekishi sono mama to rekishi banare."* 1915. 6 pages. Tr.

Darcy Murray. *The Incident at Sakai, and Other Stories.*

Poetry

"Vigorous Feet." Tr. Asataro Miyamori. *Masterpieces of Japanese Poetry, Ancient and Modern.* Maruzen, Tokyo, 1936; Taiseido, Tokyo, 1956; Greenwood Press, NY, 1971.

"In Mitsukoshi's Store." Tr. Shigeshi Nishimura. *The Current of the World,* vol. 29, no. 12, 1952.

CRITICAL STUDIES

Bowring, Richard John. *Mori Ōgai and the Modernisation of Japanese Culture.* Cambridge University Press, Cambridge, 1977.

———. "Mori Ōgai: A Re-appraisal." *Journal of the Association of Teachers of Japanese,* vol. 10, no. 2, 1975.

———. "A Study of the Works of Mori Ōgai." Ph.D. diss., Cambridge University, Cambridge, 1973.

Brazell, Karen. "Mori Ōgai in Germany." *Monumenta Nipponica,* vol. 26, no. 1, 1971.

Dower, John W. "Mori Ōgai: Meiji Japan's Eminent Bystander." *Papers on Japan,* no. 2, Harvard University, Cambridge, 1963.

Hasegawa, Izumi. "Mori Ōgai." *Japan Quarterly,* vol. 12, no. 2, 1965.

———. "The Significance of the Meiji Period in Mori Ōgai's Literature." *Acta Asiatica,* no. 40, 1981.

Johnson, Eric W. "Mori Ōgai: The Fiction from 1909 to Early 1914." Ph.D. diss., University of Chicago, Chicago, 1973.

———. "Ōgai's *The Wild Goose.*" *Approaches to the Modern Japanese Novel,* ed. Thomas E. Swann and Kinya Tsuruta. Sophia University Press, Tokyo, 1976.

Koisumi, Koichiro. "Recent Developments in Research on the Literature of Mori Ōgai." *Acta Asiatica,* no. 40, 1981.

Nakai, Yoshiyuki. "Mori Ōgai, the State of the Field." *Monumenta Nipponica,* vol. 35, no. 1, 1980.

———. "Mori Ōgai's German Trilogy: A Japanese Parody of Les Contes d'Hoffmann." *Harvard Journal of Asiatic Studies,* vol. 38, no. 3, 1978.

———. "Ōgai's Craft: Literary Techniques and Themes in *Vita Sexualis.*" *Monumenta Nipponica,* vol. 35, no. 2, 1980.

———. "The Young Mori Ōgai, 1862–1892." Ph.D. diss., Harvard University, Cambridge, 1974.

Ogata, Tsutomu. "The Charm of Mori Ōgai's Literature: His Historical Novella 'Gojiingahara no katakiuchi.'" *Acta Asiatica,* no. 40, 1981.

Rimer, John Thomas. "Mori Ōgai: 'The Dancing Girl,' 'Under Reconstruction,' 'Delusion.'" *Approaches to the Modern Japanese Short Story,* ed. Thomas E. Swann and Kinya Tsuruta. Waseda University Press, Tokyo, 1982.

———. *Mori Ōgai.* Twayne Publishers, NY, 1975.

Saito, George. "A Japanese View of George Ticknor with Reflections on Mori Ōgai." *Dartmouth College Library Bulletin,* vol. 12, no. 2, 1962.

Swann, Thomas E. "The Problem of 'Utakata no Ki.'" *Monumenta Nipponica,* vol. 29, 1974.

MUSHANOKŌJI Saneatsu
(1885–1976)

Novelist, essayist, and editor. Born in Tokyo. Lived in a utopian commune, which he founded in Hyūga, Kyūshū, 1918–26

If there is one Japanese writer upon whom Western critics heap scorn while their Japanese colleagues praise him to the skies it is Mushanokōji Saneatsu. Indeed, anyone who follows up references to Mushanokōji in the critical literature of both East and West must begin to wonder whether scholars are discussing the same person, so divergent are their views. Mushanokōji was the chief instigator of the *Shirakabaha* or "White Birch Society," a literary group formed in 1910 and consisting of well-to-do young men who had attended the Peers School before entering university. The son of a viscount, Mushanokōji was the most aristocratic of them all. Largely as a result of his efforts the group achieved an initial notoriety and eventual success. His own early novels expressed an unrestrained self-confidence and optimism which inspired the other members, including his close friend SHIGA NAOYA who went on to become the most celebrated writer of his generation.

Mushanokōji, whose name is often shortened to Mushakōji, was the youngest of eight children, of whom only three survived past the age of one. He thus had only a brother, Kimitomo – who grew up to become Japanese ambassador to Hitler's Germany – and a sister, Itako, who died when Saneatsu was fifteen. The loss of his sister, to whom he was especially close, affected him more deeply than losing his father at the age of three. In fact, he could remember his father only when reminded of certain incidents, such as being called to his bedside to be admired with the words: "If he" [Saneatsu] "is raised well he will become the greatest man in the world." Always aware of his heritage Mushanokōji took these words of his father very much to heart. Even when studying at the Peers School he rejected official lessons and read only those books that most appealed to him.

Men who believe themselves destined for greatness tend to have very few heroes, and Mushanokōji was no exception. The one person whom he regarded with awe was Count Leo Tolstoy, whose works had once been presented to him by his uncle, Kadenokōji Sukekoto. In Tolstoy he found an aristocrat like himself, but one who was both gifted and humanitarian. Tolstoy's openheartedness appealed greatly to Mushanokōji, and he was determined to follow in the master's footsteps. Perhaps fortunately he was not at liberty to redistribute his family's wealth in the Tolstoyan manner, the estate being owned by his elder brother. He did, however, finance the publication of Shirakaba (*White Birch* magazine) by persuading his brother to release some money.

After only a year at Tokyo Imperial University, Mushanokōji left, along with his friend Shiga, to start a small literary group that became the nucleus of the Shirakabaha. The group, which included Ōgimachi Kinkazu and the *tanka* poet Kinoshita Rigen, met once a fortnight and published a small, coterie magazine bearing the title *Bōya* (*Directionless Arrow*). As Mushanokōji soon realized, their number was far too small to make any impact on a literary world increasingly dominated by *Naturalist writers. Furthermore, the expression of Tolstoy's openhearted philosophy called for closer cooperation between artists, no matter how distinct their individual styles. With this in mind he began earnest negotiations with other, similar groups, hoping to bring them all under the umbrella of a single organization to be called the Shirakabaha. He was entirely successful, and the first issue of *White Birch* – its title redolent of Russian landscapes – was published in April 1910.

Among the contents of the magazine's first issue were a short story by Shiga called *"Abashiri made"* ("All the Way to Abashiri"); some *tanka* poetry from Kinoshita; a contribution from ARISHIMA

TAKEO (at thirty-two, the eldest of the group); pieces from SATOMI TON and Kiro Torahiko; and a favorable review of NATSUME SŌSEKI's recent novel *Sorekara* (*1909, And Then*) by Mushanokōji himself. The whole issue was of modest proportions, but it launched several new authors, many of whom were to become famous. As a result of his review Mushanokōji was invited by Sōseki to contribute an arts column to the *Asahi shimbun*, the daily newspaper for which Soseki was literary editor.

Mushanokōji's energy and enthusiasm were the driving force behind the Shirakabaha. He believed implicitly that he was a genius in the Nietzschean mold, and, in a sense, proved it by inspiring his colleagues to assert their individual wills. Although he made few written contributions of any importance, he influenced the direction of the magazine and attracted attention to it as no one else could have done. The critic Nakamura Mitsuo – one of the pro-Mushanokōji lobby – summarized his overall contribution by saying that he influenced the whole of *Taishō literature. Looking back on the period, Nakamura believed that Mushanokōji added the essential ingredient of self-confidence to the *I-Novel genre, enabling it to develop beyond the point where the Naturalists had taken it.

Mushanokōji's first major novel was *Omedetaki hito* (1911, *A Good-Natured Person*), a work that exudes self-confidence from every page. It describes how, in the face of despair after a broken romance, the author becomes triumphantly happy. Making no secret of his virginity, the autobiographical "I" simultaneously regards women as existing on a higher plane (on account of their desirable femininity) and on a lower one (because of their inferiority to men in the world of action). Donald Keene has pointed out the inherent contradiction in such an attitude, and indeed most Western critics become surprisingly ill-natured when referring either to this novel or to Mushanokōji's subsequent work, *Sekenshirazu* (1912, *A Puerile Person*). Stephen Kohl describes *A Good-Natured Person* as "incredibly naïve," while William F. Sibley, in discussing the nature of Mushanokōji's influence on Shiga, dismisses the whole of his thought as "a manic effusion of platitudes about humanity, art and genius." Mushanokōji, says Sibley, "is perhaps the flimsiest 'major figure' that the Japanese literary historians have established for us so far."

At this point it is worthwhile considering what the Japanese have actually said about Mushanokōji. No less a person than Satō Haruo compared him to Rousseau, prompting Nakamura to add that Japan had produced several minor Rousseaus – TSUBOUCHI SHŌYŌ and Mushanokōji among them – instead of one major figure. AKUTAGAWA, who by any standard was a literary genius and a critic of exceptional sensitivity, claimed that Mushanokōji had "opened a new skylight for the literary world." Perhaps most revealingly, Hisamatsu Sen'ichi in his *Biographical Dictionary of Japanese Literature* noted: "For all their simpleness and directness of expression, one feels that his works are constantly grappling with the fundamental problems of human existence, and it is this quality that gives their author a place of unique importance among Japanese writers and thinkers."

Clearly, one needs to find a reason why Western and Japanese scholars have disagreed so greatly in their assessment of Mushanokōji. The answer almost certainly lies in their differing cultural perspectives. Even by the early part of the twentieth century the West had had its full share of individuals proclaiming this or that philosophy of self-expression and self-fulfillment. Western culture is rich not only in egocentric outspokenness but also in the particular brand of evangelical earnestness that was Mushanokōji's stock-in-trade. It is not surprising that scholars' hackles were raised when a Japanese version of the same phenomenon was encountered. In Japan, however, all was different. The first stirrings of individualism in literature after the end of the feudal period were weak and tentative. FUTABATEI SHIMEI lacked the confidence to continue writing because he believed it diminished his identity as a Japanese citizen. Less talented but equally timid were the Naturalists who deliberately discarded their egos in order to "confess" their personal experiences. Into this self-effacing world came Mushanokōji, totally convinced of his own genius. Whether or not people agreed with him was irrelevant to their needs. They merely identified with him, perhaps even gaining in self-confidence because his work was so transparently mediocre. In evaluating his historical importance one almost has to ignore the content of his overconfident tirades; the very fact that he made them was significant.

In 1918 Mushanokōji left Tokyo, having resigned his key position in the Shirakabaha, to found a utopian commune in Kyūshū. Despite the skepticism of his friends he was intent on applying his ideas in a real social context, and chose a tract of land in Hyūga because of its legendary associations with the Emperor Jimmu. (Somewhere in the vicinity the emperor was said to have descended from the High Plane of Heaven to found Japan over two and a half thousand years previously.) With nineteen young followers Mushanokōji established his settlement, called it *Atarashiki mura* ("The New Village"), and set about making it completely self-sufficient. Perhaps surprisingly it was a qualified success, and Mushanokōji remained there for eight years until financial and personal problems obliged him to move.

Mushanokōji published two works in his first year at the New

Village, beginning with *Kōfukumono* (1919, *The Happy Man*). It depicts the life of a self-made messiah, not unlike Mushanokōji himself, who founds a village community and builds a temple for his followers. At the end, after delivering many lectures on the subject of happiness, he disappears in mysterious circumstances. However, it was the second novel of that year, *Yūjō* (*1919, Friendship*), that represented the pinnacle of Mushanokōji's writing career. Concerning an unsuccessful writer who is rejected by the girl he loves, it once more emphasized the nobility of triumphing over adversity. The novel still has an appeal for young Japanese readers, but although it has been translated into English it has long been unobtainable in the West.

After leaving the New Village, Mushanokōji, always a compulsive publisher, started a general arts magazine called *Daichōwa* in 1927. It was strongly biased towards Western and Chinese art, in accordance with his own preferences. A painter himself who rejected the "prettiness" of flowers and landscapes in favor of the "honesty" of vegetables, he was especially fond of the post-Impressionists. He loved the boldness of Cézanne and Van Gogh, saying that: ". . . compared with bygone art, the new art is extremely serious, tense and deep . . . I feel that the new art is trying to touch the hearts of others by all possible means." He exhibited his own work at the Fourth National Art Exhibit in 1929, and in the same year opened an art shop in Kanda.

At the invitation of his brother, Mushanokōji traveled to the West in 1936, visiting the United States (which he disliked) and Germany, where he attended the Olympic Games. On his return to Japan he became increasingly interested in pan-Asian politics, hoping for Asiatic unity and even joining the Great East Asian Writers' Union. During the war he wrote a book of essays entitled *Daitōa Sensō shikan* (1942, *Personal Feelings on the Greater East Asia War*), expressing a complete reversal of his previously held anti-militarist views. Ever the extremist, he denounced Britain and the United States, castigating them so vehemently that he was named as a G-category war criminal after Japan's defeat. The official classification was removed in 1951, by which time he was already publishing more peaceful essays in *Kokoro*, a magazine in which literature's elder statesmen often expressed their views.

Mushanokōji died in 1976, at the great age of ninety-one.

RECOMMENDED READING

Novels

Friendship. Yūjō. 1919. 162 pages. Tr. Ryozo Matsumoto. Hokuseido, Tokyo, 1958. His most popular novel.
Love and Death. Ai to shi. 1939. 101 pages. (1) Tr. William F. Marquardt. Twayne Publishers, NY, 1958. (2) Tr. Saburo Yamamura. Hokuseido, Tokyo, 1967. His last major novel.

WORKS IN ENGLISH TRANSLATION

Novels

Friendship. Yūjō. 1919.
Love and Death. Ai to shi. 1939.

Short Fiction

"Dawn." *"Akatsuki."* 1924. 45 pages. Tr. Takehide Kikuchi. Information Publishing, Tokyo, 1972.

"The Driving of Nails." *"Kugi o utsu oto."* 3 pages. Tr. Takehide Kikuchi. *Eigo Kenkyu,* vol. 42, no. 9, 1953.

"Even Thorns Are Beautiful." *"Toge made uruwashi."* 1930. Tr. Takehide Kikuchi. *Info,* June–Nov. 1962.

"A Happy Family." *"Kōfuku no kazoku."* 1940. Tr. Takehide Kikuchi. *Info,* Sept. 1961–May 1962.

"Judas' Explanation: John on Hearing Judas' Explanation." *"Yuda no benkai hoka."* 1921. 12 pages. Tr. Richard McKinnon. *The Heart Is Alone,* ed. Richard McKinnon. Hokuseido, Tokyo, 1957.

"Miyamoto Musashi." *"Miyamoto Musashi."* 9 pages. Tr. S. G. Brickley. *The Writing of Idiomatic English.* Kenkyusha, Tokyo, 1951.

"A Rainbow." *"Niji."* 1946. Tr. Takehide Kikuchi. *Info,* Dec. 1962–May 1963.

"Two Mice." *"Nihiki no nezumi."* 1955. 8 pages. Tr. Richard Foster. *Eigo Kenkyu,* vol. 55, nos. 11–12, 1966.

Plays

Daruma. Daruma. 1924. 11 pages. (1) Tr. G. Ogura. *Japan Times,* Oct. 28, 1928. (2) Tr. J. M. Shinshiro. *Aoba no fue.* The University Press of Hawaii, Honolulu, 1937. (3) As "Bodhidharma." Tr. Umeyo Hirano. *Buddhist Plays from Japanese Literature.* CIIB Press, Tokyo, 1962.

The Day's Episode in Ikkyu's Life. Aru hi no Ikkyū Oshō. 1913. 9 pages. (1) Tr. Fumikazu Tanaka. *Osaka Mainichi,* June 8–11, 1929. (2) As "Monk Ikkyu." Tr. Umeyo Hirano. *Buddhist Plays from Japanese Literature.* CIIB Press, Tokyo, 1962.

A Family Affair. Aru kazoku. 35 pages. Tr. Yozan T. Iwasaki and Glenn Hughes. *New Plays from Japan.* Ernest Benn, London, 1930; *Treasury of World Literature,* ed. D. D. Runes. Philosophical Society, NY, 1956.

I Don't Know Either. Washi mo shiranai. 1914. 18 pages. Tr. Umeyo Hirano. *Young East,* no.

19, Autumn 1956; *Buddhist Plays from Japanese Literature.*

The Man of the Flowers. Hanasaka jijii. 1917. 54 pages. Tr. Junichi Natori. Hokuseido, Tokyo, 1955; *Two Fables of Japan.* Hokuseido, Tokyo, 1957.

The Passion. Aiyoku. 1925. 91 pages. Tr. Noboru Hidaka. *The Passion, and Three Other Japanese Plays.* Oriental Literature Society, Honolulu, 1933; Greenwood Press, NY, 1971.

The Rabbit's Revenge. Kachi kachi yama. 1917. 57 pages. Tr. Junichi Natori. *Two Fables of Japan.*

Three Cheers for Man. Ningen banzai. 1922. 43 pages. Tr. Kenneth Strong. *Japan Quarterly*, vol. 10, no. 1, 1963.

Essay

"Kokoro no utsukushisa." *"Kokoro no utsukushisa."* Tr. Yokichi Okuma. *Chugai Eigo*, April 1920.

Poetry

"The Closed Door." Tr. Shigeshi Nishimura. *The Current of the World*, vol. 26, no. 11, 1949.

"Loneliness." *An Anthology of Modern Japanese Poetry*, ed. and tr. Ichiro Kono and Rikutaro Fukuda. Kenkyusha, Tokyo, 1957.

"Pumpkins and Potatoes." Tr. James Kirkup. *Modern Japanese Poetry*, ed. A. R. Davis. University of Queensland Press, 1978.

"Scene of Peace." Tr. Shigeshi Nishimura. *The Current of the World*, vol. 28, no. 1, 1951.

Nagai KAFŪ
(1879–1959)

Writer of short fiction and diarist. Real name, Nagai Sōkichi. Born in Koishikawa, Tokyo. Lived briefly in the United States and France, otherwise in Tokyo.

A brilliant prose stylist, Nagai Kafū enjoyed great popularity both long before and after World War II for his tales of life in the pleasure quarters of Tokyo. It was there, among the bars, cafés, and whorehouses, that he detected the last vestiges of a bygone era: the late *Edo period. He loved the humble culture of Edo's *"floating world" with a passion that was singularly absent from his relationships with women, and he spent much of his time writing nostalgic elegies from a vantage point of self-imposed exile amid contemporary society. Invariably described as an eccentric who rarely inspired affection in those acquainted with him, Kafū nonetheless projected a unique and curiously noble sensibility which continues to move his readers to this very day. Edward Seidensticker, the author of the definitive study of Kafū in the English language (1965, *Kafū the Scribbler*), believed him to be "better and more important than any one of his works." Nearly all of his stories from 1898 until his death in 1959 support the opinion that his literary gifts were more suited to the lyrical "essay-novel" than to dramatic works of fiction. Chiefly for this reason, Kafū is not as widely read in the West as some of his contemporaries, although many of his works have been rendered into English by Professor Seidensticker and other scholars. Among them are *"Sumidagawa"* (*1909,* "The River Sumida"); *Udekurabe* (1918, *Geisha in Rivalry*); and *"Bokutō kidan"* (*1937,* "A Strange Tale from East of the River"). Anyone who is entertained by the nineteenth-century prints of Hokusai or Hiroshige will find in these works a unique, twentieth-century prose equivalent.

Kafū's real name was Nagai Sōkichi, and he was born on December 3, 1879, in the Koishikawa district of Tokyo. Although he would always be proud of being a "true Edokko" (native son of Edo), both of his parents had in fact come to the capital from the province of Owari. His mother, Tsune, was the daughter of Washizu Kidō, a distinguished Confucian scholar; his father, Nagai Kagen, the son of a wealthy landowner. Since Kagen had been Kidō's disciple before marrying Tsune, it was not surprising that a strong Confucian ethic held sway in the Nagai household. While Sōkichi, their first-born son, was growing up in this emotionally cool environment, Kagen meanwhile pursued a highly successful career at the Ministry of Education, helping to draft the repressive Imperial Rescript of 1890. Educated in the West, Kafū's father was a firm believer in material progress, but by rejecting Western freedoms in favor of traditional Japanese virtues he aligned himself with the many architects of modern Japan. Through a stroke of divine irony he was blessed with a son who scorned everything he stood for; who not only despised the modern world but flouted every Confucian virtue with undisguised relish.

Even while attending high school, the young Kafū neglected his studies and spent much of his time reading pornographic literature from the Edo period. His friend Inoue Seiichi was extremely knowledgeable in this respect, the two of them sharing a taste for the fiction of *Tamenaga Shunsui (1790–1843), the creator of the *ninjōbon* genre. By the age of eighteen, Kafū and his companion were already visiting the *Yoshiwara: the pleasure quarter which, coincidentally, was even then being immortalized in literature by HIGUCHI ICHIYŌ. Determined to grasp his fair share of pleasure while still young enough to enjoy it, Kafū established the direction his life would take. He began writing stories in the manner of Shunsui, evoking the "sensuous, unthinking" world of Edo by the banks of the Sumida River.

Kafū's first story was never published, nor does the manuscript survive. It was about a nurse called O-hasu (Miss Lotus) who looked after him during one of several bouts of illness. Suffering from an intestinal complaint, upon which he was able to blame many of his academic failings, Kafū had recuperated at his father's villa in Zushi. With time on his hands and Miss Lotus in attendance he was able to pursue his interests in sex and literature at his leisure. Although nothing remains of the story he produced, the episode itself is of note because the nurse's name became his own. His literary sobriquet, Kafū, means "lotus breeze."

Kafū's first surviving story is *"Oboroyo"* ("Misty Night"), written at the end of 1898 or early the following year. Couched in the style of Hirotsu Ryūrō, an author of so-called distressing novels, whom Kafū had secured as his mentor, it tells about a girl who follows in the footsteps of her mother by becoming a prostitute, much to her mother's distress. However, it was a later work called *"Hanakago"* ("Flower Basket") that was actually the first of Kafū's stories to be published. Describing how a bride-to-be is raped by her father's employer prior to her wedding, it won a prize in a newspaper contest in 1899.

By the end of the century Kafū was leading in earnest the life of an Edo dilettante. He first apprenticed himself to a teller of *rakugo* comic stories until his family put a stop to it, whereupon he joined the Kabuki Theater as apprentice to Fukuchi Ochi, its chief playwright. Leaving to become a reporter for the *Yamato shimbun*, he came to know Jōno Saigiku (1832–1902), a writer of frivolous *gesaku* fiction who enjoyed a reputation as "one of the last true Edo dilettantes." Yet in spite of his obsession with Edo culture, Kafū began to take an interest in the works of Emile Zola, reading them first in English translation and then going to night school to learn French so that he could read them in their original language. Zola had been popular in Japan for a decade or more, appealing equally to such writers as OZAKI KŌYŌ and to the *Naturalists who opposed Kōyō. Under Zola's influence Kafū wrote three medium-length novels in the year 1902–03: *Yashin* (*Ambition*); *Jigoku no hana* (*Hell Flowers*); and *Yume no onna* (*The Woman of the Dream*). Of these early works only *The Woman of the Dream* has any real distinction, being an elegy about a girl called O-nami who becomes a prostitute in order to help her father, a samurai fallen upon hard times. Referring to this story and to Kafū's subsequent development as a writer, Professor Seidensticker comments: "It takes but a small shift for the lament upon a wasted life to become a lament upon a despoiled city and a lost tradition." Several years were to pass, however, before Kafū could enlarge the scope of his major theme.

Wishing to put an end to his frivolity, his father sent him to the United States in 1903.

Kafū spent four years in America, where, for brief periods, he felt himself to be the happiest man on earth. Unlike most Japanese traveling in the West he had no sense of inferiority: that state of mind which stems from being deprived of one's social support system. After all, even before leaving Japan he was an exile in spirit, and he was now thoroughly pleased to be away from the country of his birth. Moreover, being tall and good-looking and with a command of fluent English he was remarkably self-confident. He fully expected to make his name with the stories he would write overseas. As it happened, his expectations were justified. His years in America gave rise to *Amerika monogatari* (1908, *American Stories*), consisting of fourteen tales and ten essays, all of which were published on his return to Japan. The collection established his reputation, identifying him as a distinctive writer in a new, aesthetic tradition of modern Japanese letters.

Kafū spent his first year overseas in Seattle and Tacoma, then, after seeing St. Louis and Chicago, became a student of French and philosophy at Kalamazoo College. His movements are well-documented, for he kept a journal called *Saiyū nisshishō* (1917, *Leaves from a Journal of a Western Voyage*), in which he recorded many miscellaneous thoughts. It is a bookish memoir that shows his increasing love of French literature, while often commenting on his strained relations with his father. The issue troubling him most was his father's refusal to pay for a trip to France, the country Kafū most wanted to visit. Instead, he learned that a post had been secured for him in the New York office of the Yokohama Specie Bank. Thus, he traveled from Washington, D.C., where he had worked in a menial capacity for the Japanese legation, and began his lackluster banking career. Throughout this period he conducted an affair with an American girl called Edyth, whom he left behind when, after a year's service, the bank obligingly transferred him to their branch in Lyon.

Kafū adored France, finding it even better in reality than he had previously dared to imagine. In particular he admired the way in which the French succeeded in preserving the past, despite their embrace of the twentieth century. When he compared French cities to Tokyo he became virulent in his attacks on *Meiji Japan, lamenting the destruction of the old Edo city in the wake of progress. Indeed, his hatred of modern Japan grew to almost hysterical heights in *Furansu monogatari* (1910, *French Stories*), a series of works started in France and continued on his journey home. Financial problems alone prevented him from remaining in France, for he was dismissed by the bank and found himself quite without funds for a prolonged stay in Paris, the city of his choice. By August 1908 he was back with his family, and living in their new home in Ōkubo, on the western outskirts of Tokyo.

Kafū's rise to fame was not entirely without setbacks. Although *American Stories* had been published by the time he returned to Japan, his collection of French stories was banned because two of the pieces were deemed immoral. In fact, one of these censored works, the play *Ikyō no koi* (*Love in a Foreign Land*), failed to appear in print until 1947. Angry, but not unduly surprised, Kafū was at least left with the satisfaction of having been treated in much the same way as his hero, Tamenaga Shunsui, whose works had been banned by the Edo authorities for exactly the same reason.

Kafū's most productive year was 1909. In February he published a disturbing story called *"Fukagawa no uta"* ("A Song of Fukagawa"), in which the narrator describes his discomfort in riding a streetcar through modern-day Tokyo. When the car eventually breaks down and the man is given a transit pass that will take him on a diversion to Fukagawa, he is delighted. Unexpectedly finding himself in this ancient quarter he becomes eloquent and emotional: "His eyes, filled with the bustle of the theater teahouses, the crimson carpets of rehearsal halls, the flowered hats and lanterns of festival days, were spared the horrid streetcars and power lines and all the rest of our superficial Westernization . . ." (Seidensticker's translation). In reading these descriptions one may be reminded of the similar sensibility of TANIZAKI JUN'ICHIRŌ, a writer who followed in the tradition started by Kafū. Yet Tanizaki's evocation of the past is altogether more cerebral, more complete, and more pleasurable. In his stories (and in such essays as "In Praise of Shadows," 1933) he succeeded in making the lost world of Edo a living archetype that corresponds, in some magical fashion, to a dreamworld of psychic perfection. Kafū, on the other hand, is painful to read. His laments are all too real, and he makes us experience his own acute sensations of grief and deprivation.

Greatly impressed by "A Song of Fukagawa," Japan's leading novelist NATSUME SŌSEKI commissioned Kafū to write a newspaper serial for the *Asahi shimbun*. The result was *Reishō* (*1909–10, Sneers*), a rambling, disconnected work in which the author continued to berate "the tasteless externals of Tokyo life in 1909." Conceptually no different from his preceding story, it contrasted the delightful seediness of the back alleys with the inhuman monstrosity of mainstream Tokyo. Where it differed from Kafū's previous work was in the excellence of its lyrical passages. Those from the chapter *"Yoru no samisen"* ("The Samisen in the Night"), quoted by

Seidensticker in *Kafū the Scribbler*, are surely among the best examples of Japanese prose, their English translation echoing the quality of the original.

Kafū's first true masterpiece was also written in 1909. "The River Sumida" is a symphony of lyricism, a true classic of modern literature that can be described only in terms usually reserved for painting or music. Kafū captures perfectly the insubstantial, fading world on the banks of the Sumida, and in reading the novella one comes to recognize an aspect of his creative impulse that is easily misunderstood. Although there is little doubt that he lamented its passing, Edo culture appealed to him for the very reason that it *was* disappearing into the mists of time. He loved graveyards and twilight; shabby reed doors which allowed the air to pass through them; and the coming of autumn to stir an "indefinable restlessness" in the heart of his hero. Even when he describes an intense darkness he modifies it by noting the uncertainty one would have in detecting the presence or absence of a garden. Thus, in the pages of "The River Sumida" one is invited not only to join his lament for a lost way of life but also to take aesthetic delight in the ephemerality of all things. The novella was a remarkable achievement, and completely vindicated Kafū's tendency to suppress plot and character in favor of background.

If 1909 saw the first flowering of Kafū's genius, the following year brought him face to face with reality. Three events occurred in rapid succession. The resolutely irresponsible author became professor of French at Keio University; he was then shocked into silence when twelve anarchists were arrested in the famous May Incident; and he was dismayed when a severe flood swept away much of his beloved old city. These events combined to create a momentary seriousness in Kafū's outlook, until his frivolous temperament reasserted itself. Indeed, he later referred to the May Incident as a crisis point in his career: the moment when he felt such unbearable shame that he decided to resign himself forever to remaining a writer of *gesaku* fiction.

For all his lack of conventional morality, Kafū was a conscientious teacher who never failed to appear at the correct time to deliver his lectures. His students belonged to a private institution that was a serious rival to Waseda University, where young men from the provinces had created the literary movement known as Naturalism. Early in his career Kafū had been regarded as a Naturalist himself, but it was now clear to everyone that he was nothing of the sort. In fact, his appointment at Keio was a political ploy, engineered by MORI ŌGAI and the translator Ueda Bin, to encourage anti-Naturalist forces and so banish the dreary domesticity that was threatening to stifle Japanese literature. It was entirely successful. In rivalry to *Waseda bungaku*, Kafū edited the magazine *Mita bungaku*, and, in a famous essay, praised Tanizaki to such an extent that the younger man's reputation was assured. Ōgai, too, contributed to the Keio publication, while Kafū's own essays and sketches for the magazine were collected in 1911 under the title *Kōcha no ato* (*After the Tea*).

Kafū's halfhearted attempts to oblige his family by appearing to lead a conventional life included getting married in 1911. The unfortunate girl was a merchant's daughter for whom he cared nothing. Even when his father died suddenly in 1912, Kafū was away in the Hakone Mountains with the *geisha* Yaeji of Shimbashi and could not be contacted. Divorced in 1912, he married his *geisha* the following year, but under this more intimate arrangement they lived together for only a few months before she, too, walked out on him. Kafū's personal life was becoming even more ragged, and not just at the edges but at the center, where in his own family he feuded bitterly with his youngest brother over the division of their father's estate. Of the three Nagai brothers, only Kafū and Isaburō still belonged to the same house: the middle brother, Teijirō, having been adopted by the Washizu family many years previously. Now, with all the unpleasantness surrounding the patriarch's death, even Kafū and his mother were at loggerheads. From this period onwards the frivolous writer would find himself becoming increasingly isolated, despite his well-established fame as a novelist.

In 1913 Kafū published two novels that were later reissued in a single volume called *Yanagi sakura* (*Willow and Cherry*). Both stories are mood pieces in which language is made to serve the same purpose as the colors of theatrical costumes and settings. The autumnal "willow" story describes the last days of the Edo fiction writer, Ryūtei Tanehiko (1783–1843); while the "cherry" piece, set for contrast in the springtime, tells of the elopement of O-sen, a famous Edo beauty once depicted by that master of the brocade print, Suzuki Harunobu. During the same year Kafū also published one of his most highly regarded works: an anthology of French translations called *Sangoshū* (*Coral Anthology*). It contained poems by Baudelaire and Verlaine, together with some studies of prose writers, since grouped with other essays under the title *Taisei bungei ronshū* (*Studies of the Arts of the West*).

Kafū moved back into his family home in Ōkubo in January 1916, having recently lived in such areas as Tsukiji and Yanagibashi. He was suffering from a recurrence of his gastric complaint, and had decided not only to resign from the university but to build a cottage in the grounds of the family home and call it "Dyspepsia House." Some of the essays he wrote in this tiny garden cottage he collected under the title *Danchōtei zakkō* (1918, *Miscellaneous Manuscripts from Dyspepsia House*).

With more time on his hands Kafū began to increase his output of writings, making 1917 the most significant year in his professional life since 1909. It was now that he began to keep his famous diary, a collection of thoughts treasured by his admirers and described irreverently by Seidensticker as "a record of tasteful pursuits, suggesting an Oriental hermit gone a bit European." Perhaps more important, and certainly more accessible to Western readers, was the novel serialized in *Bummei* between August 1916 and October 1917, called *Udekurabe* (*Geisha in Rivalry*). This magnificent novel, about three *geisha* competing for the same patron, is one of Kafū's most enjoyable works. Its frank descriptions of sexual activity caused it to be heavily censored in various editions until 1956.

More sophisticated in its structure is *Okamezasa* (*1918, Dwarf Bamboo*), the story of an unsuccessful painter who becomes corrupted by the family of the artist to whom he is apprenticed. Of all Kafū's work that remains untranslated, this novel is surely the most deserving of an English version. It is realistic in the tradition of Zola and contains no moral messages whatsoever, only a tolerant portrayal of the human comedy in action. During its serial publication, Kafū began to withdraw from society as if feeling the onset of middle age. He sold his Ōkubo home, moved back to Tsukiji, and witnessed the publication of his first "complete works," which serve to punctuate this stage of his career.

As a wealthy but frugal man, Kafū never suffered from the financial problems that often plagued his contemporaries. In 1920 he built a large Western-style home in Azabu, a smart area near the American Embassy, and remained there until the air raids of 1945. He called it the *Henkikan* ("Eccentricity House") in acknowledgment of his growing tendency to reclusiveness. However, his humorous writings of this period, published as *Henkikan manroku* (1920–21, *Ruminations from Eccentricity House*), belied the fact that he was still capable of producing an occasional masterpiece. *"Ame shōshō"* (1921, "Quiet Rain") was such a work, an example of the quasi-fictional genre which dates back to *Sei Shōnagon. It is one of the finest stories in modern Japanese literature, even though it is simply an account of meetings and correspondence with a worldly male acquaintance, as recorded by a Mr. Kimpū. The latter, of course, is a somewhat exaggerated version of the author himself, while the acquaintance is a man who shares Kafū's opinions about the decline of Edo culture. These facts, however, are of minor importance, for the story is so subtle and evocative that it seems to embody the very essence of Kafū's art. A delightful humor is suggested by the improbable similarities of the two men: the aging narrator who prefers eating and sleeping to having sex, and his friend who has purchased for his mistress a new house where he intends to teach her an obscure method of playing the samisen. And all the while a perpetual rain is falling, as if washing away the angers and griefs and loves of youth.

At this point a historian has to remind himself that Kafū was still only forty-two, much younger in years than the self-caricature who appeared in "Quiet Rain." Nonetheless, it was true that most of his best fiction was now behind him, apart from one isolated masterpiece written in 1937. He seemed to have lost interest in writing fiction, despite addressing himself to the subject in a vague and confused thesis entitled *"Shōsetsu sakuhō"* (1920, "How to Write a Novel"). Influenced by the late works of Mori Ōgai he turned his attention to minor historical figures: to men like his maternal grandfather, Washizu Kidō, whom he portrayed in *Shitaya sōwa* (1924, *Shitaya Gleanings*). His chief motivation for doing so may have been his growing impatience with the colloquial language which most readers expected to find in a modern novel. If Mori Ōgai could depart from the vernacular, Kafū was prepared to follow him.

Apart from his triumph with "Quiet Rain," the 1920s were lean years in Kafū's writing career. He quarreled with many of his publishers, and with MASAMUNE HAKUCHŌ who accused him of having "literary affectations." Mori Ōgai died in 1922, and Kafū's friend Inoue Seiichi likewise returned (in Kafū's words) "to the mountains from which he came." Helping to dispel the gloom toward the end of the decade, Kafū began a long relationship with a Kōjimachi *geisha* called O-uta, purchasing her contract and subsequently setting her up in an establishment of her own. But as if to confirm a flagging inspiration during a time when only his novel *Kashima no onna* (1926, *The Woman in the Rented Room*) had any real quality, he destroyed many of his manuscripts in August 1928. On the eve of the new decade he noted in his diary the pros and cons of a writer's life. "The pronouncements of scribblers," he said, "are no different from the whining of mosquitoes." Yet he counted himself lucky to have reached his fiftieth year without any serious misfortune. "Looking back . . . I find that I have done nothing to disturb my sleep."

In 1931 there was a sudden resurgence in Kafū's writing. In *Chūō kōron* he published a novel called *Tsuyu no atosaki* (*During the Rains*), of which Tanizaki wrote warmly: "The oldness of the form stands in subtle contrast to the modern colors of the material." Tanizaki also liked *"Enoki monogatari"* ("A Tale of a Nettle Tree"), a short story about a corrupt priest who hides money in a tree and uses it to treat himself to nights of revelry. Seidensticker calls "Nettle Tree" a "sport among Kafū's works in that the element of suspense is important," and indeed its plot is of a kind beloved by KIKUCHI KAN whom Kafū often reviled in his essays and diaries.

Kafū returned to his more familiar mode in the story *"Ajisai"* (1931, "Hydrangea"). It depicts a typically dissolute narrator who, in halfheartedly attempting to murder his fickle mistress, is upstaged by a rival who actually carries out the deed. The story is familiar to many Western readers because of its inclusion in Ivan Morris's best-selling anthology, *Modern Japanese Stories* (1962).

For his novel *During the Rains* Kafū had drawn on material gathered from his visits to his favorite café, the Tiger. However, quite another source of material was often presented to famous Japanese writers when friends or admirers related their own life stories, hoping to be immortalized in prose. Such had been the genesis of Natsume Sōseki's novel *The Miner* (1908), and now it was Kafū's turn to take advantage of a similar occurrence. Based on a story told to him by the keeper of a *geisha* house, he wrote *Hikage no hana* (1934, *Flowers in the Shade*), a novel in thirteen chapters about the social outcasts of Tokyo's underworld. It was written in the same dry, "modern" style which he had used for both "Hydrangea" and *During the Rains* and was indicative of a new attempt to come to terms with the realities of modern life.

A personal link with the past was severed when Kafū's mother died in 1937. Although he did not attend the funeral because he and his brother Isaburō were still estranged, he grieved privately, and wrote some eloquent words of mourning in his diary. It was not long, however, before he was visiting his favorite haunts, Asakusa and Tamanoi, the latter having recently provided the setting for *"Bokutō kidan"* (1937, "A Strange Tale from East of the River"). A discursive "essay-novel" in the same genre as "Quiet Rain," it is generally regarded as one of his masterpieces. Here Kafū is in an unusually intimate mood, telling of his secret visits to a remote pleasure quarter east of the river where a young *geisha* has been gradually falling in love with him. Despite the story's many digressions it holds to a thin, but distinctive, narrative line. Indeed, Kafū's digressions are full-bodied chords, which, by providing contrast, actually create the narrative's plaintive, samisen-like quality. The story culminates at the point where the narrator pays one last visit to the girl, intending to be completely truthful about his identity and occupation: facts he has concealed for more or less valid reasons hitherto. Yet in the brief time he has stayed away from her, much has already changed. The old atmosphere has gone, and the girl's house is more crowded than before. He never does tell her the reasons why they should not be married, but returns home to his lonely study, his books, and his poetry.

Kafū achieved a remarkable intensity in "East of the River," chiefly by exaggerating relatively unimportant aspects of his life while understating his real emotions. The narrator's decision to "tell the truth" is surely a tacit admission of his love for the girl, and this revelation comes as a great surprise to the reader. After all, to discover real, intimate feelings in the dissolute Kafū is to stumble upon a rare treasure, as he himself was well aware. In one eloquent digression he tells exactly why he has always been an habitué of the pleasure quarters rather than a righteous husband, and his explanation harmonizes perfectly with the climax of the story. He states (quoting from a previous work): "Indignation at the hypocritical vanity of proper wives and at the fraud of the just and open society was the force that sent him speeding in the other direction, toward what was from the start taken for dark and unrighteous. There was more happiness in finding the remains of a beautifully woven pattern among castaway rags than in finding spatters and stains on a wall proclaimed immaculate." And as if to prove the point at the end of the story, he allows the reader to see something of the real Kafū amid the "castaway rags" of his frivolous nature.

A detailed discussion of Kafū's works after "East of the River" is bound to be anticlimactic. He maintained a stoic silence throughout World War II, convinced that Japan was making a big mistake with its military policies. In the final air raids he lost both his home and his magnificent library of ten thousand volumes: the books he so lovingly "aired" in his 1937 classic. The image of Kafū fleeing his home, clutching his diary and manuscripts, is captured forever in Ishikawa Jun's story *"Meigetsushu"* (1946, "Moon Gems"), translated in volume 1 of *The Shōwa Anthology* (1985). Yet the aging writer himself was by no means defeated, for in the liberal postwar atmosphere he suddenly enjoyed a great resurgence of popularity and literary acclaim. Sales of his works completely restored his fortune. During 1952 he was awarded the Imperial Cultural Decoration and became a member of the Japanese Academy of Arts two years later.

In some remote corner of its imagination, society had finally come to accept Nagai Kafū and pay homage to the values he held dear. He was certainly aware of its hypocrisy. Long ago he had said: ". . . the world has become a most inconvenient place for people who walk in the shade." He died alone, on April 30, 1959.

RECOMMENDED READING

Novel

Geisha in Rivalry. *Udekurabe. 1918.* 206 pages. (1) Tr. Kurt Meissner, with collaboration of Ralph Friedrich. Tuttle, Tokyo, 1963. (2) Extract (from Chapter 12) as "Rivalry." *Kafū the Scribbler.* The Tuttle edition of the full-length novel contains a 6-page introduction by the translators.

Short Fiction Collections

Kafū the Scribbler, The Life and Writings of Nagai Kafū, 1879–1959.
By Edward Seidensticker. 306 pages. Stanford University Press, Stanford, 1965; University of Michigan, Ann Arbor, 1990, paperback. A great work of scholarship that is also readable and entertaining. Contains many photographs and illustrations. Translations include "The River Sumida"; "Coming Down with a Cold"; "Quiet Rain"; and "A Strange Tale from East of the River."
A Strange Tale from East of the River, and Other Stories. 172 pages. Tr. Edward Seidensticker. Tuttle, Tokyo, 1971. A reprint of all the stories published in *Kafū the Scribbler.*

WORKS IN ENGLISH TRANSLATION

Novel

Geisha in Rivalry. Udekurabe. 1918.

Short Fiction

"Bill-Collecting." *"Kaketori."* 1912. 31 pages. (1) As "The Bill-Collecting." Tr. Torao Taketomo. *Paulownia, Seven Stories from Contemporary Japanese Writers,* ed. D. D. Runes, Duffield, NY, 1918; Philosophical Library, NY, 1956. (2) Tr. Roland A. Lange. *Journal-Newsletter of the Association of Teachers of Japanese,* vol. 5, no. 2, 1968.

"Coming Down with a Cold." *"Kazegokochi."* 1912. 11 pages. *Kafū the Scribbler; A Strange Tale from East of the River, and Other Stories.*

"The Dancing Girl." *"Odoriko."* Composed 1944; published 1946. 3-page extract (Chapter 10). *Kafū the Scribbler; A Strange Tale from East of the River, and Other Stories.*

"The Decoration." *"Kunshō."* Composed 1942; published 1946. 7 pages. *Kafū the Scribbler; A Strange Tale from East of the River, and Other Stories.*

"The Fox." *"Kitsune."* 1909. 25 pages. Tr. Asataro Miyamori. *Representative Tales of Japan.* Sanko Shoin, Tokyo, 1917.

"Hydrangea." *"Ajisai."* 1931. 15 pages. Tr. Edward Seidensticker. *Modern Japanese Stories,* ed. Ivan Morris. Spottiswoode, London, 1961; Tuttle, Tokyo, 1962.

"Nude." *"Ratai."* 1950. 15 pages. Tr. Mark Harbison. *Journal of*

Literary Translation, no. 17, 1986; *The Mother of Dreams,* ed. Makoto Ueda. Kodansha International, Tokyo, 1986.

"The Peony Garden." *"Botan no kyaku."* 1909. 7 pages. *Kafū the Scribbler; A Strange Tale from East of the River, and Other Stories.*

"Pleasure." *"Kanraku."* 1909. 43 pages. Tr. Ryozo Matsumoto. *Japanese Literature, New and Old.* Hokuseido, Tokyo, 1961.

"Quiet Rain." *"Ame shōshō."* Composed 1918, revised and published 1921. 24 pages. Tr. Edward Seidensticker. *Japan Quarterly,* vol. 11, no. 1, 1964; *Kafū the Scribbler; A Strange Tale from East of the River, and Other Stories.*

"The River Sumida." *"Sumidagawa."* 1909. 41 pages (1) Tr. Donald Keene. *Modern Japanese Literature,* ed. Donald Keene. Grove Press, NY, 1956; Tuttle, Tokyo, 1957. (2) Tr. Edward Seidensticker. *Kafū the Scribbler;* *A Strange Tale from East of the River, and Other Stories.*

"The Scavengers." *"Katsushika miyage."* 1949. 6 pages. *Kafū the Scribbler; A Strange Tale from East of the River, and Other Stories.*

"A Strange Tale from East of the River." *"Bokutō kidan."* 1937. 50 pages. Tr. Edward Seidensticker. *Japan Quarterly,* vol. 5, no. 2, 1958; *Kafū the Scribbler; A Strange Tale from East of the River, and Other Stories.*

"Tidings from Okubo." *"Ōkubo dayori."* 1913–14. Excerpts. 7 pages. Tr. Edward Seidensticker. *Kafū the Scribbler; A Strange Tale from East of the River, and Other Stories.*

"The Two Wives." *"Futari zuma."* 1926. 6 pages. Tr. S. G. Brickley. *The Writing of Idiomatic English.* Kenkyusha, Tokyo, 1951.

"Ukiyoe." *"Ukiyoe."* 10 pages. Tr. Torao Taketomo. *Paulownia, Seven Stories from Contemporary Japanese Writers.*

CRITICAL STUDIES

Akiyama, Masayuki. "The American Image in Kafū Nagai and Henry James." *Comparative Literature Studies,* vol. 18, no. 2, 1981.

Cheng, Ching-mao. *Nagai Kafū and Chinese Tradition.* Ph.D. diss., Princeton University, Princeton, 1971.

———. "Nagai Kafū's Concept of Fiction." *Tamkang Review,* no. 2, 1971.

Iriye, Mitsuko Maeda. *Quest for Literary Resonance: Young Nagai Kafū and French Literature.* Ph.D. diss., Harvard University, Cambridge, 1969.

Lange, Roland A. "Introduction; Kafū Nagai's 'Bill Collecting.'" *Journal-Newsletter of the Association of Teachers of Japanese,* vol. 5, no. 2, 1968.

Rabson, Steve. "Nagai Kafū: The River Sumida, A Strange Tale from East of the River." *Approaches to the Modern Japanese Short Story,* ed. Thomas E. Swann and Kinya Tsuruta. Waseda University Press, Tokyo, 1982.

Seidensticker, Edward G. "Kafū and Tanizaki." *Japan Quarterly,* vol. 4, no. 4, 1965.

———. *Kafū the Scribbler: The Life and Writings of Nagai Kafū.* Stanford University Press, Stanford, 1965.

———. "On the Diaries of Nagai Kafū and Certain of His Novels." *Transactions of the International Conference of Orientalists in Japan,* no. 2, 1957.

Natsume SŌSEKI
(1867–1916)

Novelist and scholar. Real name: Natsume Kinnosuke. Born in Tokyo. Taught in Shikoku, Kyūshū, and studied in England, otherwise a resident of Tokyo.

Natsume Sōseki is widely regarded in Japan as the greatest novelist of the twentieth century. He began his career by writing an astringent satire called *I Am a Cat* while still a professor of English Literature at Tokyo Imperial University. It was so popular (and indeed as a classic on a par with Sterne's *Tristram Shandy* it is still in print all over the world) that Sōseki became a full-time author. He went on to produce the best-loved of all Japanese novels: *Botchan* (*1906*, "The Little Master," translated as *Botchan*), and then, in a remarkable transformation, wrote the two great trilogies on which his reputation largely rests. Inevitably more somber than his humorous novels, these later works are every bit as readable as the satires. Moreover, they reveal a man gifted with profound psychological insight. In a carefully considered opinion, argued at length in a complete analysis of characters in ten of Sōseki's novels, the eminent psychiatrist Dr. Doi Takeo pronounced him the equal of Freud ". . . in the sharpness and depth of his psychological observations." A Western reader, if possessed of the wit to hold (say) both Jane Austen and Dostoievsky in high esteem, could find it possible to agree with even this assessment, provocative though it is.

Natsume Kinnosuke (Sōseki was the pen name he adopted, and by which he is universally known) was born in Edo during the last year of the *Tokugawa era. His father was a respected town official, a "ward chief" or *nanushi*, who already had a large family and was, at fifty-three, getting on in years. It is said that the Natsumes were bitterly ashamed of having another child so late in life, and for this reason the new arrival was quickly sent out for adoption. Between the ages of two and nine Sōseki was therefore brought up by foster parents, but was eventually returned home after they divorced each other. By the time he was back with his real parents, believing them to be his grandparents, he had become very confused and not a little disturbed by his loveless childhood. It was a burden he would carry throughout his life.

At school Sōseki was a late developer and had an unusually prolonged education. He was most adept at Chinese studies, showing a rare talent for composing Chinese poetry. However, in 1888, when he entered junior college, he chose English Literature as his subject and continued to pursue it at Tokyo Imperial University in 1890. By 1891 he could not only read English fluently but could translate from Japanese into English, using an ornate style which he had picked up from the Victorians. He read widely in philosophy, poetry, and fiction, becoming especially interested in the English philosophers Herbert Spencer and John Stuart Mill. For comparison, it is perhaps worth noting that at this time, far away in England, a young aristocrat was similarly being influenced by these two great thinkers. Five years Sōseki's junior, Bertrand Russell was "in broad agreement" with Spencer and "inclined to accept completely" the views expressed in Mill's *Political Economy*. Yet a great gulf between East and West is also shown by this comparison. Having learned something of esoteric Buddhism from his brother, Russell made a point of dismissing it completely. He later recalled in his *Autobiography*: "It did not offer me anything that I found of service." No wonder Sōseki with his Chinese learning would one day look upon England as a nation gripped by commercialism: surely a natural extension of the "cult of usefulness."

In 1894, Sōseki had a mild attack of tuberculosis, giving him a brush with mortality so acute as to prompt him to spend several weeks in a Zen temple. Though he failed to gain "enlightenment," the experience remained with him in a curiously persistent way. Psychologists tell us that when something is not resolved it is more likely to be remembered, and in Sōseki's case very little was ever resolved to his complete satisfaction. As he said in his autobiographical novel, *Michikusa* (*1915, Grass on the Wayside*): "Hardly anything in this life is settled. Things that happen once will go on happening. But they come back in different guises, and that's what fools us." Indeed, Sōseki always tended to accumulate and carry his experiences with him as though they were part of the perpetual present. Hypersensitive by nature and often verging on paranoia, he seems to have reexamined his past constantly, as if searching for clues which might indicate a correct path for him to follow in the future.

Sōseki was in his late twenties and appeared to have a promising career as a scholar, when, in 1895, he surprised his friends by becoming a provincial schoolmaster on the island of Shikoku. He enjoyed the job far more than one might suppose from reading *Botchan*, which is set in the village where he taught. In fact, he continued in this relatively humble occupation for several years, transferring to a school at Kumamoto in Kyūshū after his initial year in Matsuyama. Far from the centers of learning, Sōseki was happy to pursue his intellectual studies in private. When, in the summer of 1896, he married Nakane Kyōko, the daughter of the chief clerk of the House of Peers, he was able to tell her: "I am a scholar, and must therefore study. I have no time to fuss over you. Please understand this clearly." Ironically, had he taken a more chivalrous attitude towards women, his work would now seem less modern than it actually is. But a feminist sympathizer he was not.

Sōseki's marriage was filled with tensions and misunderstandings, most of them caused by the incompatibility of the two partners. Kyōko suffered from frequent attacks of hysteria, while her husband grew increasingly impatient with the burdens imposed on him by family responsibilities. There seemed to be no solution, until, at the turn of the century, Sōseki was offered an unusual opportunity to further his studies in England. Literary historians are agreed that this was a major turning point in his career, if one which almost pushed him over the edge into insanity.

The trip to England was badly conceived from the start. The Japanese authorities made no official arrangements for Sōseki to follow any specific course of study. In fact, his instructions were marvelously vague. He was simply to go to London and learn something. Consequently, he arrived in England and spent most of the next two years in complete isolation. Having insufficient money to mix with other Japanese who were studying at British universities, he stayed in the cheapest boardinghouses and became completely engrossed in reading books on science, philosophy, literature, and every other subject one might care to mention. Nonetheless, as he was the only major Japanese writer ever to spend more than a few days in England, his visit is of some historical importance. In a city where blue wall plaques commemorate the sometime presence of even second-rate writers, it is sad to find no sign remembering Sōseki, one of the great geniuses of modern literature, in Flodden Road, Camberwell. Thereabouts, even today, one may still find "questionable restaurants patronized by cabmen and laborers" such as he later described in *Michikusa*.

News reached Japan that Sōseki had gone mad. This seems to have been an exaggeration, but there is no doubt that he suffered a nervous breakdown while in England. As a lone Japanese, isolated in a foreign country, he was bound to find the situation stressful. But more than that, he underwent a severe crisis of identity: a crisis which finally turned him into a writer. Since the exact details of the problem (and indeed its brilliant solution) may be inferred from his novels almost without reference to other material, readers may feel inclined to "play detective" in attempting to understand Sōseki's complex psychology. However, he would not have been amused by such a notion. One of his more bizarre sayings was that he could think of no worse fate than being "followed through the world by farting detectives."

In the novels that Sōseki would later write, he often depicted an introverted dilettante as his central figure, whose tragically static life-style exerts a fascination on a young disciple. Sōseki coined a phrase for the dilettantes, calling them *kōtōyūmin*, or "idle intellectuals." They represent a certain class of person found in *Meiji Japan, and indeed such men are perennial figures throughout history. But above all, the characters are a projection of a self which Sōseki had at one stage become, and with which he was not at all happy. Ineffectual, and alienated from society, they quietly rejoice in the closed systems of their own psychology while weeping over the failure of other people to connect with them. Yet despite the similarities between Sōseki and the dilettantes, the reader of the novels will be struck by one outstanding difference. For all their charm, innocence, and integrity (perhaps because of these qualities) not a single one of them has the potential to become as successful as the author who created them. Somewhere within himself Sōseki found the means of transcending what appeared to be his limitations. Put succinctly, he shed his old self by postulating the new.

In some of Sōseki's novels (*Kokoro*, for example), "the new" is represented by the younger man who finds himself attracted to the dilettante. Sensing that the older person is a living example of the "right way to be," the young man is cast in the role of detective, trying to discover the secrets of his mentor's personality. He represents a "clean slate," or the possibility of starting over, learning through the mistakes of his (always reluctant) teacher but in constant peril of being condemned to repeat those mistakes himself. It is as though Sōseki had postulated the existence of a loyal, "inner" disciple to whom he had to explain his own *raison d'être* with utmost clarity and precision. By means of this technique, he could break out of the fundamentally reflective patterns of his thought and, through the gradual growth and education of the disciple, become more assured and more assertive in his activities.

On his return to Japan in 1903, Sōseki was given an opportunity to prove himself at a higher level of teaching. As had been arranged prior to his trip to England he replaced *Lafcadio Hearn as lecturer in English Literature at Tokyo Imperial University. Hearn had been immensely popular with the students, and, as a foreigner, had been regarded as an authority on the West. For Sōseki it was a hard act to follow, although his own knowledge of Western literature was undoubtedly more extensive. He took a more analytic approach than Hearn, confident that he had every bit as much right to criticize the work of English writers. At first the students were antagonistic, but when, in his second year, he began to teach a course on Shakespeare they recognized the validity of his ideas. His lectures on literary criticism, delivered during the same year (1904) were later published as *Bungakuron* (*A Study of Literature*) and *Bungaku hyōron* (*Literary Criticism*). Both works have been thoroughly examined by Matsui Sakuko in *Natsume Sōseki as a Critic of English Literature* (The Centre for East Asian Cultural Studies, Tokyo, 1975).

Although it would still be some years before Sōseki wrote his great novel *Higan-sugi made* (1912, *To the Spring Equinox and Beyond*), his first step as a writer is reminiscent of the advice given by the "idle intellectual" Matsumoto (one of the characters in the novel) to his Hamlet-like nephew, Sunaga. Aware of Sunaga's intense inwardness and the threat it poses to his sanity, Matsumoto says (to Keitarō, the "detective" figure): "He should find one thing under heaven – and a single thing is enough – which is so great or beautiful or gentle that it will engross his entire being. In a word he has to become frivolous." And later he continues: "He [Sunaga] already knew before I advised him that the only way in the world to save himself was by assuming a flippant pose. But he's struggling, still unable to put it into practice." In 1904 Sōseki was thinking exactly along these lines, realizing (apparently not for the first time) that he had a tendency to take himself too seriously. Seen from an objective viewpoint – say, from an intelligent, neutral, and non-human viewpoint – he might look slightly ridiculous with all his pretensions to the sort of knowledge which he and others like him seemed to value so highly. So Sōseki began by postulating the nonhuman viewpoint. He wrote his first novel, a brilliant satire depicting a cat's-eye view of the world.

In one sense, *Wagahai wa neko de aru* (*1905–06, I Am a Cat*) is truly a flippant novel. It is extremely funny and contains a merciless caricature of Sōseki who figures as Kushami Sensei (Master Sneeze), a professor of English Literature. Of course, part of the book's great charm is that the nameless cat is made to assume some of the author's own faults. He is not only slightly paranoid but takes himself extremely seriously, using something akin to the "royal we" in referring to himself with the archaic expression *wagahai*.

I Am a Cat first appeared in the January 1905 issue of *Hototogisu* and won such popularity for Sōseki that he had to continue it in subsequent issues. The cat duly notes: "Since New Year's Day I have acquired a certain modest celebrity . . ." and, in passing comment on the quantity of fan mail, cannot help adding: ". . . it is entirely due to me that my master, hitherto a nobody, has suddenly begun to get a name and to attract attention."

All eleven chapters of *I Am a Cat* are now available in three volumes of English translation: a testament to Sōseki's growing popularity in the West. While writing it he also produced several other stories, two of which, *"Koto no sorane"* ("The Sound of a Koto," translated as "Hearing Things") and *"Shumi no iden"* ("The Heredity of Taste") have also been published in English. The original Japanese versions were put together in book form with five other short works, and collectively called *Yōkyoshū* (1907, *Drifting Clouds*).

All of Sōseki's early works have their qualities, while some of them dwell on themes that are treated at depth in his later novels. A persistent theme is his ambivalent attitude toward Western culture. At a time when the Japanese were intent on imitating Westerners in everything from fashion and manners to ideals and philosophy, Sōseki was eager to point out the absurdities this often produced. In "Hearing Things," for example, he addresses traditional superstitions such as the favorite folktale of being bewitched by a badger, then plays a variation on it to ridicule the faddishness of contemporary society. One of the characters produces a book supposedly written by a badger. In a patient and rational manner, it not only explains how the School of Badgers has hoodwinked the Japanese public for generations, but how some of their number have recently been using "hypnotic methods" borrowed from badgers in the West. "I, for one, though secretly, deplore it," says the "author" of the book.

Sōseki, too, deplored Japan's wholesale sell-out to the West. Despite his espousal of individualism and his respect for the "free yet orderly" society of England, he was sufficiently well-grounded in traditional Japanese and Chinese studies to see the lunacy of discarding his heritage. This is not to say that he clung to traditional values with the same tenacity as, say, his contemporary MORI ŌGAI. But like Ōgai, he believed Japan should take what was desirable from the West, while retaining the essence of indigenous culture.

In this period, 1905–1907, Sōseki was acutely aware of Japan's great capacity to embrace variety in its culture. His own early work, too, shows an exceptional range of styles and themes, usually with the frivolous aspects dominating. That he was capable of quite a different sort of expression, however, is evidenced by stories of a more poetic nature: *"Yume jūya"* (*1908*, "Ten Nights of Dream") and *Kusamakura* (1906, "The Grass Pillow," translated as *The Three-Cornered World*).

"Ten Nights of Dream," composed between 1907 and 1908, is an account of ten separate dreams: all of them highly surreal, displaying the disturbing beauty of mythology. Sōseki wrote nothing else in this vein, and they pose innumerable (and probably unanswerable) questions to the author's many biographers and interpreters. In one dream, a six-year-old child rides on the back of the narrator and leads him to where he (the narrator) murdered a blind man "exactly one hundred years ago." As soon as the narrator realizes he has committed a murder, the child on his back becomes "as heavy as a god of stone." Expressed here as a powerful metaphor, the "burden of the past" recurs in most of Sōseki's work: to the extent that it may be considered the central theme of his entire *œuvre*.

The Three-Cornered World was a uniquely successful experiment in composing a novel in the form of an "extended *haiku*." In it, a young man from Tokyo travels to the country with the intention of savoring every aesthetic experience with a connoisseur's detachment. Again, the hero is satirized (albeit more gently than are others in Sōseki's work) and comes dangerously close to "real life" when he encounters a beautiful girl who always appears to be on the point of committing suicide. But the narrator sustains his detachment, observing that her life is "one continuous performance." The novel's charming and unpredictable narrative line reveals the author's growing assurance as a storyteller.

Critics love to argue about which of Sōseki's early works is the finest. Some say *I Am a Cat* is the most original, and indeed (in Donald Keene's words) it "deals apt and sometimes sharp blows at human foibles in general and at Japanese intellectuals of the late Meiji era in particular." Others, including most of Japan's reading public, prefer *Botchan*.

Botchan has long been available in English, having been translated as early as 1918 and three times thereafter. It is at once a humorous novel and a probing psychological portrait of its narrator: a largely fictional character whose deep sincerity and do-or-die bravado have been admired by readers as ideal Japanese traits. Here, Sōseki was deliberately creating a genuinely likable hero: and his success set the pattern for more complex characters (who are still basically good people) in future novels.

Botchan is the nickname given to the hero by his old family maid, Kiyo. She behaves as a surrogate mother (Botchan having lost both his parents) and is so loyal that she is the only person who really likes his foolhardy honesty. Kiyo is herself a wonderful creation and serves to connect the novel closely to Japanese tradition. When Botchan travels to Shikoku to take up his first post as a country schoolmaster, she remains his distant protector: a potential refuge if all goes wrong. Everything, of course, *does* go wrong for Botchan as soon as he arrives in the petty, back-biting world of "career teachers." Sōseki exploits the comic possibilities of the situation to the full, using a skill equivalent to that which would, many years later, be applied by Western writers to the subject of academic life. One thinks of Malcolm Bradbury's *Stepping Westward*, Tom Sharpe's *Porterhouse Blue*, and Kingsley Amis's *Lucky Jim* as humorous classics of the same stature as *Botchan*.

In many ways Sōseki was an anti-establishment figure, who, through the quirks of fate, was given prominence by the establishment he opposed. His university post was both influential and well paid yet he always had a strong distaste for those who sought to acquire only money and status. He surely agreed with Wordsworth that in "getting and spending we lay waste our powers." For this reason he depicted many of his heroes as being independently wealthy, and thus free from the constraints of earning a living. Only then, he seems to suggest, do the real issues of life come to the surface. As one might expect, they are purely existential issues: problems of being rather than problems of action. At the moral level his work addresses the questions: "What am I?" and "What should I become?" rather than "How should I behave?" or "What should I do?"

By 1907 Sōseki had still not developed the art of dramatizing his ideas in a serious mode. Extending the conversational aspects of *I Am a Cat* he wrote a minor work called *"Nihyaku tōka"* ("The Two Hundred Tenth Day") and the novel *Nowaki* (1907, *Autumn Wind*).

The latter, in the opinion of Donald Keene is "... more enjoyable than many of his more accomplished novels," owing to a fine evocation of contemporary city life. However, 1907 effected another turning point in Sōseki's career, for he suddenly abandoned teaching in order to write full-time for the Tokyo *Asahi shimbun*. This was an extremely bold move for a highly respected academic to take, though it must be said that Sōseki thoroughly secured his position by negotiating a very good contract with his friend Ikebe Sanzan, the editor of the *Asahi*. His remuneration was set at a level which today would be equivalent to (say) the salary of a bank's branch manager, and his family's security was thereby guaranteed as long as he could deliver the required quantity of work. In this respect, Sōseki proved to be far more reliable than other novelists of the era.

After writing his first serial, a very mediocre piece of romantic fiction called *Gubijinsō* (*Red Poppy*), Sōseki quickly produced *Kōfu* (*1908, The Miner*). It was commissioned at short notice in order to fill a gap left in the *Asahi* by the *Naturalist writer, SHIMAZAKI TŌSON, who had failed to complete a scheduled novel on time. Experimental, almost Modernist in tone, *The Miner* was based on a story told to Sōseki by a visitor who had called expressly to offer him material for a novel about hardships in a copper mine. Second-hand experience, however, is never likely to inspire great literature, as Sōseki was surely well aware. But he was now a working novelist with a professional duty to help fill the pages of a distinguished newspaper. He made up for his act of pragmatism by producing six great works of literature in rapid succession immediately thereafter.

Sōseki's first great trilogy is composed of *Sanshirō* (*1908, Sanshiro*), *Sorekara* (*1909, And Then*), and *Mon* ("The Gate," translated as *Mon*, 1910). The three novels can be read separately and in any order, since they are linked neither by character nor action. Their connection is rather one of spiritual development: successive heroes being older and therefore facing different kinds of life-problem as the trilogy progresses.

Sanshirō, the hero of the first novel, is characterized by his age, "san" (three) implying twenty-three and "shi" (four) implying twenty-four. He is probably based on Sōseki's observations of his students and also on his own experiences at this same transitional age. But unlike his earlier city-bred heroes (Botchan, and the narrator of *The Three-Cornered World*) Sanshirō is from the provinces, traveling to Tokyo to study at the Imperial University. On the train he meets Professor Hirota, a forty-two-year-old bachelor who, for all his cynical comments on modern society, is surprisingly unworldly. He does not even hold a teaching post. A fellow student of Sanshirō calls Hirota "The Great Darkness" because he has read everything but "doesn't give off any light." Sanshirō falls under Hirota's spell, and, like him, is clearly in danger of rejecting the society in which he must survive.

Sanshirō is Sōseki's first complete analysis of an introverted personality. The young hero has a strong tendency to idealize the unknown: not only Hirota and his sophisticated world of ideas, but also women like Mineko whom he has glimpsed in the already idealized setting of a perfect landscape. Moreover, in not grasping what others might consider a sexual opportunity, Sanshirō is not even aware of his failure. For the real world is "unreal" to an introvert because his conceptual model of it is too finely tuned. No writer has better expressed this than Sōseki in *Sanshirō*, and later in *To the Spring Equinox and Beyond*.

Daisuke, the hero of *And Then* (the second novel of the trilogy) is seven years older than Sanshirō and very different in personality: more confident, better-looking, and far more intelligent. He is Sōseki's most rounded and lifelike character, as endearing in his way as Botchan, but without the younger man's naïveté. Indeed, although a compulsive idler, he is so sure of himself that he has allowed his best friend, Hiraoka, to marry Michiyo, the girl he himself really loves. He realizes his mistake only when, for business reasons, his father presses him to marry someone else.

Daisuke's self-justification is one of the most highly reasoned accounts in all of Sōseki's novels. His outward persona is so admirable and intact, that, should any crack be discovered in it, he would be in danger of losing his mind. Inevitably, his one serious flaw is found to be his inability to detect his subconscious feelings. When the key is eventually turned, his whole world falls apart. He can only try to win back Michiyo (who does indeed love him) and piece together a life away from that society to which his persona was once so well adapted.

And Then raises some profound questions about the nature of the self and its relationship to society. After all, what is selfishness? Has Daisuke suddenly discovered how to be selfish by wanting Michiyo as his wife? Or has he discovered pure unselfishness in surrendering himself to her love? The answer is by no means obvious, and perhaps there is no clear-cut, general answer to the problem of selfishness. Here, certainly was a problem which Sōseki could not resolve, but, in a new age of individualism – an age he was helping to create – it was an issue which he clearly wanted to resolve completely. No complete resolution was forthcoming in either of the first two novels of the trilogy. In *Sanshirō*, for example, it is clear that Professor Hirota's way of life is entirely self-absorbed, yet even he can offer a justification which (as history went on to prove) could be compelling. His advice to Sanshirō is: "Don't ever surrender yourself. You may think that what you are doing is for the sake of the nation, but let something take possession of you like that and all you do is bring it down."

Sōseki's next novel, *Mon*, picks up the life story of a man who is much older than Daisuke but who has committed a similar "crime" in his youth. Having stolen the wife or mistress of his best friend (the woman's previous role is not exactly defined), Sōsuke is condemned to live away from family and friends. He and Oyone are still in love with each other, but because Oyone cannot bear children, their future appears bleak and meaningless. It is constantly overshadowed by the events of the past. Here the author has extended his concept of the single, introverted personality to depict a couple who together create a similarly closed psychological system: a case of dual introversion. Each has absorbed the other, sealing off those penetrating influences which come from the outside world to awaken and stimulate the life force within living organisms. Ironically, in the previous novel, it was only Michiyo's love for Daisuke which could break through his closed psychology and awaken his deeper instincts. Now, in *Mon*, Sōsuke must search for some other influence which might make him purposeful and decisive. He visits a Zen temple in the hope of finding a way forward, but despite his efforts, all of which are so brilliantly described in the novel, he is unable to open the gate (*mon*) to enlightenment.

"Opening the gate" would, of course, be a form of surrender: the ultimate surrender of self to everything that is not self. The reward would be enlightenment (which is given rather than taken), and the transformation would put Sōsuke in touch with the deepest sources of energy in the universe. But such a possibility is beyond his grasp because he desires it for himself.

Sōseki fell ill after completing *Mon* and, ironically, almost died while visiting the Izu Peninsula to recuperate. He had long known that his ulcerated stomach might eventually kill him, for even the nameless cat, the narrator of the first novel, often referred to "Sensei's dyspeptic condition" with considerable foreboding.

The year 1911 saw Sōseki back at work, giving a series of lectures (sponsored by the *Asahi*) in which he again attacked the craze for Westernization. He was also at work on his sixth novel (the first of a new trilogy) called *Higan-sugi made* (*To the Spring Equinox and Beyond*). It would run in the *Asahi* from New Year's Day until sometime after the spring equinox: hence its deliberately vague title. The novel is certainly his most underrated and is so ingeniously engineered that, in a sense, it undermines the whole concept of literature.

Many critics are puzzled by the curious structure of *Spring Equinox*. It begins with a young hero, Keitarō, who is possessed by the idea of living a romantic life in an exotic, faraway country. However, as he is obliged to earn his living, he can scarcely believe his good fortune when he is hired as a detective to follow and report upon the movements of an elderly man. Unfortunately, Keitarō is being tricked, but, his curiosity aroused, he continues to seek out the truth about his new acquaintances. The story then moves to a different point of view entirely, placing Keitarō even more firmly in the position of "excluded onlooker." The novel deliberately turns away from him to focus upon its true subject, his friend Sunaga: altogether a more interesting character. Sunaga is the archetypal introvert of Sōseki's stories, a young man who is completely unable to take any decisive action – even to declare his love for his cousin Chiyoko – for fear of losing his sense of self. He seems to fear "commitment," for that would mean acquiring an identity that he cannot wholly justify. He is heading toward a nervous breakdown, and, as already noted, his uncle advises him to "become frivolous" for the sake of his mental equilibrium.

Although, in *Spring Equinox*, the uncle's advice is revealing and may give the reader pause for thought, even more striking is the author's cryptic comment about Keitarō, the "decoy" hero of the early chapters. In a brief conclusion he says that Keitarō, for all his aspirations to make contact with the real world, has been doing nothing more than "proceeding here and there among various people and listening to their tales." In other words, he is a representation of the reader: the passive receptor of vicarious experience. Because the novel cannot properly be understood unless one identifies with its characters – with Keitarō, Sunaga, and the uncle, Matsumoto, in an ascending order of insight – the revelation comes as a great challenge to the reader. Indeed, it makes the reader understand that there is a real solution to Sunaga's problem, and that it lies in the great external universe itself. At this point, the thought and its mode of expression are Shakespearean in their beauty, and one begins to see the true extent of Sōseki's genius.

Kōjin (The Wayfarer) is the second novel of Sōseki's second trilogy. It was serialized in the *Asahi* during 1912 and 1913. Its central character, Ichirō, is more seriously ill than any of Sōseki's other heroes. Morose and unsociable, he deliberately provokes his own paranoia by suggesting that his wife accompany his younger brother,

Jirō, on a trip to a holiday spa. He wants to test her to see if she will remain faithful. Unfortunately, he cannot ascertain whether or not she betrays him. Beset by doubts, he gradually disintegrates until a friend, at the request of the family, takes him to the countryside in an effort to heal his mind. The friend's subsequent letter expresses Ichirō's case eloquently, and shows him for the first time in a sympathetic light. Ichirō, a brilliant university professor, is so hypersensitive that "every incident of his life is a distillation of the malaise of the whole human race." The solution is self-transcendence, but whether Ichirō can attain it is (again) problematic.

The Wayfarer is infinitely more complex and subtle than the outline of its plot suggests. Sōseki not only describes a growing psychosis with clinical accuracy, but places the victim into a family setting which (according to the psychiatrist Dr. Doi in *The Psychological World of Natsume Sōseki*) is very likely to provoke such psychosis.

Examining the characters of Sōseki's major novels, with particular emphasis on Ichirō of *The Wayfarer*, Dr. Doi demonstrates the essential role played by what he calls *amae* in Japanese life. Early in the 1950s Doi noticed that the (intransitive) verb *amaeru* (expressing an instinctive desire to be loved, and thus able, when the occasion demands, to depend on others as if taking their affection for granted) did not have an equivalent in the West. Therefore, he argued, it must be more important to the Japanese even though it is surely a universal phenomenon. He went on to write his best-selling book *Amae no kōzō* (*The Anatomy of Dependence*, 1972) and, using Sōseki's novels, not only introduced his theory of *amae* but helped to promote a better understanding of psychoanalysis in Japan.

Ichirō in *The Wayfarer* is caught in a fatal trap. Unlike his brother, he was never "spoiled or humored" as a child. Consequently he never learned how to spoil and humor others (the essential currency of human interaction, according to Doi). Instead, he identifies with his brother, believing their relationship to be above the manipulative realm of *amae* (the realm of humoring and being humored). When the identification breaks down, Ichirō is adrift in his paranoia, unable to regain contact with the outside world.

Kokoro (*1914*), the last novel of Sōseki's second trilogy, has been the most influential and is the one with which, rightly or wrongly, the author is most closely identified. In a poll conducted among graduates of four Japanese universities in 1968 it was voted second only to Dostoievsky's *Crime and Punishment* as the piece of fiction which had had the greatest effect on their thought and lives. Western readers, however, will find it more distinctively Japanese than Sōseki's other novels, especially in the way in which the central figure, Sensei, resolves his own particular life-problem.

As the "idle intellectual" of *Kokoro*, Sensei is a very believable character. Lest one think that, by now, Sōseki's readers might have become too familiar with the author's monotypal heroes, it has to be noted how different they are in personality. Sneeze, of *I Am a Cat*, is a figure of fun whose characteristics are shown in the worst possible light (so that the cat could "humor" him, as Dr. Doi might have observed had he included the novel in his study of Sōseki's works). Hirota, of *Sanshirō*, is the most negative of the heroes; while Matsumoto of *Spring Equinox* is primarily a family man whose cultured life-style must be seen in contrast to the crass commercialism of his dynamic brother. Their common features are their refusal to take an active role in life, their cultivation of good taste and useless knowledge, and their low threshold of tolerance for human foibles. Sensei, however, is more mysterious than the others. He nurses a private guilt, the exact nature of which is not revealed until late in the novel. In this respect, Sōseki was taking a bold step forward in his fiction: bringing the *éminence grise* to center stage and giving him the sort of life-problem which had hitherto plagued only the anguished heroes, Daisuke, Sōsuke, and Ichirō.

Sensei regularly visits the grave of a long-lost friend, but will tell neither his wife nor his disciple (the novel's unnamed narrator) the reason why his friend's death still obsesses him. It transpires that the dead man, K, was a rival in love whom Sensei all too easily outwitted. Deeply introverted, K committed suicide on hearing the news of Sensei's impending marriage, and, ever since, Sensei has carried with him a sense of guilt. He finally confesses to his disciple in a long letter which comprises the second half of the novel.

It is not hard to see why critics so admire *Kokoro*. Sensei's account is written with great intensity and eloquence, befitting a man who has resigned himself to die rather than continue a hopeless struggle to correct the errors of the past. Yet there is also an evasion of the central moral issue for the sake of literary aesthetics, and Sōseki could not have found this entirely satisfactory. Sensei's suicide is little more than a gesture, reminiscent of General Nogi's suicide: that archaic and almost infamous gesture, which actually figures at two critical points in the novel. In choosing death as his method of expiation, Sensei knowingly betrays his wife. By his own admission he belongs to an era that has ended, and his action carries with it the implication that his disciple, the young narrator to whom he is writing, must look elsewhere for guidance.

Sōseki's own marital relationship continued to deteriorate, as did his health. However, around the time of writing *Kokoro* he delivered another series of lectures, the most famous of which was called "My Individualism" (November 1914). Its message (treat others with respect but go your own way) seems to have been every bit as evasive as *Kokoro*'s resolution. In 1915 he went on to write *Garasudo no uchi* (*Within My Glass Doors*), a nonfiction book on wide-ranging topics, then fell desperately ill and went to Kyoto to recover.

Japanese connoisseurs of Sōseki greatly value the *dampen* ("fragments") he wrote during this period of ill health. Because many of the thoughts expressed in them show his interest in Buddhism, they have been taken as evidence of a gradual conversion to religion. Indeed, Sōseki's attitude towards religious truth has long been the subject of fierce controversy. For many years his most ardent disciples believed that a phrase used by him in conversation (namely: *sokuten kyoshi*, or "Follow heaven and forsake the self") should be taken as his central belief. Consequently, interpretations of his later work became tainted with an absurd inductive bias until the critic Etō Jun dismissed the dictum as having little relevance. Etō was surely correct in this matter, for Sōseki, more than most writers, showed a reluctance to commit himself to absolute moral principles. Rather, he explored life as it is lived and people as they are, while deferring on religious matters to those who had the proper training.

A celebrated author, Sōseki was by no means as isolated in society as the heroes of his books. For example, he enjoyed friendships with two young writers, AKUTAGAWA RYŪNOSUKE and Kume Masao, and two Zen acolytes, Kimura Genjō and Tomizawa Keidō, and he frequently exchanged letters with each of them. The translator V. H. Viglielmo has said (in his 1967 afterword to *Meian*): "It is fascinating to compare these two correspondences, for in his letters to Akutagawa and Kume he emerges as the literary master who dispenses advice and comments to the two admiring youths, whereas in his letters to Kimura and Tomizawa he is revealed as a humble seeker after religious solace."

The *sokuten kyoshi* controversy should serve as a reminder that critics are often fallible, and criticism itself often merely a matter of personal taste and opinion. Nowhere is this more obvious than in the various judgments that have been made on Sōseki's last completed novel: *Michikusa* (*1915, Grass on the Wayside*). In a brief exposition, Donald Keene begins by referring to it as "profoundly depressing," and concludes by calling it "unmitigatedly cheerless." Masao Miyoshi (in *Accomplices of Silence*, 1974) states: "To me . . . it is the only tedious work he wrote." There is no accounting for taste. As a wholly autobiographical novel – the only one Sōseki ever wrote – *Grass on the Wayside* gives a uniquely fascinating insight into the author's life. Moreover, it reads like fiction of the highest order, and is rightly acclaimed by its translator, Edwin McClellan, as "perhaps the most distinguished" autobiographical novel written in Japan this century.

Although it is an account of Sōseki's life shortly after he returned from England, *Grass on the Wayside* is written in the third person and is fully dramatized as if it were fiction. It fulfills to the utmost one of literature's most basic requirements: it is about people, and their relationships to each other, *in time*. Reading it, one is very much conscious of the flow of time; of people getting older; of changes in their circumstances. When the past catches up with Professor Kenzō (i.e., Sōseki) he handles the problem with far greater subtlety and realism than any of the heroes in previous novels. His attitude towards his foster parents, who suddenly reappear to beg for money after sixteen years of estrangement, is devoid of preconceptions. Moreover, *Grass on the Wayside* is completely free from the artifice of *Kokoro*, and has no discernible message save Kenzō's closing remark (quoted earlier): "Hardly anything in this life is settled. Things that happen once will go on happening. But they come back in different guises and that's what fools us." Given the extreme stress under which Kenzō has been living, and given the pain he feels at being unable to communicate with his wife, his remark and her response contain the greatest truth Sōseki ever wrote. Although Kenzō has spoken bitterly, his wife does not answer him directly but picks up their baby and smothers it with kisses, saying: "Nice baby, nice baby, we don't know what daddy is talking about, do we?"

At this point Sōseki should have stopped writing novels. This autobiographical scene is the pinnacle of his art. Of course, a cynic would say that Kenzō's wife is here being her usual self, using the child as a defense against her husband's moods. But be that as it may, her words are carefully chosen by the author. One day the child may very well know what his father is talking about, *but it is unlikely to have the same specific problems*, and therein lies the hope for the future. The sensitive reader may even have the intuition that, in this passage, Sōseki was describing the most important moment of his life. We know that Kenzō has had a few mediocre pieces of writing published in magazines, but nothing of any consequence. Could it have been at this point that Kenzō/Sōseki, greatly cheered by a sudden realization that there is life beyond self, returned to his study to write the first, frivolous chapter of *I Am a Cat*?

After finishing *Grass on the Wayside*, Sōseki embarked on only one other major work of prose, the long, unfinished novel *Meian* (*1916, Light and Darkness*). On this, too, critical opinion is hopelessly divided. Some scholars admire it as the greatest Japanese novel of the century; other people (most notably the novelist, TANIZAKI) have dismissed it as complete rubbish. Sōseki himself referred to it (in a letter to Nomura Kimi, May 2, 1916) as a "dull thing" which he was obliged to produce for the newspaper. Indeed, as it reads very much like a Henry James novel, one has to agree with him. *Meian* was Sōseki's first attempt at so-called true fiction, using pure invention unrelated to his own psychology. He was able to write such a work only because, during these last months of his life, he put his real genius into composing Chinese poetry (*kanshi*), very little of which has been (or ever could be) translated into English.

Sōseki's career as a writer spanned little more than a decade, from 1905 to 1916. During that time he produced the best satire, the most popular humorous novel, the best autobiographical novel, and two trilogies of the best psychological fiction in twentieth-century Japan. No one could ask for more. He should be on the reading list of every student of literature: somewhere near the top.

RECOMMENDED READING

Novels

And Then. *Sorekara.* *1909.* 304 pages. Tr. Norma Moore Field. Louisiana State University Press, Baton Rouge, 1978; G. P. Putnam's Sons, NY, 1982; Tuttle, Tokyo, 1988. Second novel of first trilogy but may be read separately.

Botchan. *Botchan.* *1906.* 176 pages. (1) As *Botchan, Master Darling.* Tr. Yasotaro Mori. Ogawa Seibundo, Tokyo, 1918. As *Botchan.* Kinshodo, Tokyo, 1963. (2) Tr. Umeji Sasaki. *Chugai Eigo*, 1919; Shunyodo, Tokyo, 1922, 1968; Tuttle, Tokyo, 1967; Prentice-Hall, London, 1967. (3) Extract, tr. Burton Watson. *Modern Japanese Literature*, ed. Donald Keene. Grove Press, NY, 1956; Tuttle, Tokyo, 1957. (4) Tr. Alan Turney. Kodansha International, Tokyo, 1972; Peter Owen, London, 1973. Sōseki's classic comedy of academic life in the provinces.

Grass on the Wayside. *Michikusa.* *1915.* 169 pages. Tr. Edwin McClellan. University of Chicago Press, Chicago, 1969; Tuttle, Tokyo, 1971. Sōseski's only autobiographical novel.

Kokoro. *Kokoro.* *1914.* 248 pages. (1) Tr. Ineko Sato. Hokuseido, Tokyo, 1941. (2) Tr. Ineko Kondo. Kenkyusha, Tokyo, 1948. (3) Tr. Edwin McClellan. Henry Regnery, Chicago, 1957; Peter Owen,

London, 1967; Tuttle, Tokyo, 1969. Considered to be his best work by many critics; final novel of second trilogy.
Sanshiro. *Sanshirō. 1908.* 248 pages. (1) Extract as "Mount Fuji." Tr. Shigeshi Nishimura. *Eigo Kenkyu,* vol. 26, no. 3, 1933. (2) Tr. W. J. Whitehouse. *Eigo no kenkyo to kyoju,* Tokyo, 1939. (3) Tr. Jay Rubin. University of Tokyo Press, Tokyo, 1977; University of Washington Press, Seattle, 1977; G. P. Putnam's Sons, NY, 1982. First novel of first trilogy. Version (3) contains 36-page essay called "Sanshirō and Sōseki" by the translator.

WORKS IN ENGLISH TRANSLATION

Novels

And Then. Sorekara. 1909.

Botchan. Botchan. 1906.

Grass on the Wayside. Michikusa. 1915.

I Am a Cat. Wagahai wa neko de aru. 1905–06. 852 pages (complete). (1) Tr. Kanichi Ando. Hattori Shoten. Tokyo, 1906–09. (2) Tr. Katsue Shibata and Motonari Kai. Kenkyusha, Tokyo, 1921; Peter Owen, London, 1971; G. P. Putnam's Sons, NY, 1982. Extract in *Asian Laughter.* Weatherhill, Tokyo, 1971. (3) Tr. Aiko Ito and Graeme Wilson. Extracts in *Japan Quarterly,* vol. 17, no. 4, 1970; vol. 18, nos. 1 and 2, 1971; and vol. 21, no. 4, 1974; complete novel in 3 volumes: Tuttle, Tokyo and Boston, vol. 1, 1971; vol. 2, 1979; vol. 3, 1986. Available in paperback.

Kokoro. Kokoro. 1914.

Light and Darkness. Meian. 1916. 397 pages. Tr. V. H. Viglielmo. University of Hawaii Press, Honolulu, 1971; Peter Owen, London, 1971; Tuttle, Tokyo, 1971; G. P. Putnam's Sons, NY, 1982.

The Miner. Kōfu. 1908. 159 pages. Tr. Jay Rubin. Stanford University Press, Stanford, 1988.

Mon. Mon. (lit: "The Gate"). 1910. 217 pages. Tr. Francis Mathy. Peter Owen, London, 1972; Tuttle, Tokyo, 1972; G. P. Putnam's Sons, NY, 1982. Third novel of first trilogy.

Sanshiro. Sanshirō. 1908.

The Three-Cornered World. Kusamakura. 1906. 184 pages. (1) As *Kusamakura.* Tr. Umeji Sasaki. *Juken Eigo,* 1924; *Kusamakura and Buncho.* Iwanami Shoten, Tokyo, 1927. (2) As *Unhuman Tour.* Tr. Kazutomo Takahashi. *Japan Times,* Tokyo, 1927. Extract in *Treasury of Japanese Literature,* ed. Takichi Watanabe. Jippohkaku, Tokyo, 1933. (3) Extract as *Grass Pillow.* Tr. Alan Turney. *Orient West,* vol. 9, no. 1, 1964; *The Japanese Image,* vol. 2, ed. M. Schneps and A. D. Coox. *Orient West,* Tokyo, 1966. (4) Tr. Alan Turney. Peter Owen, London, 1965; Tuttle, Tokyo, 1966; Henry Regnery, Chicago, 1967; G. P. Putnam's Sons, NY; 1982.

To the Spring Equinox and Beyond. Higan-sugi made. 1912. 316 pages. Tr. Kingo Ochiai and Sanford Goldstein. Tuttle, Tokyo, 1985. First novel of second trilogy.

The Wayfarer. Kōjin. 1912–13. 326 pages. Tr. Beongcheon Yu.

Wayne State University Press, Detroit, 1967; Tuttle, Tokyo, 1969; G. P. Putnam's Sons, NY, 1982. Second novel of second trilogy.

Short Fiction Collection

Ten Nights of Dream, Hearing Things, The Heredity of Taste. 203 pages. Tr. Aiko Ito and Graeme Wilson. Tuttle, Tokyo, 1974.

Short Fiction

"A Feeling of Beauty." *"Ichiya."* 1965. 12 pages. Tr. Alan Turney. *Monumenta Nipponica*, vol. 33, no. 3, 1978.

"Hearing Things." *"Koto no sorane."* 1905. 50 pages. Tr. Aiko Ito and Graeme Wilson. *Japan Quarterly*, vol. 19, no. 3, 1972. *Ten Nights of Dream, Hearing Things, The Heredity of Taste.*

"The Heredity of Taste." *"Shumi no iden."* 1906. 86 pages. Tr. Aiko Ito and Graeme Wilson. *Japan Quarterly*, vol. 20, no. 1, 1973. *Ten Nights of Dream, Hearing Things, The Heredity of Taste.*

"Nihyakutoka." *"Nihyakutōka"* ("The Two Hundred Tenth Day"). 1906. Tr. T. Johnes and H. Tomabechi. *Eigo Seinen*, vol. 36, nos. 1–12, 1916–17; vol. 37, nos. 1–12, 1917; vol. 38, nos. 1–12, 1917–18; vol. 39, nos. 4–8, 1918.

"Our Cat's Grave." *"Neko no haka."* (1) Tr. Sankichi Hata and Dofu Shirai. *Ten Nights' Dreams, and Our Cat's Grave.* Seito Shoin, Tokyo, 1934; *Treasury of World Literature*, ed. D. D. Runes. Philosophical Library, NY, 1956. (2) As "The Grave of Our Cat." Tr. Tadakuni Mizutani. *Aries.* Kansai Gakuin University, 1938.

"The Paddy Bird." *"Bunchō."* 1908. 6 pages. (1) As "Buncho." Tr. Umeji Sasaki. *Chugai Eigo*, 1923;

Kusamakura, and Buncho. Iwanami Shoten, Tokyo, 1927. (2) Tr. S. G. Brickley. *The Writing of Idiomatic English.* Kenkyusha, Tokyo, 1951.

"Record of Chips and Shavings." *Bokusetsu roku.* Excerpts, tr. Burton Watson. *Japanese Literature in Chinese*, vol. 2. Columbia University Press, NY, 1976.

"Ten Nights of Dream." *"Yume jūya."* 1908. 37 pages. (1) As "Dreams." Tr. Asataro Miyamori. *Representative Tales of Japan.* Sanko Shoten, Tokyo, 1917. (2) As "Ten Dreams." *Japan Magazine*, vol. 13, 1922. (3) As "Ten Nights' Dreams." Tr. Sankichi Hata and Dofu Shirai. *Ten Nights' Dreams, and Our Cat's Grave.* (4) As "Ten Nights of Dreams." Tr. Earl Miner and Yukio Oura. *Orient West*, vol. 6, no. 2, 1961; *The Japanese Image*, ed. M. Schneps and A. D. Coox. Orient West, Tokyo, 1965. (5) Tr. Aiko Ito and Graeme Wilson. *Japan Quarterly*, vol. 16, no. 3, 1969; *Ten Nights of Dream, Hearing Things, The Heredity of Taste.*

Reminiscence

Within My Glass Doors. Garasudo no uchi. 1915. 154 pages. (1) Extract as "The Master." Tr. Iwao Matsubara. *Osaka Mainichi*, April 26, 1928. (2) As "Natsume Sōseki's Childhood." Tr. Shigeo Inoue. *Eigo Kenkyu*, vol. 22, nos. 5–6, 1929. (3) Tr. Iwao Matsubara and E. T. Inglehart. Shinseido, Tokyo, 1928.

Criticism

"Stevenson and Meredith." Tr. Yaichiro Isobe. *Chugai Eigo*, July, 1923.

Miscellaneous

Extract from the novel *Red Poppy*. *Gubijinsō. 1907*. Tr. Kazutomo Takahashi. *Japan Magazine*, vols. 8 and 9, 1918.

Poetry

"4 Haiku." Tr. Harold Gould Henderson. *The Bamboo Broom*. J. L. Thompson. Tokyo, 1933; Kegan Paul, London, 1933.

"Haiku." Tr. Asataro Miyamori. *Haiku Poems, Ancient and Modern*. Maruzen, Tokyo, 1940.

"Haiku." Tr. Kenneth Yasuda. *A Pepper-Pod*. Knopf, NY, 1947; Tuttle, Tokyo, 1976.

"1 Haiku." *Japanese Love Poems*, ed. Jean Bennett. Doubleday, Garden City, 1976.

"1 Haiku." Tr. Lois J. Erickson. *Songs from the Land of Dawn*. Friendship Press, NY, 1949; Books for Libraries Press, Freeport, 1968.

"One Haiku." Tr. H. G. Henderson. *Modern Japanese Literature*, ed. Donald Keene. Grove Press, NY, 1956; Tuttle, Tokyo, 1957.

"7 Haiku." Tr. V. H. Viglielmo. *Japanese Literature in the Meiji Era*. Obunsha, Tokyo, 1955.

"10 Haiku." Tr. Peter Beilenson and Harry Behn. *Haiku Harvest*. Peter Pauper Press, Mount Vernon, NY, 1962.

"3 Haiku." Tr. R. H. Blyth. *Haiku*, vols. 3 and 4. Hokuseido, Tokyo, 1952.

"20 Haiku." Tr. Makoto Ueda. *Modern Japanese Haiku, An Anthology*. University of Tokyo Press, Tokyo, 1976.

"26 Haiku." Tr. Asataro Miyamori. *Anthology of Haiku, Ancient and Modern*. Maruzen, Tokyo, 1932; Taiseido, Tokyo 1947.

"2 Haiku." Tr. Joy Norton. *Poetry Nippon*, no. 55, 1981.

"Two Poems." *Atlantic Monthly*, no. 195, 1955.

CRITICAL STUDIES

Biddle, William Ward. "The Authenticity of Natsume Sōseki." *Monumenta Nipponica*, vol. 28, 1973.

Chi, Ch'iu-lang. "Sōseki as a Haiku Poet." *Tamkang Review*, no. 1, 1970.

Doi, Takeo. *The Psychological World of Natsume Sōseki*. Tr. William Jefferson Tyler. Harvard University, Cambridge, 1976.

Etō, Jun. "A Japanese Meiji Intellectual: An Essay on *Kokoro*." *Essays on Natsume Sōseki's Works*, Japan Society for the Promotion of Scientific Research, Tokyo, 1972.

———. "Natsume Sōseki: A Japanese Meiji Intellectual." *American Scholar*, no. 34, 1965.

Gunn, Giles B. "Traditions and Modernity in Modern Japanese Fiction: Variations on a Theme in Natsume Sōseki, Tanizaki Jun'ichirō and Dazai Osamu." *Japan Christian Quarterly*, no. 35, 1969.

Hasegawa, Izumi. "The Emergence of Natsume Sōseki as a Novelist: His Position and Significance in Modern Japanese Literature." *Acta Asiatica*, no. 40, 1981.

Hibbett, Howard. "Natsume Sōseki and the Psychological Novel." *Tradition and Modernization in Japanese Culture*, 1971.

Hiraoka, Toshio. "The Charm of Natsume Sōseki's Literature: Women and Love in His Early Works." *Acta Asiatica*, no. 40, 1981.

Homma, Kenshiro. *Natsume Sōseki: A Comparative Study*. The Intercultural Research Institute, Kansai University of Foreign Studies, 1990.

Iijima, Takehisa. *The World of Nats-*

ume Sōseki, ed. Takehisa Iijima and James M. Vardaman. Kinseido, Tokyo, 1987.

Itō, Sei. "Natsume Sōseki, His Personality and Works." *Essays on Natsume Sōseki's Works*, 1972.

Jewel, Mark. "A Comparative Study of Translations of Sōseki and Mishima." *Transactions of the International Conference of Orientalists in Japan*, no. 20, 1975.

Karaki, Junzō. "On *Meian*." *Essays on Natsume Sōseki's Works*, 1972.

Kuno, Shinkichi. "Sōseki Natsume and George Meredith: How Sōseki Has Read Meredith." *Hikaku Bungaku*, no. 4, 1961.

Lippit, Noriko Mizuta. "Natsume Sōseki on Poe." *Comparative Literature Studies*, vol. 14, no. 1, 1977.

McClellan, Edwin. "The Implications of Sōseki's *Kokoro*." *Monumenta Nipponica*, vol. 14, no. 3, 1958.

———. "An Introduction to Sōseki." *Harvard Journal of Asiatic Studies*, no. 22, 1959.

———. "An Introduction to Sōseki, a Japanese Novelist." Ph.D. diss., University of Chicago, Chicago, 1957.

———. *Two Japanese Novelists: Sōseki and Tōson*. University of Chicago Press, Chicago, 1969; Tuttle, Tokyo, 1971.

McClain, Yoko. "Sōseki: A Tragic Father." *Monumenta Nipponica*, vol. 33, no. 4, 1978.

———. "Sōseki and Oliver Goldsmith." *Waseda Journal of Asian Studies*, no. 7, 1985.

Matsui, Sakuko. "East and West in Natsume Sōseki: The Formation of a Modern Japanese Novelist." *Meanjin Quarterly*, no. 3, 1967.

———. *Natsume Sōseki as a Critic of English Literature*. Centre for East Asian Cultural Studies, Tokyo, 1975.

———. "Natsume Sōseki as a Critic of English Literature: A Study of Sōseki's Contribution to the English Scholarship of His Day, with Some Investigation of the Relationship Between Sōseki's Critical and Creative Writings." Ph.D. diss., University of Sydney, Sydney, 1972.

———. "View of an Elder Novelist: A Consideration of Tanizaki Jun'ichirō on Sōseki's *Meian*." *Journal of the Oriental Society of Australia*, vol. 15, no. 6, 1984.

Morita, Sohei. "On *Botchan*." *Essays on Natsume Sōseki's Works*, 1972.

Nakajima, Kunihiko. "Recent Achievements in Sōseki Studies." *Acta Asiatica*, no. 40, 1981.

Otsuka, Noyuri. "Modern Japan and Sōseki Natsume." *Japan Studies*, vol. 1, no. 4, 1964.

Pollack, David. "Framing the Self: The Philosophical Dimensions of Human Nature in *Kokoro*." *Monumenta Nipponica*, vol. 43, no. 4, 1988.

Ran, Shuh-jong. "Natsume Sōseki's Study of English Literature with Relevance to His Criticism." *Asian Cultural Quarterly*, vol. 8, nos. 2 and 3, 1980.

———. "The Nature of Natsume Sōseki's Style with Reference to Liu Hsieh's Feng-ku." *Japan Interpreter*, vol. 3, no. 4, 1976.

———. "Some English Influences on Natsume Sōseki's Criticism and Novels." Ph.D. diss., University of Minnesota, Minneapolis, 1979.

Rubin, Jay. "The Evil and the Ordinary in Sōseki's Fiction." *Harvard Journal of Asiatic Studies*, vol. 46, no. 2, 1986.

———. "*Sanshirō* and Sōseki." *Harvard Journal of Asiatic Studies*, no. 36, 1976.

———. "Sōseki on Individualism; Watakushi no Kojinshugi." *Monumenta Nipponica*, vol. 34, no. 1, 1979.

Saito, George. *Sōseki and Salinger: American Students on Japanese Fiction*, ed. George Saito and Philip Williams. Eihosha, Tokyo, 1971.

Sparling, Kathryn Wyndham. "Early Natsume Sōseki: Images and Patterns of the Absolute." Ph.D. diss., Harvard University, Cambridge, 1973.

———. "Language and Form in Sōseki's *Sorekara* and *Meian*." *Transactions of the International Conference of Orientalists in Japan*, no. 26, 1981.

———. "*Meian*: Another Reading." *Harvard Journal of Asiatic Studies*, vol. 42, no. 1, 1982.

Takemori, Tenyu. "The Emergence of Natsume Sōseki as a Novelist: His Position and Significance in Modern Japanese Literature." *Acta Asiatica*, no. 41, 1981.

Turney, Alan J. "Ateji in the works of Natsume Sōseki: A Translator's View." *Bulletin of the Asiatic Society of Japan*, no. 4, 1983.

———. "A Feeling of Beauty: Natsume Sōseki's 'Ichiya.'" *Monumenta Nipponica*, vol. 23, no. 3, 1978.

———. "Sōseki's Development as a Novelist until 1907, with Special Reference to the Genesis, Nature and Position in His Work of Kusa Makura." Ph.D. diss., University of London, London, 1978.

Vardaman, James M., Jr. "Money in the Novels of Natsume Sōseki." *Proceedings of the Second International Symposium on Asian Studies*, 1980.

Viglielmo, V. H. "The Hero in Natsume Sōseki's Novels." *Journal-Newsletter of the Association of Teachers of Japanese*, vol. 4, no. 1, 1966.

———. "An Introduction to the Later Novels of Natsume Sōseki." *Monumenta Nipponica*, vol. 19, no. 1, 1964.

———. "The Later Natsume Sōseki: His Art and Thought." Ph.D. diss., Harvard University, Cambridge, 1956.

———. "Natsume Sōseki: *Kokoro*." *Approaches to the Modern Japanese Novel*, ed. Thomas E. Swann and Kinya Tsuruta. Sophia University, Tokyo, 1976.

———. "Natsume Sōseki: 'Hearing Things,' 'Ten Nights of Dream.'" *Approaches to the Modern Japanese Short Story*, ed. Thomas E. Swann and Kinya Tsuruta. Waseda University Press, Tokyo, 1982.

Yu, Beongcheon. *Natsume Sōseki*. Twayne Publishers, Boston, 1969.

———. "A Tragedy of Character: Sōseki's *Kokoro*." *Orient West*, vol. 9, no. 2, 1964.

NIWA Fumio
(1904–   )

Novelist. Born in Yokkaichi, near Nagoya, and brought up in the precincts of the Buddhist temple, Sōgenji. Moved to Tokyo in 1932.

One of modern Japan's most prolific writers, Niwa Fumio has addressed a wide variety of subjects in his work, ranging from wartime naval battles to the lives of the Buddhist saints. He is chiefly known, however, for his "novels of passion," written in a journalistic style and invariably serialized in popular magazines. In these novels his female characters demonstrate a strong sexuality, yet the stories themselves are often set in a Buddhist milieu familiar to Niwa from his youth. As the son of a Buddhist priest he took holy orders at the age of eight and was expected to continue his family's long tradition in the priesthood. But the outside world beckoned, perhaps because his mother set an example by absconding from the temple precincts with her lover. At any rate, Niwa's unusual and almost over-colorful family background enabled him to write such novels as *Bodaiju* (*1955–56, The Buddha Tree*) and *Zeiniku* (*1934, Indulgent Flesh*). Turning his attention to social problems after World War II he produced his most controversial work: *"Iyagarase no nenrei"* (*1947*, "The Hateful Age"). In this classic study of old age he flouted Oriental convention by seeming to endorse a growing disrespect for the elderly. For good or ill, the story's title entered the Japanese language as a synonym for dotage. Niwa himself, as prolific as ever, was well short of dotage at age sixty-one, becoming a member of the Japan Art Academy in 1965, and in the same year being elected president of the Japan Writers' Association.

Niwa Fumio was born in Yokkaichi, a small port on Ise Bay near Nagoya. His father was the hereditary priest of Sōgenji, a Buddhist temple of the True Pure Land Sect. For more than two hundred years the Niwa family had been the priests of this temple, building up its wealth and influence until its status, at a peak in the early nineteenth century, suddenly declined with the onset of the *Meiji period. Niwa Fumio's father, the sixteenth in succession, did much to restore its fortunes, and he naturally expected his son to continue the tradition.

Fascinated though he was by the temple rituals, Niwa found the atmosphere oppressive after his mother left in 1912. He was surely recalling his feelings when, in *The Buddha Tree*, he described the eight-year-old Ryokun returning home from school. "A little way back from the temple gate, and overlooking it, stood the main hall of the temple. Ryokun's steps suddenly slowed down when he was through the gate; it had happened like that every day for some time now . . . this feeling of loneliness and unhappiness seemed to be waiting for him at the gate." Previously (the novel explains), his mother had taken him on exciting excursions to a Western-style inn where some of the guests were foreigners. There she would meet her lover, "an actor of some repute in the Kansai Kabuki company," and afterward would behave quite differently towards her son. "A new tenderness revealed itself in every movement she made; a side of his mother Ryokun never saw at (the temple)."

Too young to understand all the reasons why his mother might have left, Niwa used his imagination to fill in the gaps of his knowledge. However, good training though it may have been for a novelist, such speculation was poor training for a priest. After graduating from high school, Niwa was drawn toward literary studies and entered Waseda University to pursue a course in Japanese literature. There he came under the influence of OZAKI KAZUO, five years his senior, who himself had found in the works of SHIGA NAOYA an inspiration to rebel against his family's conservative values. However, unlike Ozaki and despite the passages quoted above, Niwa was not inclined to make his personal life the sole subject of his art. As the critic Nakamura Mitsuo has said: "He had almost no ambition of describing himself in his literature."

Rejecting the *I-Novel tradition, Niwa approached his work with a journalist's objectivity and a tendency to sensationalize his material. He graduated in 1929, returning home briefly to assume his duties as a priest, but finally relinquishing the priesthood in 1930. During this period he wrote many stories, eventually gaining recognition for *"Ayu"* (*1932*, "Small River Trout"). Serialized in *Bungei Shunjū*, it describes how a wife and mother becomes the mistress of a married man. Two years later he addressed much the same theme in "Indulgent Flesh," describing an adulterous affair from the point of view of the woman's son. If Niwa did not write about himself, at least he quickly discovered the novelist's technique of translating observations into fiction, even though the process seems to be only partially completed.

Niwa's early work reflects the bitterness he felt when his mother left. He sees all women as being at the mercy of their sensuous nature, a view compounded by his own affair with an unfaithful woman prior to his marriage in 1935. He does not, however, go beyond the particularity of each story to draw any firm, moral conclusions. As Kenneth Strong has said (in the introduction to his translation of *The Buddha Tree*): "A Western writer, working from a longer tradition of the novel as a philosophical criticism of life, might have made these victims of their own sensuality into universal symbols of human weakness. Niwa does not achieve this: he is still too closely involved with the experiences out of which the book grew."

Given the context in which he wrote, it is surprising that Niwa succeeded at all in fictionalizing his experience. His contemporaries, those of the second decade of *Shōwa, were men like Ozaki and DAZAI OSAMU who created literary personae for themselves in order to make sense of the world. Like actors on a stage, Ozaki's "Ogata" and Dazai's "Osamu" relive their authors' lives with such apparent veracity that the reader cannot fail to be moved. Niwa, on the other hand, chose a completely different literary method. Instead of putting himself at a distance by inventing a fictional persona, he remained in an uncomfortable netherworld, being neither wholly present in, nor completely absent from, his novels. Criticized by Japanese critics for being too detached, from a Western perspective he was "too closely involved." In other words, his literary method failed to meet either the criteria of the I-Novel or those of fully achieved fictions.

Whatever view one takes, Niwa's fiction is not literature of the highest order. One cannot help feeling that in describing his lust-tormented heroines he was simply guessing. Instead of writing from his experience, either directly through a persona or indirectly through imaginative fiction, he wrote merely from his observations. It is from this basic fallacy, from believing that a writer can "fictionalize" experience simply by inventing situations similar to those he has observed, that much of Niwa's work stems.

Ironically, the documentary aspects of Niwa's stories give them their most distinctive quality. In 1942, he wrote *"Kaisen"* ("Naval Engagement"), praised by Donald Keene as being the finest of the many documentary accounts of the war. Written as journalism it describes incidents with (Keene says) "an authority that marks Niwa unmistakably as a novelist." But if this is true, surely the converse also applies? Do not Niwa's lengthy descriptions of temple life in *The Buddha Tree* mark him unmistakably as a journalist? The novel's narrative is at its best when the author is describing the history and modern-day practice of Buddhism.

Among Niwa's other novels set in a Buddhist milieu are the semi-autobiographical *Aomugi* (1953, *Green Barley*); *Kao* (1959–60, *Face*); and *Ichiro* (1962–66, *One Road*). Mentioning these works, Nakamura Mitsuo commented: "His probing of Buddhism is as yet superficial."

More graciously received were what critics refer to as Niwa's "stories of the old and ugly." Two of these have been translated into English: "The Hateful Age" and *"Shūchi"* (1953, "A Touch of Shyness"). Appearing two years after the war, "The Hateful Age" created something of a sensation. In it, Niwa was highly critical of traditional Japanese deference to the elderly. Old Ume, the grandmother of the story, behaves quite intolerably – prompting her granddaughter's husband to say: ". . .in that little body of hers the spite, hypocrisy and dishonesty of eighty-six years have coagulated into a solid core of wickedness." Literally dumped on another branch of the family, Ume continues to misbehave, demonstrating to everyone her failure to cultivate wisdom during her active years. Niwa's portrayal of Ume as an unwelcome burden struck a particular nerve among members of the public. Recently led to defeat because of their deference to unwise leaders, the Japanese read Niwa's disrespectful portrait of old age with a sense of liberation.

In addition to his "stories of the old and ugly," Niwa continued to write the sort of novels that had made him famous, while adding a new genre of socially conscious fiction. *Hachūrui* (1950, *Reptilia*) describes the many love affairs of a businessman, but three years later, *Hebi to hato* (1953, *The Serpent and the Doves*) looks at one of the new religious cults that flourished after the war. Neither has been translated into English.

In his long career, Niwa Fumio produced hundreds of novels, short stories, and essays, none of which can be called unequivocally a masterpiece. Although he won many literary prizes, he was at heart a journalist who was better able to describe contemporary life than evoke it convincingly in dramatic terms.

RECOMMENDED READING

Novel

The Buddha Tree. *Bodaiju. 1955–56.* 230 pages. Tr. Kenneth Strong. Peter Owen, London, 1966; Tuttle, Tokyo and Boston, 1968, 1971, paperback. Includes translator's 6-page introduction.

Short Fiction Collection

The Hateful Age. 224 pages. Tr. various. Hara Shobo, Tokyo, 1965. Includes: "Indulgent Flesh," "A Touch of Shyness," and "The Hateful Age."

WORKS IN ENGLISH TRANSLATION

Novel

The Buddha Tree. Bodaiju. 1955–56.

Short Fiction

"The Hateful Age." *"Iyagarase no nenrei."* 1947. 94 pages. (1) Tr. Ivan Morris. (with cuts approved by the author). *Japan Quarterly*, vol. 3, no. 1, 1956; *Modern Japanese Stories*, ed. I. Morris. Spottiswoode, London, 1961; Tuttle, Tokyo, 1962. *The Hateful Age* (full version). (2) As "The Hateful Years." Tr. William L. Clark. *Jiji Eigo Kenkyu*, vol. 13, nos. 4–11, 1958; vol. 14, no. 2, 1959. *Various Kinds of Bugs, and Other Stories from Present-Day Japan.* Kenkyusha, Tokyo, 1958.

"Indulgent Flesh." *"Zeiniku."* 1934. 96 pages. Tr. Richard Foster. *The Hateful Age.*

"A Touch of Shyness." *"Shūchi."* 1953. 34 pages. Tr. Edward Seidensticker. *Japan Quarterly*, vol. 2, no. 1, 1955; *The Hateful Age.*

Nogami YAEKO
(1885–1985)

Novelist. Born in Ōita Prefecture, Kyūshū. Educated in Tokyo.

Still active in the 1980s when she was fast approaching a hundred years of age, Nogami Yaeko was always more widely admired than read. Only one or two of her early stories have been translated into English, but to the Japanese she presented an immense body of work, ranging from historical fiction to a complete critique of modern civilization. Ever since her first story was praised by NATSUME SŌSEKI she applied herself to literature with total dedication. She published her first full-length work, *Machiko*, in the late 1920s, and went on to write *Meiro* (1956, *The Labyrinth*), a novel of more than a thousand pages analyzing Japan's political and social history between 1936 and 1944. Her own upper-class background never deterred her from describing the pre-war Marxist movement with considerable sympathy and in inexhaustible detail. Yet she was more at home in depicting aristocratic characters, especially those who retained some of the dignity of the *Tokugawa period. She set her most highly acclaimed novel in the sixteenth century, focusing on the complex relationship between the warlord Hideyoshi and his tea master *Sen no Rikyū. Published when she was already seventy-seven, *Hideyoshi to Rikyū* (1962–63) is the work for which she will be best remembered. For some of her other work, however, she has enjoyed the attention of the feminist movement, and as a woman of great achievements who raised three sons (each of whom became distinguished scholars like their father), her example has been an inspiration. Although many critics consider her work austere, few would deny that she held enlightened, humanist attitudes. Greatly influenced by English literature, especially by the moralists of the nineteenth century, Yaeko was the "grand old lady" of modern Japanese literature for longer than anyone could remember.

The daughter of a rich wine maker in Japan's western island of Kyūshū, the fifteen-year-old Yaeko went to Tokyo to study at the Meiji Women's High School at the turn of the century. There she met the man she would later marry, Nogami Toyoichirō (1883–1950), who was to become a leading scholar of the *Nō. It was through his attendance of Sōseki's famous "Thursday meetings" (from which women were excluded) that her work came to the master's notice. Sōseki was generous with his praise and meticulous in his criticism. He arranged for her subsequent story *"Enishi"* (1909) to be published prominently in *Hototogisu*, and this was her first published work.

Yaeko's early writing was in a style of impressionistic realism, far removed from the plain, almost blunt style that she used in her later novels of social analysis. Among her early stories, *"Kaijinmaru"* (1922, "The Neptune") has been translated into English. It is a simple but convincing tale of attempted cannibalism on board a sixty-five-ton schooner that has been blown off-course during one of its voyages. The captain, a brave and intelligent man, is completely blameless in the whole affair. His ship is almost torn apart by storms, and, when the stock of food runs short, two of his crew become distrustful of the way he sensibly rations it between them. Gorōsuke and Hachizō insist on having their share in bulk, leaving the other half to the captain and his nephew, Sankichi, the only other person on board. Eventually, when the food runs out completely, Hachizō lures Sankichi to the far end of the boat and kills him with a view to eating him. His partner in crime, Gorōsuke, is overcome with guilt and changes his allegiance to help the captain subdue the murderer. They bury Sankichi at sea, and after several more days of starvation all the survivors are rescued by a much larger ship that has weathered the storms more easily. Before they reach shore, Gorōsuke dies of exhaustion, while the captain, determined to avoid any more trouble, tells the authorities that

Sankichi died of natural causes. Hachizō survives, but he, too, is now clearly feeling remorse.

"The Neptune" was first published in the *Chūō kōron* in October, 1922 and appeared in book form two years later. Given the nature of its subject matter some readers found it shocking, but it seems much less so today. It was, in fact, based on a true story told to Yaeko's brother by the captain himself. In a note at the end of the story the author records: "Since this incident, [the captain] has grown afraid of the sea and is now a ship's chandler . . . his skin was still bluish when he came home from Yokohama and made calls on his fellow villagers."

In 1911 Yaeko joined the group around Hiratsuka Raichō (1886–1971), the feminist pioneer who founded the magazine *Seitō* (*Bluestocking*), but she continued to publish in *Hototogisu* and other magazines which had a general readership. Clearly, Yaeko was an independent spirit, and she came to admire the Russian female mathematician Sonya Kovalevskaya, who also made her way in a man's world (during the 1860s) and whose autobiography Yaeko translated in 1913.

Not until 1928, however, did Yaeko produce a literary work of real importance. This was *Machiko* (*1928–30*), which was serialized in *Kaizō* (*Reconstruction*). Its heroine, Sone Machiko, is an idealist who becomes involved with the leftwing movement and makes plans to marry a revolutionary. Her discovery that he is already married to someone else is counterbalanced by her realization that a factory boss who actually loves her would be a more suitable match. The author addressed her theme with considerable intelligence, using the conflict she herself felt (between a dislike of capitalism and a distrust of revolutionary fervor) to generate the novel.

Despite Yaeko's sympathies for the ideals of the proletarian writers she could not easily assume their mantle. Had she been English she would have been classified as a so-called Hampstead intellectual – and indeed many Japanese critics have found her "too English" in her tendency to moralize from the vantage point of superior wealth and breeding. Nonetheless, Yaeko was surely right to seek alternatives for a society that was becoming galvanized by militarism, and she attempted to put all her dissatisfaction into *The Labyrinth*, the first parts of which were so heavily censored that she postponed its completion for twenty years.

Although *The Labyrinth* is far too complex to summarize here, its subject is the generation of the 1930s who were trapped in an intellectual maze because their idealism could find no effective political expression. Yaeko shared their dilemma, and perhaps for this reason the novel has often been interpreted as a projection of her ideological struggle. This is not necessarily true, according to the American scholar Donald Keene. Calling it an "impressive, but by no means flawless, novel," he comments on how markedly it departs from *I-Novel traditions, both in its scale and in its presentation of many different points of view.

In *The Labyrinth*, Yaeko attacked contemporary society not only through her Marxist characters, but even more effectively through her creation of Ejima Munemichi, an aristocratic devotee of the Nō theater who holds firm to Tokugawa ideals. Such charming anachronisms are not uncommon in Japanese literature, and one may conjecture whether or not Matsubara Hisako's equally memorable character, Father Hayato, in *Brokatrausch* (1978, *Samurai*), was based on him.

Critics are agreed that Yaeko was better able to portray such individual aristocrats as Ejima than bring to life the many would-be revolutionaries of 1930s Japan. From her husband, who was the author of *Zeami and His Theories of Noh* (translated into English in 1955) she would have learned much about Japan's traditional arts, and indeed she herself had published *Kantan*, based on the Nō drama, as long ago as 1920. She turned again to the traditional arts in her next work, focusing on one of Japanese history's most intriguing episodes.

Hideyoshi to Rikyū (1962–63, *Hideyoshi and Rikyū*) is a detailed historical novel describing the warlord Hideyoshi's conflict with his tea master, the famed Sen no Rikyū (1521-91), whom he forced to commit suicide. A mixture of fact and fiction, it naturally favored the artist in preference to the tyrant, and is generally taken to symbolize the perennial conflict between politics and the arts. For this work Yaeko won the Women's Literature Prize in 1964.

Although not many of Yaeko's works have been translated into English, the best of them is surely *"Kitsune"* (1946, "The Foxes"), a short novella in which she fully expressed her anti-militarist sentiments. It is a truly excellent work, narrated with great clarity yet in such a way that the characters come to life on the page. It tells of how Shin'ichi and Yoshiko, a young married couple from Tokyo, are persuaded by a farmer to take up the unusual occupation of fox-rearing in the mountains. The couple have, in fact, already moved to the country, partly on account of Shin'ichi's poor health but also because they both wish to avoid living with their relatives. Up in the mountains they both feel more relaxed and are amused by the idea of rearing silver foxes for their fur. It is a frivolous pursuit, especially now that the country has recently gone to war, but since there is no great need for them to earn money they can indulge their whim. As it transpires, they make a wise investment in purchasing their farm because the inhabitants of Tokyo are soon fleeing the air raids and pushing up the price of property in the mountains. Indeed, the outside world with all its unpleasantness seems to catch up with this idyllically happy couple, for Shin'ichi's illness takes such a serious turn that his friend Sasaki urgently visits him for the last time. In an eloquent speech before he dies, Shin'ichi summarizes the world situation for Sasaki and insists that he (Shin'ichi) is actually much better off than most people. "When I am neither coughing up blood nor suffering from fever, I have no particular pain. I am amply provided with food and fuel procured on the black market. Even the sound of the air raid warning bell as it comes over the plateau and through the woods sounds to me poetic rather than frightful." He concludes that he must "pay" for his selfishness in the same way that Japan is now paying for the suffering it inflicted on the Chinese earlier in the war. Curiously, this highly polemical outburst focuses rather than spoils the story, which ends with Shin'ichi's uncle – an admiral of the fleet who returns from the war injured and humiliated – caring for the foxes like an ordinary farm laborer.

Among Yaeko's other works are *Hōka Satsujinhan* (1916, *The Arsonist*); *Kanashiki shōnen* (1935, *Sad Boy*); "*Meigetsu*" (1942, "The Full Moon"); *Fue* (1964, *Flute*); and *Suzuran* (1966, *Lilies of the Valley*).

Her last years were spent in writing the long autobiographical novel *Mori* (*The Forest*), and she was awarded a Cultural Medal in 1971.

RECOMMENDED READING

Short Fiction Collection

The Neptune, The Foxes. 225 pages. Tr. Ryozo Matsumoto. Kenkyusha, Tokyo, 1957. Contains two short novels: *The Neptune, Kaijin-maru, 1922,* 103 pages; and *The Foxes, Kitsune, 1946,* 122 pages. Both translations are reprinted in *Japanese Literature, New and Old.* Hokuseido, Tokyo, 1961. Not easy to find outside of specialist libraries.

WORKS IN ENGLISH TRANSLATION

Short Fiction

"The Foxes." "*Kitsune.*" 1946. *The Neptune, The Foxes.*
"The Full Moon." "*Meigetsu.*" 1942. 22 pages. Tr. Kyoko Iriye Selden.

Stories by Contemporary Japanese Women Writers, ed. Noriko Mizuta Lippit and Kyoko Iriye Selden. M. E. Sharpe, Armonk, NY, 1982; reissued as *Japanese Women Writers,* 1991.

"The Neptune." *"Kaijin-maru."* *1922. The Neptune, The Foxes.* "Windows and an Out-of-Tune Instrument." *"Mado to onboro* *gakki."* 8 pages. Tr. Juliet W. Carpenter. *Literary Review,* vol. 30, no. 2, 1987.

CRITICAL STUDY

McClain, Yoko. "Nogami Yaeko: A Writer as Steady as a Cow." *Journal* *of the Association of Teachers of Japanese,* vol. 17, no. 2, 1982.

NOSAKA Akiyuki
(1930–   )

Novelist, scriptwriter, celebrity. Born in Kamakura. A student in Kōbe during World War II.

Nosaka Akiyuki is known in the West for three brilliant, but very different works. His subversive novel *The Pornographers* is riotously funny: a comic masterpiece about two inept pornographers who treat sex as if it were a low-value commodity like soybeans or lemons. "American Hijiki" is more sophisticated in its humor, taking cultural misunderstanding between East and West as its major theme. "A Grave of Fireflies," Nosaka's third work in translation, is a tragic chronicle describing the deaths of two orphans during the air raids on Kōbe in World War II. Together, these stories give a good insight into one of Japan's most courageous and talented postwar writers. That he is also a public figure, active in politics and well-known in his country as a pop singer who affects a stylish image, is a fact which makes Nosaka, the man, as interesting as Nosaka, the writer.

Born in Kamakura in 1930, Nosaka was brought up by his aunt

and uncle in Kōbe after his mother's early death. His childhood and adolescence could scarcely have been more traumatic. First, his uncle died and his aunt was crippled during the firebombing of Kōbe. With his sixteen-month-old sister he went to live with a distant relative in another part of the city, but within a week of the war's ending the baby girl died of malnutrition. Nosaka, by then a teenager skilled in surviving among the ruins and the black market, returned to live with his own father and stepmother after a brief period in a reform school. He entered Waseda University to study French literature, but dropped out in his senior year.

Inevitably, Nosaka's vivid wartime experiences have been a major source of his material ever since he began a career as a novelist in the early 1960s. However much he tries to shrug off these influences of his formative years, the darker themes are always present even in his most humorous work. Yet, if anything, Nosaka's acute awareness of life's cruelty has been an invaluable asset to him. It is to his eternal credit that he has been able to extract humor from tragedy, using the manner of the *Edo novelists – *Ihara Saikaku in particular – as the model for his fiction.

Nosaka's first popular novel, *Erogotoshitachi* (*The Pornographers*), appeared in 1962. The absurd antics of the two, down-at-heel pornographers are not only wonderful inventions but perfectly express the author's peculiar brand of warmhearted cynicism. So entertaining is this book that one longs for an English translation of his second erotic work, *Mayonaka no Maria* (*Midnight Maria*).

Like one or two other postwar writers, Nosaka has deliberately courted notoriety. His early work as a scriptwriter brought him into contact with television, on which he subsequently appeared both as a frequent talk-show guest and as a popular singer. However, it was perhaps his publication of an erotic story, said to have been written by NAGAI KAFŪ, that brought him the most publicity. The story became the subject of a court case: the Japanese equivalent of the *Lady Chatterley's Lover* trial in Britain. It lasted from 1973 to 1976, when a guilty verdict was finally handed down. Disgusted, but with customary humor, Nosaka criticized the "terrible literary style" in which the judges delivered their opinion.

As a perpetual maverick who delights in attacking the authoritarian aspects of Japanese culture, Nosaka refuses to be trapped by any hidebound conventions in the world of letters. He often publishes his work in quite disreputable magazines and seizes upon issues which enable him to buck the system. His 1971 novel, *Sōdōshitachi* (*The Rioters*), was based on the student riots of 1969. In it, the destruction of what he sees as an oppressive educational system is symbolized by turning Tokyo University into a heap of rubble, which then becomes a joyous playground for the children of the city.

White-suited, like Tom Wolfe, and wearing his ubiquitous "shades," Nosaka may sometimes seem to be more American than Japanese. But for all his clowning, he is a serious artist, deeply committed to continuing Japan's great tradition of populist humor.

RECOMMENDED READING

Novel

The Pornographers. *Erogotoshitachi.* 1962. 304 pages. Tr. Michael Gallagher. Knopf, NY, 1968; Secker and Warburg, London, 1969; Bantam Books, NY, 1969; Tuttle, Tokyo, 1970; Mayflower, London, 1970. Not a pornographic novel but a very humorous one.

WORKS IN ENGLISH TRANSLATION

Novel

The Pornographers. Erogotoshitachi. 1962.

"A Grave of Fireflies." *"Hotaru no haka."* 1967. 18 pages. Tr. James R. Abrams. *Japan Quarterly*, vol. 25, no. 4, 1978.

Short Fiction

"American Hijiki." *"Amerika hijiki."* 1968. 32 pages. Tr. Jay Rubin. *Contemporary Japanese Literature*, ed. Howard Hibbett. Knopf, NY, 1977.

Essay

"The Honor of a Guilty Verdict: Reflections on the Yojohan Obscenity Trial." 4 pages. Tr. Mark D. Ericson. *Japan Quarterly*, vol. 23, no. 3, 1976.

Ōba MINAKO
(1930–)

Novelist, poet, and essayist. Born in Tokyo. Traveled worldwide, lived in Alaska.

Ōba Minako exploded onto the literary scene in 1968, winning not only the Gunzō New Author Award but the Akutagawa Prize for her first published story, *"Sambiki no kani"* ("The Three Crabs"). Already in her late thirties she had been writing for many years, and indeed had wanted to be an author ever since reading Victor Hugo at the age of eleven. Following her initial success she produced a steady flow of work throughout the 1970s and 1980s, winning further prizes for her novels, stories, and essays. As many critics have pointed out, her fiction is notable for its emphasis on sex as the primitive instinct which constantly breaks through the veneers of civilization. Moreover, in her view of the natural world – gained through living for many years in Alaska – there is a sense of ferocity and wildness rarely found elsewhere in Japanese literature.

Born in Tokyo, the first daughter of a physician, Minako grew up in the shadow of war. At age fourteen she was one of many girls who were delegated to look after the A-bomb survivors of Hiroshima. Exposure to such extreme suffering at so early an age must surely have colored her outlook on the world, yet rarely has she discussed it in her work. More frequently she refers to the influence of Dostoievsky and T. S. Eliot, two authors whose work she particularly admires. Resuming her education in the postwar years she graduated from Tsuda College, and eventually married at the age of twenty-four.

Conventional marriage was never on Minako's lifetime agenda, and she insisted on retaining a measure of independence from her husband at the outset of their life together. In 1959 she went to the United States to study, first at the University of Wisconsin then on to the University of Washington. Later she moved to Paris to study art, and traveled the length and breadth of Europe by train. Throughout all this time she continued to write, but it was not until she accompanied her husband to Alaska (where he worked for the Japan-Alaska Pulp Company in Sitka) that she found the inspiration to produce work of real quality.

"The Three Crabs" was one of three stories published by Ōba Minako in 1968, the others being *"Kōzu no nai e"* ("Formless Painting") and *"Niji to ukihashi"* ("The Rainbow and the Floating Bridge"). From all three works it was apparent that a remarkable new stylist had emerged from obscurity into the spotlight of the literary world. "The Three Crabs," especially, seemed fresh and appealing, not least because it depicted Japanese people who had acquired a cosmopolitan outlook while living overseas. The loss of one's own national identity and the acquisition of a new, personal identity were to become recurrent themes in Minako's work, eventually finding full expression in her long novel, *Urashimasō* (1977, *Urashima Grass*).

In English translation "The Three Crabs" lacks the impact of some of her later stories, perhaps because her style is difficult to render into English. Nonetheless, even a foreign reader can detect the strangeness of her heroine's home life from the sharp exchanges of dialogue which compose much of the story. Hers is clearly an open marriage in which neither partner remains faithful to the other. Leaving a houseful of guests she disappears for the evening to pick up a married stranger for casual sex, afterwards recalling, with no hint of regret, the "metallic voices" of her husband and daughter. The author implies that her heroine is not unlike the faceless crabs on the seashore: a creature with no firm identity, yet one able to blend with a new environment over a long period of time.

The most striking of Minako's Alaskan stories in English translation is *"Higusa"* (1969, "Fireweed"), with its highly erotic narrative told in a unique style of prose-poetry. It appeared in the January 1969 issue of *Bungakukai*, and was included in her collection *Yūreitachi no fukkatsusai* (1970, *Easter of the Ghosts*). Set in the wilderness it opens with the death of its heroine: an elemental figure called Fireweed who has been poisoned by a member of the family with whom she lives. Fireweed's story is recounted in flashback, explaining how she came to be rescued by a village elder after her expulsion from another village. Officially the elder's mistress but involved in a torrid affair with his favorite son, she may have been killed by either of them in an attempt to restore the *status quo*. On one level, therefore, the story is a mystery tale that tries to identify Fireweed's murderer – but on quite another level it is a complex and sustained metaphor of social regeneration. Thrown out of society, Fireweed reverts to nature for her survival, and it is from nature that she draws her vitality. In turn, this attracts the attention of those who, in helping to create society, have begun to wither and die. But life-enhancing though it may be, Fireweed's passion is so strong that it destroys the social fabric and once again she must be expelled. Ironically, her death seems far less tragic than the continuing lives of those who have found it necessary to kill her.

Minako went on to write many other works in the 1970s, including *"Funakui mushi"* (1970, "Ship-Eating Insects"); *"Tsuga no yume"* (1971, "Dream of Hemlock"); *"Kokyū o hiku tori"* (1972, "The Bird that Played the Fiddle"); *"Kiri no tabi"* (1976, "Journey Through Mist"); and the novel *Garakuta hakubutsukan* (1975, *The Rubbish Museum*), which won the Fourteenth Women's Literary Prize in 1976.

Two other stories of the same period are readily available in English translation, namely *"Aoi kitsune"* (1973, "The Pale Fox") and *"Yamamba no bishō"* (1976, "The Smile of a Mountain Witch"). In the first of these, the female narrator encounters a former lover whom she calls the Pale Fox on account of his predatory nature. She seems to prefer him to her husband, the Praying Mantis, whose masochistic streak enables him to tolerate her wayward behavior. Infidelity, however, is only one aspect of the story, for woven into the narrative is an image of the heroine's father searching for his wife's grave on a remote island. Death and illicit love have thus been deliberately juxtaposed for aesthetic effect, somewhat in the manner of KAWABATA YASUNARI.

Minako added the Tanizaki Prize to her growing collection of honors when she published *Katachi mo naku* (1982, *Without Shape*), a novel that presents a more Oriental view of nature. Eleven of her short stories written since 1976 were collected into the volume *Bōshi no kiita monogatari* (1983, *Tales Heard by a Hat*), and Minako continued to delight the critics with the distinctive style of her novel *Ōjo no namida* (1987, *The Queen's Tears*). Indeed, her work appeals to many different people: to feminists who admire her liberated ideas; to traditionalists who enjoy the superb craftsmanship of her stories; and to Modernists who wish they could be equally original. In years to come, Minako will certainly be counted as one of the leading Japanese writers of the twentieth century.

RECOMMENDED READING

Short Fiction

"Fireweed." *"Higusa."* *1969*. 22 pages. Tr. Marian Chambers. *Japan Quarterly*, vol. 28, no. 3, 1981. A brilliant story, highly recommended.

WORKS IN ENGLISH TRANSLATION

Short Fiction

"Fireweed." *"Higusa."* 1969.
"The Pale Fox." *"Aoi kitsune."* 1973. 10 pages. Tr. Stephen Kohl. *The Shōwa Anthology*, vol. 2, ed. Van C. Gessel and Tomone Matsumoto. Kodansha International, Tokyo, 1985.
"Sea Change." *"Tanko."* 8 pages. Tr. John Bester. *Japanese Literature Today*, no. 5, March 1980.
"The Smile of a Mountain Witch." *"Yamamba no bishō."* 1976. 15 pages. Tr. Noriko Mizuta Lippit, assisted by Mariko Ochi. *Stories by Contemporary Japanese Women Writers*, ed. Noriko Mizuta Lippit and Kyoko Iriye Selden. M. E. Sharpe, Armonk, NY, 1982; reissued as *Japanese Women Writers*, 1991.

"The Three Crabs." *"Sambiki no kani."* 1968. 16 pages. (1) Tr. Stephen Kohl and Toyama Ryoko. *Japan Quarterly*, vol. 25, no. 3, 1978. (2) Tr. Yukiko Tanaka and Elizabeth Hanson. *This Kind of Woman, Ten Stories by Japanese Women Writers 1960–76*, ed. Y. Tanaka and E. Hanson. Stanford University Press, Stanford, 1982; G. P. Putnam's Sons, NY, 1984.

Essay

"Double Suicide, A Japanese Phenomenon." 7 pages. Tr. Manabu Takechi and Wayne Root. *Japan Interpreter*, vol. 9, no. 3, 1975.

ŌE Kenzaburō
(1935–)

Novelist. Born in Ōse Village, Ehime Prefecture, Shikoku, western Japan. Lives in Tokyo.

Despite an early affinity with ABE KŌBŌ and the continuing influence of Jean-Paul Sartre, Ōe Kenzaburō is a true original of modern Japanese letters. Since his earliest years at university he has been a highly prolific writer enjoying great popularity, wide critical acclaim, and even a fair share of condemnation from those who have tended to regard his habitual pessimism as being out of step with the mood of his contemporaries. However, his hypersensitive sensibility, penetrating intellect, and sardonic imagination have combined to give his work a conspicuously distinctive quality, and this in itself has helped sustain his literary reputation for more than three decades. Best known in English translation for his novels *Kojinteki na taiken* (1964, *A Personal Matter*) and *Man'en gannen no futtobōru* (1967, *The Silent Cry*), Ōe has, in the opinion of this writer at least, never improved upon the standard he achieved with *"Shiiku"* (1958, *"The Catch"*). In this short novella, written at the age

323

of twenty-two, he created an allegory of lost innocence, the power and perfection of which would have been difficult for any writer to repeat.

Ōe Kenzaburō was born, far from the literary world that revolves around Tokyo, in Ōsemura (Ōse Village, now Uchiko-chō) on the island of Shikoku in western Japan. He grew up in this somewhat isolated rural environment, the third son in a family of seven, during one of the most difficult periods of Japan's recent history. He was six years old when the war in the Pacific started, and ten when it finished. During the intervening period, at the age of nine, he lost both his father and grandmother. Nonetheless, he survived the privations of the wartime era, and, as a gifted linguist, entered Tokyo University in 1954 to study French literature.

Ōe himself claims that the book that most inspired him to become a writer was not French, but American: Mark Twain's *Huckleberry Finn*. He first encountered Twain's novel at the age of fifteen, finding in its hero many qualities which he considered truly admirable. He was particularly moved by Huck's steadfast refusal to betray his friend, no matter what the cost to himself in terms of pain and suffering. Equally, Huck's tenacity and will to survive were qualities that Ōe himself required in order to overcome his own fears and disabilities. Always prone to shyness and stuttering, he was very much an outsider wherever he went, constantly seeking refuge either in literature or in the inventions of his imagination.

Ōe's early readings in American literature gave way to an intensive study of modern French writers when he moved to university. Outsiders all, Camus, Sartre, and their followers were highly fashionable at the time. Ōe wrote his graduation thesis on Jean-Paul Sartre, and it was in the leftwing writings of Sartre that he found arguments to support his own political attitudes. Throughout his career, Ōe has maintained a leftist position, frequently speaking on behalf of groups directly opposed to Japan's prevailing conservatism.

All of Ōe's earliest stories have leftwing themes dealing with the various predicaments of students obliged to face what is clearly a hostile and dangerous world. Indeed, Ōe was often referred to as "the student writer," partly on account of his precocious development while still at college and partly because he wrote about the feelings of students beset with various problems. "*Kimyō na shigoto*" (1957, "An Odd Job") describes how one college student takes a job slaughtering dogs for use in laboratory experiments. It was the first of his stories to be published and it appeared in the university's literary magazine. In comparing the passive dogs awaiting their fate to "us ambiguous Japanese students" his attitude was clear, and, it has to be said, totally unambiguous.

One of Ōe's chief characteristics is his tendency to recycle themes and ideas, playing ever more complex variations on them. This use of repetition is central to his literary method and dates back to his earliest writings. For example, his focus upon "unsuitable jobs for students" was extended to the more accomplished story, "Shisha no ogori" (1957, "Lavish Are the Dead"). Here, a male and a female student independently accept temporary jobs in the morgue of the university's medical center. It would be hard to imagine less congenial work than transferring dozens of bloated corpses from one huge vat of alcohol to another, and Ōe is at pains to emphasize its nastiness with his customary attention to detail. English readers may find a full analysis of this work, by Robert Rolf, in *Approaches to the Modern Japanese Short Story* (ed. Thomas E. Swann and Kinya Tsuruta; Waseda University Press).

The ideas expressed in "Lavish Are the Dead" are complex and provocative, a combination that can be identified as another hallmark of Ōe's writing. The young man who is also the narrator of the story (a literary student when he is not handling lifeless corpses) is fascinated by his temporary job because the bodies have reached a state of "perfect objectivity." They are no longer threatening, like real human beings. The student, who normally has difficulty in communicating with other people, can therefore hold imaginary conversations with the corpses, as though their very objectivity has given them a kind of life within his consciousness.

If there is one overriding emotion within "Lavish Are the Dead" it is the feeling of futility which is shared by all the characters. The girl, prior to an accident that causes her to miscarry, speaks of her coming baby in terms of "giving birth to a new uncertainty." By contrast, the superintendent of the morgue has had futility thrust upon him. Normally an easygoing man, he is outraged when he learns that all the corpses are now too old for medical research and must be buried. As for the narrator, he is constantly threatened by "an unbearable feeling, like chronic indigestion," which threatens to overwhelm him. For all of them, the futility of life has been accentuated rather than expunged by contact with inanimate death.

Although it is a highly accomplished story, "Lavish Are the Dead" reveals a remarkably negative turn of mind. It points an accusing finger at the establishment and finds nothing whatsoever to celebrate in the human spirit. In this respect the author's nihilism is quite unlike that of, say, DAZAI OSAMU, who always succeeds in uplifting his readers' spirits rather than deliberately depressing them.

Ōe himself worked hard at university, writing, studying, and, in order to earn some money, tutoring. There is no evidence to suggest that he or any other student in the mid-1950s was forced to slaughter dogs or shuffle corpses in order to make ends meet. Writers, however, are permitted a degree of exaggeration, and it was in writing that Ōe found the freedom that was so obviously lacking in his everyday life.

The great milestone of Ōe's early career was certainly "The Catch," the story that won him the thirty-ninth Akutagawa Prize. As already mentioned, it remains one of his best pieces, being lyrical, profoundly felt, and beautifully written with neither the obscurity nor the self-conscious cleverness that mars some of his later work.

The story is set in a remote mountain village, not unlike the village in which the author was raised, during World War II. The narrator is a young boy who has a friend called Harelip, a kid brother, and a father who makes a living by hunting weasels. Into their midst the war intervenes sharply when a black American pilot is taken prisoner. To the undernourished children of the village the black man is a magnificent giant who inspires both fear and insatiable curiosity. Awaiting instructions from the local prefecture, the village elders lock him in a cellar attached to the narrator's living quarters. There the villagers feed and tend him quite lovingly as if he were an especially prized breed of domestic animal.

After several weeks, the children lose their fear of the black man completely. They even unlock him and take him to the river to bathe, all the time marveling at his immense physique. The narrator says: "How can I describe how much we loved him, or the blazing sun above our wet, heavy skin that distant, splendid summer afternoon, the deep shadows on the cobblestones, the smell of the children and the black soldier, the voices hoarse with happiness, how can I convey the repletion and the rhythm of it all?"

The above-quoted passage is one of the few truly joyful expressions in the whole of Ōe's work, despite its implication of tragedy to come. And with all the inevitability of tragedy, the children's age of innocence passes when the villagers decide to turn their prize over to the authorities. Acting very unlike Huckleberry Finn, the black pilot takes the narrator hostage and is swiftly killed by the boy's father. For the boy, the black man's single act of betrayal is sufficient to eradicate all the myth and magic of childhood, and Ōe's genius makes us feel the enormity of the event. "Bloody fights with Harelip, hunting small birds by moonlight, sledding, wild puppies, these things were for children." Suddenly, the boy perceives the pilot as having been an ordinary mortal instead of a mythical beast. It is akin to the loss of divinity in the emperor (felt by most

Japanese in 1945), or, in Western myth, to mankind's expulsion from the Garden of Eden.

Ōe published many other pieces in 1958, including *"Miru maeni tobe"* ("Leap Before You Look"), *"Tatakai no konnichi"* ("Today the Struggle"), and his first attempt at a full-length novel, *Memushiri kouchi* (*Plucking Buds and Shooting Kids*). The last-named, an extended version of "The Catch," varies the plot by characterizing the boy and his friends as juvenile delinquents at odds with authority rather than as ordinary members of a village community.

"Ningen no hitsuji" ("Sheep") also dates from 1958 and is readily available in English translation. Set during the Occupation, it describes how some passengers on a bus, including a poor student, are publicly humiliated by a group of drunken American soldiers. The story's dark humor becomes apparent when the student, having been forced to expose his buttocks to fellow passengers on the bus, is pursued by a teacher who wishes him to lodge a complaint with the authorities. Nothing, of course, could be more distasteful to the student, whose embarrassment is already unbearable. The teacher, however, regards social justice in purely abstract terms and refuses to see the incident from the younger man's point of view. His hypocrisy is revealed in the final paragraph when, although exhausted by the chase, he vows to continue it until he finds out the student's name. He declares: ". . . I'll heap shame on both you and the soldiers so that you'll want to die." Clearly, his own sense of humiliation can be assuaged only by making sure that the student is seen by others as being the one true victim of the incident.

Such are the subtleties and complexities of Ōe's writing that many readers find his later works difficult and obscure. Moreover, the Japanese themselves have to contend with the additional barrier of the author's peculiar style. John Nathan, who has translated several of Ōe's works, has described Ōe's style in these terms: "Like a floor covered with fragments of broken glass, his sentences glitter with adjectives and adverbs. They excite the reader's eye and lead him on with their sparkling; bewitched by the eccentricities of the style, he is drawn into the abnormal world portrayed by the author before he has time to take in properly the meaning of each sentence and paragraph. It is extremely difficult to get across in translation the peculiar fascination of such a style."

In Ōe's style and in the complexity of his literary technique, 1965 represents a landmark year. The events leading up to this year, however, were both sad and, in another sense, triumphant. In the early sixties Ōe had published a number of works on sexual themes, including *"Sevuntiin"* (1961, "Seventeen"), *"Sakebigoe"* (1962, "Outcries"), and *"Seiteki ningen"* (1963, "The Sexual Man"). In his story *"Seiji shōnen shisu"* (*1961*, "The Death of a Political Boy") he had slyly taunted MISHIMA YUKIO by portraying a rightwing fanatic as sublimating his sexual impulse in futile political activity. Such obsessive interest in futile sexuality had perhaps been triggered by Ōe's marriage in 1960 to Yukari, the daughter of the writer Itami Mansaku, for he explored the subject with a remarkable freedom from inhibition, often portraying the sex act with a vivid and almost brutal objectivity. These works and their treatment of sex are described in some detail by Hisaaki Yamanouchi in *The Search for Authenticity in Modern Japanese Literature* (Cambridge University Press, 1978).

The two events that changed Ōe's life irrevocably were the birth of a son with severe brain damage in June 1963, and a visit to Hiroshima in August of that year to attend the Ninth World Conference Against Atomic and Hydrogen Bombs. The experience of these two events – the encounter with the A-bomb survivors and the birth of his son – became inextricably linked in Ōe's imagination. In coming to terms with them he would go on to write many works of fiction in which themes based upon them would constantly recur. Indeed, in the pivotal year of 1965 he published two works simultaneously: *Hiroshima nōto* (*Hiroshima Notes*), describing his meeting with the survivors of the A-bomb holocaust; and *Kojinteki na taiken* (*A Personal Matter*), a full-length novel in which he writes about his "personal holocaust" in fictional form.

A Personal Matter is a brilliant and imaginative novel, considered by many to be a classic of postwar Japanese fiction. In it, and as if to punish himself still further, Ōe succeeds in making his grim theme highly entertaining, extracting from tragic events an essence of humor which serves to heighten the tragedy. The distressed hero, nicknamed Bird for his hunched shoulders ("like folded wings") and general birdlike appearance, teaches English literature and grammar to cram-school students. He might well have gained a better job had he not dropped out of university some years previously to indulge in a wild bout of drunkenness. However, having shaken off the craving for drink, he remains addicted to his childhood dream of visiting Africa – a continent that represents adventure and mystery, and which is also a place so remote that it acts as an imaginary refuge to which Bird can escape from his problems. Not surprisingly, Africa looms large when his young wife gives birth to a deformed child. It is almost more than Bird can bear. Gratefully he accepts a bottle of whiskey from his father-in-law, gets drunk, and proceeds to initiate a sexual relationship with his friend Himiko.

Until the appearance of Himiko, the novel, for all its amazing use of language, is no more remarkable than one of YOKOMITSU RIICHI's tales of neurotic young men and their suicidal tendencies. But with Himiko's sympathetic presence acting both as antidote and stimulus to Bird's precarious state of mind, the novel begins to ferment with all the vigor of a spectacular chemical reaction.

Himiko is a wonderfully likelike character. Formerly a brilliant classmate of the "hero" at college, she spends all day alone in her chaotic room philosophizing about pluralistic universes. By night she cruises Tokyo in a red sports car, seeking (and finding) sexual adventure. Her one previous sexual encounter with Bird was on an occasion when, unknown to the hero, she lost her virginity. Since then she has become an expert, investigating every sexual practice with the same thoroughness she has brought to philosophy, and finding "something genuine" in each experience.

Bird, satiated with sex, must now face up to his terrible moral dilemma: should he hasten the baby's death or must he try to ensure that everything be done to save this child, even though it may well grow up retarded, helpless, unhappy, and in pain? Every aspect of the problem is examined in the course of the book. Bird is acutely aware that his fainthearted conspiracy with one of the doctors to allow the child to weaken slowly is really an evasion of the problem. He should either kill it with his bare hands or else wholeheartedly pray for its recovery and spend all his money (saved for his African trip) on medical expenses.

The author resolves the problem, ethically if not aesthetically, in the last chapter. Yet there is something truly unsatisfying about Bird's return to conventionality, especially when all the life of the novel exists in the man's relationship with Himiko. Despite this, the book provides an extraordinary reading experience, not least because of Ōe's virtuosity in plucking unusual similes out of thin air.

A Personal Matter has stood the test of time and is as poignant today as when it was written. If anything, social concern about the problem it addresses has grown rather than diminished. However, literary historians may detect some voguishness in the novel, as though Ōe were too highly steeped in the films and literature of the European avant garde. When Bird, as he passes an open door in the hospital, catches an enticing glimpse of an adolescent nymphomaniac are we not seeing again an Antonioni movie (1960, *La Notte*) and peering over the shoulder of Marcello Mastroianni? Not only are the images identical, they are used in much the same way: as cameos of loneliness and disorientation.

There are many Western echoes in most of Ōe's novels, so perhaps it is not surprising that this Japanese writer's search for values and orientation in a brave new international world should, in this one instance, be similar in feeling to that of an Italian film director. Being lost in one's own city of Tokyo – with the added irony of having only a route map of Africa in the car – is, after all, not that much different from being Italian and stranded spiritually in Milan.

After 1965 Ōe's fiction begins to grow progressively more difficult, moving away from realistic drama to depict various worlds of fantasy where cause and effect are deliberately disconnected. Mystification certainly triumphs over common sense in his 1967 novel *Man'en gannen no futtobōru* (literally: "Football in the Year 1860," translated as *The Silent Cry* in 1974). It would be difficult indeed to invent a plot more convoluted than that which provides structure to this psychological melodrama, set in a densely forested valley in western Japan. Returning to their ancestral home are two brothers, one of them, Taka, a former actor who has recently toured America, the other the narrator, Mitsu, a scholarly and reclusive translator of English zoological books. Their uneasy relationship generates the fundamental tension of the novel, although each is weighed down with personal problems of a very different kind. Mitsu is gradually degenerating for two reasons: first because of the birth of a severely retarded son and second because his closest friend has recently committed suicide in a bizarre and obscene manner. Taka, on the other hand, is simply a masochist with fascist leanings, whose dearest wish is to reinstate the reputation of an ancestor who once supposedly betrayed a peasant's rebellion in 1860. The events of that year figure largely in the novel, as Ōe (who actually won the Tanizaki Prize for this work) tries to outdo TANIZAKI JUN'ICHIRO himself in linking historical narrative to present-day events.

It rapidly becomes clear that Taka is hell-bent on emulating the achievement of his ancestor by igniting a rebellion among the young people of the valley. With their cultural traditions disintegrating and their enterprises failing, the local population have fallen under the dominance of a Korean capitalist known ironically as the Emperor of the Supermarkets. Only Taka can offer leadership and salvation, but his reason for doing so remains ultimately obscure.

The result is a confusing *melée* of disturbed psychologies, morbid ideas, and semi-allegorical events which may or may not have been intended to symbolize the state of contemporary Japanese society. Moreover, the novel's basic unpleasantness is apparent on every page. For example, it is plainly obvious to the reader that Taka is a psychotic criminal with no redeeming features whatsoever. Outrageously, Ōe treats him with sympathy, as if, through Taka's fantasies of violence (possibly inspired by Norman Mailer), he may be striving for some important but unspeakable truth, knowledge of which will benefit mankind in general. Although a factual truth about the mysterious ancestor seems in the end to vindicate Taka's (now terminated) existence, the "silent cry" of his suicide merely emphasizes his brother's evasive attitudes – and these scarcely require any further elucidation.

The Silent Cry was well-received by Western critics, yet more than any other book it reveals Ōe's weaknesses as a novelist during his post-1965 career. Trading as he does in the grotesque, the bizarre, and the obscene, he inhabits a world of private anguish into which no external reality can intrude unless it be given a personal and pessimistic coloration. For example, animals abound in this and in other works, but they do not truly exist in Ōe's world. Their characteristics are merely abstracted by the author for his own purposes – as if the natural world were nothing more than a storehouse of convenient similes. In this respect, the solipsistic Ōe stands quite outside the great traditions of Oriental literature and sensibility.

Western readers may judge these aspects of Ōe for themselves by reading the collection of novellas published under the title *Teach Us to Outgrow Our Madness*. Although the collection includes "The Catch" – already noted above as the best of his early work – the other stories exhibit a startling range of solipsistic inventions, lurid similes, and disturbing, dreamlike narratives. In *"Sora no kaibutsu Aguii"* (1964, "Aghwee the Sky Monster"), Ōe shuffles his pack of ideas and deals them in an unusual hand. The novel's eighteen-year-old student narrator is obliged to solve the problem of his employer's apparent insanity following the death of his baby son. At various times during the day the man sees a phantom in the sky: "a fat baby in a white cotton nightgown, big as a kangaroo." At first believing that his employer is being haunted because he arranged to have the baby killed, the student comes to realize that the man has all the time been devising a convenient excuse for committing suicide. Here and in other stories too (like Himiko in *A Personal Matter*) Ōe creates parallel universes in which he can ask "What if? What if?" over and over again. His ultimate aim appears to be the eradication of each alternative so that he may eventually return to an acceptable normality.

Ōe visited India and Southeast Asia in 1970, and during those visits recorded that he felt his Japanese identity was "something of only relative importance." This is a very revealing comment, not least because most Westerners – Christians especially – would feel that such an observation is a mere truism. Each person, surely, is first a human being and only second the citizen of a nation or a member of a particular race. However, the idea appears to have hit

Ōe with some force, indicating that the Japanese feel an especially strong racial identity. As Hisaaki Yamanouchi has pointed out, Ōe, despite his extensive borrowings from Western literature, has been conducting a search not only for his individual identity but for the whole Japanese nation.

Two other novels by Ōe that are readily available in English translation (and published in the above-mentioned collection that includes "The Catch") are *Mizukara waga namida o nuguitamau hi* (1972, *The Day He Himself Shall Wipe My Tears Away*) and "*Warera no kyōki o iki nobiru michi o oshieyo*" (1969, "Teach Us to Outgrow Our Madness").

The Day He Himself is a ghastly parody of Mishima Yukio, a 100-page tirade that would have horrified Mishima, whose death by *seppuku* prompted Ōe to write it. The story completely reverses Mishima's ideals and logic, portraying a self-loathing hero who believes himself to be dying of cancer. From his hospital bed he dictates an account of an armed insurrection, supposedly undertaken by his father (always referred to obliquely as "a certain party"). However, this plot to blow up the emperor is probably a fake, for the rebel officers merely steal the family's money, while the narrator, who is ten years old at the time, witnesses a lone aircraft strafing the soldiers and killing "a certain party."

As a factual account, a bare outline of the story gives no indication of the unusual manner of its telling. For example, the narrator in his bed is wearing "cylinder-type underwater goggles covered with cellophane," identical to those worn by his father at the end of the war (as protection against the glare of atomic explosives?). Moreover, since his supposed "cancer" is eating away "the layers of body and soul which have concealed his true essence since August sixteenth, 1945," the narrator believes he is finally recapturing his "Happy Days" (shades of Beckett), the days before the Japanese emperor admitted his own mortality.

The climax to the novel, and indeed the whole point of it, is the (blurred) identification of "a certain party" with "He Himself" (the emperor). However, the route by which this lost innocence is to be regained is inglorious in the extreme. Instead of a sudden, spectacular death in the manner of Mishima, the narrator relies upon his own protracted disease (actually cirrhosis of the liver) to carry him off. Indeed the layers of his body and soul are being peeled away by corruption itself, and a full resolution requires him to take neither personal responsibility nor action of any kind.

A less complex and more readable story is "*Teach Us to Outgrow Our Madness*," which draws on similar material. Told in the third person, with the author characterizing himself as "an outlandishly fat man," it is structured around a terrifying incident at a zoo. The fat man, learning from an eye specialist that his retarded son can see no farther than three feet in front of him, takes the boy to the zoo in the hope of disproving the diagnosis. Unfortunately, the visit is a disaster because the man is set upon by a group of laborers who pretend to heave him bodily into the polar bear pit. When father and son become temporarily separated for the first time, the man is appalled to discover that the child survives quite adequately on his own.

Ōe adds an historical dimension to the story, exploring once again the relationship between his hero and the (equally obese) father of his hero – a man who, at the end of his life, retreated from a world he could no longer face. Now, with the knowledge of his father's sense of shame and his own son's ability to survive alone, the hero feels that he is being "hurled to the polar bear of madness" – a symbol of his psychological extremity. The story is full of comic pathos, especially in the way in which the man feels driven to inflict obesity on his child, taking him each day to a special Chinese restaurant. By carrying out this odd ritual he tries to preserve at least one link between the three generations.

Although several other stories by Ōe have been translated into English, many more remain which have not been translated, including such major works as *Kōzui wa waga tamashii ni oyobi* (1973, *The Flood Has Reached My Soul*) and *Dōjidai gēmu* (1979, *A Contemporary Game*). The absence of these works from the bookshelves of Western stores makes one realize that Ōe is not quite as popular as ENDŌ SHŪSAKU, KAWABATA YASUNARI, Mishima, or Tanizaki with American and English readers. This is not surprising, in view of the difficulties which many of his novels present. However, there are other reasons, too, and they all suggest that Ōe's appeal will always be greater in Japan than in the West. First, his development as a writer has been inextricably linked with Japan's recent history, while his political stance, too, is chiefly a reaction to conditions at home. Second – and this may be the most compelling reason – Ōe's translated works do not, even after patient study, strike every reader as being a fully achieved body of literature. Although "The Catch" is a masterpiece and *A Personal Matter* a *tour de force*, Ōe's other works betray a disturbing lack of distinction between the author's inner world and the reality surrounding it. If only Ōe could clarify this distinction, his translated work would speak more directly of the human condition instead of being constrained by the Japanese *milieu*.

RECOMMENDED READING

Novel

A Personal Matter. Kojinteki na taiken. 1964. 165 pages. Tr. John Nathan. Grove Press, NY, 1968; Weidenfeld and Nicholson, London, 1969; Tuttle, Tokyo, 1969.

Fiction Collection

Teach Us to Outgrow Our Madness: Four Short Novels by Kenzaburō Ōe. 261 pages. Tr. John Nathan. Grove Press, NY, 1977, paperback; M. Boyars, London, 1978; Serpent's Tail, London, 1989. Includes "Aghwee the Sky Monster"; and Ōe's excellent (and highly recommended) early story "The Catch," here translated as "Prize Stock."

WORKS IN ENGLISH TRANSLATION

Novels

The Day He Himself Shall Wipe My Tears Away. Mizukara waga namida o nugui tamau hi. 1972. 110 pages. *Teach Us to Outgrow Our Madness*.

Hiroshima Notes. Hiroshima nōto. 1964. 181 pages. Tr. Toshi Yonezawa. *Hiroshima Notes*, ed. David L. Swain. YMCA Press, Tokyo, 1981.

A Personal Matter. Kojinteki na taiken. 1964.

The Silent Cry. Man'en gannen no futtobōru. 1967. 274 pages. Tr. John Bester. Extracts as "A Game of Football." *Japan Quarterly*, vol. 20, no. 4, 1973; vol. 21, nos. 1–2, 1974. Complete work: Kodansha International, Tokyo and NY, 1974, 1981; Serpent's Tail, London, 1988.

Short Fiction

"Aghwee the Sky Monster." *"Sora no kaibutsu Aguii."* 1964. 40 pages. Tr. John Nathan. *Evergreen Review*, no. 54, 1968. *Teach Us to Outgrow Our Madness*, in *Contemporary Japanese Literature*, ed. Howard Hibbett. Knopf, NY, 1977.

"The Catch." *"Shiiku."* 1958. 45 pages. (1) Tr. John Bester. *Japan Quarterly*, vol. 6, no. 1, 1959; *The Shadow of Sunrise*. Kodansha International, Tokyo, 1966; Ward Lock, London, 1966; *New Writing in Japan*. Penguin Books, Harmondsworth, 1972. (2) As "Prize Stock." Tr. John Nathan. *Teach Us to Outgrow Our Madness*.

"The Clever Rain Tree." *"Atama no ii rein tsurii."* 1980. 19 pages. Tr. Brett de Bary and Carolyn Haynes. *The Shōwa Anthology*, vol. 2, ed. Van C. Gessel and Tomone Matsumoto. Kodansha International, Tokyo, 1985.

"Lavish Are the Dead." *"Shisha no ogori."* 1957. 18 pages. Tr. John Nathan. *Japan Quarterly*, vol. 12, no. 2, 1965.

"An Odd Job." *"Kimyō na shigoto."* 1957. 12 pages. As "A Strange Job." Tr. Ruth W. Adler. *Journal of the Concerned Asian Scholars*,

vol. 12, no. 3, 1980; *Stone Lion Review*, vol. 9, no. 2, 1982.
"Sheep." *"Ningen no hitsuji."* *1958*. 10 pages. Tr. Frank Motofuji. *Japan Quarterly*, vol. 17, no. 2, 1970.
"Someone Else's Feet." *"Tanin no ashi."* 7 pages. Tr. Ruth W. Adler. *Journal of the Concerned Asian Scholars*, vol. 14, no. 2, 1982.
"Teach Us to Outgrow Our Madness." *"Warera no kyōki o iki nobiru michi o oshieyo."* *1969*. 50 pages. Tr. John Nathan. *Japan Quarterly*, vol. 19, no. 2, 1972; *Teach Us to Outgrow Our Madness.*
"Unexpected Muteness." *"Fui no*

oshi."* 10 pages. Tr. William Wetherall. *Japan Quarterly*, vol. 36, no. 1, 1989.
"Women Who Listen to the Rain Tree." *"Rein tsurii o kiku onna tachi."* *1982.* 15 pages. Tr. Mark Harbison. *Journal of Literary Translation*, vol. 17, 1986.

Essay

"Introduction to *The Crazy Iris, and Other Stories of the Atomic Aftermath.*" *1984.* 8 pages. Tr. David L. Swain. *The Crazy Iris, and Other Stories of the Atomic Aftermath*, ed. Kenzaburō Ōe. Grove Press, NY, 1985.

CRITICAL STUDIES

De Bary, Brett. "Ōe Kenzaburō: Voice of the Postwar Generation." *Papers on Japan*, no. 5, Harvard University, 1970.
Hirano, Ken. "Kenzaburō Ōe." *New Japan*, no. 24, 1972.
Iwamoto, Yoshio. "The Mad World of Ōe Kenzaburō." *Journal of the Association of Teachers of Japanese*, vol. 14, no. 1, 1979.
————. "Ōe Kenzaburō's Existentialist Novel: *A Personal Matter.*" *Papers of the C.I.C. Far Eastern Language Institute*, no. 4, 1973.
Jackson, Earl., Jr. "Toward a Phenomenology of Ōe Kenzaburō: Self, World, and the Intermediating Microcosm." *Transactions of the International Conference of Orientalists in Japan*, no. 25, 1980.
Napier, Susan Jolliffe. "Death and the Emperor: Mishima, Ōe and the Politics of Betrayal." *Journal of Asian Studies*, vol. 48, no. 1, 1989.
————. "In Search of Intensity, Heroes of Action and Inaction in the Works of Mishima Yukio and Ōe Kenzaburō". Ph.D. diss., Harvard University, Cambridge, 1984.
Rabson, Steve. *Approaches to the*

Modern Japanese Novel, ed. Thomas E. Swann and Kinya Tsuruta. Sophia University, Tokyo, 1976.
Rolf, Robert. "Ōe Kenzaburō: 'Lavish Are the Dead,' 'Prize Stock.'" *Approaches to the Modern Japanese Short Story*, ed. Thomas E. Swann and Kinya Tsuruta. Waseda University Press, Tokyo, 1982.
Wilson, Michiko Niikuni. *The Marginal World of Ōe Kenzaburo: A Study in Themes and Techniques.* Sharpe, London, 1986.
————. "Ōe's Obsessive Metaphor, Mori, the Idiot Son: Toward the Imagination of Satire, Regeneration, and Grotesque Realism." *Journal of Japanese Studies*, vol. 7, no. 1, 1981.
Yamanouchi, Hisaaki. "Abe Kōbō and Ōe Kenzaburō: The Search for Identity in Modern Japanese Literature." *Modern Japan: Aspects of History, Literature and Society*, 1975.
————. *Ōe Kenzaburō and Contemporary Japanese Literature*, Nissan Institute of Japanese Studies, Oxford, 1986.

Okamoto KANOKO
(1889–1939)

Writer of short fiction and poetry. Born and resided in Tokyo.

Speaking of the work of Okamoto Kanoko, Japan's Nobel Prize-winning author KAWABATA YASUNARI wrote: "In Mrs. Okamoto I see a realm that I have always been seeking – in vain." In itself, Kawabata's comment should alert Western readers to Kanoko's unique genius. But if further testimony is needed, translator Yukiko Tanaka has spoken of "the aura of mystery" that still surrounds Kanoko in both life and art, adding: "Her fiction contains passages of unparalleled beauty and an underlying sense of awe."

For triggering pure aesthetic sensations, no Japanese writer in English translation – with the notable exceptions of *Sei Shōnagon and TANIZAKI JUN'ICHIRŌ – can match Okamoto Kanoko. Her art is deeply beautiful, working at a subliminal level while giving every appearance of being spontaneously ephemeral. Subjectively, it may be said to touch the *anima* in man. In a more objective sense, it makes an original and harmonious contribution to all that is most admirable in traditional Japanese culture.

Born to a wealthy, upper-class family, Kanoko was brought up as though she were a princess of the feudal era. One feels that this would have happened even had she not been an intelligent and beautiful child, who, early on, showed a remarkable talent for writing *waka poetry. However, her parents recognized her unique qualities and took exceptional care with her tutoring. In turn, she was introduced to the Chinese and Japanese classics, and to music, dance, calligraphy, and poetry. As a result she became highly accomplished, and developed a charismatic personality that would one day be projected into her fiction.

Kanoko did not, however, become a writer of fiction early in life. First she had, one might say, various incarnations: as a capable wife and mother, as a scholar of esoteric Buddhism, and as a *femme fatale*. These roles, admittedly, add up to an extraordinary combination: but then, Kanoko was far from being an ordinary woman.

Surprisingly, having taken so much trouble with her upbringing, Kanoko's parents allowed her to make an unsatisfactory marriage. An impoverished art student, Ippei, had been ardent in his courtship, but, once married, offered no support to his wife and family. For a while he even deserted them completely, leaving Kanoko to fend for herself at a time when her own parents were in severe financial difficulties. On top of this, two of Kanoko's three children died within their first year, contributing to a growing neurosis that led Kanoko to a nervous breakdown.

Only gradually did life come together again, apparently by Kanoko's own transformation into an indomitable force. Having immersed herself in Buddhism, publishing several books on the subject, she made an extended trip to Europe in 1929, reunited with a much-reformed Ippei. Two other men, with whom Kanoko had meanwhile fallen in love, went with them. It should be added that she preferred romantic to sensual affairs, and appeared to relish the pain which this caused her.

Now began a long and careful preparation for the art of writing fiction. Rather than experiment, as do most aspiring storytellers, by publishing a "first novel" with all its ungainly imperfections, Kanoko studied literature for more than a decade before allowing others to see her work. Already in her late forties, and with only two or three years to live, she wrote all of the stories that have since secured her ever-growing literary reputation.

The magazine *Bungakukai* (*Literary World*), which was started in 1933 by Kobayashi Hideo, gave Kanoko's first story an enthusiastic review. It was called *"Tsuru wa yamiki"* ("The Crane Was Frail") and was about the writer AKUTAGAWA RYŪNOSUKE, whom she had met on several occasions. However, not until her second work was published in 1937 did Kanoko attract widespread attention. *"Boshi jojō"* ("Mother's Love") is an autobiographical story that examines her feelings towards her son, Tarō, when she herself was having an affair during Ippei's absence. It is ornate, intense, and eloquent, and touches that melancholic note which one generally associates with the *Nō.

Many of Kanoko's stories have been translated, notably in *The Tale of an Old Geisha, and Other Stories* (Capra Press, 1985). The title story (*1938, "Rōgishō"*) is one of her best known. It is slightly sinister in its plot line, for it describes how an old geisha siphons the life force from a young man by encouraging his unattainable dreams of becoming a scientist. It ends with a poem written by the geisha: "Year after year / Sadness deepens in me, / And my life flourishes / Ever more."

The women of Kanoko's stories are frequently compared to the beautiful and dangerous *femmes fatales* created by Tanizaki. Although the resemblance is striking, translator Yukiko Tanaka claims that Kanoko's female characters are more conscious of their strength: "heroines in the true sense," rather than projections of male fantasy figures. This is debatable, not least because their consciousness of strength is precisely an awareness of their power over the male psyche.

Quoted (and translated) by Makoto Ueda in *Modern Japanese Writers* (Stanford University Press, 1976), Kawabata Yasunari had this to say of Kanoko's women: "Needless to say, all the beautiful women conjured up by Mrs. Okamoto are crystallizations of life and symbolize the eternal virgin and mother. They exude rays of almost religious light. This is what I meant when I once said 'Her flowers, while rooted deep in the ground, bloom as radiantly as if they belonged to the water or the clouds.' Those women, somewhat resembling the Virgin Mary or the Mona Lisa, are products of the Western tradition that idolized women. Japanese literature has had no such tradition – or, if one argues it had one in *The Record of Ancient Matters* or *A Tale of a Bamboo-Cutter* or *The Tale of Genji*, it is a tradition that has long since withered away. But without it, no art can boast true youthfulness."

RECOMMENDED READING

Short Fiction Collection

The Tale of an Old Geisha, and Other Stories. 78 pages. Tr. Kazuko Sugisaki. Capra Press, Santa Barbara, 1985. Includes: "Sushi," "The Old Geisha," and "North Country." This volume is in the Capra

Back-to-Back Series, i.e., books that you turn upside down to read the second author – in this case an additional 47 pages of Anaïs Nin. Although a paperback, it is a collector's item, design and typography being of the highest quality.

WORKS IN ENGLISH TRANSLATION

Short Fiction

"A Floral Pageant." *"Hana wa tsuyoshi."* *1937.* 20 pages. (1) As "Scarlet Flower." Tr. Edward Seidensticker. *Japan Quarterly,* vol. 10, no. 3, 1963. (2) Tr. Hiroko Morita Malatesta. *To Live and to Write, Selections by Japanese Women Writers, 1913–1938,* ed. Yukiko Tanaka. The Seal Press, Seattle, 1987.

"Komori, The Bat." *"Komori."* 5 pages. *Nippon.* vol. 28, 1940.

"A Mother's Love." *"Boshi jojō."* *1937.* 46-page extract (approx. half of novella). Tr. Phyllis Birnbaum. *Rabbits, Crabs, Etc., Stories by Japanese Women.* University of Hawaii Press, Honolulu, 1982.

"The Old Geisha." *"Rōgishō."* *1938.* 26 pages. *The Tale of an Old Geisha, and Other Stories.*

"Sushi." *"Sushi."* *1939.* 24 pages. *The Tale of an Old Geisha, and Other Stories.*

Poetry

"1 Tanka." *The Burning Heart,* tr. and ed. Kenneth Rexroth and Ikuko Atsumi. Seabury Press, NY, 1977.

"1 Tanka." *The Moment of Wonder,* ed. Richard Lewis. Dial Press, NY, 1971.

Tanka: "The Sound of Waves," "At the Foot of Mount Fuji," and "The Golden Bee." Tr. Asataro Miyamori. *Masterpieces of Japanese Poetry, Ancient and Modern.* Maruzen, Tokyo, 1936; Taiseido, Tokyo, 1956; Greenwood Press, NY, 1971.

CRITICAL STUDIES

Ohkoso, Yoshiko. "Kanoko Okamoto and Foreign Literature." *Haiku Bungaku,* no. 16, 1973.

Sugisaki, Kazuko. "Harmonious Motion of Life: A Comparative Study of the Works of Katherine Anne Porter and Kanoko Okamoto." Ph.D. diss., Occidental College, LA, 1973.

ŌOKA Shōhei
(1909–1988)

Novelist, critic, and translator. Born in Tokyo. Lived in Ōiso, a coastal town near Tokyo.

Ōoka Shōhei established his reputation in the West when his war novel, *Nobi* (1952, *Fires on the Plain*), was translated by Ivan Morris. This powerful work, which was based on the author's experiences in the Philippines, is not only outstanding for its depiction of the horrors of war, but is peculiarly disturbing for its strange, metaphysical imagery. Four years previously, Ōoka had published "*Furyo ki*" (1948, "Prisoner of War"), an autobiographical account of being taken prisoner-of-war by the Americans, and had won the Yokomitsu Prize for it in 1949. Critics were impressed by what they saw as technical originality in this forerunner to *Fires on the Plain*, perhaps not fully appreciating the extent to which Ōoka – an authority on French literature – had been influenced by Western narrative techniques. Although he turned to other themes in the 1950s, Ōoka had not yet completed his work on World War II, for he embarked on a massive documentary study of the campaign he knew best: in *Reite senki (1967–70, The Battle for Leyte)*. The author of many novels and essays, Ōoka lectured extensively on French literature, in Japan and overseas.

Born in Tokyo, Ōoka Shōhei received private lessons in French at an early age from Kobayashi Hideo, the celebrated critic who was renowned for his opposition to Japan's indigenous *I-Novel tradition. Accomplished as a scholar, Ōoka went on to study French at Kyoto University, graduating in 1932. Being especially interested in Stendhal, he began translating *La Chartreuse de Parme* into Japanese, and the subsequent volume established him as a scholar, enabling him to continue his career as a professional translator and critic. Indeed, Ōoka seemed to be following in the footsteps of Kobayashi until the day came in 1944 when he was conscripted into the army as a private. Sent to the Philippines, he was to experience one of the most disastrous campaigns of World War II.

Ōoka's attitude during the war was a mixture of stoic endurance and conventional loyalty. When taken prisoner by the Americans he attempted to kill himself in order to avoid dishonoring his country. Only in retrospect did he try to come to terms with the horror of war, and in this effort he produced his first masterpiece of creative writing.

In *Furyo ki*, Ōoka recounted his experiences in precise, almost matter-of-fact language, avoiding all sentimentality. Although auto-biographical, the novel is much more sophisticated in its narrative technique than a conventional *shishōsetsu* (I-Novel), and in this respect Ōoka may have been influenced by two factors. First, from Kobayashi he was aware of all the arguments against simplistic *Naturalism and the I-Novel tradition; second, he knew that he himself, having had an excellent education, was far from being a typical foot soldier. Unless he departed slightly from tradition there was a danger that the novel would end up as an eccentric autobiography without any universal qualities. Thus he made the hero of *Furyo ki* quite distinct from himself, a technique he took even further in his subsequent work. The critic Nakamura Mitsuo has commented on Ōoka's method, saying: "The distance between author and hero, or the coexistence of lyricism and observation, creates a literary breadth which had never existed in [Japanese] novels up to that time."

After the success of *Furyo ki*, Ōoka went on to address contemporary life in *Musashino fujin (1950, The Woman of Musashino)*, but he returned to his still vivid wartime experiences for *Fires on the Plain* in 1952. This novel represented the pinnacle of his career as a writer. It was first published serially in *Buntai (Literary Style)*, the high-quality magazine founded by UNO CHIYO and Kitahara Takeo in

1941 (and, after a long closure, restarted by them as a quarterly in 1947). From this prominent position, *Fires on the Plain* was soon recognized as one of the very few postwar masterpieces of literature. It won the Yomiuri Prize in 1952, and was made into a film by Ichikawa Kon in 1959.

In its essence, *Fires on the Plain* is a metaphysical novel rather than a wartime history. The action takes place on the island of Leyte in the Philippines, after nearly half of the Japanese troops have been killed in American air attacks. Because those who survive have insufficient food to remain alive, the novel's hero, Tamura, is expelled from his squadron and left to wander alone on the island's central plain. He is now, in a sense, free (". . . free to spend these last days of my life, not as a soldier under orders, but as I myself wished.")

While walking through the unfamiliar countryside, Tamura suddenly becomes aware of the "unrepeatability" of life, and for the first time realizes that such an insight may reveal something of inherent value which is otherwise concealed. He notes: "In our country, even in the most distant or inaccessible part, this feeling of strangeness never comes to us, because subconsciously we know that there is always a possibility of our returning there in the future." No such possibility exists for Tamura. Isolated from his group – and thus deprived of the social mechanisms which confirm his identity – he is first disoriented by the chaotic beauty of the island and then drawn inexorably toward a small, Christian church whose spire rises above the landscape.

Throughout the novel, Ōoka's symbolism is ambiguous and understated, but remarkably powerful nonetheless. The image of a lone Japanese soldier being drawn "spontaneously" toward Christianity is very moving, and one fully expects that some kind of salvation awaits him. However, although the church looks inviting from a distance, at close quarters it is seen to be littered with corpses. Tamura himself, reacting to a sudden interruption, kills a woman – and at this point his gradual decline into madness begins. He comes across some deserters who have survived by cannibalizing their fellow soldiers. Eventually, after killing them too, he is picked up by American soldiers. Suffering from amnesia, Tamura remains in a mental hospital long after the war has ended, obsessed by an image of "fires on the plain" – strongly suggestive of the judgment of God.

In fiction, Ōoka never equaled the achievement of *Fires on the Plain*. However, like his hero Tamura, he felt obliged to ponder his relationship to the events of the war for many years afterward. During the 1960s he compiled a detailed documentary account of the Leyte campaign, *Reite senki*, carefully examining the notebooks, diaries, and letters of individual soldiers in addition to standard military and historical records. His interest in war literature was further underlined by publication of *Sensō to bungaku to* (1972, *War and Literature*), a series of interviews with leading writers, addressing this topic.

Ōoka did, however, write many other novels, including *Kaei* (*1958–59, The Shadow of Flowers*) and *Jiken* (1977, *Incident*), the latter being one of the few examples of courtroom fiction in Japanese literature. After a year as Fulbright Visiting Professor at Yale University, Ōoka resumed his academic career in Japan, lecturing in French Literature at Meiji University in Tokyo.

Writing in *Japan Quarterly* in 1969 (vol. 16, no. 1), Ōoka drew attention to the fact that many readers of Japanese fiction in translation are attracted by qualities they perceive as being distinctively Japanese. However, these qualities, he said, often go unnoticed in Japan because of their very familiarity. By the same token, Ōoka himself has gained attention in his own country by using unfamiliar techniques, while in the West he has been equally successful (with *Fires on the Plain*) by presenting a strangely foreign interpretation of Christianity. In the same essay ("World View of Japanese Literature") he noted: "Modern Japan has made a name for itself in the world for its high level of economic development . . . but our literature would seem to be in hiding. There is room here for action on our part."

RECOMMENDED READING

Novel

Fires on the Plain. *Nobi.* 1952. 246 pages. Tr. Ivan Morris. Knopf, NY, 1957; Secker and Warburg, London, 1957; Transworld, London, 1959; Tuttle, Tokyo, 1967; Panther, London, 1968; Penguin, Harmondsworth, 1969; Greenwood, Westport, CT, 1978; Corgi, London, 1980. A classic war novel.

WORKS IN ENGLISH TRANSLATION

Novel

Fires on the Plain. Nobi. 1952.

Short Fiction

"The Mother of Dreams." *"Haha rokuya."* 1966. 7 pages. Tr. Aga-tha Haun. *The Mother of Dreams, and Other Short Stories: Portrayals of Women in Modern Japanese Fiction*, ed. Makoto Ueda. Kodansha International, Tokyo and NY, 1986.

Essays

"Prisoner of War." *"Furyo ki."* *1948.* 30 pages. Tr. Sakuko Matsui. *Solidarity,* vol. 2, no. 7, 1967.

"World View of Japanese Literature." 3 pages. *Japan Quarterly,* vol. 16, no. 1, 1969.

CRITICAL STUDIES

Korges, James. "Abe and Ōoka: Identity and Mind–Body." *Critique: Studies in Modern Fiction,* vol. 10, no. 2, 1968.

Motofuji, Francis Toshiyuki. "Ōoka's *Fires on the Plain.*" *Approaches to the Modern Japanese Novel,* ed. Thomas E. Swann and Kinya Tsuruta. Sophia University, Tokyo, 1976.

Polameri, Veikko. "Ōoka Shōhei's Reflections on *dentō* and *gendai.*" *European Studies on Japan,* 1979.

OSARAGI Jirō
(1897–1973)

Novelist. Real name, Nojiri Kiyohiko. Born in Yokohama. Lived in Kamakura.

Osaragi Jirō was the pen name of Nojiri Kiyohiko, one of the most talented and successful novelists in Japan this century. Often classified as a "popular writer," with all the connotations such an epithet implies, he will undoubtedly be read long after many of Japan's mainstream novelists have been forgotten. He was a leading figure of the *taishū bungaku* ("mass literature") movement of the 1920s, contributing, with other writers, to Shirai Kyōji's magazine *Taishū bungei*. For a few years, this enterprising journal provided an outlet for writers who wished to reach a larger public than if they were locked into the narrow confines of the **bundan* (literary world). Encouraged by TANIZAKI JUN'ICHIRO's approval, Osaragi developed fictional skills that won him a vast readership through mass-market newspapers and paperback books. He wrote thirty novels about the adventures of a swordsman called Kurama Tengu, and later turned his attention to serious fiction with contemporary themes. Known in the West for his brilliant postwar novels, *Kikyō* (*1948, Homecoming*) and *Tabiji* (*1956, The Journey*), Osaragi Jirō fully achieved his goal of raising popular fiction to the highest standards. His last major work was *Tennō no seiki* (*1967–73, The Century of the Emperor*), a monumental account of events leading to the restoration of the *Meiji Emperor in the nineteenth century. Of this extraordinary novel, with its several *thousands* of characters, the critic Katō Shūichi has written: "In scale and depth it is greater than most other works in the history of Japanese literature."

Born in Tokyo, Osaragi Jirō was the son of a senior official of a shipping company. From this secure, if unexciting family background, he made his way in the world via the traditional route of Tokyo Imperial University, studying political science together with French law and literature. On graduating he entered the Foreign Office, where he was well placed in the Treaty Bureau to provide an effective liaison for his father's company. However, his desire to publish some of the fiction he had been writing prompted him to take a pen name in 1924. His pseudonym, which suggests that he hails from the proximity of the Great Buddha in Kamakura, enabled him to circumvent the restriction on government employees that prevented them from publishing works under their own names.

In the mid–1920s, Japanese literature was facing a crisis. Whereas earlier writers like TSUBOUCHI SHŌYŌ never imagined the possibility of an elitist literature, the guildlike functioning of the *bundan* unwittingly encouraged it. Great artists like AKUTAGAWA RYŪNOSUKE were becoming isolated from society, while the mass media provided a forum for cheap and often badly written fiction. Inevitably, someone would come along to fill the gap. Responding to the ideas of *Taishō democracy, the socialist Shirai Kyōji appeared with the slogan "art for the people," and started the magazine *Taishū bungei* in 1925. Through its pages he attempted to liberate literature from the monopoly of the *bundan*, chiefly by attracting contributions from writers who had experience of other occupations. Among those who wrote for *Taishū bungei* were Edogawa Rampo, the author of detective fiction and horror stories; *Yoshikawa Eiji (1892–1962), who became famous for his novel *Miyamoto Musashi* (1935–39); and, of course, Osaragi himself. Many of their works were published in book form, in a series called *Gendai taishū bungaku zenshū*. When this collection appeared in 1927, the expression *taishū bungaku* entered the language, denoting a new and special category of modern literature.

Osaragi was helped in his career by several factors which worked to his advantage. First, the demand for fiction was steadily growing as newspapers and magazines expanded their circulations in the late twenties and early thirties. Second, one or two distinguished writers, notably KIKUCHI KAN, had defected from so-called pure literature and were in favor of raising the standard of popular fiction. Even Kume Masao, who strongly held to the idea of purity, recommended the writing of potboilers as a useful means of earning a living. Osaragi's pursuit was therefore almost respectable, even though his work was unlikely to be taken seriously by critics. Like Yoshikawa Eiji he appealed to the public's love of adventure stories. He created the character Kurama Tengu, a freelance swordsman who owed allegiance to no one but himself (and possibly his author). Set in the last days of the samurai period, the Kurama Tengu stories show the hero fighting sometimes for the shōgunate, sometimes for the opposing monarchist faction. *Akō rōshi* (1927–28, *The Masterless Samurai of Akō*) was one of Osaragi's earliest works in this genre, and it became immensely popular. In producing such tales Osaragi acquired a wide knowledge of the period, which stood him in good stead when later he came to write his masterpiece, *The Century of the Emperor.*

If one were to seek a parallel in Western literature, Osaragi's career developed very much like that of the English novelist Michael Moorcock, who began as a writer of "sword-and-sorcery" tales, then outshone many of his more seriously minded contemporaries in his later work. Osaragi made a similar improvement, applying his finely honed narrative skills to thoughtful novels of contemporary life. His postwar novel, *Kikyō*, was an exceptional achievement. Translated as *Homecoming* in 1954, it was the first major work of Japanese fiction to be published in the United States since the outbreak of World War II.

Osaragi's sophisticated narrative technique in *Homecoming* keeps one guessing about which of the four characters introduced at the beginning will become the central figure. Each of them embodies either the faults or the virtues of the pre-war generation, and we meet them all on foreign soil. Kyōgo Moriya, a former naval officer, has been forced to flee the country after taking the blame for a gambling scandal. His friend Captain Ushigi is a narrow-minded militarist, fighting in Manchuria. Onozaki, representing the bohemian class, is an artist dwelling in self-imposed exile. And finally, the beautiful Saeko, a ruthless black marketeer, travels abroad merely in order to purchase diamonds for smuggling into Japan.

In the manner of popular fiction, Osaragi inserts elements of intrigue, suspense, and coincidence. Saeko meets Moriya and falls in love with him. When he refuses to return with her to Japan (where he has a wife and children of his own), she denounces him to the secret police. He is arrested and thrown into prison where he remains until the end of the war. Only much later do all the characters meet again, Onozaki giving Saeko a clue to the where-abouts of Moriya's daughter from whom Moriya has long been estranged. Aware that she must continue to protect her interests, Saeko tries to influence Moriya through the younger girl. In arranging for father and daughter to meet, she brings about the most powerful scene in the novel.

Within the context of an exciting narrative, *Homecoming* reveals a vivid picture of postwar society. The intense emotions of Moriya and his daughter, Tomoko, who meet at the Golden Tower Shrine in Kyoto, are in sharp contrast to the tranquility of the temple gardens. In this scene Osaragi succeeded in giving the impression that there was much to be thankful for after the war. Amid all the chaos and selfishness of modern society there was still the spiritual beauty of Japanese culture, and, in the person of Tomoko, the potential for renewal.

Osaragi continued to chronicle the contemporary period in *The Journey*. In this novel he showed how World War II and the American Occupation had led not only to a newfound materialism, but, in some cases, to a complete reversal of the social order. On one side there are casualties such as the impoverished Baron Iwamuro and the despairing figure of Okamoto who has lost his only son. But there are also those who, in their different ways, are survivors. Taeko is an ordinary but spirited girl, determined to find a secure place for herself in the new society. More ruthless is Iwamuro's wife (Taeko's improbable rival in love), who uses her charms to extract money from foreign businessmen. Between these two extremes is the center ground, held by those with academic and literary sensibilities. There is Professor Segi, an elderly teacher whose remarkable wit is one of the chief delights of the novel; and there is his disciple, Sutekichi, a man of genuine qualities who will find society hostile whatever changes may occur.

Professor Segi is the final arbiter of moral values in *The Journey*. At one point he says, sadly: "The real scum in this world are the people who only think about themselves. It's they who make this extremely difficult world of ours even more difficult." Such is the novel's intricacy that Professor Segi never encounters the most selfish character, Taeko's fiancé, Ryōsuke. He typifies those who perceive the need to amass capital in a capitalist society, but who will go to any lengths to achieve it. A small-time trader, he embezzles money belonging to Iwamuro's wife, provoking Taeko to steal its replacement in a moment of weakness. The whole chain of events might lead to tragedy (and would probably do so in real life or in many another novel) but here the counterbalancing effect, the goodwill generated by Professor Segi, actually produces a positive result. One is left with the feeling that life will carry on beyond the closing chapter, and that a new and more stable society will emerge.

Osaragi wrote many other novels in his long career, including *Munakata kyōdai* (1949, *The Munakata Sisters*) and *Pari moyu* (*1961–63, Paris Burns*). For the latter he drew upon his knowledge of French history to evoke the period of the Paris Commune. In his last work, *The Century of the Emperor*, he finally returned to Japanese history, filling the novel with innumerable characters, many of whom are foreign. He was especially interested in examining the foreign pressures brought to bear upon Japan during the period of the Meiji Restoration, and he showed clearly that the emperor was manipulated by those who sought to place him once more at the center of political power.

Unlike many of his contemporaries Osaragi made a small fortune from his writing. He lived in two large, adjacent homes in Kamakura, with his wife, children, relatives and (according to Harold Strauss) eighteen cats. A famous cat lover, Osaragi once wrote a delightful essay, "Cats and Kabuki." In it he sent a message to actors: "If a cat visits you on the stage you can be sure it is the best of omens." Described by Strauss as "a gentle, sensitive, cosmopolitan man," Osaragi Jirō died at the age of seventy-six, his last masterpiece fully completed.

RECOMMENDED READING

Novel

Homecoming. *Kikyō. 1948.* 303 pages. Tr. Brewster Horwitz. Knopf, NY, 1954; Secker and Warburg, London, 1955; Tuttle, Tokyo, 1955; Berkley Pub., NY, 1961; Greenwood Press, NY, 1977. Extract in *Treasury of World Literature*, ed. D. D. Runes. Philosophical Library, NY, 1956. Contains 8-page introduction by Harold Strauss. The first contemporary Japanese novel to be translated into English after World War II.

WORKS IN ENGLISH TRANSLATION

Novels

Homecoming, Kikyō. 1948.
The Journey. Tabiji. 1956. 342 pages. Tr. Ivan Morris. Knopf, NY, 1960; Secker and Warburg, London, 1961; Tuttle, Tokyo and Boston, 1967.

Essays

"Cats and Kabuki." 2 pages. *Japan Quarterly*, vol. 7, no. 2, 1960.
"Murders Every Night." 3 pages. *This Is Japan*, vol. 11, 1964.

CRITICAL STUDY

Kimball, Arthur G. "Crisis in Identity: Osaragi's *Homecoming*." *Japan
Christian Quarterly*, vol. 35, no. 3,
1969.

OZAKI Kazuo
(1899–1983)

Writer of short fiction. Born in Ujiyamada, Ise, Kanagawa Prefecture. Lived in Tokyo, then in Shimosoga.

By most literary standards, Ozaki Kazuo would be considered a minor writer whose autobiographical works bear little comparison to the great fictional structures of his contemporaries. Yet on closer examination this most loyal disciple of SHIGA NAOYA is revealed as being one who appeals greatly to the connoisseur of modern Japanese literature. Moreover, his work is easily understood and presents few difficulties to anyone who reads it. Admired by so different a writer as MISHIMA YUKIO, Ozaki created a literary persona for himself and sustained it throughout his career. As "Ogata Shōkichi" he narrated the story of his domestic life, including his wayward adolescence, his long struggle with illness, and his happy marriage to a woman, who, through his portrayal of her, became one of the most endearing and lifelike characters of literature. For his "Yoshibei" stories – Yoshibei being one of the names he invented for his wife – Ozaki was awarded the fifth Akutagawa Prize in 1937.

Ozaki Kazuo was born to a family that could trace its lineage back for more than five hundred years. Both of his parents were from Shintō families, his father a professor of history at the seminary in Ise, his mother the second daughter of a Shintō priest who was also a scholar of classical Japanese. As the eldest son, Ozaki was expected to pursue a respectable career, but he caused a serious rift in the family when he informed his father, an otherwise tolerant man, that he wished to become a writer.

Already interested in literature, the young Ozaki had come across Shiga Naoya's 1912 story *"Ōtsu Junkichi"* in 1916, finding it a powerful inspiration both for his life and for what he hoped would be his career. He later said (in *"Ano hi kono hi,"* 1970–73, "This Day, That Day"): "If I had not read *"Ōtsu Junkichi,"* I might never have become a writer. . . . It taught me that a *shōsetsu* [novel or story], which I had thought of as only an entertaining mixture of fact and fiction, need not be that at all, and that if one had a grievance against one's father, then one should be bold enough to air it. . . ." And air it he did, by demanding to go to Waseda College, a liberal establishment that his conservative father detested. The battle of wills was at its height, when, in 1918, Ozaki's father died suddenly of Spanish influenza. Ozaki was not yet twenty.

In a 1935 story entitled "Land of My Fathers," Ozaki shows great affection for the man whose protection he once rejected. His father, he wrote, "was a typical gentleman of the feudal age. I am not capable of making fun of such ascetic convictions." At the time he may have felt differently. Committed to a literary career, and, as the new head of the family, suddenly released from parental constraints, he entered Waseda Academy in preparation for going on to Waseda College. At this point, he encountered both a tragedy and a severe misfortune. First, his sister died of tuberculosis, an event which became the subject of an early published work. Second, he himself contracted the disease, weakening his constitution and making him vulnerable in the future. Nonetheless, he enrolled at Waseda College in 1923 and in July of that year was introduced to Shiga, the writer who was becoming acknowledged as the greatest in Japan. Because students were not normally expected to address contemporary authors in their graduation theses, Ozaki raised more than a few eyebrows in his faculty when he wrote a thesis on the works of Shiga.

In those years, many aspiring writers came under the spell of the Sage of Nara. Shiga represented the pinnacle of the modern *I-Novel movement, and was an eloquent prose stylist who could turn his life into art in such a convincing manner that his works appeared beautifully "transparent" to his admirers. Ozaki said (again in "This Day, That Day"): "The language took me by surprise. I had never encountered its like before. It was as though nothing came between the reader and the events described."

There was, of course, one snag in being a disciple of Shiga. If nothing came between the reader and the incidents portrayed, one thing did come between the aspiring writer and the events of his own life: namely, the literary method of Shiga himself. Very few writers ever produced work of outstanding quality once they had fallen under Shiga's influence, so distinctive were his style and method. Ozaki, however, proved to be the one great exception. In the cumulative self-portrait that emerges from his collected works, he comes across as being not only more likable than Shiga but far less self-absorbed. Moreover, his inspiration did not evaporate once he had eliminated the problems of his adolescence and early manhood. Even late in life, as he says in one story, "ambition and passion still survived in him."

At Waseda, however, Ozaki's problems were still in their embryonic state. Having discovered that he was richer than the other students he spent his money freely and was generous to a fault. Even when he left college he saw no reason to earn a living and moved in with his lover, a widow called Hikida Sumie who owned a nearby coffee shop. But the money dwindled, Sumie became impatient, and the stock market crash of 1929 eliminated what little of Ozaki's property remained. His family in Shimosoga began to insist that he do something to stem the tide of misfortune.

Still intent on being a writer, Ozaki did nothing that might have been financially constructive. He burned his mother's letters, deserted Sumie, and left Tokyo to visit Shiga for moral support. In this instance, Shiga was very helpful. Working under the master's supervision, Ozaki began translating the works of *Ihara Saikaku (1642–93) into modern Japanese. At the same time (around 1931) he shared lodgings with his friend Shirai Hiroshi, and through him met Yamahara Matsue, a schoolfriend of Shirai's wife. Immediately, Ozaki was entranced by the spontaneity of the teenage Matsue, and thus began a lifelong relationship in which, as he put it, he was the "sinker" (presumably plumbing the mysteries of life and art) while she was the "float" who kept them firmly connected to reality.

With her irrepressible good humor, Matsue did not seem to mind being married to a penniless author. His unconventional life style suited her very well, for he was obviously so fascinated by her that he took the trouble to relate to his wife more assiduously than most Japanese husbands are inclined to do. Not merely an emotional support and potential mother of his children, Matsue was an inspiration: an inexhaustible source of amusing incidents that became the lifeblood of Ozaki's art.

The stories that Ozaki wrote in the mid–1930s are among his best. He made his name with *"Nonki megane"* (*1933*, "Rosy Glasses") a brilliant work in which he first introduced the character Yoshibei, based on Matsue. She appears as an eccentric optimist, a naïve, appealing girl who is eager to please but quite unaware that some of her social *faux pas* might be considered offensive if anyone more conventional should commit them. In this story, too, Ozaki establishes a successful literary method: inserting references to his narrator's decline into poverty and expressing his determination to improve in the future. Looming over the story is the narrator's constant fear that hardship may destroy Yoshibei's joyful attitude to life. But in a wonderful resolution he finally admits that it is he, in his unwavering attempt to be a writer, who views the world through rose-colored spectacles. For all her naïveté, Yoshibei sees life as it really is.

Although Ozaki went on to write many other stories, he never improved greatly on the techniques he established in "Rosy Glasses." Unashamedly an I-Novel, it belongs to the subclassification of that genre, called *shinkyō shōsetsu*, or "novels of contemplation." Another translation is "state-of-the-mind stories," since the *shin* of *shinkyō* is derived from the Chinese reading of the character for *kokoro*, meaning the (human) spirit, heart, or mind. It carries connotations of life directed by feeling rather than by intellect alone, a fair description of Ozaki's work and one he himself readily accepted. "I have a free view of the novel," he wrote in 1955, "and most of my work contains elements of the essay. I have not yet come upon a compelling reason for abandoning this variety of fiction."

Ozaki's self-criticism and desire for self-improvement are always set within the immediate social context of his family and friends. He is deeply concerned with the morality of his thoughts and actions, and sees them in direct relationship to other people. At the same time he reserves one small, private corner for himself where he alone exists and feels the pain and joy of life quite independently of others. In one of his most famous stories, *"Yaseta ondori"* (*1949*, "The Thin Rooster"), he receives a plaintive message from a young literary critic, who says: "The baby is crying, my wife is in a huff, and I've got a mountain of chores piling up – so these days I really wish I could become a Buddhist priest and flee the world." Ozaki's narrator replies: "If it's just a matter of fleeing your family and society, you can do that much right at home." All he need do is create a "private cell" in his mind where he may confront the task of making sense of life through contemplation. Yet even in this respect, Ozaki seems to create his own cell out of a desire to protect his family from unnecessary grief.

During World War II, Ozaki was kept extremely busy by the authorities who organized lecture programs and other activities, including a grueling forty-day trip to Manchuria. As a result of wartime privations and overwork, he suffered a ruptured stomach ulcer at the end of August 1944, and, perhaps fortunately, was obliged to remove his family from Tokyo to the relative safety of his ancestral home in Shimosoga. Some years previously, his mother had managed to borrow money to save their home at the height of her son's "dissolute period," and now, with three children to support, Ozaki at least had somewhere to live. His illness, however, was so serious that he nearly died. For the next five years he was confined to his bed.

Many of Ozaki's later stories emerge from his experience of illness, but although they often refer to the pain he suffered they also contain minute observations of the life around him. Most notable is his thrice-translated *"Mushi no iroiro"* (*1948*, "This and That About Bugs"), in which he makes ingenious connections between the behavior of insects and man's place in the universe. The story is a particularly good example of his art because it gives the impression of being a rambling collection of spontaneous thoughts, until, at the end, a very human resolution brings all the themes into focus. After commenting with apparently objective interest in the behavior of various types of insects, the narrator is led by his sixteen-year-old daughter into a conversation about the immensity of the universe. He then questions whether he himself resembles any of the insects he has discussed, carefully failing to give any definitive answer. Rather, he ends the story by describing how, while lying in bed, he catches a fly in the wrinkles of his forehead: a feat that amazes his children because they, being youthful and smooth-skinned, are quite unable to match it.

The I-Novelist is often criticized for abbreviating the artistic process, for attempting the impossible task of depicting a reality unmediated by the human imagination. But in Ozaki's case, such criticism is pointless because of the high degree of artistic organization in his stories. He is extremely selective in what he chooses to portray, and yet he includes just as many fictional elements as, for example, does DAZAI OSAMU. In fact, there are many resemblances between the literary methods of these two writers, Ozaki's narrator, Ogata Shōkichi, being a persona who serves much the same function as Dazai's Osamu. Both characters are essentially fictional projections of their authors' real selves, and they both invite the reader to adopt protective attitudes toward them. There, however, the similarity ends, for although Ogata often parades his weaknesses he is far less inclined than Osamu to excuse or indulge them. Neither does he have any need to flirt with death in order to extend his experience beyond that of the reader. After all, Ozaki's narrator has been running a "three-legged race with death" for as long as he can remember.

There is an English expression, "a creaking door swings longest," and it surely applies to Ozaki Kazuo. He died at the age of eighty-four, having outlasted most of his contemporaries despite his long period of illness. In the postwar period he had written the above-mentioned stories, "This and That About Bugs" and "The Thin Rooster," together with *"Utsukushii bochi kara no nagame"* (1948, "The Beautiful View from the Cemetery"), in direct reaction to his brush with death. He went on to write many more stories, including *"Monoui haru"* (1950, "Languid Spring") and *"Namekuji yokochō"* (1951, "Snail Alley"), extending his career several decades beyond that of his mentor, Shiga, who long ago had lapsed into silence. Yet only recently, and chiefly through the painstaking translations of Robert Epp, has a good selection of Ozaki's works become widely available to the West. Fortunately, it is never too late to discover a writer of Ozaki's quality. As Mishima Yukio said: "The I-Novel has always been with us, and even though it has been bathed by the waves of time, it has clung to its existence unwaveringly." For his tolerance, humor, and uncompromising search for authenticity, Ozaki Kazuo will always occupy a special niche in the history of the I-Novel, that most distinctive genre of Japanese prose literature.

RECOMMENDED READING

Short Fiction Collection

Rosy Glasses and Other Stories by Kazuo Ozaki. 150 pages. Tr. Robert Epp. Paul Norbury Publications, Ashford, Kent, England, 1988. Contains 28-page introduction by the translator. Includes: "Yoshibei – On Conventions," "Various Kinds of Bugs" (tr. as "This and That About Bugs"), and "The Thin Rooster" (tr. as "The Skinny Rooster"). Excellent translations of Ozaki's stories: highly recommended.

WORKS IN ENGLISH TRANSLATION

Short Fiction

"Crickets." *"Kōrogi."* 1946. 10 pages. *Rosy Glasses.*

"The Day of the Wedding." *"Kashoku no hi."* 1957. 11 pages. (1) Tr. Hiroo Mukai. *Hemisphere,* vol. 11, Jan. 1967. (2) As "Day of the Nuptials." *Rosy Glasses.*

"Entrance Bath." *"Genkan buro."* 1937. 6 pages. *Rosy Glasses.*

"Guile." 1934. 16 pages. *Rosy Glasses.*

"Land of My Fathers." *"Fuso no chi."* 1935. 10 pages. *Rosy Glasses.*

"Putting in for Retirement." *"Taishoku no negai."* 1964. 12 pages. *Rosy Glasses.*

"Rosy Glasses." *"Nonki megane."* 1933. 16 pages. *Rosy Glasses.*

"The Thin Rooster." *"Yaseta ondori."* 1949. 20 pages. (1) Tr. Edward Seidensticker. *Japan Quarterly,* vol. 2, no. 2, 1955. *Modern Japanese Short Stories.* Japan Publications Trading Co., Tokyo, 1960; revised edition 1970. (2) As "The Skinny Rooster." *Rosy Glasses.*

"Various Kinds of Bugs." *"Mushi no iroiro."* 1948. 23 pages. (1) As "Insects of Various Kinds." Tr. Hiroo Mukai. *Pacific Spectator,* vol. 5, Autumn 1951. (2) Tr. William L. Clark. *Jiji Eigo Kenkyu,* vol. 12, no. 11, 1957. *Various Kinds of Bugs, and Other Stories.* Kenkyusha, Tokyo, 1958. (3) As "Entomologica." Tr. Chris Brockett. *Japan Echo,* vol. 12, Special Issue, 1985. (4) As "This and That About Bugs." *Rosy Glasses.*

"Yoshibei – On Conventions." *"Yoshibei."* 1934. 8 pages. *Rosy Glasses.*

Ozaki KŌYŌ
(1867–1903)

Novelist. Real name, Ozaki Tokutarō. Born in Shiba, Tokyo. Lifelong resident of Tokyo, living in Ushigome Yokoderachō after his marriage in 1891.

At the turn of the century Ozaki Kōyō was not only the most popular novelist in Japan, but, by virtue of his leadership of the *Ken'yūsha ("Friends of the Inkstone"), had dominated literary society for more than a decade. He first established his reputation in 1889 with his novel *Ninin bikuni iro zange* (*The Amorous Confessions of Two Nuns*), the success of which brought him literary editorship of the *Yomiuri shimbun*, the largest newspaper in Tokyo. From this prominent platform he thrilled a whole generation of readers with a succession of realistic, Romantic novels written in a highly polished and eloquent style of his own devising. Greatly influenced by *Ihara Saikaku (1642–93), the master of early *Edo period literature, Kōyō emphasized the pathos of romantic love in nearly all of his works. As a consequence, his popularity among readers of the *Yomiuri* was phenomenal. Critics hailed *Tajō takon* (*1896,*

Passions and Griefs) as a masterpiece, while his last, unfinished novel, *Konjiki yashiya* (*1897–1903, The Gold Demon*) was a long-running sensation with the public. Much loved, even by those men (like MORI ŌGAI) who thought his writing frivolous, Ozaki Kōyō died at age thirty-five from stomach cancer.

Born Ozaki Tokutarō, the son of a famous ivory carver in Tokyo's fishing port of Shiba, Kōyō was an intelligent and quick-witted boy who found his *terakoya* (temple school) very dull indeed. He hated English and mathematics, the two subjects given most attention in the 1870s. Much more to his liking was a book he discovered for himself in a cheap, roadside library: a romance by the master of the *ninjōbon* genre, *Tamenaga Shunsui (1790–1843). Such tales about daily life in Edo and of the romantic intrigues of its younger citizens appealed greatly to him, and he went on to read the works of Shunsui's teacher, Shikitei Samba (1776–1822), and the popular fiction of Santō Kyōden (1761–1816). Eventually Kōyō entered Tokyo Imperial University, first to study law then switching to literature, but he failed to obtain a degree and left without completing any of the courses. He was, however, already committed to a career as a writer, and as early as 1883 founded an association called Bun'yūkai ("Friends of Literature"), a forerunnner of the Ken'yūsha.

When the Ken'yūsha itself was started in 1885 it was little more than a high-spirited group of precocious teenagers who shared a common interest in popular fiction. Other founding members were Ishibashi Shian (1867–1927) and Maruoka Kyūka (1865–1927). Their magazine *Garakuta bunko* was filled with comic verse, a few Chinese translations, and some original stories – none of which was very good. But as Kōyō matured and began to assert his strong personality, the group grew larger and became more influential. In fact, it gradually assumed the dimensions of society-in-microcosm, with individual members being bound by loyalty to the group and even suffering some restrictions because of their relative degrees of status. As the most talented of its originators, Kōyō was in the best position at the top. He took his responsibilities very seriously, doing all he could to help younger writers while struggling to perfect his art. In this way, the *Meiji *bundan* flourished, taking literature away from its traditional milieu of the demimonde, and elevating it to the high status that TSUBOUCHI SHŌYŌ (in his 1885 treatise, *Shōsetsu shinzui*) had demanded for it.

In the view of Nakamura Mitsuo and many other literary historians, the Ken'yūsha's rise accompanied that of Japanese nationalism. Its members reacted strongly against the early Meiji obsession with European culture, preferring instead to look to Japan's indigenous writers for their inspiration. They found it in the works of Saikaku, whose particular brand of realism was an adequate substitute for fictional techniques imported from the West. Ignoring the efforts of FUTABATEI SHIMEI to make the great Russian writers the chief paragons of literary excellence, they also turned away from Futabatei's new colloquial style of language to cultivate various archaic styles that were more in keeping with their artistic goals.

By the time Kōyō published the novel that made him famous, *Ninin bikuni iro zange*, the Ken'yūsha was already the "operational center of the *bundan*." This phrase was quoted by Tsubouchi Shōyō in his introduction to Kōyō's novel, when *Iro zange* appeared as volume 1 of a series called *Shincho hyaku shu* (*Hundred Novels by New Authors*). It identified the *bundan* as a literary phenomenon: a clique which stood slightly apart from, and perhaps slightly above, society at large. Looking back on that era from the vantage point of 1962, the critic Itō Sei wrote: "The Meiji *bundan* was a small, half-feudal literary establishment, in which young writers were supposed to learn not only how to write, but also how to live." As acknowledged master, Kōyō had a number of pupils, including those called *shosei* who actually lived in his house, where they occupied a small, front room, busily writing fiction. In 1891, Kōyō formed a special branch of the Ken'yūsha for his protégés: the *Seishunsha* (Youth Society), entrusting his colleague Emi Suiin (1869–1934) with editorship of the society's magazine, *Senshibankō* (*A Thousand Purples, Ten Thousand Crimsons*).

The influence of Saikaku was much in evidence in Kōyō's *Iro zange*. In its preface Kōyō stated: "The principal aim of this novel is tears." Whether or not this was a nod in Tsubouchi Shōyō's direction, acknowledging human emotion as being the essential aim of a novel, it certainly suggested Kōyō's awareness of himself as an entertainer of the public. Then as now, people enjoyed weeping over Romantic fiction, and Kōyō was expert at finding characters and plots to satisfy their craving. However, where he differed from today's writers of this genre was in the polished excellence of his style. Developed from the prose of Saikaku, his style was so appealing that his devoted admirers often committed their favorite passages to memory. Translators, on the other hand, have always been deterred by it. Only one major novel by Ozaki Kōyō has been rendered into English, and that, *The Gold Demon*, was described by its translators as having been "rewritten in English" rather than translated.

Praised by the critic Ishibashi Ningetsu for depicting "the many and varied kinds of love," *Iro zange* set a high standard for Kōyō to maintain. As it brought him the literary editorship of the *Yomiuri* he had no financial worries, and was assured of a large readership through the pages of the newspaper. Selling over 30,000 copies daily, the *Yomiuri* was read by everyone who mattered. It gave prominence to Kōyō's novel *Kyara makura* (*1890, The Perfumed Pillow*), which ran simultaneously with KŌDA ROHAN's "Hige otoko" ("Man with a Moustache"). Critics were fascinated by the contrast between Rohan's mode of "idealism" and Kōyō's more relaxed, less moralistic "realism." Both men had now replaced the first, avant-garde wave of modern literature with a less adventurous form of fiction which had its roots firmly in Oriental tradition.

In 1891, a golden year for Kōyō, he married Kabashima Kiku on March 21 and moved from Kitamachi to a much larger house in Yokoderachō. It was there that the young TAYAMA KATAI first called on him, a visit he described vividly in his memoir *Thirty Years in Tokyo* (1917). Katai wrote: "[I remember] being greatly impressed by his luxurious life-style, his lordly magnanimity, and especially by his beautiful wife Kikuko." One can well imagine the scene. Kiku plied the impressionable (and, being impoverished, the somewhat envious) Katai with delicacies, while her husband spoke of the need for Japanese writers to emulate Zola's detailed descriptions and psychological insights. He also mentioned the novel on which he was then working: *Yakitsugijawan* (*1891, The Mended Tea Cup*), which came to be collected in his complete works as *Sodeshigure* (*Tear-Soaked Sleeves*).

Kōyō believed that style was the most important aspect of a novel. He continued to write in the manner of Saikaku, while occasionally experimenting with the *gembun itchi (unified speech and writing) style, applying the same rigorous methods of writing and rewriting in order to perfect it. His famous comment: "The descriptive style is a paintbrush; *gembun itchi* is a camera," tells us that his heart remained with the more elegant styles of language. He criticized *gembun itchi* for being "utterly materalistic," saying: "It can cope with everything to the last detail, but it has no warmth." Perhaps it was because he wanted to match Zola's density of description that he felt obliged to experiment with *gembun itchi* despite his unease with it.

Kōyō's novel *Futari nyōbō* (*1891–92, Two Wives*) was written in the colloquial style, while in *Sannin zuma* (*1892, Three Wives*) he reverted to the descriptive manner of Saikaku. As always, his themes and characters were clear-cut, even a trifle obvious, but his handling of them showed great artistic sense. In *Three Wives* he dwelled on one of the themes for which he is best remembered: the lure of money in matters of romance. Its hero, Yonosuke, is loved by many women because of his great wealth. Following naturally from this idea is the tragedy of "true love" prevented by circumstances from reaching consummation. This was the theme of *Kokoro no yami* (*1893, Darkness in the Heart*), in which a young, blind masseur falls hopelessly in love with the daughter of an innkeeper. Donald Keene, in *Dawn to the West*, has written: "Kōyō was able to create within the framework of a simple but effective plot a portrait of a blind man that is psychologically believable and curiously moving."

Given the scale of Kōyō's responsibilities, it is a measure of his energy that he found time to develop and perfect his art. He worked long hours and admired people of similar dedication. His 1894 story, *Murasaki*, describes how a young man fails his examinations for medical school, until, through his persistent efforts, he finally passes. Among his younger pupils, Kōyō tended to favor IZUMI KYŌKA (1873–1939), not only for his enthusiasm and application, but for his taste in literature. Kyōka was the most talented of his disciples, and went on to create some of the most striking tales of the supernatural in modern Japanese fiction.

Less loyal to Kōyō was his contemporary, YAMADA BIMYŌ (1868–1910), whom he expelled from the Ken'yūsha for editing the rival magazine, *Miyako no hana* (*The Flower of the Metropolis*). An advocate and one of the pioneers of the *gembun itchi* style, Bimyō acquired a brief reputation before going into rapid decline. His argument with Kōyō undoubtedly harmed him, but few historians have extended him their sympathy. Kōyō was normally a generous man and went out of his way to help writers, such as Tayama Katai, with whom he did not wholly agree. Even after rejecting Katai as a pupil he later cooperated with him in writing the novel, *Fuefukigawa* (1895, *Fuefuki River*).

From 1895 onwards, Kōyō was faced with increasing competition from several quarters. Most notably, Mori Ōgai was emerging as a great, alternative prose stylist, and he was completely independent of the Ken'yūsha. Kōyō redoubled his efforts to keep one step ahead, aware that his reputation was at stake. After writing *Ao budō* (*1895, Green Grapes*), an unfinished novel about the temporary illness of his disciple Oguri Fūyō – a false alarm in more ways than one – he embarked on his masterpiece *Tajō takon* (1896, *Passions and Griefs*). In this story of a geology professor who falls into a fit of lonely depression when his wife dies, Kōyō created a character with true depth and a believably human psychology. The professor, invited to stay at the home of a friend, falls in love with his friend's wife. Charmingly, he is unaware of his infatuation, but the woman's proximity does much to lift his spirits. Even today, *Passions and Griefs* is admired by critics who are not necessarily among Kōyō's devotees.

For devotees themselves, of whom there are still a surprising number even in the West, the favored novel will always be *The Gold Demon*. As already mentioned, this has been rendered into English: in a beautifully written 1905 version by A. Lloyd. The translator's nineteenth-century constructions go some way toward suggesting the beauty of Kōyō's prose, described by Donald Keene as a mixture of "Saikaku and *Bakin with a touch of *Heian romance." On its original publication in the *Yomiuri*, it became the most popular of all Kōyō's works. Indeed, one young woman who was dying of consumption was said to have been so enthralled by the novel that she demanded future installments be buried with her.

The Gold Demon is a "cliff-hanger romance" in the grand style. Its hero, Kan'ichi, adopted into another family on his father's death, has been brought up to believe that his beautiful stepsister, Miya, will one day become his wife. He is deeply in love with her, and is devastated when he learns that she has consented to marry Tomiyama, a banker whom most men regard as vulgar for openly displaying his wealth. In a dramatic scene on a beach, Kan'ichi parts from Miya in anger and despair, cursing her for being seduced by money. He leaves his adopted family, and, as if to hurt himself as much as possible, becomes a ruthless moneylender intent on nothing but the acquisition of wealth. It is a perennial theme, even more relevant in times of prosperity, and in a sense treated by F. Scott Fitzgerald in *The Great Gatsby*. But no one could be less Gatsby-like than Kan'ichi, who remains frugal, mean-minded, and quite unyielding even when Miya crawls to him with her anguished apologies. More flamboyant is the other female figure, the beautiful Mitsue, who is herself a successful moneylender, and who, in attempting to seduce Kan'ichi, plays a role that is tailor-made for a Japanese Joan Collins. As one can gather, *The Gold Demon* is the very stuff of popular fiction. It is so exhilarating to read that one stands in awe of Kōyō's ability to entertain.

Alas, *The Gold Demon* was never completed. Kōyō fell ill with a stomach complaint that had first troubled him in 1899. It was diagnosed as cancer when he was admitted to the university's hospital in March 1903. He died later that year, on October 30.

To the younger generation, Kōyō's passing was greeted with a mixture of sorrow and relief. Neither KUNIKIDA DOPPO nor Tayama Katai cared much for his fiction, the latter commenting: "On the outside his works were beautiful brocade, but on the inside they were faded artificial flowers." Attending Kōyō's funeral he recalled thinking: "This splendid ceremony, this public sympathy, this grief based on a sense of duty and humanity, this sorrow shown by friends and colleagues and pupils alike – I wonder how it would all look in the light of new ideology? Isn't the ceremony simply a display of old morality? . . . In a world where new ideology reigned there would be none of this strength of formalism and obligation. . . .We have been too bound up with standardized morality. From now on we must live our lives as our own individual selves."

Katai's comments applied less to Kōyō the writer than to Kōyō the leader of the literary world. As an individual writer he would probably have shone in whatever age he found himself. Among his dying words was a subtle reference to the last words of the thirteenth-century General Kusunoki Masashige. Said Kōyō: "Had I but seven lives to live I should devote them all to the service of literature." The general himself had, of course, referred to serving the emperor rather than literature – but then, Ozaki Kōyō (as Nakamura suggested) was always "just half a step ahead of the times in which he lived."

RECOMMENDED READING

Novel

The Gold Demon. *Konjiki yashiya. 1897–1903.* 562 pages. Rewritten in English by Arthur and Mary Lloyd. Seibundo, Tokyo, 1905. Extract in *The Treasury of Japanese Literature*, ed. Tokichi Watanabe. Jippohakaku, Tokyo, 1933. As "The Demon of Gold and Love." *Info*, in 40 parts, Feb. 1968–June 1971. Koyo's great unfinished novel; 1905 edition sometimes available from rare book dealers. Contains 13-page translators' introduction.

WORKS IN ENGLISH TRANSLATION

Novel

The Gold Demon. Konjiki yashiya. 1897–1903.

Miyamori. *Representative Tales of Japan.* Sanko Shoten, Tokyo, 1917.

Short Fiction

"The Japanese Desdemona." *"Higashi nishi tanryo no yaiba."* 28 pages. Tr. T. Kimoto. Shunyodo, Tokyo, 1902.
"Larboard." *"Tori kaji."* Tr. T. Kimoto. *The Orient*, vol. 14, 1899.
"A Wonderful Legacy." *"Fumi nagashi."* 1890. 12 pages. Tr. Asataro

Miscellaneous

Extract from the novel *Shiobara.* 5 pages. Tr. F. J. Daniels. *Japanese Prose.* Lund Humphries, London, 1944.

Poetry

"11 Haiku." Tr. R. H. Blyth. *A*

History of Haiku, vol. 2. Hokuseido, Tokyo, 1964.

"4 Haiku." Tr. Asataro Miyamori. *Anthology of Haiku, Ancient and Modern*. Maruzen, Tokyo, 1932.

"Harvest Moon." Tr. Kenneth Yasuda. *A Pepper-Pod*. Tuttle, Tokyo, 1976.

"The Harvest Moon; A Pilgrim in the Spring." Tr. Asataro Miyamori. *Haiku Poems, Ancient and Modern*. Maruzen, Tokyo, 1940.

"The Neighbour." Tr. Harold Steward. *A Net of Fireflies*. Tuttle, Tokyo, 1960.

"1 Haiku." Tr. Peter Beilenson. *Japanese Haiku*. Peter Pauper Press, Mount Vernon, NY, 1955.

"1 Haiku." Tr. Peter Beilenson and Harry Behn. *Haiku Harvest*. Peter Pauper Press, Mount Vernon, NY, 1962.

"1 Haiku." Tr. Harold Gould Henderson. *The Bamboo Broom*. J. L. Thomson, Tokyo, 1933; Kegan Paul, London, 1933.

"Perfection." Tr. Harold Gould Henderson. *From the Bamboo Broom*. Japan Reference Library, NY, 1940.

"3 Haiku." Tr. V. H. Viglielmo. *Japanese Literature in the Meiji Era*. Obunsha, Tokyo, 1955.

CRITICAL STUDIES

Itō, Sei. "Ozaki Kōyō and His Circle." Tr. V. H. Viglielmo. *Japan Quarterly*, vol. 2, no. 3, 1955.

Kornicki, Peter Francis. "The Novels of Ozaki Kōyō: A Study of Selected Works with Special Reference to the Relationship Between the Fiction of the Tokugawa and Early Meiji Periods." Ph.D. diss., University of Oxford, Oxford, 1978.

———. "Ozaki Kōyō and Edo Fiction." *Transactions of the International Conference of Orientalists in Japan*, no. 22, 1977.

Taeusch, Carl F. "Ozaki Kōyō and His Approach to the Modern Novel." Ph.D. diss., University of Michigan, Ann Arbor, 1977.

———. "Realism in the Novels of Ozaki Kōyō." *Journal of the Association of Teachers of Japanese*, no. 10, 1975.

SATOMI Ton
(1888–1983)

Writer of fiction. Real name, Yamauchi Hideo. Born in Yokohama, a lifelong resident of Tokyo.

Just as Evelyn Waugh is virtually unread in Japan, so Satomi Ton is little known in the West. Perhaps this is because neither the English nor the Japanese have ever lifted import restrictions on each other's snobberies. More likely, it is because of the difficulty of translating eloquent prose styles which combine complexity of language with clarity of expression. Satomi, a first-rate stylist but a second-rate novelist, was ten years younger than his brother, the writer ARISHIMA TAKEO (1878–1923), and bore even less resemblance to him than either of them did to Evelyn Waugh. They were, in fact, brought up separately and their careers took very different paths although both of them became members of the celebrated *Shirakabaha* (White Birch Society). This group of young, wealthy, and precocious literati included SHIGA NAOYA and MUSHANOKŌJI SANEATSU, both of whom became leading writers of their era. Individuals all, they were united only in their opposition to the

366

*Naturalists: ". . .that crowd cooped up in lodgings around Waseda University," as Satomi characterized the men from the provinces who had dominated Tokyo's literary world for the past few years. His remark is still refreshing, despite its ill-concealed condescension. Japanese literature needed new input, and Satomi was among those writers who once more attended to pleasure instead of poverty. In a succession of short stories, novellas, and full-length novels he demonstrated his preoccupation with the senses and his complete indifference to social problems. His best work is generally reckoned to be *Kiribatake* (1921, *Grove of Tulip Trees*), although he established a reputation as early as 1915 with *Osoi hatsukoi* (*Late Virgin Love*). Only one of his stories has been translated into English: the brilliant *"Tsubaki"* (1923, "The Camellia"), which may be found in Ivan Morris's yet-to-be-equaled anthology *Modern Japanese Stories* (1962).

Satomi Ton was born in Yokohama and brought up in Tokyo. As a youngest son he was adopted by his mother's family rather than being raised in the household of his father, a Kyūshū samurai who held an important post in the Ministry of Finance. At the Peers' School he mixed with boys from similar, wealthy backgrounds, and then furthered his education, as many of them did, at Tokyo Imperial University. Although he never completed his course in English Literature and left university without a degree, he undoubtedly gained much from the company of his creative friends. Yet it was he, in conjunction with Sonoike Kinyuki, who had published one of the forerunners of the *Shirakaba* while still at the Peers' School. At the same time, a slightly older group consisting of Shiga, Mushanokōji, Kinoshita Rigen, and Ōgimachi Kinkazu were already meeting and discussing their writings at the university, while a younger group at the Peers' School, led by Yanagi Muneyoshi and Kōri Torahiko were publishing yet another broadsheet of their own. In 1909 they all joined forces to produce the highly professional magazine *Shirakaba*, the first issue of which appeared in April 1910. It contained Shiga's story *"Abashiri made"* ("As Far as Abashiri") together with poetry by Mushanokōji and a translation of a Chekhov story by Satomi, whose pen name appeared in print for the first time.

Critical reaction to *Shirakaba* was mainly favorable, the most helpful praise coming from NATSUME SŌSEKI, whose own recent novel, *Sorekara* (1909, *And Then*), had been discussed in the first issue. There were to be many more issues of the magazine, which reached a peak of influence in 1916–17 and continued to be published until 1923. Satomi began to contribute fiction in 1911, going on to write such stories as *"Fugu"* (1913, "Blowfish") and *"Zenshin akushin"* (1916, "Good and Evil Intentions"). Through these works, together with *"Niwaka ame"* (1916, "The Sudden Storm"), *"Chichioya"* (1917, "The Father") and *"Ginjirō no kataude"* (1917, "Ginjirō's One Arm"), he gained a reputation as a writer of psychological fiction with a strong imaginative element. Indeed, he won praise from IZUMI KYŌKA (1873–1939), the *Ken'yūsha novelist who became a master storyteller with his tales of the supernatural. Although Satomi anchored his own stories much more firmly in reality he often paid homage to Kyōka by including a few ghostly embellishments. His fine novella "Grove of Tulip Trees" portrays a hero so overcome by jealousy that he hallucinates the murder of his unfaithful wife and her lover, his best friend. Such an extension of human emotion into the realm of the supernatural would have been borrowed directly from Kyōka, who in turn had taken it from the *Nō.

With varying degrees of success, Satomi tried to make the typical, upper-class male chauvinist of the era a figure of heroic proportions. Cultivating a philosophy of *magokoro* (sincerity), he equated it with what is now called philandering. In other words, to be sincere was to admit, quite frankly, one's fondness for women and to indulge oneself without any trace of hypocrisy. Satomi's long novel *Tajō busshin* (1923, *Passions and Piety*) contains just such a hero, and he was certainly based on the author himself.

During the years of military oppression and throughout World War II Satomi kept a low profile, venting his spleen on the military leaders only when the war was over. His brother Arishima Takeo, who once played an active role in the *Shirakaba* movement, had committed suicide as long ago as 1923. Never especially close to Arishima, Satomi severely criticized him in *"Anjōke no kyōdai"* (1931, "The Brothers of the Anjō Family"), and revealed his dislike of the older man's tendency to dramatize himself in life as well as art. After the war, Satomi carried on writing fiction, beginning with *"Obasute"* (1946, "Deserting an Old Woman") and continuing with many other stories including *"Migoto na shūbun"* (1947, "A Splendid Scandal") and *"Iro-otoko"* (1947, "A Handsome Man"). His last major work was *Gokuraku tombo* (1961, *A Happy-Go-Lucky Fellow*), another entertaining novel about the long and happy life of a womanizer.

Critical opinion of Satomi is virtually unanimous in judging him to be a minor writer. According to Nakamura Mitsuo he was "a conscientious artisan," while Donald Keene (referring to Satomi's role in the *Shirakabaha*) calls him "an immoralist among earnest men." His qualities included a gift for writing dialogue (clearly apparent even in the translation of "The Camellia"). He always wrote within his abilities and acquired a loyal following in the course of his productive career.

RECOMMENDED READING

Short Fiction

"The Camellia." *"Tsubaki."* *1923.* 6 pages. Tr. Edward Seidensticker. *Modern Japanese Stories*, ed. Ivan Morris. Spottiswoode, London, 1961; Tuttle, Tokyo and New York, 1962 and 1977. Were it not for Ivan Morris's superb anthology, there would not be a single work by Satomi Ton in English translation.

SHIGA Naoya
(1883–1971)

Writer of short fiction and one novel. Born in Ishinomaki, in Miyagi Prefecture, northern Honshū. Lived in various parts of Japan.

Coming to terms with the life and works of Shiga Naoya can be one of the most frustrating experiences in literary studies. Not only was his life exceedingly undramatic, but many of his works appear so banal as to be unrewarding to all but the most conscientious scholar. Indeed, were it not for the fact that some of his stories are unequaled in their perfection, one might be tempted to move on quickly to other, more consistently entertaining writers.

In one of his most brilliant essays ("The 'Pure' and the 'In-Between' in Modern Japanese Theories of the Novel"), Edward Seidensticker admits that he once asked: "What in the world do the Japanese see in Shiga Naoya?" For even though Shiga wrote little of any consequence between 1927 and his death in 1971, he was regarded by most critics throughout that period as the greatest living writer in Japan. He was said to be "the god of the novel,"

370

the only true exponent of pure literature. Other writers threw down their pens in despair at not being able to match the sincerity of his style. Even outward-looking proletarian writers were inspired, paradoxically, by the inward-looking Shiga Naoya.

Like *tōfu*, a dish which most Westerners find insipid, Shiga's fiction is an acquired taste. Most of it is autobiographical, continuing the *I-Novel tradition of the *Naturalist writers who preceded him. It is also clearly the work of a man who confined himself to a world where his material would be strictly limited. Occasional flights of imagination are held in check by rigorous self-questioning. Every step taken in literature is seen as if it were a step taken simultaneously in life. Eventually, his work forces one to examine the whole relationship of art to reality.

Shiga was born in 1883, in a provincial town in northern Honshū, to parents of the *shizoku* (ex-samurai) class. At the time, his father worked for the Dai-ichi Bank, although only two years later he resigned in order to take up a much more lucrative position with a Tokyo firm. Thus, Shiga grew up in the capital, enjoying security in a family that was becoming increasingly wealthy. Although his mother died when he was thirteen, his stepmother treated him as her own child and gave him a brother and five sisters.

From 1889 to 1906, Shiga attended the famous Peers' School where he mixed with sons of the nobility and with others like himself who came from families successful in business. He excelled at sports such as swimming and gymnastics, but did poorly in his studies, especially in languages and literature. Far from being a child prodigy, he did not even shine at Tokyo Imperial University, an institution which he left in 1910 after four years' study of English and Japanese literature.

There is, however, a sharp distinction to be drawn between official academic success and those private achievements which can make one successful later in life. As early as 1904, Shiga had written "A Little Girl and a Flowering Colza," a charming short story which is strongly suggestive of his mature style. In his last year at college he joined some of his old Peers' School friends in producing a journal called *Shirakaba* (*White Birch*), to which he contributed many other stories and quickly established a literary reputation.

The *Shirakabaha* group was composed of privileged and self-confident young men who had a diversity of interests in the arts. Among them were MUSHANOKŌJI SANEATSU, ARISHIMA TAKEO, and SATOMI TON, each of whom would eventually become famous. Although Shiga and his friends differed in their approaches to literature, they shared a common belief in the greatness of the individual self. In fact, self-realization was the clarion call of the *Shirakabaha*, and it undoubtedly gave Shiga the support he needed in developing his unique genius.

Seeking his own way in life, Shiga inevitably quarreled with his father, a man whom he tended to view as a philistine. The conflict between them had been growing for years, and had first become apparent when Shiga's father forbade him to take part in a protest over an environmental issue. Shiga had wanted to visit a copper mine that had been poisoning the Watarase River. However, his father privately feared embarrassment because the Shiga family had actually opened the mine many years previously. Shiga was unaware of this, and resented the intervention. Equally, in 1907 when he had his first love affair he again felt the full weight of paternal disapproval. His father dismissed the family maid who was the object of Shiga's affections.

Ambitious and willful, the young author responded to the stimulus of conflict, and produced some of his best work in the years 1910 to 1914. He wrote *"Seibei to hyōtan"* ("Seibei's Gourds") in 1913, a story since translated so frequently into foreign languages that it has become representative of early modern Japanese literature to the world at large. Perfectly constructed, it tells of a boy who collects gourds, selecting them for their aesthetic beauty with an unerring eye. Forced to give up his hobby by both his father and schoolmaster, Seibei never discovers that his prize specimen is later sold for a vast sum of money, gaining in price still further as it moves from one dealer to another. But, ever optimistic, he switches his attention to painting, until such time as his father intervenes.

In 1913, Japan's greatest contemporary writer, NATSUME SŌSEKI, then literary editor of the *Asahi shimbun*, invited Shiga to write a full-length novel for serial publication. This was a golden opportunity, for the novel was to follow Sōseki's own *Kokoro* which was currently running in the newspaper. Having already started a full-length work, Shiga readily agreed. Unfortunately, he was unable to make much progress, and in the following year when he failed to deliver the manuscript he felt an unbearable shame that continued to haunt him for most of his life.

Shiga is often criticized for being self-absorbed and unable to enter imaginatively the sufferings of other people. Yet in his early work there is strong evidence of his desire to make contact with the "otherness" of the world. In *"Shōji"* (*1911*, "The Paper Door"), for example, he depicts two families sharing a large room at an inn, separated by a flimsy paper partition. Whereas the small children and the maids from each family become acquainted, the older members remain aloof. In another story, entitled *"Dekigoto"* (*1913*,

"An Incident"), passengers on a tramcar spontaneously make friends with each other after a child, hit by the car, is miraculously discovered to be unhurt.

Here, and in several of his other stories, Shiga appears to be reaching out for a truth that lies beyond himself. By fatal coincidence, on the very same day that he wrote "An Incident," he was himself struck by a tramcar in Tokyo and very nearly killed. He recuperated at Kinosaki hot spring, later recalling his thoughts and feelings in his 1917 piece, *"Kinosaki ni te"* ("At Kinosaki"). In this essay-like story, he projects so strongly into the otherness of the world that his prose takes on a mystical dimension. He mentions how, when he accidentally killed a lizard, he was struck forcibly by the loneliness of existence. "I who had not died was walking here. I knew I should be grateful. But the proper feelings of happiness refused to come. To be alive and to be dead were not two opposite extremes. There did not seem to be much difference between them."

Shiga is generally credited with being the master of the "I-Novel" (*shishōsetsu*), that form of writing which grew out of Naturalism and went on to become the most distinctive mode of expression in modern Japanese literature. The term "I-Novel" in its Japanese usage is said to have originated with MORI ŌGAI who used the German words "Ich roman" to refer to his story *"Maihime"* (*1890*, "The Dancing Girl"). Nothing more was intended by him than a simple identification of the fact that his story was written in the first person, but the expression itself lingered, almost as if portending a new literature of the self. TAYAMA KATAI produced the first significant I-Novel when he wrote *"Futon"* (1907, "The Quilt"), a confessional story that was so well-received that many other writers followed his example. Eventually, the I-Novel acquired a kind of cult following, and although its readers numbered only a few thousand – far less than the readership commanded by works of entertaining fiction – the genre became established at the top end of the literary spectrum. It appealed to the connoisseur, to the person who felt he or she could recognize quality, sincerity, and authenticity. In this respect lovers of I-Novels were not unlike those who valued the simple earthenware vessels used in the traditional Japanese tea ceremony. The admired object, whether cup or story, needed to be subtle without being dishonest, simple without being obvious, and above all tangible in its authenticity. In the early part of the century only Shiga's work appeared to fulfill all the criteria for the perfect I-Novel.

In his excellent study of the Japanese I-Novel, *The Rhetoric of Confession* (University of California Press, Berkeley, 1988), Edward Fowler shows that the genre has always been controversial, despised by some critics and lauded by others. He himself takes the view that a "myth of sincerity" has been perpetuated by both sides and that an I-Novel embodies sincerity only to the extent that its author possesses sufficient artifice to be convincing. "That a writer like Shiga really does sound more sincere than others . . . is a tribute not to his honesty but to his mastery of the rhetoric (the intimate voice, ellipses, allusions, etc.) of authenticity." There is, he claims, an "act of faith" required of the reader. "The critic's only recourse in determining the author's credibility, other than relying on documentation that is never fully verifiable, is to appeal to the author's style." Shiga's style, and that of the other accomplished I-Novelists, is, according to Fowler, "the literary equivalent of acting."

Readers must decide for themselves whether such an interpretation is unduly cynical, even though it identifies the problem perfectly. After all, many people who enjoy a favorite author are very much inclined to discover every recorded detail about that author's life. The I-Novelist, especially, is subject to the scrutiny of his peers – as witness the hundreds of books that have been written about Shiga and DAZAI OSAMU, the two Japanese novelists who are most famous for having written about themselves. Ultimately, one's enjoyment of an I-Novel is dependent upon the extent to which one approves or disapproves of the author himself and one's attitude is formed by an intuitive leap of the imagination rather than by a mere act of faith.

In 1914, Shiga married Kadenokōji Sadako, a cousin of his *Shirakaba* friend, Mushanokōji. Once more, his father disapproved, but this time Shiga severed relations with him by renouncing his inheritance. Troubled by the family quarrel, the couple moved to Kyoto, then to Kamakura, and on to Mt. Akagi where proximity to nature greatly helped Shiga's writing. *"Takibi"* (*1920*, "The Bonfire") recalls his brief period in Akagi.

His brush with death, his marriage, his quarrel with his father, and constant moving from one dwelling to another completely disrupted Shiga's work on his novel. He had begun writing it in 1912, with the working title *"Tokitō Kensaku"* and the intention of celebrating his growth towards self-realization. But even though he put a prodigious effort into its creation, he was unable to finish it for many years. Ironically, the succession of events which prevented him from meeting Sōseki's deadline gave way to a quiet married life-style equally unconducive to work. Even the conflict with his father, once intended as the focus of the novel, was finally set aside when the two became reconciled in 1917. Like most writers, Shiga needed the stimulus of conflict, yet he was now secure, well-off, happily married, and highly revered. His inspiration evaporated.

Shiga eventually completed parts I and II of the novel, now renamed *An'ya kōro* (*A Dark Night's Passing*), in 1921 and 1922. He reworked his original text, introducing some new fictional elements to avoid making the hero's conflict with his father the central theme. Instead, Kensaku's journey to self-knowledge is prompted by the discovery that his own existence is the result of his mother's affair with her father-in-law: the man whom he had thought to be his grandfather. It is an adequate technical device, but one suspects that Shiga was loath to use it.

Part III of the four-part novel followed in 1923. Like the preceding sections, it appeared in the magazine *Kaizō* and confirmed the author's already great reputation. Where parts I and II alternate between self confidence and pessimism, Part III finds the hero at peace: a novelistic structure which exactly reflects Shiga's own life. If, today, critics find this approach too esoteric for their taste, one has to acknowledge Shiga's genius for dwelling on the very boundary that separates life from art. Throughout the novel, which he completed finally in 1937, he depicts his personal feelings and his reactions to the events of his life with the greatest sensitivity, clarity and insight.

Edwin McClellan, the translator of *A Dark Night's Passing*, has emphasized its qualities by writing: "... Self-centred or not, it is an extraordinarily bold novel for the time and place in which it was written. For against the reality of family and the order and conventions that it represents, Shiga affirms the greater reality of his own sexuality, his own search for love, his own communion with nature and participation in myth, his own fantasies and dreams."

AKUTAGAWA RYŪNOSUKE, shortly before his suicide, wrote in his story "*Haguruma*" (1927, "Cogwheels"): "I stretched myself out on the bed and began to read *A Dark Night's Passing*. Every stage of the hero's spiritual battle moved me deeply. When I compared myself to him, I realized what a fool I had been, and I found myself crying. But the tears brought with them a feeling of peace."

Such an endorsement by Akutagawa, whom most people would now identify as the greater writer, causes one to look again at the content of Shiga's work. Is it really as vacuous as it seems? Is it not rather the work of a man who was so uncompromising in his integrity that he would go to any lengths to avoid using artifice? To Shiga, artifice meant self-deception. He hoped, by setting an example, that he could win people's trust, and in so doing could forge an unbreakable contact with the world around him. In one sense he succeeded, for, at least in the reader's imagination, the "immortality" of a writer seems to remove the barrier of death.

Shiga believed implicitly in the instinctive wisdom of nature and had no doubt that it extended to the imagination. To him, this wisdom was the ultimate control, but it had to be cultivated with the utmost care. In *Modern Japanese Writers* (Stanford, 1976), Makoto Ueda shows how this belief, and Shiga's ability to embody it in literature, made him a writer of fiction rather than a diarist or essayist. "The prime function of a diary, like most other genres of personal nonfiction, was to record only what one actually did. A work of fiction, on the other hand, could present what one 'would do, or would wish to do' in various imaginary situations. It described man not only as he had been or was, but as he might be or might want himself to be."

Ueda goes on to say: "Shiga's characters are never faced with such agonizing choices as either eating human flesh or starving to death." Such "imaginary situations" were not even remotely considered as potential subjects by Shiga, who once said: "It is hazardous to health to be frequently exposed to the ugliness and folly in human life." His refusal to address the least pleasant aspects of existence may be seen either as a serious weakness or as his greatest strength.

Above all, Shiga hoped that his work would elate people: by expressing a powerful spiritual rhythm completely in tune with nature. He admired *Ihara Saikaku (1642–93) for this very reason, saying of his works: "The subject matter is the events of ordinary people's lives. They do not make particularly moving stories, and yet the impressions they create in me are marvelously powerful and vigorous, filling me with spiritual elation."

Between 1929 and 1937 Shiga wrote just three or four pieces, after which he completed his novel and then fell silent for the whole of World War II. He had never been prolific and indeed had published only five short nature sketches between January 1914 and April 1917, a period almost equivalent to World War I. This meager output is inexplicable until one considers the nature of Shiga's art. Writing was a spiritual exercise for him: a therapy by which he could resolve inner conflict. It was evidently successful. He attained the tranquility he sought, and, in the calm, domestic years of his later life, had scarcely any inner conflicts to express.

There was, however, one exception. The habit of writing dies hard, and Shiga felt strangely dissatisfied with his quiet life. In his early forties he struck up a relationship with a woman half his age, admitting to everyone that he needed the stimulus of conflict to sustain his art. But in his story *"Kuniko"* (1927) he postulated the worst that could happen: the suicide of his wife through jealousy and despair. Thus he resigned himself to his marriage commitment, and, as far as is known, remained faithful to his wife until his death in 1971.

Solution by resignation is characteristic of Shiga, and of the Oriental tradition in which he stands. He judiciously resigned himself to life. Perhaps for this reason his work seems to lack the life-enhancing energy that we find in MISHIMA YUKIO, Dazai, and Akutagawa: writers who make us recoil from death because they themselves embrace it. As for Shiga, for all his avowed intentions and nobility of purpose, he rarely elates the reader.

RECOMMENDED READING

Novel

A Dark Night's Passing. An'ya kōro. 1921–37. 408 pages. Tr. Edwin McClellan. Kodansha International, Tokyo and NY, 1976; paperback edition 1979; Fontana, London, 1980. Shiga's only long novel. Contains translator's 5-page preface.

Short Fiction Collections

The Paper Door and Other Stories. 173 pages. Tr. Lane Dunlop. North Point Press, San Francisco, 1987. Contains translator's 5-page preface and 17 stories, including: "Seibei's Gourds" (as "Seibei and His Gourds"), "Han's Crime," "The Razor," "The Shopboy's God," and "At Kinosaki." An excellent collection, sensitively translated and superbly presented.

The Shiga Hero. By William F. Sibley. 221 pages total; 82 pages of translations. University of Chicago Press, Chicago, 1979. Contains a biography of Shiga, an analysis of his work, and ten stories including: "At Kinosaki," "For Grandmother," and "The Bonfire" (tr. as "Night Fires"). An intelligent thesis, supplemented with well-chosen stories.

WORKS IN ENGLISH TRANSLATION

Novel

A Dark Night's Passing. An'ya kōro. 1921–37.

Mixed Anthology

A Late Chrysanthemum: Twenty-One Stories from the Japanese. 178 pages total; 34 pages devoted to four stories by Shiga. Tr. Lane Dunlop. North Point Press, San Francisco, 1986. Tuttle, Boston, 1991. Contains "Infatuation," "A Gray Moon," "At Kinosaki," and "The Razor."

Short Fiction

"Akanishi Kakita." *"Akanishi Kakita."* *1917.* 21 pages. (1) Tr. Saburo Haneda. *The Reeds,* vol. 2, 1956. (2) Tr. Elizabeth Schultz and Tadanobu Sakamoto. *Literature East and West,* vol. 21, 1977. (3) *The Paper Door, and Other Stories.*

"Araginu." *"Araginu."* *1908.* 9 pages. Tr. Eric S. Bell and Eiji Ukai. *Eminent Authors of Contemporary Japan,* vol. 1, Kaitakusha, Tokyo, 1930.

"As Far as Abashiri." *"Abashiri made."* *1908.* 9 pages. (1) As "Abashiri Made." Tr. C. S. Bavier. *The Pen,* 1932. (2) *The Paper Door, and Other Stories.*

"At Kinosaki." *"Kinosaki ni te."* *1917.* 6 pages. (1) Tr. Ineko Sato. *Eigo Seinen,* vol. 90, nos. 5–6, 1944. (2) Tr. Saburo Haneda. *The Reeds,* vol. 1, 1955. (3) Tr. Edward Seidensticker. *Modern Japanese Literature,* ed. Donald Keene. Grove Press, NY, 1956; Tuttle, Tokyo, 1957; Grove Weidenfeld, NY, 1989, paperback. (4) *The Shiga Hero.* (5) *A Late Chrysanthemum.*

"Autumn Wind." *"Akikaze."* *1949.* Tr. Michihiro Niijima. *Eigo Kenkyu,* vol. 41, nos. 8–11, 1952; vol. 44, no. 5, 1955.

"The Bonfire." *"Takibi."* *1920.* 7 pages. (1) As "Fires." Tr. S. F. Richards. *Literature East and West,* vol. 15, no. 4; vol. 16, nos. 1–2, 1972. (2) Tr. Dennis Keene. *Japan Quarterly,* vol. 22, no. 2, 1975. (3) As "Night Fires." *The Shiga Hero.*

"The Case of Sasaki." *"Sasaki no baai."* *1917.* Tr. A. L. Sadler. *The Far East,* no. 24, 1951.

"Death of a Hermit Crab." *"Yadokari no shi."* *1917.* 6 pages. Tr. S. G. Brickley. *The Writing of Idiomatic English.* Kenkyusha, Tokyo, 1951.

"Dwelling by the Moat." *"Horibata no sumai."* *1924.* 8 pages. (1) Tr. Edward Fowler. *Monumenta Nipponica,* vol. 32, no. 2, 1977. (2) As "The House by the Moat." *The Paper Door, and Other Stories.*

"For Grandmother." *"Sobo no tame."* *1911.* 10 pages. *The Shiga Hero.*

"The Gray Moon." *"Haiiro no tsuki."* *1945.* 5 pages. (1) Tr. Ineko Sato. *Eigo Seinen,* vol. 92, no. 8, 1946. (2) As "A Gray Moon." Tr. Saburo Haneda. *The Reeds,* vol. 2, 1956. (3) As "The Ashen Moon." Tr. Stephen W. Kohl. *Monumenta Nipponica,* vol. 32, no. 2, 1977. (4) As "Under an Ashen Moon." *The Shiga Hero.* (5) As "A Gray Moon." *A Late Chrysanthemum; The Paper Door, and Other Stories.*

"Han's Crime." *"Han no hanzai."* *1913.* 10 pages. (1) As "The Murder." Tr. Eiji Ukai and Eric S. Bell. *Japan Times,* August 28, 1927. As "A Murder Case." *Eminent Authors of Contemporary Japan,* vol. 2. Kaitakusha, Tokyo, 1930. (2) Tr. Ivan Morris. *Japan Quarterly,* vol. 2, no. 4, 1955; *Modern Japanese Literature,* ed. Donald Keene. Grove Press, NY, 1956; Tuttle, Tokyo, 1957; *Modern Japanese Short Stories.* Japan Publications Trading Co., Tokyo, 1960; revised edition 1970; *Murder in Japan,* ed. John L. Apostolou and Martin H. Greenberg. Dembner Books, NY, 1987. (3) Tr. Ryozo Matsumoto. *Japanese Literature, New and Old.* Hokuseido, Tokyo, 1961. (4) *The Paper Door, and Other Stories.*

"An Incident." *"Dekigoto."* *1913.* 6 pages. (1) As "An Accident." *The Shiga Hero.* (2) *The Paper*

Door, and Other Stories.

"An Incident on the Afternoon of November Third." *"Jūichigatsu mikka gogo no koto."* *1918.* 8 pages. (1) Tr. Iwao Matsubara. *Osaka Mainichi*, Nov. 29, 1925. (2) *The Paper Door, and Other Stories.*

"Infatuation." *"Chijo."* *1926.* 9 pages. *A Late Chrysanthemum; The Paper Door, and Other Stories.*

"The Kidnapping." *"Ko o nusumu hanashi."* *1914.* 18 pages. *The Shiga Hero.*

"Kuniko." *"Kuniko."* *1927.* 33 pages. *The Paper Door, and Other Stories.*

"A Little Girl and a Flowering Colza." *"Nanohana to komusume."* *1904.* 5 pages. (1) Tr. Michihiro Niijima. *Eigo Kenkyu*, vol. 44, no. 9, 1955. (2) As "The Little Girl and the Rapeseed Flower." *The Paper Door, and Other Stories.*

"The Man and Wife." *"Kōjinbutsu no fūfu."* *1916.* 15 pages. Tr. Nobuyuki Honna. *Kinjo Gakuin Daigaku Ronshu*, no. 36, 1968.

"Manazuru." *"Manazuru."* *1920.* 6 pages. (1) Tr. Stephen W. Kohl. *Monumenta Nipponica*, vol. 32, no. 2, 1977. (2) *The Shiga Hero; Asia*, vol. 2, no. 4, 1979.

"A Memory of Yamashina." *"Yamashina no kioku."* *1925.* 7 pages. *The Paper Door, and Other Stories.*

"A Moorhen." *"Ban."* 8 pages. Tr. Eric S. Bell and Eiji Ukai. *Eminent Authors of Contemporary Japan*, vol. 2. Kaitakusha, Tokyo, 1930.

"An Old Man." *"Rōjin."* *1911.* 5 pages. Tr. Arthur L. Sadler. *Selections from Modern Japanese Writers*, ed. A. L. Sadler. Australian Medical Publications, Sydney, 1943.

"The Paper Door." *"Shōji."* *1911.* 9 pages. *The Paper Door, and Other Stories.*

"Rain Frogs." *"Amagaeru."* *1923.* 13 pages. *The Paper Door, and Other Stories.*

"The Razor." *"Kamisori."* *1910.* 16 pages. (1) Tr. Eric S. Bell and Eiji Ukai. *Eminent Authors of Contemporary Japan*, vol. 1. (2) Tr. Francis H. Mathy. *Monumenta Nipponica*, vol. 13, nos. 3–4, 1957. (3) Tr. Nobuyuki Honna. *Kinjo Gakuin Daigaku Ronshu*, no. 36, 1968. (4) *The Shiga Hero; Murder in Japan.* (5) *A Late Chrysanthemum; The Paper Door, and Other Stories.*

"The Righteous." *"Seigiha."* *1912.* 6 pages. Tr. Kenji Takahashi. *Contemporary Japan*, vol. 3, Dec. 1937.

"Seibei's Gourds." *"Seibei to hyōtan.* *1913.* 8 pages. (1) As "Seibei and Hyotan." Tr. Taro Ito. *Jokyu Eigo*, Dec. 1929–March 1930. (2) As "Seibei and the Gourd." Tr. A. L. Sadler. *Selections from Modern Japanese Writers.* (3) As "The Artist." Tr. Ivan Morris. *Modern Japanese Stories*, ed. I. Morris. Spottiswoode, London, 1961; Tuttle, Tokyo and New York, 1961. (4) As "Seibei and His Gourds." Tr. Saburo Haneda. *The Reeds*, vol. 2, 1956. (5) As "Seibei and Gourds." *The Shiga Hero.* (6) *The Paper Door, and Other Stories.*

"The Shop-boy's God." *"Kozō no kamisama."* *1919.* 9 pages. (1) As "The Patron Saint of a Shop-Boy." Tr. Eric S. Bell and Eiji Ukai. *Eminent Authors of Contemporary Japan*, vol. 2. (2) *Selections from Modern Japanese Writers.* (3) As "The Guardian God of an Apprentice." Tr. Saburo Haneda. *The Reeds*, vol. 1, 1955. (4) As "The Apprentice's Patron God." Tr. Shigeru Tadokoro. *Wakayama Daigaku Gakugei*

Gakubu Kiyo, no. 6, 1956. (5) As "The Patron Saint." Tr. Michael Y. Matsudaira. *The Heart Is Alone*, ed. Richard McKinnon. Hokuseido, Tokyo, 1957; *The Mentor Book of Modern Asian Literature*, ed. D. B. Shimer. New American Library, NY, 1969. (6) *The Paper Door, and Other*

Stories.
"Tensho." *"Tenshō"* or *"Tensei."* 1924. 6 pages. (1) As "Reincarnation." Tr. Shigeru Tadokoro. *Wakayama Daigaku Gakugei Gakubu Kiyo*, no. 7, 1957. (2) Tr. Wenkai Kung. *The East*, vol. 13, nos. 1–2, Nov. 1976. (3) As "Reincarnation." *The Shiga Hero*.

CRITICAL STUDIES

Kohl, Stephen. "Shiga Naoya: A Critical Biography." Ph.D. diss., University of Washington, Seattle, 1974.
———. "The White Birch School (*Shirakabaha*) of Japanese Literature: Some Sketches and Commentary." *Occasional Paper*, no. 2, University of Oregon, 1975.
———. "Shiga Naoya and the Literature of Experience: Manazuru and The Ashen Moon." *Monumenta Nipponica*, vol. 32, no. 2, 1977.
Lee, Yang Hi. "Shiga Naoya: His Life and Works." Ph.D. diss., Columbia University, NY, 1966.
Mathy, Francis. *Shiga Naoya*. Twayne Publishers, NY, 1974.
Morris, Ivan. "Introductory Note: Shiga and Akutagawa." *Japan Quarterly*, vol. 2, no. 4, 1955.
Power, John. "Individualism in the Works of Shiga Naoya." Ph.D. diss., University of Sydney, Sydney, 1973.
———. "Shiga Naoya and the *Shishōsetsu*." *International Congress of Orientalists*, no. 28, 1974.
Seidensticker, Edward G. "The 'Pure' and the 'In-Between' in Modern Japanese Theories of the Novel." *Harvard Journal of Asiatic Studies*, no. 26, 1966; *This Country, Japan*. Kodansha International, Tokyo and NY, 1979 and 1984.
Sibley, William F. "The Shiga Hero." Ph.D. diss., University of Chicago, Chicago, 1971.
———. *The Shiga Hero*. University of Chicago Press, Chicago, 1979.
Swann, Thomas E. " 'Han no Hanzai': Another Look." *Literature East and West*, vol. 8, no. 4, 1964.
Usui, Yoshimi. "Shiga and Akutagawa." *Japan Quarterly*, vol. 2, no. 4, 1955.

SHIMAKI Kensaku
(1903–1945)

Novelist. Real name, Asakura Kikuo. Born in Hokkaidō. Active in politics at Tōhoku University, Sendai.

In one of his last stories, *"Kuroneko"* (1945, "The Black Cat"), Shimaki Kensaku created an especially vivid character: a black cat that refuses to accept the deprivations of wartime. Rather than eke out a living it throws caution to the wind and raids the kitchen when everyone is asleep. During daylight, however, it looks the narrator in the eye with all the audacity of a skilled poker player. Discovering the cat's double life the narrator realizes the animal must be killed, yet he cannot help but admire its heroic attitude. It has an indomitable spirit, quite unlike that of the other cats: those "servile-looking" creatures who continue to "move sluggishly around the garden" after the hero has been executed. Says the narrator in retrospect: the black cat was more like the very last Sakhalin lynx observed by a traveler and described in a book. Rather than flee or fight when attacked by a hunter, the lynx simply urinated on him from his perch in a tree.

Although one may quickly grasp the meaning of this powerful story, its exact emotional quality is hard to explain without reference to the details of Shimaki's life. For Shimaki was wholly identified as being the archetypal *tenkō writer of the modern, military period. Like many other intellectuals he was forced to renounce his socialist beliefs under threat of imprisonment, torture, or death. In order to survive, all he had to do was to undergo (or "commit") tenkō, a word which is variously translated as "apostasy," "conversion," or "reorientation." Such were the physical and social pressures to conform, few people avoided tenkō when it was forced upon them and nearly all experienced a second, voluntary tenkō when they realized that Communism was "the god who failed." Among literary men KOBAYASHI TAKIJI was one who resisted completely and he paid for it with his life. According to the critic Kamei Katsuichirō he may well have been the black cat of Shimaki's story.

Born Asakura Kikuo, Shimaki grew up in poverty in his native Hokkaidō. His father died when he was two years old and his mother struggled to give him an education until her poor eyesight forced her to stop work. As a consequence, Shimaki left school when he was fourteen years old and took a job as an office boy for a daily wage of fifteen sen. Had one of his colleagues not then given him a large caseful of books, Shimaki might have remained a menial employee for the rest of his life. As it was, he read voraciously day and night, eventually deciding to go to Tokyo to study English.

Shimaki's trips to Tokyo were dogged by disaster. On his first visit in 1920 he caught tuberculosis and was obliged to return home. Three years later he made a second visit only to be seriously injured in the *Great Kantō Earthquake. Although he recovered he never enjoyed good health. Photographs of him taken at Tōhoku University in the mid–1920s show him to have been a frail and studious person: almost a caricature of the pallid but intense intellectual familiar to readers of Russian literature. Indeed, Shimaki himself read a lot of Soviet pamphlets and very soon helped to organize the first labor union in Sendai.

Shimaki joined the Japanese Communist Party at the end of 1927 and was arrested at the beginning of 1928. Thrown into solitary confinement he was not tried until the following year. To make matters worse, even after commiting tenkō he was still found guilty of inciting the farm workers of Shikoku, and was returned to solitary confinement – in a cell adjacent to that of a leper – for another three years.

As if turning misfortune to advantage, Shimaki became immediately famous for a story he wrote after leaving prison. It was called *"Rai"* (*1934*, "Leprosy"), and along with *"Mōmoku"* (1934, "Blindness") it was recognized as being a powerful evocation of prison life. Each of these two stories describes a sorely afflicted man who is nonetheless steadfast in his convictions. Both pieces were included in Shimaki's widely acclaimed collection, *Goku* (1934, *Prison*).

Invited to become an associate of the magazine *Bungakukai*, Shimaki continued to describe himself as "a soldier of proletarian literature." He was, however, still under police surveillance and encountered serious problems with the censor when his first novel, *Saiken* (*Reconstruction*), was published in 1937. Like his other stories of this period, *Saiken* portrayed a hero of "nonconversion," but since the book was wholly banned ten days after its publication Shimaki decided to try another approach. He realized that the complex *tenkō* issue could be dealt with from another angle. Thus, in *Seikatsu no tankyū* (1937–38, *In Quest of Life*, two vols.), he concentrated on its ethical rather than political implications. Although the novel was often criticized harshly for its uneven style, it enabled him to continue writing throughout World War II, emphasizing the value of life rather than the importance of abstract principles.

In Quest of Life struck a chord with the Japanese public. It ran to over a hundred printings and its popularity continued even after the war had ended. Shimaki could look back on the furious controversy which first greeted the novel in the 1930s and feel that he had been exonerated. "I do not feel ashamed of anything I have written," he had said in 1939. "I cannot be a great author ... but I should like to be one who, small and weak though he may be, is honest and free of taint."

Shimaki may have been altogether *too* unambitious in his later novels, for they were dismissed by Nakamura Mitsuo (one of the few critics who had praised *In Quest of Life*) as being "nothing but lay sermons." Two of them were set in Manchuria. *Manshū kikō* (1940, *Manchurian Journey*) was an account of his journey to the new Japanese colony on the mainland, and *Ishizue* (1944, *Foundation*) the story of how a young man, somewhat in the manner of a latter-day Tolstoy, establishes a model village there.

Seemingly oblivious of Japan's militaristic oppression overseas, Shimaki clearly ran the risk of being deemed a supporter of the discredited regime, despite his failure to endorse "Japanism" in all its patriotic aspects. In fact, he survived the war by only two days, succumbing to a final attack of tuberculosis on August 17, 1945. Before he died he wrote a set of famous short stories based on his intimate observations of the animals in and around his home. Four of them, including *"Aka gaeru"* (1946, "The Red Frog"), *"Mukade"* ("The Centipede"), and *"Jigabachi"* (1945, "The Wasps"), have been translated into English and are widely regarded as his finest works. By far the best is "The Black Cat," a story which not only embodies the agonizing conflicts of Shimaki's life but transcends them memorably.

RECOMMENDED READING

Mixed Anthology

A Late Chrysanthemum: Twenty-One Stories from the Japanese. 178 pages total; 27 pages devoted to four stories by Shimaki. Tr. Lane Dunlop. North Point Press, San Francisco, 1986. Tuttle, Boston, 1991. Anthology also contains stories by KAWABATA YASUNARI, HAYASHI FUMIKO (title story), DAZAI OSAMU, and others.

WORKS IN ENGLISH TRANSLATION

Short Fiction

"The Black Cat." *"Kuroneko."* 1945. 10 pages. *A Late Chrysanthemum.*
"The Centipede." *"Mukade."* 4 pages. *A Late Chrysanthemum.*
"The Red Frog." *"Aka gaeru."* 1945. 8 pages. (1) As "A Red Frog." Tr. Tadao Katayama. *The Reeds,* no. 3, 1957. (2) As "A Frog." Tr. John Bester. *Japan P.E.N. News,* no. 10, 1962. (3) *A Late Chrysanthemum.*
"The Wasps." *"Jigabachi."* 1945. 6 pages. Tr. John Bester. *A Late Chrysanthemum.*

Shimazaki TŌSON
(1872–1943)

Novelist and poet. Real name, Shimazaki Haruki. Born in Magome (now Misaka Magome, Nagano Prefecture). Lived in Tokyo and northeast and central Japan.

More than any other Japanese author, Shimazaki Tōson needs to be liberated from the confines of university studies. Apart from many of his early poems there are now three major prose works by him in English translation. They are, in chronological order: *Hakai* (1906, *The Broken Commandment*, tr. 1974); *Ie* (1911, *The Family*, tr. 1976); and *Yoake mae* (1929–35, *Before the Dawn*, tr. 1987). No three works could be more dissimilar from one another. *The Broken Commandment* is pure fiction, telling of how a young schoolteacher is torn between revealing or concealing the fact that he comes from an *eta*, or outcast, family. By contrast, the second novel is purely autobiographical. It is a detailed account of the author's early married life and of the unwelcome responsibilities thrust upon him when various branches of his family encounter financial problems. Although critical opinion is divided, many readers who find the first book enjoyable will probably dislike the second for its unrelieved tedium and absence of structure. Indeed, after encountering *The Family*, only the stouthearted will wish to address Tōson's third full-length work in English translation: the 800-page historical novel *Before the Dawn*. But if at first glance this book appears to be a long and difficult work, it soon proves to be as compulsively readable as *The Broken Commandment*. Moreover, in being a fictionalized account of the life of Tōson's father during the turbulent years of the mid-nineteenth century, the novel combines the literary methods used in producing the other two works. *Before the Dawn* is one of the world's greatest historical novels and gives a unique insight into Japan's transition from feudalism to the modern era.

Shimazaki Haruki (Tōson is a pen name) was born in Magome in the mountainous region of central Japan. His father, Shimazaki Masaki, was a village headman who also held the hereditary offices of *honjin* (posthouse keeper) and *toiya* (freight forwarder) in the feudal administration of the Kiso Road. This road, part of the famous Nakasendō Highway between the imperial city, Kyoto, and the shōgunal headquarters in Edo, was an alternative route to the more direct Tōkaidō further to the south. Both routes were frequently used by *daimyō* (lords) and their vast retinues of soldiers during their long treks to and from Edo, fulfilling the obligatory four-month periods of attendance at the shōgun's castle. Thus, being strategically placed in both social and geographic terms, the Shimazaki family were an important link in the feudal order. They had accumulated considerable wealth during the *Tokugawa period and were regarded as "country gentry" by the local farming community. Only with the the advent of the *Meiji Restoration, in an upheaval that was strongly supported by Tōson's father, did the family's fortunes decline. The hereditary offices were abolished, and, as if in acknowledgement that there was no future in Magome, Masaki sent his fourth son, Haruki, to be educated in the newly-named city of Tokyo at the tender age of nine.

Tōson was intensely lonely in the unfamiliar environment of the big city, even though he was cared for by friends of the family who were kind and considerate. His father, who paid him only one visit (in 1884) before his death in 1886, soon became a remote figure from the past. His brief presence in Tokyo had caused an agony of embarrassment for the young boy, and rarely can a father and son have been made more acutely aware of a "generation gap" than on that occasion. After his father's death Tōson entered the Meiji Gakuin, a Christian school renowned for its teaching of English. He graduated in 1891 and in the following year joined the staff of Meiji Jogakkō, the school's sister institution for girls. There he not only became romantically involved with one of the students, but he also met the young poet Kitamura Tōkoku (1868–94), who, in an all-too-brief career, was soon to become the leading exponent of Romanticism in modern Japanese poetry.

Tōson's first love affair ended in disaster. The student he admired was already pledged to marry someone else and was thus unable to return his affections. As a consequence, Tōson resigned his position at the school after only a year of teaching English. Like some latter-day Bashō he wandered aimlessly around the country for nine months before finally returning to Tokyo to join Tōkoku's Romantic circle. Greatly influenced by the powerful personality of the young poet, the group began to publish *Bungakukai* (*World of Literature*), a coterie magazine which ran from January 1893 to January 1898.

In literature, as in life, Tōson's romantic yearnings were not easily fulfilled. As a poet he was frustrated by what he thought were the limitations of the Japanese language. It would not allow him to say all that he wished to say while still remaining within the bounds of accepted poetic form. According to his acquaintance KUNIKIDA DOPPO (as reported by TAYAMA KATAI in *Thirty Years in Tokyo*), Tōson was "too caught up with form," although other critics praised him for extending the language of poetic expression. At any rate, Tōson remained a poet for several years, continuing his art in the more peaceful surroundings of Sendai in northeast Japan after the sudden trauma of Tōkoku's suicide in 1894.

Supporting himself by teaching, Tōson wrote his first collection of verse during his ten-month stay in Sendai. When published, the volume was called *Wakanashū* (1897, *A Collection of Young Leaves*), and it was well received for the lyricism and freshness of its language. Kenneth Strong, the translator of Tōson's first novel *The Broken Commandment*, comments upon them thus: "rather naïve, but conveying even today the excitement, the vivid delight in a rediscovery of the external world and of the self, that marked *Wakanashū* as the first clear utterance of Japanese Romanticism."

Having returned briefly to Tokyo, a city from which he was rarely absent for long, Tōson married Hata Fuyuko in April 1899, and the couple immediately left for Komoro where Tōson began teaching at the local academy. Situated at the northern edge of the mountainous region where he had spent his infancy, Komoro now became his home for five difficult years of intellectual toil and a growing marital crisis. Tayama Katai, who recalled that his first impression of Tōson was of "a pale, quiet, pleasant enough young man," remarked in his memoirs that the Komoro period was a time when "art and life clashed" for the young author. At first, writing under the influence of John Ruskin (from whose *Modern Painters* he had made some translations in 1896), Tōson began a series of impressionistic prose sketches of local places and later published them under the title *Chikumagawa no suketchi* (1913, *Chikuma River Sketches*). These brief descriptions of one of the most beautiful parts of Japan showed a rare talent for lyrical evocation. It was a skill which he continued to use throughout his writing career. As Edwin McClellan (in *Two Japanese Novelists*, 1969) has said: "What gives his sometimes heavily written novels their peculiar power is the seemingly incongruous presence of the poet in the background." Indeed, had Tōson remained single, he might well have continued to write only poetry and lyrical prose, but under the stimulus of needing to support his family he wanted to produce a more substantial work that would bring some financial rewards.

Controversy still surrounds the story of Tōson's early struggle to survive as a novelist, for once he had embarked on writing *The Broken Commandment* nothing would deflect him from his task – not even the undernourishment of his three children. Tragically, all three of them died, the first in April 1905 just weeks after Tōson had given up his teaching post in order to devote himself full-time to his novel. When he eventually published the book, borrowing money so that he could have it printed privately, the newspapers said that he had sacrificed the lives of his children in the cause of art. Notwithstanding such notoriety, or perhaps because of it, *The Broken Commandment* was an instant success.

By any standards, *The Broken Commandment* is an excellent novel. Although Western critics invariably dislike its happy ending, they all agree it is one of the finest works of Meiji literature. Donald Keene goes so far as to say: "Its only predecessor among works of realism was FUTABATEI SHIMEI's *Drifting Cloud*." This is praise indeed, but even more generously it was acknowledged by NATSUME SŌSEKI as being the first true novel of the modern period. Reading it today in Kenneth Strong's translation, one is immediately struck by the brisk pace of its narrative, the realism of its dialogue, and the tight structure of its plot. Even its ending, overly melodramatic though it may be for some tastes, is completely plausible and not nearly as unsatisfying as critics would have us believe.

Ushimatsu, the hero of *The Broken Commandment*, is a young schoolteacher who has successfully passed through training college without revealing his family's terrible secret. Should anyone discover that he is an *eta*, a nonperson in the eyes of society, his whole life will be ruined. In the opening scene the author takes care to impress on the reader how callously the *eta* are treated. Ushimatsu sees a fellow resident expelled from his lodging house after being identified as a member of the outcast minority, even though the man is sick and has more than enough money to pay for his keep. Clearly, any revelation that the young teacher is himself an *eta* will cause immense problems, and he must therefore at all costs observe his father's commandment: "Do not tell!"

To the hero the admonition is exactly like a commandment from God. Over and over again the old man's words echo in his mind, and much of the novel's power seems to stem from this relatively simple device. However, having already been alerted by the novel's title that Ushimatsu is likely to break the commandment, the reader is kept in suspense wondering in what manner such an unthinkable betrayal could be engineered. Fortunately, the author has complete control over his readers' anticipations (incidentally an essential skill for writers of fiction, but one which critics are always inclined to label as "manipulative"), and Tōson carefully builds a scenario in which telling the secret suddenly becomes preferable to not telling it. When Ushimatsu's father dies one begins to feel that even though it was motivated by good will and common sense the admonition no longer represents a viable policy. And when the secret is actually discovered by a ruthless politician whose wife is acquainted with Ushimatsu's family, the choice between keeping or breaking the commandment begins to look irrelevant.

The brilliance of Tōson's plot is now made apparent because, far from being irrelevant, breaking the commandment assumes the dimension of being a psychological necessity for Ushimatsu. He is a great admirer of Inoko Rentarō, an *eta* who has risen above the cruel burden of his outcast status to become a distinguished author and a campaigner for *eta* rights. Ushimatsu would like to confide in him, but cannot bring himself to utter the words "I too am an *eta*," however hard he tries. He is clearly in danger of suffering a severe mental breakdown, his moral torment akin to that of Dostoievsky's Raskolnikov (the character on whom he is loosely modeled). As for the reader, who was once hoping against hope that Ushimatsu would never reveal his secret: he is now experiencing a complete reversal of attitude, praying that the young teacher will find the strength to unburden his soul. For a first novel it was a remarkable performance, and one wishes that Tōson could have written a dozen such books instead of being diverted into the stagnant waters of his autobiography. Yet had he not made a radical change in his literary method he might never have risen above the level of ingenious fiction to create the masterpiece *Before the Dawn*.

Tōson's first venture into autobiography was *Haru* (1908, *Spring*) in which he recounted his early, Romantic years and his friendship with Kitamura Tōkoku. Representing himself in the person of

Kishimoto, a man in his early twenties who is suffering from unrequited love, Tōson kept closely to the facts of his life. What he failed to do, however, was to probe beneath superficial, outward appearances in order to reveal any depths of character or motivation. For example, Kishimoto's slightly older friend, Aoki (Tōkoku), is portrayed as being deeply disillusioned with life, despite being married and having a small daughter of his own. But why? Tōson does not give an adequate answer. As Edwin McClellan writes: "The novel . . . is weak because the characters' actions are never based on sufficient motive."

For *Spring* Tōson used an impressionistic technique that was quite at variance to his more detailed exploration of psychology in *The Broken Commandment*. Impressionism is, of course, part of nearly every Japanese writer's stock-in-trade, but it takes many forms and may be used either with precision (by TANIZAKI JUN'ICHIRŌ) or with vagueness (as here, by Tōson). One cannot help coming to the conclusion that when impressionism is used with vagueness the writer often has very little to say. This could well be true in Tōson's case, for, after all, his strongest inclination was to observe the external world rather than probe the depths of his own soul. In fact, his sudden switch to autobiographical writing may have been prompted solely by the success of Tayama Katai's "Futon" (1907, "The Quilt"), a confessional story which appeared soon after Tōson's first work of fiction and proved to be even more popular.

Undaunted by the inadequacy of *Spring*, Tōson continued in an autobiographical vein by writing *Ie* (1911, *The Family*), a long, descriptive novel covering the period 1898–1910. It is a curious work, with few discernible literary qualities. Unimaginative in content, uneven in technique, and with poor and often banal dialogue, it fails to stimulate more than half-a-dozen of the thousand-and-one nerve endings of a modern literary sensibility. Nonetheless, it is considered to be one of the best works of Japanese *Naturalism: a movement which played a significant role in the early development of modern Japanese literature.

It is hard to understand why an author who was so capable of entertaining his readers in *The Broken Commandment* could tolerate the sheer tedium of *The Family*. One can only suppose that Tōson lost all sense of objectivity during its writing, despite some attempt to portray himself, this time as Sankichi, with a measure of detachment. Burdened by family obligations, Sankichi has to support nephews, nieces, aunts, and uncles in addition to his own wife and children. Not surprisingly, and completely at odds with the author's attempt at detachment, a note of self-righteousness often creeps into the text. It is as though Tōson wrote *The Family* in order to apportion credit or blame to his family's individual members rather than create, as was his avowed aim, a realistic portrait of family life. Simply by writing at great length and piecing the story together page upon page, Tōson fully expected to achieve his goal: ". . . exactly as if I were building a house."

The Family would be a poor novel indeed if it had no redeeming features, and it certainly gives us a detailed insight into the daily life of a Meiji family. However, given the unusual social background of the Shimazakis there is no reason to suppose that they in any way typified the society of their time. Yet Tōson, writing as though his characters were wholly typical, made no attempt to individuate their personalities and failed to attribute any characteristic dialogue to them. Too much is left to the reader's imagination: a faculty which is already taxed to the utmost in trying to distinguish the outlines of the relatives in the blandness of the text. Only the unfortunate brother Sōzō, Sankichi's elder by three years and a chronic invalid, can be readily pictured in the mind's eye. Everyone despises him, for he is said to have brought about his own misfortune by catching syphilis at an early age. In the novel's only amusing line, the second oldest brother, Morihiko, comments on Sōzō's unique blend of helpless dependency and undiminished appetite: "If he were an animal, he'd have been eaten a long time ago."

Tōson persisted in using the vague, impressionistic technique developed in *Spring* when writing *The Family*. So understated are the emotional lives of its characters that one has to read between the lines to sense what they might be feeling. Emotion is never evoked, but only mentioned. In a revealing passage near the end of the book Tōson wrote: "Sankichi looked around the house. The passions and the furies that had stirred him and his wife had long since passed. Love and desire no longer preoccupied him. He was able to regard both himself and Oyuki [his wife] with the objectivity of a connoisseur enjoying sculpture or the taste of good wine. They had come to be quite inseparable – bound to each other." The thought is gracefully expressed (in Cecilia Segawa Seigle's translation). But passions? Furies? There has been no sign of them previously, except by implication. *The Family* is as flat and meandering as a broad river making its way to the sea.

By 1911, when *The Family* had been published in its entirety, Tōson's own nuclear family had been diminished by the death of his wife in childbirth. Of the seven children born to Fuyuko only four remained, and Fuyuko herself was now no longer alive to look after them. Facing a severe test of personal character Tōson tried to bring up his two older sons with the aid of his niece, but the arrangement led to a crisis of breathtaking proportions. Not only did he sleep with his niece, making her pregnant, but he was completely unable to face the consequences. Instead of confessing his dilemma to her father, (Hirosuke in real life; Morihiko in *The Family*; Yoshio in *Shinsei*), he decided to flee the country. That he chose to live in France in the middle of World War I rather than face the censure of his brother gives some idea of the shame he must have felt.

Tōson, it must be said, does not emerge from this episode as an honorable or even likable man. As on the occasion earlier in his life when his children were starving, he had a habit of compounding his error. This time, from the safety of Paris, he wrote a frank confession to Hirosuke, who generously and unexpectedly forgave him, promising never to speak of the matter again. However, on returning to Japan after three years abroad, Tōson decided to publish a complete account of his affair in the novel *Shinsei* (*1918–19, A New Life*). Hirosuke was deeply offended, not least by the disgraceful revelation that his brother had resumed sexual relations with the girl quite recently, after arriving back from France.

In order to appreciate Tōson the writer, one must set aside the sordid details of his life and concentrate on those works which are most removed from them. Few scholars would agree with this suggestion because the bulk of his work, the novels produced in his middle years, are wholly concerned with himself in relationship to his family. Subtract them from the total picture and one is left with a few travel sketches, some slim volumes of Romantic poetry, an early work of fiction and one great historical novel. Yet how refreshing it becomes to think of Tōson as the author of these varied and uplifting works, rather than as a man who catalogued the misery of his family life. The novels of his middle years are embarrassing examples of self-justification and they contain more than a little hypocrisy as a result. Indeed, after reading "A New Life," AKUTAGAWA said he had never encountered a more hypocritical hero than Kishimoto, the novel's Tōson-figure.

During his three years in France, Tōson wrote the first half of *Sakura no mi no jukusuru toki* (*1914–1918, When the Cherries Ripen*), and completed it on his return to Japan. He had hoped to make faster progress on this second novel about his student days, but he felt ill at ease in the unfamiliar surroundings of Paris. Quickly recognizing that his intellectual relationship with the West did not extend naturally to contact at a social level, Tōson resigned himself to thinking nostalgically of Japan. Many years previously he had become a Christian, but now he recalled how he had come to doubt his Christian faith, and with it, had rejected nearly everything that had given his life hope and meaning. Ever since then he had tried to espouse humanist values, but the difficulties of filling the spiritual void were, as we have seen, not easily overcome.

That an important element was lacking from Tōson's spiritual life is suggested by *Etoranzee* (1920–21, *L'Étranger*), a story in which the hero, a Japanese living by himself in Paris, is visited by an imaginary creature who talks to him in his lonely room. The concept itself carries an ineffable sadness, not least because Tōson was at his best when observing the real world outside. Yet in Paris, far from his homeland, all he could "see" were other Japanese exiles. The rest, including the French themselves, made no sense to him and he was blind to their existence.

Throughout his life Tōson read widely in the literature and philosophy of the West. While noting that he was not the intellectual equal of Sōseki or MORI ŌGAI, Cecilia Segawa Seigle (in the introduction to her translation of *The Family*) says he was "unique in his understanding of European philosophers." He liked their humanism and positive attitude toward life, and "sincerely believed that life and art were inseparable, that no single phase of existence should be neglected." Among the European writers Tōson most admired were Shakespeare, Goethe, Tolstoy, Flaubert, and Zola: all of them men in whom the life force was strong and resilient. He may even have regarded them as father figures, as substitutes for the father he had never really known.

Eventually Tōson came to recognize the problem which had cast a shadow over much of his life. He decided to learn more about the man who had sent him away from home at the age of nine and whom he could still remember saying: "Haruki is my son, my spiritual heir." Through meticulous research in public libraries and family records Tōson began a quest in search of his father. Helped by the fact that he was now financially secure and no longer obliged to support so many dependents, he even decided to purchase a house for his eldest son, Kusuo, in the ancestral village of Magome. For two years prior to beginning the notes that would become the basis of his masterpiece *Before the Dawn*, Tōson repaired and refurbished the house, acquired additional farmland, and helped to put everything in working order for the Shimazakis' return to their traditional home. As William Naff comments (in his introduction to *Before the Dawn*), these activities "seem to have played an important role in renewing his sense of connection to Magome and its history."

Before the Dawn was written between 1927 and 1935, and was published in quarterly installments in the monthly journal *Chūō kōron* between April 1929 and October 1935. While it was appearing, critics failed to understand the radical change Tōson had wrought in his literary method, nor did they appreciate the scope, scale, and grandeur of his conception. Most people regarded it as "too historical" to be considered seriously as mainstream literature: a prejudice against historical fiction which prevails to this day. Only after its complete publication did one or two enlightened critics such as Kobayashi Hideo recognize its exceptional quality. Divided into two volumes it was eventually published in book form: Book One appearing in 1932; Book Two in 1935.

The narrative of *Before the Dawn* begins with news of the arrival of Commodore Perry's "Black Ships" in Edo harbor in 1853, and covers all the major events of Japanese history until 1886, the year in which Tōson's father died. In storytelling technique the author provides both oblique and direct views of the political turmoil surrounding the Meiji Restoration. He makes excellent use of Magome's midway position between Kyoto and Edo in presenting the oblique view, consisting of the fragmentary information that comes to his father from people traveling between the two cities. But then he rounds out this incomplete picture by transporting us directly to the centers of action, to diplomatic meetings, battles, banquets, and assassinations. The result is impressive, for not only is the life of the village set within the context of national history, but the late Tokugawa and early Meiji periods are themselves illuminated from a unique, provincial perspective.

The central figure of *Before the Dawn* is Aoyama Hanzō, who, as previously mentioned, is a vivid fictional re-creation of Tōson's father, Shimazaki Masaki. At the beginning of the novel he is still preparing to take over the responsibilities of village headman and posthouse keeper from *his* father, Kichizaemon (Tōson's grandfather and the sixteenth head of the Magome Shimazakis). Hanzō, however, is not an unquestioning follower of family traditions, having become intensely interested in "National Learning," the Shintō revivialist movement started by four great scholars including Motoori Norinaga (1730–1801) and Hirata Atsutane (1776–1843). In their writings, to which he is introduced by an older man whom he greatly respects, Hanzō discovers a new sense of national identity and the inspiration to return to the pre-Buddhist roots of Japan.

Tōson's presentation of the chauvinistic ideas promulgated by the National Learning movement has been criticized as being too one-sided in their favor. Such criticism, however, does not take into account the artistic aspects of *Before the Dawn*. It is primarily a dramatic work that tries to evoke the unique spirit of Tōson's father. The National Learning, therefore, is seen almost entirely from his point of view during much of the novel. Only in one pivotal scene towards the end are we given an alternative view. Hanzō goes to the local Buddhist temple to remove his ancestors' tablets in accordance with the new policy on separating Shintō from (what the National Scholars believed was) the pernicious influence of Buddhism. But so skillfully does Tōson portray the deep spirituality of the priest that the reader is now inclined to see Hanzō in a different light. The priest's Buddhist religion transcends national boundaries, and he finds Atsutane's followers cold and arrogant. Suddenly, the novel is given a whole new dimension as Hanzō's dreams of a reborn Japan are placed in a wider context.

Hanzō's encounter with the priest is a pivotal scene because he is persuaded to leave untouched the two tablets belonging to the temple's founder and his wife: that is, those of the original Aoyamas (Shimazakis) in Magome. His lack of any personal animosity towards the priest is another example of his fundamentally generous nature. Unfortunately, when he later becomes bitterly disillusioned by the failure of the new Meiji government to institute much-needed agricultural reforms, he begins to regret his decision. Tōson, as usual, forces us to read between the lines, but the implication is clear. By attempting to burn down the temple in what appears to be an act of madness, Hanzō is simply trying to make amends for being too halfhearted in his adherence to the National Learning. Not surprisingly, the incident brings about his final downfall.

To say that *Before the Dawn* is "a good read" is an understatement. It requires days of patient study, yet its contents are remarkably easy to assimilate. In no other book will one find a more complete introduction to Japan's turbulent nineteenth century, and nowhere else are the labyrinthine politics of the era more entertainingly explained. Far from being a rambling narrative, it is a vast and soaring edifice as tightly structured as *The Broken Commandment*. Ultimately, its powerful effect on the reader stems from the way in which Tōson contrasts the feudal era to the Meiji period. He re-creates the feudal era as vividly as a dream, then goes on to portray his hero awakening from the dream to the cold realities of the modern world. The novel abounds in irony, for Hanzō himself is one of the grass-roots supporters of the revolution and yet his idealism is crushed by directives from above. So convincingly is this thesis embodied in action that the novel attains the level of tragedy. No one who reads it in William Naff's excellent translation can fail to be impressed.

After completing his masterpiece, Tōson immediately embarked on another major project which he was unable to finish. Having so successfully contrasted feudal and modern eras in *Before the Dawn*, he now wished to apply a similar technique by comparing the cultures of East and West. Taking notes as he traveled, he made a trip around the world in 1936–37 and then returned to Japan to begin his research. He studied the ideas of those who were instrumental in the Westernization of Japan: men such as *Fukuzawa Yukichi (1834–1901), the founder of Keio University. However, Tōson completed only three chapters of this last novel, called *Tōhō no mon* (*The Eastern Gate*), before his death in 1943. As he appeared to be building an argument for Japan's continued presence in Manchuria (among other topics addressed in the novel), several critics have expressed their relief that *The Eastern Gate* was never finished.

Tōson died on August 22, 1943, at the age of seventy-two. Together with SHIGA NAOYA and a handful of other writers he was one of the most influential novelists in Japan in the twentieth century. His ancestral village of Magome has become virtually a national shrine, and is visited by thousands of tourists each year. In the West, too, his reputation must surely rise with the 1987 publication of *Before the Dawn* in English. This work alone sets him alongside his great contemporaries, Sōseki and Ōgai. It wholly redeems his otherwise uneven career.

RECOMMENDED READING

Novels

Before the Dawn. *Yoake mae. 1929–35.* 759 pages. Tr. William E. Naff. University of Hawaii Press, Honolulu, 1987. Contains 12-page introduction by the translator and 38-page glossary. A magnificent historical novel covering the years 1853–86, and a landmark in Japanese–English translation.
The Broken Commandment. *Hakai.* 1906. 249 pages. (1) Extract, tr. Edward Seidensticker. *Modern Japanese Literature*, ed. Donald Keene, Grove Press, NY, 1956; Tuttle, Tokyo, 1957; Grove Weidenfeld, NY, 1989, paperback. (2) Tr. Kenneth Strong. University of Tokyo Press, Tokyo, 1974. UTP edition of this still very readable novel contains 19-page introduction by translator. A finely produced volume, ideal for the collector.

WORKS IN ENGLISH TRANSLATION

Novels

Before the Dawn. Yoake mae. 1929–35.

The Broken Commandment. Hakai. 1906.

The Family. Ie. 1911. 311 pages. Tr. Cecilia Segawa Seigle. As *An Integral Translation with an Introduction of Ie.* University Microfilm, Ann Arbor, 1971. As *The Family.* University of Tokyo Press, Tokyo, 1976.

Short Fiction

"Awakening." *"Nobi jitaku."* 1925. 11 pages. Tr. Eric S. Bell and Eiji Ukai. *Eminent Authors of Contemporary Japan,* vol. 1. Kaitakusha, Tokyo, 1930.

"Breakfast." *"Asameshi."* 1906. (1) As "The Breakfast." Tr. Osamu Nakamura and H. P. Holt. *Eigo Seinen,* vol. 31, nos. 10–12, 1914. (2) Tr. Kanichi Ando. *Osaka Mainichi,* Nov. 1 and 2, 1923.

"A Domestic Animal." *"Kachiku."* 1906. 15 pages. Tr. Torao Taketomo. *Paulownia, Seven Stories from Contemporary Japanese Writers.* Duffield, NY, 1918.

"First Journey." *"Hatsutabi."* 7 pages. Tr. S. G. Brickley. *The Writing of Idiomatic English.* Kenkyusha, Tokyo, 1951.

"Ryokan Sho-nin, or Saint Ryokan." *"Orokana uma no hanashi."* 6 pages. Tr. Yoshitaro Takenobu. *Eigo Kenkyu,* vol. 18, no. 7, 1925.

"Should She Have Told Him?" *"Haha."* 1911. 21 pages. Tr. Asataro Miyamori. *Representative Tales of Japan.* Sanko Shoten, Tokyo, 1917.

"Storm." *"Arashi."* 1926. Tr. Ineko Sato. *Eigo Seinen,* vol. 90, nos. 11–12, 1944; vol. 91, nos. 2–3, 1945.

"Tsugaru Strait." *"Tsugaru kaikyō."* Tr. Torao Taketomo. *Paulownia, Seven Stories from Contemporary Japanese Writers.*

Poetry

"At Komoro's Old Castle; Beside the Chikuma River." Tr. Shigeshi Nishimura. *The Current of the World,* vol. 28, nos. 3–4, 1951.

"By the Old Castle at Komoro" (extract). *Modern Japanese Poetry,* tr. Donald Keene. Center for Japanese Studies, University of Michigan, Ann Arbor, 1964.

"By the Old Castle at Komoro; Song of Travel on the Chikuma River; Coconut." Tr. Geoffrey Bownas and Anthony Thwaite. *The Penguin Book of Japanese Verse.* Penguin Books, Harmondsworth, 1964.

"Drunken Song." Tr. Shigeshi Nishimura. *The Current of the World,* vol. 15, no. 6, 1938.

"First Love; By the Ancient Castle at Komoro." Tr. S. Sato and C. Urdang. *Poetry,* May 1956.

"In a Birdless Land." Tr. Shigeshi Nishimura. *The Current of the World,* vol. 30, no. 7, 1953.

"Kani no kodomo." Tr. Howard Norman. *The Youth's Companion,* vol. 3, no. 3, 1948.

"Like a Fox; A Coconut." *An Anthology of Modern Japanese Poetry,* ed. and tr. Ichiro Kono and Rikutaro Fukuda. Kenkyusha, Tokyo, 1957.

"Mountain Spirit; Tree Spirit." *The Spirit of Japanese Poetry.* Tr. Yone Noguchi. John Murray, London, 1914.

"On the Carved Vines and Squirrel at the Zuiganji Temple of Matsushima." Tr. Shigeshi Nishi-mura. *The Current of the World,* vol. 28, no. 12, 1951.

"Otsuta." Tr. D. J. Enright. *Bulletin of the Japan Society of London,* no. 20, Oct. 1955.

"Otsuta; In the Birdless Country; Crafty Fox; First Love; A Coco-nut." *The Poetry of Living Japan,* by Takamichi Ninomiya and D. J. Enright. John Murray, Lon-don, 1957.

"The Six Maidens." Tr. Shigeshi Nishimura. *Eibungaku Shicho,* vol. 25, no. 1, 1952.

"Song on Traveling the Chikuma River." Tr. Donald Keene. *Modern Japanese Literature,* ed. D. Keene. Grove Press, NY, 1956; Tuttle, Tokyo, 1967; Grove Wei-denfeld, NY, 1989, paperback.

"Songs of Labour." Tr. Shigeshi Nishimura. *Eibungaku Shicho,* vol. 24, no. 2, 1952, Aoyama Gakuin University.

"2 Poems." Translated from the French by Unity Evans. *Japanese Literature.* Walker, NY, 1965.

"Wakanashu, Collection of Young Names." *Introduction to Classic Japanese Literature.* Kokusai Bunka Shinkokai, Tokyo, 1948.

"Shimazaki Tōson's Four Collec-tions of Poems." 44 pages. Tr. James R. Morita. *Monumenta Nipponica,* vol. 25, nos. 37–38, 1977.

"A Coconut." Tr. Hisayuki Ide-maru. *Poetry Nippon,* nos. 37–38, 1977.

"First Love; Tide Sounds; Voyage Over a Sea of Clouds." Tr. James Kirkup. *Modern Japanese Poetry,* ed. A. R. Davis. University of Queensland Press, St. Lucia, Australia, 1978.

"Song for the Burial of my Mother; Birdless Country; The Coconut; Thoughts of a Traveler on the Chikuma River." Tr. Burton Watson. *From the Country of Eight Islands.* 1981.

Essays

"The Art of Writing." Tr. Takamasa Sasaki. *Eigo no Kenkyu to Kyoju.* Tokyo, 1940.

Chikuma River Sketches. *Chiku-magawa no Suketchi.* 1901–1904. 288 pages. Tr. William E. Naff. University of Hawaii Press, Honolulu, 1991.

CRITICAL STUDIES

McClellan, Edwin. "The Novels of Shimazaki Tōson." *Harvard Journal of Asiatic Studies,* no. 24, 1962–63.

———. "Tōson and the Autobio-graphical Novel." *Tradition and Modernity in Japanese Culture,* 1971.

———. *Two Japanese Novelists: Sōseki and Tōson.* University of Chicago Press, Chicago, 1969; Tuttle, Tokyo, 1971.

Naff, William Edward. *Shimazaki Tōson: An Introduction.* University of Washington Press, Seattle, 1973.

———. "Shimazaki Tōson: A Critical Biography." Ph.D. diss., Univer-sity of Washington, Seattle, 1965.

Roggendorf, Joseph. "Shimazaki Tōson, A Maker of the Modern Japanese Novel." *Monumenta Nip-ponica,* no. 7, 1951.

Seigle, Cecilia Segawa. "An Integral Translation with an Introduction of 'Ie' by Shimazaki Tōson." Ph.D. diss., University of Pennsylvania, Philadelphia, 1971.

Walker, Janet Anderson. "The East-West Context of Shimazaki Tōson's *Shinsei* (The New Life): A Study in the Modern Confessional Novel." Ph.D. diss., Harvard Uni-versity, Cambridge, 1974.

TANIZAKI Jun'ichirō
(1886–1965)

Novelist and essayist. Born in Tokyo. Moved to the Osaka area after the *Great Tokyo Earthquake in 1923.

Tanizaki Jun'ichirō was a literary genius whose brilliance as a writer of fiction earned him a worldwide reputation. Yet, although he was frequently nominated for the Nobel Prize for Literature, he was never awarded it, perhaps because the committee found his novels so pleasurable to read. Hardly ever did he address a social, political, or philosophical issue. Rather, he wrote about men's obsessions with cruel and beautiful women, deriving from this perennial theme an astonishing number of variations. He wove complex plots, created lifelike characters, and commanded an exceptionally wide range of expressive prose styles. Indeed, so complete was his mastery of the essential elements of fiction that a convincing argument can be made for ranking him as one of the finest of all the world's great storytellers.

In English, there is scarcely any inferior work by Tanizaki despite the fact that he is one of the most widely translated of modern

Japanese novelists. His classic story *"Shisei"* (*1910*, "Tattoo") was the first to reach the West (in 1917), eventually to be followed in 1935 by *Shunkin shō* (*1933, A Portrait of Shunkin*) and in the following year by *Ashikari* (*1932, Ashikari*, first translated as *Autumn Moon*). In the postwar years many of his later novels were also translated, first by Edward Seidensticker who produced an immaculate version of the vast, 530-page domestic saga, *Sasame yuki* (*1943–48, The Makioka Sisters*), and then by Howard Hibbett who in the 1960s translated not only the daringly experimental novel *Kagi* (*1956, The Key*), but also many stories collected in a volume called *Seven Japanese Tales*, and finally the last, sublime work, *Fūten rōjin nikki* (*1961–62, Diary of a Mad Old Man*).

There followed a lull in the translation of Tanizaki's works at this point, for a fair cross section of his work had already been made available. Yet just as the elderly protagonist of *Diary of a Mad Old Man* refused to die and thus satisfy all the requirements of Western literary taste, so Tanizaki's popularity continued to grow in the West. His delightful early novel *Chijin no ai* (*1925, Naomi*) appeared on both sides of the Atlantic and even became the basis for a play in London's fringe theater. Even into the 1990s hitherto unpublished stories continued to appear, Paul McCarthy becoming the latest in a long line of translators to carry the torch for this most entertaining, sophisticated, and resilient of novelists.

Some of the qualities for which Tanizaki is most admired are apparent in his extended essay *"In'ei raisan"* (*1933–34*, "In Praise of Shadows"). It is one of the finest essays in *any* language, and the reader who wishes to understand traditional Japanese aesthetics is urged to seek it out. Discussing such topics as architecture, drama, and the complexions of women after bathing, Tanizaki here reveals a sensibility that is at once vigorous and sensitive in equal proportions. It is for contact with such an exceptional sensibility that one reads and enjoys him, for no one is more uncompromising or more subtle than Tanizaki. Both these aspects of his genius find expression in this, his greatest essay, as indeed they always do in his fiction. His masculine vitality is controlled and directed by a feminine delicacy in such a way that it seems to echo the most fundamental processes of nature itself. As a prose writer, this remarkable combination is his greatest strength. His essays and stories unfold like healthy ferns achieving their intricate patterns in smooth but unpredictable movements.

Tanizaki was born in 1886 into a merchant family that had lived in Edo (Tokyo) for many generations. His mother was very beautiful by the standards of Old Japan, and she undoubtedly had an influence on her son that came perilously close to provoking an

Oedipal complex in him. "Mother loved to dress me up," he wrote in his memoir *Yōshō jidai* (posthumously published in 1966–68, and later translated as *Childhood Years*), "and almost anything could be made an occasion for a display of my finery. 'Today let's make you look really nice,' she'd say, opening a chest of drawers and taking out some carefully wrapped garment. As the cool silk of the singlet touched my skin, my whole body would start to tingle." In such terms does Tanizaki describe his formative influences, always with humor and often with intense but typically understated emotion. For example, he ends this passage by saying: "It all made me very happy; and Mother seemed happier still, turning me this way and that as she gazed at me."

With his appearance thus enhanced by his mother's attention, Tanizaki was often the butt of sexual innuendo at school, yet he remained strongly, even obsessively, heterosexual. He was also extremely precocious, though one must allow for the fact that in penning his memoirs the mature writer may have embellished the infant's sensibility. His admiration for beautiful women, for example, was by no means limited to his mother. He was especially influenced by the *geisha* O-sumi who came to live with the family as the mistress of his uncle. She tended to behave very naturally in front of Tanizaki because he was "too young to count." As a result, his image of femininity was greatly enriched. ". . . I sensed something in O-sumi, despite her air of diligence as she performed household tasks, her kimono sleeves tied back for work. In the way she held herself and the movements of her hands and feet, I was aware of a sensuous charm that I had never found in my mother or my aunts. Now for the first time I realized the difference between a geisha and an ordinary woman."

The Tanizaki family's fortune had been originally founded by his maternal grandfather Kyūemon, who was also notable for being a member of the Russian Orthodox Church and for keeping a mistress "without Grandmother's knowing anything about it." A onetime kettle-maker and innkeeper, Kyūemon had switched to printing and publishing – making a lot of money from his daily price list for rice dealers – before going on to start a lamp-lighting business. This latter concern was entrusted to Tanizaki's father, an adopted husband who married the youngest of Kyūemon's three daughters. It was promptly sold because Tanizaki's father was hopeless at business. Only the energetic efforts of an uncle, the one who "had an eye for beautiful women" and who introduced O-sumi into the family, preserved the family's fortune for an all-too-brief period.

Tanizaki began his school career at the Kogishi Kindergarten, followed, in 1892, by the Sakamoto Primary School where on the first day he created "endless problems" for the headmaster by crying (". . . there was no other crybaby quite on my scale"). As time went by, however, it became apparent to everyone that little Jun'ichirō was exceptionally intelligent and remarkably creative. Four years older than his brother, Seiji, he always remained ahead of him in most areas of life. Although his brother, too, entered the literary world in later life, he made no lasting impact on it. From the outset it was Jun'ichirō who developed rapidly, becoming a star pupil at school, and writing poems in classical Chinese to praise a victory over the enemy in the Sino-Japanese war of 1894–95.

Few incidents are more telling of Tanizaki's approach to life and literature than his description (again in *Childhood Years*) of an earthquake in the summer of 1894. He describes how it struck at around two o'clock in the afternoon, and how, clutching a writing brush, he ran out into the middle of the road with his mother, terrified of being crushed by falling buildings. "As we stood in the middle of the intersection, holding on to one another as we swayed back and forth, I began to move the brush, tracing lines in black ink upon my mother's breast." Apart from the fact that only Tanizaki could successfully bring sex and a hint of incest into a description of a natural disaster, there is also a curious sense that he is reinventing a half-remembered historical episode for the benefit of his readers. In later life, Tanizaki became the preeminent historical novelist of his day, and he always considered history – even academic history – to be virtually a branch of fiction. He believed that the past was gone forever and that no amount of historical research could ever produce more than a plausible semblance of it.

Taught by a Mr. Inaba at the beginning and end of his primary school career, Tanizaki was introduced to a wide range of literature, including Ueda Akinari's *Ugetsu monogatari* (1768, *Tales of Rain and Moonlight*) and the novels of Yano Ryūkei (1850–1931). He was also struck by *Bakin's *Chinsetsu Yumiharizuki* (*The Crescent Moon*), and recalled that "Mr. Inaba's own skill in the telling was enough to make our palms begin to sweat." If one believes that a love of stories is inculcated at an early age, then Japanese letters owes much to the immortalized Mr. Inaba whose educational methods, according to Tanizaki, were "designed to produce a kind of child prodigy." As regards literature, however, it was Iwaya Sazanami's *New Hakkenden*, which began its serialization in a children's magazine in 1898, that was the most important early influence on Tanizaki. He said: "It was the work that gave me my first real taste of the pleasures of fiction – the creation of an imaginary world, and the joys of entering into it and wandering freely there."

The other major influences on the young Tanizaki were the novels of KŌDA ROHAN, especially *Tai dokuro* (1890, *Encounter with a Skull*), and the *Kabuki theater, to which he was often taken by his grandmother. A decline in the family fortunes from 1896 onwards prevented him from frequenting the theater as much as he would have liked, but by this time he had already seen many of the great actors of the day. He graduated from elementary school in 1901, passed from junior high to high school in 1905, and entered Tokyo Imperial University in 1908. By this time he had already published his first story, *"Shumpū shūu roku"* (1903, "Account of Spring Breezes and Autumn Roads"). Written from personal experience in a style influenced by Rohan and OZAKI KŌYŌ, it describes how his father tried to dissuade him from continuing his education. Predictably, the boy had burst into tears, lamenting the thought of entering military or business life. He wrote: "Ever since I was a small child I had disliked military men most of all human beings, and businessmen next." His insistence on pursuing literature at university – giving up the legal studies of his high school period – suggests a strong will and a clear vision of his potential as a writer.

At this point it must be said that the idea of Tanizaki's "pursuing literary studies" at university is somewhat misleading, for he was notoriously lax in attending his classes. He much preferred exploring the pleasure quarters of Tokyo, where he consorted with prostitutes and eventually found himself requiring medical treatment for venereal disease. In a bid to make amends he began writing seriously, hoping to make money from his efforts. Although money was slow in coming, his first effort was very successful from an artistic point of view. *"Shisei"* ("Tattoo") was first published in the 1910 issue of the university literary magazine *Shinshichō* (*New Thought Tides*). Set in the *Tokugawa period so that its decadent and highly charged atmosphere would be suitably enhanced, the story tells of how a tattooer becomes enslaved by a beautiful girl whom he selects originally to be the victim of his cruel skill. We are told that the tattooer, Seikichi, is a former painter who still preserves "the true spirit of an artist with great sensitivity." His secret ambition is "to have under his needle the lustrous skin of some beautiful girl, on which he dreamed of tattooing, as it were, his very soul." He finds his ideal woman on a summer's evening when he catches a glimpse of "a feminine foot of dazzling whiteness disappearing behind the curtains of a palanquin." Later, he meets her again, puts her to sleep with a narcotic, and tattoos a large vermilion spider on her back. When she awakes, bathes, and dresses, and comes to Seikichi, she says: "Master, my heart is now free from all fear. And you. . .you shall be my first victim."

"Tattoo" is an enduring classic partly because, being set in the past and containing a strong supernatural element, it was never tainted with the everyday reality of the "here and now." Its author recoiled strongly from the prevailing *Naturalism of the period and championed the otherwise lonely cause of IZUMI KYŌKA, a former *Ken'yūsha writer who continued to spin intricate stories of the supernatural in ornate, and by all accounts, "untranslatable" language. Kyōka's influence on Tanizaki was greater even than that of Rohan or Kōyō, and one has only to read the older man's famous story "Sannin no mekura no hanashi" (1912, "The Tale of Three Who Were Blind") to glimpse the imaginative world that so excited the young Tanizaki.

Having conjured up a *femme fatale* from the netherworld of his own psyche, Tanizaki found that she positively reveled in taking her revenge. It was a wholly natural process. Throughout his life he maintained a sado-masochistic relationship with his *anima*, each of them taking turns to be cruel to the other. In nearly all of his stories, from the first to the last, he and his feminine projection are engaged in their duet of cruelty, a duet which, sometimes inexplicably, never seems to lapse into bad taste.

Accomplished though it was, "Tattoo" did not bring instant recognition to Tanizaki. He went on to write other stories with similar, sadistic elements, producing *"Shōnen"* (1911, "The Children") in which a group of boys and one girl, Mitsuko, play games of dominance and subjection. Victimized by the boys in their earlier games, Mitsuko eventually makes them her slaves, inducing them in the end to commit quite unpleasant acts of coprophilia. In another story of the same year, called *"Kirin"* (1911, "The Kylin"), Tanizaki created a historical narrative, depicting the sojourn of Confucius in the dukedom of Wei. With this seemingly unpromising material he soon arrived at his favorite topic, for under the sage's influence the Duke neglects his consort, Nan-tzu, and she in turn threatens to seek a cruel revenge. Unable to allow Nan-tzu to inflict torture on the visiting sage, the Duke is obliged to give up the good work on which he had embarked and return to his consort's bed. Nan-tzu's victory is complete and Confucius quietly leaves them, having had a very narrow escape.

As the months went by, 1911 was rapidly becoming a tumultuous year for Tanizaki, with highs and lows that he never anticipated. He was devastated by the death of his sister who succumbed to tuberculosis; he suffered a nervous breakdown; and, to make matters worse, was expelled from university because he failed to pay his tuition fees. However, on the good side, he remained highly creative and published an erotic story called *"Hyōfū"* (1911, "Whirlwind") in the October issue of *Mita bungaku* (*Mita Literature*). Unfortunately, it was so explicit that the police authorities banned it and confiscated all the issues of the magazine. Tanizaki's career did not suffer unduly from the misadventure and the notoriety may even have brought him more quickly to the attention of other editors. Shortly afterwards he was invited by Takita Choin to contribute to *Chūō kōron* (*Central Review*), for which he wrote a story called *"Himitsu"* ("A Secret"). In this the main protagonist dresses up as a woman, goes to the theater, and accidentally encounters his former mistress who, to his dismay, outshines him in elegance. Clearly, Tanizaki had no intention of diluting his audacious themes more than was necessary.

Already popular with editors and readers alike, Tanizaki received a valuable accolade from the novelist NAGAI KAFŪ in November of 1911. Writing in *Mita bungaku*, Kafū praised three specific characteristics of Tanizaki's fiction: its "profound beauty distilled from carnal terror," its urbanity, and the perfection of its style. He stated that Tanizaki was an original and even unique writer who had the genius to venture into territory neglected by others. To Kafū the younger man's fiction was genuinely refreshing after the repetitive efforts of the Naturalists with their insistence on the humdrum aspects of daily life. Indeed, by singling out Tanizaki's "urbanity" he was deliberately attacking the Naturalists whom he (and, for that matter, Tanizaki) considered to be bumpkins up from the country, out of their depth in the big city.

In later years, Kafū and Tanizaki did not always see eye to eye, but each enjoyed reading the other's works. Looking back on his life in one of his last essays, Tanizaki noted some of the differences in their background and outlook. Kafū, he said, had quite a different attitude to women, regarding them as inferior instead of looking up to them as he, Tanizaki, did. Moreover, Kafū was much more wealthy and thus able to travel extensively in the West. Tanizaki himself never traveled far abroad, visiting only China, in 1918 and 1926. Indeed, the only vital connection between the two writers was their mutual belief in "art above all." In 1916 Tanizaki had written that art came first and life second, and in this Kafū wholeheartedly concurred.

Jōtarō (1914, *Jōtarō*) was Tanizaki's next major work, a short novel that was highly praised by his friend Satō Haruo. Like many of the early stories it has not been translated into English although it is especially interesting from a biographical point of view. The central figure, Izumi Jōtarō, is a celebrated writer who is inclined towards laziness and nihilism. Only in the discovery of sensuous beauty does he find anything of value. To amuse himself he tries to corrupt his disciple, Shōji, but without much success. Eventually he decides that what he really wants is fulfillment of his masochistic urges, and to this end he finds Onui, a girl who is willing to whip and beat him in exchange for money. Her wickedness gives him immense pleasure, which is enhanced rather than spoiled when he finds out that she and Shōji were once lovers. Now reunited, Shōji and Onui all but destroy Jōtarō, until, driven to penury by Onui's demands, the writer retreats to his family home for comfort and protection.

Jōtarō merely confirmed Tanizaki's reputation as an "immoralist" or "diabolist," and although it is clearly a work of fiction there is little doubt that it portrays his essential feelings and sexual preferences. In view of these aberrations it is perhaps surprising that Tanizaki chose to get married when he did. The marriage, needless to say, was not a success. He and his first wife were divorced in 1930 in circumstances that can only be described as unusual. According to Satō Haruo, the writer who so admired *Jōtarō*, Tanizaki turned to him one evening after dinner and suggested: "How would you like to marry O-Chiyo?" This was not entirely an off-the-cuff remark, for Satō had been in love with O-Chiyo for years. However, it did help to heal a long-standing rift between the two friends and enabled Satō to marry the first Mrs. Tanizaki.

After the publication of *Jōtarō*, Tanizaki produced some other works that were more directly autobiographical, including *Oni no men* (1916, *The Devil Mask*) and *Itansha no kanashimi* (1917, *The Sadness of the Rebel*). The latter, as Tanizaki explained, was much more faithful to real life and to actual people than anything else he had written. It was, he said, "My only book of confessions." He described the years in which he had struggled to become a writer, when he lived in squalid conditions, argued with his father, and consistently borrowed money from his friends to indulge his deviant sexuality. The entire work shows him in a very bad light, as if he were determined to expose the worst side of his character in an act of self-humiliation.

The work that changed the course of Tanizaki's career was *Chijin no ai* (1925, *A Fool's Love*, translated as *Naomi*). The Great Earthquake of 1923 had obliged him to move from the Yokohama "Bluff" – the heart of the foreign community – to Osaka, where he intended to stay for a short period while life in the Tokyo area returned to normal. In the event, he stayed in Osaka for the rest of his life, settling there to produce works of fiction that were altogether more balanced, more fully imagined, and more successful as works of art than anything he had produced previously.

Naomi was the culmination, and, in a sense, a rejection of Tanizaki's recent infatuation with all things Western. It is a contemporary tale of an engineer called Kawai, a man in his early thirties who decides to acquire a teenage mistress. He finds a girl called Naomi, a fifteen-year-old who comes from a poor family and has the engaging qualities of long limbs, Eurasian looks, and a playful personality. Rapidly, Kawai becomes addicted to her as though to a powerful drug. She, in turn, demands expensive clothes and begins to torment him with jealousy when she flirts with other men. In fact, although Kawai is never aware of it, Naomi understands perfectly his sexual psychology and has no hesitation in using it to her advantage. Not until the end do we see how strong, balanced, and therefore beautiful is their relationship. For not only is Naomi the perfect partner for Kawai; the reverse is also true. Without Kawai, Naomi's sexual exploits with other men would be unrewarding in the extreme.

Throughout *Naomi* there are many ironical allusions to Japan's obsession with Western culture. In particular, the scenes that depict dancing lessons with Madame Shlemskaya are unforgettable. Yet it would be wrong to overemphasize the satirical aspects, for the novel is primarily an investigation of sexual "balance and imbalance." On this level *Naomi* is as valid today as when it was first written. Issued by Western publishers some sixty years after its appearance in Japan, it was a welcome addition to the growing library of Tanizaki's translated works.

The story of *Naomi*'s original publication is perhaps also worth noting because the novel caused a sensation in Japan during the 1920s. It began its serial publication in the Osaka *Asahi shimbun* in 1924 and was not only widely read but also widely condemned. Conservative elements of society were not quite ready for a story of a young temptress, who, in superficially mimicking Western ways, leads a life of complete amorality. The newspaper was forced to cease its publication of the story and readers had to wait nine months before chapter 16 could be resumed in the magazine *Josei*. One doubts if Tanizaki was upset by the delay. After all, the torture of sexual tantalization was the mainspring of the novel, and prolonging the agony of its publication only enhanced its notoriety. So successful was it that "Naomism" entered the Japanese language as a legitimate word.

A remarkable change had come over Tanizaki since his removal to Osaka. He had completely lost his infatuation with Western culture and had fallen in love with the food, the customs, and especially the women of the Kansai region. This change in his attitude greatly affected both the content and the style of his novels. For example, *Manji* (1928–30, *Whirlpool*) is narrated in the Osaka dialect and is set squarely among the upper classes of the region. Its plot, made devious by the machinations of the novel's four main protagonists, is intended to resemble the shape of the Chinese character *manji*, a Buddhist swastika or "whirlpool." In showing the same events from different points of view, the novel is more intricate than anything Tanizaki had created hitherto: evidence that his powers as a storyteller were growing.

Tade kuu mushi (1929, *Some Prefer Nettles*), the novel that followed *Manji*, shows Tanizaki at his best. It is the story of how Kaname, a Tokyo man whose marriage is failing, discovers the fleeting, nostalgic beauty of Old Japan when he is introduced to the culture of Osaka by his father-in-law. In turning back to the indigenous culture of Japan he also discovers much within himself that he has not previously recognized, especially in matters of aesthetic taste. For example, he begins to neglect the more obvious attractions of his Eurasian mistress, Louisa, and becomes fascinated by the wan beauty of O-hisa, his father-in-law's introverted and very old-fashioned mistress. The author shows Kaname in the process of rediscovering his true identity, as suggested by the title which is taken from an old proverb: "Every worm to his taste; some prefer nettles." (*Tade* is actually a bitter herb which the Japanese sometimes eat as a garnish with raw fish).

As the novel's translator, Edward Seidensticker, points out: "The real theme of *Some Prefer Nettles* is the clash between the new and the old, the imported and the domestic." Furthermore, the reader's interest is no longer held only by the actions of the characters but by their cultural context as well. "Unhurried, isn't it?" remarks Kaname's father-in-law as they watch a traditional puppet theater. Kaname agrees, and the narrative continues: "Relaxed, unhurried – the words quite took in the mood of the place." So magical is the mood that Kaname finds himself recalling a visit to a temple when he was a child. "The voices of the children playing outside, the awnings of the little festival shops, the candy shops and the comic-mask shops, shining like stained glass in the sun – all the sounds and impressions from the street and the temple yard melted into the slow, genial sounds of the recitation and the twanging accompaniment on the stage with one quiet, liquid movement. . . . It was as if a hundred formless and uncollected dreams were passing through his mind, the dreaming and the waking fused one into the other. . . . Call it a taste of the joys of great peace, call it a transport to some fairyland, it was a feeling of serene removal from the world such as Kaname had not felt since the day he had been taken, still a child, to see the Kagura dancing at the Shrine of the Sea God in the old downtown section of Tokyo."

The above passage (which has been abbreviated) is quoted because it typifies the hypnotic charm of Tanizaki's best fiction.

Here he communicates, as he so often does, a sense of falling
through many planes of memory until life is connected and made
whole again. He makes his appeal to all the senses, bringing in the
"lazy warmth" of the sun, the various sounds, and the freshness of
the air. The experience is, of course, a momentary escape into
childhood memories, but it is much more than a mere description
of it. It is an evocation of the experience so finely constructed that
it can trigger exactly the same feeling in the reader. The pleasure
that it gives is similar to that which can be obtained from reading
the classics of the *Heian period. Entering that world, too, is like
visiting the Garden of Eden. It reverses the expulsion.

Attention has already been drawn to the combination of vigor
and sensitivity in Tanizaki's fiction. These masculine and feminine
elements find their expression, respectively, in the structure of his
stories and in the impressionistic techniques he uses for creating
character. Tanizaki's vigorous sense of structure is one of his
strongest assets. In a famous controversy with AKUTAGAWA RYŪNO-
SUKE he stated: "The greatest weakness of Japanese novelists is that
they have no power to construct, no talent for the geometry of
building up a complicated plot." He was impatient with Akutagawa
for always writing on a small scale and considered that only Izumi
Kyōka among living writers had any talent for plot construction. In
this aspect of fiction Tanizaki can match any Western writer and
his ingenuity is boundless.

In characterization, however, he shows a completely different
aspect of his genius. Far from seeking to emulate Western techniques
he is altogether more natural and intuitive. His characters spring
to life, not because he delineates them exactly but because he leaves
so much to our imagination. On one occasion, when someone
criticized him for not explaining a character's inner thoughts and
motivations, he remarked: "But why should I discuss his psychology?
Can't the reader guess from what I've already told him?" Indeed,
his approach to characterization parallels that of a dramatist who
seeks to reveal character entirely through dialogue and action. He
goes, perhaps, one stage further, combining the talents of both
dramatist *and* actor, and in so doing can indicate a person's inner
nature by the slightest gesture. The opening lines of J. C. Powys's
Confessions (1916) can well be applied to Tanizaki's technique: "It
is the little thing, the unrehearsed gesture, the catch in the breath,
the droop of the lip, the start of surprise, which really reveals. We
may analyze ourselves in volumes and remain undiscovered; and
then – by a yawn, a tilt of the head, a sob of exhaustion, a flash of
hate – we are betrayed and unmasked forever."

Brilliant as he was at plot construction and characterization,

Tanizaki also excelled in one other aspect of writing fiction. As a prose stylist he had command of an extraordinary variety of styles. Like the connoisseur he was, he would select whichever style he felt was most appropriate to the task in hand and employ it consistently throughout. Fascinated by this subject he went on to write a textbook on style called *Bunshō tokuhon* (1934, *The Composition Reader*) in which he identified "flowing," "airy," "craggy," "laconic," "conversational," and even "military" styles: any one of which might, on the right occasion, be used profitably by an aspiring writer. In his own fiction he showed a marked preference, first for the flowing style, which is akin to that found in *The Tale of Genji*, and second, for a freer conversational idiom through which his distinctive voice could be heard more easily.

Tanizaki's belief that every novel should, as a basic prerequisite, hold the reader's attention in a vicelike grip, led him into the realm of popular literature. He conceived a gigantic saga called *Rangiku monogatari* (*1930, A Cascade of Chrysanthemums*) which, although running to 148 installments, never reached the point at which the main character was supposed to appear. The novel is notable chiefly for being the author's first major attempt to set his fiction in the distant historical past. He chose the sixteenth century because not many people knew much about it, thus allowing himself the freedom to embellish and invent.

In the early 1930s Tanizaki's work became much more polished, complex, and accomplished. Literary historians usually point to *Yoshino kuzu* (*1931, Arrowroot*) as representing a turning point, although several of his previous stories had foreshadowed the change. For example, the episode quoted earlier from *Some Prefer Nettles*, in which Kaname falls through the different planes of memory, is very much like the structure of *Yoshino kuzu*. Not only do childhood memories form the inspiration for the novel, but many different layers of historical time are either represented or referred to, including the twelfth, fifteenth, eighteenth, and nineteenth centuries. The narrator, like many of the narrators in Tanizaki's later works, finds himself witness to a strange and intricate story in which recent history is linked, through theater and literature, to the myths of the distant past.

Not only were there changes to Tanizaki's art in the early 1930s, in his life, too, there was rearrangement. His divorce of 1930 has already been mentioned, and he remarried in 1931. Again, it appears that he made the same mistake as before in choosing a woman who could be too easily dominated. Within months of his wedding to Tomiko he was already writing to the woman who would become his third wife and confessing his love for her. She, Mrs. Nezu

Matsuko, was the inspiration for much of his best work from this time onwards. In admitting that he needed her in order to survive as an artist he said: "Please do not misunderstand me. It is not that you exist for the sake of my art but that my art exists for you." They began living together and were eventually married in 1935.

Tanizaki's great historical stories of the 1930s are classics of modern literature. They are also, alas, too complex to be analyzed here in the detail they deserve. *Mōmoku monogatari* (*1931, A Blind Man's Tale*) is narrated by an old, blind masseur who has, since the events of the tale, become a wandering entertainer who goes from inn to inn recounting his story while massaging his clients. There is a wonderful irony in "seeing" the tumultuous events that led to the Tokugawa shōgunate "through the eyes" of a blind man. The device is especially effective because the narrator, as the favorite servant to Oda Nobunaga's sister, has been uniquely acquainted with the personal lives of the great feudal lords, including both Nobunaga and his successor Toyotomi Hideyoshi (1536–98). The novel is a miracle of storytelling, given the intricacies of Japanese medieval history. Without giving away too much one can draw attention to its graceful ending: for the whole account is at that point revealed as the reminiscence of the masseur long after the events he has described have retreated into the dim recesses of history. Indeed, the entire era of Tokugawa Ieyasu (1542–1616) has since come and gone. It is as though the narative has, with the aid of a magical telescope, taken us right into the midst of Japan's most famous historical period – so close that we can actually touch the characters, vicariously, through the masseur's fingers. Then, by reversing the instrument, the author compels us to see it all from a different perspective: as a view of a distant time re-created by a powerful imagination.

Bushūkō hiwa (*1931–32, The Secret History of the Lord of Musashi*) is the first of Tanizaki's historical "detective" stories, in which the narrator locates secret documents that give us a new insight into some aspect of history. In this case, the documents reveal the true sexual psyche of the protagonist, a sixteenth-century samurai hero called Terukatsu. As a boy of thirteen he is witness to a great battle during a siege of the castle in which he is staying. In a remarkable scene he is taken deep into the castle to see women washing the severed heads of dead enemy soldiers. He is particularly struck by the sight of one girl who handles a head with its nose cut off. Clearly, the image is intended to remind us of castration, for the girl refers to it as a "woman-head." From that moment onwards Terukatsu is obsessed with a desire to re-create the scene and "see her smiling face again." In later life, as the story goes on to relate, he succeeds in persuading his gentle wife to commit an act of mutilation on their priest, Doami. We are informed: "To the end of his forty-two years, the lord sought out new women, one after the other, with whom to share his bizarre stimulus and revolting dissipation."

Ashikari (1932, *Ashikari*) is an equally compelling and richly evocative work. In it, Tanizaki finds yet another way to approach the past, by having his narrator travel to the site of the Minabé Palace where the Emperor Gotoba lived before being exiled to the island of Oki. While reading poems written by the emperor, the man is approached by a stranger who proceeds to tell him a story. He describes how, as a ten-year-old boy, he had often been taken by his father to a great mansion thereabouts so that his father could catch a glimpse of the lady of the house. We learn that the Lady Oyū, although merely the daughter of a merchant, was such a beauty that she had been brought up with all the fastidious care once lavished on ladies of the court. Having being left widowed with a son at the age of twenty-two she was forced by social propriety to remain faithful to the memory of her husband. However, the stranger's father had fallen in love with her, and to overcome social convention had married her sister with whom he had "an arrangement." When the young son died, the family compelled Oyū to marry someone other than the stranger's father, who finally consummated his marriage with Oyū's sister. The stranger himself is the product of that marriage – and that very night he is making his annual pilgrimage to watch Oyū from a distance, just as he did as a boy.

So perfect is *Ashikari* that it needs little critical elucidation. Its magic is entirely the result of a subtle evocation of memories, linking, by implication, the life the Emperor Gotoba to that of the Lady Oyū, and in so doing it brings the most distant memories of the past right into the present moment. Written in an archaic style it not only has the mysterious quality of the *Nō but also uses some of the Nō's conventions. Nonetheless, it is distinctively original and very typical of Tanizaki's mature work.

If *Ashikari* is "perfect" one finds oneself running out of words to describe *Shunkin shō* (1933, *A Portrait of Shunkin*). It is a masterpiece of an even higher order: more rich, more varied, and yet still perfectly controlled. Shunkin is a blind *samisen* teacher whose exceptional beauty causes the virtual enslavement of her disciple Sasuke. Their love affair is the only subject of the novel but it takes such unexpected twists and turns that the reader's attention is held from the first page to the last. Along the way one is introduced to a variety of old Japanese customs, such as songbird contests and the many subtleties associated with playing the *koto* and *samisen*. The whole story is infused with the spirit of music, while the author's perennial theme of sexual subjugation is here given an almost divine interpretation.

From 1935 to 1941 Tanizaki worked on his modern-language version of *The Tale of Genji*, a monumental work that left him virtually no time for creating fiction of his own. Since he never ventured into the political arena there was no external reason compelling him to turn from fiction to translation. But clearly the work of rendering *Murasaki's classic into modern prose was one that satisfied something deep within him. Like the narrators of his stories he needed a vital connection with the past and wanted his name to be linked forever with Japan's greatest writer. The first version of his translation appeared between the years 1939 and 1941, on the eve of war in the Pacific.

During the war, Tanizaki set himself another huge task: the creation of his longest and in many ways most remarkable work, *Sasame yuki (1943–48, The Makioka Sisters)*. It was actually a historical novel, not of the distant past but of 1930s Osaka society. As such it was, and is, a complete picture, so carefully drawn that the reader is transported to that particular time and place for the duration of its narrative. A lengthy work by any standards, *The Makioka Sisters* provides one of the most sustained and enjoyable reading experiences in the whole of Japanese fiction.

That such a distinguished historical novelist as Tanizaki, writing in the 1940s, should set his most ambitious novel in the previous decade was an indication (if any were needed) of the pace of change in Japan this century. Because the world around him was changing so quickly Tanizaki wished to preserve a picture of it before it faded in his memory. He also had the great advantage of having observed his material at first hand, for many of the events of the novel were drawn from his own experience. Indeed, Sachiko, the second eldest of the four sisters, is based on his third wife, Matsuko.

Readers who are more accustomed to European or American novels may, at first acquaintance, find *The Makioka Sisters* relatively formless in its structure. There appears to be no plot whatsoever, although the author clearly has innumerable ways of moving his story forward without resorting to ostensible contrivance. This apparent formlessness is, however, quite deliberate – as one would expect from such a master of structure. Tanizaki wanted his novel to flow as smoothly as does *The Tale of Genji*, the classic that was etched permanently in his imagination, and the structure of his novel had to be so transparent that it could contain the real lives of his characters.

From the very beginning of the novel the personalities of the four sisters are evoked with magical skill. Tsuruko, the eldest with a large family of her own, lives with her husband in what is considered to be the "main house" of the Makioka family in Osaka. If tradition were to be rigidly upheld, both Yukiko and Taeko, the two unmarried sisters (aged thirty and twenty-five, respectively), would live there too, yet they both prefer to stay in the more congenial and less crowded home of Sachiko and her husband, Teinosuke. The novel's plot, such as it is, is entirely concerned with finding a suitable husband for Yukiko, for until that has been accomplished, the youngest daughter cannot in turn be married. Yukiko, although beautiful, has remained a spinster by virtue of an unfortunate series of circumstances, and for the past ten years every single marriage proposal has been rejected by the proud Makiokas. The family are, of course, much *too* proud and too intent on keeping up appearances since the death of their patriarch and the subsequent sale of their business. They realize that they cannot aim "too high" in finding a match for Yukiko, yet their breeding makes them acutely aware of aiming "too low." To compound the difficulty, Yukiko herself is totally intractable. Although she has only the power of veto in this matter of a husband, she has frequently used it. She is also quite stubbornly old-fashioned, being as passive and "correct" in her behavior as any high-born lady of the past.

Even though *The Makioka Sisters* has little or no intellectual content it compels our attention for the artistry expended on its characterization. Its female characters are among the most convincing ever created in literature. Into each of them Tanizaki has breathed the breath of life, and each one is a unique spirit. Indeed, the author is so confident of his ability to evoke personality that he is able to attribute tastes to his characters that are wholly "out of character" – and does so without any danger of the inconsistencies becoming unacceptable. Thus, we learn halfway through the book that the ultra-traditional Yukiko actually prefers Western food. This is an extraordinary revelation, given that she may be said to represent all those ancient virtues that were even then disappearing from Japanese life. Equally, we are surprised to discover that the home-loving Sachiko (whose life revolves around the family and whose family revolves around her) takes a great interest in world affairs by reading the newspapers avidly. No previous hint has been given that she has any such interest, and in another novel it might well sound a jarring note. But here such revelations only add to the characters' reality. Each unexpected piece of information brings another dimension to them, increasing the illusion that we know them as real human beings.

Another element that contributes to the artistic success of *The Makioka Sisters* is the presence of a foreign family next door to Sachiko's home. Mr. and Mrs. Stolz and their children are German, and their behavior is more adaptable than that of their Japanese neighbors. Although they can be rigidly polite and formal when the occasion calls for it, they are much less hidebound in their attitudes. As a foil to the Makioka family they are ideal. They even help to tie the novel into its proper period by returning to Germany shortly before the outbreak of war, thus giving rise to an excuse for an exchange of correspondence (one of the author's favorite novelistic ploys).

As in most of Tanizaki's later work, Western culture is nonetheless kept at a distance. Most Western things, from dress to "stiff Western stationery" that crackles "like a movie sound effect" when one opens it, are, while not condemned outright, looked upon disapprovingly. For example, the youngest sister Koi-san is shown as having two distinct sides to her. The "good" Koi-san looks best in kimono and makes traditional Japanese dolls, while the "bad" Koi-san is more suited to Western clothes and instructs her boyfriend to steal Western jewelry from his family's shop. Solid Japanese virtues, exemplified in Yukiko and surviving in Osaka rather than Tokyo, comprise the implied morality of the novel. In comparison with Western novels, however, morality is not unduly emphasized. There is nothing puritanical about Yukiko's reluctance to walk unaccompanied with a prospective suitor. One feels that her coolness towards men is nothing more than an accepted formality, and that she will one day become a loving wife like her sister Sachiko. Yukiko's virginity is the "thin snow" of the novel's original Japanese title. In this, and in all other respects, the book lovingly documents an age that had, for its author, already passed.

The only one of Tanizaki's masterpieces never to have been translated fully into English is *Shōshō Shigemoto no haha* (1949–50, *The Mother of Captain Shigemoto*). This is a pity, because, although it is considered to be a difficult work, in Japan it has also been one of the most highly regarded of his novels. As in *The Secret History of the Lord of Musashi*, Tanizaki introduces his tale by depicting an historian uncovering strange secrets of the past. (Incidentally, his oblique method of beginning novels in this way is amazingly successful, and is probably not unconnected with his desire to tantalize the reader before satisfying him in full.) The novel's main story is set in the Heian period and concerns Shigemoto's search for his mother from whom he has been separated since childhood. Like the stranger in *Ashikari* who still seeks a glimpse of his late father's paramour, Shigemoto, too, is acting on his father's behalf.

Robbed of his beloved wife by the statesman Shihei, his father suffered deeply and tried every means – including poetry, wine, and religion – to distract himself from his grief. As Makoto Ueda has said: "It is with relief that one finally reads of his son, Captain Shigemoto, being reunited with his mother, and so saving the old man's soul."

Several years passed before Tanizaki produced another work of fiction, because, between 1951 and 1954, he produced a second translation of *The Tale of Genji*. In 1956, however, he created a sensation with his novel *Kagi* (*The Key*), an intimate account of the sex life of a middle-aged professor and his wife, told in an experimental narrative style. Each of the two main characters keeps a diary and each is aware that the other reads it. The novel is therefore composed entirely of diary extracts: an audacious and risky technique that Tanizaki handled very well. Although it is a minor work, being little more than a diverting entertainment, its original format confirms Tanizaki's status as a virtuoso storyteller.

Tanizaki's urge to experiment continued into his old age and did not end with *The Key*. Shortly before his death he wrote a final masterpiece called *Fūten rōjin nikki* (1961–62, *Diary of a Mad Old Man*). This celebration of senile sexuality is again couched in the form of a diary, written by seventy-seven-year-old Tokusuke who is rapidly failing in health. His chief motivation for clinging to life is his secret erotic obsession with his young daughter-in-law, Satsuko, an ex-chorus girl. She is frivolous, acquisitive, somewhat cruel, and provocatively conceited. The old man, being the author's perverse alter ego, enjoys these qualities in a woman, greatly favoring her over his daughters whose genuine concern for his well-being leaves him exasperated. All he wants is a glimpse of Satsuko's ankle . . . permission to touch her body . . . a fleeting kiss – any one of which may send his blood pressure soaring and increase the pain in his arm.

Diary of a Mad Old Man contains some of Tanizaki's most delightful inventions. For example, Tokusuke decides that his tombstone must be decorated with an image of the Buddha's footprints, an idea supposedly inspired by the famous stone in the Yakushiji Temple at Nara. Actually, he intends that the model for the footprints will be Satsuko's dainty feet! "When she treads on my grave and feels as if she's trampling on that doting old man's bones, my spirit will still be alive, feeling the whole weight of her body, feeling pain, feeling the fine-grained velvety smoothness of the soles of her feet." The author cunningly leads us to believe that Tokusuke's prodigious efforts will finish him off. But no, the novel does not end with the old man's death. It ends with his making plans to reconstruct his Western-style home (Tanizaki had by now resigned himself to Westernization) in order to gain a better view of his daughter-in-law's legs when she bathes in the new swimming pool. No writer ever ended his career with a more triumphant, more cussedly human *adieu*.

RECOMMENDED READING

Novels and novellas

Diary of a Mad Old Man. *Fūten rōjin nikki. 1961–62.* 203 pages. Tr. Howard Hibbett. Knopf, NY, 1965; Secker and Warburg, London, 1966; Tuttle, Tokyo, 1967; G. P. Putnam's Sons, NY, 1981; Oxford University Press, Oxford, 1988; Vintage Paperback, NY, 1991. Tanizaki's last work and one of his best.

The Makioka Sisters. *Sasame yuki* (lit: "Thin Snow"). *1943–48.* 530 pages. Tr. Edward Seidensticker. Extract as "The Firefly Hunt." *Modern Japanese Literature*, ed. Donald Keene. Grove Press, NY, 1956; Tuttle, Tokyo, 1957; Complete novel: Tr. Anthony H. Chambers. Knopf, NY, 1957 and 1985 (tr. Edward Seidensticker); Tuttle, Tokyo, 1958; Grosset Press, NY, 1966; Putnam Publishing Group, NY, 1981 and 1986; Secker and Warburg, London, 1983; Pan Books, London, 1983; North Point Press, San Francisco, 1990, paperback. Highly entertaining saga of an Osaka merchant family.

Naomi. *Chijin no ai. 1925.* 237 pages. Tr. Anthony H. Chambers. Knopf, NY, 1985; Secker and Warburg, London, 1986; Pan Books, London, 1987, paperback. Collectors may wish to obtain both U.S. and U.K. hardcover editions: strikingly different in appearance although each depicts a teenage *femme fatale* on the cover.

A Portrait of Shunkin. *Shunkin shō. 1933.* 81 pages. (1) As "The Story of Shunkin." Tr. Roy Humpherson and Hajime Okita. (Mimeograph). Shanghai, 1935. *Ashikari, and The Story of Shunkin* (details as for *Ashikari*, following). (2) Tr. Howard Hibbett. *Seven Japanese Tales* (see short fiction collections, below). *A Portrait of Shunkin*. Hara Shobo, Tokyo, 1965. A short novel that approaches perfection in its form and imagery.

Essay

"In Praise of Shadows." *"In'ei raisan." 1933–34.* 48 pages. (1) As "Beauty in Shadows." *Contemporary Japan*, vol. 11, no. 1, 1942. (2) Tr. Edward Seidensticker. *Atlantic Monthly*, Jan. 1955; *Japan Quarterly*, vol. 1, no. 1, 1955. (3) Tr. Thomas J. Harper and Edward

Seidensticker. Leete's Island Books, New Haven, 1977; Tuttle, Tokyo, 1984; Jonathan Cape, London, 1991. One of the best essays in *any* language. Frequently published on its own, it lends itself to imaginative production. John Caple's design for the Jonathan Cape paperback is especially good. All versions of (3) contain a 6-page afterword by Thomas J. Harper.

WORKS IN ENGLISH TRANSLATION

Novels and Novellas

Arrowroot. Yoshino kuzu. 1931. 55 pages. Tr. Anthony H. Chambers. *The Secret History of the Lord of Musashi, and Arrowroot.* Knopf, NY, 1982; Secker and Warburg, London, 1983; Putnam Publishing Group, NY, 1983; North Point Press, San Francisco, 1991, paperback; *Some Prefer Nettles, Arrowroot and The Secret History of the Lord of Musashi.* Pan Books, London, 1985.

Ashikari. Ashikari. 1932. 67 pages. As "Autumn Moon." Tr. Roy Humpherson and Hajime Okita. (Mimeograph). Shanghai, 1935. *Ashikari, and The Story of Shunkin.* Hokuseido, Tokyo, 1936; Stechert, NY, 1936; Greenwood Press, NY, 1970.

A Blind Man's Tale. Mōmoku monogatari. 1931. 94 pages. Tr. Howard Hibbett. *Seven Japanese Tales* (see short fiction collections, below).

Diary of a Mad Old Man. Fūten rōjin nikki. 1961–62.

The Key. Kagi. 1956. 183 pages. Tr. Howard Hibbett. Knopf, NY, 1961; Secker and Warburg, London, 1961; Tuttle, Tokyo, 1962; New American Library, NY, 1962; New American Library of Canada, NY, 1962; Berkley Pub., NY, 1971; Putnam Publishing Group, NY, 1981; Vintage Paperback, NY, 1991.

The Makioka Sisters. Sasame yuki. 1943–48.

Naomi. Chijin no ai. 1925.

A Portrait of Shunkin. Shunkin shō. 1933.

The Secret History of the Lord of Musashi. Bushūkō hiwa. 1931–32. 142 pages. (Details as for *Arrowroot*, above).

Some Prefer Nettles. Tade kuu mushi. 1929. 202 pages. Tr. Edward Seidensticker. Extract in: *Mademoiselle*, April 1955. Complete novel: Knopf, NY, 1955; Secker and Warburg, London, 1956; Tuttle, Tokyo, 1956; Penguin Books, Harmondsworth, 1970; Putnam Publishing Group, NY, 1981. Collected in: *Some Prefer Nettles, Arrowroot and The Secret History of the Lord of Musashi.* Pan Books, London, 1985. Further extract in: *The Treasury of World Literature*, ed. D. D. Runes. Philosophical Society, NY, 1956.

Short Fiction Collections

A Cat, a Man, and Two Women. 164 pages. Tr. Paul McCarthy. Kodansha International, Tokyo and NY, 1990, paperback 1991. Contains translator's 7-page preface and three stories: "The Little Kingdom"; "Professor Rado"; and "A Cat, a Man, and Two Women."

Seven Japanese Tales. 298 pages. Tr. Howard Hibbett. Knopf, NY,

1963; Secker and Warburg, London, 1964; Tuttle, Tokyo, 1967; Putnam Publishing Group, NY, 1981. Contains: "A Portrait of Shunkin," "Terror," "The Bridge of Dreams," "The Tattooer" (more frequently tr. as "Tattoo"), "The Thief," "Aguri," and "A Blind Man's Tale."

Short Fiction

"Aguri." *"Aoi hana."* 1922. 20 pages. *Seven Japanese Tales.*

"A Blind Man's Tale." *"Mōmoku monogatari."* 1932. 94 pages. *Seven Japanese Tales.*

"The Bridge of Dreams." *"Yume no ukihashi."* 1959. 33 pages. *Seven Japanese Tales; The World of Japanese Fiction.* Dutton, NY, 1973; *Contemporary Japanese Literature.* Knopf, NY, 1977.

"A Cat, a Man, and Two Women." *"Neko, to Shōzō, to futari no onna."* 1936. 100 pages. (1) As "A Cat, One Man, and Two Women." Tr. Anthony H. Chambers. *Journal of Literary Translation*, no. 17, 1986. (2) As "A Cat, Shozo, and Two Women." Tr. Sakuko Matsue. Wild Peony, New South Wales, 1988. (3) *A Cat, a Man, and Two Women.*

"Hokan." *"Hōkan."* 1911. 11 pages. Tr. Edilberto N. Alegre. *Asian Studies*, vol. 4, no. 1, 1966. University of Philippines, Manila.

"The House Where I Was Born." *"Haha o kouru ki."* 1919. 12 pages. (1) Tr. S. G. Brickley. *The Writing of Idiomatic English.* Kenkyusha, Tokyo, 1951. (2) As "Longing for Mother." Tr. Edward Fowler. *Monumenta Nipponica*, vol. 35, no. 4, 1980.

"The Little Kingdom." *"Chiisana ōkoku."* 1918. 36 pages. *A Cat, a Man, and Two Women.*

"The Piscatorial Li Tai-Po." *"Sa-*

kana no Ri Taihaku." Tr. Glenn Shaw. *Eigo Seinen*, vol. 46, nos. 2–9, 1921–22.

"Professor Rado." *"Rado sensei."* Part One 1925; Part Two 1928. 26 pages. *A Cat, a Man, and Two Women.*

"Tattoo." *"Shisei."* 1910. 8 pages. (1) As "The Young Tattooer." Tr. Asataro Miyamori. *Representative Tales of Japan.* Sanko Shoin, Tokyo, 1917. (2) As "Shisei." Tr. Sumimasa Ijichi. *Herald of Asia*, April 7, 1923. (3) Tr. Ryozo Matsumoto. *Japanese Literature, New and Old.* Hokuseido, Tokyo, 1961. (4) Tr. Ivan Morris. *Modern Japanese Stories*, ed. I. Morris. Spottiswoode, London, 1961; Tuttle, Tokyo and Boston, 1962. (5) As "The Tattooer." Tr. Howard Hibbett. *Show*, vol. 3, May 1963; *Seven Japanese Tales.*

"Terror," *"Kyōfu."* 1913. 10 pages. *Seven Japanese Tales.*

"The Thief." *"Watakushi."* 1921. 16 pages. *Seven Japanese Tales; Murder in Japan*, ed. John L. Apostolou and Martin H. Greenberg. Dembner Books, NY, 1987.

"The White Fox." *"Byakko no yu."* Tr. Eric S. Bell and Eiji Ukai. *Eminent Authors of Contemporary Japan*, vol. 1. Kaitakusha, Tokyo, 1930.

Play

Okuni and Gohei. Okuni to Gohei. 1922. 30 pages. (1) Tr. Isamu Suzuno. *Tokyo Nichinichi*, Sept. 20, 1924. (2) Tr. Eric S. Bell and Eiji Ukai. *Eminent Authors of Contemporary Japan*, vol. 2. Kaitakusha, Tokyo, 1931.

Autobiography

Childhood Years, A Memoir. Yōshō jidai. First published posthumously in Tanizaki's *Collected*

Works, 1966–68. 181 pages. Tr. Paul McCarthy. Kodansha International, Tokyo and NY, 1988; Collins, London, 1990; Fontana, London, 1991.

Miscellaneous

Extract from the novel *The Mother of Captain Shigemoto. Shōshō Shigemoto no haha. 1949–50.* 10 pages. Tr. Edward Seidensticker. *Modern Japanese Literature*, ed. Donald Keene. Grove Press, NY, 1956; Tuttle, Tokyo, 1957; Grove Weidenfeld, NY, paperback, 1989.

Essays

"In Praise of Shadows." *"In'ei raisan." 1933–34.*
"Kyoto, Her Nature, Food . . . And Women." *This Is Japan*, vol. 12, 1965.
"Postscript to *A Portrait of Shunkin." Shunkinshō gokō.* Tr. Anthony H. Chambers. *Monumenta Nipponica*, vol. 35, no. 4, 1980.

CRITICAL STUDIES

Berry, Margaret. "Meredith and Tanizaki on Modern Love." *Asian Profile*, vol. 11, no. 3, 1983.

Chambers, Anthony. "A Study of Tanizaki's *Shōshō Shigemoto no haha." Harvard Journal of Asiatic Studies*, vol. 38, no. 2, 1978.

———. "A Study of Tanizaki's 'Yoshino Kuzu.'" *Harvard Journal of Asiatic Studies*, vol. 41, no. 2, 1981.

———. "Tanizaki Jun'ichirō's Historical Fiction." *Journal of the Association of Teachers of Japanese*, vol. 8, no. 1, 1972.

———. "Tradition and Innovation in Tanizaki's 'Ashikari.'" *Studia Asiatica*, 1975.

———. "Tradition in the Works of Tanizaki Jun'ichiro." Ph.D. diss., University of Michigan, Ann Arbor, 1974.

Daly, Saralyn. "Tanizaki's West: a Fable of the Occident." *Discovering the Other*, 1984.

Furukawa, Hiroyuki. "Tanizaki Says, 'I Am Not a Great Admirer of Oscar Wilde': A Note on Tanizaki's Translation of *Lady Windermere's Fan." Gaikoku Bungaku Kenkyu*, vol. 23.

Gangloff, Eric John. "Tanizaki's Use of Traditional Literature: a Comparison of *Manji* and *Shinjū Ten no Amijima." Journal of the Association of Teachers of Japanese*, vol. 11, no. 2, 1976.

Geddes, John. "Dialect in Tanizaki's *Shunkinshō." Monumenta Nipponica*, vol. 39, no. 4, 1984.

Gunn, Giles B. "Traditions and Modernity in Modern Japanese Fiction: Variations on a Theme in Natsume Sōseki, Tanizaki Jun'ichirō and Dazai Osamu." *Japan Christian Quarterly*, no. 35, 1969.

Hyman, Stanley. "A Japanese Master: Tanizaki Jun'ichirō." *New Leader*, no. 46, 1963.

Ito, Ken K. *Visions of Desire: Tanizaki's Fictional Worlds.* Stanford University Press, Palo Alto, 1991.

Lippit, Noriko Mizuta. "Tanizaki and Poe: The Grotesque and the Quest for Supernatural Beauty." *Comparative Literature*, vol. 29, no. 3, 1977.

McCarthy, Paul Francis. *The Early Life and Works of Tanizaki Jun'ichirō.* Harvard University Press, Cambridge, 1975.

———. "Images of Women as Mother in Tanizaki's Fiction." *Transactions of the Asiatic Society of Japan*, vol. 4, no. 1, 1986.

———. "The Madonna and the Harlot: Images of Woman in Tanizaki." *Japanese Journal of Religious Studies*, vol. 9, no. 2, 1982.

McDonald, Keiko I. "A Reassessment of *Some Prefer Nettles.*" *Journal Newsletter of the Association of Teachers of Japanese*, vol. 12, no. 2, 1977.

———. "Rhetorical Stance in Tanizaki's *The Key.*" *Japan Interpreter*, vol. 11, no. 2, 1976.

Matsui, Sakuko. "View of an Elder Novelist: A Consideration of Tanizaki Jun'ichirō on Sōseki's *Meian.*" *Journal of the Oriental Society of Australia*, vol. 15, no. 6, 1984.

Merken, Kathleen Chisato. "The Evolution of Tanizaki Jun'ichirō as a Narrative Artist." Ph.D. diss., University of British Columbia, Vancouver, 1979.

Newton, Michael C. "The Autobiography of Illusion: Tanizaki's 'Ame.'" *Transactions of the International Conference of Orientalists in Japan*, no. 22, 1977.

Olson, Lawrence. "*The Makioka Sisters*: A Japanese Family Novel." *East Asia*, vol. 11, no. 5, 1964.

Peterson, Gwenn Boardman. *The Moon in the Water: Understanding Tanizaki, Kawabata and Mishima.* University Press of Hawaii, Honolulu, 1979.

Seidensticker, Edward G. "Kafū and Tanizaki." *Japan Quarterly*, vol. 4, no. 4, 1965.

———. "Tanizaki Jun-ichirō." *Monumenta Nipponica*, vol. 21, no. 3, 1966.

Tayama KATAI
(1872–1930)

Novelist. Real name, Tayama Rokuya. Born in Tatebayashi (modern-day Gumma Prefecture). Resident of Tokyo.

One of the most influential figures in early modern Japanese literature, Tayama Katai renounced an early flirtation with Romanticism to embrace the *Naturalist movement, eventually becoming its most admired writer. Many of his stories, including the epoch-making *"Futon"* (*1907*, "The Quilt"), have been translated into English. Readers who do not have fluency in Japanese are greatly indebted to Kenneth G. Henshall, not only for these translations but also for bringing us Katai's magnificent volume of memoirs, *Tokyo no sanjū-nen* (1917, *Thirty Years in Tokyo*). This volume, with its myriad of references to major and minor figures, gives us a unique, insider's view of the Japanese literary world during the years 1885–1915.

When Katai was only five years old, his father, a former samurai, was killed during the government campaign to quell the Satsuma rebellion. His death left a once-proud family in the uncomfortable position of having to subsist on a meager war pension. Yet, even had he lived, it is doubtful whether the Tayamas would ever have enjoyed prosperity. The *Meiji Restoration of 1868 had brought sweeping changes in its wake, including the abolition of feudal status. Indeed, Katai's father had been driven by penury to volunteer for action in the Seinan Civil War, and his death – to the sensitive young writer, his son – may well have seemed fated.

Katai sought refuge in literature, reading all of the Japanese literary classics in his early teens and going on to learn both Chinese and English. He composed poetry and prose in Chinese, and studied *waka* (Japanese verse) with a poet of the traditional Keien school. Exploring various career choices he considered taking a law degree, but found law school beyond his means. The army, too, was beyond reach on account of his poor eyesight. Katai was therefore left with the prospect of a literary career, and, in 1891, sought patronage from OZAKI KŌYŌ (1867–1903), the leading literary figure of the era.

Kōyō's response could not have been more advantageous to Katai. Instead of accepting him as a disciple into the stifling atmosphere of the inner *Ken'yūsha circle, he sent him to Emi Suiin (1869–1934), the editor of a new magazine called *Senshibankō* (*A Thousand Purples, Ten Thousand Crimsons*). Suiin accepted Katai's stories and even arranged for him to publish in other magazines and newspapers.

Although he gradually became established as a professional writer, Katai made very little money from his early work. Stylistically his stories were influenced by FUTABATEI SHIMEI's translations of Turgenev, while in content they were based on themes drawn from his own life or from the lives of his friends. Literary historians may condemn him on both counts, but in fact this was a powerful combination at the time. Indeed it is difficult to fault Katai, an exceptionally fine writer, on purely literary grounds. If there is a weakness in his work, it is one that stems from his inability to avoid self-pity in real life.

Throughout the 1890s, Katai continued to write in a lyrical and Romantic vein, invariably making his protagonists suffer at the hands of fate while letting them subsequently find solace in nature. The use of this formula ended in 1901 when he read the complete works of de Maupassant. In words that are reminiscent of AKUTAGAWA RYŪNOSUKE's famous description of KUNIKIDA DOPPO, Katai later recalled: "Until then I had only looked longingly at the heavens – I didn't know a thing about the earth. I knew nothing at all. I'd been a feeble idealist."

What most impressed Katai in de Maupassant's stories was the way in which the French writer presented "life in the raw" without any petty embellishments of his own. His approach suggested a complete theory of subjectivity which Katai would later develop and put to use. Claiming that there were two kinds of subjectivity – "natural" and "petty" – Katai believed that the former (expression of the author's individuality) was essential to literature, while the latter (opinionated embellishment) was to be avoided completely.

Another major influence was Nietzsche's philosophy, introduced into Japan in 1897 by the critic Hasegawa Tenkei (1876–1940). Seen as a Naturalistic rather than Romantic writer, Nietzsche was admired by Katai for his strength in overcoming restrictions imposed by society upon the natural impulses of the individual. Inspired by Sudermann's Nietzschean story "*Der Katzensteg*" (1890, "The Cat's Bridge"), Katai wrote "*Jūemon no saigo*" (1902, "The End of Jūemon"), based on an incident in which Nagano villagers murder a man whom they find anti-social. It is an excellent story, written in an otherwise unproductive period when Katai was feeling frustrated by married life.

In considering writers such as Katai it is always worth remembering that Naturalism in Japan bore little resemblance to the European movement of the same name, even though it was partially inspired by it. This is because the Japanese had their own agenda. They wanted to write novels that would be considered wholly realistic, hence they argued that the novelist should stick closely to the facts of his own experience. Although they were sympathetic to the pessimism of Zola and de Maupassant, especially in the way in which the French writers regarded people as being at the mercy of heredity, environment, and other forces beyond their control, they turned upon themselves those "dissecting scalpels" with which Zola and others were laying bare the supposedly animal nature of human beings. As a result, the works of Japanese Naturalism make quite a different impression upon the reader from those of the West. Less vivid and less energetic, they are essentially the product of a separate literary tradition with its own internal dynamics.

In 1899, Katai had agreed to an arranged marriage with a nineteen-year-old girl called Risako, the sister of a literary friend. However, he soon realized his mistake, for his wife was far too submissive and conventional to provide him with the emotional stimulus he needed. Eventually, fate intervened. An attractive and thoroughly "modern" girl, Okada Michiyo, expressed a desire to become his private pupil. Little did she know that she would inspire one of the greatest stories of unrequited love ever written. In "*Futon*," Katai perfected his art and recounted a frustrating master-pupil relationship with such veracity that he changed the course of Japanese literature for many years to come.

Later describing himself as "a wolf wearing a mask of gentle timidity," Katai wrote "*Shōjobyō*" (*1907*, "The Girl Watcher") as a prelude to "*Futon*." He feared that if he were to express immediately his desire for Michiyo it would offend her family and ruin his chances of having an affair with her. Michiyo had lived with the Tayamas between 1904 and 1906, and Katai fully expected to see her again.

Psychological pressures built up in Katai's mind as he first witnessed the success of his friends SHIMAZAKI TŌSON and Doppo, and then struggled with his newfound awareness of Nietzschean powers. Suddenly, in July 1907, he wrote "*Futon*" from start to finish in ten days. It appeared in *Shinshōsetsu* (*New Novel*) magazine in September of that year, and was an immediate sensation. Moreover, as critics began to evaluate the novel they acknowledged its author as the first Japanese who had been brave enough to express the truth of his personal life without regard to social convention. "*Futon*" therefore became one of the classics of early modern Japanese literature.

Katai's achievement with "*Futon*" can be appreciated only if one considers its influence on several generations of writers who followed him. Single-handedly he established the dominant mode of literature in Japan (one which continues to this day) called the *I-Novel tradition. Others have since expanded the mode, or refined it, or even, like DAZAI OSAMU and MISHIMA YUKIO, turned it inside out in order to reach more definitive truths. But it was Katai who did most to reconcile the Japanese psyche with Western individualism. He did it by examining his own social behavior with all the rigor that society itself would normally apply. Indeed, translator Kenneth Henshall makes the point that, although a conventional interpretation of Katai's work suggests "anti-societal individualism propounded in the name of 'nature,'" at the same time, "it should always be borne in mind that the individual never seems to triumph in Katai's works."

In real life, Katai himself may have felt triumphant at the success of "*Futon*," yet his professional achievement was not matched by personal happiness. He twice contracted typhoid, becoming ill while covering the Russo–Japanese War in 1904, and he became increasingly disillusioned not only with society but with the deeper workings of nature. In his war stories, such as "*Ippeisotsu*" (*1908*, "One Soldier") and "*Kuruma no oto*" (*1908*, "The Sound of Wheels"), he depicted individual people as being helplessly caught in the machine of fate.

There was no end, either, to Katai's marital problems. While publication of "*Futon*" ended whatever prospects he may have had with his pupil Michiyo, scholars now believe that a truly passionate affair with a *geisha* called Iida Yone may have given him the strength to write *"Futon."* The affair, which lasted for many years, is said to have caused him more pain than pleasure. It was typical of a man who, though he had a natural zest for living despite his gloomy outlook, was above all else committed to his art.

Striving as ever for complete authenticity, Katai continued to write Naturalist "fictions." The serial publication of his novel *Sei* (*Life*) was in 1908 in the *Yomiuri shimbun*. His mother was the model for the central character, and the story reveals much about the dominating role she was obliged to assume when her husband was killed. As the novel was another popular success, Katai decided to continue his life story with *Tsuma* (1908, *The Wife*) and *En* (1910, *The Bond*).

Throughout these years Katai was developing his theoretical ideas concerning literature while also attempting to put them into practice. Stylistically, he wanted to eradicate even the relatively small element of analysis and explanation that had appeared in *"Futon."* He called his ideal style "single-plane depiction" (*heimen byōsha*), which demanded that the author be completely passive towards his material. Underlying the theory was the perception that nature is largely unknowable, and hence an author should not attempt to pass judgments, nor should he influence the reader by suggesting the relative significance of various incidents depicted. In both *Sei* and *Tsuma* he attempted to put this theory to work, combining it with the I-Novel technique. However, since the I-Novel is recounted from a specific viewpoint, the passive method of writing tended to weaken it considerably. To overcome this problem, Katai departed from the I-Novel in his full-length work *Inaka Kyōshi* (*1909, Country Teacher*).

In *Country Teacher*, the author appears only as a minor character, while the central figure is based on a man whom Katai had met briefly while visiting his brother-in-law, the writer-turned-priest, Ōta Gyokumei. He had not taken much notice of the country schoolteacher at the time, but on a subsequent visit to the priest's temple where the young man lodged he saw a freshly-dug grave bestrewn with flowers. He found it especially poignant because the teacher had died in complete obscurity at the very moment when Japan was celebrating its great victory over Russia.

Piecing together a highly realistic portrait of the country school-teacher, Katai made extensive use of the man's diaries, and gathered firsthand material from friends and relatives. The result was an extremely well-written novel suffering from that inevitable dullness which comes from writing about a very dull person. Only when

Katai injected real fiction, contriving a secret love life for his hero, does the story escape from the claustrophobic limitations imposed by its subject.

Katai's later career remains largely mysterious to English readers because little of any importance following *Country Teacher* has been translated. Donald Keene has described *Toki wa sugiyuku* (1916, *Time Goes By*) as Katai's "most completely Naturalistic novel." Based on the life of the author's uncle, it is said to fulfill the ideal of "pure observation" which was one of the central tenets of Naturalism. In this work, and in *Ippeisotsu no jūsatsu* (1917, *A Soldier Shot to Death*), Katai demonstrated an increasingly pessimistic view of nature, emphasizing its destructive rather than its restorative powers.

For several months in 1913, and again in 1916, Katai went into retreat to meditate: episodes that formed the basis of *Zansetsu* (1918, *Lingering Snow*). Inspired by the novel *En Route* by Joris-Karl Huysmans (a writer who had left behind Zola's brand of naturalism to embrace religion), *Zansetsu* was neither a popular nor a critical success. Kenneth Henshall refers to it (and other stories in the same vein) as "full of obscure and esoteric Buddhist philosophy." He also makes the perceptive observation that Katai had finally given up being assertive in life in order to harmonize with his passivity in literature.

Alienated from his family and largely abandoned by his public, Katai continued to write essays and historical fiction. *Minamoto no Yoshitomo* (1926) suggested a certain sympathy with the cruel warlord who was defeated by Taira no Kiyomori in the twelfth century. Returning to direct autobiography, Katai also produced *Momoyo* (1927, *The Hundred Nights*), describing the many facets of love that can exist between a man and a *geisha*: a topic which critics dismissed as irrelevant to the age. Nonetheless, it was a sincere work, based on his improved relationship with Iida Yone whom he had rescued from the ruins of the *Great Kantō Earthquake in 1923.

Limited in imagination and with a tendency to ignore literary structure, Katai is not widely read today. However, it would be a shame if his work were relegated entirely to the field of historical studies. At least "*Futon*" may still be read with enjoyment, while his work as a whole is surely of interest to anyone who wants to address fundamental issues of literary theory.

Tayama Katai died in hospital in 1930, following a long illness.

RECOMMENDED READING

Novel

Country Teacher. Inaka kyōshi. 1909. 256 pages. Tr. Kenneth G. Henshall. University of Hawaii Press, Honolulu, 1984. An attractive volume, with photographs and other illustrations. Contains translator's 5-page preface and an 8-page extract from Katai's memoirs.

Short Fiction Collection

The Quilt, and Other Stories by Tayama Katai. 204 pages. Tr. Kenneth G. Henshall. University of Tokyo Press, Tokyo, 1981. Contains 33-page introduction by the translator, together with eight works by Katai, including: (the epoch-making story) "The Quilt," "The End of Jūemon," "One Soldier," and "Girl Watching." A finely printed and bound volume, potentially a collector's item.

WORKS IN ENGLISH TRANSLATION

Novels

Country Teacher. Inaka kyōshi. 1909.
A Soldier Shot to Death. Ippeisotsu no jūsatsu. 1917. 169 pages. Tr. Kenichiro Honma. Yamaguchi Shoten, Kyoto, 1982.

Short Fiction

"The End of Jūemon." *"Jūemon no saigo."* 1902. 53 pages. *The Quilt, and Other Stories.*
"The Girl Watcher." *"Shōjobyō."* 1907. 17 pages. *The Quilt, and Other Stories.*
"One Cold Morning." *"Samui asa."* 1914. 5 pages. *The Quilt, and Other Stories.*
"One Soldier." *"Ippeisotsu."* 1908. 19 pages. (1) As "A Mere Private." Tr. Asataro Miyamori. *Representative Tales of Japan.* Sanko Shoin, Tokyo, 1917. (2) Tr. G. W. Sargent. *Modern Japanese Literature,* ed. Donald Keene. Grove Press, NY, 1956; Tuttle,

Tokyo, 1957; Grove Weidenfeld, paperback, 1989. (3) As "A Soldier." Tr. William E. Naff. *The Heart Is Alone,* ed. Richard McKinnon. Hokuseido, Tokyo, 1957. (4) *The Quilt, and Other Stories.*
"The Photograph." *"Shashin."* 1909. 6 pages. *The Quilt, and Other Stories.*
"The Quilt." *"Futon."* 1907. 52 pages. (1) As "Futon." Tr. Yoko Fukano. University of Queensland, Brisbane, 1978. (2) *The Quilt, and Other Stories.*
"The Railway Track." *"Senro."* 1912. 5 pages. *The Quilt, and Other Stories.*
"The Sound of Wheels." *"Kuruma no oto."* 1908. 6 pages. *The Quilt, and Other Stories.*

Autobiography

Literary Life in Tokyo 1885–1915. Tayama Katai's Memoirs (Thirty Years in Tokyo). Tokyo no sanjū-

nen. 1917. 292 pages. Tr. with full annotations and an introduction by Kenneth G. Henshall. E. J. Brill, Leiden, The Netherlands, 1987.

CRITICAL STUDIES

Henshall, Kenneth George. "A Study of the Writings of Tayama Katai with Particular Regard to Their Naturalistic Elements." Ph.D. diss., University of Sydney, Sydney, 1979.

Loftus, Margaret. "Two Soldiers: A Comparative Study of Stephen Crane's *The Red Badge of Courage* and Tayama Katai's *One Soldier.*" *Chu-Shikoku America Bungaku Kenkyu*, no. 7, 1970.

Richter, Frederick. "A Thematic Analysis of Representative Works by Tayama Katai." Ph.D. diss., Indiana University, Bloomington, 1972.

Tokuda SHŪSEI
(1871–1943)

Novelist. Born in Kanazawa, Ishikawa Prefecture. Lived in Tokyo.

Although poorly educated, Tokuda Shūsei came to be respected for his realistic novels and his objective, almost "artless" style. His career falls into two phases, separated, more or less, by his fortieth birthday. In each of these phases (perhaps somewhat confusingly for students of early modern Japanese literature) he is referred to by historians as being one of the "big four." As a follower of OZAKI KŌYŌ, the celebrated master of the *Ken'yūsha, Shūsei is usually ranked as one of Kōyō's four outstanding disciples: the others being IZUMI KYŌKA, Oguri Fūyō, and Yanagawa Shun'yō. But on the eve of the *Taishō era, Shūsei found his true vocation as a Naturalist. Throughout the rest of his career he continued to develop humanistic *Naturalism, eventually becoming recognized as the writer who brought it to its full maturity. In this he is reckoned to have surpassed his three great colleagues: TAYAMA KATAI, SHIMAZAKI TŌSON, and MASAMUNE HAKUCHŌ. Despite all his achievements, however, little of his work has been translated into English.

After leaving Kanazawa Middle School and studying briefly at a college near his home in Ishikawa Prefecture, Shūsei began work in the offices of a magazine publisher, later moving to a newspaper. He is thought to have joined Kōyō's circle in the mid–1890s at the same time as his friend Kyōka, who also came from Kanazawa. It was an excellent opportunity for both of them. After all, the Ken'yūsha not only set the standard in literature but had a virtual monopoly on it during the height of its influence around the year 1898. Even though its relatively low-brow approach was soon to become discredited, it provided Shūsei with both a social context and an identity as a writer.

Shūsei's first novel, *Kumo no yukue* (*1900, Where The Clouds Go*), brought him to the attention of the public, but because of its plain style it was never considered outstanding by the critics. Attitudes changed, however, when the age of Naturalism dawned. Now, ornate styles were rejected in favor of blunt and even clumsy forms of expression: a process that went hand in hand with the defictionalizing of literature, and led, eventually, to the *I-Novel. Naturalism, however, predated the I-Novel with which it is so closely identified. Its patron saint was Emile Zola who was much admired by the Japanese for representing nature "as it is," rather than rearranging it to suit the dictates of fiction. Certainly, Zola's *Thérèse Raquin* is thought to have been the (unacknowledged) model for Tayama Katai's "*Futon*" (*1907*, "The Quilt"), a story which became so popular that it prompted many other writers – including Shūsei – to tap a similar vein. In 1908 Shūsei published *Arajotai* (*The New Home*), describing the deprivations of a Tokyo housewife in starkly realistic terms. For the first time, Shūsei's artless style came into its own, exemplifying Katai's own statement that: "A commonplace style suits commonplace material; a blunt style suits blunt ideas."

Never very original, Shūsei saw that his next step forward would have to be in the direction of the confessional I-Novel itself. To this end he wrote *Ashiato* (*1910, Footprints*), based on the life of his wife, going on to describe how he met and married her in *Kabi* (*1911, Mildew*). As in other I-Novels, the hero-protagonist – in this case Sasamura – is unequivocally a representation of the author. Like KUNIKIDA DOPPO (whose defictionalized stories were the progenitors of the I-Novel) Sasamura/Shūsei frankly admitted to having no answers to the great questions of life. Yet unlike Doppo, neither did he display any poetic sentiments nor hint at any grand moral vision. His aim was simply to describe the misery of his married life with all the realism he could muster.

Fortunately, Shūsei did not fall into the trap of becoming completely self-centered, as many Naturalists did. Indeed, he outlived the movement by more than two decades and continued to broaden and deepen his art right up until World War II. That he was outstandingly successful in doing so is shown by the generous comments of Nakamura Mitsuo, one of the most outspoken critics of Naturalism. He says: "This nonchalant, most 'natural' naturalist of all left works presenting the best of his talent and even the distinctiveness of a great writer . . ." and he goes on to name *Tadare* (*1913, The Sore*) and *Arakure* (*1915, The Daredevils*) as exceptional works written during the decline of Shūsei's adopted school.

Shūsei's understanding of feminine psychology may well have been the saving factor which rescued his work from artistic atrophy in the early Taishō period. Whereas *Kabi* described marriage from the author's own point of view, *Arakure* viewed it from a female perspective. Although neither of these novels has been translated into English, a 1935 story entitled "*Kunshō*" ("The Order of the White Paulownia") can be found in Ivan Morris's *Modern Japanese Stories*. Told in Shūsei's typically blunt style it describes how an overworked wife is prevailed upon to "keep up appearances" in her marriage, despite her husband's drinking and gambling. In the end, all her meager savings are spent in celebrating the Order of the White Paulownia, a war decoration unexpectedly conferred by the government on her ne'er-do-well spouse.

In his later years Shūsei produced two important works, both of them described as "masterpieces" by Nakamura Mitsuo. *Kasō jimbutsu* (*1938, Men in Disguise*) is an I-Novel recounting a love affair that Shūsei had after the death of his wife. *Shukuzu* (*1943, The Epitome*) is an unfinished novel about the life of a *geisha*. Although briefly banned by the authorities when it was first serialized, the latter came to be regarded as one of Shūsei's greatest works and was much admired by younger writers.

There is no reason to suppose that Shūsei will ever become well known in the West, not least because Japanese Naturalism is much more austere in its artlessness than the European Naturalism of Zola and de Maupassant. Yet in his feminist sympathies and his mastery of the I-Novel technique, Shūsei has surely influenced such a writer as TSUSHIMA YŪKO whose work is frequently translated and anthologized. As one of the four great Naturalist writers, Tokuda Shūsei belongs to the mainstream of modern Japanese literature with its preference for simplicity of style and a direct, "unmediated" observation of life through the eyes of a single character.

RECOMMENDED READING

Short Fiction

"The Order of the White Paulownia." "Kunshō." 1935. 20 pages. (1) As "The White Order of the Paulownia." *Contemporary Japan*, vol. 2, 1936. (2) Tr. Ivan Morris. *Modern Japanese Stories*, ed. Ivan Morris. Spottiswoode, London, 1961; Tuttle, Tokyo and NY, 1962, paperback 1977. Readily obtainable in version (2).

WORKS IN ENGLISH TRANSLATION

Short Fiction

"The Order of the White Paulownia." *"Kunshō." 1935.*
"The Shoiage." *"Shoiage."* 13 pages. Tr. Asataro Miyamori. *Representative Tales of Japan*. Sanko Shoin, Tokyo, 1917.

CRITICAL STUDY

Rolf, Robert. "Shūsei, Hakuchō, and the Age of Literary Naturalism 1907–1911." Ph.D. diss., University of Hawaii, Honolulu, 1975.

Tokutomi ROKA
(1868–1927)

Novelist and translator. Born in Kumamoto Prefecture, Kyūshū. From 1907, lived in Chitose, near Tokyo.

The author of several best-selling works, Tokutomi Kenjirō (who is always referred to as Roka) was the younger brother of the historian and essayist, *Tokutomi Sohō (1863–1957). Brought up in the Christian faith, both men were identified with Japan's growing nationalism at the turn of the century. Later, the brothers disagreed over politics, Sohō leaning to the right; Roka to the left. Always high-minded and idealistic, Roka was also a gifted storyteller and made his name with the novel *Hototogisu* (1898–99, literally: "Cuckoo," translated as *Namiko*), a tragic love story in which the personal lives of the protagonists are outshone (rather than overshadowed) by the Sino–Japanese War of 1894–95. Translated into many foreign languages, it was widely read in the West, and indeed the sales of Roka's books made him the wealthiest writer of his era. *Omoide no ki* (1901, *Footprints in the Snow*) and "*Shizen to jinsei*" (1900, "Nature and Man") were both immensely popular, the latter running to over two hundred printings in the *Taishō period. Completely independent of contemporary literary fashions, Roka has often been ignored by historians, yet his work was well-crafted and is still highly readable today.

Born in the first year of *Meiji in the western island of Kyūshū, Roka was five years younger than his brother Iichirō (Sohō). They both attended Dōshisha, the Christian college founded by Niijima Jō in Kyoto, which later became Dōshisha University. Roka was a favored pupil, proving himself not only adept at languages but also keenly interested in the Christian religion. When he was seventeen years old he was baptized into the Methodist Church and was active in recruiting other converts to the faith. However, rather than pursue a career as a teacher or minister he followed his brother to Tokyo. There he began working for Min'yūsha, a publishing company founded by Sohō in 1887.

There is little doubt that Roka's ambitions were stimulated by the growing fame of his elder brother. Sohō had already written several essays about the younger generation, and had attracted highly favorable attention as a consequence. His long essay *"Shōrai no Nihon"* ("Japan of the Future") was published by the Keizai Zasshi company and it confirmed his reputation. Roka, on the other hand, had done little except for a few translations inspired by the example of FUTABATEI SHIMEI (whose translations of Russian literature were to become the major influence on Roka's career). But Roka was already caught up in the dynamic spirit of the age. Looking back on that period (in *Omoide no ki*), he described it as "a truly delightful time" when young men, "unaware of the price of progress," were rushing headlong into a "bright, idealistic world."

When Sohō founded the magazine *Kokumin no tomo* (*The People's Friend*), Roka contributed first as a proofreader, then as a translator, and eventually as the author of many original works. The magazine quickly became popular among the younger generation, espousing as it did the cause of democratic radicalism and being written in a lively, readable prose style. Through its pages, many people were introduced to Western ideas and literature for the first time. TAYAMA KATAI, for example, wrote in *Thirty Years in Tokyo*: ". . . of particular benefit to me was the introduction to foreign literature through Roka's translations, which appeared in number six type [i.e., very small type] in *Kokumin no tomo*." The magazine's success was equaled by that of a newspaper, subsequently launched by Sohō, called the *Kokumin shimbun*. With their aggressive political stance, these two journals were in striking contrast to the ailing publications of the Ken'yūsha, and they helped to nurture such talents as KUNIKIDA DOPPO, and, of course, Roka himself.

Not until the end of the century did Roka become really famous. His novel, *Hototogisu*, was published serially in the *Kokumin shimbun* during 1898–99 and was an instant success. Even in translation it is still immensely readable today, and paints a vivid picture of upper-class society during the Sino–Japanese War of 1894–95. The story centers on the marriage of Namiko, the daughter of General Kataoka, to Takeo, a young naval officer. Ideally suited to each other, the couple are idyllically happy and would undoubtedly remain so, were it not for the interference of Takeo's mother. Being quite unlike her good-natured son, she has become extremely irascible after losing her husband. Under his domination she had been quiet and submissive, but now she has changed out of all recognition. She terrifies her servants and makes Namiko miserable. Worse still, when Namiko falls ill with tuberculosis, Takeo's mother ensures that she is promptly sent back to her parents, thereby causing this happiest of marriages to be annulled. Her cruel act, which is provoked in part by another young officer who wants Namiko for himself, is carried out when Takeo is at sea fighting the Chinese.

Roka's accurate portrayal of human motivations, especially the base motivations, greed and jealousy, earned him the reputation of being a realist. In fact, overriding all considerations of human emotion in *Hototogisu* is a new sense of national pride and identity, embodied in the ideals of General Kataoka and his son-in-law, Takeo. Yet perhaps most striking is the author's insistence on women's equality and his awareness that the suppression of women was one of the worst aspects of contemporary society.

Many of Roka's stories and essays were collected in *Shizen to jinsei*, a volume in which his talent for describing nature (already apparent in *Hototogisu*) was shown to the full. It was followed by the autobiographical *Omoide no ki* ("Recollections," translated by Kenneth Strong and published in 1970 under the title: *Footprints in the Snow*). Both works were enormously successful, enabling Roka to become independent of his brother whom he now surpassed in reputation. The hero of *Omoide no ki* was accepted by the public as a likable young man whose longing for individual freedom in a society riddled with restrictions was perfectly justified. Indeed, Roka's ability to create fundamentally good characters was matched only by his skill in drawing those who were superficially bad.

The novel which Roka intended as his masterpiece was *Kuroshio* (*1904, The Black Tide*), but although it was supposed to be a work in six volumes the author never progressed beyond volume 1. Told from the point of view of Tozaburō, a retired soldier, it was to cover the period 1887–1901, examining the consequences of Westernization and ending with the formation of the Social

Democratic Party in April 1901. However, Roka quarreled with his brother while writing it and decided to put it to one side in favor of foreign travel.

In more than one sense, Roka could be characterized as the Paul Theroux of Japan in the early years of the century. He had already helped to popularize the notion of rail travel in *Shizen to jinsei*, and now, in 1906, he set sail for the West with the intention of calling on his literary and spiritual hero, Tolstoy. The trip was a great success. Roka met the Russian writer at Yasnaya Polyana and was so deeply impressed by the encounter that, on his return to Japan, he began to emulate Tolstoy's preference for rustic seclusion. To achieve this in 1907 he had only to move five miles west of Shinjuku (a Tokyo suburb) to the village of Chitose. His descriptions of country life were later collected in a volume called *Mimizu no tawagoto* (1913, *The Prattling of an Earthworm.*)

Like many writers, Roka was deeply affected by the treason trials of 1910. The execution of Kōtoku Shūsui and eleven others for supposedly conspiring against the emperor shocked liberal intellectuals throughout Japan, and was cited by NAGAI KAFŪ (in a famous remark) as the sole reason for his retreat into nostalgia. Kafū also noted that Tokutomi Roka was the only writer who had the courage to speak out openly against the government. In an address to the First Higher School in 1911 Roka said that those executed had not been ordinary rebels but "men of high ideals who sacrificed themselves to a dream of a new world of liberty and equality." It seems likely that he could speak in this manner because of the relative security afforded by his considerable wealth and status.

Highly critical of society, Roka became more and more reclusive, living quietly with his wife, Aiko, in their country retreat. When rustic life bored him he would set off on his travels again, sometimes going far afield, as in 1919 when he made a world trip. On his return he wrote an account of the journey in "From Japan to Japan" (1910), and subsequently embarked on his last major work, his autobiography, *Fuji*. As if to demonstrate once and for all the equality of women, Roka and Aiko wrote it together, the first volume appearing in 1924. Although the entire work was never completely finished, the final part was published posthumously in an unrevised state. Roka died in 1927, and his collected works (in twenty volumes) were published in the following year.

In retrospect it may seem strange that a man as patriotic as Roka could be so vehemently opposed to the government of his country. Yet in many ways he reminds one of the early British socialists with whom, by virtue of his knowledge of English literature, he shared a common intellectual heritage. He wanted to eliminate social injustice, and at the same time make the arts a focal point of people's lives and aspirations. Finding that his idealism exceeded his capacity for influencing society, he adopted a pose of Tolstoyan aloofness. He and Aiko were "Adam and Eve," regaining their lost innocence at a time when everyone else was rushing towards the militarism of the 1930s. The same, quixotic attitude is detectable in most of Roka's writing – and it is this which makes his stories still appealing today.

RECOMMENDED READING

Novel

Namiko*. Hototogisu. 1898–99*. 313 pages. Tr. Sakai Shioya and E. F. Edgett. Extract in: *The Literary World*, July 1, 1904; *Eigo Seinen*, August 1904. Complete novel: Yurakusha, Tokyo, 1904; G. P. Putnam, London, 1904. Further extract as "The Hototogisu, The Heart of Nami-ko." *The Treasury of Japanese Literature*, ed. Tokichi Watanabe. Jippohkaku, Tokyo, 1933. A best-seller in its day; 1904 versions available from rare book dealers.

WORKS IN ENGLISH TRANSLATION

Novels

Footprints in the Snow. Omoide no ki. 1901. 442 pages. Tr. Kenneth Strong. Allen and Unwin, London, 1970; Tuttle, Tokyo, 1971. Note: the author is referred to by his real name (in reverse order) on this volume: Kenjiro Tokutomi.

Namiko. Hototogisu. 1898–99.

Nature and Man. Shizen to jinsei. 1900. 313 pages. Tr. Arthur Lloyd, H. von Fallot, and H. Ono. Kogakukan, Tokyo, 1913; Kobunsha, Tokyo, 1948.

Short Fiction

"Five Days at Yasnaya Polyana."

"*Junrei kikō*." 1906. 30 pages. Tr. Laurence Kominz. *Monumenta Nipponica*, vol. 41, no. 1, 1986.

"Glowing Embers." "*Kaijin*." 1990. 56 pages. Tr. Asataro Miyamori. *Representative Tales of Japan*. Shanko Shoten, Tokyo, 1917.

Essays

"An Autumn Morning at the Tone." 2 pages. Tr. Sumimasa Ijichi. *Eigo Seinen*, vol. 19, no. 7, 1908.

"Five Minutes' Dream." 2 pages. *Seinen*, vol. 8, no. 7, 1902.

"The Poor Child." 3 pages. Tr. Takeo Fujino. *Eigo Seinen*, vol. 22 nos. 2–3, 1909.

"Raiau." Tr. Yaichiro Isobe. *Chugai Eigo*, July 1920.

CRITICAL STUDY

Asahara, Jōhei. *Roka Garden: Kenjiro Tokutomi and His Wife*. Rokuroku Kai, Tokyo, 1957.

Tsubouchi SHŌYŌ
(1859–1935)

Critic, novelist, and translator. Real name, Tsubouchi Yūzō. Born in Ōta, near Nagoya. Moved to Tokyo in 1876.

Rightly acclaimed as the founder of modern Japanese literature, Tsubouchi Shōyō was the author of *Shōsetsu shinzui* (*1885–86, The Essence of the Novel*), the first comprehensive analysis of fiction to be written in Japan. His treatise, calling upon writers to introduce elements of Western psychological realism, inspired several generations of novelists and became a formative influence on Japanese twentieth-century fiction. Its immediate impact on FUTABATEI SHIMEI triggered a lifelong friendship and a working relationship that enabled Futabatei to write *Ukigumo* (*1887–88, Drifting Clouds*), Japan's first modern novel. Shōyō's own love of Edo fiction, however, was often at odds with the new literary theories he argued so eloquently. Of the nine novels that he wrote and published, only six were fully completed and none of them was especially realistic. Yet, by his example, he did more than anyone else to raise the status of the novel to that of a high art form, inspiring not only the Romanticist

OZAKI KŌYŌ but later generations of *Naturalists and *I-Novelists.
Turning away from fiction in his later years to concentrate exclusively
on theater, Shōyō translated all the works of William Shakespeare,
drawing upon a knowledge of *Nō, *Kabuki, and *Bunraku theater
to make them comprehensible to a Japanese audience. At Waseda
University, where he founded the Faculty of Letters in 1890 and
edited the literary journal *Waseda Bungaku*, the Shōyō Memorial
Dramatic Museum was built to commemorate his 1928 completion
of the Shakespeare translations. By this time, modern Japanese
literature – originally seeded by the ideas contained in his treatise
– had already flowered with a brilliance that must have exceeded
his wildest expectations.

Shōyō's success owed much to an unusual blend of elements in
his personality. Although a privileged scholar he rejected a career
in government service to champion the cause of fiction, and did so
at a time when novels were considered to be mere low-brow
entertainment. In his personal life, too, his choices were equally
perverse. A man of striking good looks with an upper-class background
he nonetheless selected a wife from the gay quarters, purchasing
her contract from a house of prostitution. There can be no doubt
that Shōyō's life was governed by his emotions, and that he was
constantly developing his intellect – chiefly by reading and writing
about fiction – in order to make sense of it. Even today, both the
example he set and the works that he wrote continue to be
stimulating for these very reasons.

Born towards the end of the Edo period, Tsubouchi Shōyō was
the son of an official in the administration of the Owari *han*, a large
province under the *Tokugawa system of government. His father,
a man with strong religious convictions, was in charge of the
community of Ōta, near Nagoya. In all, there were three boys and
three girls in the family, each of whom appears to have been highly
caring of each other and of their parents. Shōyō's mother, a woman
from the merchant class, may well have softened the Confucian
austerity of the household by encouraging her son's obsession with
the popular arts.

During his boyhood Shōyō became completely engrossed in Edo
fiction, borrowing books from the same Daisō lending library in
Nagoya that his favorite author, *Bakin, had once frequented. The
extent of his reading was phenomenal. His college friend, Ichijima
Shunjō, later mentioned that Shōyō had shown him a list of over
one thousand titles, all of which had been read. The critic Nakamura
Mitsuo has attributed much of Shōyō's success in bringing about a
revolution in literature to his vast knowledge of *gesaku* fiction
(popular literature of the late Edo period).

At the same time, Shōyō was gradually becoming proficient in English. He started to learn it in 1872, around the year when it was becoming part of the standard school curriculum. Studying at the English prefectural school, the Aichi Eigo Gakkō, he was one of only eight boys chosen to go to Tokyo to further his education at Kaisei Gakkō, a private establishment which evolved into Tokyo University. There, by his own admission, he freely enjoyed himself, carousing with friends, drinking, and frequenting the theater. While this was all good experience for an aspiring novelist, it was not helpful to his studies. Shōyō, who would later become Japan's greatest Shakespearean scholar, actually failed his final examinations, receiving poor marks for not writing a decent essay about the character of Gertrude in *Hamlet*.

It appears that Tsubouchi completely misunderstood the question. Asked to write about Gertrude's character he wrote about her behavior, and even when his tutor, the American scholar William Houghton, tried to explain, he was puzzled by the distinction. Accepting the challenge when lesser men would have given up, he began to study Western literature in earnest. Now the hardworking, Confucian side of his own character showed itself. He made notes as early as 1880 for the treatise which, by its emphasis on psychological realism, would one day change the course of Japanese literature.

Shōyō finally graduated from Tokyo University in 1883, met the woman who later became his wife, Kato Sen, in 1884, and began publishing *Shōsetsu shinzui* in 1885. As part of his grand design, he intended the launch of his treatise on literature to coincide with that of his first novel, but unfortunately a delay in the printing of the treatise prevented such a *coup de grâce*. It probably made no difference, because his novel, *Tōsei shosei katagi* (1885, *The Character of Present Day Students*) fell far short of embodying all the insights of *Shōsetsu shinzui*. Its complex plot, about a *geisha* called Tanoji whose true parentage is in question until the final chapter, owes more to *gesaku* fiction than to Western literature. Indeed, it is fair to say that all of Shōyō's creative writing stemmed from his love of Edo tales, while his theoretical work, despite some borrowing from the eighteenth-century Japanese scholar Motoori Norinaga (1730–1801), was based on what he knew of Western culture. Both books, however, were well received. His close friend Takada Sanae, who later became Minister of Education and President of Waseda University, compared the novel favorably to the works of Dickens and Thackeray, while admitting that it lacked pathos.

It is for his treatise on fiction that Shōyō is best remembered today. Although Western scholars are inclined to find it superficial, it is nonetheless a statement about art by a creative mind. It rings true in much the same way as E. M. Forster's *Aspects of the Novel* (1927), having behind it the benefit of an artist's practical experience. This is its greatest strength, and the main reason why writers were inspired by it. The message he communicated was the idea that life should be allowed to speak through literature without being manipulated to justify the writer's moral preconceptions. In other words, a novel should show why men behave as they really do, rather than depicting them in idealized terms designed to edify the reader.

Shōyō built a comprehensive argument around his basic idea. Dividing creative works into the visual and abstract arts he wrote: "The perfect novel depicts what is difficult to paint in a painting; makes palpable what is difficult to express in a poem; portrays the mysterious which is impossible to project on the stage." Its primary aim was to seek out the truth of human emotions, while, as a secondary aim, picturing the life and customs of whatever society was chosen as its subject. Emotional truth was far more important than the secondary goal, for it was the means by which the reader could gain a greater understanding of himself and his relationship to others. This was not to suggest that novels had any specific purpose beyond delighting the reader with their truth and beauty. Shōyō wrote: "An artist seeks only to give his reader an awareness of beauty and gladden his heart . . ."

Some critics have found these ideas contradictory. After all, not only does Shōyō go on to admit the validity of didactic fiction, but he also lists so many by-products of the artistic novel – his other main category – that anyone might be forgiven for thinking it a "useful" form of art. Shōyō, however, would not have agreed. Even though a reader might become ennobled by absorbing beauty, or wise through learning to distinguish good from evil, or merely well informed by reading about other people's lives and customs, still the novel should never be thought of as utilitarian in its function. It needed no justification for itself. It was art for art's sake.

Examined in these terms, Shōyō's treatise seems to ignore much of literature's potential for making political, philosophical, or religious statements. However, this is not necessarily true. It must never be forgotten that Shōyō was writing about the *essence* of the novel: its fundamental identity. Seen from the perspective of the late twentieth century when every literary experiment, style, and -ism has been explored, Shōyō's ideas are refreshingly simple and alive. For in its essence the novel is indeed a re-creation of life, rather than a mere description of it. This is surely what he meant when he wrote: "Once the author has presented [the hero] in the world of the novel, he cannot make him move as he, the author wishes. He must think of him as a real person and portray his life as it would naturally progress." If, along the way, political, philosophical, or religious truths are revealed, so much the better. But in essence, the aim of the artistic novel is "solely to picture the state of the world" by bringing characters to life on the page.

Anyone caring to write a "nonutilitarian" novel would have found Shōyō's treatise extremely useful, for it goes on to discuss the constituent parts of novel writing in some detail. First, authors should select realistic subjects: ordinary people in preference to heroes who defy the laws of nature. Second, they should think carefully about the motivations of their characters, revealing these motivations in the course of the story. Plots should be tightly constructed with a clear, logical development, and on no account should the story be twisted so that, for example, bad characters get their comeuppance automatically. Indeed, a vigorously bad character may triumph in art as in life, while his good but weaker opponent may be vanquished.

In matters of literary style, a vexed issue at the time, Shōyō quickly got to the root of the problem. He wrote: "In China and in the West, the written and spoken languages are for the most part the same, and there is no particular necessity to choose either as a literary form. In our country, however, the situation is different. There are several literary styles. Each has its flaws and its merits, its advantages and disadvantages, and they vary according to where they are used. This is why we must select a literary style for the novel." As potential candidates he identified three main styles used in fiction: *gabuntai*, the "rhetorical" style in which *The Tale of Genji* is written; *zokubuntai*, or "colloquial" style used (for example) by *Tamenaga Shunsui (1790–1843), the great chronicler of everyday life in Edo; and *gazoku setchū buntai*, a combination of the other two. As a temporary measure, Shōyō recommended the last of these, that is, the use of *gabuntai* for narrative and *zokubuntai* for dialogue, until a fully integrated style could be developed.

There can be no doubt that stylistic considerations proved to be the biggest hurdle preventing anyone from writing a "perfect" modern novel in Japan. Shōyō's own first novel, *Tōsei shosei katagi* was weak stylistically although it did show his genuine talent for writing dialogue. A more rigorous approach was needed, preferably by someone who was even more skilled as a linguist than Shōyō himself. As it happened, in late January 1886, an intense young man wearing thick spectacles came to call on him. His name was Hasegawa Tatsunosuke, who later adopted the unusual pseudonym, Futabatei Shimei.

Even though Shōyō was supposedly the mentor in their relationship, he was somewhat intimidated by Futabatei's fearsome brilliance. Assiduously cross-examined by this young student of Russian
literature, he began to feel that his theories were superficial.
Futabatei completely rejected his call for a style in which rhetorical
and colloquial elements would peacefully coexist. He wanted to
develop a new, integrated style immediately, asking for – and
obtaining – Shōyō's assistance in creating the famous *gembun itchi
style to unify the written and spoken languages. It was in this style
that Futabatei wrote Ukigumo, a novel which, for its embodiment
of all the qualities Shōyō most admired, came to be recognized as
Japan's first modern work of fiction.

Like the occasion on which Shōyō was awarded a black mark for
Hamlet, Futabatei's progress was enough to make anyone despair.
Yet, for a few years at least, Shōyō held fast to his course and
continued writing fiction of his own. His second novel, Imotose
kagami (A Mirror of Marriage) was published between January and
September 1886. Paying much more attention to characterization
(Futabatei's greatest strength) Shōyō portrayed a young, upper-class
man who marries a fishmonger's daughter. By means of a complex
subplot, in which the hero becomes obsessed with repaying his
father's debts to a prostitute, the author set a stage where suspicion,
jealousy, and marital discord could flourish. The novel's best scenes
are those between the inarticulate wife, Otsuji, and her manipulative,
domineering sister, Oharu, who bends Otsuji's will to suit her own
purposes.

In her detailed study The Development of Realism in the Fiction of
Tsubouchi Shōyō (1975), Marleigh Grayer Ryan notes a marked
improvement in his technique. She says: "In this second novel
Shōyō shows himself to be the master of the incisive scene." She
also explores the attractive idea that the author was agonizing over
whether or not to marry Kato Sen, a woman below his social class
like Otsuji in the novel. Marleigh Ryan identifies Shōyō's sympathy
for lower-class women as being one of the most appealing qualities
in his work. "He understood their pettiness, their ignorance, and
their greed in a way that bespeaks long and close observation. Most
of all, he recognized the reality of their suffering."

Before producing his next major novel, Tsubouchi worked for two
years making four translations and wrote a political allegory and
two minor novels. Early in his career (in 1880) he had published a
summary translation of Scott's 1819 novel The Bride of Lammermoor
with the evocative title Shumpū jōwa (Spring-breeze Love Story). A
free translation with many embellishments but with culturally

specific information faithfully rendered, it introduced Sir Walter Scott to the Japanese public. With his friend Takada Sanae he also translated Scott's *The Lady of the Lake* as *Shunsō kiwa* (*Romance of the Spring Window*), where again the Japanese title was designed to appeal to the reader. In 1884, his painstaking version of *Julius Caesar*, made in the **jōruri* style perfected by *Chikamatsu, was hailed as "the first real translation in the Far East" (i.e., the first real translation of any Western literature, not just of *Caesar* or Shakespeare). And in the same year he published a partial version of one of his favorite novels, Bulwer-Lytton's *Rienzi* (1835), under the title *Gaiseishi den* (*Biography of a Patriot*).

Shōyō's translations of Shakespeare have long since been superseded by other, more modern versions, but in their day they provided an extensive repertory for the new movement in Japanese theater. They were also sufficiently well crafted to demonstrate the truth of Shōyō's assertion that Western literature was far better than anyone had supposed, previous translations having been all too inadequate. Moreover, his confidence in the value of translation may still, today, give heart to Western readers who do not understand the Japanese language. Much of the literature he inspired is readily accessible by anyone who reads English: its settings, plots, characters, and even subtle nuances accurately conveyed.

Shōyō's own attempts at original composition were far less successful than his translations and criticism. The first of many political allegories, *Seijiyu no kōshaku* (1882, *Lectures of the Pure Administration Tea Shop*) promoted the idea of democracy and poked fun at traditional Japanese reliance on oligarchy. His novels of 1887, *Kokoya kashiko* (*Here and There*) and *Tanehiroi* (*Seed Picking*) showed that he had taken to heart Takeda's criticism about the lack of pathos in his fiction. Yet only his last finished novel, *Saikun* (1889, *The Wife*), came close to achieving the sort of realism he had called for in his famous thesis.

A tragedy in four, long chapters, *Saikun* depicts a young bureaucrat, his wife, her rigidly anti-feminist stepmother, and an apprentice maid called Osono. Unhappily married, the wife is imposed upon by her stepmother to raise some money, which she does by sending Osono to the pawnbroker with her kimonos. In having the money stolen from her on the way home, Osono is forced to explain her mission to the head of the household. Furious with his wife for stooping to a moneylender, he threatens divorce, reducing his wife to a state of collapse. Believing it to be her own fault the innocent Osono commits suicide by drowning herself in a well.

Even in synopsis *Saikun* is appealing, not least because it shows the plight of two very different women and their respective destinies. Yet in the year of its publication, not only Shōyō but his great friend Futabatei gave up writing fiction altogether.

Having gone so far along the road to realism, it is strange that both men should have stopped writing at the same time. As far as Futabatei was concerned, a literary career was still inferior to other occupations. Shōyō had no such qualms, but he may well have been influenced by his friend's despair at failing to make a living from creative writing. Ever the brooding pessimist, Futabatei actually felt guilty whenever he received money for his art, so perhaps he argued that they were both doomed to fail. Shōyō, too, for all his audacious appeals in *Shōsetsu shinzui* must have felt social pressures acting against his inclination to entertain the public. After all, on the publication of *Tōsei shosei katagi*, the great Meiji intellectual *Fukuzawa Yukichi is supposed to have commented: "It is quite beneath the dignity of a person holding a Bachelor of Arts degree to engage in such a vulgar occupation as the writing of novels." And as Marleigh Ryan has pointed out, neither Futabatei nor Shōyō "conceived of the possibility of an elitist literature." In identifying popularity with artistic success both men struggled with their art, but were too far ahead of their time to get the recognition they deserved.

Shōyō went on to complete his Shakespearean translations, a gargantuan task that occupied much of his time until 1928. In 1905 he founded a literary association called Bungei kyōkai. Dissolved in 1913 it proved to be very helpful to aspiring playwrights. Generously and with characteristic modesty, Tsubouchi Shōyō dedicated his whole life to improving the status of the literary arts in Japan. History rewarded him, for he lived to see a remarkable flowering of fiction. He even outlived Ozaki Kōyō, NATSUME SŌSEKI, and AKUTAGAWA RYŪNOSUKE – all of them masters of fiction who owed much to Shōyō's unique initiative.

RECOMMENDED READING

Criticism

The Essence of the Novel. *Shōsetsu shinzui.* 1885–86. (1) Extract, tr. Donald Keene. *Modern Japanese Literature*, ed. D. Keene. Grove Press, NY, 1956; Tuttle, Tokyo, 1957. (2) Extracts, tr. Marleigh Grayer Ryan. *Japan's First Modern Novel: Ukigumo of Futabatei Shimei.* Columbia University Press, NY, 1965. (3) Complete version, tr. Nanette Twine. University of Queensland, Brisbane, 1983.

WORKS IN ENGLISH TRANSLATION

Literary Criticism

"Chikamatsu and Shakespeare." *Eigo Seinen*, vol. 61, nos. 1–6, 1929.

The Essence of the Novel. Shōsetsu shinzui. 1885–86.

History and Characteristics of Kabuki. 292 pages. Tr. Ryozo Matsumoto. Yamagata, Yokohama, 1960.

Play

Kiri-hitoha. Kiri hitoha (Paulownia Leaf). 1894–95. Tr. Arthur Lloyd. *Far East,* vol. 2, nos. 7–8, 1897–98; vol. 3, no. 25, 1898.

Urashima. Shinkyoku Urashima. 1904. 92 pages. Tr. Kwanshu M. Furusawa. Furusawa, Urawa, 1936.

CRITICAL STUDIES

Ryan, Marleigh Grayer. *The Development of Realism in the Fiction of Tsubouchi Shōyō.* University of Washington Press, Seattle, 1975.

Yanagida, Izumi. "Tsubouchi Shōyō." *Japan Quarterly,* vol. 11, no. 3, 1964.

TSUSHIMA Yūko
(1947–   )

Novelist and writer of short fiction. Real name, Tsushima Satoko. Born in Mitaka City, Tokyo, and a resident of the capital.

Tsushima Yūko was born the daughter of a famous novelist, her father being DAZAI OSAMU, author of *The Setting Sun* and one of the most gifted men of his generation. In 1948, when she was only one year old, Dazai committed what the Japanese call *shinjū* ("love suicide") with his mistress. Too young, therefore, to have acquired any direct memories of her father she could scarcely avoid the voluminous literature about him, for every aspect of his life has since been repeatedly sifted, argued over, and published. Now widely hailed as one of Japan's most accomplished writers herself, Tsushima reveals certain stylistic affinities with her father while having a more resilient psychology and a much more practical outlook on life. In a career that began in the late 1960s she has won several major prizes for novels and short stories that deal mainly with the problems of feminine identity in the modern world. Two of her best-known works are the novel *Chōji* (1978, *Child of Fortune*), a penetrating study of a thirty-six-year-old woman that won praise from feminists in the West, and *Yama o hashiru onna* (1980, *Woman Running in the Mountains*), a work which has a wider appeal and is arguably her finest in translation.

Tsushima was brought up by her mother, Michiko, Dazai's second wife, whose marriage in 1939 had been arranged by the distinguished author IBUSE MASUJI, Dazai's friend and mentor. Satoko, as Tsushima was named, was the second daughter and third child born to the couple. Her brother, three years her elder, was mentally retarded and died in 1959 at the age of fifteen. Throughout her early years Tsushima was the constant companion of her brother and in her work she has often portrayed characters based upon him.

The fatherless family occasionally moved their home when Tsushima was small, first to her uncle's house in Bunkyo ward, and again when she was two years old and ten years old, respectively. She attended a music school for children until the age of six, going on to junior high school in 1959 and high school in 1962. In April 1965 she was enrolled at the Shirayuri Women's University in Tokyo to study English literature. She graduated in March 1969, whereupon she started a postgraduate course of study at Meiji University. Student strikes were rife at the time, so she rarely attended.

Tsushima began writing while still an undergraduate and suc-ceeded in having her first story, "*Requiem: Inu to otona no tame ni*" (1969, "Requiem for a Dog and an Adult"), published in the Keiō University magazine *Mita bungaku* (*Mita Literature*, so-called because the Keiō campus is in the Mita district of Tokyo). As a student of literature she had acquired a knowledge of the technical aspects of writing, yet her inspiration came – as she herself later said – from an inner need to express herself in language. A childhood in which nonverbal communication with her brother had played such a major part had left her emotionally inarticulate, and the act of writing was therapeutic quite apart from the intrinsic value of the stories themselves.

In much of Tsushima's work there is a strong element of self-exploration. Her novels and stories are subjective even when she appears to move away from the *shishōsetsu* (*I-Novel) genre to write in the third person. In this, she follows the example of her father, who was one of the most skillful of all modern Japanese writers in projecting a carefully constructed literary persona. She tends not to exaggerate as Dazai certainly did, but like him she uses a variety of techniques to uncover emotional truth even when she fictionalizes her material.

Tsushima's first novel, *Ikimono no atsumaru ie* (1973, *The House Where Living Things Are Gathering*), has not been translated into

English, but is based closely on the experiences of her early life. Its heroine, Rutsuko, has had a sheltered childhood in the city and wishes to discover her roots by seeking out her father's former home in the country. It would be some years before Tsushima would attempt another long novel, but in the meantime she established her reputation by becoming a prolific writer of short stories.

One of her earliest stories in English translation is *"Shateki"* (1975, "The Shooting Gallery"). Packed with vivid imagery it is the title story of a collection that was well received on both sides of the Atlantic. It is typical of her early style, and features, as many of her stories do, a mother who is bringing up two children on her own. However, the author deliberately makes it difficult for us to visualize her heroine, for neither her external appearance nor her personality is indicated. All we are given is an interior landscape – and, indeed, the English expression "interior landscapes" precisely identifies much of Tsushima's work.

The figure of the solo mother with young children appears frequently in her stories not only because her mother was such a figure but also because she herself was faced with similar circumstances shortly after she began writing. Tsushima married in 1972, but separated from her husband after they had already started a family. She raised two children by herself while continuing to write, and she naturally drew upon this experience for her short stories and novels.

Tsushima's stories appeared in rapid succession and were collected into volumes that appeared on almost a yearly basis during the 1970s. The best known are *Mugura no haha* (1974, *The Mother in the House of Grass*), which won the Tamura Toshiko Prize, her first, in 1976, and *Kusa no fushido* (1977, *A Bed of Grass*), which took the Izumi Kyōka Prize. The title story of the latter has been translated into English, and is a sixty-page novella told in the first person by a narrator who has recently lost her first child. Using many digressions and flashbacks it creates convincing portrayals of its feminine characters, yet, because the men are so weak and ineffectual, the story gives the impression of presenting an unbalanced view of the world. Some readers may find its atmosphere disturbing for that very reason.

The narrator of the story "A Bed of Grass" has moved back into her mother's dilapidated house soon after the death of her child. Although she continues to see Takashi, her lover who teaches at a university, she has clearly grown apart from him and can no longer tolerate his selfishness. Instead, she spends much of her free time with her friends Kuni and Suwan. Kuni, physically strong but emotionally confused, is a single mother whose priority is to find men who will sleep with her, whereas Suwan is a young Thai student who greatly misses his mother in Bangkok. Neither is a suitable friend for the narrator, and indeed the reader may be surprised that she persists in seeing them. Yet there is a large measure of realism in the story, as there is in nearly all of Tsushima's work. Families disintegrate; friends drift apart. "A Bed of Grass" has all the quirkiness and untidiness of reality, and if its characters are strange bedfellows, their relationships are more than plausible: they are imperfect and real.

Tsushima gained many readers in the West when her second full-length novel, *Child of Fortune*, was published in translation in 1983. In Japan it had won the Women's Literature Prize in 1978, the year of its original publication. Its heroine is Mizuno Kōko, a music teacher who is fast approaching middle age, having drifted into her profession without that wholehearted conviction that makes for a rewarding career. She is not unduly distressed by her circumstances, for her working hours are relatively short and she makes sufficient money to support herself and her only child, Kayako. Rather, it is in her personal life that her tendency to drift, without getting in touch with what might be called the "springs of motivation," is more seriously damaging.

There have been three men in Kōko's life: Doi, her college boyfriend whose child she aborted with scarcely a moment's thought; Hatanaka, whom she married and who became the father of Kayako; and Osada, her most recent lover. None of these men is necessarily an ideal life partner, and together they must surely bear some of the responsibility for Kōko's confusion. By implication it is Doi who has been the most influential. He is described as being light, flippant, and superficial: a man some years Kōko's senior at college whom she regarded with both "fear and admiration." Unaware of his real feelings he has unwittingly curbed Kōko's development, and although quiet and intelligent is possessed of a cynicism which (the narrator admits) "sometimes deflated other people's dreams in what seemed a deliberate way."

Unfortunately, Kōko never finds a greater love than Doi. She marries Hatanaka, an emotional and charming scrounger, after Doi suddenly decides to marry another woman who is expecting his child. One suspects that had Kōko been more open and perhaps less selfish in her attitude to motherhood then Doi might well have married her instead. As it is, her relationship with Hatanaka is a failure, even though it produces Kayako who has grown up to be a likable if somewhat willful teenager by the time the narrative begins.

Tsushima forces the reader to work hard at piecing together her heroine's biography, dropping hints and clues without necessarily drawing attention to their significance. Her narrative technique reveals Kōko's state of mind by reverting to the past in flashback at every opportunity. We learn that Kōko's affair with Doi was resumed after her divorce; that the two of them would go on holiday together, taking Kayako with them. We also learn that Kōko took renewed enjoyment in the "momentary, evanescent pleasure" of sex with Doi, while being terrified of again becoming pregnant by him. "Even as she clutched Doi's body, believing she knew after all this time what it meant to love one man, she was hating and despising the instincts within her." Eventually we discover, too, that history has repeated itself. When she hears that Doi's wife is expecting another baby, Kōko is prompted to end the relationship for good.

A crucial aspect of the plot of *Child of Fortune* has deliberately been omitted from the outline, above, so as not to spoil readers' enjoyment of the novel. However, it can be noted that if there is a single root cause of Kōko's dilemma it is in the social pressures holding back those desires that might otherwise lead to a more fulfilling life. Kōko's relationship with Doi has been trampled underfoot: ". . . under the dirty feet of respectability." Even the support of her own daughter is undermined by a sanctimonious elder sister who persuades Kayako to live with "the family" rather than with her single parent. Ultimately the author levels blame neither at Kōko's weakness nor at Doi's superficial character. She blames society.

Child of Fortune is a fine novel and much less depressing than many of Tsushima's short stories. There is even a note of optimism at the end when Kōko emerges from a confrontation a clear winner for the first time. Despite all the odds she is taking charge of her own destiny, aware at last that this is within her power.

Tsushima's stories and novels are very appealing to women readers who seek a greater measure of independence and a more clearly defined identity for themselves. Perhaps chiefly for this reason she has become popular in the West, especially among feminists who regard her as one of their own. Tsushima, however, has never been stridently feminist herself, even though she has addressed most of the issues which concern the women's movement. She is a personal rather than a political writer: one who comes to terms with events in her own life by turning them into fiction and looking at them from every angle. In this, she is not unlike the novelist ŌE KENZABURŌ, although her work is utterly different in style.

Woman Running in the Mountains is easily Tsushima's best work in English translation. It is very far from being a feminist statement, although it depicts in unsparing detail the life of an unmarried mother. Despite its title – which suggests movement and freedom – it begins slowly, reminding one of the novels of Japanese *Naturalism that were written in the early part of the century. Its heroine, the twenty-one-year-old Takiko who lives in what is described as "certainly a gloomy neighborhood," never walks but "trudges" to the bus stop. Having disgraced her family by conceiving a child after casual sex with a man from her office she has to endure frequent beatings from her father, who is lame, unemployed, and alcoholic. Her brother avoids her, while her long-suffering mother keeps telling her to have an abortion. To her credit Takiko is sufficiently spirited to have her baby – whatever her family or the neighbors might say – and gives birth to Akira, a healthy boy. In a further display of independence she transfers the official records of herself and her baby to a separate family register, although financial constraints compel her to remain living with her parents.

The first half of *Woman Running in the Mountains* is so low-key in its emotional content that the reader may begin to question its purpose and direction. The novel is filled with the minutiae of baby care, every bath and bowel movement being recorded in a deliberately factual manner. Only gradually are we made aware of Takiko's personality, of the nature of her loneliness, and the mysterious purity of her aspirations. She recalls a childhood dream of a vast, frozen sea, and this in itself suggests that one part of her psyche remains untouched by the life around her. While she is not exactly "sex-crazed," as her father insists, in her friendships with the opposite sex she has obviously said yes more often than not. Nonetheless, her sexual relationships have always been unsatisfying. Her attitude to men is expressed in these terms: "Though she couldn't have said why, Takiko responded to a man's desire with sympathy. She could think of it only as pitiful, and thus not for her to violate. Maeda's desire [Maeda being the absent father of her baby] seemed somehow not to belong to Maeda himself." It therefore comes as a surprise – and indeed as a joy – when Takiko, in her hopeless attempts to sell cosmetics door to door, becomes fascinated by the sight of tropical flowers growing in a greenhouse. For the first time she seems to recognize that desire is a force to be reckoned with, and not merely one to be pitied. She relishes the life and vigor of the plants, and by chance is able to secure a job working for the nursery that grows them. There she falls in love with Kambayashi, one of the gardeners, who, by happy coincidence, comes from the "frozen north" of her dreams.

With the appearance of Kambayashi, a male character who is not in the least inadequate, Tsushima's novel acquires a balance, a direction, and an energy that have been lacking in the narrative until this point. One feels that the author has overcome a barrier that hitherto has prevented her from depicting a rounded and encompassing view of life. On being deserted and rejected by men the heroines of many of her stories attempt to rebuild their lives independently of either lovers or husbands. Takiko herself is set upon such a course until her instincts lead her to Kambayashi. The difference is remarkable because instead of *writing about* her heroine, as she normally does, the author succeeds in bringing her to life.

Tsushima's other works have included the novels *Moeru kaze* (1980, *Burning Wind*) and *Yoru no hikari ni owarete* (1986, *Driven by the Light of the Night*), and the series of short stories entitled *Hikari no ryōbun* (1979, *Realm of Light*), which stands directly in the I-Novel tradition. *Realm of Light*, which won the Noma Prize in Japan in 1979, has been translated into French and was published in France in 1986.

It is still too early to judge whether Tsushima will come to be regarded as one of the leading Japanese writers of the century. Although she has explored areas of human experience that others – even other women writers – have neglected, her imagery is sometimes obscure while her descriptions of daily life often seem all too obvious. She is, however, one of the most popular Japanese writers in English translation, and it is therefore clear that she has the power to communicate across cultural boundaries. Besides the English and French versions of her novels and stories, some of her work has been translated into German, Dutch, and Swedish, while *Child of Fortune* has even been rendered into Finnish. Moreover, no anthology of contemporary Japanese women's fiction now seems complete without one of her works, for she is established both as a recognizable voice and as a representative writer of her generation. Her readers in the West can almost certainly look forward to many more translations of her work.

RECOMMENDED READING

Novels

Child of Fortune. *Chōji.* 1978. 161 pages. Tr. Geraldine Harcourt. Kodansha International, Tokyo, 1983; Women's Press, London, 1986. Contains 4-page translator's introduction.
Woman Running in the Mountains. *Yama o hashiru onna.* 1980. 275 pages. Tr. Geraldine Harcourt. Pantheon, NY, 1991.

WORKS IN ENGLISH TRANSLATION

Novels

Child of Fortune. Chōji. 1978.
Woman Running in the Mountains. Yama o hashiru onna. 1980.

Short Fiction Collection

The Shooting Gallery, and Other Stories. 138 pages. Tr. Geraldine Harcourt. The Women's Press, London, 1988; Pantheon Books, NY, 1988. Includes: "The Silent Traders," "The Chrysanthemum Beetle," "The Shooting Gallery," and five others.

Short Fiction

"A Bed of Grass." "*Kusa no fussido.*" 1977. 62 pages. Tr. Yukiko Tanaka and Elizabeth Hanson. *This Kind of Woman,* tr. and ed. Yukiko Tanaka and Elizabeth Hanson. Putnam, NY, 1984.

"The Chrysanthemum Beetle." "*Kikumushi.*" 1983. 35 pages. *The Shooting Gallery, and Other Stories.*

"Clearing the Thickets." "*Kusamura.*" 1976. 14 pages. *The Shooting Gallery, and Other Stories.*

"An Embrace." "*Hōyō.*" 1984. 17 pages. Tr. Geraldine Harcourt. *Journal of Literary Translation,* no. 17, 1986; *The Shooting Gallery, and Other Stories.*

"Island of Joy." "*Yorokobi no shima.*" 1978. 7 pages. Tr. Lora Sharnoff. *Japan Quarterly,* vol. 27, no. 2, 1980.

"The Magic Words." "*Jumon.*" 6 pages. Tr. Susan Bouterey Hulston, Gillian Kinjo, and Chigusa Kimura Steven. *The Magazine,* vol. 3, no. 2, 1988.

"The Marsh." 12 pages. Tr. Yukiko Tanaka. *Unmapped Territories.* Women in Translation (formerly an imprint of The Seal Press), Seattle, 1991.

"Missing." "*Yukue fumei.*" 1973. 11 pages. *The Shooting Gallery, and Other Stories.*

"The Mother in the House of Grass." "*Mugura no haha.*" 1974. 31 pages. Tr. Sara Dillon. *The Literary Review,* vol. 30, no. 2, 1987.

"A Sensitive Season." "*Hatsujōki.*" 1974. 21 pages. *The Shooting Gallery, and Other Stories.*

"The Shooting Gallery." "*Shateki.*" 1975. 15 pages. *The Shooting Gallery, and Other Stories.*

"The Silent Traders." "*Dammari ichi.*" 1982. 10 pages. Tr. Geraldine Harcourt. *Japanese Literature Today,* no. 9, 1984; *The Shōwa Anthology,* vol. 2, ed. Van C. Gessel and Tomone Matsumoto. Kodansha International, Tokyo, 1985; *The Shooting Gallery, and Other Stories.*

"South Wind." "*Minamikaze.*" 1978. 13 pages. Tr. Geraldine Harcourt. *Japan Quarterly,* vol. 33, no. 1, 1986; *The Shooting Gallery, and Other Stories.*

"To Scatter Flower Petals." 1977. 13 pages. Tr. Lora Sharnoff. *Japan Quarterly,* vol. 27, no. 2, 1980.

UNO Chiyo
(1897–   )

Novelist, publisher, and fashion designer. Born in Iwakuni, Yamaguchi. Lived briefly in Hokkaidō, then in Tokyo.

If a full-length biography of Uno Chiyo were published in English, it might, perhaps, dispel the myth that Japanese women always remain in the shadow of the men they marry. In Uno's case, nothing could be further from the truth. Far from being a passive stereotype, she was an assertive and enterprising woman. She founded Japan's first fashion magazine, *Sutairu* (*Style*), in 1936, and made a fortune from it. She became a kimono designer, successfully promoting her creations all over the world. Her love life was notorious, and she was married four times, mostly to famous and gifted men. Nonetheless, she outshone all of her achievements, and indeed those of her men, with the brilliance of her literature. For it was into her writing that she put her experience of love, her knowledge of its difficulties and complications, its pleasures, partings, heartaches, and nostalgia. The scholar Yukiko Tanaka rates her story *Iro zange* (*1933–35, Confessions of Love*) as "one of the finest novels

treating the theme of love written in the pre-World War II period."
Preferring her later work, Donald Keene has written: "Her stories
tended to be brief but, starting with *Ohan* (completed 1957), they
were flawlessly fashioned." She ranks alongside HAYASHI FUMIKO,
ENCHI FUMIKO, and OKAMOTO KANOKO as one of the outstanding
Japanese women writers of the twentieth century.

Unconventional even as a child, Uno Chiyo was born and brought
up in Yamaguchi. In her story *"Mohō no tensai"*(1936, "A Genius of
Imitation") she recalled: "Influenced by the spirit of the times and
my surroundings, I grew up as a child who wanted to go to the
battlefields despite my sex: I aspired to be a kind, gentle nurse like
Florence Nightingale or an officer as brave as Joan of Arc . . ." She
also recalled reading many stirring war songs, written in the
vernacular and printed in books that sold for five sen. She wrote:
"It was these war songs, now I come to think of it, that introduced
me to literature."

The young Uno Chiyo displeased both her teachers and her parents
by becoming absorbed in reading newspapers and magazines. Her
father actually banished them from the house, but still she read
them secretly, not always understanding what they contained yet
allowing "the mystery of the adult world" to swell in her imagination
"like a dangerous boil." At school, too, she was reprimanded, not
just for reading magazines but for "publishing" one of them. "I
trust this writing doesn't reflect what you girls really believe," said
the principal to Uno and her friends. It did, for Uno was a modern
girl even then.

Despite her wayward nature, Uno was exceptionally diligent in
her studies. She is said to have copied over a hundred textbooks
in order to prepare for a single examination. Wishing to become a
teacher, she would have been qualified for senior schools had she
actually taken this examination, but she suddenly opted for working
in a nearby elementary school. Off she went ("wearing white powder
on my face and a long, blue *hakama* skirt over my tight-sleeved
kimono . . .") to begin her independent life at age eighteen. In rapid
succession, she fell in love, scandalized her conservative colleagues
with her flamboyant dress (and matching behavior), then promptly
fell out of love and moved to Tokyo. Complaining that the only
men who appeared in her life "were poor, uninteresting and short,"
she worked at menial jobs until her cousin, one of her several
lovers, asked her to marry him and move to Sapporo.

"It snowed a lot in Sapporo," Uno recalled with meaningful
brevity. Becoming bored with knitting socks for her husband, she
began to write fiction. She sent her stories to local newspapers and
won two first prizes in succession, one of them for *"Shifun no kao"*

(*1921*, "The Face with Makeup Powder"). Gaining in confidence, she remembered having once met Takita Choin, the editor of *Chūō kōron*, whom she had served while working as a waitress in a Tokyo restaurant. With this lofty target in mind she wrote "*Haka o abaku*" (*1922*, "To Open a Grave") and sent it to him. She later said: "It was a story with a clear theme and had a young idealistic teacher, clearly resembling the author, as the heroine; it depicted the heroine's struggles against the public education system, which did not treat handicapped children with due consideration."

One can safely assume that not many an ex-waitress would send a story to the *Chūō kōron*, and fewer still would make a personal visit to complain when it failed to appear in print. Uno had no hesitation. She left Sapporo, arrived in Tokyo, and called at the publisher's offices where she was given an enormous check for four hundred yen, together with the news that her story was typeset for the spring issue. She said: "I was so absorbed in myself that I forgot about returning to my home in Hokkaidō." She remained in Tokyo, divorced her first husband, and married Ozaki Shirō, the novelist, in 1926.

Living with Ozaki in the suburb of Ōmori, Uno became an *I-Novelist, although she looked at the world through the eyes of her husband and wrote in his style. Once again she was bored. ("My dog got sick and I wrote about it in a story; a new neighbor moved in next door and I wrote about *that*.") Yet there was a part of Uno that always wanted to be "a good wife," and this aspect of her complex personality often gained the upper hand. When it did, she found herself suppressing her natural drives. Even more than security she wanted fame, excitement, and money of her own, all of which she rightly guessed were in her stars.

Working as a journalist, Uno went to call on the artist Tōgō Seiji (1897–1978), in order to discover some morbid details about his attempt to commit "double suicide" with a lover. The newspapers had been full of the scandal in 1929, and Uno, now separated from Ozaki, was sure to find a good story in it. This she did, although perhaps not in the way she anticipated. Not only did she sleep with Tōgō that night but she actually moved in with him on the following day. From the very long tale that Tōgō had to tell, she pieced together a remarkable work of fiction: *Confessions of Love*. Much of it was written towards the end of her five-year relationship with the artist, and it depicts him in a somewhat unfavorable light. Weak and apathetic, the "hero" is jilted by two women but loved by Tsuyuko, with whom he tries to commit suicide. The novel is greatly admired for its narrative technique and its vivid description of Tokyo life in the 1920s.

Several of Uno's works date from 1935–36, including not only the above-mentioned *Confessions of Love* and "A Genius of Imitation," but two short stories describing her breakup from Tōgō: "*Wakare mo tanoshi*" (*1935*, "Parting Is Also Pleasurable") and "*Miren*" (*1936*, "Lingering Attachment"). She often remarked that her fiction was a useful by-product of failed romance: an attitude which undoubtedly sustained her after many a separation. However, for some time after 1936 there was a steep decline in her literary output as her activities in publishing began to take over. Never a prolific writer, Uno now became a full-time businesswoman. Her enterprise attracted much attention, and she herself became a subject whom journalists liked to interview.

One journalist who came to see her was Kitahara Takeo, who was then working for the *Miyako shimbun*. Although ten years younger than Uno he became the most important man in her life. They were married in 1939, worked together in the publishing house that Uno had founded, and traveled across Manchuria and China in 1941. Wartime paper shortages forced the suspension of *Style*, but in September 1941 the couple started a literary magazine called *Buntai* (*Literary Style*) together with the poet Miyoshi Tatsuji. This, too, had to cease publication during the war when Kitahara was conscripted into the armed forces. Left to her own devices, the ever-resourceful Uno went back to writing, producing an excellent story in dialect called "*Ningyōshi Tenguya Hisakichi*" (*1942*, "The Doll Maker Tenguya Hisakichi"). In order to obtain the interviews on which it was based, Uno traveled all the way to the island of Shikoku to meet with an elderly maker of puppet dolls whose work she admired. So good was the story that the author tried to repeat her new formula in "*Nichiro no Sentōsho*" (1943, "Memoir of the Russo–Japanese War"), based on conversations with Kitahara's father. However, this second wartime work did not quite match the quality of the first.

After the war, everything came together for Uno in a spectacular way. Her husband returned, and the couple revived both magazines: *Style* as a full-color publication in February 1946; *Literary Style* as a quarterly in 1947. In their respective markets they were both very successful. *Buntai* carried such masterpieces of postwar literature as ŌOKA SHŌHEI's *Nobi* (*1947*, *Fires on the Plain*), while *Sutairu* grew to a massive 100,000 circulation at its peak a few years later. Uno was now a very rich woman. She built a home in fashionable Tsukiji, bought a villa in Atami, then switched her attention to fashion design, starting a completely new business designing kimonos and marketing them to the West.

With so much activity in her life, Uno had little time for writing, yet she started her most famous novel, *Ohan* (*The Wife*, translated as *Ohan*), in 1947. Towards the end of the 1950s when all her business ventures collapsed, she completed *Ohan* and made it ready for publication. It not only brought her new fame as an author, but won the 1958 Women's Literary Award and the Noma Prize. Furthermore, it was translated into English in 1961 by Donald Keene.

Ohan is based on a further tale from Shikoku, this time told to Uno by the owner of an antiques shop. In Uno's novel he becomes the narrator, explaining how he has left his wife, Ohan, to live with his mistress, an ex-*geisha* called Okayo. When he encounters his wife after their long separation she tells him about their son, Satoru, and he feels a sudden desire to reunite the family. However, his attempt ends in tragedy, leaving the way clear for Okayo to assert her possessive instincts. The whole story is beautifully crafted and has a timeless quality suggesting that its drama is by no means limited to a particular time or place.

Uno projected herself into each of the characters of *Ohan*, a fact which may account for its success as a work of art. She shared the narrator's fantasy of respectability as much as she identified with Okayo's feminine guile and Ohan's resignation. When the novel was published in book form in 1957 it marked a new phase in Uno's career as a serious writer.

The emotional atmosphere surrounding the collapse of Uno's business enterprises is well shown in "*Sasu*" (1963–66, "To Stab"). Under the circumstances, separation from Kitahara was inevitable. They quarreled over whether or not to publish a new magazine, Uno being in favor of expansion, Kitahara opposed to it. The whole story is in "To Stab," where Uno ruefully reflects on her reckless nature, comparing herself to the scorpion who kills a swimming turtle on whose back she rides. Once again, the conflicts of her life become the essential material for her literary work, this time in a directly autobiographical manner.

Uno went on to write many more excellent stories, including "*Teisetsu*" (1970, "Chastity") and "*Ame no oto*" (1974, "The Sound of the Rain"). Her 1970 story "*Kōfuku*" ("Happiness") brought her a second Women's Literature Award. In English, it may be found in Phyllis Birnbaum's volume *Rabbits, Crabs, Etc.* (1982), and is a charming self-portrait of a woman, who, in the guise of the heroine, Kazue, looks back on a turbulent life without any regrets whatsoever.

RECOMMENDED READING

Novel

Confessions of Love. *Iro zange. 1935.* 155 pages. Tr. Phyllis Birnbaum. 17-page extract as "Passion and Repentance." *Journal of Literary Translation,* no. 17, 1986; complete work: University of Hawaii Press, Honolulu, 1989; Peter Owen, London, 1990; Tuttle, Tokyo, 1990. Contains translator's 6-page introduction. UHP paperback is an attractive volume, produced to a high standard of design and binding.

WORKS IN ENGLISH TRANSLATION

Novels

Confessions of Love. Iro zange. 1935.
Ohan. Ohan. 1957. 67 pages. Tr. Donald Keene. *The Old Woman, The Wife, and The Archer, Three Modern Japanese Short Novels.* Viking Press, NY, 1961; Constable, London, 1962. The other two short novels in this volume are "The Songs of Oak Mountain," by Fukasawa Shichiro; and "Asters," by Ishikawa Jun.

Short Fiction

"A Genius of Imitation." *"Mohō no tensai."* 1936. 8 pages. Tr. Yukiko Tanaka. *To Live and To Write, Selections by Japanese Women Writers 1913–1938,* ed. Yukiko Tanaka. The Seal Press, Seattle, 1987.

"Happiness." *"Kōfuku."* 1970. 14 pages. Tr. Phyllis Birnbaum. *Rabbits, Crabs, Etc., Stories by Japanese Women.* University of Hawaii Press, Honolulu, 1982.

"Shopgirl." *"Garasu no naka no musume."* 18 pages. Tr. Mitsugi Teshigawara. *Young Forever, and Five Other Novelettes.* Hokuseido, Tokyo, 1941.

"To Stab." *"Sasu."* 1963–66. 13 pages. Tr. Kyoko Iriye Selden. *Stories by Contemporary Japanese Women Writers,* ed. Noriko Mizuta Lippit and Kyoko Iriye Selden. M. E. Sharpe, Armonk, NY, 1982; reissued as *Japanese Women Writers,* 1991.

CRITICAL STUDY

Copeland, Rebecca L. *The Sound of the Wind: The Life and Works of Uno Chiyo.* University of Hawaii Press, Honolulu, 1992.

Yamada BIMYŌ
(1868–1910)

Novelist, poet, and scholar. Real name, Yamada Taketarō. Born in Kanda, Tokyo, and a lifelong resident in the capital.

Described by Hisamatsu Sen'ichi as "the earliest novelist to use the colloquial language in his creative work," Yamada Bimyō enjoyed a brief reputation in the 1880s but is now almost forgotten. Only one of his works has been translated into English: a short poem taken from an earlier French version. There appears to be no good reason for correcting the perspective thus given, for Bimyō was so preoccupied with stylistic considerations that his novels had few other qualities. He is included here solely because many Japanese scholars (like Hisamatsu, above) believe that it was he, rather than FUTABATEI SHIMEI (1864–1909), who published the first example of *gembun itchi*, the style unifying spoken and written languages. Bimyō strenuously (and perhaps wisely) denied any such suggestion, although he was certainly the first to use Western-style punctuation. He also experimented with new styles of poetry, and has been described (by Nakamura Mitsuo) as a Jack-of-all-trades but master of none. In 1910, much of his life having been blighted by the domination of his tyrannical grandmother, Bimyō died in poverty at age forty-two.

A contemporary of OZAKI KŌYŌ (1867–1903), Bimyō was a friend of both Kōyō and Futabatei in their boyhood. While he was still at the first high school he joined with Kōyō, Ishibashi Shian (1867–1927), and Maruoka Kyūka (1865–1927) in founding the *Ken'yūsha in 1885. Sharing a common love for the works of *Bakin, they started a magazine called *Garakuta bunko* (*Trash Library*) which ran until 1889. It was in this coterie magazine that Bimyō published his first story, "*Tategoto zōshi*" (*1885*, "Tale of the Harp"). Written in Bakin's style (*Bakin-cho*) it described how Alfred the Great halted the Danish invasion of England in the ninth century.

In the following year, Bimyō published some new-style poetry in the collection *Shintaishi sen* (1886, *Anthology of New-Style Poems*), along with works by Kōyō and Kyūka. Quite unlike *waka* or *haiku, Bimyō's verse used a vocabulary not normally acceptable in traditional poetic forms. Most of the poems were, however, original compositions rather than translations, and Bimyō later spent much effort analyzing prosody in a number of theoretical works. His treatise "*Nippon imbun ron*" (*1891–92*, "On the Prosody of Japanese Poems") was the first work to address Japanese poetry from a technical viewpoint, even though it was roundly criticized by MORI ŌGAI. Unfortunately, Bimyō himself lacked the sensibility to be a successful poet, a fact which did not go unnoted by his contemporaries.

According to Marleigh Grayer Ryan in her critical analysis to Futabatei's *Ukigumo*, Bimyō first used the colloquial language for fiction in "*Fūkin shirabe no hitofushi*" (*1887*, "A Song to Be Played on the Organ"). Donald Keene in *Dawn to the West*, on the other hand, draws attention to Bimyō's satire "*Chōkai shōsetsu tengu*" (1886–87, "Mockery and Reproof for a Braggart Novelist"), which he says is "written entirely in the colloquial language," and predates *Ukigumo* by six months. However, not only was the earlier work (as Keene says) "no more than an abortive sketch," but Bimyō himself denied that even "A Song to Be Played on the Organ" could lay claim to being his first example of *gembun itchi*. Rather, he thought that his first stories written in this style were those in the collection *Natsu kodachi* (1888, *A Summer Grove*). These were actually submitted to – and rejected by – the publishers of *Ukigumo* before Futabatei delivered the manuscript for part one of his famous novel.

Such arcane details as those mentioned above are, perhaps, of interest only to the literary historian. Nonetheless, Bimyō has to be given his due. If one finally accepts the conventional view of

Futabatei's prior claim, it is chiefly because TSUBOUCHI SHŌYŌ had already called for unification of the written and spoken languages in his 1886 treatise, *Shōsetsu shinzui* (*The Essence of the Novel*), and since its publication had been working closely with Futabatei in developing the new *gembun itchi* style.

Bimyō's story "*Musashino*" (*1887*, "The Musashi Plain") was serialized in the *Yomiuri shimbun* shortly before being anthologized in *A Summer Grove*. Set in the fourteenth century it describes how a young woman searches for her husband who is reported dead in battle. If this sounds somewhat like a modern-day soap opera, rest assured that she is not disfigured in an automobile accident, but is eaten by a bear. Moreover, Bimyō's style is not in the least bit anachronistic. Quite reasonably, his story is narrated in a contemporary "colloquial" style while all the characters speak in a "written" language appropriate to the period. Needless to say, such a curious reversal did not catch on.

Bimyō persisted with his odd mixture of styles in *Kochō* (*1889, The Butterfly*). This, his most famous novel, may well have been responsible for the major disaster that befell *Meiji letters in the same year. Published in the New Year's supplement of *Kokumin no tomo* (a very prestigious intellectual magazine), and set in the *Heian period, it contains a scene in which a young lady tries to escape being raped by a burly fisherman. Moreover, the scene was depicted in a frontispiece that showed the heroine almost completely naked. As a result, the story attracted far more attention than it deserved, quite eclipsing Tsubouchi Shōyō's best novel, *Saikun* (*The Wife*), which appeared in the same issue. One need look no further than TAYAMA KATAI's *Literary Life in Tokyo* (1917) to gauge the public's reaction. Katai said: "I'll never forget the . . . supplement with a story by Yamada Bimyō that was illustrated with a picture of a naked woman. I've forgotten the title, but it dealt with little-known facts about Emperor Antoku, and I was filled with surprise and admiration that such *virgin soil* was being tilled in Japanese literature." As an afterthought, he added: "Dr Tsubouchi's story *Saikun* was in the same issue."

Historians have suggested that Tsubouchi gave up writing realistic fiction while on the very brink of success because no one paid any attention to *Saikun*. If so, Watanabe Seitei's illustration for Bimyō's story, rather than the story itself, may have changed the course of Japanese literature. For not only Tsubouchi, but Futabatei himself – the author of Japan's first modern novel – stopped writing at the same time, discouraged by the climate of opinion.

In 1888 Bimyō had been appointed editor of *Miyako no hana*, a literary magazine issued by the Kinkōdō, who published *Ukigumo*.

But although he was mistakenly hailed by Uchida Roan as a "Japanese Shakespeare" for *The Butterfly*, he fell rapidly from favor in the years that followed. Towards the end of his life he wrote *Jirō Tsunetaka* (*1908*) and *Taira no Shigehira* (1910), but by this time everyone had lost interest in him. Diverted by many different interests, he lacked both direction and encouragement. The new rising star of Japanese letters, KUNIKIDA DOPPO, had denounced the Ken'yūsha for dressing their literature in a Western style, and for all his experimentation Bimyō had no real achievements to show in his defense. He had, in any case, been expelled from the Ken'yūsha for accepting the editorship of *Miyako no hana*, a rival magazine to the Ken'yusha's ailing publication, *Garakuta bunko*. In his personal life he was believed to have been responsible for driving his wife to suicide, and he died a virtual outcast from literary society in 1910.

WORK IN ENGLISH TRANSLATION

Note: The only work by Bimyō in English translation is a single poem, translated from the French by Unity Evans. *Japanese Literature*. Walker, NY, 1965.

CRITICAL STUDY

Morita, James R. "Yamada Bimyō as Novelist." Ph.D. diss., University of Chicago, Chicago, 1968.

YASUOKA Shōtarō
(1920–   )

Novelist, essayist, and writer of short fiction. Born in Kōchi, in Shikoku. After service in Manchuria, returned to live in Kugenuma, Kanagawa.

A brilliant storyteller and one of Japan's most endearing writers of humorous fiction, Yasuoka Shōtarō did not become famous until 1953. In that year he won the Akutagawa Prize for his stories *"Inki na tanoshimi"* ("Gloomy Pleasures") and *"Warui nakama"* ("Bad Company"). Both were written under distressing conditions, for, at the end of the war, Yasuoka was stricken with Pott's disease (curvature of the spine) and obliged to spend six years in bed. His achievement is thus all the more remarkable, and furthermore, the stories written during this period are deeply funny. Anyone studying a connection between tragic experience and the humorous response to life which it sometimes provokes would do well to read Yasuoka.

Born in the island town of Kōchi in 1920, Yasuoka spent most of his youth traveling with his father, a veterinary officer in the Japanese army. Being the son of a "horse doctor" was a constant embarrassment to the boy, and his mother felt much the same way. Yasuoka would later express the family relationships in his stories, often exaggerating them for comic effect. At the time, however, he undoubtedly suffered because of his father's unusual line of work. Forced to change schools six times in twelve years, he frequently played truant, coming perilously close to delinquency but also acquiring a streetwise mentality which may have increased his resilience to misfortune. It certainly added a subversive element to his writing.

Yasuoka was eventually accepted into Keiō University to study literature, despite his undistinguished academic record at school. Called up into the army in 1944, he was prevented by illness from seeing active service. He was shipped home from Manchuria in a body cast in March 1945, and placed in the care of his mother. When his father also returned from the war a few months later, the family was faced with extreme poverty and little likelihood of overcoming it. Yet Yasuoka returned to his studies, graduated, and began writing the stories that have brought him so much success.

The first of Yasuoka's stories to attract attention was *"Garasu no kutsu"* (*1951*, "The Glass Slipper"), which earned him a nomination for the Akutagawa Prize. Growing in confidence he went on to write not only *"Aigan"* (*1952*, "Prized Possessions") but the two stories already mentioned that won him the prize in 1953. Suddenly, Yasuoka was seen as that comparatively rare kind of writer: one whose work has a broad popular appeal and yet is sophisticated and profound.

Recovering from his illness, Yasuoka married in 1954 and began to enjoy an active social life with many literary friends. He carried on working as hard as ever, producing a novel based on his war experiences, *Tonsō* (1956, *Flight*). His English translator, Karen Wigen Lewis, claims: "[*Tonsō*] anticipated the M.A.S.H. view of war by a couple of decades."

The death of Yasuoka's mother in 1957 was another cruel blow, but it provided the impetus for him to write his masterpiece: the novel *Umibe no kōkei* (*1958*, *A View by the Sea*). This account of his mother's death in an insane asylum was hailed as one of the greatest achievements of Japanese postwar literature. It won both the Mombushō Geijutsu senshō (Ministry of Education commendation) and Noma literary prizes in 1958.

Following the success of *A View by the Sea*, and, to a lesser extent, *Shita dashi tenshi* (*The Angel Who Stuck Out His Tongue*) Yasuoka turned to writing shorter fiction and essays. He visited the United States in 1958 by invitation of the Rockefeller Foundation and published "*Amerika kanjō ryokō* ("Sentimental Journeys in the United

States") in 1962. His essays on literary figures, including SHIGA NAOYA, IBUSE MASUJI, and TANIZAKI JUN'ICHIRŌ, are notable for their off-beat, unconventional style of interpretation. But not until 1967 did Yasuoka write another major novel, this time winning the Mainichi Prize for *Maku ga orite kara* (*After the Curtain Falls*).

Yasuoka's growing versatility as an all-around man of letters has helped to make this somewhat idiosyncratic writer into a member of the literary establishment. He won yet another prize (the Yomiuri) for his 1973 story collection *Hashire Tomahōku (Run, Tomahawk)* and went on to translate Alex Haley's *Roots* into Japanese. Taking his cue from the American author in the well-established Japanese tradition of borrowing, then improving upon, Western achievements – Yasuoka produced his own "Roots saga" called *Ryūritan (A Tale of Wandering Ancestors)*. It won him the ultimate Japanese literary award: the Grand Prize for Literature, in 1981.

Like his friend ENDŌ SHŪSAKU, Yasuoka has become one of the half-dozen (or so) acknowledged giants of contemporary Japanese fiction. He deserves to be more widely read in the West, for his humor is universal and his stories capture the essence of life. It is hoped that much more of his work will be translated.

RECOMMENDED READING

Short Fiction Collection

A View by the Sea. 196 pages. Tr. Karen Wigen Lewis. Modern Asian Literature Series. Columbia University Press, NY, 1984. Has 5-page foreword by Van C. Gessel, and a 4-page introduction by the translator. Contains the 91-page novella "A View by the Sea," "Bad Company," "Gloomy Pleasures," and three other stories.

WORKS IN ENGLISH TRANSLATION

Short Fiction

"Bad Company." "*Warui nakama.*" 1953. 26 pages. Tr. Karen Wigen Lewis. *A View by the Sea; The Shōwa Anthology*, vol. 1, ed. Van C. Gessel and Tomone Matsumoto. Kodansha International, Tokyo, 1985.

"Circus Horse." "*Sākasu no uma.*" 2 pages. Tr. Leon Zolbrod. *The East*, vol. 1, no. 6, 1965.

"The Glass Slipper." "*Garasu no kutsu.*" 1951. 12 pages. Tr. Edward Seidensticker. *Japan Quarterly*, vol. 8, no. 2, 1961. Yasuoka's debut work.

"Gloomy Pleasures." "*Inki na tanoshimi.*" 1949. 12 pages. *A View by the Sea.*

"The Moth." "*Ga.*" 1960. 13 pages. *A View by the Sea.*

"The Pawnbroker's Wife." "*Shichiya no nyōbō.*" 1960. 10 pages. Tr. Edward Seidensticker. *Japan Quarterly*, vol. 8, no. 2, 1961;

New Writing in Japan. Penguin Books, Harmondsworth, 1972.

"Prized Possessions." *"Aigan."* 1952. 8 pages. Tr. Edwin McClellan. *Contemporary Japanese Literature,* ed. Howard Hibbett. Knopf, NY, 1977, paperback; Tuttle, Tokyo, 1978.

"Rain." *"Ame."* 10 pages. *A View by the Sea; Murder in Japan,* ed. John L. Apostolou and Martin H. Greenberg. Dembner Books, NY, 1987.

"Thick the New Leaves." *"Aoba shigereru."* 1958. 30 pages. *A View by the Sea.*

"A View by the Sea." *"Umibe no kōkei. 1959.* 91 pages. (1) 3-page extract as "View of the Bay." Tr. Joyce Ackroyd and Mikio Hiramatsu. *Hemisphere,* vol. 3, no. 6, June 1964. (2) *A View by the Sea.*

Miscellaneous

Three-page synopsis of the novel *A Tale of Wandering Ancestors. Ryuritan. 1981. Japanese Literature Today,* no. 8, 1983.

CRITICAL STUDIES

Gessel, Van Craig. "The Literature of Kojima Nobuo, Yasuoka Shōtarō and Endō Shūsaku: Cripples, Clods and Cowards in Contemporary Japanese Fiction." Ph.D. diss., Columbia University, NY, 1979.

———. "The Loss of Home: Yasuoka Shōtarō." *The Sting of Life.* Columbia University Press, NY, 1989.

———. "War and Postwar in the Writings of Kojima Nobuo, Yasuoka Shōtarō and Endō Shūsaku." *Transactions of the International Conference of Orientalists in Japan,* no. 23, 1978.

YOKOMITSU Riichi
(1898–1947)

Writer of short fiction. Born in Higashiyama, Fukushima Prefecture (northeast Japan). Moved to Tokyo at age eighteen.

Yokomitsu Riichi was a pivotal figure in the literary world of Japan in the 1920s and 1930s. He was a founder member of that loosely knit group (to which, incidentally, the young KAWABATA YASUNARI also belonged) called the *Shinkankakuha*: the "new sense-impression school." These writers, and none more so than Yokomitsu, wanted to escape from the prevailing tradition of autobiographical literature started by the *Naturalists (TAYAMA KATAI and SHIMAZAKI TŌSON) and continued by the *Shirakabaha (SHIGA NAOYA, MUSHANOKŌJI SANEATSU, and SATOMI TON). The underlying idea of the *Shinkankakuha* was to develop a style that would address reality without the intervention of the author's sensibility. By this means, Yokomitsu believed they could transcend personal experience – which nonetheless remained as the essential content of literature – and effectively "fictionalize" reality in the manner of great Western novelists.

Despite a heroic attempt, Yokomitsu never succeeded in bridging the gap between theory and practice. His disconnected, impression-istic, and indeed *haiku*-like style of writing is not only difficult to read but fails to produce the cumulative effect of great fiction. Although it sometimes captures the imagination with a powerful image, only rarely (as in his 1925 story, "The Depths of the Town") does it offer a sustained reading experience.

English readers, however, may gain from Yokomitsu some fascinating insights into the creative process of writing fiction. Much of his work has been translated by Dennis Keene, who is also the author of the definitive study, *Yokomitsu Riichi, Modernist* (Columbia University Press, New York, 1980). Professor Keene argues convinc-ingly that Yokomitsu was misled by his own theories, and that, far from being a writer who sought a sense-impression style in which objects could be "given back" their identity, he was really attempting to become a Symbolist, imposing his own view on the world within a closed system of perception.

Yokomitsu was born in 1898 at a hot spring resort called Higashiyama. His father was a thirty-one-year-old civil engineering contractor whose work called for frequent moves to various parts of the country. His mother was a member of the Matsuo family and supposedly descended from the famous *haiku* poet, Matsuo Bashō. With only one sister, a girl four years his senior who married at the early age of seventeen, Yokomitsu had a lonely but otherwise unremarkable upbringing. He showed no special talent for literature until the end of his school career, but excelled in such sports as judo and baseball. In fact, the picture that emerges of the young Yokomitsu from others' recollections is that of a curiously mixed personality: part introvert, part extrovert. After just eighteen months at Waseda University, he returned home with a nervous breakdown.

Disentangling the biography of a writer who tried to fictionalize reality is no easy task and scholars are not entirely clear about what happened to Yokomitsu at Waseda in 1916. However, his friend, the novelist Nakayama Gishū, recalled some forty years later that Yokomitsu had discovered his girlfriend in bed with another man. Highly possessive by nature (perhaps because of his closeness to his sister and her subsequent "desertion") Yokomitsu was deeply affected by the incident. It formed the basis of an early work: "*Kanashimi no daika*" (1920, "The Price of Unhappiness"), a story that was later rewritten (i.e., "fictionalized" in the author's *Shinkankakuha* style) as "*Maketa otto*" (1924, "The Defeated Husband").

Yokomitsu returned to Waseda in 1918 with renewed confidence and entered the English Department where he was described as being conspicuous on account of his "arrogant bearing." In the interim he had already begun to write short stories, producing such works as *"Onmi"* ("Love") which describes a man's obsession with his sister's baby, and *"Warawareta ko"* ("The Child Who Was Laughed At") about a peasant boy who is forced by his parents to become a clog maker because he shows some skill for carving masks. The latter story is truly excellent. It ends with the clog maker as an old man: catching sight of the mask he made in his childhood and smashing it to pieces as if in revenge for causing him a lifetime of menial work. Regaining his composure, the man, like an automaton, begins to make clogs out of the broken fragments of the mask.

By the time Yokomitsu came to write "The Price of Unhappiness" (it was not actually published in its original form until 1955) he had already met the girl who was to become his first wife. Kojima Kimiko, whom he married in 1924, was only fourteen in 1920, and was certainly not the inspiration for the story. Rather, the author was recalling the painful incident that ended his first attendance at Waseda. In an attempt to fictionalize the experience, he modeled his heroine on Kimiko, perhaps because she provoked similar anxieties of jealousy, or, more likely, because his memory of the first girl had faded. Thus, "The Price of Unhappiness" is plotted as a complete novel, and tells of a hero who, distrusting his wife, is eventually given confirmation of her infidelity when he discovers her in the arms of their lodger. He feels a curious relief – an ambivalent sense of freedom – and like Yokomitsu in 1916 he walks away from the problem. The remaining two-thirds of the story describe the hero's (rejected) proposal of marriage to a former sweetheart, a long debate about the nature of human relationships, and a final, uneasy reconciliation with his wife.

Critical opinion is divided on the merits of "The Price of Unhappiness." Kawabata Yasunari referred approvingly to "the violent intensity, gravity, and unadorned truth" that he said runs through the novel. Dennis Keene speaks of its "slightly clumsy and convoluted style," its "nagging tone" and "continual worrying over the same few themes." Whatever its merits or defects, the work is available to English readers only in the rewrite, "The Defeated Husband": "a botched rewrite," according to Kawabata. This version, published in the October 1924 issue of *Bungei jidai*, is thought by many critics to be the first *Shinkankakuha* work.

Between the first draft and the rewrite of "The Price of Unhappiness" Yokomitsu produced several stories (one of which was extremely controversial), and a longer work of historical fiction called *"Nichirin"* (written 1920–22, published 1923, "The Sun in Heaven"). Although well received in its day, *"Nichirin"* is said to be stylistically atrocious, having been written under the influence of Ikuta Chōkō's deliberately stilted translation of Flaubert's *Sal-*

ammbo. Just as Flaubert wanted to make ancient Carthage seem remote and alien by portraying brutal action with clipped, staccato prose, so Yokomitsu applied a similar technique to a tale about Princess Himiko's vengeance on men in Old Japan. With his customary wit, Professor Donald Keene in *Dawn to the West* remarks: "The uncouth short sentences are reminiscent less of Flaubert than of Tarzan; at best they suggest a primitive people who had yet to discover subordinate clauses . . ." Yokomitsu's translator, on the other hand, makes the point that Yokomitsu's sporadic style never matches the cumulative effects of Flaubert's descriptions. The simple reason he gives is that Japanese is a "short-breathed language." In other words, this is a classic example of a writer failing to assimilate a Western influence because of the nature of Japanese linguistic tradition. The same problem was to follow Yokomitsu right into his *Shinkankakuha* period.

For all his serious intent, there can be little doubt that Yokomitsu was fatally inclined to "voguishness," and fully realized the advantages of being controversial. His 1924 story, "*Atama narabi ni hara*" ("Heads and Bellies") began: "It was noon. The crowded express train raced at full speed. The small wayside station was ignored like a stone." Writing in a subsequent issue of *Bungei jidai*, Kataoka Teppei (another *Shinkankakuha* member) took an unnamed critic to task for daring to say that "ignored like a stone" was bad writing. Kataoka's defense of Yokomitsu's phrase emphasized "sensation," describing it as being "that expressionistic power which mediates between the object and the writer's existence, and which gives this existence its life . . ." In other words, if the "I" of the author interfered, nothing would be added except a "secondary existence" which would actually diminish the power of the image. Moreover, as Kataoka said, it is the image that defines the implied "I" (i.e., to a human onlooker, the emotional impact of seeing an express train pass through a now disused station would be akin to the "ignored like a stone" simile). This is a very acute observation, if one which is taken so much for granted in Western literature that readers may have trouble recognizing its validity. Dennis Keene further clarifies the idea by saying: "The *Shinkankakuha* removed the viewpoint from the individual, and made it abstract or attached to things in the world, thus rejecting the idea that the world is revealed through the individual and replacing it by the idea that man is revealed through the world." In the example of Yokomitsu, the approach led to a finely polished surface which concealed rather than revealed his emotional life.

The mid–1920s were turbulent years in Japan's literary world. With his Modernist approach Yokomitsu was better placed than others to cope with the modernization of Tokyo following the city's virtual destruction in the *Great Kantō Earthquake of September 1923. Whereas TANIZAKI JUN'ICHIRŌ, for example, retreated to the Kansai where traditional Japanese ways were more in evidence, Yokomitsu faced the prospect of a new Tokyo, a new Japan, and new forms of literature. In his personal life, however, he was beset by tragedy. His young wife, Kimiko, died of consumption in 1926 at the age of twenty. Her illness became the subject of two stories: "*Haru wa basha ni notte*" (1926, "Spring Riding in a Carriage") and "*Hanazono no shisō*" (1927, "Ideas of a Flower Garden").

In the stories concerning his first wife, and in those that refer to his father's death in 1922, Yokomitsu used direct personal experience as basic content for his narratives. The Western reader may wonder why he did not make the effort to invent parallel situations and use his personal experience to infuse them with the truth of emotion. This would have given him greater freedom of expression and might have enabled him to create the sort of fiction to which he obviously aspired. The fact that he did not do so is revealing of Japanese psychology, for Yokomitsu never really stepped outside the fundamental worldview of the Naturalists. He could not escape from their insistence that only the self is knowable.

In 1927 Yokomitsu was happily married, with the birth of a son in November, and was enjoying a degree of fame that might have seemed out of all proportion to his achievement, especially in the year of Akutagawa's suicide. Having reestablished his home life, he traveled to Shanghai in 1928 and began to write his first full-length novel in the *Shinkankaku* style. *Shanghai* centers upon the May 30th Movement of 1925, which was remarkable for being the first major strike by Chinese workers against their Japanese employers. In addressing this topic, Yokomitsu was well aware that it was exactly the sort of material which proletarian authors treated, and he hoped to show that a true "literary" approach would produce a more revealing account and possibly a great work of art. It did not. The novel merely provided his proletarian rivals with ammunition to attack those who, like KIKUCHI KAN, still believed in art for art's sake.

Yokomitsu did, however, create a literary sensation in 1930 when he published a short story called "*Kikai*" ("Machine"). It has been translated twice into English: always a good indication of a work's critical appeal and very helpful to readers who want a second insight into the original. Gone are the short, staccato sentences, and in their place is a densely constructed narrative, described by Tanigawa Tetsuzō as an "arabesque-like, associationist method of writing."

At the time, no one noticed its similarities to various examples of European Modernism which had recently been appearing in the quarterly magazine *Shi to shiron* (Poetry and Poetics). For the first time, Joyce, Proust, Valéry, Eliot, and Gide had been offered to Japanese readers in good translations, and the fashion-conscious Yokomitsu had adopted a style that was more in accord with them. The story itself has many fine qualities: a nightmarish setting in a nameplate factory that stinks with corrosive smells; the untimely death of a worker (who drinks acid, mistaking it for water); and a suggestion that some kind of mechanistic fate has invaded the life, and indeed the moral sensibility, of the narrator.

A few other stories followed in the new style of *"Kikai,"* notably *"Jikan"* (*1931*, "Time") and *"Basha"* (*1932*, "The Carriage"). However, as the intensity of these stories might indicate, Yokomitsu was now reaching crisis point. In 1929 he had discovered Paul Valéry's *L'Introduction à la méthode de Léonard de Vinci*, and was overwhelmed by its nihilistic message. It was certainly the inspiration of *"Kikai,"* where Yokomitsu's closing image ("All I feel is that there is the sharp point of some machine coming slowly toward me . . .") is strongly suggestive of what he understood as Valéry's "nihilism at the center of individual consciousness."

Increasing demands came as a result of Yokomitsu's prominence and he produced a great quantity of work during the early 1930s. His second long novel, *Shin-en* (*The Garden of Sleep*), was serialized in two parts in 1930 and 1932. *Hanabana* (*Flowers*) and *Gaka* (*Song of Songs*) appeared during 1931. Although none of these has been translated, Japanese critics refer to them as being representative of the "new psychological novel," suggesting a greater emphasis on character and motivation. But as Dennis Keene says: "The modern Japanese novel is not remarkable for psychological analyses," and he describes *Shin-en* as "a disappointment." A story of two men in love with one woman, *Shin-en* set the pattern for Yokomitsu's later work. The men are (in Keene's words) "ideological ciphers representing two opposed ways of life."

Yokomitsu was becoming completely disillusioned with serious writing, and set about preparing the way for yet another modification of his literary philosophy. In 1935 he published a critical essay titled *"Junsui shōsetsuron"* ("A Theory of the Pure Novel"), in which he claimed that Japanese literature had reached an impasse. It was the old story: on the one hand, the *I-Novelists writing diaries, and, on the other, the proletarians writing ideological tracts. Caught in between them was himself, the one from whom so much was expected. He argued that if critics and public both wanted a Japanese

Dostoievsky, they would have to tolerate an "in-between literature" containing such elements of the popular novel as coincidence and sentiment.

It is at this point in Yokomitsu's biography that one is most likely to judge his entire career as predicated on a total misunderstanding of the nature of literature. This would be a mistake, for he tried very hard to create true fictions without losing any of the authenticity that comes from direct personal experience. What he misunderstood was the creative process itself. He would have done better to have taken the genre of popular fiction and refine it for his expressionistic purposes. But he rejected both of Japan's great literary traditions: the *monogatari* tradition (**Genji*) and the diary tradition (**Pillow Book*), finding them both trivial in comparison to what he saw from the West. He really wanted to have them merged into a single, more powerful form, but could not find the means of doing it.

It is possible that Yokomitsu believed he had found a solution by assigning different and opposing life-styles to his main characters. He used it again in his 1934 novel *Monshō* (*The Family Crest*), and yet again in the novel he wrote on his return from a European trip, *Ryoshū* (*1937, Travel Sadness*). The latter reveals how the author had also changed his political views, turning away from the left-wing leanings of his youth towards the nationalism which was almost universal before World War II. One of his characters, Yashiro, is appalled by Europe and finds everything there either distasteful or incomprehensible.

Deeply depressed by Japan's defeat in the war, Yokomitsu was taken ill during the summer of 1946. He recovered briefly to write what many people consider to be one of his finest works, a short story called "*Bishō*" (1947, "Smile"). It is set in a period towards the end of the war when defeat seemed inevitable, and centers upon a brilliant young mathematician who has invented a death ray that he claims will win victory for Japan. The narrator, entranced by the man's "guileless and innocent smile," has complete faith in him and says: "I was wondering just what part the concept of zero, of nothing, plays in your system. I have always thought that it should be completely central . . ." Because the mathematician agrees so enthusiastically, the reader may assume that Yokomitsu was suggesting some kind of synthesis of Western science (demonstrably so powerful in the destruction of Hiroshima) and Oriental mysticism, albeit in a sketchy and intuitive form. He was not, however, actually recommending such a synthesis, for, in his last paragraph, he admits to the inhuman nature of the mathematician's spirit. The man's perfect smile reflects the coldness of his heart, whereas, in its turn, the real world smiles *coldly* on such ambitious enterprise.

With this brilliant paradox and all its life-affirming implications, Yokomitsu ended his career. He died shortly after completing "Smile" in 1947.

RECOMMENDED READING

Short Fiction Collections

Love, and Other Stories of Yokomitsu Riichi. 266 pages. Tr. Dennis Keene. University of Tokyo Press, Tokyo, 1974; 1979, paperback. Columbia University Press, NY, 1979, paperback. Contains 14-page introduction by the translator. Includes: "The Defeated Husband," "After Picking Up a Blue Stone," "The Depths of the Town," "Spring Riding in a Carriage," and "The Machine." An excellent volume containing a cross section of Yokomitsu's best work.
Time, and Others. 92 pages. Tr. various. Hara Shobo, Tokyo, 1965. This volume contains both Japanese and English texts. The translations, all by Western scholars, are: "Time," "The Machine" (as "Machine"), "Silent Ranks," and "Spring Riding in a Carriage" (as "Spring, in a Surrey").

WORKS IN ENGLISH TRANSLATION

Short Fiction

"After Picking Up a Blue Stone." "*Aoi ishi o hirotte kara.*" 1925. 25 pages. *Love, and Other Stories.*
"The Carriage." "*Basha.*" 1932. 43 pages. *Love, and Other Stories.*
"The Child Who Was Laughed At." "*Warawareta ko.*" 1927. 7 pages. *Love, and Other Stories.*
"The Defeated Husband." "*Maketa otto.*" 1924. 38 pages. *Love, and Other Stories.*
"The Depths of the Town." "*Machi no soko.*" 1925. 4 pages. *Love, and Other Stories.*
"The Fly." "*Hae.*" 1923. 7 pages. (1) As "Hae." Tr. Ken Chikui. *Shin Ei-Bei Bungaku,* 1932. (2) Tr. John Nathan. *Japan Quarterly,* vol. 12, no. 1, 1965. (3) As "Hae." Tr. Tsutomu Fukuda. *The Azaleas,* no. 3, 1969.
"Ideas of a Flower Garden." "*Hana-zono no shisō.*" 1927. 17 pages. Tr. Dennis Keene. *Japan Quarterly,* vol. 20, no. 2, 1973; *Love, and Other Stories.*
"Love." "*Ommi.*" 1921. 19 pages. *Love, and Other Stories.*
"Machine." "*Kikai.*" 1930. 20 pages. (1) Tr. Edward Seidensticker. *Modern Japanese Stories,* ed. Ivan Morris. Spottiswoode, London, 1961; Tuttle, Tokyo and NY, 1962; 1977, paperback; *Time, and Others; The World of Japanese Fiction,* Dutton, NY, 1973. (2) As "The Machine." *Love, and Other Stories.*
"Mount Hiei." "*Hiei.*" 1935. 13 pages. Tr. Lane Dunlop. *Journal of Literary Translation,* no. 17, 1986.
"The Pale Captain." "*Aoi taii.*" 1927. 10 pages. *Love, and Other Stories.*
"Silent Ranks." "*Shizuka naru ra-*

retsu." 1925, 35 pages. Tr. John
Bester. *Japan P.E.N. News,*
no. 12, Feb. 1964; *Time, and
Others.*
"Smile." *"Bishō."* 1947. 35 pages.
Love, and Other Stories.
"Spring Riding in a Carriage."
"Haru wa basha ni notte." 1926.
14 pages. (1) As "Spring Came
on a Horse-Drawn Cart." Tr.
Mary M. Suzuki. *The Heart Is
Alone,* ed. Richard McKinnon.
Hokuseido, Tokyo, 1957. (2) As
"Spring in a Surrey." Tr. John
Nathan. *Japan Quarterly,* vol. 12,
no. 1, 1965; *Time, and Others.*
"Time." *"Jikan."* 1931. 17 pages.
(1) Tr. Donald Keene. *Modern
Japanese Literature,* ed. Donald
Keene. Grove Press, NY, 1956;

Tuttle, Tokyo, 1957; Grove Weidenfeld, NY, 1989, paperback.
(2) Tr. Tadao Katayama. *The
Reeds,* vol. 10, 1965. (3) Tr. Richard Foster. *Time, and Others.*
"Young Forever." *"Seishun."* 1936.
19 pages. Tr. Habuku Kodama.
*Young Forever, and Five Other
Novelettes,* ed. Japan Writers'
Society. Hokuseido, Tokyo,
1941.

Plays

*The Curtain Would Not Draw. Shi-
maranu kāten.* 1926. 24 pages.
Tr. Kazuo Yamada. *Shin Ei-Bei
Bungaku,* 1933.
*The Roof-Garden, and Other One-
Act Plays.* Shijo Shobo, Toyo,
1934.

CRITICAL STUDIES

Keene, Dennis. "Flaubert and Yoko-
mitsu: Does Stylistic Influence
Take Place?" *Transactions of the
International Conference of Orien-
talists in Japan,* no. 17, 1972.
———. "The *Shinkankakuha*: A Japan-
ese Literary Movement of the
Nineteen Twenties." *Transactions
of the International Conference of
Orientalists in Japan,* no. 16, 1971.

———. "Yokomitsu Riichi and the
Shinkankakuha." Ph.D. diss.,
Oxford University, Oxford, 1973.
———. *Yokomitsu Riichi, Modernist.*
Columbia University Press, NY,
1980.
Viglielmo, V. H. "Yokomitsu Riichi's
'Jikan': An Allegorical Interpre-
tation." *Essays on Japanese Litera-
ture,* 1975.

YOSHIYUKI Junnosuke
(1924–   )

Novelist. Born in Okayama. Resident of Tokyo.

Not exactly a chronicler of the demimonde (an epithet that fits better the name of NAGAI KAFŪ) Yoshiyuki Junnosuke used the demimonde as a kind of mirror in which he discovered his own psychology. Variously described as "urbane," "sophisticated," "cool," and "nihilistic," Yoshiyuki's writing is also thoughtful, probing, sensitive, and sensual. An aura of eroticism is nearly always present, even when his world-weary heroes are talking about art or food. Only when they actually perform erotic sex does it tend to disappear. The narrator of *Anshitsu* (1970, *The Dark Room*) comments, for example: "Her body looked sexy with the black 'brands' on it. But in the end I only made love to her twice with them on. Not that I didn't believe what she said. I just got tired of it after the second time."

The extract quoted is not untypical. Yoshiyuki is a stylish writer whose quasi-personal fictions approach the quality of those by

Albert Camus, to which they bear some resemblance. MISHIMA YUKIO rated him very highly, saying in his introduction to *New Writing in Japan* (Penguin Books, 1972): "The delicacy of Yoshiyuki's language and sensibility is probably more subtle and sophisticated than that of any Japanese writer since the war. . . . The *idée fixe* of Japanese youth today – that love is impossible and impracticable – lies deep at the root of Yoshiyuki's thinking."

Born in the provinces, Yoshiyuki was brought up in Tokyo by successful, if unconventional, parents. His father was himself a writer of avant-garde literature before becoming a stockbroker, while his mother was a fashionable beautician, renowned for her introduction of Western beauty techniques to Japan. In 1943, young Junnosuke was drafted into the army: a career which lasted only three days because he suffered from bronchial asthma. Two years later he entered Tokyo University to study English literature.

Yoshiyuki developed early as a writer, having joined several literary groups before leaving college to take up journalism. His first paid job was on a scandal magazine called *Modan Nihon* (*Modern Japan*), but he worked hard in his spare time to write short stories, including "*Bara hambainin*" (*1950*, "The Rose Seller"). However, recognition did not come until publication of "*Genshoku no machi*" (*1952*, "Street of Primary Colors"), which earned him a nomination for the Akutagawa Prize. Later that year he was hospitalized with tuberculosis, and in 1954 his left lung was removed.

Given his experience of hospitals one might have expected him to dwell on them in the manner of ENDŌ SHŪSAKU, but Yoshiyuki had quite another milieu that he wished to make his own. The neon-lit underworld of Tokyo with its brothels and prostitutes attracted him strongly. In a sense, he made it his home, yet he retained at least an illusion of being detached from it in order to keep his freedom. "Street of Primary Colors" was set in this milieu, and so was "*Shūu*" (*1954*, "Sudden Shower"), a story of a young man who fights against his inclination to fall in love with a prostitute. This work finally won him the Akutagawa Prize when he was in the hospital recovering from his operation.

Yoshiyuki's narratives, though resembling the traditional *I-Novel form of personal confession, are in fact more subtle. Emotionally, they conceal more than they confess, but intellectually they are models of pristine clarity. Thus he deals with the experiences of the everyday consciousness, indicating what lies below the surface of the male psyche only by the most oblique hints and suggestions. And it is the female characters of his stories – the wayward outcasts of society with whom a man can feel totally at ease – who succeed in disturbing the surface, perhaps because nothing could be further from their intentions.

Yoshiyuki won the Tanizaki Prize for *The Dark Room*, a novel in which the hero, now middle aged, again finds himself falling in love with a prostitute. The brilliance of its dialogue and the lifelike animation of its characters deliberately lighten an atmosphere of futility, making it seem more romantic and alluring.

In going some way towards combining the Romantic dissipation of DAZAI OSAMU with the erotic eloquence of KAWABATA YASUNARI, Yoshiyuki has made a significant contribution to postwar Japanese literature. As critics have noted, his characters could just as well be American and the setting Paris, not least because he has become closely acquainted with the work of Henry Miller, an American-in-Paris whose life-style was not dissimilar from that of Yoshiyuki's narrators. Nonetheless, to a Western eye, Yoshiyuki's narrative line is spun with an almost abstract sensitivity (far more economically than Henry Miller's), and is characteristically Japanese.

RECOMMENDED READING

Novel

The Dark Room. *Anshitsu. 1970.* 170 pages. Tr. John Bester. Kodansha International, Tokyo and NY, 1975, 1980, paperback. A sophisticated and intriguing novel, typical of Yoshiyuki's style.

WORKS IN ENGLISH TRANSLATION

Novel

The Dark Room. Anshitsu. 1970.

Short Fiction

"Are the Trees Green?" *"Kigi wa midori ka." 1958.* 23 pages. Tr. Adam Kabat. *The Shōwa Anthology,* vol. 1, ed. Van C. Gessel and Tomone Matsumoto. Kodansha International, Tokyo and NY, 1985.

"Birds, Beasts, Insects and Fish." *"Chōjū chūgyo." 1959.* 12 pages. Tr. Maryellen Toman Mori. *Japan Quarterly,* vol. 28, no. 1, 1981.

"In Akiko's Room." *"Shōfu no heya." 1958.* 10 pages. Tr. Howard Hibbett. *Contemporary Japanese Literature,* ed. H. Hibbett. Knopf, NY, 1977, paperback; Tuttle, Tokyo, 1978.

"Sudden Shower." *"Shūu." 1954.* 24 pages. Tr. Geoffrey Bownas. *Japan Quarterly,* vol. 19, no. 4, 1972. *New Writing in Japan.* Penguin Books, Harmondsworth, 1972.

"Three Policemen." *"Sannin no keikan." 1974.* 6 pages. Tr. Hugh Clarke. *Seven Stories of Modern Japan,* ed. L. Morton, Wild Peony, New South Wales, Australia.

CRITICAL STUDY

Docherty, Miyoko Uraguchi. "A Presentation of Personal Consciousness Through the External World: A Study of *Anshitsu* by Yoshiyuki Junnosuke." *European Studies on Japan*, 1979.

GENERAL READING

Some books in English that discuss a number of modern Japanese novelists in one or more volumes are listed below.

Fowler, Edward. *The Rhetoric of Confession, Shishōsetsu in Early Twentieth-Century Japanese Fiction.* University of California Press, Berkeley, 1988. 333 pages. A major study of the **I-Novel** and its exponents.

Gessel, Van C. *The Sting of Life: Four Contemporary Japanese Novelists.* Columbia University Press, NY, 1989. 326 pages. Contains chapters on YASUOKA SHŌTARŌ, SHIMAO TOSHIO, KOJIMA NOBUO, and ENDŌ SHŪSAKU.

Hisamatsu, Sen'ichi. *Biographical Dictionary of Japanese Literature.* Kodansha International, Tokyo and NY, 1976. 437 pages. Approximately one third of the entries are devoted to writers of the modern era.

Katai, Tayama. *Literary Life in Tokyo: 1885–1915.* Tr. and annotated by Kenneth G. Henshall. E. J. Brill, Leiden, The Netherlands, 1987. 292 pages. A translation of the novelist's anecdotal memoirs, *Thirty Years in Tokyo.*

Katō, Shuichi. *A History of Japanese Literature, vol. 3, The Modern Years.* Tr. Don Sanderson. Macmillan, London, and Paul Norbury Publications, Tenterden, Kent, 1983. 307 pages. Covers the period from the **Meiji Restoration** to the early 1980s. An excellent and wide-ranging survey by one of Japan's leading scholars.

Keene, Donald. *Dawn to the West: Japanese Literature in the Modern Era.* Holt, Rinehart, Winston, NY, 1984; Henry Holt and Company, NY, 1987. Highly acclaimed as the definitive work in English on modern Japanese literature. In two volumes: "Fiction," and "Poetry, Drama, Criticism." 1,327 and 685 pages respectively.

Kimball, Arthur G. *Crisis in Identity and Contemporary Japanese Novels.* Tuttle, Tokyo, 1973. 190 pages. The search for identity, examined through ten major novels.

Lippit, Noriko Mizuta. *Reality and Fiction in Modern Japanese Literature.* M. E. Sharpe, NY, 1980. 217 pages. A study of modern writers and their relationship to society.

Miyoshi, Masao. *Accomplices of Silence: The Modern Japanese Novel.* University of California Press, Berkeley, 1974. 194 pages. A penetrating study of selected novels by six major writers: FUTABATEI, ŌGAI, [NATSUME] SŌSEKI, KAWABATA, DAZAI, and MISHI-MA.

Nakamura, Mitsuo. *Modern Japanese Fiction 1868–1926.* Kokusai Bunka Shinkōkai, Tokyo, 1966 (part 1), 1968 (part 2); revised edition (both parts) 1968. 119 and 61 pages. A broad study of literary movements, with discussion of both major and minor writers. Contains many excellent black-and-white photographs.

————. *Contemporary Japanese Fiction 1926–1968.* Kokusai Bunka Shinkōkai, Tokyo, 1969. 185 pages. The companion volume to *Modern Japanese Fiction.*

Powell, Irena. *Writers and Society in Modern Japan.* Macmillan, London. 1983; Kodansha International, Tokyo and NY, 1983. 149 pages. An analysis of the social and historical contexts of modern Japanese literature.

Rimer, J. Thomas. *A Reader's Guide to Japanese Literature from the Eighth Century to the Present.* Kodansha International, Tokyo and NY, 1988. 208 pages. An excellent introduction in which 30 of the 50 works selected for elucidation are from the modern era.

————. *Modern Japanese Fiction and Its Traditions, An Introduction.* Princeton University Press, Princeton, 1978. 313 pages. Discusses the influence of such classics as **The Tale of Genji** and *The Tale of the Heike* on modern writers, with in-depth analysis of major works.

Swann, Thomas E., and Tsuruta, Kinya, eds. *Approaches to the Modern Japanese Short Story.* Waseda University Press, Tokyo, 1982. 341 pages. Various scholars discuss selected stories by 15 writers.

Ueda, Makoto. *Modern Japanese Writers and the Nature of Literature.* Stanford University Press, Stanford, 1976. 292 pages. A brilliant study of eight major writers: [NATSUME] SŌSEKI, KAFŪ, TANIZAKI, SHIGA, AKUTAGAWA, DAZAI, KAWABATA, and MISHIMA.

Yamanouchi, Hisaaki. *The Search for Authenticity in Modern Japanese Literature.* Cambridge University Press, Cambridge, 1978. 214 pages. Addresses major writers, from FUTABATEI onwards, and their struggle to cope with rapid changes in society.

GLOSSARY

Bakin. See **Takizawa Bakin**.

Bundan. The "literary world" or "literary establishment," a collective term referring to those who, at any given time, are engaged in writing, editing, and publishing literary works.

Bunraku. The traditional puppet theater of Japan, which began during the sixteenth century and was developed in the early **Edo period** when it was known as ***jōruri***. See that entry and also **Chikamatsu Monzaemon**.

Chikamatsu Monzaemon (1653–1724). The great playwright of the **Edo period** whose works for the ***jōruri*** puppet theater were unsurpassed. He began his career as a poet but made his name with the play *Yotsugi Soga* (1683, *The Soga Heir*). Between 1688 and 1703 he wrote mainly for the ***Kabuki***, but turned back to the puppet theater when his favorite actor retired. His play *Sonezaki shinjū* (1703, *The Love Suicides at Sonezaki*) was based on a real-life incident and gave rise to a new and important dramatic genre called *sewamono* (domestic tragedies). His greatest masterpiece was *Shinjū ten no Amijima* (1721, *The Love Suicides at Amijima*), which, like many of his works, addressed the feudal theme of *giri* (duty) versus *ninjō* (human feeling). Chikamatsu has inspired many generations of writers right up to the present day.

Edo period. 1603–1867. The period when the shōgunal government was situated in Edo. Corresponds exactly to what is often called the **Tokugawa period**. The leading fiction writers of the early, middle, and late years of the Edo period were respectively **Ihara Saikaku**, Ueda Akinari (1734–1809), and **Takizawa Bakin**. Despite their achievements it is acknowledged that fiction rarely aspired to the highest levels of art during the Edo period. Only with the revolution in writing prompted by TSUBOUCHI SHŌYŌ during the following **Meiji period** did fiction gain in status and quality.

Floating world. *Ukiyo*. The uncertain but exciting world of the **Tokugawa period**, enjoyed especially by the inhabitants of Edo who placed a high value on momentary pleasures. The spirit of the times was reflected in the *Ukiyo-e* (paintings of the floating world) which greatly influenced such Western artists as Manet, Degas, Gauguin, and Van Gogh. See also **Yoshiwara**.

Fukuzawa Yukichi (1834–1901). Scholar, educator, publisher. One of the most influential men of the early **Meiji period**, he did much to transform Japanese culture by promoting changes in education. He opened a private school of Western studies in 1858 and lived to see it become a university (later called Keiō University) in 1890. In the 1870s he issued a series of pamphlets called *Gakumon no susume* (*The Encouragement of Learning*, tr. David A. Dilworth and Umeyo Hirano. Sophia University, Tokyo, 1969), outlining his ideas in terms that any literate person could understand. He urged students to learn Western languages and thus, indirectly, helped to bring about a transformation in literature. He wrote many books, the most famous of which are *Bunmeiron no gairyaku* (1875, *An Outline Theory of Civilization*, tr. David A. Dilworth and G. Cameron Hurst. Sophia University, Tokyo, 1973) and *Fukuō jiden* (1898, *The Autobiography of Fukuzawa Yukichi*, tr. Eiichi Kiyooka. Hokuseido, Tokyo, 1934; revised editions 1940, 1948; new tr. 1960).

Gembun itchi. The "unity of speech and writing" style, developed around 1886–87 by FUTABATEI SHIMEI in association with TSUBOU-CHI SHŌYŌ and independently by YAMADA BIMYŌ. Literary historians are not agreed upon which writer was first. The style was called for in an 1886 essay by Mozume Takami (1849–1928) and eventually transformed written Japanese by adding spoken-language syntax and vocabulary and a set of Western-style punctuation marks, none of which had previously been used in Japanese literature.

Gesaku. The fiction that was produced by writers between 1770 and the end of the **Edo period**. Meaning "playful" or "humorous," the term was originally used by the samurai-playwright Hiraga Gennai (1728–79) to describe his puppet play *Shinrei Yaguchi no watashi* (1770, *The Miracle at the Yaguchi Ferry*). As a professional soldier Gennai wanted to indicate that he was a mere amateur in the arts, yet even professional writers found his epithet appealing at a time when writing fiction was considered an inferior occupation. For a brief but excellent introduction to *gesaku* fiction, see Chapter 17 of Donald Keene's *World Within Walls* (Secker and Warburg, London, 1976). See also **Takizawa Bakin**.

Gossamer Years, The (tenth century, *Kagerō nikki*). The earliest surviving diary by a woman, written by the mother of Fujiwara no Michitsuna (real name unknown). It has been translated by Edward Seidensticker as *The Gossamer Years: The Diary of a*

Noblewoman of Heian Japan (Tuttle, Tokyo, 1964). The author was the concubine of Fujiwara no Kaneie, an assistant minister whose unfaithfulness caused her great distress during the period 954–74.

Great Kantō Earthquake (September 1, 1923). The Great Earthquake which affected the Tokyo area near the end of the **Taishō period** was a disaster of immense proportions. It occurred on a hot, windy day, causing fires to spread and thus compound the damage. More than half of Tokyo was destroyed, as was the whole of Yokohama and many other towns in the region. At least a hundred thousand people were killed.

Haikai. A very broad term, encompassing all types of literature (including prose) written in the spirit of *haiku.* The word was first used to denote the comic poetry of the *Kokinshū,* a *waka* collection dating from the year 905.

Haiku. A seventeen-syllable poem that is complete in itself, unlike a *hokku,* which denotes the opening verse of a comic linked-verse (see *renga*) sequence. Both forms are arranged in a 5-7-5 syllable pattern. The greatest *haiku* poet was undoubtedly Matsuo Bashō (1644–1694). In the **Meiji period**, Masaoka Shiki (1867–1902) did much to reinvigorate the *haiku* form. Among modern Japanese novelists, NATSUME SŌSEKI composed distinguished *haiku,* many of which have been translated into English.

Hearn, Lafcadio (1850–1904). Author and journalist, born of mixed Irish–Greek parentage, Lafcadio Hearn was educated in England and France, and then emigrated to America shortly before he was twenty. Working as a crime reporter for the *Times–Democrat,* he became one of the best-known journalists in the South. After a brief sojourn in the West Indies he finally moved to Japan in 1890, where he married a Japanese woman and began collecting and retelling folktales in English. Maturing greatly as a prose stylist, he produced, at the height of his powers, *Kwaidan* (literally "weird tales"), the 1904 collection that has an almost Dostoievskian power. He was held in the highest esteem by the Japanese themselves who knew him as Koizumi Yakumo. One of his many achievements was his successful period as the first lecturer in English Literature at Tokyo Imperial University, a post in which he was succeeded by NATSUME SŌSEKI in 1903. Said to be shy, restless, morbidly sensitive, and unusually quick-tempered, he was a figure of legendary proportions. All his most important books are readily obtainable, in various editions, as they have been for most of the twentieth century. They include: *In Ghostly Japan* (1899); *Shadowings* (1900); and *Japan: An Interpretation* (1904).

Heian period. 794–1185. The period that began with the establishment of the court at Heiankyō (now Kyoto) and ended when the military government of Minamoto no Yoritomo took charge. Japanese literature reached its zenith during this period in the works of **Murasaki Shikibu** and **Sei Shōnagon**.

Hoshi Shin'ichi (b. 1926). Japan's greatest writer of science fiction. Born into a scientific family, he studied agricultural chemistry and took over his father's pharmaceuticals business in 1947. Obliged to leave because of the company's debts, he eventually took up writing and published his first story in 1957. Immensely prolific – and loved by some people in the West as he is by many in Japan for his refreshingly jaundiced view of technology – he writes with great wit and imagination. Among his translated collections are *The Spiteful Planet and Other Stories*, tr. Bernard Susser and Tomoyoshi Genkawa (The Japan Times, Tokyo, 1978); *The Capricious Robot*, tr. R. Matthew (Kodansha International, Tokyo, 1986); and *A Bag of Surprises*, tr. Stanleigh H. Jones (Kodansha International, Tokyo, 1989).

Ihara Saikaku (1642–93). Poet, novelist, and a master of the elliptical utterance, Saikaku was one of the two or three greatest literary geniuses of Japan. A poet of astonishing productivity (he once composed 23,500 verses in a single day-and-night session), he is today remembered chiefly as a novelist. His first novel, *Kōshoku ichidai otoko* (1682, *The Life of an Amorous Man*), has been seen as a parody of **The Tale of Genji**. Its hero, Yonosuke, embodied the new ideals of the **floating world** in which pleasure – especially sexual pleasure – replaced the gloom of medieval times. This elegantly phrased novel, difficult to read but nonetheless popular, established a new genre called *ukiyo zōshi* (stories of the floating world). Saikaku went on to write many other books, including *Kōshoku gonin onna* (1686, *Five Women Who Loved Love*), a tragicomedy of adultery and punishment. Among the many writers of modern Japan whom he influenced were HIGUCHI ICHIYŌ, KŌDA ROHAN, and OZAKI KŌYŌ.

I-Novels. *Shishōsetsu*, or, alternatively, *watakushi shōsetsu*. Novels *or* short stories that are largely confessional, revealing the author's own thoughts, experiences, or actions. The first- or third-person narrator of such works will usually be a true representation of the author, but not always. MORI ŌGAI's *Maihime* (1890, *The Dancing Girl*) was a forerunner of the genre while TAYAMA KATAI's "*Futon*" (1907, "The Quilt"), a masterpiece of Japanese **Naturalism**, was arguably the first true I-Novel. To a greater or lesser degree, respectively, fictional elements exist in both of these works, as indeed they do in many of the I-Novels that followed. Defined in various ways by the critics (usually according to how much fiction or "untruth" they will tolerate) the I-Novel is a broad category and may even include such a work as MISHIMA YUKIO's apparent parody of the genre, *Kamen no kokuhaku* (1949, *Confessions of a Mask*). SHIGA NAOYA was a master of the mainstream I-Novel; while his disciple OZAKI KAZUO produced some charming stories that exemplify the genre. DAZAI OSAMU developed it further, largely by exaggerating; and of the many women practitioners, HAYASHI FUMIKO with her autobiographical novel, *Hōrōki* (1927, *Vagabond's Song*), is especially worth noting. So adaptable and ubiquitous is the I-Novel that it is often called the characteristic genre of modern Japanese literature.

Iwano Hōmei (1873–1920). A poet, essayist, and novelist who, unlike other exponents of Japanese **Naturalism**, expressed philosophical ideas. These he culled from a variety of sources, including Emerson and Schopenhauer, presenting them in such essays as *"Shimpiteki hanjū shugi"* (1906, "Mystical Semi-Bestialism"). He believed that existence was without purpose and was given meaning only by momentary pleasures. He is most famous for a series of five autobiographical novels which critics have described as being cruel in their lack of sentiment. They are: *Hōrō* (1910, *Roaming*); *Dankyō* (1911, *Broken Bridge*); *Hatten* (1912, *Growth*); *Dokuyaku o nomu onna* (1914, *The Woman Who Took Poison*); and *Tsukimono* (1910–18, *The Possessed*). Some of his poems (but not his novels) have been translated into English.

Jōruri. The traditional puppet theater of Japan, later called **Bunraku**. It took its original name from that of the Princess Jōruri, the subject of *Jōruri monogatari*, a romantic tale that was popular during the late Muromachi period (1392–1568). Consisting of puppet "actors," a chanted narrative, and a *samisen* accompaniment, *jōruri* was developed into a high art form by **Chikamatsu Monzaemon** (1653–1725) who also wrote the first *Kabuki* plays of any distinction. The term **Bunraku** is more commonly used today, but strictly speaking refers to that refined form of the genre that was developed in Osaka (by Chikamatsu and others) from the seventeenth century onwards. Many modern writers have depicted practitioners of the *jōruri* in their works, or have used it in other ways. Notably, TANIZAKI JUN'ICHIRŌ made it a key element in his novel *Tade kuu mushi* (1929, *Some Prefer Nettles*).

Kabuki. The form of drama originated by itinerant women entertainers at the end of the sixteenth century. From the outset it was notable for its elaborate costumes and its great popular appeal. In 1629, when the shōgunal government forbade women to appear on the stage because their presence encouraged prostitution, young men and boys took their place – until they, too, were banned for the same reason in 1652. In the absence of overt sexual enticements, *Kabuki* was obliged to become more subtle and sophisticated. Plots were borrowed from literature and from the already established **Nō** and Kyōgen forms of theater (Kyogen being mainly a humorous genre, often performed during interludes of the Nō) and the plays began to be written down. The earliest surviving ones are those from the Genroku era (1688–1703), and the new genre developed alongside the *jōruri* (puppet theater) to become one of Japan's most distinctive cultural traditions.

Ken'yūsha. "The Society of the Friends of the Inkstone." A famous literary group founded in 1885 by OZAKI KŌYŌ, together with Ishibashi Shian (1867–1927), Maruoka Kyūka (1865–1927), and YAMADA BIMYŌ. The Ken'yūsha took the **Edo period** writer Bakin (**Takizawa Bakin**) as their ideal; rejected the Western pretensions of their contemporaries; enjoyed composing in classical Chinese; and were delightfully frivolous and apolitical. At the time of the group's founding most of its members attended Tokyo University. For three years they circulated a private journal called *Garakuta bunko* (*Trash Library*) before launching it as a public magazine in May 1888.

Konjaku Monogatari shū. (Completed c. 1120. *Tales of Times Now Past*). A collection of over 1,000 brief tales, collected by an anonymous compiler (or compilers) during the twelfth century. It is divided into 31 *maki* (chapters), beginning with tales about the founding of Buddhism in India, moving on to China, and finally to Japan where the last 11 chapters are entirely secular in content. Used by AKUTAGAWA RYŪNOSUKE as a source for his stories, the *Konjaku monogatari* have exerted a fascination on many modern writers. A fine selection of sixty-two of the stories has been translated into English by Marian Ury (*Tales of Times Now Past*. University of California Press, Berkeley, 1979; paperback 1985).

Meiji period. 1868–1912. Corresponds to the reign of the Meiji Emperor, Mutsuhito. During the Meiji period Japan was transformed from a largely agrarian society to a modern industrial state that was able to defeat Russia in naval warfare shortly after the turn of the century. In literature, the changes were no less dramatic. Following TSUBOUCHI SHŌYŌ's 1885 treatise, *The Essence of the Novel*, writers recognized the need for greater realism in their work. FUTABATEI SHIMEI began the process of rejuvenating Japanese fiction; and within a few years NATSUME SŌSEKI and MORI ŌGAI brought it to full fruition.

Meiji Restoration. 1868. The reintroduction of direct imperial rule that brought to an end the 268-year-old Tokugawa shōgunate and its rigid system of medieval government. Mutsuhito, the Meiji emperor who was born in 1852 and reigned until his death in 1912, was the figurehead of the new administration. Although he did not wield great personal power he presided over an era of tumultuous change, the dominant characteristic of which was the Westernization of Japan.

Murasaki Shikibu (c. 976–c. 1031). The author of the world's first novel, **The Tale of Genji**, and a diary composed between 1008–10. A member of a minor but highly literary branch of the Fujiwara family, Murasaki vied with her rival, **Sei Shōnagon**, for literary supremacy during the **Heian period**. Well versed in Chinese literature, she benefited from the fact that her husband, who died in 1001, left her a large library of Chinese books. Shortly afterwards she began *The Tale of Genji*, a task that occupied much of her time for the next twenty years. Few factual details are known about her life, although it is clear that she had at least one daughter. It is thought that she may have died in a convent at the age of about fifty.

Naturalism. A literary movement that flourished in the years 1906–10 and remained influential long afterwards. Centered on Waseda University in Tokyo, its chief exponents were TAYAMA KATAI, SHIMAZAKI TŌSON, TOKUDA SHŪSEI, Chikamatsu Shūkō, **Iwano Hōmei**, and the critic MASAMUNE HAKUCHŌ. The Naturalist writers believed in reporting the everyday reality of their lives, usually in a bleak and pessimistic manner. In their search for identity they wrote personal confessions notable for their frankness, and in so doing created the **I-Novel** genre that continues to be developed to this day. See especially Masamune Hakuchō.

Nitobe Inazō (1862–1933). Christian educator; author. Well known in the West for his book *Bushidō: The Soul of Japan*, Nitobe was a Quaker who sought to promote international understanding. His lectures had a great if not always a lasting influence on many young writers. In the late 1890s ARISHIMA TAKEO studied under him at Sapporo Agricultural School and lodged with his family.

Nō. The Nō theater is the classical drama of Japan that evolved from various sacred rituals and festival entertainments. It reached a peak of excellence during the fifteenth century, especially in the work of Zeami Motokiyo (1363–1443), author of *Sanemori*, *Kiyotsune*, *Tōboku*, and many other plays. Notable for its spiritual power and ghostly themes, the Nō has been constantly refined over the years, while innumerable books (many of them in English) have been written about it. Modern versions of Nō plays were created by MISHIMA YUKIO in the 1950s. For students of the classical drama the key works are those by Zeami himself, translated into English as *On the Art of the Nō Drama: The Major Treatises of Zeami*, J. Thomas Rimer and Masakazu Yamazaki (Princeton University Press, 1984). The reader's attention is also drawn to an excellent historical novel, *The House of Kanze*, written in English by Nobuko Albery (Century Publishing, London, 1985), which follows the fortunes of the Kanze School of Nō (Zeami's family name was actually Kanze) throughout the fourteenth and early fifteenth centuries.

The Pillow Book (992–1000, *Makura no sōshi*). Written by **Sei Shōnagon**, a collection of notes, impressions, character sketches, anecdotes, and delightful lists of "likes and dislikes" that is one of the great classics of Japanese literature. It begins: "In spring it is the dawn," an elliptical opening which the reader is meant to complete with ". . . that is most beautiful." Indeed, as far as beauty is concerned there can surely be few works in any language to match *The Pillow Book*. The author's civilized wit is apparent on every page. One example, from Ivan Morris's translation: "The heron is an unpleasant-looking bird with a most disagreeable expression in its eyes. Yet, though it has nothing to recommend it, I am pleased to think that it does not nest alone in Yurugi Wood."

Renga. Linked poetry. Originally a game, *renga* developed into a serious art form after the twelfth century. Its composition required two or more poets taking turns to add verses of their own while observing certain rules and conventions.

Restoration. See **Meiji Restoration**.

Saikaku. See **Ihara Saikaku**.

Sei Shōnagon (c. 968–c. 1025). With **Murasaki Shikibu** one of the two great classical writers of Japan and author of *Makura no sōshi* (992–1000, **The Pillow Book**). The daughter of an official of the Kiyohara clan who was also a poet and scholar. Sei Shōnagon served at the court of the Empress Sadako as a lady-in-waiting. Little is known of either her life or the circumstances of her death, yet through her work her exceptional wit and sensibility are as alive today as they ever were. She was more learned than Murasaki and, in the opinion of no less an authority than Arthur Waley, a much better poet. Her influence on Japanese literature continues to this day.

Sen no Rikyū (1522–91). Tea master to the warlord Hideyoshi in the sixteenth century and one of the great figures of Japanese history. He was born in Sakai into a family of fish wholesalers and studied the art of the tea ceremony under Jōō, the famed tea master of the late Muromachi period. First employed by Oda Nobunaga, the warlord who preceded Hideyoshi, he rose to become an arbiter of taste in aesthetic matters, at the same time wielding great political influence. He eventually fell out with Hideyoshi, who, enraged by his "arrogance," obliged him to commit suicide. Many modern writers have depicted him in their historical fiction, among them INOUE YASUSHI and NOGAMI YAEKO.

Shingeki. The "new theater" of the twentieth century, inspired initially by translations of Western plays, especially those of Shakespeare and Ibsen. Among the early *shingeki* playwrights were Nagata Hideo (1885–1949) and Nakamura Kichizō (1877–1941), the latter being so addicted to Ibsen that he was nicknamed "Henrik."

Shinkankakuha. The "new sense-impression" group of writers in the latter half of the 1920s, of whom the most prominent were YOKOMITSU RIICHI and KAWABATA YASUNARI. Variously translated also as the "neo sensationalist" or (less satisfactorily) "neo sensualist" group, these writers wished to create a "literature of sensations" in which reality would be represented without the interference of intellectual or emotional bias. They were associated with the magazine *Bungei jidai* (*Literary Age*).

Shirakabaha. The White Birch Society. A literary group founded in 1910 by SHIGA NAOYA, MUSHANOKŌJI SANEATSU, Kinoshita Rigen, and Ōgimachi Kinkazu. Its aristocratic and upper middle class members, who came to include the brothers SATOMI TON and ARISHIMA TAKEO, were opposed to **Naturalism** but very much in favor of Western thought, aesthetics, and individualism. Writing retrospectively, Mushanokōji said: "Shirakaba valued highly the will of nature, the will of man, and was a movement which tried to find out how the individual could best live." The group's magazine, *Shirakaba* (*White Birch*), was first published in April 1910 and ran until 1923.

Shōwa period. 1926–1989. Corresponds to the reign of the Emperor Hirohito who was born in 1901 and officially enthroned in 1928. During this long and turbulent period of Japanese history, the rise of militarism in the 1930s culminated in the war in the Pacific and Japan's defeat in 1945. This was immediately followed by the American Occupation which ended with the signing of the 1952 San Francisco Treaty of Peace. In the postwar years a sustained period of economic expansion turned Japan into a financial and economic superpower. These vastly different eras within the Shōwa period have each been reflected in literature, while some writers (most notably, TANIZAKI JUN'ICHIRŌ) transcended their times to create works that will endure for centuries to come.

Taishō period. 1912–1926. Corresponds to the reign of the Emperor

Yoshihito (born 1879). Culturally, the period is far from being an artificial or arbitrary division of history. The demise of the *Meiji* Emperor and the subsequent suicide of General Nogi who, in a gesture to the feudal past, "followed his emperor into death," left many people in a state of shock and prompted them to reflect deeply on the benefits and disadvantges of Westernization. In literature, the period is dominated by AKUTAGAWA RYŪNOSUKE, whose own suicide in 1927 brought the period to a very definite end.

Takizawa Bakin (1767–1848). One of the greatest Japanese storytellers, a prolific **Edo period** *gesaku* writer who is most famous for *Chinsetsu yumiharizuki* (1806–10, *Crescent Moon*) and *Nansō Satomi hakkenden* (1814–41, *Biographies of Eight Dogs*). In *Crescent Moon*, an historical epic set in the twelfth century, the author's didactic aim ("encouraging virtue, punishing vice") is made palatable by his inclusion of much fantasy and romance. At age forty-seven he started *Eight Dogs*, which became the longest work of Japanese fiction, in 106 volumes. It exemplifies samurai ideals, the author himself being of samurai origin. Influenced by Chinese fiction and deeply Confucian in his philosophy, Bakin provided inspiration to many writers of the modern era.

Tale of Genji, The. Generally considered to be the greatest work of Japanese literature and the world's first true novel, *Genji* was composed by **Murasaki Shikibu** (c. 976–c. 1031) between the years 1001 and c. 1015. Originally consisting of 54 chapters that were bound separately, it contains 430 characters (excluding servants, etc.), most of whom are interrelated. The narrative tells of the loves and sorrows of Prince Genji, an attractive and life-enhancing figure who was a fictional creation, though modeled on various heroes of the **Heian period**. The work is remarkable for the beauty and breadth of its conception, for its tightly constructed narrative, and for a psychological dimension that was entirely new in literature. The elucidation of its text has prompted the creation of a vast library of scholarly works, no less than 10,000 full-length books being listed by Professor Ikeda Kikan, writing in the 1950s. Today, most Japanese read either "Tanizaki Genji" or "Enchi Genji," the translations from classical to modern Japanese made respectively by TANIZAKI JUN'ICHIRŌ and ENCHI FUMIKO. The most important English translations are those by Arthur Waley (1956) and Edward Seidensticker (1976), both of which are easily obtainable.

Tamenaga Shunsui (1790–1843). Novelist of the late **Edo period**. Born Sasaki Sadataka, he was the proprietor of a bookstore and did not become famous until he began writing the popular romances of *ninjōbon* fiction, a genre that he developed to its full potential. His masterpiece was *Shunshoku umegoyomi* (1832–33, *Colors of Spring: The Plum Calendar*), a tale in twelve volumes set in the **Yoshiwara**. In 1841 he was hauled before the magistrates for suspected pornography, found guilty, and put in handcuffs for fifty days. The incident brought his career to an end, but his works remained to inspire OZAKI KŌYŌ and other writers of the modern period.

Tanka. Short poem. *Tanka* is the classic form of Japanese poetry, being composed of thirty-one syllables, divided into five lines of five, seven, five, seven and seven syllables respectively.

Tenkō Bungaku. "Apostasy" or "conversion." The so-called *tenkō* literature of the 1930s began after KOBAYASHI TAKIJI was murdered by the authorities in 1933. As a consequence, many other leftwing writers who were either imprisoned or threatened with imprisonment came to realize that their situation was hopeless. The vast majority of them issued statements declaring that they had changed their political beliefs. Their subsequent works often reflected guilt and confusion. Some, like SHIMAKI KENSAKU, wrote powerful descriptions which identified the pressures they were under.

Togawa Masako (b.1933). A brilliant thriller writer who has acquired a certain popularity in the West through her novels, *Oi naru genrei* (1962, *The Master Key*. Dodd, Mead, NY, 1984; Century, London, 1985; Penguin, Harmondsworth, 1986); *Ryojin nikki* (1963, *The Lady Killer*. Century, London, 1986; Dodd, Mead, NY, 1986; Penguin, Harmondsworth, 1986); and *Hi no seppun* (1985, *A Kiss of Fire*. Dodd, Mead, NY, 1988; Chatto and Windus, London, 1988; Mandarin, London, 1988). All three have been translated by Simon Grove.

Tokugawa period. 1603–1867. Dates from the 1603 founding of the Tokugawa shōgunate by Tokugawa Ieyasu (1542–1616) to its overthrow in 1867 and the subsequent restoration of the **Meiji** Emperor in 1868. Corresponds to the **Edo period** because Ieyasu established the shōgunal government in Edo (present-day Tokyo).

Tokutomi Sohō (1863–1957). Critic; editor; publisher. The elder brother of TOKUTOMI ROKA, Sohō was one of the most prolific journalists of modern Japan. Early in his career he was a radical supporter of the democratic cause and founded the magazine *Kokumin no tomo* (*The People's Friend*) at the end of the 1880s. Much later, however, he became completely discredited on account of his willing cooperation with the military regime before and during World War II.

Uchimura Kanzō (1861–1930). An influential Christian thinker and activist whose lectures were attended by such distinguished writers as SHIGA NAOYA and ARISHIMA TAKEO during their formative years. He came from the American Protestant tradition, having been educated at Sapporo Agricultural School where W.S. Clark (1826–86), the dean of Amherst College, had recently been teaching. A graduate in marine biology, Uchimura studied theology in the United States and returned to Japan in 1888 to preach the revolutionary idea that there was one God who transcended both emperor and state. He founded the magazine *Seisho no kenkyū* (*Bible Studies*) and believed that Christianity could flourish without an established church. A pacifist and a socialist who nonetheless took a realistic view of the world, he is chiefly known outside Japan for his 1895 English-language memoir, *How I Became a Christian.*

Waka. The conventional Japanese verse form in which thirty-one syllables are arranged in lines of five, seven, five, seven, and seven syllables. It came to be called **tanka** (meaning "short poem") during the **Meiji period**, by which time the form was already over a thousand years old.

Yoshikawa Eiji (1892–1962). A popular writer, best known for his sword-play epic, *Miyamoto Musashi*, which was serialized in the *Asahi shimbun* 1935–37 and 1938–39. Nearly 1,000 pages long, it was translated into English by Charles S. Terry and published as *Musashi* by Kodansha International, Tokyo, 1981. Yoshikawa, OSARAGI JIRŌ (who wrote similar works), and KIKUCHI KAN pioneered Japanese literature with mass appeal in the twentieth century.

Yoshiwara. The pleasure quarters of Edo (in the modern era, Tokyo) which existed from the early seventeenth century until just after World War II. More charming than the "red light districts" of Western cities, it was not only a location for brothels but also a center for theater, visual arts, and literature. The old Yoshiwara district burned down in 1657 in the so-called Fire of the Long-Sleeved Garment (started accidentally by a priest burning clothes in a brazier), and a new one was built immediately afterwards on an 18-acre site near the Asakusa temple. In the late **Edo period** it became the focus of the **floating world** (*ukiyo*), when people greatly indulged themselves in the momentary pleasures of song, *sake*, and sex, although not necessarily in that order. It is said that the atmosphere of Old Japan lingered on in the Yoshiwara long after it had disappeared elsewhere. Readers interested in the subject are referred to the writings of HIGUCHI ICHIYŌ and NAGAI KAFŪ, and also to a more recent (and highly readable) social history called *Yoshiwara, The Pleasure Quarters of Old Tokyo*, by Stephen and Ethel Longstreet (Tuttle, Tokyo, 1988).

About the Author

John Lewell was born on a farm in Suffolk, England, shortly after the end of World War II. With a scholarship from his school, Framlingham College, he went to Peterhouse, Cambridge University, where he graduated in English Literature and Fine Art in 1967. He has traveled and lectured extensively in North America and is the author of several books on technological subjects, including two on computer graphics. He currently lives in London with his Thai-born wife and their baby son.